Study Guide and SPSS Manual

to accompany

Susan A. Nolan / Thomas E. Heinzen
Statistics for the Behavioral Sciences

Robert Weathersby
Eastern University

Robin Freyberg
Stern College for Women
Yeshiva University

WORTH PUBLISHERS

Study Guide and SPSS Manual
by Robert Weathersby and Robin Freyberg
to accompany
Susan A. Nolan and Thomas E. Heinzen: *Statistics for the Behavioral Sciences*

ISBN-10: 1-4292-0635-7
ISBN-13: 978-1-4292-0635-8

First Printing 2008

Worth Publishers
41 Madison Avenue
New York, NY 10010
www.worthpublishers.com

CONTENTS

CONTENTS

PREFACE

This **Study Guide** is designed for use with *Statistics for the Behavioral Sciences* by Susan A. Nolan and Thomas E. Heinzen. It is intended to help you learn the material in the textbook, evaluate your understanding of that material, and to review any problem areas. Each chapter contains an outline, learning objectives, a chapter review (organized by major textbook section), and study questions accompanied by correct answers and text page references, all designed to help you master introductory statistics.

The **SPSS Manual** shows you how to perform the statistical procedures discussed in *Statistics for the Behavioral Sciences* using SPSS. It provides applications and exercises for nearly all chapters of the text. Step-by-step instructions describing how to carry out statistical analysis using SPSS are also provided. The data sets which accompany some of the exercises within this manual can be downloaded from the book's companion Web site: www.worthpublishers. com/nolanheinzen1e

Acknowledgments

We would like to thank the Worth Publishers team, including Christine Ondreicka, Jenny Chiu, and Stacey Alexander for their dedication in coordinating various aspects of the editorial and production processes.

Robert Weathersby
Robin Freyberg

CHAPTER ONE

AN INTRODUCTION TO STATISTICS AND RESEARCH DESIGN

The Basic Elements of Statistical Reasoning

CHAPTER OUTLINE

Two Branches of Statistics: Growing Our Knowledge about Human Behavior
- Descriptive Statistics: Organizing, Summarizing, and Communicating Numerical Information
- Inferential Statistics: Using Samples to Draw Conclusions about a Population
- Distinguishing Between a Sample and a Population

Variables: Transforming Observations into Numbers

Independent and Dependent Variables: The Main Ingredients of Statistical Thinking
- Putting Variables to Work: Independent, Dependent, and Confounding Variables
- Developing and Assessing Variables: The Reliability and Validity of Tests

An Introduction to Hypothesis Testing: From Hunch to Hypothesis

Types of Research Designs: Experiments, Nonexperiments, and Quasi-Experiments
- Experiments and Causality: Control the Confounding Variables
- Research Designs Other than Experiments: Nonexperiments and Quasi-Experiments
- One Goal, Two Strategies: Between-Groups Designs vs. Within-Groups Designs

Curiosity, Joy, and the Art of Research Design
- Digging Deeper into the Data: Variations on Standard Research Designs
- Outlier Analyses: Does the Exception Prove the Rule?
- Archival Studies: When the Data Already Exist

LEARNING OBJECTIVES

After studying this chapter, you should be able to:

1. Define each of the following terms and provide examples that are not in the text: *variable*; *construct*; *discrete observations* and *continuous observations*; *nominal, ordinal, interval* and *ratio variable*; *independent, dependent, confounding*, and *extraneous variable*; *noise*; *reliability* and *validity*, including *test–retest reliability* and *predictive validity*; *hypothesis testing, operational definition, experiment, random assignment, single-blind* and *double-blind experiment, placebo effect, demand characteristics, nonexperiments* and *quasi-experiments*; *correlation and correlational studies*; *between-* and *within-groups research design*; *order effects* and *counterbalancing*; *outlier analysis* and *archival studies*.

2. Distinguish between descriptive and inferential statistics, as well as between samples and populations by defining and providing examples of each. It is particularly important that you develop an appreciation of the distinction between the average person's understanding of statistics as a collection of numerical facts about people, cities, sports, the stock market, etc., and the behavioral scientist's use of statistics to organize, summarize, and analyze data in a systematic program of research.

3. Describe the process of *hypothesis testing* in terms of its purpose, under-lying logic, and methodology. Your description should display an understanding of the basic vocabulary of research design, including the manipulation or observation of *independent variables* and the measure-ment of *dependent variables*—including an assessment of their *reliability* and *validity*—in the context of a research design in which *confounding* and *extraneous variables* are controlled or at least accounted for.

4. Explain the essential (defining) differences between *experiments, quasi-experiments, nonexperiments* and *correlational studies*, and describe the general circumstances under which researchers might employ each one in the practice of *hypothesis testing*.

5. Compare and contrast *between-* and *within-groups research designs*, including an explanation of *order effects* and how they may be controlled by the use of *counterbalancing*.

6. Describe *outlier analysis* and *archival studies* as methods of "digging deeper into the data."

CHAPTER REVIEW

> ### Two Branches of Statistics: Growing Our Knowledge about Human Behavior

The text that this study guide accompanies is about the ways in which behav-ioral and social scientists use statistics in the service of asking and answering questions about individuals, groups, and the social environment.

Statistics is both a branch of formal mathematics (theoretical statistics) and an indispensable set of tools used by researchers in the behavioral and social sciences to make sense of the world (applied statistics). This text is about the application of statistics to solve research problems in the social and behavioral sciences. There are two major branches, or divisions, of statistics: **descriptive statistics** and **inferential statistics**. The purpose of descriptive statistics is to organize, summarize, and communicate detailed information about a collection of numbers called data. Note that a descriptive statistical analysis includes the construction of tables and graphs to organize data, as well as the calculation of statistics as a means of summarizing data.

The goal of most research in the social and behavioral sciences is to use the information in a sample of data to form a conclusion—that is, make an *inference*—about an entire population. This process of using the information in a sample to make an inference about a population defines the task of inferential statistics. A **sample** is a set of data that a researcher has collected from a much larger set of data called a **population**. Ideally, the sample should be representative of the population.

> Variables: Transforming Observations into Numbers

The term *data* was described briefly above as a collection of numbers. More formally, a *datum* (as noted in the text, *data* is the plural form of *datum*) is a value of a variable that was obtained by observing, or measuring, the variable. A **variable**, in turn, is any characteristic of the unit of study (typically a person) that varies. The term **construct** (short for hypothetical construct) is used to refer to a variable that is not directly observed but whose existence is inferred to explain what is observed. Psychologists explain individual differences in behavior by appealing to a variety of constructs, including intelligence, introversion, sensation-seeking, anxiety, creativity, depression, and so forth. Researchers use the terms *data*, *measures*, and *observations* somewhat interchangeably, but in each instance they are referring to the values of a variable.

Variables are most basically classified according to one of the four scales applied to measure them: **nominal**, **ordinal**, **interval**, and **ratio**. The scale names are listed according to the level of quantitative precision they represent. Thus a nominal scale represents the lowest level of quantitative precision (none at all), whereas the ratio scale represents the highest level. (The French word "noir" is a useful mnemonic to help you remember this order.) Identifying a variable's scale of measurement determines the statistical test used for data analysis.

The values of **nominal variables** are names or labels. For example, the values "female" and "male" represent different categories of the nominal variable gender. The only property of the real number system used in a nominal scale of measurement is the property of *difference*. Coded values (e.g., "1" = "female" and "2" = "male") have the appearance of quantity but reflect only qualitative difference.

The values of **ordinal variables** are usually ranks (e.g., class rank or order of finish). The values of ordinal variables may also be codes (e.g., 0 = *never*, 1 = *weekly*, and 2 = *daily*) representing differences in responses to a question about the frequency of some behavior such as: "How often do you read the newspaper?" The ordinal scale includes the properties of difference (1 ≠ 2) and magnitude (1 < 2).

Most variables studied by psychologists are regarded as **interval variables**. The interval scale includes the number system properties of *difference* (1 ≠ 2), *magnitude* (1 < 2), and *equal intervals* (2 − 1 = 3 − 2).

The most sophisticated scale of measurement is used to measure **ratio variables**. Examples of ratio variables include any variable whose values are counts, such as number of siblings and number of times engaging in a particular behavior. Physical measurements such as height, weight, time (age, reaction time, number of hours worked per week) are also ratio variables. The ratio scale of measurement includes the number system properties of *difference* (1 ≠ 2), *magnitude* (1 < 2), *equal intervals* (2 − 1 = 3 − 2), and an absolute zero scale value that permits ratio comparisons (8 / 4 = 4 / 2). To help you to distinguish between interval and ratio variables, you may remember that negative values are possible on an interval scale but they are not possible on a ratio scale (because of the true, or absolute, zero). However, the distinction between these scales is not important for most statistical analyses. For example, SPSS[1] refers to ratio and interval variables as **scale** variables, because the same statistical procedures are used to analyze the values of either type of variable. Similarities and distinctions among the four scales of measurement are summarized in Table 1.

Variables may also be categorized as either **discrete** or **continuous**, depending upon limits imposed by the scale of measurement. The values of discrete variables are always integers and usually whole numbers, whereas continuous variables have values that are, at least conceptually, unlimited. Variables measured on a nominal or ordinal scale are always discrete[2], whereas interval and ratio variables may be either discrete or continuous. The rule of thumb is this: Continuous variables may have fractional values but discrete variables may not.

> Independent and Dependent Variables: The Main Ingredients of Statistical Thinking

Variables are also categorized according to their functional role in research designs. An **independent variable** is conceptualized as the "cause" whereas a

---

[1] According to the company's Web site, SPSS was an acronym for "Statistical Package for the Social Sciences" when the company was founded in 1968. The computer program is now known simply as "SPSS" and the company is "SPSS, Inc." Familiarity, if not facility, with this software is expected by most graduate programs in the social and behavioral sciences.

[2] An exception to this general rule is the use of fractional ranks to resolve ties. For example, two individuals who "tie" for second place might each be assigned the rank of 2.5: (2 + 3) / 2 = 2.5.

Table 1 *Differences between the four types of variables in terms of the scales used to measure them*

Scale	Scale Properties	Example of Scale Properties	Example of Variable Illustrating Scale Properties
Nominal	Difference	1 = "fiction" 2 = "nonfiction" $1 \neq 2$	A person who reads fiction is expressing a preference that *differs* from that of a person who reads nonfiction.
Ordinal	Difference Magnitude	1 = "1 or 2 books a year" 2 = "at least 1 book each week" $1 < 2, 2 > 1$	A person who reads "at least 1 book each week" reads a *greater* number of books than a person who reads "1 or 2 books a year."
Interval	Difference Magnitude Equal Intervals	$2 - 1 = 3 - 2$	The difference between reading 2 books a week and 1 book a week is the same as the difference between reading 3 books a week and 2 books a week.
Ratio	Difference Magnitude Equal Intervals Absolute Zero (enables ratio comparisons)	$4 / 2 = 2 / 1$	A person who reads 4 books a week reads twice as many books as a person who reads 2 books a week, etc.

dependent variable is measured as the "effect" of that cause. A third category of variables, called **confounding variables**, produce effects that may be mixed up, or *confounded*, with those of the independent variable. Researchers must be able to control confounding variables if they are to conclude that the independent variable and dependent variable are causally related.

Investigators are also concerned about the effects of variables that partially obscure the relationship between independent and dependent variables. Such variables, called **extraneous variables**, add **noise** to a study that can make detecting the "signal" (effect) of the independent variable difficult. Unlike the effects of confounding variables, the effects of extraneous variables are randomly, and thus about equally, distributed across all levels of the independent variable.

Dependent variables in behavioral and social science research are frequently measured by instruments that were developed to assess constructs such as intelligence, extraversion, or test anxiety. Researchers are obligated to describe the *reliability* and the *validity* of such instruments in the method sections of published reports. A **reliable** instrument is one that produces consistent scores from one administration to another, whereas a **valid** instrument is one that accurately measures the construct it was designed to measure. There are several forms of reliability and validity, but the ones that capture the essence of these properties are test–retest reliability and predictive validity. A test or instrument that produces similar scores in the same group of participants on two occasions is said to have good **test–retest reliability**, whereas a test or instrument that accurately predicts performance on a related measure is said to have good **predictive validity**. For example, the SAT was designed to predict academic performance in college, and to the extent that it does so, it has predictive validity. Please note that reliability and validity are related in the sense that a valid measure must also be a reliable measure. After all, an instrument that does not yield consistent results (is not reliable) can not be considered accurate (valid). However, an instrument need not be valid to be reliable. A watch that is consistently 10 minutes fast is reliable but is hardly a valid (accurate) measure of the time of day.

> An Introduction to Hypothesis Testing: From Hunch to Hypothesis

The purpose of research in the behavioral and social sciences is to discover relationships between variables, and the process that accomplishes this purpose is called **hypothesis testing**. A hypothesis is a formal statement about a relationship between variables that exists in some population(s) of interest. Hypothesis testing, then, is the process of making an inference (drawing a conclusion) about variable relationships in populations based on evidence observed in samples that are representative of those populations.

Researchers must be ever aware of the possibility of drawing an erroneous inference about a population. This may occur, for example, when chance factors cause a sample to be unrepresentative of the population. However, this possibility is rendered less likely by the successful *replication* of original research findings; the greater the number of successful replications, the greater the confidence in the findings. As a general rule, the successful replication of any study depends critically on the extent to which the variables manipulated and measured in the original study were the same variables that were manipulated and measured in the replication. For this reason, researchers are obligated to describe their independent and dependent variables with sufficient precision and clarity. These descriptions are so important they have a special name: operational definitions. An **operational definition** of a variable is always expressed in terms of the procedures (operations) used to manipulate or measure the variable.

> Types of Research Designs: Experiments, Nonexperiments, and Quasi-Experiments

Experiments

In a true **experiment**, the effects of most potentially confounding variables are controlled by randomly assigning participants to conditions. As long as the groups of participants are sufficiently large, random assignment virtually guarantees that the groups are equivalent before the independent variable is manipulated. The use of random assignment thus enables the researcher to more confidently conclude that her manipulation of the independent variable *caused* any observed differences in the dependent variable.

Placebo effects and demand characteristics are confounding variables that require additional control procedures. A **placebo effect** occurs when the effect of a treatment is confounded with a participant's beliefs or expectations about the effect of a treatment. The effect is so well-documented that clinical trials of any new medication are routinely conducted as single-blind experiments. A **single-blind experiment** is so-named because participants can not detect (have been made "blind" to) the condition to which they have been randomly assigned. This "blindness" is accomplished by including a placebo (e.g., a "fake" medication enclosed in a capsule that appears identical to the capsule containing the "real" medication) so that participants can not tell whether they were assigned to the experimental (treatment medication) condition or the control (placebo) condition. The idea is that participants' expectations about the effectiveness of the treatment medication (the placebo effect) will be about the same in the experimental and control conditions. Any difference between the two conditions must therefore be due to the actual effect of the medication. However, a single-blind experiment can not control for the **demand characteristics** that occur when researchers communicate their expectations to participants. To control for both the placebo effect and demand characteristics, investigators employ a **double-blind experiment** in which neither the researcher who administers the treatment/placebo nor the participant knows the condition to which the participant was assigned.

Nonexperiments

A study that does not include a control group is termed a **nonexperiment.** The simplest nonexperimental design is one in which a single group of participants are administered a treatment of some kind and then measured on a dependent variable. An improvement on this design, called the *one-group pretest–posttest design*, enables a comparison of scores before and after a treatment or intervention, but the lack of a control group renders suspect any inference that the treatment caused any observed difference between pretest and posttest scores. The one-group, pretest–posttest design (also called a before–after design) is shown below:

| **One-Group** | **Pretest** | **Treatment** | **Posttest** |

Quasi-Experiments

The prefix *quasi* means "resembling," and quasi–experiments resemble true experiments in several important respects. Like experiments, quasi-experiments include an independent variable that is conceptualized as the "cause" and a dependent variable conceptualized as the "effect." In addition, the independent variable has at least two levels, one of which functions as the experimental condition and the other as the control condition. However, random assignment is not a characteristic of quasi-experiments, so there is no way of knowing whether changes in the dependent variable were caused by the independent variable or by some preexisting differences between the participants in the two conditions. A traditional quasi-experimental design is the *nonequivalent control group design with pretest and posttest*. This design is depicted below:

	Dependent Variable Measure	Independent Variable Levels	Dependent Variable Measure
Group 1	Pretest	Treatment	Posttest
Group 2	Pretest	Control	Posttest

As the name of the design indicates, the control group is not equivalent to the treatment group, so any change in the dependent variable from pretest to posttest in Group 1 may be due to preexisting group differences that are confounded with treatment effects.

Correlational studies represent the largest category of quasi-experimental research. The term **correlation** refers to an association between at least two, usually interval, variables. A correlational study, then, is any study in which the correlation between at least two variables is assessed. However, it is important to note that the variables analyzed in a correlational study are *observed* rather than *manipulated*—that is, the researcher simply measures the variables as they exist.

Between- and Within-Groups Research Designs

Experiments and quasi-experiments may be broadly categorized as either between-groups research designs or within-groups research designs. In a **between-groups research design**, each participant is randomly assigned (experiments) or assigned in some nonrandom way (quasi-experiments) to one and only one condition (level or combination of levels of the independent variable). A between-groups design may not be the best choice if you are trying to detect a small treatment effect, particularly if you have a limited number of participants.

A better choice in this case would be a **within-groups research design** in which each participant experiences all the conditions of the study. When the same individuals experience all the conditions within a study, the variability in the dependent measure that is due to individual differences is eliminated, thus removing the single largest source of noise from the results. With this reduction in the level of noise, the signal (effect of the independent variable) is easier to detect. So, within-groups research designs are more *powerful* (statistical power is discussed in Chapter 12 of the text) than between-groups research designs because within-groups designs are more *sensitive* to the effect of the independent variable. However, unlike between-groups designs, within-groups designs must employ a special control procedure called counterbalancing to control for order effects. **Order effects** occur when participants' scores on the dependent variable are affected by the order in which they experience the conditions of the study. For example, when all participants experience the same order of conditions scores may improve in the control condition because of *practice effects* or scores might decline because of *fatigue effects*. Researchers use **counterbalancing** to control for order effects by randomly assigning half the participants to one order (e.g., treatment followed by control) and half to the other order. The practice effects adding to the control condition scores in the treatment-control order of conditions will be *countered* or *balanced* by the practice effects adding to the treatment condition scores in the second (control-treatment) order of conditions.

> Curiosity, Joy, and the Art of Research Design

Digging Deeper Into the Data: Variations on Standard Research Designs

Outliers are data values that are unusual—often so unusual that they invite a further analysis into the cause(s) of their difference relative to the majority of a data set. As described in the text, John Snow's **outlier analysis** provided further evidence that the contamination of the water from the Broad Street well (the independent variable) was responsible for the cholera epidemic (the dependent variable). In this case, the outliers were the apparent exceptions that proved the rule.

Hospital records, school records, and the census are just a few of the sources of data that are analyzed in **archival studies**. The work of the late Seymour Kety on the etiology of schizophrenia is particularly illustrative of the value of archival studies. Kety and colleagues (e.g., Kety, Rosenthal, Wender, & Schulsinger, 1968; Kety, Rosenthal, Wender, & Schulsinger, 1976) reasoned that if schizophrenia were caused by environmental factors, then the incidence of the disorder should be approximately the same among the adoptive and biological families of individuals with schizophrenia who had been adopted as infants. A national sample of archival data in the form of records of adopted persons with and without schizophrenia showed that this was decidedly not the case. The adoptive families of normal and schizophrenic adoptees showed approximately the same low lifetime rate of the disorder, whereas the rate was significantly elevated among the biological families of schizophrenic adoptees.

STUDY QUESTIONS

1. The two branches of statistics are _____ and _____.
   a. theoretical statistics; applied statistics
   b. research design; data analysis
   c. numerical methods; graphical methods
   d. descriptive statistics; inferential statistics

2. Social and behavioral scientists use _____ statistics to organize, summarize, and communicate a group of numerical observations.
   a. theoretical
   b. inferential
   c. descriptive
   d. applied

3. In _____ statistics, sample data are used to make general estimates about the larger population.
   a. inferential
   b. theoretical
   c. descriptive
   d. applied

4. The _____ includes all possible observations of interest to a researcher, whereas the observations available for study comprise the _____.
   a. sample; population
   b. population; sample
   c. experimental group; control group
   d. control group; experimental group

5. The term **variable** refers to a:
   a. physical, attitudinal, or behavioral characteristic that can take on different values.
   b. number or label assigned to an observation according to a rule or system.
   c. single value that summarizes and describes a sample of data values.
   d. numerical value assigned to an observation.

6. Variables that are *not* directly observable are called _____.

7. A _____ has an infinite number of possible values.
   a. discrete observation
   b. continuous observation
   c. construct
   d. nominal variable

8. The values of a(n) _____ variable are names or categories.
   a. nominal
   b. ordinal
   c. interval
   d. ratio

9. Which one of the following is a measurement of a **nominal variable**?
   a. reaction time of an adult male measured before and after drinking an ounce of alcohol
   b. a high school senior's first, second, and third choice of colleges to attend
   c. classification of psychiatric patients as either "neurotic" or "psychotic"
   d. estimation of the number of red blood cells in a laboratory sample

10. Which one of the following is an **ordinal variable**?
    a. noon temperature in Boston measured in degrees Fahrenheit
    b. number of first-year college students enrolled at University X
    c. number of stocks sold on the New York Stock Exchange on a given day
    d. military rank from private to four-star general

11. Which one of the following is an **interval variable** but *not* a **ratio variable**?
    a. height (in inches or centimeters)
    b. weight (in pounds or kilograms)
    c. age (in years or days)
    d. temperature (°F or °C)

12. Which one of the following is a **ratio variable**?
    a. the number of times a laboratory monkey presses a bar in an experimental chamber during a one-hour period
    b. the temperature in degrees Celsius of a hospital patient
    c. a driver's order of finish in an automobile race
    d. a patient's rating of his own anxiety level on a scale in which 10 represents "low anxiety" and 100 represents "extreme anxiety"

13. The widely used computer program SPSS refers to _____ variables as scale variables, probably because measures of these variables may be analyzed using the same statistical procedures.
    a. nominal and ordinal
    b. ordinal and interval
    c. interval and ratio
    d. ordinal, interval, and ratio

14. Match each term on the left with a description on the right. (A description may be used more than once.)
    a._____ nominal variable   1. may be discrete or continuous
    b._____ ordinal variable   2. may only be discrete
    c._____ interval variable   3. may only be continuous
    d._____ ratio variable   4. may be neither discrete nor continuous

15. An educational psychologist is interested in whether performance on an achievement test is affected by classroom conditions. Accordingly, she administers the test to one group of students in a noisy environment and to another group of students in a quiet environment. Which of the following is the independent variable in this proposed study?
    a. intelligence
    b. achievement test score
    c. classroom conditions
    d. the gender of the student

16. In a certain study, participants in an experimental condition received an injection of the hormone epinephrine (adrenalin) whereas control-group participants received a placebo. Half the participants who received epinephrine were told that the treatment was a vitamin supplement and half were told the truth. Later, each participant was instructed to wait in a room with an individual who, unknown to the participant, was a confederate of the experimenter ("stooge"). Within a few minutes, the stooge began behaving according to a script—either in an obviously euphoric manner or an obviously angry manner. In this study, the dependent variable is:
    a. not described.
    b. the injection (epinephrine vs. placebo).
    c. the behavior of the stooge (angry vs. euphoric).
    d. whether the participant was told the truth or not.

17. A(n) _____ variable is any variable that systematically varies with the independent variable and makes it impossible to determine the cause of any observed changes in the dependent variable.
    a. confounding
    b. extraneous
    c. operational
    d. moderator

18. _____ influences an experiment by making the relations between variables less clear than they really are.

19. In a study of the effect of manipulations of variable M on variable N, _____ is (are) the dependent variable(s).
    a. variable M
    b. variable N
    c. both variable M and variable N
    d. neither variable M nor variable N

20. A(n) _____ scale or instrument is one that is consistent.
    a. operationally defined
    b. reliable
    c. valid
    d. ratio

21. A(n) _____ scale or instrument is one that measures what it was intended to measure.
    a. operationally defined
    b. reliable
    c. valid
    d. ratio

22. A large group of students received similar scores on the Stanford-Binet IQ test when it was administered in the eighth grade and again during their junior year of high school. The consistency of the scores observed at the two time points is most specifically a measure of _____.
    a. test bias
    b. test-retest reliability
    c. internal consistency
    d. predictive validity

23. Suppose that every individual who earns a passing score on a test of mechanical aptitude is hired by a very large automobile repair company. If these same individuals' scores on the test turn out to be strongly related to their supervisors' evaluations of their work at the end of their first year of employment, then the mechanical aptitude test has adequate _____.
    a. test-retest reliability
    b. predictive validity
    c. hypothetical validity
    d. construct reliability

24. A test that is:
    a. not reliable can not be valid.
    b. not valid can not be reliable.
    c. valid is also reliable.
    d. reliable is also valid.

25. The term _____ refers to the process of drawing conclusions about whether a particular relation between variables is supported by the evidence.
    a. hypothesis testing
    b. sampling
    c. validity
    d. reliability

26. An **operational definition** of a variable is a definition of the variable in terms of:
    a. its relationship to the independent and dependent variables.
    b. the procedures or operations used to measure or manipulate the variable.
    c. whether it is being used as the independent variable or the dependent variable.
    d. the network of theoretical constructs to which the variable is related.

27. In a study of the effectiveness of a certain new therapy for depression, 30 depressed individuals are randomly assigned to receive the new therapy and 30 other depressed persons are randomly assigned to receive a standard therapy for depression. After six months of therapy, the Beck Depression Inventory and structured interviews are used to assess each individual. Which one of the following indicates that this study is an **experiment**?
    a. random assignment of participants to conditions
    b. exposing the two groups to different forms of therapy
    c. the use of a double-blind procedure to control confounding variables
    d. This study is not an experiment.

28. The use of **random assignment** of participants to different conditions enables an investigator to:
    a. generalize the results of a study to other settings and populations.
    b. measure the relationship between two naturally-occurring variables.
    c. control for the effects of other variables that might affect the dependent variable.
    d. separate the actual effects of a treatment from belief in the effect of the treatment.

29. To control for the confounding of participants' expectations about the effects of an experimental treatment with its actual effects, a _____ is used in which participants do not know the condition to which they have been assigned.
    a. double-blind experiment
    b. quasi-experiment
    c. nonexperiment
    d. single-blind experiment

30. Participants exhibit a **placebo effect** when they:
    a. respond to subtle cues from the experimenter about how they should react to a treatment.
    b. show a greater response to the control condition than to the experimental condition.
    c. respond to a treatment according to their expectations of the treatment's effects.
    d. respond evasively to questions they deem to be too sensitive or personal.

31. Which one of the following reduces the possibility that an experimenter may unintentionally influence participants to respond in a certain manner?
    a. single-blind experiment
    b. double-blind experiment
    c. counterbalancing
    d. a pretest-posttest design

32. Researchers are exhibiting _____ when they inadvertently cue participants to respond to an experimental condition in a particular way.
    a. placebo effects
    b. demand characteristics
    c. interaction effects
    d. order effects

33. A researcher proposed to conduct an experiment to determine whether playing the Scrabble board game improves vocabulary. She suspected that individuals with higher IQs, more education, and higher incomes might have more extensive vocabularies. In this proposed study, IQ, education level, and income are _____ variables.
    a. dependent
    b. potentially confounding
    c. independent
    d. archival

34. A **quasi-experiment** may include all of the following *except*:
    a. a control group.
    b. random assignment of participants.
    c. manipulation of an independent variable.
    d. measurement of a dependent variable.

35. A *nonequivalent control group design with pretest and posttest* is an example of a(n):
    a. experiment.
    b. quasi-experiment.
    c. nonexperiment.
    d. double-blind experiment.

36. A **correlation** is:
    a. used to assess a cause-effect relationship between variables.
    b. an association between two or more, usually interval, variables.
    c. an association between two or more variables, both of which have been manipulated.
    d. an association between two or more variables, only one of which has been manipulated.

37. In correlational studies:
    a. the independent variable is manipulated.
    b. participants are randomly assigned to conditions.
    c. an association between two or more variables is assessed.
    d. at least one variable must be measured on a nominal scale.

38. A _____ is one in which participants experience only one level of the independent variable.
    a. between-groups research design
    b. within-groups research design
    c. counterbalanced design
    d. correlational design

39. Which of the following is (are) correct regarding **within-groups research designs**?
    a. Each participant experiences only one condition of the experiment.
    b. Each participant experiences all the conditions of the experiment.
    c. Within-groups designs are far more common than between-groups designs.
    d. Random assignment is frequently used to control order (e.g., practice) effects.

40. **Order effects** are unique to _____ research designs, and may be at least partially controlled by _____.
    a. between-groups; counterbalancing
    b. within-groups; random assignment to conditions
    c. between-groups; random assignment to conditions
    d. within-groups; counterbalancing

41. Which one of the following is *not* used in between-groups research designs?
    a. counterbalancing
    b. unbiased selection of participants
    c. inclusion of appropriate control groups
    d. random assignment of participants to conditions

42. Which of the following analyze existing records or documents instead of collecting new data?
    a. archival studies
    b. nonexperiments
    c. correlational studies
    d. quasi-experiments

ANSWERS TO CHAPTER 1 STUDY QUESTIONS

Question Number	Correct Answer	Question Number	Correct Answer
1	d, p. 3	20	b, p. 15
2	c, p. 3	21	c, p. 15
3	a, p. 3	22	b, p. 15
4	b, p. 3	23	b, p. 15
5	a, p. 6	24	a, p. 15
6	constructs (p. 6)	25	a, p. 17
7	b, pp. 6–7	26	b, p. 18
8	a, p. 7	27	a, p. 22
9	c, p. 7	28	c, p. 22
10	d, p. 7	29	d, p. 22
11	d, pp. 7–8 (Note that the Fahrenheit and Celsius scales do not include a true zero—that is, both scales include sub-zero values.)	30	c, p. 22
		31	b, p. 22
		32	b, p. 22
		33	b, p. 23
		34	b, p. 24
12	a, pp. 8–9	35	b, p. 24
13	c, p. 9	36	b, p. 25
14	a (2), b (2), c (1), d (1) p. 9	37	d, p. 25
		38	a, p. 26
15	c, p. 11	39	b, p. 26
16	a, p. 12	40	d, p. 26
17	a, p. 12	41	a, p. 26
18	Noise (p. 12)	42	a, p. 30
19	b, p. 12		

REFERENCES

Kety, S. S., Rosenthal, D., Wender, P. H., & Schulsinger, F. (1968). The types and prevalence of mental illness in the biological and adoptive families of adopted schizophrenics. In D. Rosenthal & S. S. Kety (Eds.), *The transmission of schizophrenia* (pp. 345–362). Oxford: Pergamon.

Kety, S. S., Rosenthal, D., Wender, P. H., & Schulsinger, F. (1976): Studies based on a total sample of adopted individuals and their relatives: why they were necessary, what they demonstrated and failed to demonstrate. *Schizophrenia Bulletin*, *2*, 413–428.

CHAPTER TWO

DESCRIPTIVE STATISTICS

Organizing, Summarizing, and Graphing Individual Variables

CHAPTER OUTLINE

Organizing Our Data: A First Step in Identifying Patterns
- Distributions: Four Different Ways to Describe Just One Variable
- Applying Visual Depictions of Data: Generating Research Questions

Central Tendency: Determining the Typical Score
- The Need for Alternative Measures of Central Tendency
- Mean: The Arithmetic Average
- Median: The Middle Score
- Mode: The Most Common Score
- The Effect of Outliers on Measures of Central Tendency
- An Early Lesson in Lying With Statistics: Which Central Tendency is "Best?"

Measures of Variability: Everyone Can't Be "Typical"
- Range: From the Lowest to the Highest Score
- Variance: The First Step in Calculating Standard Deviation
- Standard Deviation: Variation from the Mean

Shapes of Distributions: Applying the Tools of Descriptive Statistics
- Normal Distributions: The Silent Power Behind Statistics
- Skewed Distributions: When Our Data Are Not Symmetrical
- Bimodal and Multimodal Distributions: Identifying Distinctive Populations
- Kurtosis and Distributions: Tall and Skinny Versus Short and Wide

Digging Deeper into the Data: Alternate Approaches to Descriptive Statistics
- The Interquartile Range: An Alternative to the Range
- Statistics That Don't Focus on the Mean: Letting the Distribution Guide our Choice of Statistics

LEARNING OBJECTIVES

After studying this chapter, you should be able to:

1. Define each of the following terms and provide examples that are not in the text: *raw scores, distribution, frequency table, cumulative percentage, grouped frequency table, histogram, frequency polygon, central tendency, mean, statistics, parameters, median, mode, unimodal, bimodal, multimodal, outlier, range, standard deviation, deviation from the mean, variance, sum of squares, normal distribution, skewness, kurtosis, positively skewed data, floor effect, negatively skewed data, ceiling effect, mesokurtic, leptokurtic, platykurtic, interquartile range, first quartile, third quartile.*

2. Explain how a *frequency table, grouped frequency table, histogram,* and *frequency polygon* are constructed and describe the kinds of data distributions for which each of these techniques would be appropriate.

3. Describe the kinds of data distributions for which the *mean, median,* and *mode* would be appropriate (and inappropriate) as measures of *central tendency,* and explain how each of these descriptive statistics are determined from a distribution of raw data.

4. Explain how the *range, variance,* and *standard deviation* are computed, and describe the kinds of data distributions for which the range and standard deviation would be appropriate (and inappropriate) as measures of *variability*.

5. Compare and contrast *normal* and *nonnormal* distributions with respect to the properties of *modality, skewness,* and *kurtosis*.

6. Discuss the relation between *positively* and *negatively skewed* data distributions and the presence of *floor* and *ceiling effects*.

7. Explain how the *interquartile range* (*IQR*) is determined from the *first* and *third quartiles*. Discuss the advantage of reporting the *IQR* instead of the range as the preferred measure of variability within data distributions for which the *second quartile,* or median, is the most appropriate measure of central tendency. Explain how the *IQR* is used to determine the presence of outliers.

CHAPTER REVIEW

> Organizing Our Data: A First Step in Identifying Patterns

Descriptive statistics include tabular, graphical, and statistical methods of organizing and summarizing the information contained in samples of data. Tables and graphs offer visually appealing methods of organizing distributions of data and four are discussed in your text: frequency tables, grouped frequency tables, frequency histograms, and frequency polygons. A **frequency table** lists scores in one column and the frequencies with which each score was observed in the next column. An optional third column may be used to list cumulative percentages. A **grouped frequency table** is used to organize scores into intervals when the range of scores is too large to list each one. Frequency histograms and polygons are graphs used to display scores that have been organized into frequency or grouped frequency tables. Review your text for the steps to make a frequency table.

Frequency tables are used to organize and summarize data from any scale of measurement as long as the values are discrete and the range is limited. However, for interval and ratio data that represent values of continuous variables, a grouped frequency distribution is usually required.

Frequencies may also be displayed in a variant of a bar chart called a **histogram**. A histogram of the math anxiety ratings looks like this:

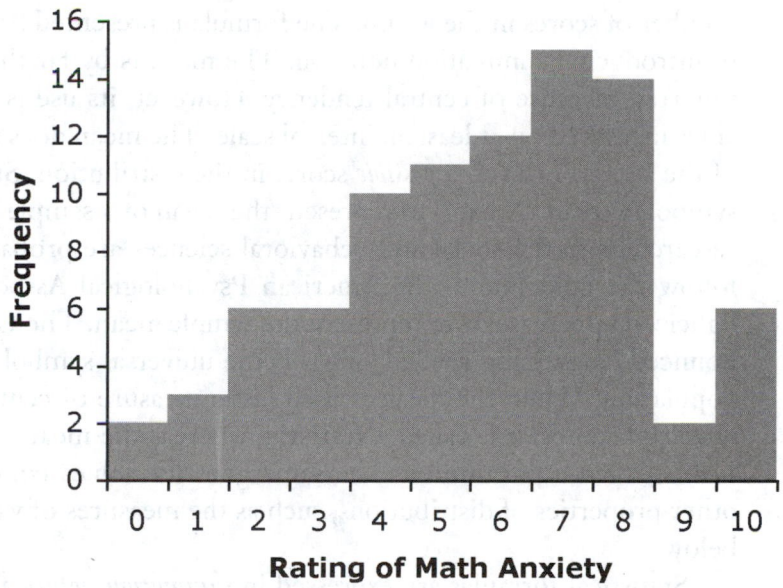

The frequency of each rating is represented by the height of the bar above that rating. The bars in a histogram are usually displayed with no gaps between them. There are no gaps between adjacent ratings because most, if not all, psychological variables that are measured on an interval or ratio scale are thought to have an underlying distribution that is continuous. It is only the limits of the measuring instrument that make the values appear to be discrete.

> Central Tendency: Determining the Typical Score

So far we've seen that samples of data may be *organized* using tables and graphs. Samples of data may be also be *summarized* by single values called descriptive statistics. Generally, two values are computed to summarize a group of scores: a measure of *central tendency* (or *center*) and a measure of *variability* (or *spread*).

Statistics that measure the **central tendency** of a group of scores are values considered to be *typical* or *representative* of all scores in the group. The *mean*, *median*, and *mode* all measure the center of a group of scores, but each defines "center" differently. The statistic used frequently depends upon the shape of the distribution and the scale of measurement.

Mean: The Arithmetic Average

The mean is probably the most familiar measure of central tendency, although you probably know it as the "average," a relatively general term that can refer to any measure of central tendency. The full name of the mean is the *arithmetic* mean, to distinguish it from the *geometric* mean and the *harmonic* mean, two measures of center that are almost never used as descriptive statistics. The arithmetic mean is computed by summing all of the scores and dividing by the number of scores in the group. The formula is presented below in the context of introducing summation notation. The mean is by far the most commonly reported measure of central tendency. However, its use is restricted to variables measured on at least an interval scale. The mean does not have to be one of the scores, or even a *possible* score, in the distribution. Statisticians use the symbol $\overline{X}$ (read "X bar") to represent the mean of a sample of scores, whereas researchers in the social and behavioral sciences are probably more likely to follow the guideline of the American Psychological Association and use an italicized uppercase M to represent the sample mean. The Greek letter μ (pronounced "mew" and spelled "mu") is the universal symbol for the mean of a population. When the mean is used [as] a measure of central tendency for a *sample* of scores, it is called a **statistic**, whereas the mean of an entire *population* is called a **parameter**. The same goes for values computed to describe other properties of distributions, such as the measures of variability described below.

Statistical formulas are expressed in *summation notation*, a system of symbols that represent scores, statistics, and the operations used to compute them. For example, the formula for the mean is:

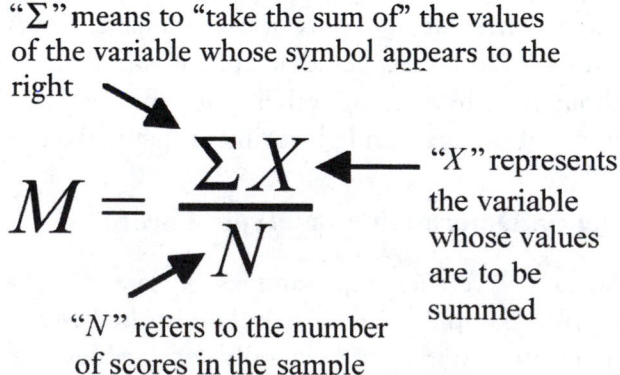

"Σ" means to "take the sum of" the values of the variable whose symbol appears to the right

$$M = \frac{\Sigma X}{N}$$

"X" represents the variable whose values are to be summed

"N" refers to the number of scores in the sample

Median: The Middle Score

The **median** is the *ordinal center* of a distribution, that is, the median is the middle score of a distribution in which the scores have been ranked in order. Thus half of the scores in a distribution are ranked below the median and half are ranked above the median. The symbol for the median is *Mdn*.

To determine the median, first arrange the scores in ascending or descending order, and locate the score that has the same number of scores above and below it. If N is even, then the median is the arithmetic mean of the two scores in the middle; if N is odd, then the median is the score in the middle; that is, no other steps are necessary.

Mode: The Most Common Score

Of the three most frequently used measures of central tendency, the mode is the easiest to determine and the least informative: The **mode** is simply the most frequently occurring score in the sample. In the array of scores below, the mode is 6, because this score was observed two times and no other score occurred more than once. If no score is observed more than once in a distribution, then there is no mode. If there are two scores that occurred with equal frequency, then the distribution is said to be **bimodal**. If more than two scores are observed with equal frequency, then the distribution is described as **multimodal**. The mode is the *only* measure of central tendency that may be used when the variable is measured on a nominal scale. The mode may also be used when the variable is measured on either an ordinal or equal-interval scale, but is less informative in these instances than either the mean or the median.

The Effect of Outliers on Measures of Central Tendency

The mean is sensitive to the *interval value*, whereas the median is sensitive only to the *ordinal position*, of each score in a distribution. Consider the following array of scores:

| 2, | 3, | 5, | 6, | 6, | 7, | 11, | 14, | 16, | 17, | 21 |

If the score "21" is changed to "210," the median remains the same (*Mdn* = 7), but the mean is markedly increased (from 9.82 to 27.00). Because the mean is sensitive to the value of each score in a distribution, it will always be "pulled" in the direction of extreme scores, or **outliers**. In contrast, the median is sensitive only to the ordinal position, or rank, of each score and will not be pulled toward outliers. For this reason, the mean is *not* the preferred measure of center for distributions that include outliers.

> Measures of Variability: Everyone Can't Be "Typical"

Range: From the Lowest to the Highest Score

A measure of central tendency is usually accompanied by a measure of **variability**, because distributions can be similar with regard to one of these measures but very different with regard to the other. The simplest to determine, but least informative measure of spread is the range. The **range** is computed by simply subtracting the smallest score from the largest. It is a crude measure of variability because it ignores all but the two most extremes scores.

$$Range = X_{max} - X_{min}$$

Variance: The First Step in Calculating Standard Deviation

The most commonly reported measure of variability is the **standard deviation.** This statistic is computed as the square root of the **variance**, a less commonly reported descriptive statistic but one that figures prominently in the calculation of several important inferential statistics. Both statistics measure the deviation of scores from the mean and thus require that the scores in the sample be measured on at least an interval scale. The symbol and definitional formula[1] for the variance is as follows:

$$SD^2 = \frac{\sum(X - M)^2}{N}$$

At the heart of the formulas for computing the variance and the standard deviation is the **sum of squares** (**SS**), a foundational concept for much of descriptive and inferential statistics. As you can see from the following formulas, the sum of squares is exactly what its name indicates: the sum of squared deviations of each score from the mean. The variance, then, is computed as the mean of these squared deviation scores:

$$SS = \sum(X - M)^2$$

$$SD^2 = \frac{SS}{N}$$

Following are the steps in computing the variance, using the definitional formula above:

1. Compute the mean.
2. Subtract the mean from each score, then square the difference.
3. Sum the squares that you computed in Step 2.
4. Divide the result of Step 3 by N, the number of scores.

---

[1] As the name suggests, a *definitional formula* for a statistic is closely related to its definition and thus facilitates learning to calculate, interpret, and use the statistic. Prior to the widespread availability of computing devices, statisticians used a computational formula to compute the variance and thereby avoided the rounding error that sometimes occurred when the mean was subtracted from each score.

Standard Deviation: Variation from the Mean

The shortcoming of the variance as a descriptive statistic is that it is an average of *squared* deviation scores and thus appears to inflate the spread in a distribution. To obtain a measure of spread that looks more like the unsquared data values themselves, the square root of the variance is taken, and the resulting statistic is called the **standard deviation**. The definitional formula describes the standard deviation as a sort-of-but-not-really "average" deviation score:

$$SD = \sqrt{\frac{\sum (X - M)^2}{N}}$$

Like M and $\overline{X}$, SD^2 and SD are symbols for sample statistics. Following is an abbreviated version of Table 2-7 from p. 70 in the text, showing the symbols for sample statistics and the corresponding symbols for population parameters. The symbols s and s^2 represent unbiased estimates of population parameters and will be introduced in Chapter 9.

	Sample Statistics	Population Parameters
Mean	$M, \overline{X}$	μ
Variance	SD^2, s^2	σ^2
Standard Deviation	SD, s	σ

> Shapes of Distributions: Applying the Tools of Descriptive Statistics

Normal Distributions: The Silent Power Behind Statistics

The normal, or "bell," curve is perhaps the most famous (or infamous) symbol in statistics. Its use in statistical analysis is demonstrated by noting that the values of most variables of interest to behavioral and social scientists are distributed in a manner that may be well-approximated by a normal curve. There are many normal curves, each one described by its mean and standard deviation. However, all normal curves share the following characteristics.

- *unimodal*: a single mode or peak
- *symmetric*: the half of the distribution to the left of the center is the mirror image of the half to the right of center
- *bell-shaped*: the shape follows in part from the first two properties, but there are other shapes that are unimodal and symmetric (e.g., an equilateral triangle has a single peak, is symmetric about the center, but is clearly not bell-shaped)
- *central tendency convergence*: the mean, median, and mode are located at the same point along the horizontal axis of a normal curve

Please note that the properties listed above are also descriptive of distributions that are not exactly normal in shape. This fact serves as a useful reminder that the normal curve is a mathematical function as opposed to a distribution of actual measurements. That's why we should always be careful to say that the normal curve is *well-approximated* by many distributions of various measures of interest to scientists from a variety of disciplines.

Skewed Distributions: When Our Data Are Not Symmetrical

Skewness refers to how the frequencies of the scores are distributed along the horizontal axis. Distributions are **positively skewed** if most of the scores are bunched at the low end of the range of scores with progressively fewer scores falling near the high end. The long "tail" extends to the *right*. In a positively skewed distribution, the mode is less than the median, and the median is less than the mean:

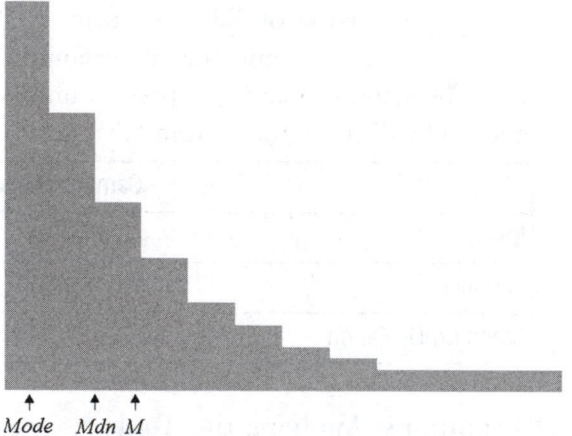

Distributions may be *positively skewed* because of a **floor effect.** A floor effect occurs when most of the scores "pile up" at the lower end of the distribution; because of the presence of a lower limit or "floor."

Distributions that are **negatively skewed** extend in the opposite direction; that is, most of the scores are bunched at the high end of the range, with the tail extending to the *left*. In a negatively skewed distribution, the mode is greater than the median, and the median is greater than the mean:

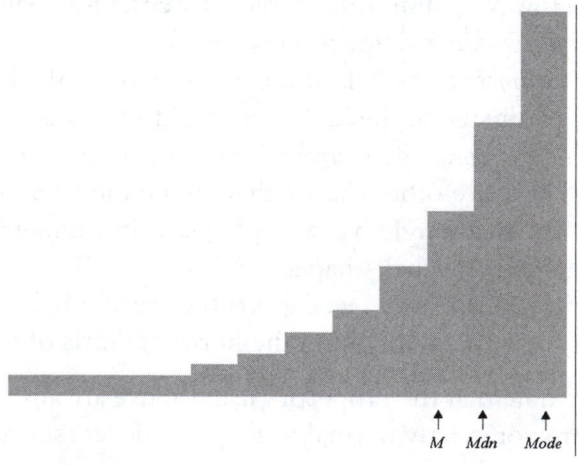

Distributions may be *negatively skewed* because of a **ceiling effect**. A ceiling effect occurs when most of the scores are clustered at the high end of the distribution because of the presence of an upper limit or "ceiling."

Bimodal and Multimodal Distributions: Identifying Distinctive Populations

The modality of a distribution refers to the number of distinct peaks. A peak represents a score occurring with a high frequency, and the term "mode" refers to the score with the highest frequency of occurrence. A **unimodal** distribution has only one distinct peak, whereas a **bimodal** distribution has two distinct peaks. A distribution with several distinct peaks is described as **multimodal**.

Kurtosis and Distributions: Tall and Skinny Versus Short and Wide

The **kurtosis** of a distribution is a statistic that expresses the concentration of scores in the center and the tails relative to a normal distribution. A distribution that has fewer scores in the center has a flatter peak and its tails tend to be relatively short and thin compared to the peak and tails of a normal distribution. Distributions with flatter peaks and shorter, thinner tails are described as **platykurtic**. In contrast, a distribution that has a taller peak and longer, thicker tails than a normal distribution is termed a **leptokurtic** distribution.

The kurtosis statistic for a platykurtic distribution has a negative value, whereas the kurtosis statistic for a leptokurtic distribution has a positive value. A normal distribution is described as **mesokurtic** and has a kurtosis of 0.

Kurtosis may refer to either the tails or the center of a distribution, but the statistic is more sensitive to the relative "heaviness" of the tails. All skewed distributions are leptokurtic, so kurtosis is almost always described as an attribute of distributions that are unimodal and more or less symmetric.

> Digging Deeper into the Data: Alternate Approaches to Descriptive Statistics

The Interquartile Range: An Alternative to the Range

As just noted, the mean and standard deviation are sensitive to the values of every score in a distribution and thus should not be used to describe distributions that are badly skewed by outliers. The range is not a suitable alternative measure of variability, because this statistic is sensitive only to the minimum and maximum scores, completely ignoring the spread of scores between these two, perhaps outlying, extremes. An alternative measure of spread is the **interquartile range**, a statistic that defines the middle half of the scores and is thus insensitive to the scores at the extreme ends of a distribution. As its name suggests, the interquartile range is a range of scores between (*inter* = *between*) two quartiles. *Quartiles* are scores that divide a distribution into four equal groups. The first quartile ($Q1$) is the score that equals or exceeds 25%

of the scores; the second quartile ($Q2$) equals or exceeds 50% of the scores (as you can see, $Q2$ is also the median); and the third quartile ($Q3$) is greater than or equal to 75% of the scores. The interquartile range (IQR) is the range of scores between the first and third quartiles; $IQR = Q3 - Q1$. The IQR shares with the median an insensitivity to scores at the extreme ends of a distribution, and for this reason is usually reported as a measure of variability when the median is reported as a measure of center.

The interquartile range is often reported as a derived component of a descriptive set of statistics called the five-number summary. The five numbers that comprise this summary are the minimum and maximum values as well as $Q1$, $Q2$, and $Q3$. The inclusion of the minimum and maximum data values in the five-number summary provides information about the tails of a distribution that the quartiles ignore.

The five-number summary provides a measure of center ($Q2$, or the median), a measure of spread within the middle half of the scores (IQR), and a measure of the entire range of scores (the minimum and maximum values). Notice, however, that no single statistic conveys a complete sense of the skewness of this distribution. This illustrates the importance of graphic displays of data; there is no other way to view a complete "picture" of what's going on.

The IQR is also used to identify outliers. An outlier is defined as any data value that is more than 1.5 IQRs above $Q3$ or more than 1.5 IQRs below $Q1$. For the current events scores displayed above, an outlier in the right tail is any value that is more than 1.5(3) = 4.5 units above $Q3$. So, an outlier in the right tail of the distribution must exceed $Q3 + (1.5)IQR = 6 + (1.5)(3) = 6 + 4.5 = 10.5$. The three scores, 15, 17, and 19 are all outliers according to this criterion. There are no outliers in the left tail, because there are no negative scores: $Q1 - (1.5)IQR = 3 - (1.5)(3) = 3 - 4.5 = -1.5$.

Statistics That Don't Focus on the Mean: Letting the Distribution Guide Our Choice of Statistics

The text discusses several examples of distributions that suggest analyses that focus on statistics other than the mean. For example, a graph of the death rate recorded for the pandemic of 1918–1919 showed a multimodal distribution, with predictable peaks occurring for infants and the elderly, the two most vulnerable age groups within any society. However, in marked contrast to the plot of mortality rates for different ages during the flu pandemic of 1928–1929, a third peak was observed for young adults in the 25–30 age range—a group that would ordinarily be regarded as least vulnerable to disease (see Figure 2-16 on p. 81 in the text). As noted by the authors of your text, focusing on the mean mortality rate in a multimodal distribution such as this one ignores the most important aspect of the data. Other examples cite a comparison of the variability within distributions as the focus of interest.

STUDY QUESTIONS

1. Which of the following may be displayed in a **frequency table**?
   a. the different values of a variable
   b. the number of times each variable value was chosen by a participant ✓
   c. a variable value with a frequency of zero (i.e., no scores match this value)
   d. All the answers are correct. p. 42-43

2. A frequency table may be used to describe _____ data.
   a. nominal
   b. ordinal
   c. interval or ratio
   d. All the answers are correct.

3. A **grouped frequency table** is required when working with measures of a(n) _____ variable.
   a. continuous
   b. interval or ratio   p. 46
   c. ordinal or nominal
   d. All the answers are correct.

4 . A **histogram** may be constructed from:
   a. any sample of data as long as there are at least two scores for each individual. ✗
   b. a frequency table but not a grouped frequency table. OR
   c. a grouped frequency table but not a frequency table.
   d. either a frequency table or a grouped frequency table. ✓ P. 49

5. *Unlike* a bar graph, a histogram:
   a. displays points connected by lines to represent frequencies.
   b. is used to display frequencies for nominal variables. ✓
   c. is used to display frequencies for interval variables. P. 49-50
   d. does all of these.

6. A **frequency polygon** is a type of _____.
   a. table ✓
   b. line graph   P. 51
   c. bar graph
   d. descriptive statistic

7. The _____ is the most commonly used measure of central tendency.
   a. mean ✓
   b. median   p. 56.
   c. mode
   d. range

8. Consider the following sample of scores:
   13, 18, 9, 27, 15, 28, 5, 16, 21, 23, 29, 15, 15
   What is the **mean**?
   (a.) 18
   b. 13
   c. 15
   d. 16

9. Which of the following is *not* a symbol for the mean?
   (a.) X
   b. M
   c. $\overline{X}$
   d. μ

10. Complete the analogy: *Population* mean is to _____ as *sample* mean is to _____.
    a. statistic; parameter
    (b.) parameter; statistic
    c. descriptive statistic; inferential statistic
    d. inferential statistic; descriptive statistic

11. What does the symbol **ΣX** tell you to do?
    (a.) Find the sum of the scores in the distribution of the variable X.
    b. Find the mean of the scores in the distribution of the variable X.
    c. Find the square root of the scores in the distribution of the variable X.
    d. Subtract the mean from each of the scores in the distribution of the variable X.

12. The _____ of a group of scores is the score that is greater than half the scores and less than half the scores.
    a. mode
    (b.) median   *isn't it interquartile range?*   *Pg. 59*
    c. mean
    ✗ (d.) None of these answers are correct.

13. Consider the following sample of scores: *5, 9, 13, 15, 15, 15, 15, 16, 18, 21, 23, 27, 28, 29*
    13, 18, 9, 27, 15, 15, 28, 5, 16, 21, 23, 29, 15, 15
    What is the **median**?
    a. 18
    b. 15
    (c.) 15.5
    d. 16

14. For any group of scores ordered from lowest to highest, the _____ is the value that results when you divide the number of scores by 2 and add 0.5 to the quotient.
    a. mean   *P. 59*
    ✗ (b.) median
    c. mode   *b/c it's odd #.*
    (d.) ordinal position of the median

15. The _____ is the most frequently occurring score in a group of scores.
   a. mean
   b. mode
   c. median
   d. None of these answers are correct.

16. A(n) _____ distribution has more than one mode.
   a. unimodal
   b. bimodal
   c. multimodal
   d. bimodal or multimodal

17. When the data are values of a(n) _____ variable, the mode is the only appropriate measure of central tendency.
   a. interval
   b. nominal
   c. ordinal
   d. None of these answers are correct.

18. Consider the following ages of undergraduate students enrolled in a senior seminar on the psychology of aging:
   21, 22, 22, 23, 24, 22, 21, 63, 22, 24, 22, 25, 23, 22
   Which measure(s) of central tendency is (are) representative of these data?
   a. the mean
   b. the median
   c. the mode
   d. the median and the mode

19. A(n) _outlier_ is an extreme score that is either very low or very high in comparison to the other scores in a sample.

20. When your data do not indicate a clear preference for one measure of central tendency over another, you should report the:
   a. mean.
   b. median.
   c. mode.
   d. mean, median, and mode.

21. Which of the following measures of variability depend(s) on only two scores?
   a. the standard deviation
   b. the variance
   c. the range
   d. the standard deviation and the variance

22. The variance is most closely related to which of the following statistics?
    a. the range
    ✓ b. the interquartile range
    c. the median
    (d.) the standard deviation

23. Because the _____ is based on squared deviation scores (which do not give an at-a-glance sense of how spread out the original raw scores are), it is reported only occasionally as a descriptive statistic.
    a. standard deviation
    b. range
    (c.) variance
    ✗(d.) average deviation

✗ 24. The deviation is the typical amount by which the scores in a sample vary from the mean. Stanard

25. The most commonly used measure of variability is the:
    ✓ a. variance.
    b. range.
    c. interquartile range.
    (d.) standard deviation.

26. To compute the **sum of squares** for a sample of scores you would:
    ✗ (a.) sum all of the scores, square the sum, and divide this sum by the number of scores.
    b. square each score, subtract the mean from each squared score, and sum the differences.
    (c.) subtract the mean from each score, square each difference, and sum the squared differences.
    d. square each score, sum the squared scores, and divide this sum by the number of scores.

27. Which of the following is a (are) symbol(s) for the sample variance?
    a. s^2 and σ^2
    ✓ b. SD^2 and σ^2
    (c.) s^2 and SD^2
    d. σ^2, s^2, and SD^2

28. Which one of the following is a formula for the variance?
    ✓ a. $\sqrt{\dfrac{\Sigma(X-M)^2}{N}}$ (b.) $\dfrac{\Sigma(X-M)^2}{N}$

    c. $\Sigma\sqrt{\dfrac{(X-M)^2}{N}}$ d. $\dfrac{\Sigma(X-M))}{N}$

29. The standard deviation is the:
    a. square of the variance.
    b. square root of the variance. ✓
    c. average deviation score.
    d. sum of squared deviations.

30. Which of the following describe(s) a **normal distribution**?
    a. unimodal, symmetrical, and bell–shaped
    b. bimodal, symmetrical, and bell–shaped ✓
    c. unimodal, asymmetrical, and positively skewed
    d. unimodal, asymmetrical, and negatively skewed

31. The values of most variables that are of interest to researchers in the social and behavioral sciences have a _____ distribution.
    a. normal
    b. positively skewed ✓
    c. negatively skewed
    d. bimodal

32. A _____ distribution is one in which most of the scores are at the high end of the scale with relatively few scores in the middle and lower end.
    a. platykurtic
    b. positively skewed   p.74 ??
    c. negatively skewed
    d. mesokurtic

33. The tail of a _____ distribution extends to the left.
    a. normal
    b. positively skewed   negatively skewed ✓
    c. positively skewed
    d. mesokurtic

34. When a distribution is **positively skewed**, the:
    a. median is greater than the mean.
    b. mean and median are the same. ✓
    c. mean is greater than the median.
    d. mean is platykurtic and the median is leptokurtic

35. The presence of a **ceiling effect** is usually indicated by a _____ distribution of scores.
    a. positively skewed ✓
    b. negatively skewed
    c. symmetric and unimodal
    d. rectangular

36. Whether a distribution is called *unimodal*, *bimodal*, or *multimodal* depends upon the:
    a. thickness of the tails.
    b. number of high points or peaks. ✓
    c. location of the high points or peaks.
    d. range of scores, from lowest to highest.

37. A single frequency polygon that displays the heights of a large representative sample of men and a large representative sample of women would be described as _____.
    a. positively skewed
    b. negatively skewed ✓
    c. unimodal
    d. bimodal

38. The term **kurtosis** refers to whether a distribution has _____ than a normal distribution.
    a. more extreme scores (outliers)
    b. thicker or thinner tails ✓
    c. more negative or positive scores
    d. more or fewer peaks

39. The **interquartile range** is the:
    a. middle 50% of the scores. ✗
    b. range of scores within one standard deviation of the mean.
    c. range of scores within two standard deviations of the mean.
    d. difference between the maximum score and the minimum score divided by 4.

Dosen't make sense

ANSWERS TO CHAPTER 2 STUDY QUESTIONS

Question Number	Correct Answer
1	d, pp. 42–43
2	e, pp. 42–43
3	a, p. 46 (Not all interval or ratio data are measurements of a continuous variable. For example, number of siblings or number of times voted in the last five years are discrete variables, and the limited range of values of these variables would be displayed in a frequency table.)
4	d, p. 49
5	c, pp. 49–50
6	b, p. 51
7	a, p. 56
8	a, p. 56
9	a, p. 57
10	b, pp. 57–58
11	a, p. 58
12	b, p. 59
13	c, p. 59 (The median is 15.5, the average of the two middle scores: 5, 9, 13, 15, 15, 15, **15, 16**, 18, 21, 23, 27, 28, 29)
14	d, p. 59 (The formula results in the ordered position, or rank, of the median—not the median, itself—for an odd number of scores. When there is an even number of scores, the formula will result in a value that lies midway between the ordered positions of the two middle scores. The average of these two scores is the median.)

Question Number	Correct Answer
15	b, p. 59
16	d, p. 60
17	b, pp. 61, 63
18	d, pp. 61–62 (The median and the mode are both 22. The mean is pulled in the direction of the outlier and thus misrepresents the typical student's age.)
19	outlier (p. 62)
20	d, p. 63
21	c, p. 67
22	d, p. 67
23	c, pp. 68–69
24	standard deviation (p. 67)
25	d, p. 67
26	c, p. 68
27	c, p. 69
28	b, p. 69
29	b, p. 69
30	a, p. 72
31	a, p. 72
32	c, p. 74
33	b, p. 74
34	c, p. 74 (see Figure 2-12)
35	b, p. 74
36	b, p. 75
37	d, p. 75
38	b, pp. 72, 75
39	d, p. 79

CHAPTER THREE

VISUAL DISPLAYS OF DATA

Graphs That Tell a Story

CHAPTER OUTLINE

Uses of Graphs: Clarifying Danger, Exposing Lies, and Gaining Insight
- Graphing in the Information Age: A Critical Skill
- "The Most Misleading Graph Ever Published": The Cost and Quality of Higher Education
- "The Best Statistical Graph Ever Created": Napoleon's Disastrous March to Moscow

Common Types of Graphs: A Graph Designer's Building Blocks
- Scatterplots: Observing Every Data Point
- Line Graphs: Searching for Trends
- Bar Graphs: An Efficient Communicator
- Pictorial Graphs: Choosing Clarity over Cleverness
- Pie Charts: Are Pie Charts Passé?

How to Build a Graph: Dos and Don'ts
- APA Style: Graphing Guidelines for Social Scientists
- Choosing the Type of Graph: Understanding Our Variables
- The Limitations of Graphic Software: Who is Responsible for the Visual Display?
- Creating the Perfect Graph: General Guidelines

Graphing Literacy: Learning to Lie Versus Creating Knowledge
- Lying with Statistics and Graphs: Eleven Sophisticated Techniques
- The Future of Graphs: Breaking the Fourth Wall
- The Uses and Misuses of Statistics: It's Not Just What You Draw, It's How You Draw It

Digging Deeper into the Data: The Box Plot

LEARNING OBJECTIVES

After studying this chapter, you should be able to:

1. Define each of the following terms and provide examples that are not in the text: *scatterplot, range-frame, linear relation, nonlinear relation, line graph, time plot or time series plot, bar graph, Pareto chart, pictorial graph, pie chart, table, figure, defaults, chartjunk, Moiré vibrations, grids, ducks, sparklines, box plot, whiskers.*

2. Discuss how graphs are used to inform and to mislead. Include in your discussion a brief description of each of the four "lies" depicted in "the most misleading graph ever published."

3. Describe the kinds of variable relationships that are appropriately displayed in scatterplots, line graphs (including time series plots), and bar graphs (including Pareto charts). Discuss the limitations of pictorial graphs and pie charts.

4. Explain the distinction between *tables* and *figures*, including the conditions that recommend the use of one over the other and how each should be constructed according to the editorial guidelines of the American Psychological Association. Your explanation should include an identification of some elements (e.g., *chartjunk, moiré patterns, grids,* and *ducks*) that clutter and thereby obscure the story told by a figure.

5. Discuss the importance of graphing literacy as it relates to recent developments in computer technology and the increasing access to information associated with these developments. Include in your discussion an identification and brief description of the 11 ways in which graphs may be used inappropriately to distort information and deceive consumers of that information. Wrap up your discussion with a brief description of some recent advances in graphing tools, including *sparklines* and interactive graphs.

6. Discuss the use of *box plots* as graphical displays of the five-number summary discussed in Chapter 2. Your discussion should include an explanation of how box plots are constructed as well as how the *whiskers* of a box plot may be used to identify outliers in a data set.

CHAPTER REVIEW

> ### Uses of Graphs: Clarifying Danger, Exposing Lies, and Gaining Insight

An ability to inform, or even persuade, with pictorial descriptions of information is becoming increasingly important as advances in computer technology enable access to information that was almost unfathomable just a few decades ago. Viewed in this context, it is very important that students in the behavioral sciences become critical consumers of that information as they acquire the skills to create effective graphs and interpret visual displays of data encountered routinely in the popular media and the professional literature.

A few basics should establish a solid foundation as you pursue the goal of graphic literacy. A useful starting point is to examine a graph that Michael Friendly of York University labeled "the most misleading graph ever published." The graph appeared on the cover of the December 7, 2000 edition of the *Ithaca Times* and is reproduced in Figure 3-1 on p. 96 in your text. The graph/cover purports to relate the rising cost of an education at Cornell University to changes in the quality of that education but does so in an alarmingly misleading fashion. You should review the complete discussion in the text of the deceptions and distortions in the graph.

Graphic literacy is a critical thinking skill. Remember also that the details of a graph's appearance are determined by you, the graph's creator. There are default choices built into graphics software programs, but it is your responsibility to override those defaults as you build your graph with its major purpose in mind: to clearly and effectively depict the relations between variables. During the construction of a graph, each seemingly trivial decision point is an opportunity to engage rather than dupe, enlighten rather than mislead. The graph that you create says something about you. What would you like that message to be?

> Common Types of Graphs: A Graph Designer's Building Blocks

The histograms and polygons introduced in Chapter 2 are graphic displays of the frequencies of single variables measured on either an interval or ratio scale. As such, they are used most frequently during the initial steps of data analysis to identify patterns in raw data and are very rarely encountered in either the popular media or the professional literature. The histograms and polygons that appear in the published literature are most likely to be displays of the distributions of demographic characteristics of research participants such as age, income, or years of formal education. However, these are more commonly described in the text of the report with statements that include the mean, median, and standard deviation. The results sections of published articles are far more likely to include graphs that depict the relation between two or more variables. These multivariable graphs include *scatterplots*, *line graphs*, *bar graphs*, and (less frequently) *pictorial graphs* and *pie charts*.

A **scatterplot** is used to portray the relation between two variables that are measured on an interval or ratio scale. The variable designated as the "X" variable is conceptualized as the *independent variable* (the variable whose values are used to predict the values of the other variable), and the horizontal (X) axis of the scatterplot should be titled with the name of the independent variable. The other variable, designated as "Variable Y," is the *dependent variable* (the variable whose values may be predicted by, and thus depend on, those of the independent variable), and the title of the vertical (Y) axis should be the name of the dependent variable. Each pair of scores for a given participant is plotted as a single point at the intersection of the score on the independent variable and the score on the dependent variable.

The problem of determining the minimum values used to label the axes of a scatterplot is solved by a range-frame. A **range-frame** defines the range of values displayed on the axes of a scatterplot or similar graph by the minimum and maximum scores observed in the sample. This means that scores that are beyond the range of scores in the sample and scores that are impossible (e.g., an SAT section score below 200) will not be represented on the axes of the graph. The idea is to increase the ratio of data ink to total ink by erasing unnecessary ink—in this case, the parts of the axes that are not within the score ranges. The following figure contrasts a scatterplot of the relation between scores on the math section of the SAT and final grade in an introductory statistics course with a range-frame depicting the same relation.

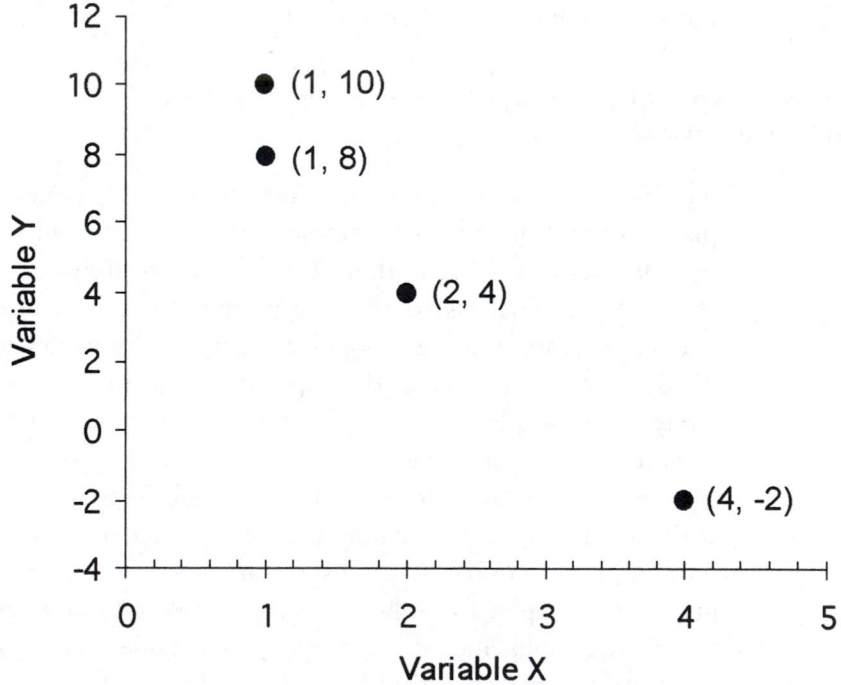

Although scatterplots sometimes appear in research articles, they are constructed primarily to determine whether there is a **linear relation** between the variables. A linear relation is observed if the points in a scatterplot may be approximated by a straight line as in the scatterplot on the previous page. If the relation appears to be linear, the statistical methods described in Chapters 5 (correlation) and 6 (regression) may be applied to determine the degree to which the variables are linearly related (correlation) and to predict values of the dependent variable from values of the independent variable (regression). A scatterplot will also reveal a **nonlinear relation** between variables, such as the relation between arousal and performance described by the Yerkes-Dodson law. In addition to disclosing a pattern of bivariate relation, a scatterplot reveals outliers that may be distorting or inflating the degree of linear association between the variables.

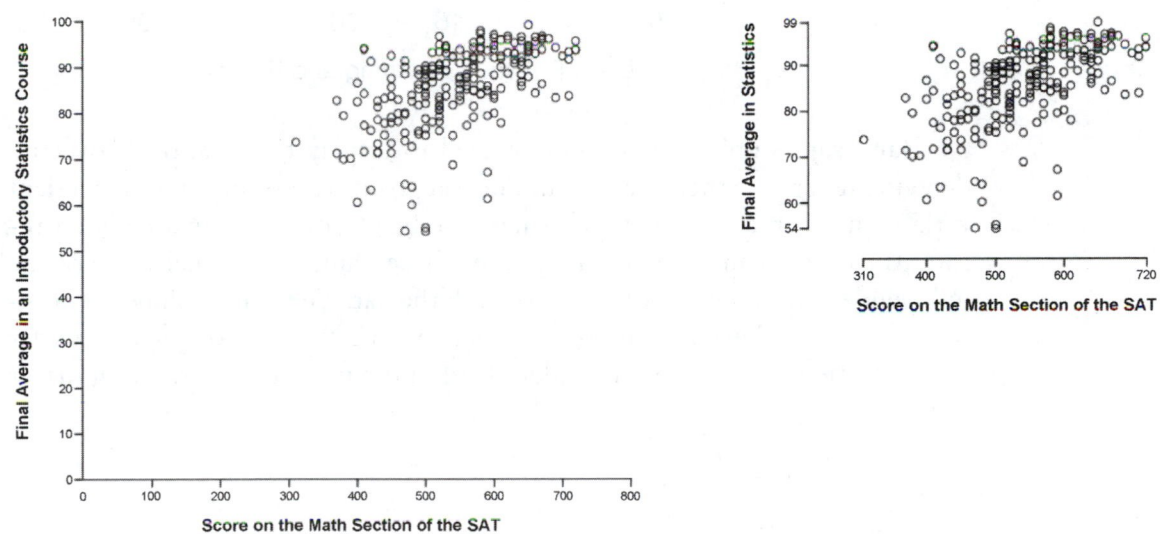

Like a scatterplot, a **line graph** depicts the relation between variables measured on an interval or ratio scale. A key difference, of course, is that a line graph features a continuous line to represent changes in the dependent variable as a function of changes in the independent variable. Fitting a line to the points in a scatterplot transforms the scatterplot into a kind of line graph that may be used to predict values of the dependent variable from values of the independent variable. However, the line graphs that appear in research articles generally depict changes in the dependent variable over time (a **time-series plot**) or some other continuously distributed interval or ratio variable such as temperature. A line graph that figures prominently in the history of psychology is the "forgetting curve" constructed from data recorded by Hermann Ebbinghaus, a nineteenth-century experimental psychologist who used himself as his experimental subject. The graph can be seen on the following page.

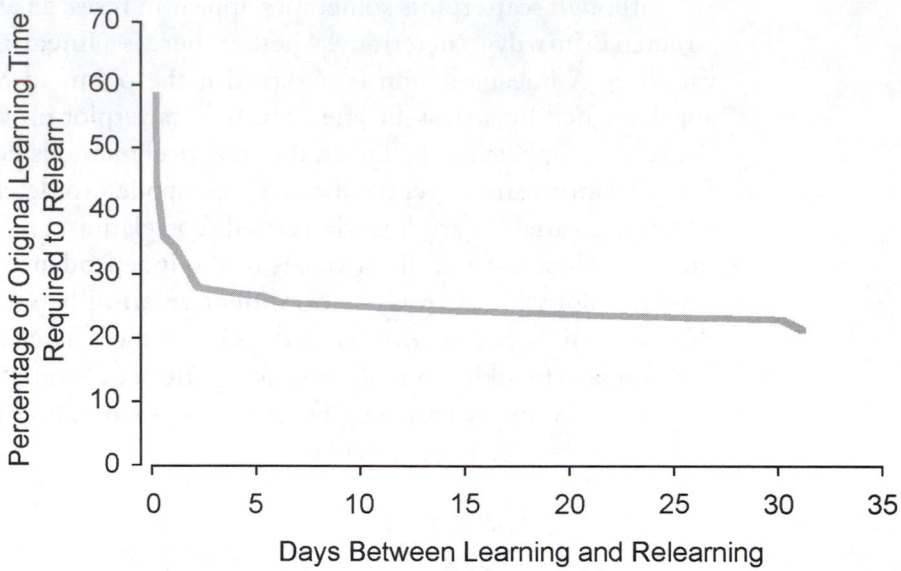

Bar graphs are most commonly used to display the relation between a dependent variable measured on an interval or ratio scale and an independent variable measured on a nominal scale. The height of each bar usually corresponds to the mean score for the group whose name (a nominal value of the independent variable) appears just beneath the bar. The bar graph below compares the mean departure times for drivers exiting their parking spaces under two conditions: alone ("No Intruder") and in the presence of a waiting driver ("Intruder").

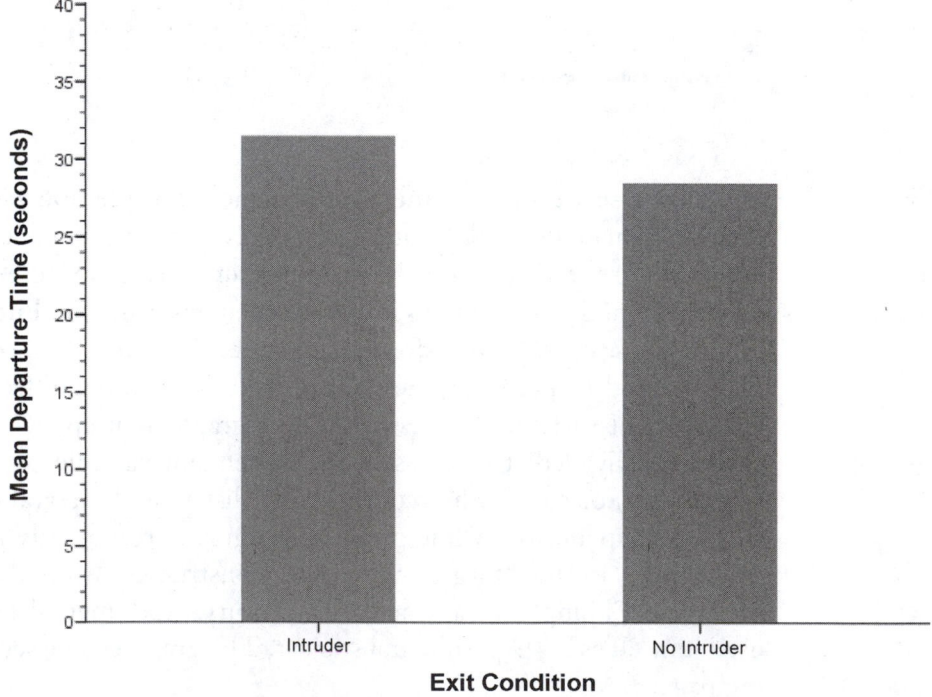

The versatility of bar graphs is illustrated by **Pareto charts**, bar graphs in which the bars are arranged in order with the highest bar on the left and the lowest bar on the right. Pareto charts are used when there are several categories of an independent variable. The world's 11 most populous countries (http://www.nationmaster.com/) are arranged in alphabetical order in the bar graph below on the left. The Pareto chart on the right facilitates a more direct comparison by ordering the countries according to population (see also Figure 3-12 on p. 113 in the text).

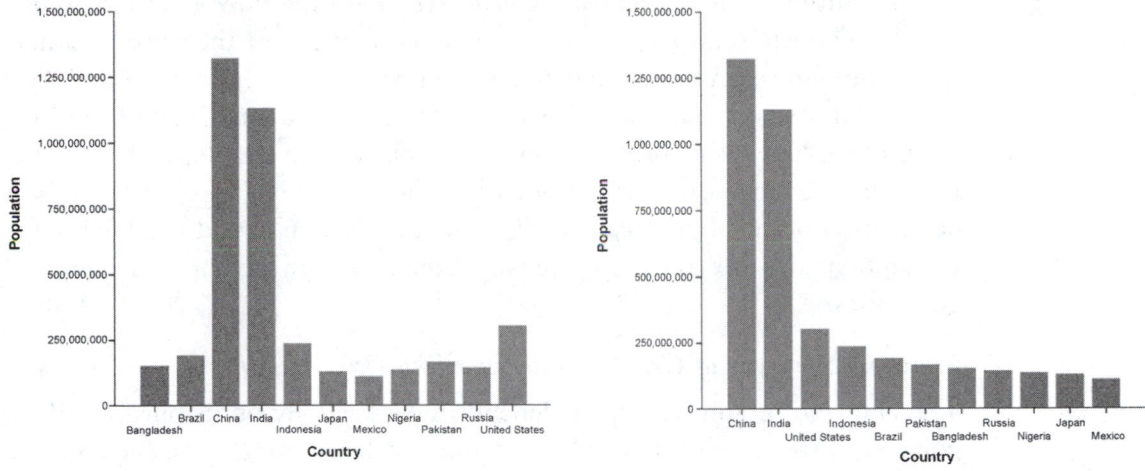

Pictorial graphs and pie charts appear in the popular media but should not be used to present research results. As its name suggests, a **pictorial graph** uses a picture or symbol instead of a bar to indicate the value of the dependent variable for each category of the independent variable. A **pie chart** is divided into slices that represent the categories of a single independent variable. The area of each slice represents the proportion, or percentage of cases in that category. Because proportions and percentages may be more clearly presented in a bar graph, pie charts are indeed passé.

> ### How to Build a Graph: Dos and Don'ts

If a graph is worth constructing, then the following guidelines should be observed:

- Follow the basic rules of graph construction.
- Make sure that the graph effectively addresses your hypothesis.
- Include all of the data that you included in your analysis.
- Include only the independent and dependent variables in your graph.
- Do not substitute a confounding variable for the independent variable.
- If the graph requires a key to symbols (figure legend), make sure that it is easy to interpret.

- Construct a "clean" graph that communicates the message in your data in an orderly, efficient manner, without resort to "gimmicks" such as ducks and other forms of chartjunk.
- Assume responsibility for the graphs that you create.

APA Style: Graphing Guidelines for Social Scientists

Authors who wish to submit research or review articles for publication in one of the behavioral sciences generally adhere to the editorial guidelines found in the 5th edition of the *Publication Manual of the American Psychological Association* (2001). The APA editors provide detailed instructions for the construction of tables and figures. A **table** is defined in the text as "a presentation of data, typically quantitative, that is typed as text in rows and columns" (text page 119). A **figure** is "any visual presentation of data other than a table, such as a photograph, drawing, or, most frequently, a graph" (text page 119). A brief description of each figure, called a *figure caption*, is numbered to match the figure and typed as text on a separate page. Refer to your text for details on APA guidelines.

Choosing the Type of Graph: Understanding Our Variables

The choice of graphical display depends most basically on its purpose. If the purpose of the graph is to display a frequency distribution, then the choice is between a bar graph and a histogram or frequency polygon. Use a bar graph if the variable is measured on a nominal or ordinal scale, and a histogram or polygon if the variable is measured on an interval or ratio scale. If the purpose of the graph is to display the relation between an independent variable and a dependent variable, then the choice depends on the type of independent variable—that is, the scale on which the independent variable is measured. (We are assuming that the dependent variable is measured on an interval or ratio scale. Methods of analysis used when the dependent variable is measured on a nominal or ordinal scale are discussed in Chapters 13 and 14, respectively.) If the independent variable is measured on an interval or ratio scale, then the appropriate display is a scatterplot or a line graph. If the independent variable is measured on a nominal scale, then a bar graph is used to display the relation between the variables. A bar graph can accommodate a second, or even a third, independent variable.

The Limitations of Graphic Software: Who is Responsible for the Visual Display?

The GIGO ("garbage in, garbage out") acronym reminds us that a computer is a tool, the effectiveness of which is determined by the skill of the person wielding it. If you abandon responsibility for the appearance of your graph to the computer software's **default** (built-in, pre-selected) options ("garbage in"), you should not be surprised when the graph that results is completely unsuitable for your purpose ("garbage out"). The graph on the left reflects the default settings for creating a line graph in the Macintosh edition of the spreadsheet program Microsoft Excel. The version on the right was edited to meet APA specifications.

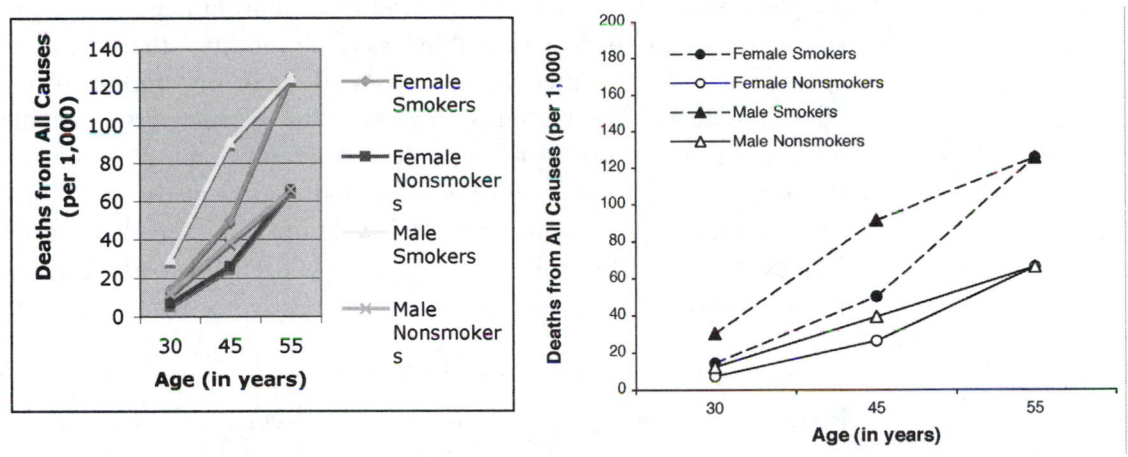

Creating the Perfect Graph: General Guidelines

Two general guidelines to keep in mind as you prepare to create a graph are:

1. The terms that appear in the graph (e.g., the names of the independent and dependent variables, the terms used to label the symbols in the figure legend, and any terms in the figure caption) should match those used in the text of your report.

2. The graph should be a clearly presented, complete representation of the relation between the variables displayed therein. If the reader has to return to the text to understand your graph, then you have not met this basic requirement.

Default options in computer software are likely to place *chartjunk* in your graph. **Chartjunk** is a term coined by Edward Tufte that refers to "any unnecessary information or feature in a graph that detracts from a viewer's ability to understand the data" (text page 122). Examples of chartjunk include *moiré vibrations*, *grids*, and *ducks*. **Moiré vibrations** are "any of the patterns that computers provide as options to fill in bars" (text page 122). Grids and at least one duck are included among the default options displayed in the graph on the left above. The **grids** are the thin lines extending horizontally across the graph, whereas the *duck* is the dark gray shadows outlining the symbols and the lines connecting them. More generally, a **duck** is any feature added to the graph that is intended to "dress up" the data but which more often obscures it. Additional examples of graphical ducks include the use of "fancy fonts" and "cutesy pictures."

> ## Graphing Literacy: Learning to Lie Versus Creating Knowledge

Lying with Statistics and Graphs: Eleven Sophisticated Techniques

1. *The false face validity lie.* This method of deception occurs when the operational definition of a variable lacks face validity—that is, the way the variable is measured or manipulated does not appear (on its "face") to be an honest attempt to capture the essence of the variable's conceptual (i.e., more abstract, or general) definition.

2. *The biased scale lie.* A biased scale is one that elicits mostly favorable or unfavorable responses and thereby results in a skewed distribution. For example, the following 5-point scale will elicit mostly favorable responses because the scale's anchors are mostly positive adjectives.

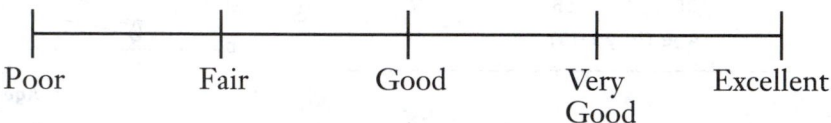

Poor   Fair   Good   Very   Excellent
                                          Good

3. *The sneaky sample lie.* Here, the culprit is a sample that is self-selected. Any method of participant selection that is not random will result in a biased sample, and self-selected samples are the most biased of all. The most common example of a self-selected sample is one that is composed of individuals who complete a survey or questionnaire because they have strong feelings about the topic.

4. *The pull-polling lie.* Otherwise legitimate surveys sometimes include questions that make use of strategies used in push polls, political tele-marketing schemes masquerading as surveys of public opinion. An example of one such strategy is to bias responses to a survey question by combining the question with a statement intended to "push" the respondent to choose a particular answer to that question as well as bias responses to subsequent questions.

5. *The limited range lie.* The range of data values may be limited for any number of reasons, but the result is the same: an incomplete or even distorted depiction of a sample distribution or relation between vari-ables. Reasons for a limited range of data include the practice of excluding outliers[1] or other values that would alter a predicted rela-tion if they were included, forcing survey respondents to select from among a narrow range of choices, and the intentional use of instru-ments or samples that result in a limited range of scores.

6. *The interpolation lie.* Interpolation occurs when a linear relation is assumed to obtain between widely separated clusters of data points.

---

[1] Outliers may be legitimately excluded as long as the rule defining their exclusion is in wide-spread use and was established prior to data collection. Researchers carry an obligation to pro-vide the rule of exclusion and to retain a record of the outliers that were excluded.

This is an ill-advised practice inasmuch as it is speculative at best and deceptive at worst. If the relation between two variables can be approximated by a straight line, then this linear pattern should be apparent over the full range of values of both variables.

7. *The extrapolation lie*. Extrapolation occurs when an observed relation between variables is assumed to extend beyond the range of data in the sample. It is quite possible that a relation apparent in a sample of data may not hold for values beyond this observed range. Thus, like interpolation, extrapolation is speculative and potentially deceptive. It is rarely, if ever, advisable to generalize beyond the range of data within a sample.

8. *The false impression lie*. This method of deception is illustrated by the graph on the cover of the *Ithaca Times* and reproduced in Figure 3-1 on p. 96 in the text. The graph displays a line representing Cornell University's rising tuition cost (as a share of the median family income of its students) over a 34-year period, from 1965 to 1999, above a second line depicting Cornell's ranking as an elite university fluctuating somewhat erratically before plummeting sharply in 1999. The most striking false impression in the graph is the depiction of Cornell's rank falling precipitously when it had in fact improved to its highest ranking ever over the 11 (not 34!) years that *U. S. News and World Report* had been ranking colleges and universities.

9. *The change the interval lie*. In addition to portraying a false impression of the relation between Cornell's tuition and its *U. S. News and World Report* ranking, the *Ithaca Times* graph depicted Cornell's ranking over an 11-year period with a line of the same length as the line representing changes in Cornell's tuition over a 34-year period. The graph maker must have realized that rankings and changes in tuition as a proportion of median student family income were measured in very different units and thus chose to place them on a graph with no vertical scale. So, in addition to misrepresenting the horizontal time scales, vertical distances used to represent year-to-year changes in both variables were apparently arbitrarily chosen.

10. *The inaccurate values lie*. This error is most likely to occur when pictures or other symbols are used to represent data values. Figure 3-23 on p. 129 in the text is an example of how the proportional changes in the dimensions of the picture-graphic misrepresent the proportional changes in the values of the variable.

11. *The outright lie*. Given the pressure to "publish or perish" that exists in many large research universities, it is hardly surprising that the history of science is rife with cases of outright data fabrication. Most recently, as noted in the text, Korean scientist Hwang Woo Suk authored a paper published in *Science* in which he claimed to have extracted stem cells from human embryos cloned in his lab. He

resigned from Seoul National University after colleagues told university officials that he has falsified the data.

The Future of Graphs: Breaking the Fourth Wall

The most striking advances in the visual display of information take advantage of the user's ability to interact with digital media, including links on Web pages that grant access to information at multiple levels.

Other innovative strategies include the creation of new graphic elements such as sparklines and Internet mapping tools that enable users to click on a data link (e.g., a description of a house or land for sale) to gain access to a map and pinpoint the location of the data. **Sparklines** are defined in the text as "datawords that are data-intense, design-simple, word-sized graphics that may be inserted into sentences" (text page 131). The combination of sparklines and text facilitate a more efficient consumption of information by enabling readers to peruse documents without ever lifting an eye from the page. The greatest potential for the use of Internet mapping tools is thought to lie in business applications, but the authors of your text think that this use of geographical information systems will find its way into social science research as sociologists, epidemiologists, organizational psychologists, and others link behavioral data (e.g., physical and psychological disorders, voting behavior, blood donations) to maps and other visual displays that relate the prevalence of such behaviors to specific geographic areas.

Forensic graphing and the use of graphs to monitor therapy represent the application of more standard graphic techniques to practical problems. For example, a basic bar chart may be used to resolve custody battles by contrasting custody support that is due against custody payments that have been received over a period of several months (see Figure 3-24, p. 131 in the text). Clinical psychologists and other therapists can enlist the help of standard line graphs to track clients' rates of improvement over time against expected rates of improvement for clients with particular profiles (see Figure 3-25, p. 133 in the text).

> The Uses and Misuses of Statistics: It's Not Just What You Draw, It's How You Draw It

One of the central themes of this chapter may be encapsulated in the pithy saying, "Figures don't lie, but liars figure." This bit of folk wisdom means, of course, that graphs can be used to tell a story that may not accord with the facts. A graph that faithfully reflects the data and that captures the viewer's imagination requires the skills of an artist and a statistician.

> Digging Deeper into the Data: The Box Plot

Box plots (sometimes called *box-and-whisker plots*) are graphic displays of the five-number summaries that were introduced in Chapter 2. The top of the box corresponds to the third quartile ($Q3$) and the bottom of the box marks the first quartile ($Q1$). So, the height of the box displays the interquartile range, or the middle 50% of the data values. The line inside the box indicates the location of $Q2$, the median. The lines that extend from the top and bottom of the box are called **whiskers**. The whiskers of a traditional box plot extend to the maximum and minimum data values in the sample, but some statistics software (notably SPSS) extend the whiskers to the largest and smallest values that are not outliers. (Recall from Chapter 2 that the interquartile range is used to define an outlier as any score that is more than 1.5 $IQRs$ below $Q1$ or above $Q3$.)

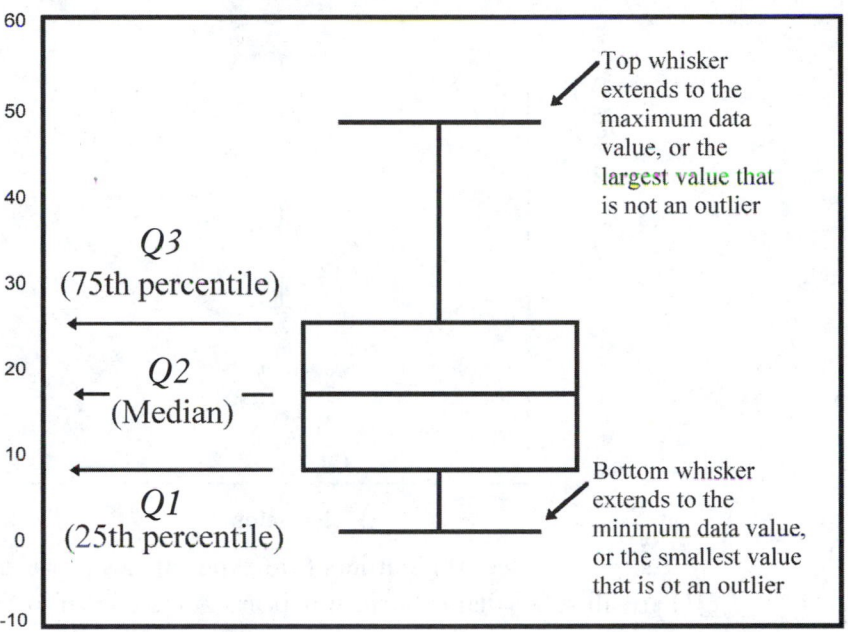

The position of the median relative to $Q1$ and $Q3$ provides an indication of skewness:

The median is closer to $Q3$ than to $Q1$, indicating *negative* skewness

The median is closer to $Q1$ than to $Q3$, indicating *positive* skewness

The box plot below (from SPSS) describes the most recently available data on the life expectancies of the female and male citizens of 220 nations (http://www.nationmaster.com/).

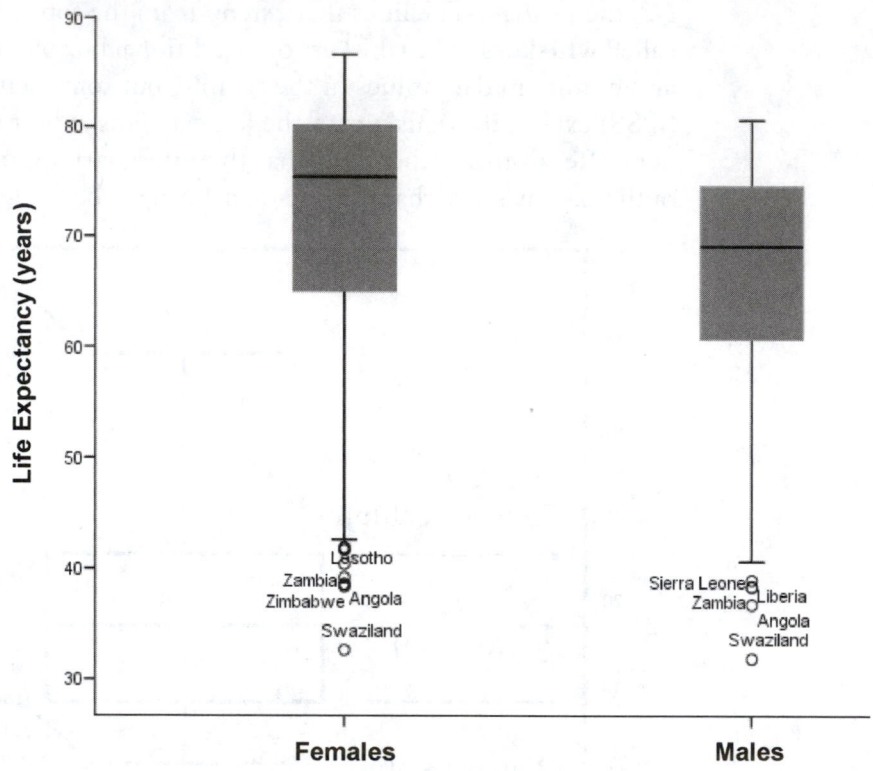

As you can see, the outliers (life expectancies more than 1.5 *IQR*s below *Q1*) are all sub-Saharan African nations. A male born in Swaziland, for example, can expect to live just a little over 30 years. The presence of outliers in the low end of the distribution gives it a negative skew, as indicated by the position of the median relative to *Q1* and *Q3*. As a reminder that "the tail tells the tale" (see p. 136 in the text), rotating the box plot 90 degrees clockwise shows the tail extending to the right in the direction of negative skewness.

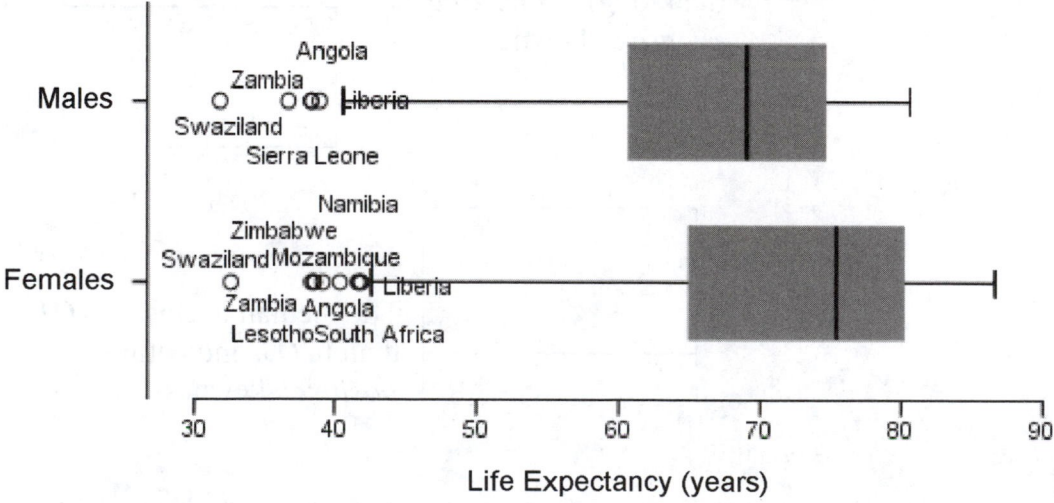

STUDY QUESTIONS

1. Which of the following statements regarding graphs is most clearly false?
   a. The purpose of a graph is to reveal and clarify relations between variables.
   b. A graph can sometimes reveal more about the person creating the graph than it does about the data it represents.
   c. Once a particular type of graph is selected, details related to the appearance of the graph are determined by software.
   d. It is possible to construct a graph that is deliberately misleading.

2. Which of the following statements regarding rules for the construction of graphic displays of data is most accurate?
   a. There are no rules. It is up to the graph creator to decide how to construct the graph.
   b. Rules for the construction of graphs have been rendered obsolete by graphic software.
   c. There are conventional rules, and failing to adhere to them frequently results in misleading graphs or graphs that obscure information that may be of vital importance.
   d. The rules vary markedly from one academic field to another, so it would be incorrect to say that there are conventional rules that apply across disciplines.

3. *Histograms* and *polygons* are:
   a. frequently presented in the results sections of published research articles.
   b. commonly used to display the relation between two or more variables.
   c. frequently presented in media accounts of scientific research.
   d. used to display frequency distributions.

4. A researcher who wishes to present demographic information (e.g., ages and incomes) about research participants usually does so in:
   a. a table in which each participant is listed in the left column and demographic information about that participant is presented in the columns to the right.
   b. a graphic display that depicts the relation between two or more demographic variables.
   c. the text with a simple report of means, medians, and standard deviations.
   d. a graphic display of a frequency distribution such as a histogram.

5. What do *scatterplots*, *line graphs*, and *bar graphs* have in common?
   a. They are all used to display the relation between two or more variables.
   b. They are all used to display the frequency distribution of a single variable.
   c. They are all used to display the frequency distributions of two or more variables.
   d. They are examples of older graphic displays that have been rendered obsolete by modern computer software.

6. A _____ is a graph that depicts the relation between two interval variables.
   a. pie chart
   b. bar graph
   c. histogram
   d. scatterplot

7. In a **scatterplot**, the variable doing the predicting is called the _____ variable.
   a. dependent
   b. independent
   c. interval
   d. moderator

8. A **range-frame** is a scatterplot or related graph that:
   a. indicates only the range of the data on each axis.
   b. is designed to decrease the data-ink ratio: less data, more ink.
   c. includes grids and Moiré vibrations to enhance the presentation.
   d. replaces the plotted points with an oval to indicate the pattern of relation.

9. To convert a scatterplot to a range-frame, you would:
   a. begin the axes at zero and extend them to the highest possible scores on the variables.
   b. erase the axes below the minimum scores and above the maximum scores.
   c. begin the axes with the lowest possible scores on the variables.
   d. erase the titles, labels, and tic marks on both axes.

10. An important feature of a scatterplot is its ability to identify:
    a. a causal relation between variables.
    b. confounding variables.
    c. extraneous variables.
    d. outliers.

11. There is a _____ relation between two variables when the pattern of points in a scatterplot roughly resembles a straight line.
    a. positive
    b. linear
    c. nonlinear
    d. negative

12. A _____ may used to represent change in a(n) _____ variable over time.
    a. line graph; interval
    b. line graph; nominal
    c. bar graph; interval
    d. bar graph; nominal

13. Which of the following should be used to predict job performance from an applicant's score on a vocational aptitude test?
    a. a scatterplot with a line of best fit
    b. a time-series plot
    c. a bar graph with applicants' aptitude scores measured on the horizontal axis
    d. a bar graph with applicants' job performance measured on the horizontal axis

14. In a **time series plot**, the horizontal axis is labeled with the name of the _____ variable; the values of this variable are _____.
    a. independent; measures of a variable that changes over time
    b. dependent; measures of a variable that changes over time
    c. independent; increments of time
    d. dependent; increments of time

15. In a **bar graph** depicting the relation between two variables, the height of each bar typically represents the:
    a. median score on the dependent variable.
    b. mean score on the dependent variable.
    c. level of the independent variable.
    d. frequency of responses.

16. A **Pareto chart** is a type of _____ that orders the categories of an independent variable along the horizontal axis for easier comparisons.
    a. bar graph
    b. line graph
    c. pictorial graph
    d. scatterplot

17. Identify the error, if there is one, in the graph below.

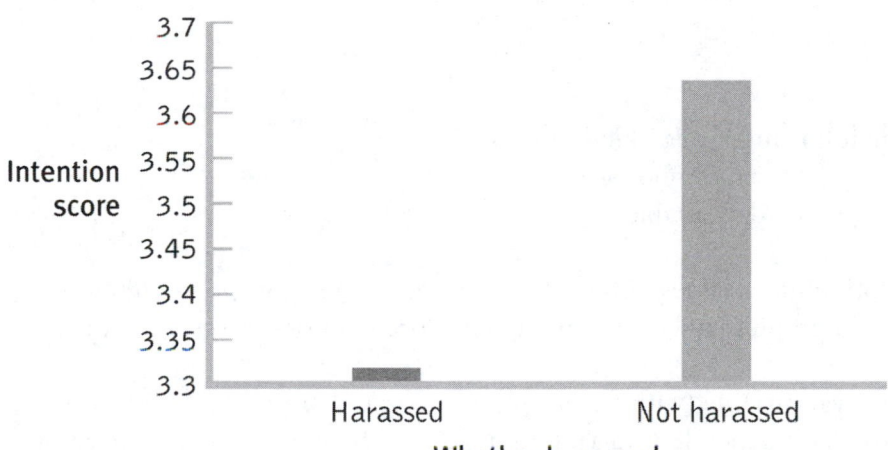

Effect of Sexual Harassment Status on Female Navy Officers' Intentions to Stay in the Navy

a. The graph is correct as is.
b. The vertical axis is too busy.
c. The vertical axis does not begin at zero.
d. The horizontal axis is labeled incorrectly.

18. Which one of the following uses a picture or symbol to represent the value of the dependent variable for each level of the independent variable?
    a. Pareto chart
    b. bar graph
    c. pie chart
    d. pictorial graph

19. Which one of the following is a graph in the shape of a circle?
    a. pie chart
    b. pictorial graph
    c. Pareto chart
    d. Moiré display

20. Suppose that a **pie chart** is constructed to represent responses to a survey question. The size of each slice in the chart represents the:
    a. mean score for each category of participants.
    b. median score for each category of participants.
    c. proportion or percentage of individuals choosing each response.
    d. proportion of variability in the dependent variable that is explained by the independent variable.

21. Which one of the following graphs most effectively depicts the relation between an interval variable and a nominal variable?
    a. pictorial graph
    b. pie chart
    c. bar graph
    d. line graph

22. Which one of the following is *not* a kind of **figure**?
    a. a chart   c. a photograph
    b. a graph   d. a table

23. Match the description of variables in the left column with the appropriate graph from the right column. (A graph may be appropriate for more than one description of variables.)
    a. _____ one interval variable (with frequencies)   1. bar graph
    b. _____ one interval independent variable and   2. line graph or scatterplot
       one interval dependent variable
    c. _____ one nominal independent variable and   3. histogram or polygon
       one interval dependent variable   4. pie chart
    d. _____ two or more nominal independent variables
       and one interval dependent variable

24. T F   A graph should use the same terms that were used in the body of the paper.

25. T F   Computer defaults are the choices selected by the user when using software to construct a graph.

26. Tufte (2001/2006) coined the term _____ to refer to any unnecessary information or feature in a graph that detracts from a viewer's ability to understand the data.
    a. chartjunk
    b. Moiré vibrations
    c. ducks
    d. grids

27. T F   **Moiré vibrations** are background patterns on which the data representations, such as bars, are superimposed.

28. Graphical **ducks**:
    a. refer to any of the patterns that computers provide as options to fill in bars.
    b. are symbols or pictures used to represent values of the dependent variable.
    c. are features of the data that have been dressed up to be something other than data.
    d. refer collectively to all the default options that are implemented by graphics software.

29. Of the 11 sophisticated techniques for lying with statistics and graphs, which one refers to the use of an operational definition of a variable that doesn't represent the variable's conceptual definition (e.g., using the frequency or duration of shouting as an operational definition of *aggression*)?
    a. the biased scale lie
    b. the false face validity lie
    c. the false impression lie
    d. the sneaky sample lie

30. A phone researcher asks "How aware are you that Senator So-and-So has been accused of child abuse? Very aware, somewhat aware, or unaware?" Merely asking the question in this way makes you "somewhat aware" of the accusation, thus biasing your response to the question as well as to others that may follow. This technique of lying with statistics and graphs is called the _____ lie.
    a. push-polling
    b. biased scale
    c. false impression
    d. extrapolation

31. To spot the _____ lie, check to see that the graph includes data over the full range of the independent variable, including a reasonable number of in-between data points.
    a. change the interval
    b. limited range
    c. interpolation
    d. extrapolation

32. Korean scientist Hwang Woo Suk's confession that he fabricated much of the data, statistics, and graphs in his highly publicized cloning and stem cell research is a relatively recent example of a technique of deceiving with statistics and graphs called the _____ lie.
    a. outright
    b. false impression
    c. extrapolation
    d. inaccurate values

33. **Sparklines** are:
    a. a type of graphical duck that involves adding eye-catching features to graph lines such as shadows to produce a 3-dimensonal effect.
    b. thin vertical lines that extend from the top of a bar or the edges of a box in a box-plot to indicate the amount of variability in the data.
    c. any variation on a solid graph line that graphics software provides as a means of displaying trends in a line graph.
    d. data words that are data-intense, design-simple, word-sized graphics that may be inserted into sentences.

34. A five-number summary of a distribution of scores is graphically displayed in a:
    a. scatterplot.
    b. bar graph.
    c. line graph.
    d. box plot.

35. The **box plot** was invented by:
    a. George E. P. Box in the 1940s.
    b. Karl Pearson in the 1920s.
    c. John Tukey in the 1960s.
    d. E. R. Tufte in the 1980s.

36. In a box plot in which the values of a measured variable are displayed on the vertical axis, the width (measured horizontally) of the box represents:
    a. the range.
    b. the interquartile range.
    c. the variance.
    d. nothing.

37. In a box plot, the **whiskers** are lines that extend to:
    a. the first and third quartiles.
    b. the maximum and minimum scores in the sample.
    c. two standard deviations on either side of the mean.
    d. two standard deviations on either side of the median.

ANSWERS TO CHAPTER 3 STUDY QUESTIONS

Question Number	Correct Answer	Question Number	Correct Answer
1	c, p. 9	18	d, p. 116
2	c, p. 101	19	a, p. 117
3	d, p. 101	20	c, p. 117
4	c, p. 101	21	c, p. 117
5	a, p. 102	22	d, p. 119
6	d, p. 102	23	a (3), b (2), c (1), d (1) [p. 120]
7	b, p. 102	24	t, p. 122
8	a, p. 103	25	f, p. 122
9	b, p. 103	26	a. p. 122
10	d, p. 104	27	f, p. 122
11	b, p. 104 (A linear relation may be positive or negative, but you can't tell which from the description in this question stem.)	28	c, p. 123
		29	b, p. 127
		30	a, p. 127
		31	c, p. 128
12	a, p. 107	32	a, p. 129
13	a, p. 107	33	d, p. 131
14	c, p. 108	34	d, p. 135
15	b, p. 112	35	c, p. 135
16	a, p. 113	36	d, p. 136 (see Figure 3-26)
17	c, p. 114	37	b, p. 135

REFERENCES

Robinson, W., Boisjoly, R., Hoeker, D., & Young, S. (2002). Representation and misrepresentation: Tufte and the Morton Thiokol engineers on the *Challenger*. *Science and Engineering Ethics, 8*, 59–81.

Tufte, E. R. (1997). *Visual explanations: Images and quantities, evidence and narrative.* Cheshire, CT: Graphics Press.

CHAPTER FOUR

PROBABILITIES AND RESEARCH
The Risks and Rewards of Scientific Sampling

CHAPTER OUTLINE

Samples and Their Populations: Why Statisticians Are Stingy
- Decision Making: The Risks and Rewards of Sampling
- Random Sampling: An Equal Chance of Being Selected
- Variations on Random Sampling: Cluster Sampling and Stratified Sampling
- Convenience Sampling: Readily Available Participants
- Random Assignment: An Equal Chance of Being Assigned to a Condition
- Variations on Random Assignment: Block Design and Replication

Sampling in the Behavioral Sciences: Why Sampling Is Both an Art and a Science
- Neither Random Selection, Nor Random Assignment: A Study of Torture
- Random Assignment, But Not Random Selection: A Study of Expert Testimony
- Random Selection, But Not Random Assignment: A Study of Children's Literature

Probability Theory: Distinguishing Between Mere Coincidence and Real Connections
- Coincidence and Probability: Why Healthy Skepticism Is Healthy
- Beyond Confirmation Biases: The Dangers of Groupthink

Probability Theory: The Basics
- Expected Relative-Frequency Probability: The Probability of Statistics
- Independence and Probability: The Gambler's Fallacy
- Statistician Sleuths: The Case of Chicago's Cheating Teachers

Statistics and Probability: The Logic of Inferential Statistics
- Using Probability to Make Decisions: Dead Grandmothers
- Developing Hypothesis: Consideration of Future Consequences
- Making a Decision about Our Hypotheses: Consideration of Future Consequences

Type I and Type II Errors: Statistical Inferences Can Be Wrong
- Type I Errors: Sins of Commission
- Type II Errors: Sins of Omission

Statistics in Everyday Life: Tying It All Together
- The Case of Lush: Testimonial to a Moisturizer
- Understanding the Meaning of Proof: Statistical Literacy in Consumer Research

Digging Deeper into the Data: The Shocking Prevalence of Type I Errors
- Estimating Type I Error in the Medical Literature: Does That Pill Really Work?
- Medical Findings and Confirmation Biases: Science Versus Self-Deception

LEARNING OBJECTIVES

After studying this chapter, you should be able to:

1. Define each of the following terms and provide examples that are not in the text: *generalizability, random sample, convenience sample, cluster sampling, stratified sampling, volunteer sample, randomized block design, replication, confirmation bias, illusory correlation, groupthink, subjective probability, expected relative-frequency probability, trial, outcome, success, gambler's fallacy, control group, experimental group, null hypothesis, research hypothesis, Type I error, Type II error.*

2. Explain the concepts of generalizability and external validity in the context of sampling as they relate to the notion that statisticians are "stingy."

3. Distinguish between *random samples* and *convenience samples*, and explain why it is difficult to obtain a random sample. Explain the similarities and differences among *simple random, cluster,* and *stratified random samples.* What are some special concerns with *volunteer samples*?

4. Contrast *random selection* and *random assignment* and explain how a source of random numbers may be used to assign participants to different levels of an independent variable. Include in your discussion an explanation of the importance of *replication* in studies in which random assignment, but not random selection, is used.

5. Discuss the importance of developing sound statistical reasoning as a safeguard against judgments based on cognitive errors such as *illusory correlation, confirmation bias,* and *groupthink.* Your discussion should include an elucidation of the roles played by illusory correlation and confirmation bias in perceiving meaning in statistical inevitability (coincidence) as well as an identification of *groupthink* as a serious consequence of abandoning statistical reasoning.

6. Distinguish between *subjective* and *expected relative-frequency probability* and explain how the *gambler's fallacy* represents a violation of the assumption of independence in predicting the *outcomes* of independent *trials.*

7. Discuss the procedure and logic of hypothesis testing, including the random assignment of participants to *experimental* and *control groups,*

the formulation of statements of the *null* and *research hypotheses*, and the possible decisions regarding the null hypothesis that are dictated by the outcome of a study. Be sure to include in your discussion an explanation of *Type I* and *Type II errors*.

8. Identify the shortcomings of traditional hypothesis testing as identified in the discussion of the article by Sterne and Smith (2001). Explain how medical findings may be filtered through confirmation bias.

CHAPTER REVIEW

> Samples and Their Populations: Why Statisticians Are Stingy

In Chapter 1 you learned the distinction between a *sample* and a *population*. You also learned that the purpose of *inferential statistics* is to use the information in a sample of data to draw inferences (make general estimates) about a larger population. More specifically, you learned that *statistics* computed for samples of data may be used to estimate the values of corresponding population *parameters*. A researcher is interested in a sample of individuals only to the extent that the sample is representative of the larger population. For example, a researcher who proposes to study a sample of students from William Patterson College in New Jersey will compute sample statistics as reasonable estimates of the corresponding parameters determined for the population of students attending the college. Researchers working at other institutions have the same goal: to study a sample of individuals who are representative of the larger population.

In this chapter, you were introduced to the terms *generalizability* and *external validity* and the importance of studying representative samples. **Generalizability** refers to the extent to which a researcher's findings may be applied to other samples and contexts. If the findings may be generalized from, say, a sample of students attending the University of Iowa to a sample of students attending William Patterson College in New Jersey, then the findings are said to be high in *external validity*.

If the samples are high in external validity and they are representative of their respective populations, then it follows that findings from either study may be generalized to either population. Ideally, all researchers would like to *generalize* their findings as broadly as possible. Thus the goal of a researcher at Institution X is seldom simply to study a sample that is representative of Institution X or to produce findings that may be generalized to Institution Y. More often the goal is to study a sample that is representative of the national population of college and university students. According to this "big picture" scenario, the results of a single representative sample of participants may be generalized to any other sample from any other institution in the nation.

The "big picture" is an ideal founded on a fundamental goal of science: to discover principles (sometimes called "laws") that hold under a wide range of conditions. Not all problems are of a general nature, however. Sometimes the goal is simply to generalize to a more limited population or set of conditions. Either way, the laws of probability enable researchers to make inferences about an entire population from the information provided by a representative sample.

The two general categories of samples discussed in the text are *random samples* and *convenience samples*. A **random sample** is the result of a process that gives every member of the population an equal chance of being selected. The prototypical method of random sampling is called *simple random sampling*, where "simple" refers to a population that is not first divided into clusters or strata. Simple random sampling is rarely used for two reasons: (1) Few, if any, large target populations exist as lists of identifiable units, and (2) even if such lists were available, the cost of accessing each randomly selected unit limits this method to large research organizations with a national scope. For these reasons, most researchers in the behavioral sciences gather information from a **convenience sample** of individuals who are nearby and thus readily available.

Variations on Random Sampling: Cluster Sampling and Stratified Sampling

Variations of random sampling that are usually much easier to implement include *cluster sampling* and *stratified random sampling*. **Cluster sampling** is "a selection method in which all of the clusters in a population are identified and a certain number of these clusters are selected randomly; everyone in the selected clusters would then be recruited to participate in the study" (text page 157). National survey organizations frequently use *multistage cluster sampling* to select individuals to be interviewed.

Stratified random sampling "is a sampling method in which strata, usually levels of a nominal variable, are identified, and then a random sample of the same size is taken from each stratum" (text page 157). Stratified random sampling is a more efficient method of ensuring that all groups are represented in the sample. For example, stratification of a population by gender would require selecting separate simple random samples from the females and males in the population. The two samples would be combined to produce the final sample. The advantage of stratified random sampling is that smaller samples are needed from groups (strata) that include similar individuals. The more similar the individuals, the smaller the sample size needed to adequately represent the stratum.

Convenience Sampling: Readily Available Participants

As noted above, most behavioral science research is based on convenience samples. At some larger research universities, the list of available participants is composed of students who sign up for various studies as a requirement of the major. Students who elect not to be research participants must choose some alternative exercise that is deemed to be equivalent in terms of time and effort to complete as well as educational value. Convenience samples may also be composed of individuals who passively volunteer as members of intact groups (e.g., classes or meetings of some sort) who need only remain in the room to participate. Because convenience samples were not randomly selected from a population, the extent to which findings based on such samples may be generalized to the population—that is, the external validity of the results—is usually limited. However, the most important findings are almost always replicated by other researchers, using different convenience samples of individuals in places that may differ culturally as well as geographically from the location of the original study. A failure to replicate the basic findings of an original study usually means that those findings may not be generalized beyond the context in which they were obtained. On the other hand, successful replication of a finding using different convenience samples extends the generalizability of that finding.

A **volunteer**, or *self-selected*, **sample** is a special kind of convenience sample composed of individuals who choose to sign up for an experiment or to complete a mailed, telephone, or online survey without additional prompting. Findings based on volunteer samples are particularly suspect because the personality and demographic characteristics of volunteers tend to differ from those of individuals who do not actively volunteer. Indeed, the differences between a volunteer sample and a sample of randomly selected individuals are usually more exaggerated than the differences between a more typical convenience sample and a randomly selected sample. Note here that such volunteer samples should not be confused with students who "volunteer" to participate in a study to satisfy a course or major requirement or with randomly selected individuals who agree to participate by signing an informed consent agreement.

Random Assignment: An Equal Chance of Being Assigned to a Condition

As you learned in Chapter 1 (see text page 22), the defining characteristic of an experiment is the random assignment of participants to groups or conditions. **Random assignment** ensures that each participant has an equal chance of being assigned to each experimental condition. So, random *assignment* shares with random *selection* the use of a random process, but the procedures are used for different reasons and should not be confused. Random assignment is the most effective means of accomplishing two objectives: (1) to eliminate experimenter bias in the assignment of participants to experimental conditions, and (2) to evenly distribute potentially confounding participant characteristics (education, gender, income, intelligence, personality, sensory acuity, etc.) across the different conditions of an experiment. Recall from Chapter 1 that a confounding variable is one whose effects are "mixed up" or "confounded" with those of the independent variable. If some random process is not used to assign participants to groups, the study will likely be confounded at the outset by preexisting group differences. After administering the independent variable manipulation, any differences between the dependent variable scores in the groups may be due to the effect of the independent variable, or to preexisting group differences, or to both. The results are thereby confounded, and any conclusions regarding the effect of the independent variable are rendered suspect by the ambiguity of the research design. A research design that is compromised in this way is said to have low *internal* validity. We may conclude, then, that *random assignment* is the single best method of increasing the *internal validity* of a research design. In contrast, a research design that uses a biased, and thus unrepresentative, sample of participants is said to be low in *external* validity because the results may only be generalized to individuals like those who participated in the study. *Random selection* thus increases a study's *external validity*.

A variation on random assignment called a **randomized block design** "creates equivalent groups by matching the participants with regard to important characteristics and then using randomization only within blocks, or groups, of participants who are similar on one or more of these characteristics" (text page 159). The advantage of a randomized block design over simple random assignment is an increased likelihood of detecting an effect of the independent variable.

> Sampling in the Behavioral Sciences: Why Sampling Is Both an Art and a Science

The text describes three studies that illustrate variation in the use of random selection and random assignment. For ethical reasons, neither random selection nor random assignment could be used in the first study. In this quasi–experiment conducted by Basoglu and colleagues (1997), various dimensions of the mental health of a convenience sample of Turkish torture survivors were examined in two groups of survivors who differed primarily in terms of whether they had been political activists prior to their experience of torture. The researchers found that, despite experiencing more severe torture, survivors who had been political activists were generally less depressed, less anxious, and less likely to be diagnosed with post–traumatic stress disorder than survivors in the nonactivist group. Basoglu et al. concluded that the activists' greater psychological preparedness—they anticipated being imprisoned and tortured for their political activities and prepared themselves as well as they could—reduced the long–term impact of torture on their mental health. Because Basoglu and colleagues could not randomly assign torture survivors to different groups, they anticipated that group differences other than a history of political activism may have influenced the outcome. Accordingly, they reported that gender as well as level of education and income were associated with better psychological outcomes in the sample they studied. The results may be generalized to Turkish torture survivors who are similar to the individuals in this sample. With the exercise of appropriate caution, the findings may also be generalized to survivors of torture and other severe trauma in similar regions of the world.

In the second study (Leippe et al., 2004), *random assignment* but not *random selection* was used. More than 350 undergraduate students comprising a convenience sample were randomly assigned to one of five conditions. Four of the conditions were defined by the timing of expert testimony about the validity of eyewitness memory (before vs. after the evidence was presented) and by whether the judge did or did not remind jurors of that testimony. In the last (control) condition, there was no testimony and thus no reminder of that testimony. The use of random assignment enabled Leippe et al. to conclude that the timing of expert testimony about the flawed nature of eyewitness memory is causally related to the probability of jury conviction, regardless of the overall strength of the case against the defendant. However, it is difficult to know the extent to which these results may be generalized from a convenience sample of college students to an older population of jurors hearing such testimony in actual trials. Although college students will be called upon to serve on juries, they are not representative of other populations of individuals who will serve as jurors. Replications of the Leippe et al. study using samples of students from other colleges and universities would be a useful first step toward strengthening the external validity of these findings. More useful still would be replications based on samples of potential jurors representing a wider range of ages and levels of education.

The last study in this group, an archival study of children's literature, used *random selection* but not *random assignment*. Diekman and Murnan (2004) randomly selected 10 books from each of two populations of children's books: those that had been categorized by both publishers and researchers as sexist and those that were designated nonsexist. The researchers could not randomly assign authors to write either sexist or nonsexist books and then examine them to see if they were indeed free of gender stereotypes, but they could randomly select books from a population archive and determine whether the labels sexist and nonsexist were valid.

Regardless of whether a study includes random selection, random assignment, both, or neither, the goal of statistical inference remains the same: to discover something about populations from the information available for study in samples. Because of the practical difficulty involved in accessing entire populations, random selection is rarely encountered in published research in the social and behavioral sciences. Random assignment is much more common, but is clearly limited to studies of independent variables that do not harm research participants.

> Probability Theory: Distinguishing Between Mere Coincidence and Real Connections

Unaided by statistical reasoning, our own perceptual biases more often than not lead us astray. Chief among our cognitive foibles is **confirmation bias**, which refers to a tendency to selectively attend to observations that confirm what we already believe while ignoring events that contradict those beliefs. A seemingly pervasive confirmation bias serves to support **illusory correlation**, or our tendency to perceive unrelated events as correlated. Armed with a belief that dreams foretell important events in our lives (an illusory correlation), we selectively remember dreams that seemed to do just that while ignoring all the important events that were not the subjects of remembered dreams and all the dreams about events that never happened (a confirmation bias). Confirmation bias and illusory correlation contribute to **groupthink**, "the overconfident, biased decision making that occurs when a group of people confirm one another's beliefs rather than relaying on objective evidence" (text page 171).

Probability Theory: The Basics

A contestant on the "Who Wants to Be a Millionaire" television program phones a friend to get an answer to a question that has her stumped. When the friend offers an answer, the contestant asks her friend how certain she is that her answer is correct. A typical response is usually expressed as a percentage such as "I'm about 70 percent sure." This answer is an example of a **subjective probability**, an intuitive feeling about the chance that a successful outcome will occur (such as providing a correct answer). In statistics, the probability of an outcome is determined objectively by observing the frequency with which an outcome occurs over a very large number of trials. You may wonder why it is necessary to observe the outcomes of a very large number of independent trials. A coin has two sides, so why isn't the probability that it will land on one side or the other equal to 0.5? Expressed more formally, why not just compute the probability of a success (e.g., a coin landing heads) as the number of ways that a success can occur over the total number of possible outcomes?

$$p(\text{success}) = \frac{\text{number of ways a success can occur}}{\text{number of possible outcomes}} = \frac{1}{2} = .5$$

The answer is that this method of determining probability assumes that the coin is perfectly balanced. There is simply no way to test that assumption apart from flipping the coin an infinitely large number of times. Because no one can flip a coin an infinite number of times[1], statisticians settle for the "long-run" (i.e., a repetition of many, many trials) interpretation of expected-frequency probability.

---

[1] There have been some valiant efforts by some notable people in the history of statistics. For example, Karl Pearson flipped a coin 24,000 times and counted heads 12,012 times (50.05%). South African mathematician John Kerrich spent much of World War II in a prison camp in Jutland, courtesy of the Nazi regime. While there, he flipped a coin 10,000 times and counted 5,067 heads (50.67%).

The familiar example of flipping a coin will be used to provide examples of the following definitions:

- A **trial** is a single coin flip.
- An **outcome** is the result of a trial; a coin can land either heads or tails.
- A **success** is an outcome of interest such as a coin landing heads.
- The *frequency* of a particular outcome, usually the one defined as a success, is the number of times the outcome was observed in a given set of independent trials.
- An *independent* trial is one whose outcome is not influenced by the outcome of any previous trial.
- The *relative frequency* of a success is the number of times the outcome occurred relative to the number of times it could have occurred. If the frequency of heads is 47 out of 100 trials, then the relative frequency of heads is 47 / 100 = 0.47.
- *Proportion* is another name for relative frequency.
- *Percentage* is a proportion expressed as frequency per 100 trials. Multiplying any proportion by 100 converts the proportion to a percentage.
- *Expected relative frequency* is the relative frequency of successes that would be expected to occur in a very large number of independent trials—in "the long run."
- **Expected relative frequency probability** is the likelihood of observing a success expressed as an expected relative frequency.

When expressed as a *proportion*, a probability value ranges between 0 and 1. When expressed as a *percent chance*, a probability can be any value between 0 and 100. The following are equivalent statements:

- The probability of selecting 1 of 800 winning tickets for a lottery in which 1,000,000 tickets were sold is .0008.
- The proportion of winning lottery tickets is .0008.
- The percentage of winning lottery tickets is .08.
- There is a .08 percent chance of purchasing 1 of the winning lottery tickets.
- The odds are 9,992 to 8 against winning the lottery.

The expected relative frequency probability of an outcome of interest (a success) is determined as follows:

$$p(\text{success}) = \frac{\text{number of successes}}{\text{number of trials}}$$

Please do not miss the point that expected relative frequency probabilities are defined over a very large number of *independent* trials. The coin does not "remember" whether it landed heads or tails on the previous trial or the ones before that, so each flip results in an outcome that is not affected in any way by the result of any previous trial. A failure to remember this basic principle leads to a cognitive bias called the **gambler's fallacy**, "a type of biased thinking in which an individual believes that a previous occurrence has an effect on an ensuing occurrence, when in fact the two events are unrelated" (text page 176). The term refers to a gambler's tendency, after losing several games in a row, to wager a larger sum on the next game in the mistaken belief that he or she is due for a win.

> Statistics and Probability: The Logic of Inferential Statistics

Developing Hypotheses: Consideration of Future Consequences

Hypothesis testing begins with data collection which, in turn, involves an identification of a target population, sampling from that population, assigning participants to two or more groups or conditions, and selecting an independent variable and a dependent variable. In the example described in the text, a researcher randomly selects a sample of 60 students from the sophomore class of a university then randomly assigns half the students to an experimental group and half to a control group. The students assigned to the **experimental group** will be exposed to the experimental treatment, a semester-long program administered through the university's career center that features weekly hour-long meetings during which they learn about various graduate school and career options. Students assigned to the **control group** also attend weekly hour-long meetings over the course of the semester, but they do not receive information about career and graduate school options. The independent variable in this study is the kind of program the students are assigned to attend, and its two levels are defined by the presence and absence of information about career and graduate school options. Because the students are randomly assigned to the two groups, the only difference between them is the level of the independent variable to which they are exposed. At the end of the semester, both groups complete the Consideration of Future Consequences (CFC) scale. Their scores on the CFC scale serve as the dependent variable.

The **null hypothesis** to be tested in this study is that attending the weekly career center program meetings will not affect CFC scores—that is, the mean CFC score in the population of students who are exposed to information about career and graduate school options is the same as that of the population of students who are not exposed to such information. The null hypothesis is described in the text as the "boring" hypothesis, because it is the hypothesis that says nothing is going on: no effect of the independent variable and thus no difference between the mean scores in the two populations of students. The university administrators hope that the evidence will permit a rejection of the null hypothesis in favor of the alternative called the research hypothesis. The **research hypothesis** in this example states that the mean CFC score in the population of students who are exposed to information about career and graduate school options is *not* the same as that of the population of students who are not exposed to such information. The research hypothesis could also be expressed as a directional statement: The mean CFC score in the population of students who are exposed to information about career and graduate school options is *greater than* that of the population of students who are not exposed to such information. If the research hypothesis is a directional statement, then the null hypothesis must be a directional statement as well: The mean CFC score in the population of students who are exposed to information about career and graduate school options is *less than or equal to* that of the population of students who are not exposed to such information. The research hypothesis is the "exciting hypothesis" in the sense that it declares that providing students information about their post-graduation plans will encourage them to get a head start researching and planning for their futures—actions that indicate a consideration of future consequences.

An analysis of the data will disclose whether the group means are "significantly different"; that is, the difference is considered to be too large to have occurred by chance. The larger the difference between the group (sample) means, the more likely it is that the population means are different as stated in the research hypothesis. Researchers typically use a criterion of statistical significance that permits a rejection of the null hypothesis if the difference between the group means is so large that it may expected to occur by chance less than 5% of the time. The value 5% (.05) is the criterion of statistical significance as well as the maximum probability of committing a Type I error.

The sample evidence thus requires that the researcher make a decision to either *reject* or *fail to reject* the null hypothesis. Please note that failing to reject the null hypothesis is not the same as "accepting" it. It is never appropriate to "accept" or "conclude support for" the null hypothesis. If the null hypothesis is not rejected, then the results are *inconclusive* regarding the validity of the null hypothesis. Of course, the university administrators hope to be able to reject the null hypothesis because doing so will allow them to conclude support for the research hypothesis. This is the somewhat convoluted logic of hypothesis testing. A researcher is obligated to test a hypothesis that she does not believe to be true and hopes to be able to reject so she can conclude support for its logical opposite—the research hypothesis. This logic is not entirely strange, however. A prosecuting attorney goes through a similar procedure when he is obliged to assume that a defendant is innocent even while he attempts to persuade the jury with compelling logic and evidence that the defendant is guilty beyond a reasonable doubt.

In making a decision regarding the null hypothesis, it is possible that the decision is in error. The two types of errors are discussed in the next section, but for now you should note that it is impossible to avoid decision errors. The only way for researchers to know whether they are making a decision error is to know whether the null hypothesis is true. Of course, if this were known, then there would be no reason to test the null hypothesis. Thus, researchers can not know whether they are making a decision error when they reject or fail to reject the null hypothesis, so they can not avoid committing decision errors. For this reason, it is never appropriate to use any forms of the words "prove" or "true" when interpreting the results of a hypothesis test. The possibility of making an error when deciding whether to reject or to fail to reject the null hypothesis means that it is not possible to "prove" that the null hypothesis is "true" or "false." If the null hypothesis is rejected, the appropriate conclusion is that the results support the research hypothesis. If the null hypothesis is not rejected, then the researcher should conclude simply that the results do not support the research hypothesis.

Type I and Type II Errors: Statistical Inferences Can Be Wrong

As discussed above, each test of a null hypothesis requires a decision to either reject, or fail to reject, the hypothesis. As shown in the following table, two errors are possible. A **Type I error** occurs when a true null hypothesis is rejected, whereas a **Type II error** is committed when a researcher fails to reject a false null hypothesis.

Status of the Null Hypothesis

Researcher's Decision	The null hypothesis is true	The null hypothesis is false
Reject the null hypothesis	Type I Error	Correct Decision
Do not reject the null hypothesis	Correct Decision	Type II Error

Hypothesis testing in science has traditionally regarded a Type I error as more serious than a Type II error. The relative seriousness with which science regards the two errors is reflected in what are regarded as acceptable probabilities of committing each type of error. The maximum probability of committing a Type I error has traditionally been set at .05 (5%), whereas an acceptable probability of committing a Type II error is about 0.2 (20%). This is a conservative position that regards our current state of knowledge as something worth defending against new, perhaps "half-baked" ideas.

The relative seriousness of a Type I error vs. a Type II error is encapsulated by Blackstone's ratio which states that it is "better that ten guilty persons escape than that one innocent suffer." In other words, a Type I error is regarded as at least 10 times worse than a Type II error.

> Statistics in Everyday Life: Tying It All Together

This section of the chapter pits a single individual's testimony about the effectiveness of a cosmetic against statistical reasoning. How should an intelligent consumer evaluate a product that is endorsed in this fashion? Following the logic of statistical inference, one might consider the following questions:

- Is the sample, one 60-year-old woman, representative of the population of individuals who might benefit from using the product?
- How likely is a positive report if the product is really no better than any other product of its kind?

Regarding the first question, the report of a single individual, no matter how glowing, can never be a representative sample. The problem of sample bias is compounded in this instance by the fact that this is a volunteer (self-selected) sample of one individual who, at 60 years of age, is using a product targeted for a much younger group of consumers and is therefore unlikely to be representative of her age group. The second question can not be separated from the first: If the sample is a single biased testimonial, the likelihood of a positive response to a product that is no better than its competition is high. Any decision about the effectiveness of a product that is based on an unusual sample is likely to be a Type I error.

> Digging Deeper into the Data: The Shocking Prevalence of Type I Errors

Writing in the *British Medical Journal*, Sterne and Smith (2001) estimate that only about 10% of studies of treatment effectiveness in the medical literature reported positive outcomes—that is, only about 10% of the treatments really work. This means that the null hypothesis is false in just 100 of every 1,000 studies and true—that is, the treatment really does not work—in the remaining 900. Of the 900 studies of ineffective treatments, 45 (5%) will nevertheless reject a true null hypothesis (commit a Type I error) as a consequence of testing each null hypothesis at the traditional significance level of 5%. The authors also estimated that, of the 100 studies that examined effective treatments, only half (50%) will correctly reject the null hypothesis; the other half will fail to reject a false null hypothesis (commit a Type II error) because the study methods were not powerful enough (did not include a sufficiently large number of patients, etc.) to detect a treatment effect. These estimated probabilities result in a situation in which just 53% (50 of 95) of the studies that result in a rejection of the null hypothesis are correct rejections; the remaining 47% are Type I errors.

When the public digests media report after media report of the medical research findings that turn out to be Type I errors, a certain level of skepticism, or even cynicism, is to be expected. What is to be done about the "shocking prevalence of Type I errors" that foment so much public skepticism in the findings of scientific research? A remedy, endorsed by Sterne and Smith as well as the American Psychological Association, is to improve the methodology of studies by using adequate sample sizes and reducing measurement error. In addition, the magnitude of treatment effects should be emphasized rather than the "statistical significance" of the effects.

STUDY QUESTIONS

1. The **generalizability** of research findings refers to the application of those findings:
   a. to solve problems in theoretical fields such as experimental psychology.
   b. from one sample or in one context to other samples or contexts.
   c. to solve problems in applied fields such as clinical psychology.
   d. from a population to a sample of individuals.

2. Which one of the following statements about sampling is most accurate?
   a. The laws of probability require that a representative sample include at least 50% of the units in a population.
   b. A large sample is always more representative than a smaller sample, regardless of how the units are sampled.
   c. When a sample is used to represent a population, there is always a risk of reaching an inaccurate conclusion about the population.
   d. A sample of one individual may sometimes be representative of an entire population.

3. A(n) _____ sample is one in which every member of the population has an equal chance of being selected to participate in a study.

4. A _____ sample is composed of participants who were selected because of their ready availability.
   a. random
   b. quota
   c. probability
   d. convenience

5. The goal that underlies every sampling technique is to:
   a. produce a diverse sample of individuals, regardless of the makeup of the population.
   b. give each individual in the population an equal chance of being selected.
   c. include simple random sampling at some stage in the process.
   d. produce a sample that is representative of the population.

6. Which of the following sequences of numbers would be considered the *least* random by people who do not understand randomness?
   a. 35963
   b. 61962
   c. 75246
   d. 33351

7. Which one of the following is *most* likely to be a random sequence?
   a. 01010101
   b. 11110000
   c. 11111111
   d. These sequences are equally likely.

8. If a school psychologist obtained a list of all 2000 students enrolled in a certain high school and randomly selected 50 students from the list, her sample would most accurately be termed a _____ sample.
   a. convenience
   b. simple random
   c. stratified random
   d. cluster

9. In _____ sampling, a simple random sample is taken from each of several subgroups (e.g., four age groups) within a population.
   a. convenience
   b. stratified random
   c. cluster
   d. quota

10. What is the essential difference between stratified random sampling and cluster sampling?
    a. Unlike stratified random sampling, cluster sampling does not involve random selection at any stage in the process.
    b. Each individual in a selected cluster is recruited to be a participant, whereas many individuals in an identified stratum will not be recruited to be participants.
    c. Cluster sampling involves simple random sampling, whereas stratified random sampling does not.
    d. A stratum is always a level of nominal variable, whereas a cluster is never a level of nominal variable.

11. Which one of the following statements about random samples is *most* accurate?
    a. Random samples are composed of individuals who had the highest probability of being selected.
    b. Random samples are almost never used because researchers almost never have access to an entire population.
    c. The results of studies based on random samples of participants are generally very low in external validity.
    d. Random samples are common in the social and behavioral sciences, but are extremely rare in the natural sciences.

12. Suppose that a student researcher distributes surveys to her friends, students who live on her hall, and fellow members of campus clubs. This student's method of selecting participants for her research project is most similar to the procedure used to select a _____ sample.
    a. cluster
    b. convenience
    c. simple random
    d. stratified random

13. A **volunteer sample**:
    a. is a kind of convenience sample.
    b. is a kind of stratified random sample.
    c. may be distinguished from a self-selected sample.
    d. is more similar to a random sample than to a convenience sample.

14. Who among the following students would be *least* likely to bias the results of a study in which he or she volunteered to participate?
    a. Susan, who responded to an advertisement in a student newspaper to earn some extra money
    b. Dan, who signed an informed consent agreement after being randomly selected from a list of eligible students
    c. Mary, who thought that participating in a faculty member's research project as a course requirement would be easier than the alternative—writing a 10-page research paper
    d. Phil, who needed the extra credit points to earn a passing grade in his statistics class

15. Random assignment:
    a. is used to select a representative sample from a population.
    b. is used only when it is not feasible to randomly select participants from the population.
    c. guarantees that each participant has an equal chance of being assigned to one of the conditions of an experiment.
    d. guarantees that each individual within a population has an equal chance of being selected to participate in an experiment.

16. According to the text, the "activity that reduces the risks and increases the rewards of scientific sampling more than any other" is _____.
    a. replication
    b. random sampling
    c. random assignment
    d. using a randomized block design

17. The **replication** of a scientific study:
    a. is a form of plagiarism.
    b. should ideally be as identical as possible to the original study.
    c. can compensate to some degree for an inability to sample randomly from a population.
    d. is not possible unless participants are randomly selected from the population of interest.

18. Which one of the following statements is *most* accurate?
    a. Random assignment requires a sample of research participants who were randomly selected from the population of interest.
    b. Random assignment almost always results in a sample that is adequately representative of the population of interest.
    c. Research findings are generally replicated only if both random selection and random assignment are used.
    d. Random selection is almost never used, whereas random assignment is frequently used in behavioral science research.

19. The goal of sampling is to obtain _____ sample.
    a. a representative
    b. a simple random
    c. the largest possible
    d. the smallest possible

20. In their study of whether psychological preparedness protected against post-traumatic stress disorder among torture survivors in Turkey, Basoglu and colleagues (1997):
    a. randomly selected their participants from the population of torture survivors in Turkey, then compared those who had decided to become political activists to those who had not.
    b. selected a convenience sample of torture survivors, then randomly assigned them to undergo different levels of psychological preparedness training.
    c. randomly selected their participants, then randomly assigned them to undergo different levels of psychological preparedness training.
    d. compared convenience samples of torture survivors who either did or did not have a history of political activism.

21. Diekman and Murnan (2004) looked for the presence of female stereotypes in samples of children's books that had been classified by publishers and researchers as either sexist (10 books) or nonsexist (10 books). The populations of sexist and nonsexist children's books were small enough to permit _____, but the fact that the books were from populations that had already been labeled either sexist or nonsexist meant that the researchers could not use _____.
    a. random assignment; random selection
    b. random selection; random assignment

22. What do the studies by Basoglu et al. (1997), Leippe et al. (2004), and Diekman and Murnan (2004) have in common?
    a. random assignment of participants to experimental conditions, but not random selection from a population of interest
    b. random selection of participants from a population of interest, but not random assignment to experimental conditions
    c. random selection from the population, random assignment to conditions, and the study of samples to make inferences about populations
    d. the study of samples to make inferences about populations

23. Negative stereotypes about various ethnic groups are examples of _____ that are maintained by _____.
    a. groupthink; illusory correlation
    b. illusory correlation; confirmation bias
    c. confirmation bias; groupthink
    d. confirmation bias; illusory correlation

24. Which one of the following is an example of **subjective probability**?
    a. The probability of drawing a face card from a standard deck of playing cards is 12 / 52.
    b. There is a 70% chance of rain today, because it has rained on 70% of days like this in the past.
    c. Of the winners of the 41 Super Bowls, 8 teams won in consecutive years; therefore, the chance that the Indianapolis Colts will repeat as Super Bowl champions is 8 out of 41.
    d. Peyton Manning is 90% confident that the Indianapolis Colts will repeat as Super Bowl champions.

25. Aunt Sophie thinks that there is a 100% chance that it will rain because she "feels it in her bones." Aunt Sophie's belief is an example of:
    a. the gambler's fallacy.
    b. an expected relative frequency probability.
    c. a subjective probability.
    d. a confirmation bias.

26. Rex is flipping a coin to see how often it lands heads. In the language of probability, each flip of the coin is called a(n) _____.
    a. success
    b. trial
    c. outcome
    d. event

27. Rex is flipping a coin to see how often it lands heads. In the language of probability, each time the coin lands either heads or tails is called a(n) _____.
    a. success
    b. trial
    c. outcome
    d. event

28. Which of the following is an example of an **expected relative-frequency probability**?
    a. There are 52 cards in a standard deck, so the chance of drawing an ace of spades is 1 in 52.
    b. Mary estimates that there is a 75% chance that her best friend will have a baby girl because Mary has guessed correctly on three out of the last four pregnancies.
    c. Joe expects that 10 flips of a fair coin will result in 5 heads and 5 tails.
    d. If you keep flipping a coin, the proportion of heads will eventually be very close to 0.5.

29. In statistics, **probability** is defined as the:
    a. number of times a particular outcome has occurred in the past.
    b. number of times a particular outcome will occur in the future.
    c. level of confidence that a particular outcome will occur.
    d. expected relative frequency of a particular outcome.

30. When asked to write down a random sequence of the digits 0 and 1, most people:
    a. produce lists that frequently include more than three 0's or three 1's in a row.
    b. produce lists like those that would be produced by a random number generator.
    c. write down the next "random" digit with the immediately preceding digits in mind.
    d. produce lists showing a pattern of perfect alternation—that is, 1, 1, 0, 0, 1, 1, 0, 0, 1, 1, etc.

31. Individuals who commit the gambler's fallacy do not realize that any outcome in a game of chance is:
    a. determined by the previous as well as the next outcome.
    b. determined by the previous but not the next outcome.
    c. predictable by complex mathematical models.
    d. independent of the previous as well as the next outcome.

Use the following passage to answer questions 32–35.

One hundred students were randomly selected from the sophomore class of a mid-sized university to participate in a study designed to increase student interest in pursuing internships and research opportunities before their junior year. Fifty of the students were randomly assigned to attend weekly hour-long meetings during which counselors from the university's career center would discuss with them career opportunities for employment and graduate school options. The remaining 50 students also attended weekly hour-long meetings during which various campus issues were discussed, but there were no discussions of graduate school or career options. At the end of the fall semester, the Consideration of Future Consequences (CFC) scale was administered to the students in both groups.

32. The students assigned to attend weekly meetings during which they discussed career opportunities and graduate schools options with career center counselors comprised the:
    a. control group.
    b. experimental group.
    c. population of interest.
    d. research hypothesis group.

33. Which one of the following is an appropriate null hypothesis for this study?
    a. The CFC scores of the students assigned to the experimental group are not the same as those of the students assigned to the control group.
    b. The CFC scores of the students assigned to the experimental group are the same as those of the students assigned to the control group.
    c. The CFC scores of the students assigned to the experimental group are higher than those of the students assigned to the control group.
    d. The CFC scores in the populations represented by students in the experimental and control groups are the same.

34. Suppose that the mean CFC scores for the experimental and control groups are almost identical. The researcher should decide to:
    a. reject the research hypothesis.
    b. accept the null hypothesis.
    c. reject the null hypothesis.
    d. fail to reject the null hypothesis.

35. Suppose that the mean CFC score for the experimental group is much higher than the mean CFC score for the control group. In fact, the difference between the two group means is so large that it would occur by chance in fewer than 5 in 10,000 studies like the one described. Which one of the following is an appropriate conclusion?
    a. This result proves that the null hypothesis is false.
    b. This result proves that the research hypothesis is true.
    c. The results of this study were probably due to chance factors.
    d. The null hypothesis is almost certainly false and should be rejected.

36. Which of the following is a (are) correct statement(s) regarding the **null hypothesis**?
    a. The null hypothesis is sometimes called the alternative hypothesis.
    b. The null hypothesis is the one that a researcher cares the most about.
    c. The null hypothesis claims the opposite of what the researcher predicts.
    d. The null hypothesis is usually more accurate than the research hypothesis.

37. Which of the following is the most accurate description of a **research hypothesis**?
    a. It usually indicates a situation in which there is no difference between two populations.
    b. It is usually a more specific statement that the statement of the null hypothesis.
    c. It is also called the alternative (to the null) hypothesis.
    d. It is usually not as exciting as the null hypothesis.

38. A **Type I error** occurs when the:
    a. null hypothesis is incorrectly rejected.
    b. research hypothesis is incorrectly rejected.
    c. experimental group mean is not higher than the control group mean.
    d. data do not support either the research hypothesis or the null hypothesis.

39. A researcher who rejects a false null hypothesis has made a _____.
   a. Type I error
   b. Type II error
   c. correct decision
   d. Type I error as well as a Type II error

40. Suppose that a parole board has to decide whether a prisoner, a convicted murderer, is to be released. The null hypothesis states that the prisoner has not been rehabilitated. Which one of the following decisions represents a Type I error?
   a. The prisoner is released and kills a family of five in cold blood within 48 hours.
   b. The prisoner is released and becomes a model citizen.
   c. The prisoner is denied release when in fact he has been totally rehabilitated.
   d. The prisoner is denied release when in fact he remains an extremely dangerous man.

41. Suppose that a parole board has to decide whether a prisoner, a convicted murderer, is to be released. The null hypothesis states that the prisoner has not been rehabilitated. Which one of the following decisions represents a correct acceptance of the null hypothesis?
   a. The prisoner is released and becomes a model citizen.
   b. The prisoner is denied release when in fact he has been totally rehabilitated.
   c. The prisoner is denied release when in fact he remains an extremely dangerous man.
   d. The logic of hypothesis testing does not permit acceptance of the null hypothesis.

ANSWERS TO CHAPTER 4 STUDY QUESTIONS

Question Number	Correct Answer	Question Number	Correct Answer
1	b, p. 153	25	c, p. 173
2	c, pp. 154–155	26	b, pp. 173–174
3	random (pp. 154–155)	27	c, p. 174
4	d, p. 155	28	d, p. 174
5	d, p. 155	29	d, p. 175
6	d, p. 157	30	c, p. 175
7	d, p. 157	31	d, pp. 175–176
8	b, p. 157	32	b, p. 179
9	b, p. 157	33	d, p. 179 (Hypothesis statements are always about populations.)
10	b, p. 157		
11	b, p. 158	34	d, pp. 180–181
12	b, p. 158	35	d, pp. 188–189
13	a, p. 158	36	c, p. 179
14	b, p. 158	37	c, p. 179
15	c, p. 158	38	a, p. 183
16	a, p. 161	39	c, pp. 183–184
17	c, p. 161	40	a, pp. 183–184
18	d, p. 162	41	d, pp. 183–184 (The logic of hypothesis testing requires that the null hypothesis either be rejected or not rejected; it does not permit the acceptance of the null hypothesis.)
19	a, p. 162		
20	c, p. 163		
21	b, p. 166		
22	d, p. 167		
23	d, pp. 169–170		
24	d, p. 173		

REFERENCES

Freedman, D., Pisani, R., & Purves, R. (2007). *Statistics* (4th ed.) New York: W. W. Norton & Company.

Quinn, D. M., & Spencer, S. J. (2001). The interference of stereotype threat with women's generation of mathematical problem-solving strategies. *Journal of Social Issues, 57*(1), 55–71.

Strathman, A., Gleicher, F., Boninger, D. S., & Edwards, C. S. (1994). The consideration of future consequences: Weighing immediate and distant outcomes of behavior. *Journal of Personality and Social Psychology, 66*(4), 742–752.

CHAPTER FIVE

CORRELATION

Quantifying the Relation Between Two Variables

CHAPTER OUTLINE

Correlation: Assessing Associations Between Variables
- The Need for Standardization: Putting Two Different Variables on the Same Scale
- The z Score: Transforming Raw Scores into Standardized Scores
- The Characteristics of Correlation: Understanding the Coefficient at a Glance

The Pearson Correlation Coefficient: Quantifying a Linear Association
- Everyday Correlation Reasoning: Asking Better Questions
- Calculation of the Pearson Correlation Coefficient: Harnessing the Power of z Scores

Misleading Correlations: Understanding the Limits of Causal Reasoning
- Correlation is Not Causation: Invisible Third Variables
- A Restricted Range: When the Values of One Variable Are Limited
- The Effect of an Outlier: The Influence of a Single Data Point

Reliability and Validity: Correlation in Test Construction
- Correlation, Psychometrics, and a Super-Heated Job Market: Creating the Measures Behind the Research
- Reliability: Using Correlation to Create a Consistent Test
- Validity: Using Correlation to Determine Test Whether We Are Measuring What We Intend to Measure

Digging Deeper into the Data: Partial Correlation

LEARNING OBJECTIVES

After studying this chapter, you should be able to:

1. Define each of the following terms and provide examples that are not in the text: *z score, correlation coefficient, positive correlation, negative correlation, Pearson correlation coefficient, outlier analysis, outlier, psychometrics, psychometricians, practice effect, split-half reliability, coefficient alpha, criterion-related validity, postdictive validity, concurrent validity, partial correlation.*

2. Explain how *z* scores may be used to compare raw scores from different scales.

3. Discuss the limits of a correlation coefficient as it may be used to describe the relation between two variables.

4. Demonstrate facility with the calculation and application of the Pearson correlation coefficient.

5. Describe how psychometricians use correlation to determine the reliability and validity of various instruments.

CHAPTER REVIEW

> ### Correlation: Assessing Associations between Variables

The z Score: Transforming Raw Scores into Standardized Scores

In this chapter you were introduced to the *z* score as a means of providing a common scale of measurement, or standard, that enables comparisons between scores from different scales. A **z score** (also called a standard score) expresses a raw score in terms of the number of standard deviations it deviates from the mean of the raw scores in the population of interest. Put another way, a *z* score is used to locate a raw score (*X*) on a scale that uses standard deviations as its unit of measurement. A distribution of *z* scores is called the *z* distribution. The *z* distribution has a mean of 0 and a standard deviation of 1. The formula for transforming a raw score to a *z* score is as follows:

$$z = \frac{X - \mu}{\sigma}$$

where, μ and σ are the mean and standard deviation, respectively, of the population of interest.

The *sign* of a *z* score indicates whether it is above or below the mean, whereas the *magnitude* of a *z* score indicates how far it is above or below the mean. Note that most *z* scores fall in the range of −3 to 3. That's because most of the data gathered in research studies are within 3 standard deviations of the mean. Scores that are more than 3 standard deviations from the mean may be may tagged as *outliers* and removed from the data set because they are too extreme.

As just noted, transforming raw scores to z scores allows a direct comparison between different scales. The transformation process is depicted graphically in the following figure:

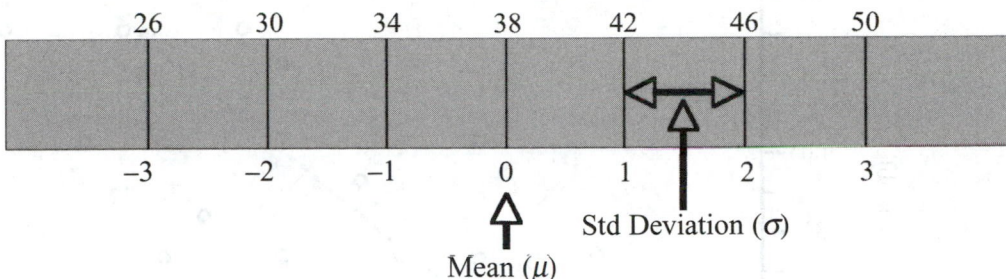

A glance at the scale measured in raw score units shows that the mean is 38 (the value that corresponds to a z score of 0) and the standard deviation is 4 (the distance between any two consecutive z scores). Without doing any calculations, you can see that a raw score of 32 corresponds to a z score of –1.5.

The Characteristics of Correlation: Understanding the Coefficient at a Glance

A **correlation coefficient** is a precise quantitative measure of the *strength* and *direction* of a *linear* association between two variables, both of which are usually measured on an interval scale. A linear relation between two variables is disclosed in a scatterplot like the one on the next page. (Recall from Chapter 3 that each point in a scatterplot represents the intersection of a single participant's scores on each of two variables.) Note that the pattern of points may be approximated by the broken line that slopes upward from left to right.

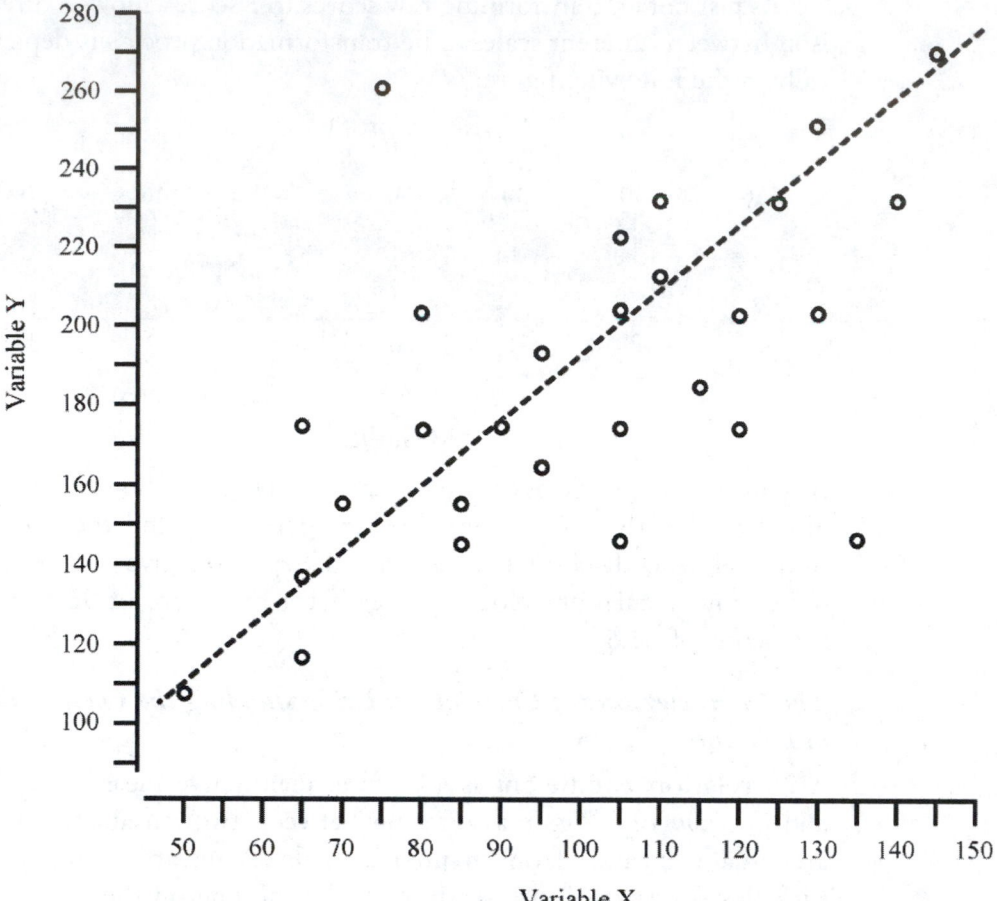

The *sign* of the correlation coefficient indicates the *direction* of the linear relation. The scatterplot above depicts a **positive correlation**. Two variables are positively correlated when participants with high scores on one variable tend to have high scores on the other variable (and those with medium and low scores on one variable tend to have medium and low scores, respectively, on the second variable). In contrast, a **negative** (also called an *inverse*) **correlation** is one in which higher scores on one variable are associated with lower scores on the other variable. A scatterplot displaying a negative linear relation is like a mirror image of a scatterplot showing a positive correlation.

The range of possible values of a correlation coefficient is −1 to 1. The values −1 and 1 represent perfect correlations which, in turn, reflect perfect linear relations between variables. A perfect linear relation is one in which all of the points in a scatterplot fall along a straight line that has either a positive or negative slope. As noted in the text, correlations of exactly ±1 or 0 are almost never encountered in the "real world," and there are no perfect correlations between variables studied in the social and behavioral sciences. However, you can imagine a class in which the grade is determined only by attendance; there are 25 classes and each one attended adds 4 points to the grade. As long as there is at least some variability in class attendance, the correlation between class attendance and final grade will be 1.

The *magnitude*, or absolute value, of the correlation coefficient is a precise measure of the *strength* of the linear relation: the closer the correlation coefficient to 1, the stronger the linear relation between the variables, *irrespective of the sign of the coefficient*. Don't miss the point that the strength of a linear relation is completely independent of the direction of that relation. For example, a correlation of −.46 indicates a stronger linear relation than a correlation of 0.37.

The strength of a linear association may also be estimated from the pattern of points in a scatterplot. The greater the strength of the relation, the smaller the average vertical distance between the points and a line drawn to fit them. Conversely, the greater the average vertical distance between the points and the line, the weaker the linear relation between the variables. To illustrate these points, lines were drawn to fit the patterns of data in each of the scatterplots below. The correlation coefficient computed for the scatterplot on the left is −.45; for the scatterplot on the right, the correlation coefficient is −.94.

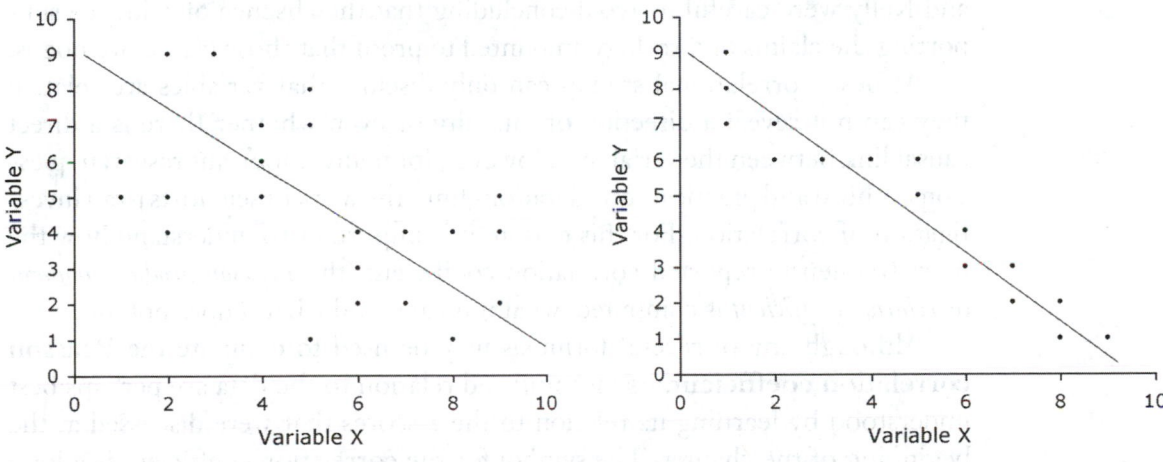

Of the linear relations displayed above, which one do you suppose to be more common in the behavioral and social sciences? If you said the one on the left, then you are correct. Correlations between variables studied in the social and behavioral sciences typically do not exceed 0.4 in absolute value. As noted in the text, Cohen (1988) reported that a correlation considered "large" by social science standards must be at least 0.5; a correlation of "medium" or "moderate" size is around 0.3; and a "small" correlation is near 0.1.

If the correlation coefficient is close to zero, then there is essentially no *linear* relation between the two variables; the variables may be related, but that relation can not be linear. A much-cited nonlinear relation in psychology is depicted in the Yerkes-Dodson inverted "U" curve relating arousal and performance. According to this function, when arousal is either very low or very high, performance is relatively low; the highest levels of performance are observed over a range of moderate levels of arousal.[1] Using a correlation coefficient to describe a *curvilinear* pattern of data such as might be observed in a test of the Yerkes-Dodson effect would be very misleading.

> ## The Pearson Correlation Coefficient: Quantifying a Linear Association

The relation between the positions of stars and planets and the affairs of earthly life is discussed in the text as an example of an *illusory correlation*. As defined in Chapter 4, an illusory correlation is just that—a correlation that only appears to exist. In their review of studies of the validity of astrology, Dean and Kelly (2003) described "time twins," unrelated individuals born at around the same time, as "the definitive test of astrology because errors or uncertainties of birth chart interpretation are avoided" (text page 187). The results of a study of 110 variables measured at ages 11, 16, and 23 on 2,101 individuals born an average of 4.8 minutes apart in London between March 3 and March 9, 1958 disclosed similarities that were almost exactly what would be expected by chance. Dean and Kelly were careful to avoid concluding that the absence of evidence supporting the claims of astrology amounted to proof that those claims are bogus.

At best, correlational studies can only disclose that variables are related; they can not reveal a direction of causality or even whether there is a direct causal link between the variables. However, for many important research questions, ethical and practical considerations limit the work of scientists to an investigation of correlation. For this reason, it is important to understand how the most frequently reported correlation coefficient, the *Pearson product-moment correlation coefficient* is computed, what it means, and what it does not mean.

Although any of several formulas may be used to compute the **Pearson correlation coefficient**, its meaning and relation to the data are perhaps best understood by learning its relation to the z scores that were discussed at the beginning of the chapter. The symbol for the correlation coefficient is a lowercase "r" (for regression, the subject of the next chapter), so the formula will be expressed as a solution for r.

$$r = \frac{\sum z_X z_Y}{N}$$

The Pearson correlation is thus computed as the average of the product of the z scores for each participant. As you learned earlier, z scores are raw scores

---

[1] The source of this function is a study (Yerkes & Dodson, 1908) in which mice required the fewest trials to learn to enter the correct white compartment when the electric shock administered for entering the incorrect black compartment was of intermediate intensity. Lower or higher intensities of shock were associated with slower learning (more trials to reach a criterion performance). The Yerkes-Dodson "hypothesis" has received limited support in studies of human performance on a variety of tasks (see Watters, Martin, & Schreter, 1997).

expressed in terms of standard deviations from the mean of the comparison group. So, the first step in computing a Pearson r is to convert each pair of raw scores to z scores. The second step is to compute the product of each participant's z scores (these are called *cross-products*). The final step is to compute the mean of the cross-products of z scores by summing them and dividing the sum by N, the number of participants. An example based on fictional data follows:

Case	VAR X	VAR Y	z_X	z_Y	$z_X z_Y$
1	6	5	1.581	1.414	2.236
2	4	4	0.527	0.707	0.373
3	3	3	0.000	0.000	0.000
4	1	1	−1.054	−1.414	1.491
5	1	2	−1.054	−0.707	0.745
M	3.00	3.00		$\Sigma z_X z_Y =$	4.845
SD	1.90	1.41		$r = \Sigma z_X z_Y / N =$	0.969

You may note that the first two cases have raw scores above the mean on both variables, whereas the last two cases have raw scores below the mean on both variables. Raw scores that are above the mean convert to positive z scores, whereas those below the mean convert to negative z scores. Thus, with the exception of the score equal to the mean, the cross-products of the z scores are positive, as is the correlation coefficient.

The example below illustrates the calculation of the Pearson correlation coefficient when higher scores on VAR X are associated with lower scores on VAR Y; that is, scores that are above the mean on VAR X are paired with scores that are below the mean on VAR Y (and vice versa). With one exception, the cross-products of the z scores are negative, resulting in a negative correlation coefficient.

Case	VAR X	VAR Y	z_X	z_Y	$z_X z_Y$
1	6	1	1.581	−1.414	−2.236
2	4	2	0.527	−0.707	−0.373
3	3	3	0.000	0.000	0.000
4	1	4	−1.054	0.707	−0.745
5	1	5	−1.054	1.414	−1.491
M	3.00	3.00		$\Sigma z_X z_Y =$	−4.845
SD	1.90	1.41		$r = \Sigma z_X z_Y / N =$	−0.969

Misleading Correlations: Understanding the Limits of Causal Reasoning

As just noted, a correlation between variables does not mean that the variables are causally related. If an increase in the values of one variable causes an increase (or a decrease) in the values of a second variable, then the variables are strongly correlated, but it does not follow that strongly correlated variables are causally related. Why not? It may be that strongly correlated variables are not causally related to each other, but are both causally related to a third variable. In short, a correlation between two variables, A and B, may result from any of the following:

1. Changes in the values of Variable A cause changes in the values of Variable B.
2. Changes in the values of Variable B cause changes in the values of Variable A.
3. Changes in the values of Variables A and B are caused by changes in Variable C.

The point is that correlation alone does not disclose which of these alternatives is correct. Consider the following problem. For a large sample of middle-aged men, the correlation between income and blood pressure is 0.74. Does this mean that men with higher incomes tend to have jobs that involve greater responsibility, and this greater responsibility causes stress that manifests as higher blood pressure? If you agree with this interpretation, then you've just endorsed the idea that a correlation between two variables means that changes in one variable cause changes in the other. You've agreed that the relatively high correlation between income and blood pressure is evidence of a causal chain: an increase in job responsibilities causes stress, and one sign of increased stress is an increase in blood pressure. This interpretation is reasonable, but only as an alternative among several. A more parsimonious interpretation is that the correlation between income and blood pressure is a product of aging. As men age, their incomes increase as does their blood pressure. More specifically, income increases with experience, and it is impossible to acquire experience apart from aging. An increase in blood pressure is a result of physical changes associated with aging. The correlation between Variable A (income) and Variable B (blood pressure) is probably caused by Variable C (age). Again, the correlation may be explained by any of a number of interpretations, but the correlation, alone, does not enable a determination of which of them is correct.

Interpreting a correlation to be evidence of causation is arguably the most prevalent misrepresentation of a correlation coefficient. However, the correlation coefficient itself may be misrepresentative. For example, a correlation coefficient computed for a *restricted range* of data misrepresents those data by underestimating the degree of linear relation between the variables. The range of values of a variable may be restricted by the use of samples that are not representative of an entire population. For example, job applicants' scores on tests of vocational aptitude are often used by employers to make hiring decisions. The rather low correlation between test scores and subsequent job performance is a result of restricting the range of test scores to include only the top-scoring applicants who were hired. A restricted range of data also explains why the correlation between scores on the Graduate Record Exam

(GRE) and first-year grades in graduate school is much lower than the correlation between scores on the SAT and first-year grades in college. Undergraduates who are admitted to graduate school tend to have higher scholastic aptitude than those who are not admitted (or do not apply), so the range of GRE scores tends to be smaller than the range of SAT scores. In addition, the range of first-year grades in graduate school is restricted to A's and B's (D's and F's are not typically given in graduate school; a C is tantamount to an F).

The presence of one or more outliers can also alter the magnitude and/or the sign of a correlation coefficient (see Figures 3-6 and 5-14 in the text for examples of scatterplots showing an outlier). As defined in the discussion of outlier analysis in Chapter 1, an **outlier** is a data value that lies outside the range of most of the values in a sample of data. Outliers[2] that represent valid measures present an opportunity, via **outlier analysis**, for a more complete understanding of the relationship between the variables under study. However, because an outlier can distort the correlation between variables, it is important to decide how extreme an outlier must be before it is excluded before any data are collected. A rule adopted by many researchers is to exclude any data value that is more than two standard deviations from the mean. For variables whose distributions are well-approximated by a normal curve (the normal distribution was introduced in Chapter 2), this rule excludes the most extreme 5% or so of the data values.

Reliability and Validity: Correlation in Test Construction

The operational definitions of many of the dependent variables studied by social scientists have been scores generated by the use of instruments (scales, tests) that were developed to measure various constructs. The development of the various instruments used by social science researchers has largely been the task of **psychometricians**, statisticians and psychologists who are also experts in the assessment of the *reliability* and *validity* of the data generated by those instruments. The branch of statistics or psychology concerned with psychological measurement is called, appropriately enough, **psychometrics**, and reliability and validity together comprise the *psychometric properties* of measurement.

The most widely used statistical tool of the psychometrician is the Pearson correlation coefficient. You were introduced to *test-retest reliability* and *predictive validity* in Chapter 1. Both are assessed by computing a Pearson correlation coefficient. To review, test-retest reliability refers to the consistency of scores on the same test administered to the same sample of participants at different times, whereas predictive validity is assessed by determining the correlation between scores on a test and level of performance on some criterion measure assessed later.

---

[2] Some outliers result from errors in measurement or data entry. However, the outliers examined in an outlier analysis represent valid measures of the dependent variable.

In addition to assessing the consistency of scores over time, it is important to assess the consistency of responses to items that purport to measure the same construct. This assessment, called **internal consistency reliability**, measures the extent to which responses to the items comprising an instrument are correlated with each other. The earliest assessment of internal consistency reliability was termed **split-half reliability**, because a test was first split into two halves—usually the odd- and even-numbered items—and the Pearson correlation between responses to the items from the two halves was computed. **Coefficient alpha** (or *Cronbach's alpha*, after its inventor) is currently used to assess internal consistency reliability. This statistic (the symbol is the Greek letter α) is based on the average of the correlations between responses to all possible pairs of items (also called item-to-item or inter-item correlations). This average of inter-item correlations is like computing the average correlation for *all possible* split halves of an instrument. Thus, coefficient alpha differs from a split-half reliability coefficient in that it is not affected by the order of the items. Internal consistency reliability coefficients are expected to be higher than test-retest reliability coefficients unless the test-retest interval is extremely short. An alpha coefficient of 0.8 is considered adequate for an instrument used in research, but the internal consistency reliability coefficient for an instrument used for diagnostic purposes must be at least 0.9.

The Pearson correlation coefficient is also used to assess various forms of validity. **Criterion-related validity** refers to the degree to which scores on an instrument (test or questionnaire) are correlated with certain *criteria*, which may be scores on instruments that measure the same, or a related, construct, or behavioral expressions of the construct. There are three forms of criterion-related validity, each one defined according to when the criterion is evaluated. **Concurrent validity** is measured by how well scores on an instrument correlate with a criterion assessed *at about the same time*. For example, in the Method section of their study of rejection and depression in adolescents, Nolan, Flynn, and Garber (2003) wrote: "After developing the adolescent-, mother-, and teacher-report rejection scales ..., the scales were correlated with an established measure of rejection to examine concurrent validity" (p. 747). Similarly, scores on a new short version of an instrument may be correlated with scores on the established longer version administered at about the same time. **Postdictive validity** is measured by how well scores on an instrument correlate with a criterion assessed *at some time in the past*. Roy and Wormith (1985; cited in Mills & Croner, 1997) administered the Criminal Sentiments Scale (CSS) to a sample of federal inmates and reported the scale "to be postdictive once age of the offender was controlled for" (p. 400). In other words, the inmates' responses to items in the scale were consistent with their current status as persons with a history of criminal behavior. **Predictive validity**, introduced in Chapter 1, is measured by how well scores correlate with a criterion measured *at some future time*. For example, the predictive validity of the SAT is assessed by computing the correlation between SAT scores and GPA for the first semester or first year of college. Note that assessments of postdictive and predictive validity depend upon the relative stability of the construct of interest. For example, Roy and Wormith found that the postdictive validity of the CSS was higher for younger inmates whose attitudes toward the law and society had presumably not yet been reformed.

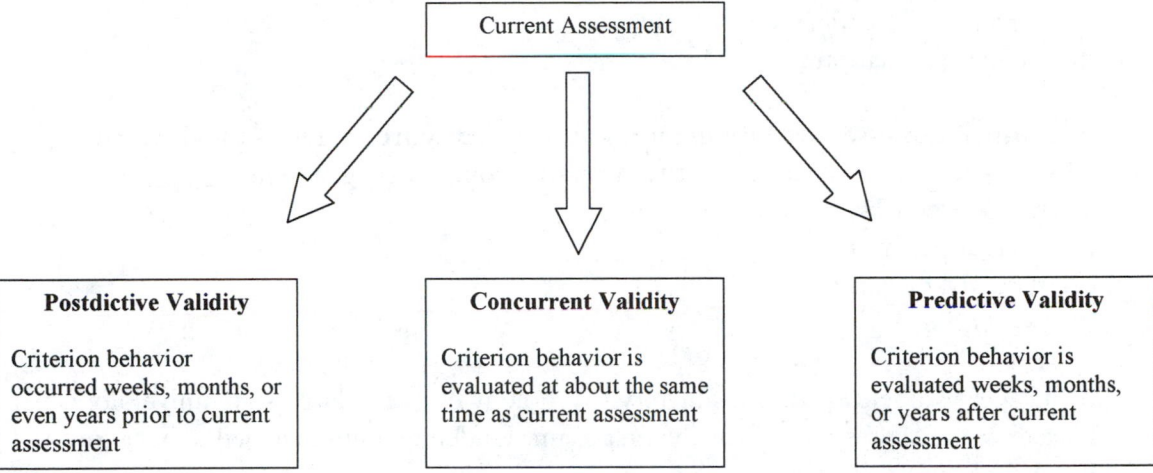

Digging Deeper into the Data: Partial Correlation

A **partial correlation** is computed to measure the degree of linear association between two variables after statistically removing the correlation between each of these variables and a third variable. For example, in their study of the relation between rejection and depression in adolescents, Nolan, Flynn, and Garber (2003) also collected data on the relation between externalizing behaviors (acting out) and anxiety. The correlations between externalizing behaviors, anxiety, and depression are shown in the table below.

		X	Y	Z
		Externalizing	Anxiety	Depression
X	Externalizing	---		
Y	Anxiety	0.356	---	
Z	Depression	0.635	0.368	---

The Z symbol is used here to identify depression as the variable to be controlled in the calculation of the partial correlation between externalizing (X) and anxiety (Y).

STUDY QUESTIONS

1. Which one of the following tells how many standard deviations a particular individual scored above or below the mean of his or her comparison group?
   a. deviation score
   b. z score
   c. correlation coefficient
   d. standard deviation

2. A yardstick expresses distance in inches or feet. A **z score** expresses the distance between an individual score and the mean of a comparison group in _____.
   a. raw score units
   b. deviation scores
   c. standard deviations
   d. percentiles

3. A first-year student in an introductory psychology class at a large state university is perplexed by the scores posted for the first exam. Under a column labeled z, her score is 0.5. What does this score mean?
   a. She scored at the 50th percentile.
   b. She answered only half of the questions correctly.
   c. She scored above the mean.
   d. She scored below the mean.

4. The mean number of words recalled correctly in an experiment examining free recall from long-term memory is 18, with a standard deviation of 6. If a participant recalled 18 words, her z score would be _____.
   a. 3
   b. 12
   c. 18
   d. 0

5. Which one of the following is the formula used to compute a z score?
   a. $z = \dfrac{(X - \mu)^2}{N}$ b. $z = \dfrac{\mu - X}{\sigma}$

   c. $z = \dfrac{X - \mu}{N}$ d. $z = \dfrac{(X - \mu)^2}{\sigma}$

6. In a certain population of scores, the mean is 100 and the standard deviation is 10. Which one of the following scores corresponds to a z score of −1.5?
   a. 85
   b. 15
   c. 115
   d. 150

7. A **correlation coefficient** describes the strength and direction of a _____ relation between two variables.
   a. linear
   b. nonlinear
   c. causal
   d. exponential

8. The range of possible values for a correlation coefficient is:
   a. determined by the means and standard deviations of the two correlated variables.
   b. interpreted directly from a scatterplot depicting the relation between two variables.
   c. determined by the range of scores for the two variables.
   d. between –1 and 1.

9. There is a _____ relation between two variables when the pattern of points in a scatterplot roughly resembles a straight line.
   a. positive
   b. linear
   c. curvilinear
   d. negative

10. There is a **positive correlation** between two variables when individuals with _____ scores on one variable tend to have _____ scores on the other variable.
    a. two or more; two or more
    b. high; low
    c. positive; negative
    d. high; high

11. The pattern of data points in a graph depicting the relation between scores on the scholastic aptitude test (SAT) and first-year college grade point average (GPA) tends to slope upward and to the right, indicating a _____ correlation between these variables.
    a. weak
    b. strong
    c. positive
    d. negative

12. There is a **negative correlation** between two variables when cases with _____ scores on one variable tend to have _____ scores on the other variable.
    a. high; high
    b. low; low
    c. high; low
    d. negative; negative

13. In a study of 174 factory workers, Bardsley and Rhodes (1996) found that workers who were most often late to work tended to be the ones who scored the lowest on job satisfaction. This is an example of a _____ correlation.
    a. near-zero
    b. curvilinear
    c. positive
    d. negative

14. A *perfect correlation*:
    a. has a value of either 1 or –1.
    b. has zero variability around the mean of both variables.
    c. exists only in theory and may not be computed for actual data.
    d. results when the mean of one variable is 1 and the mean of the other variable is –1.

15. The *strength* of the correlation between two linearly related variables is indicated by the:
    a. magnitude (absolute value) of the correlation coefficient.
    b. sign (positive or negative) of the correlation coefficient.
    c. length of the line in a scatterplot.
    d. number of points in a scatterplot.

16. Correlations that are _____ are fairly common in everyday life.
    a. greater than 1
    b. less than –1
    c. approximately 0
    d. approximately 1 or –1

17. Correlations that are considered "large" by Cohen's (1988) standards are _____ in the social sciences.
    a. fairly common
    b. fairly uncommon
    c. almost unheard of
    d. routinely reported

18. Which of the following variable pairs are *least* likely to be correlated?
    a. amount of time studying and amount learned
    b. the price and quality of purchased goods
    c. intelligence and physical strength
    d. shoe size and glove size

19. Choose the best description of the correlation displayed in the scatterplot below:

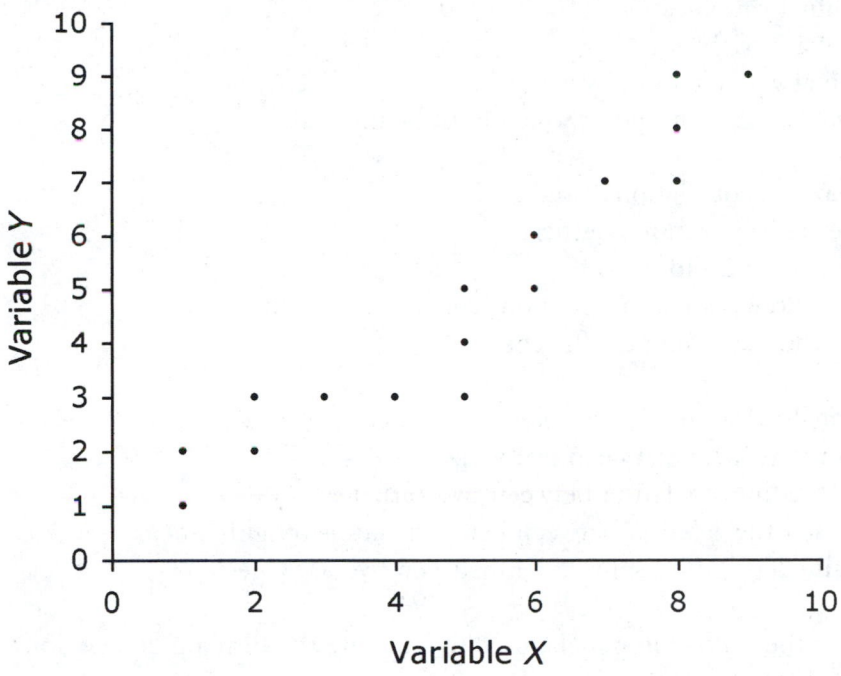

   a.   strong, positive   b.   strong, negative
   c.   moderate, positive   d.   moderate, negative

20. Choose the best description of the correlation displayed in the scatterplot below:

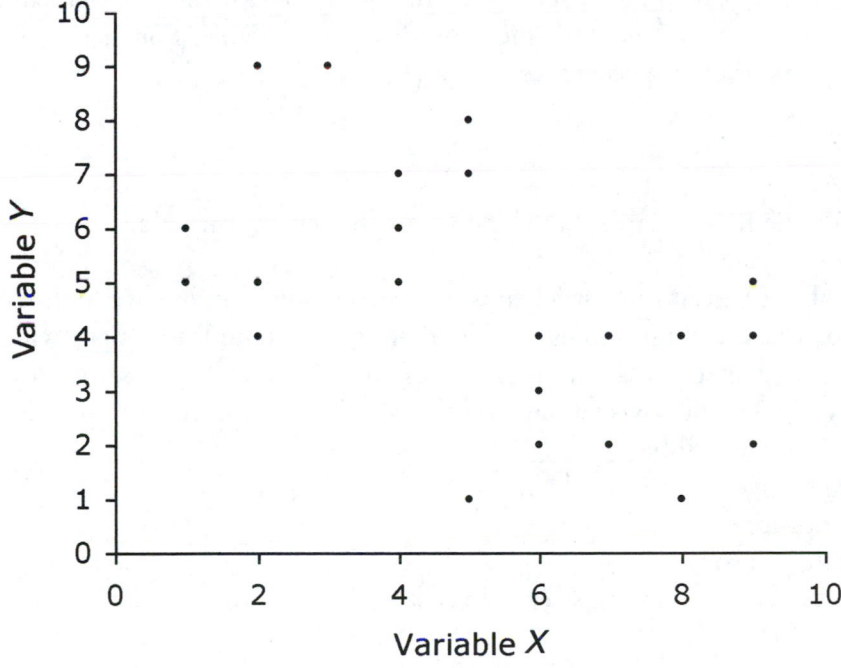

   a.   strong, positive   b.   strong, negative
   c.   moderate, positive   d.   moderate, negative

21. The **Pearson correlation coefficient** quantifies a linear relation between:
    a. two nominal variables.
    b. two interval variables.
    c. two ordinal variables.
    d. two variables, at least one of which must be interval.

22. The first step in a correlational study is to:
    a. compute the correlation coefficient.
    b. construct a scatterplot.
    c. convert the raw scores to deviation scores.
    d. compute the regression coefficient.

23. In correlational research, a scatterplot is used to:
    a. quantify the relation between two variables.
    b. quantify the linear relation between two variables.
    c. confirm that the relation between two variables is roughly linear.
    d. graphically depict a causal relation between two variables.

24. Which one of the following may be used to compute the Pearson correlation coefficient?

    a. $\dfrac{\sum z_X}{\sum z_Y}$
    b. $\dfrac{\sum z_X z_Y}{N}$
    c. $\dfrac{\sqrt{z_X z_Y}}{N}$
    d. $\dfrac{\sqrt{\sum z_X z_Y}}{N}$

25. Several of the participants in a correlational study recorded scores that were above the mean on one variable, but below the mean on the other variable. For these participants, the cross-products of their z scores were:
    a. positive.
    b. negative.
    c. zero.
    d. positive for the first variable, but negative for the second variable.

26. Suppose that about half of the participants in a correlational study have high scores on one variable paired with high scores on the other variable (and lows paired with lows), and the remaining participants have high scores on one variable paired with low scores on the other variable (and lows paired with highs). The sum of the cross-products of z scores for this sample will be _____.
    a. large and positive
    b. large and negative
    c. approximately zero
    d. insufficient information to answer

27. The direction of causality for a correlation between two variables can only be specified if:
    a. the correlation coefficient is statistically significant.
    b. the absolute value of the correlation coefficient is greater than 0.5.
    c. a third variable that is related to both variables has been identified.
    d. False premise: A correlation can not disclose whether two variables are causally related.

28. Which of the following is a possible explanation for a high correlation between two variables, A and B?
    a. Variable A causes Variable B, but Variable B does not cause Variable A.
    b. Variable B causes Variable A, but Variable A does not cause Variable B.
    c. A third variable causes the high correlation between Variables A and B, but Variables A and B can not be causally related.
    d. Either Variable A causes Variable B, or Variable B causes Variable A, or the correlation between Variables A and B is caused by a third variable.

29. A manager finds that the correlation between scores on a test administered to job applicants (a test of vocational aptitude) and ratings of actual job performance is lower than he expected. If the manager hired only those applicants who performed very well on the test, then the low correlation is probably due to:
    a. the low predictive validity of the test.
    b. the low postdictive validity of the test.
    c. inadequate internal consistency reliability.
    d. a restriction in the range of test scores.

30. An **outlier** is a score that:
    a. lies outside the range of most of the scores.
    b. can distort the direction, but not the strength, of the correlation between two variables.
    c. can distort the strength, but not the direction, of the correlation between two variables.
    d. always artificially inflates the magnitude of a correlation coefficient.

31. Removing the outlier from the data plotted in the figure below would _____ the correlation between the variables.

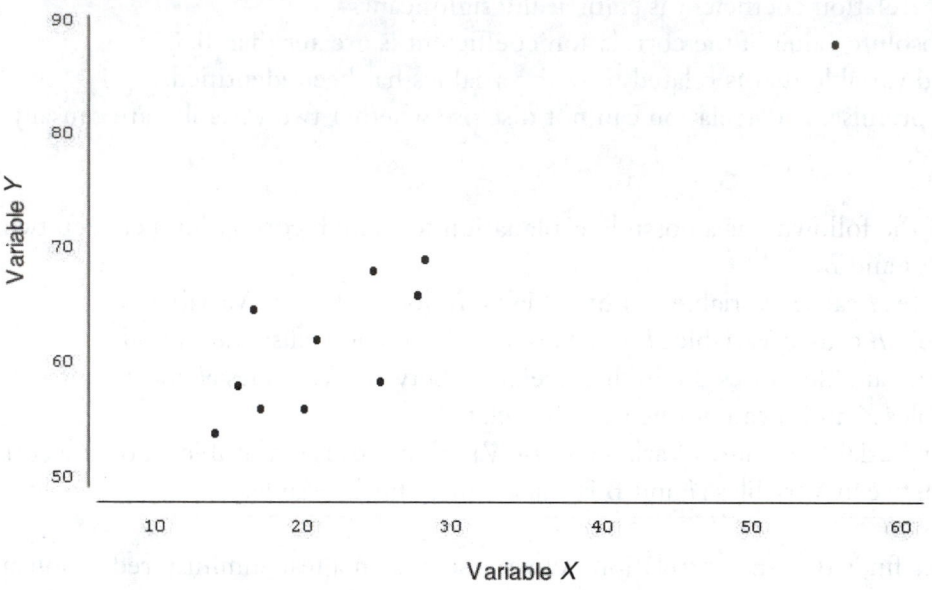

a. increase the magnitude of
b. decrease the magnitude of
c. reverse the sign of
d. have no effect on

32. **Psychometrics** is a branch of _____.
a. statistics
b. clinical psychology
c. education
d. experimental psychology

33. Which of the following is the *most* accurate statement regarding **psychometricians**?
a. The demand for psychometricians has increased markedly as a result of a widespread increase standardized testing.
b. The demand for psychometricians has decreased markedly as a result of a widespread reduction in standardized testing.
c. Despite the increasing demand for their services, psychometricians are underpaid relative to other professionals in statistics, education, and psychology with similar levels of education and training.
d. The demand for psychometricians has declined in recent years as many of the duties that formerly required training in psychometrics have been assumed by professionals in other fields.

34. The fact that scores often improve on tests that are taken a second time presents a problem for assessing:
    a. predictive validity.
    b. split-half reliability.
    c. postdictive validity.
    d. test-retest reliability.

35. Initially, researchers determined the *internal consistency* of a test by computing:
    a. the correlation between responses to the even-numbered and odd-numbered items.
    b. the correlation between scores following repeated administrations.
    c. split-half reliability using the formula for Cronbach's alpha.
    d. the average inter-item correlation.

36. **Coefficient alpha** is:
    a. used to assess the internal consistency of a test.
    b. used to assess test-retest reliability.
    c. used to assess predictive validity.
    d. generally regarded as inferior to the split-half method.

37. Which one of the following is determined by calculating the average of all split-half correlations among the items that comprise a test?
    a. coefficient alpha
    b. split-half reliability
    c. criterion-related validity
    d. practice effects

38. **Criterion-related validity** may be established by determining the correlation between:
    a. scores on a scale or measure and performance on some relevant external standard.
    b. scores on the items from one half of a scale with scores on the items from the other half of the scale.
    c. scores from the same from of the same scale administered to the same individuals at different times.
    d. scores from different forms of the same scale administered to the same individuals at the same time.

39. If a test designed to measure construct X has adequate _____, then individuals who have high scores on this test should behave in other ways that clearly express construct X.
    a. criterion-related validity
    b. internal consistency
    c. test-retest reliability
    d. split-half reliability

40. In an assessment of _____, scores on a measure of interest are correlated with a criterion measured at about the same time.
    a. test-retest reliability
    b. postdictive validity
    c. predictive validity
    d. concurrent validity

41. According to an analysis of the first-year academic performance of the freshman class at a small college, the students ranked 1 to 25 on high school SAT scores had the same ranks for their first-year GPA. For these 25 students, the SAT has very good _____.
    a. test-retest reliability
    b. postdictive validity
    c. internal consistency
    d. predictive validity

42. The degree of association between two variables, after statistically removing the association of both variables with a third variable, is quantified by a technique called

    _____.
    a. partial correlation
    b. tetrachoric correlation
    c. bivariate correlation
    d. point-biserial correlation

ANSWERS TO CHAPTER 5 STUDY QUESTIONS

Question Number	Correct Answer
1	b, p. 207
2	c, p. 207
3	c, p. 209
4	d, p. 209
5	a, p. 210
6	a, pp. 208–210
7	a, p. 211
8	c, p. 211
9	b, p. 211
10	d, pp. 211–212
11	c, pp. 211–212
12	c, p. 212
13	d, p. 212
14	a, p. 212
15	a, p. 213
16	c, p. 214
17	b, p. 214
18	c, p. 214
19	a, pp. 219–222
20	d, pp. 219–222
21	b, p. 222
22	b, p. 222
23	c, p. 222
24	b, p. 225
25	b, p. 225
26	c, p. 225 [The sum of the cross-products of z scores will be positive for half of the participants (those who have high scores paired with high scores and those who have low scores paired with low scores), but the sum will be negative for the other half (participants who have high scores paired with low scores and those who have low scores paired with high scores). The positive and negative sums of cross-products of z scores will cancel each other, resulting in a sum of cross-products of z scores that is near zero.]
27	d, p. 227 (A correlation alone cannot disclose whether two variables are causally related.)
28	d, pp. 227–228
29	d, pp. 228–229
30	a, p. 229
31	b, p. 230
32	a, p. 232
33	a, p. 232
34	d, pp. 232–233
35	a, p. 233
36	d, p. 233
37	a, p. 233
38	a, p. 234
39	a, p. 234
40	d, p. 234
41	d, p. 234
42	a, p. 236

REFERENCES

Mills, J. F., & Kroner, D. G. (1997). The Criminal Sentiments Scale: Predictive validity in a sample of violent and sex offenders. *Journal of Clinical Psychology, 53,* 399–404.

Nolan, S. A., Flynn, C., & Garber, J. (2003). Prospective relations between rejection and depression in young adolescents. *Journal of Personality and Social Psychology, 85,* 745–755.

Watters, P. A., Martin, F. & Schreter, Z. (1997). Caffeine and cognitive performance: The nonlinear Yerkes-Dodson Law. *Human Psychopharmacology: Clinical and Experimental, 12,* 249–257.

Yerkes, R. M., & Dodson, J. D. (1998). The relation of strength of stimulus to rapidity of habit-formation. *Journal of Comparative Neurology and Psychology, 18,* 459–482.

CHAPTER SIX

REGRESSION

Tools for Predicting Behavior

CHAPTER OUTLINE

Regression: Building on Correlation
- The Difference Between Regression and Correlation: Prediction Versus Relation
- Linear Regression: Calculating the Equation for a Line Using z Scores Only
- Reversing the Formula: Transforming z Scores to Raw Scores
- Linear Regression: Calculating the Equation for a Line by Converting Raw Scores to z Scores
- Linear Regression: Calculating the Equation for a Line with Raw Scores

Drawing Conclusions from a Regression Equation: Interpretation and Prediction
- Regression: Quantifying Common Sense
- What Correlation Can Teach Us about Regression: Correlation Still Isn't Causation
- Regression to the Mean: The Patterns of Extreme Scores
- The Effect Size for Regression: Proportionate Reduction in Error

Multiple Regression: Predicting from More than One Variable
- Multiple Regression: Understanding the Equation
- Stepwise Multiple Regression and Hierarchical Multiple Regression: A Choice of Tactics

Digging Deeper into the Data: Structural Equation Modeling (SEM)

LEARNING OBJECTIVES

After studying this chapter, you should be able to:

1. Define each of the following terms and provide examples that are not in the text: *simple linear regression, regression to the mean, intercept, slope, standard error of the estimate, proportionate reduction in error, orthogonal variable, multiple regression, stepwise multiple regression, hierarchical multiple regression, structural equation modeling, statistical (or theoretical) model, path, path analysis, manifest variable, latent variable, longitudinal study.*
2. Describe the similarities and differences between correlation and regression.

3. Determine the regression equation for both z scores and raw scores and use either equation to predict values of the dependent variable for known values of the independent variable.

4. Discuss the limits of prediction using a regression equation, including problems of interpolation and extrapolation as well as potentially confounding variables.

5. Compute the proportionate reduction in error as a measure of effect size and relate this statistic to the correlation coefficient.

6. Distinguish between simple and multiple linear regression and discuss the circumstances under which stepwise and hierarchical multiple regression are typically used.

7. Describe structural equation modeling as an evolution of path analysis and explain how it is used by researchers to model complex relationships between latent variables via measures of manifest variables.

CHAPTER REVIEW

> Regression: Building on Correlation

Regression and correlation may be conceptualized as two sides of the same coin. *Correlation* focuses on the relation between variables and does not assign labels to them, whereas *regression* is more concerned with the functions of the variables in the relation and labels them accordingly. When computing a Pearson correlation coefficient, either variable may be regarded as the "X" or the "Y" variable; that is, changing the order of the variables does not change the value of the correlation coefficient. When developing a regression equation, one variable is designated as the independent (or predictor) variable, and the other as the dependent (or criterion) variable.

Think of correlation as enabling linear regression, or prediction. If two variables are correlated, then the values of one variable may be used to predict values of the second variable. **Simple linear regression** refers to the prediction of the values of the dependent variable from values of one independent variable. For example, many colleges and universities use a student's high school SAT score to predict his or her grade point average (GPA) for the first year of study. The tool used for prediction is called the *regression equation*.

In Chapter 5, you learned to convert raw scores to z scores, and then you learned to compute the correlation coefficient as the average of the cross-products of z scores. In Chapter 6, you learned that the regression equation could be expressed in terms of z scores. To predict values of Variable Y, the dependent variable, from values of Variable X, the independent variable, you first converted the raw scores on both variables to z scores. Then you multiplied an individual's z score on Variable X (z_X) by the correlation coefficient (r_{XY}) to compute the predicted z score on Variable Y ($z_{\hat{Y}}$) for that individual:

$$z_{\hat{Y}} = (r_{XY})(z_x)$$

The "hat" above the subscript is used to represent a predicted value. You are using the regression equation to predict a z score on the Y variable from a z score on the X variable. Here is an example, based on real data. A certain college requires all psychology majors to take the Major Field Test (MFT) in Psychology published by the Educational Testing Service (ETS) during January of their senior year. A student who fails to score at or above the 10th percentile must pass an oral exam in order to graduate, and students who wish to graduate with honors must score at or above the 50th percentile. A senior student with a GPA of 2.32 is apprehensive about the MFT. She wonders whether her total score on the MFT will be above the minimum score (139) required for graduation. Since implementing the policy requiring senior majors to take the MFT, the Psychology Department at this institution has compiled the following statistics:

	GPA	MFT
M	3.175	160.122
SD	0.492	12.977
r	0.665	

As shown in the table, the correlation between cumulative GPA and total score on the MFT in Psychology at this school is 0.665. Predict this student's total MFT score. Will she achieve the minimum total score on the MFT and avoid the oral examination?

1. Convert the student's GPA to a z score.

$$z_{GPA} = \frac{2.32 - 3.175}{0.492} = -1.738$$

2. Use the regression equation to predict this student's z score on the MFT.

$$z_{MFT} = (r_{XY})(z_{GPA}) = (0.665)(-1.738) = -1.156$$

3. Convert this student's predicted z score on the MFT to a total (scale) score on the MFT.

$$X_{MFT} = z_{MFT}(SD_{MFT}) + M_{MFT} = -1.156(12.977) + 160.122 = \mathbf{145.121}$$

According to the regression equation, this student should be able to avoid the oral examination.

Now, we'll examine the steps required to predict this student's total MFT score using the regression equation for raw scores. The raw-score regression equation is similar to the equation for a straight line that you learned in high school geometry: $y = mx + b$. In geometry you learned that y is a linear function of x; more specifically, y is the ordinate (or vertical axis coordinate) that you determine by multiplying x, the abscissa (or horizontal axis coordinate), by m (the slope of the line) and adding this product to b, the y-intercept, or point where the line intersects the vertical axis when x = zero. The raw-score regression equation used for prediction in the social sciences has a slightly different form and uses different symbols:

$$\hat{Y} = a + bX$$

where,

$\hat{Y}$ is the symbol for the predicted value of the dependent variable,
a represents the intercept, or the predicted value of the dependent variable when $X = 0$,
b is the symbol for the slope, or the amount of change in the dependent variable that corresponds to an increase of 1 unit in the independent variable, and
X represents a known value of the independent variable.

You will encounter the terms *regression constant* and *regression coefficient* in the social science literature as well as statistical analysis software such as SPSS. The term *regression constant* is simply another name for the intercept, whereas *regression coefficient* refers to the slope.

    Developing the raw-score regression equation requires determining the slope and the intercept. The following formulas may be used when descriptive statistics for both variables and the correlation coefficient are available:

$$b = r\frac{SD_Y}{SD_X}$$

$$a = M_Y - bM_X$$

1. Compute the slope: $b = (0.665)\left(\dfrac{12.977}{0.492}\right) = (0.665)(26.376) = 17.54$

2. Compute the intercept: $a = 160.122 - (17.54)(3.175) =$
$$160.122 - 55.69 = 104.432$$

3. The raw-score regression equation is thus: $\hat{Y} = 104.432 + (17.54)(X)$

4. Substituting this student's GPA in the regression equation, her predicted total score on the MFT = 104.432 + (17.54)(2.32) = 104.432 + 40.693 = **145.125**.

The small difference in the total MFT scores predicted from the z-score and raw-score regression equations is due to rounding error.

    As just noted, the basis of simple linear regression is the correlation between two variables. Both correlation and regression may be depicted in a scatterplot such as the one on the next page showing the regression of MFT total score on cumulative GPA. (The axes are scaled as they are because MFT total scores range from 120 to 200, and no student had a GPA below 2.0.)

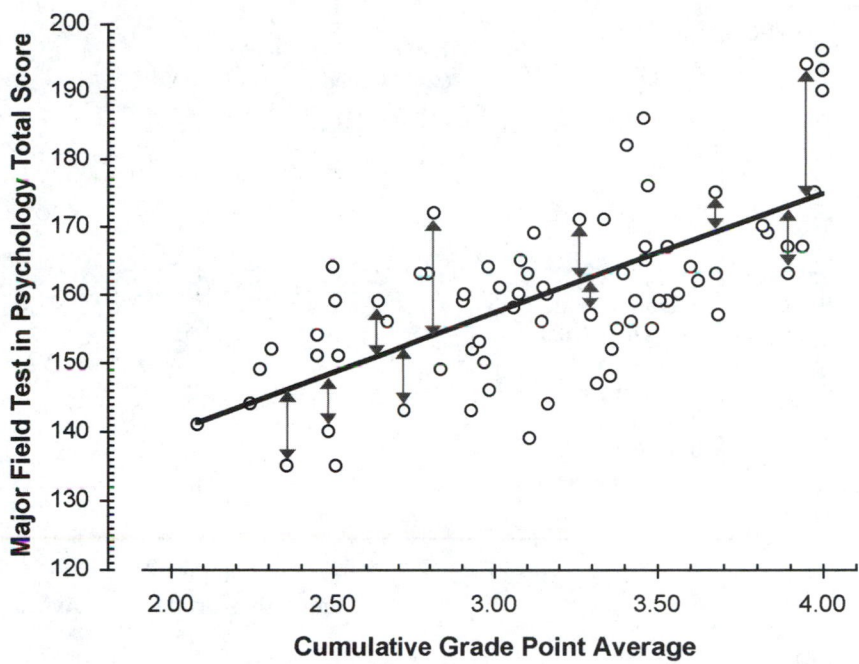

The line in the figure is the *regression line*, also called the *least squares line* and the *line of best fit*. It is the line that corresponds to the regression equation. The regression line is called the least squares line because it minimizes the sum of squared vertical distances between the points and the line (some examples are shown in the scatterplot). It is called the line of best fit because there is no other line that could be drawn to "fit" the data points that could further reduce the sum of the squared vertical distances between the points and the line.

To draw the regression line, you need to determine two points. The simplest method is to solve the regression equation for two values of X, plot the two points, $(X_1, \hat{Y}_1)$ and $(X_2, \hat{Y}_2)$, and draw a straight line through them. A second method uses the point of means and the slope that you computed for the regression equation. The regression line always passes through the point of means, so use M_X, M_Y (3.175, 160.122) as the first point (see the scatterplot on the next page). To determine the X coordinate of the second point, begin at the point of means and either add 1 unit to, or subtract 1 unit from, M_X. Adding 1 unit to M_X would result in a value (4.175) off the scale, so we will subtract 1 unit: $M_X - 1 = 3.175 - 1 = 2.175$. By definition, the slope is the amount of change in the Y variable for every unit of change in the X variable, so we'll determine the Y coordinate for the second point by subtracting the slope (17.54) from M_Y: $160.122 - 17.54 = 142.582$. The second point is thus (2.175, 142.582). A line connecting the points (2.175, 142.582) and (3.175, 160.122) is the regression line.

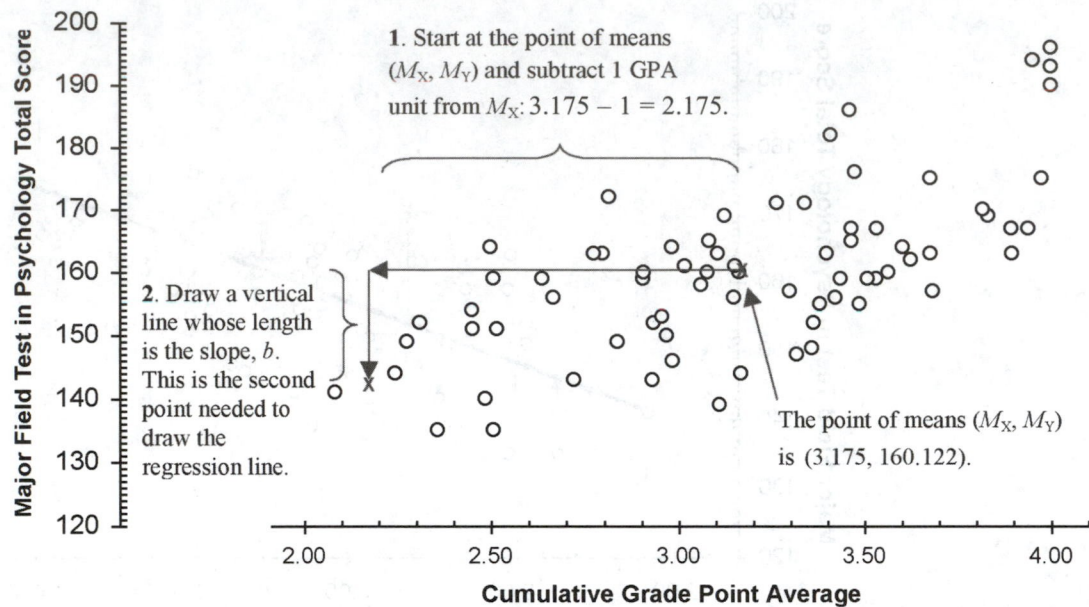

> Drawing Conclusions from a Regression Equation: Interpretation and Prediction

Regression is a powerful statistical tool, but it shares many of the limitations associated with correlation. You know from your study of Chapter 5 that there may not be a direct causal link between correlated variables. There are any number of other variables that may be responsible for an observed correlation. So, as was true for correlation, regression does not imply causality. As you will be reminded repeatedly in this course and others, a causal relation between an independent variable and a dependent variable may be observed only when participants are randomly assigned to different levels of the independent variable.

The presence of extreme data values (outliers) and a restriction in the range of one of the variables are additional problems that can distort the true correlation between variables and thus limit the accuracy of predictions. These potential problems serve as a further reminder that constructing a scatterplot should always be the initial step in the analysis of correlational data. In addition to revealing nonlinearity, a scatterplot will disclose the presence of potential outliers as well as a restricted range.

Regression to the Mean: The Patterns of Extreme Scores

A final observation about drawing conclusions from regression involves a statistical artifact that is frequently misinterpreted. You may have noticed that the hypothetical student's predicted z score on the MFT (-1.156) is closer to the mean than her GPA expressed as a z score (-1.738). This statistical consequence of multiplying the z score on the independent variable by a correlation coefficient that is less than 1 is called **regression to the mean**. More formally, when the variables in a correlational study are not perfectly correlated, the predicted score on the dependent variable will, on average, always be less extreme than the score on the independent variable; that is, the predicted score will regress toward the mean of the scores on the dependent variable. A failure to appreciate the inevitability of regression to the mean can easily result in flawed interpretations of changes in scores over time.

> The Effect Size for Regression: Proportionate Reduction in Error

Look at the scatterplot of the regression of MFT total scores on GPA.

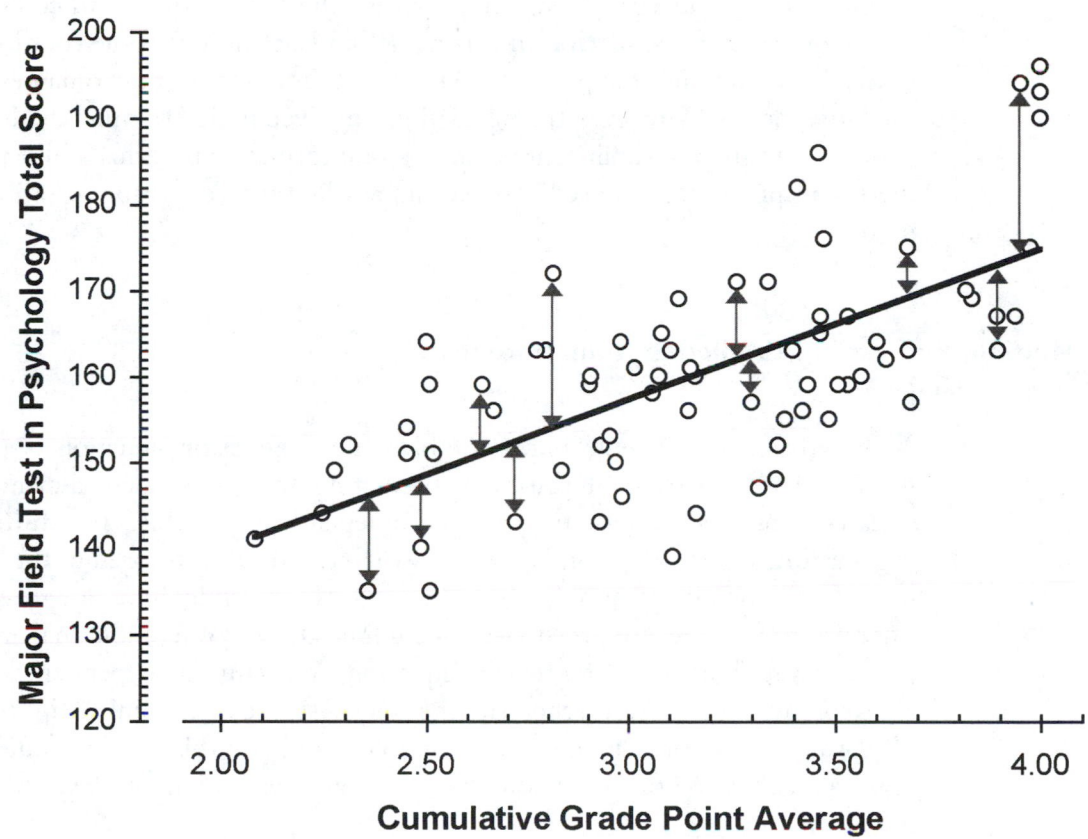

You may think of the vertical distances as errors of prediction, because they represent the differences between the predicted and actual values of the Y variable. In fact, the **standard error of the estimate** (s_{est}), a statistic based on these vertical distances, is computed as a measure of the typical error associated with predicting Y values using the regression equation. The greater the magnitude of the correlation between the variables, the closer the points to the regression line, and the smaller the standard error of the estimate. This inverse relation between s_{est} and r is evident in the formula used to compute the standard error of the estimate from group statistics:

$$s_{est} = SD_Y \sqrt{\frac{N(1-r^2)}{N-2}}$$

The standard error of the estimate is, in turn, related to the measure of effect size for regression. The effect size for simple linear regression is a measure of the increase in the accuracy of predictions that is achieved by basing those predictions on the correlation between X and Y. In fact, the effect size for regression may be obtained by simply squaring the correlation coefficient (r^2) to produce a statistic called the *coefficient of determination*. However, effect size is perhaps better understood by going through the steps required to compute the **proportionate reduction in error** (*PRE*). Please note that the coefficient of determination and the proportionate reduction in error are two names for the same statistic. However, the calculations involved in determining the PRE, while more time-consuming, are much more informative in terms of illustrating the improvement in prediction accuracy when the regression equation is used.

> Multiple Regression: Predicting from More than One Variable

As noted above, a simple linear (or bivariate) regression equation is used when the researcher's interest is in predicting the values of a dependent variable from the values of a single independent variable. In **multiple regression**, two or more independent variables are used to predict the values of a dependent variable. In other words, multiple linear regression extends simple linear regression by including at least one additional independent variable in the regression equation. Virtually all dependent variables of interest to researchers in the social sciences are linked in complex ways to multiple independent variables, and for this reason, multiple regression is far more common than bivariate regression in the research literature.

The goal of any regression analysis is to explain as much of the variability in the dependent variable as efficiently as possible. An ideal multiple regression equation includes independent variables that uniquely account for this variability. Such variables are said to be **orthogonal**. In other contexts, "orthogonal" means "at right angles," and this idea is expressed in the context of multiple regression as well when we observe that orthogonal independent variables are related to the dependent variable "from different angles." Conversely, independent variables that overlap in their predictive associations with the dependent variable are said to be *nonorthogonal*.

In multiple regression, the term *slope* is replaced by *partial regression coefficient* and the *intercept* is called the *regression constant*. The form of a raw-score multiple regression equation with three independent variables is as follows:

$$\hat{Y} = a + b_1 X_1 + b_2 X_2 + b_3 X_3$$

where,

$\hat{Y}$ is the predicted value of the dependent (criterion) variable,
a is the regression constant (similar to the y-intercept in simple linear regression),
$b_1 - b_3$ are the unstandardized partial regression coefficients, and
$X_1 - X_3$ are the values of the independent (predictor) variables.

The multiple regression equation shows each independent variable (X) being multiplied (weighted) by an unstandardized partial regression coefficient (b). The *magnitude* (absolute value) of each partial regression coefficient is the amount of change in the predicted value of the dependent variable ($\hat{Y}$) for each increase of one unit in the associated independent variable, *with the effects of all other independent variables held constant*. The *sign* of the partial regression coefficient indicates the *direction* of change in the predicted value of the dependent variable: a positive sign denotes an increase, whereas a negative sign indicates a decrease.

With multiple predictors, the regression *line* is now a multidimensional *plane*, and computations required to determine the regression constant and partial regression coefficients that minimize $\sum (Y - \hat{Y})^2$ can be difficult if not tedious. For this reason, the matrix algebra required to determine these values is almost always done by computer software. However, the logic remains the same: Values of each independent variable are plugged into the multiple regression equation to predict a value of the dependent variable.

Stepwise Multiple Regression and Hierarchical Multiple Regression: A Choice of Tactics

Stepwise multiple regression is a method in which computer software selects the independent variables for entry into the multiple regression equation according to the simultaneous execution of two criteria: one for adding variables and one for removing them.[1] In the first step, the software selects the independent variable that results in the largest increase in R^2. At each step that follows, an independent variable is added to the equation only if doing so significantly increases the value of R^2. At the same time, an independent variable is removed if it no longer significantly increases the value of R^2. The steps are complete when the remaining variables do not meet the criterion for admission, and the variables in the model do not meet the criterion for removal.

---

[1] This is the procedure implemented in SPSS. It is a combination of forward and backward stepwise regression called simultaneous stepwise regression.

Although stepwise regression is perhaps the most commonly used regression procedure, there is a trend afoot, endorsed by the authors of your text, to encourage limiting its use to research for which there are no guiding theoretical models. This category of statistical analysis is sometimes termed *exploratory data analysis*, because the data are being "explored" to see what's there. In contrast, researchers engage in *confirmatory data analysis* with the goal of supporting, or confirming, some theoretical model of interest.

The theory-driven, confirmatory alternative to stepwise regression is called **hierarchical multiple regression**, a term that refers to the practice of entering independent variables into the regression equation according to a hierarchy (order) dictated by logic, theory, and previous research. Prediction models resulting from a theory-driven approach to multiple regression are likely to remain stable across samples and are less likely to be based on one or more Type I errors. For this reason, hierarchical regression is recommended over stepwise regression unless the area of research is one about which little is known. However, there is no known litmus test for what constitutes a well-established theory or area of research, and researchers sometimes plunge headlong into research on a topic that has not been as well-researched as they may have supposed. The use of hierarchical regression in this instance is ill-advised and constitutes its most serious misuse.

> Digging Deeper into the Data:
Structural Equation Modeling (SEM)

Structural equation modeling (**SEM**) is a procedure that quantifies the degree to which sample data fit a particular model. Here "model" refers to a **statistical** (or **theoretical**) **model**, which may be defined as a sophisticated network of relations hypothesized to exist among a set of variables. The network of variables in an SEM model is usually depicted graphically as an arrangement of geometric figures (squares, rectangles, or circles) connected by arrows to indicate the direction(s) or "paths" of influence among the variables. It is important to note that the variables in a statistical model are not conceptualized as having fixed functions such as the independent and dependent variables in a multiple regression equation. Rather, the variables should be thought of as being interrelated in ways that require them to function simultaneously as independent and dependent variables. An example of a relatively simple model to explain the development of an addiction to nicotine was presented in the text (Figure 6-9, p. 283 in the text) and is reproduced here for

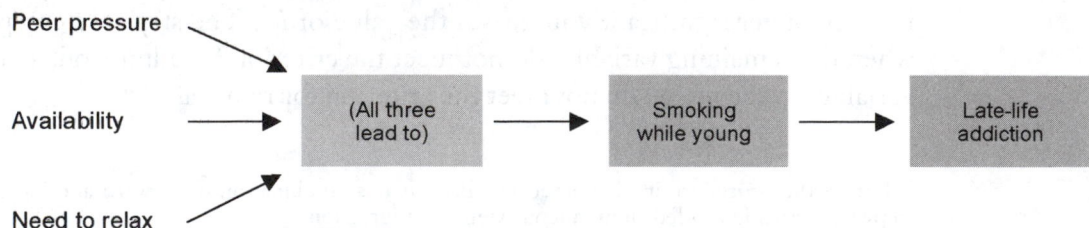

convenience:

The model is typical of the sort that would have been analyzed using the method of **path analysis**, a subset of structural equation modeling that uses regression analyses to quantify the relation between the variables connected by the arrows or **paths** in the model. SEM builds upon simpler path models such as this one by identifying additional variables as well as measuring each variable in multiple ways. SEM also includes a single statistic that measures how well the data fit the model. See Tickle, Hull, Sargent, Dalton, and Heatherton (2006) for a theoretical model of the influences on adolescent smoking analyzed with SEM.

The variables that are observed and measured in SEM are called **manifest variables**. These variables, in turn, are used to operationally define constructs that are not directly observable. The constructs are called **latent variables**. In the path model on the previous page, *peer pressure*, *availability*, and *need to relax* are constructs, ideas that are not observable, but may be inferred from various measures, or manifest variables, such as responses to questionnaires or structured interviews. In their SEM of influences on adolescent smoking, Tickle et al. (2006) described *media exposure to smoking* as "an endogenous latent construct with multiple indicators" (p. 121). One of those "indicators," or manifest variables, was frequency of exposure to films that had been analyzed for "smoking content … quantified in two primary ways: seconds of on-screen exposure to tobacco use in the film and a count of episodes (or scenes) in which tobacco use appeared during the film" (p. 121). In SEM, each latent variable is typically "indicated" by at least three manifest variables.

The authors of your text described a longitudinal study of rejection and depression in children (Nolan, Flynn, and Garber, 2003) that was analyzed using SEM. A **longitudinal study** is one in which the same participants are measured at different time points separated by several weeks, months, or even years to assess developmental changes. (Longitudinal studies are often contrasted with *cross-sectional studies* in which different age groups, called cohorts, are examined at the same time. Although they take much longer and are much more expensive to conduct, longitudinal studies have the advantage over cross-sectional studies of avoiding the confounding influence of cohort effects—differences in people born at different times, often a generation apart.) A diagram of the SEM (Figure 6-10, p. 285 in the text) used in that study shows the constructs *rejection* and *depression* measured by three manifest variables at each of three time points. The network of quantified relations between the constructs revealed that experiences of rejection in the 6th and 7th grades predicted depression in the 7th and 8th grades, but depression experienced during the earlier grades did not predict rejection a year later. However, the authors were careful to note that "such a relation cannot be ruled out because of strong cross-sectional correlations between depression and rejection" (p. 745).

In summary, structural equation models use path analyses and other methods to test theoretical (statistical) models by quantifying the relations among constructs called latent variables, each of which is operationally defined by at least three measures called manifest variables. Structural equation modeling represents an advance over other correlational methods, including multiple regression and path analysis, by providing an index of how well sample data fit a theoretical model that includes complex interrelations among multiple variables.

STUDY QUESTIONS

Please label the following statements as either True or False.

1. In simple linear regression, values of the dependent variable are predicted from values of one independent variable.

2. Simple linear regression is not used if a scatterplot of the data reveals a pattern that is curved rather than well-approximated by a straight line.

3. In a scatterplot that includes a regression line, the distance between the data points and the line is indicated by the magnitude of the correlation coefficient: the higher the absolute value of the correlation coefficient, the closer the points to the line.

4. As long as the correlation between two variables is less than perfect, a predicted z score will be closer to the mean than the z score used to predict it.

5. The phrase regression to the mean refers to the fact that scores on the dependent (Y) variable are generally closer to M_Y than scores on the independent (X) variable are to M_X.

6. In simple linear regression, the *intercept* is the value of the dependent (Y) variable when $X = M_X$.

7. In simple linear regression, the *slope* of the regression line is a measure of the amount of change in the dependent variable for each unit of change in the independent variable.

8. If values of one variable may be used to predict values of another variable, then the variables must be causally related.

9. In both simple and *multiple linear regression*, the symbol for the measure of effect size is R^2.

10. The term *path analysis* refers to a hypothesized network of relations, often portrayed graphically, among multiple variables.

11. In structural equation modeling, *latent variables* are observed and measured.

Multiple-Choice Questions

12. Complete the analogy: *Correlation* is to *regression* as:
    a. relation is to causality.
    b. relation is to prediction.
    c. prediction is to relation.
    d. causality is to relation.

13. In **simple linear regression**, scores on _____ independent variable(s) are used to predict scores on _____ dependent variable(s).
    a. one; one
    b. one or more; one
    c. one; one or more
    d. two or more; one

14. A scatterplot shows that two variables, X and Y, appear to be linearly related, and the Pearson correlation coefficient computed to quantify this relation is $-.71$. From this information, you know that the **slope** of a line drawn to fit the points in the scatterplot is _____.
    a. positive
    b. negative
    c. approximately zero
    d. insufficient information to answer

15. For a small sample of survey respondents, the correlation between number of years of formal education ($M_X = 13.8$, $SD_X = 2.86$) and age when first married ($M_Y = 22.2$, $SD_Y = 5.00$) is 0.844. Chris has never been married and has just completed his 16th and last year of formal education. What age (in years) would you predict for Chris when he marries?
    a. 18.96
    b. 24.06
    c. 25.66
    d. 25.44

16. In the equation $\hat{Y}$, what is the symbol for the **intercept**?
    a. $\hat{Y}$
    b. a
    c. b
    d. X

17. In the equation $\hat{Y}$, what is the symbol for the **slope**?
    a. $\hat{Y}$
    b. a
    c. b
    d. X

18. In the equation $\hat{Y}$, what does the symbol represent?
    a. actual value of Y when $X = 0$
    b. predicted value of Y when $X = 0$
    c. actual value of Y for a given value of X
    d. predicted value of Y for a given value of X

19. The *regression line:*
    a. is used to predict values of the independent variable from values of the dependent variable.
    b. has a positive slope if an increase in the independent variable is associated with a decrease in the dependent variable.
    c. represents a visual equivalent of the equation used to compute the Pearson correlation coefficient.
    d. has a positive slope if an increase in the independent variable is associated with an increase in the dependent variable.

20. In the equation, $\hat{Y} = a + b(X)$, the symbol *a* represents the:
    a. predicted value of Y when $X = 0$.
    b. predicted value of X when $Y = 0$.
    c. predicted change in Y when X changes by one unit.
    d. change in X when the predicted value of Y changes by one unit.

21. A certain college requires all psychology majors to take the Major Field Test (MFT) in Psychology published by the Educational Testing Service (ETS) during January of their senior year. Psychology majors may graduate summa cum laude if they have a cumulative GPA of at least 3.75 and a total MFT score at or above the 90th percentile based on national norms published by the ETS. Since implementing this policy, the Psychology Department at this institution has compiled the following statistics:

	MFT Total Score	GPA
M	164.358	3.273
SD	13.892	0.385
r	0.596	

What is the *slope* of the regression line for predicting MFT total score from GPA?
    a. 0.017
    b. 21.506
    c. 93.970
    d. 164.304

22. A certain college requires all psychology majors to take the Major Field Test (MFT) in Psychology published by the Educational Testing Service (ETS) during January of their senior year. Psychology majors may graduate summa cum laude if they have a cumulative GPA of at least 3.75 and a total MFT score at or above the 90th percentile based on national norms published by the ETS. Since implementing this policy, the Psychology Department at this institution has compiled the following statistics:

	MFT Total Score	GPA
M	164.358	3.273
SD	13.892	0.385
r	0.596	

What is the predicted MFT total score for a student who has a cumulative GPA of 3.75?
a. 181.57
b. 188.311
c. 174.616
d. 164.366

23. For two linearly related variables, X and Y, the regression equation is $\hat{Y} = 10 - 0.2(X)$ For each 10-unit increase in X, what is the predicted change in Y?
a. increase of 8 units
b. decrease of 8 units
c. increase of 2 units
d. decrease of 2 units

24. A *positive* value for the slope of a regression line indicates that:
a. as the values of one variable increase, the values of the other variable decrease.
b. as the values of one variable increase, the values of the other variable also increase.
c. a large change in the independent variable results in a small change in the dependent variable.
d. a small change in the independent variable results in a large change in the dependent variable.

25. A *negative* value for the slope of a regression line indicates that:
a. as the values of one variable increase, the values of the other variable decrease.
b. as the values of one variable increase, the values of the other variable also increase.
c. a large change in the independent variable results in a small change in the dependent variable.
d. a small change in the independent variable results in a large change in the dependent variable.

26. Ignoring sign, a *large* value for the slope of a regression line indicates that:
    a. as the values of one variable increase, the values of the other variable decrease.
    b. as the values of one variable increase, the values of the other variable also increase.
    c. a large change in the independent variable results in a small change in the dependent variable.
    d. a small change in the independent variable results in a large change in the dependent variable.

27. When $X = 0$, the predicted value of Y is _____.
    a. always 0
    b. always 1
    c. the intercept
    d. the slope

28. The statistic that measures the typical distance between the regression line and the data points in a scatterplot is called the _____.
    a. regression constant
    b. regression coefficient
    c. standard error of the estimate
    d. proportionate reduction in error

29. In simple linear regression, SS_{Error} and SS_{Total} are the same value when:
    a. the slope is large and positive.
    b. $r^2 = 1$.
    c. the slope is large and negative.
    d. $r^2 = 0$.

30. Two or more independent variables are **orthogonal** if they:
    a. make separate and distinct contributions in the prediction of the dependent variable.
    b. are positively correlated with each other as well as with the dependent variable.
    c. are positively correlated with each other but not correlated with the dependent variable.
    d. are negatively correlated with each other but positively correlated with the dependent variable.

31. The symbol for effect size in multiple regression is:
    a. r^2.
    b. R^2.
    c. b.
    d. R.

32. In multiple regression, the direction of the relation between an independent variable X_1 and the dependent variable Y is given by the sign of:
    a. the square of the multiple correlation coefficient (R^2).
    b. its associated unstandardized regression coefficient (b_1).
    c. the multiple correlation coefficient (R).
    d. the standard error of the estimate.

33. In **stepwise multiple regression**, the order in which the independent variables are entered into the regression equation is determined by:
    a. the researcher, according to the amount by which the entered variable changes R^2.
    b. the researcher, according to theory, logic, and previous research.
    c. computer software, according to the amount by which the entered variable changes R^2.
    d. computer software, according to theory, logic, and previous research.

34. In **hierarchical multiple regression**, the order in which the independent variables are entered into the regression equation is determined by:
    a. the researcher, according to the amount by which the entered variable changes R^2.
    b. the researcher, according to theory, logic, and previous research.
    c. computer software, according to the amount by which the entered variable changes R^2.
    d. computer software, according to theory, logic, and previous research.

35. Which one of the following is a weakness associated with the hierarchical approach to multiple regression?
    a. By "fishing" for the best combination of predictors, the model may capitalize on chance and thus inflate the probability of committing a Type I error.
    b. The value of R^2 increases with the addition of each new independent variable, even though the variable may actually decrease the efficiency of the prediction model.
    c. Orthogonal and nonorthogonal independent variables receive equal weight in the determination of the most efficient prediction model.
    d. Researchers may not have a theory to guide the selection of independent variables.

36. Which one of the following refers to a statistical method in which a series of regression analyses are used to quantify hypothesized connections between variables at successive steps in a theoretical model?
    a. stepwise multiple regression
    b. path analysis
    c. factor analysis
    d. hierarchical multiple regression

37. In structural equation modeling, combinations of _____ variables are measured as a means of quantifying the relations between _____ variables, constructs that are not directly observed.
    a. independent; dependent
    b. dependent; independent
    c. manifest; latent
    d. latent; manifest

38. In a **longitudinal study**, _____ sample(s) of participants is (are) observed at _____ time(s).
    a. two or more; different
    b. two or more; the same
    c. a single; different
    d. a single; the same

ANSWERS TO CHAPTER 6 STUDY QUESTIONS

Question Number	Correct Answer	Question Number	Correct Answer
1	T, p. 254	16	b, p. 259
2	T, p. 255	17	c, p. 259
3	T, p. 256	18	d, p. 259
4	T, p. 257	19	d, pp. 261–263
5	F, pp. 257–258 [Regression to the mean refers to predicted, not actual, scores on the dependent variable.]	20	a, p. 259
		21	b, pp. 260–261
		22	b, pp. 260–261
6	F, p. 259 [The intercept is the value of Y when $X = 0$.]	23	d, pp. 259–261 [The slope is the amount of change in the Y variable for each 1-unit change in the X variable, so if X changes by 10 units, Y changes by (slope)(10) units. Just multiply the slope, –0.2, by 10.]
7	T, p. 259		
8	F, p. 267		
9	F, pp. 273, 278 [In simple linear regression, the symbol used to represent effect size is r^2.]		
		24	b, pp. 259–261
10	F, p. 282	25	a, pp. 259–261
11	F, p. 284	26	d, pp. 259–261
12	b, p. 254	27	c, p. 259
13	a, p. 254	28	c, p. 265
14	b, pp. 255–256	29	e, p. 274
15	d, p. 256 [First convert Chris's years of formal education to a z score: $(16 - 13.8) / 2.86 = .769$. Then multiply this z score by the correlation coefficient: $(.844)(.769)$ to obtain the predicted age when married expressed as a z score $(.649)$. Finally, convert this z score to an age by multiplying it by SD_Y and adding this product to M_Y: $(.649)(5) + 22.2 = 25.44$ years.]	30	a, p. 275
		31	b, p. 278
		32	b, p. 278
		33	c, pp. 278–279
		34	b, p. 279
		35	d, p. 280
		36	b, p. 283
		37	c, p. 284
		38	c, p. 284

REFERENCES

Campbell, D. T., & Kenny, D. A. (1999). *A primer on regression artifacts*. New York: The Guilford Press.

Tickle, J. M., Hull, J. G., Sargent, J. D., Dalton, M. A., & Heatherton, T. F. (2006). A structural equation model of social influences and exposure to media smoking on adolescent smoking. *Basic and Applied Social Psychology, 28*, 117–129.

CHAPTER SEVEN

INFERENTIAL STATISTICS

The Surprising Story of the Normal Curve

CHAPTER OUTLINE

LEARNING OBJECTIVES

After studying this chapter, you should be able to:

1. Define each of the following terms and provide examples that are not in the text: *normal curve, ubiquity of the normal curve, meta-analysis, standardization, z distribution, standard normal distribution, central limit theorem, distribution of means,* and *standard error.*

2. Identify the individual who derived the formula for the normal curve and discuss the importance of this discovery to inferential statistics.

3. Explain how the process of *standardization* may be used "to compare apples to oranges"; that is, you should be able to explain how individual scores from different normal distributions may be converted to standard (z) scores and directly compared as percentiles of the *standard normal distribution.*

4. Paraphrase the *central limit theorem* and identify the two important principles demonstrated by the theorem. In particular, you should be

able to explain the principle that specifies a normal *distribution of means* of samples that were randomly selected from a population of individual scores that are not distributed in the form of a normal curve. In addition, you should be able to explain why a distribution of sample means is less variable than a distribution of individual scores.

5. Distinguish between the standard deviation of a population of individual scores (σ) and the standard deviation of the population of all possible means of samples of a fixed size that are randomly selected with replacement from that population (called the *standard error* and symbolized with a subscript: σ_M).

6. Demonstrate how the mean of a sample of N scores may be compared to all other means of samples of N scores by first converting the mean to a z statistic, then using a table of normal curve percentages to express the z statistic as a percentile.

CHAPTER REVIEW

> ### The Normal Curve: It's Everywhere!

The normal curve is probably the most familiar figure in statistics. The curve's widespread use in the behavioral and social sciences is based on studies showing that the shapes of the frequency distributions of a number of variables are well approximated by the normal curve. However, it is important to remember that the curve itself was derived mathematically, apparently before anyone noticed that a large number of variables seemed to have a bell-shaped distribution. The French expatriate Abraham De Moivre (1667-1754) is credited with deriving the formula used to draw the normal curve, although a sketch of the curve does not appear in any of his published work. The normal curve depicted on the next page was created in SPSS and is presented here to illustrate the curve's properties as discussed in the text.

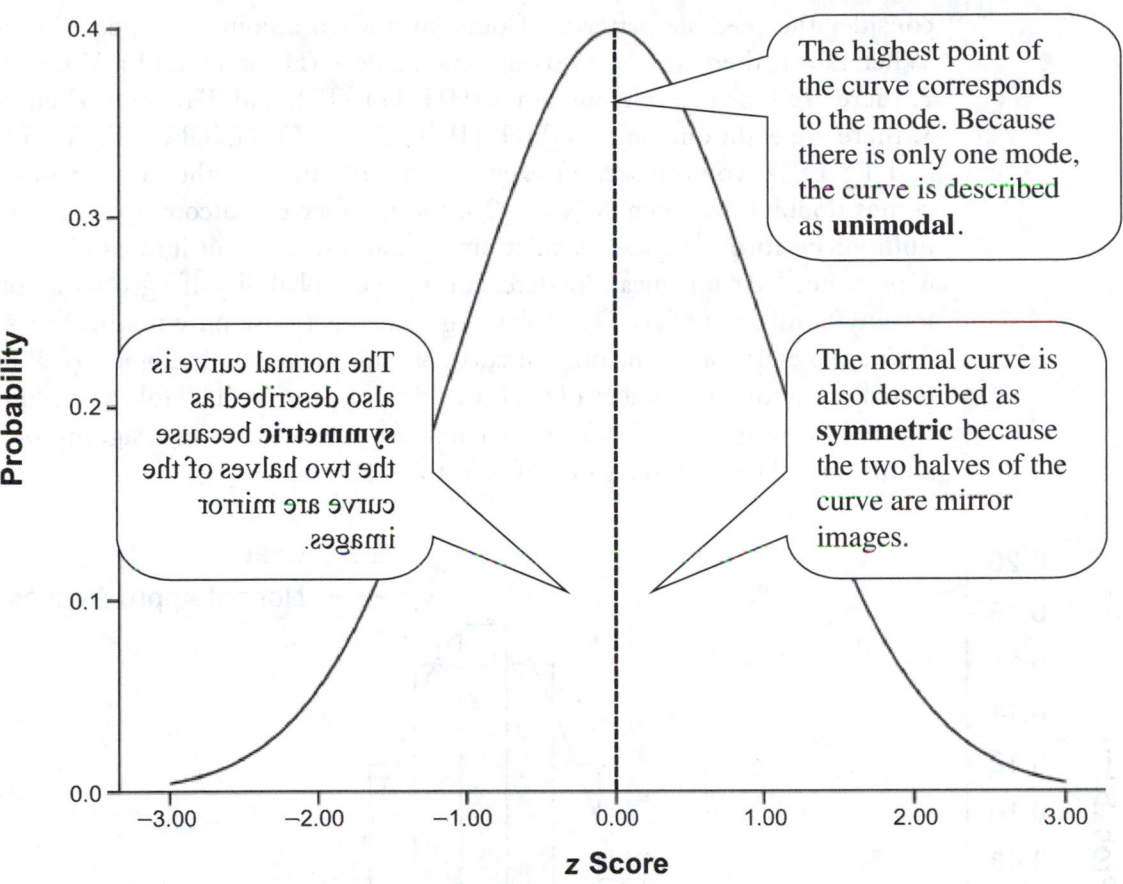

The highest point of the curve corresponds to the mode. Because there is only one mode, the curve is described as **unimodal**.

The normal curve is also described as **symmetric** because the two halves of the curve are mirror images.

The normal curve is also described as **symmetric** because the two halves of the curve are mirror images.

Think of a variable (a characteristic that varies) and the chances are good that the distribution of that variable has a shape that is very similar to the normal curve. This phenomenon is what is meant by the phrase, the **ubiquity of the normal curve**. The normal curve seems to be *ubiquitous* or everywhere at once. Practically speaking, the ubiquity of the normal curve means that the curve and its associated percentiles may be applied to the frequency distributions (histograms or polygons) of a very large number of variables that are of interest to scientists in a variety of disciplines.

In De Moivre's case, the practical application of the normal curve was in providing a foundation for determining the probability of various outcomes in games of chance. De Moivre earned a meager living as a math tutor and as a consultant to gamblers ("adventurers" or "gamesters" as he called them) who frequented Slaughter's Coffee House in London. It was in this latter role that he developed the equation for the normal curve as the limit of a probability distribution of chance outcomes.[1] To get an idea of De Moivre's problem,

---

[1] A probability distribution of chance outcomes was introduced in Chapter 4 in the context of flipping a coin. A distribution that specifies the probabilities for a variable number of outcomes (e.g. a coin landing heads) in N trials of a process that has same probability P of occurrence on each trial is called a binomial distribution. De Moivre showed that the binomial distribution approaches the form of the normal curve as N increases.

consider the possible patterns of outcomes when a coin is flipped N times. When $N = 1$, there are just two outcomes, a head (H) or a tail (T). When $N = 2$, there are four possible outcomes (HH, HT, TH, and TT), and when $N = 3$, there are eight outcomes (HHH, HHT, HTH, THH, TTH, THT, HTT, and TTT). As you can see, for each addition of one trial, the number of outcomes doubles, so when N is just 20, the number of outcomes exceeds one million! Performing these calculations by hand was all but impossible, so de Moivre needed some means of determining the probability of a given outcome for any number of trials. De Moivre's genius was to use pure mathematics to derive the equation of the normal curve as a means of specifying a probability distribution for any number of trials of a chance process. The following figure shows how well De Moivre's normal approximation works in assigning probabilities to outcomes in a game of coin toss.

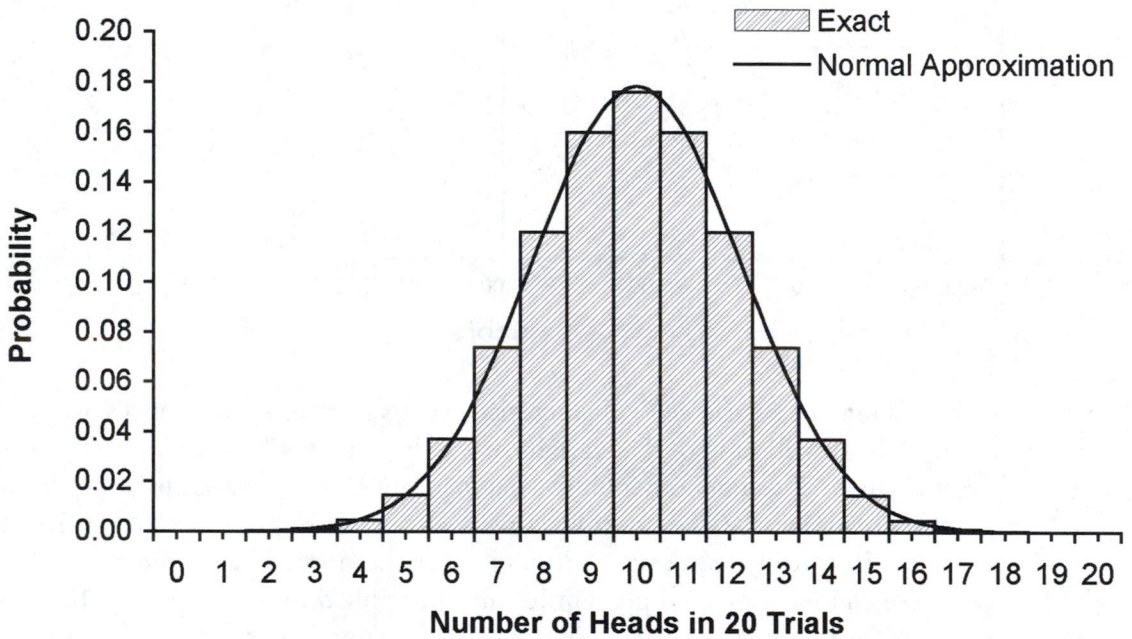

The histogram in the figure is the theoretical probability distribution of the frequency of heads in 20 trials if the coin is perfectly balanced and other ideal conditions are met. Notice how closely the shape of the probability histogram conforms to the normal curve. De Moivre showed that for an infinitely large number of trials, the probability of observing any number of heads is specified precisely by the normal curve. More practically, the probability distribution becomes progressively similar to the normal curve as the number of trials increases. This is shown in the following table:

Trials	Heads	Exact Probability	Normal Approximation	Difference
20	10	0.1762	0.1784	0.0022
40	20	0.1254	0.1262	0.0008
80	40	0.0889	0.0892	0.0003
160	80	0.0630	0.0631	0.0001
320	160	0.0446	0.0446	0.0000

When $N = 160$, the probability histogram is very closely approximated by a normal curve:

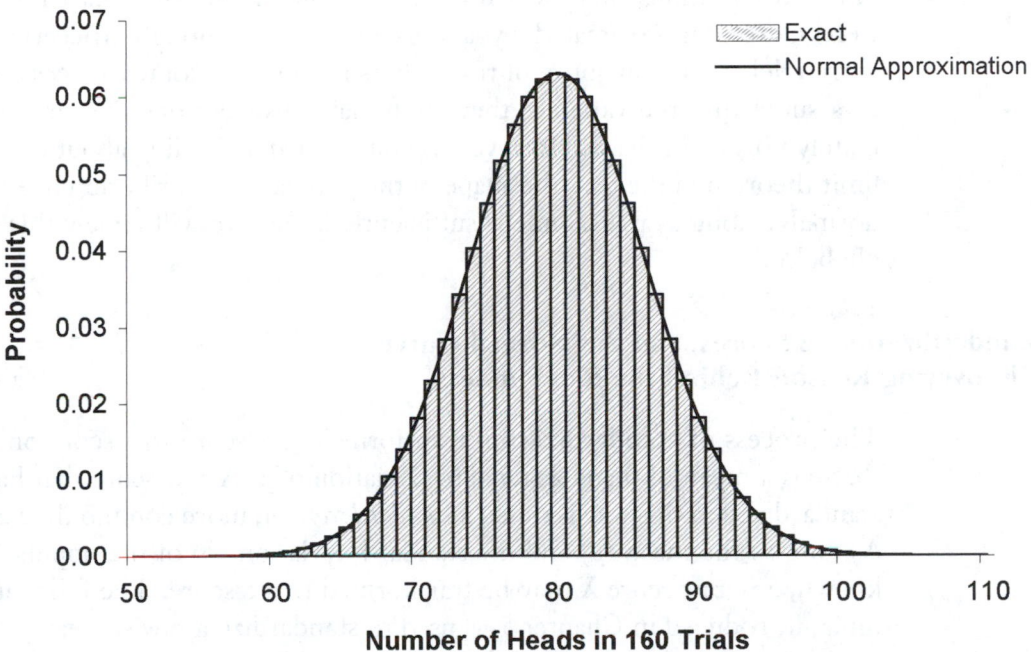

This illustrates an important point emphasized in your text: If the underlying population of individual measures is normally distributed, the shape of the distribution of a sample of measures from that population will more closely resemble a normal curve as the size of the sample increases. This principle applies to any measurable variable, from the outcome of a coin flip to an individual's IQ score.

Probability distributions such as these form the foundation of inferential statistics, because they provide a standard against which research observations may be compared. For example, you may make an inference about whether a coin is fair by tossing it for a sufficiently large number of trials and comparing the resulting frequency distribution of outcomes to a theoretical probability distribution like the one displayed above. If the frequency distribution is sufficiently similar to the theoretical probability distribution, then it is reasonable to infer that the coin is fair. This is why the authors of your text observed that De Moivre's derivation of the formula used to draw the normal curve "opened the door to inferential statistics" (text page 300). Although De Moivre's motivation to develop the equation of the normal curve was more narrowly focused, his work made it possible to test hypotheses about a very large number of variables whose frequency distributions are very well approximated by the normal curve.

The authors of your text also note that a report by Micceri (1989) failed to provide evidence of the ubiquity of the normal curve. Micceri examined the distributions of 440 variables that are commonly measured in psychology and education (e.g., SAT and GRE scores, MMPI scores) and reported that *none* of the distributions, all of which were based on samples of at least 190 scores, were closely approximated by a normal curve. Although Micceri's report stirred debate, the majority of researchers in the behavioral sciences continue to assume that the variables they study have distributions that are approximately normal in shape. However, as you learned in reading about the central limit theorem in the text, the shape of the population distribution need not be normal as long as the sample is sufficiently large. We will review this principle below.

> ## Standardization, z Scores, and the Normal Curve: Discovering Reason Behind the Randomness

The process of **standardization** transforms a raw score to a score on a scale that has a mean of 0 and a standard deviation of 1. A raw score that has been standardized in this way is called a *standard score* or, more commonly, a *z* score. As long as the mean (μ) and the standard deviation (σ) of the population are known, any raw score X may be transformed to a z score. The following formula, introduced in Chapter 5, is used to standardize a raw score:

$$z = \frac{X - \mu}{\sigma}$$

Expressed as a z score, the mean of any distribution of raw scores has a value of 0. Because the standard deviation of the z score scale is 1, any raw score that is 1 standard deviation above the mean has a value of 1, whereas a raw score that is 1 standard deviation below the mean has a value of -1. Suppose, for example, that the mean height in the population of female college students in the United States is 64.2 inches with a standard deviation of 2.57 inches. A student whose height is 66.77 inches is 1 standard deviation above the mean, so her height transformed to a score on the z scale is 1.

$$z = \frac{X - \mu}{\sigma} = \frac{66.77 - 64.2}{2.57} = 1$$

Similarly, a student who is 61.63 inches tall is 1 standard deviation below the mean, so her score on the z scale is –1.

$$z = \frac{X - \mu}{\sigma} = \frac{61.63 - 64.2}{2.57} = -1$$

Standardization enables meaningful comparisons between measures of different variables or between measures of the same variable between individuals from different populations. For example, a female college student who is 5 feet 8 inches tall may be meaningfully compared to a male college student who is 6 feet tall only after standardizing the height of each student. Using the means and standard deviations above, this works out to:

$$z_{Female} = \frac{68 - 64.2}{2.57} = 1.48 \qquad z_{Male} = \frac{72 - 69.6}{2.69} = 0.89$$

Relative to the appropriate comparison groups, the female student is taller than the male student by almost a half standard deviation.

Measures that are approximately normally distributed may also be compared by expressing their standard score equivalents as percentile ranks. The *percentile rank* of a normally distributed z score may be determined by using Table B.1 in your text to locate the percentage of scores to the left of that z score. A few of these percentages are displayed in the figure below:

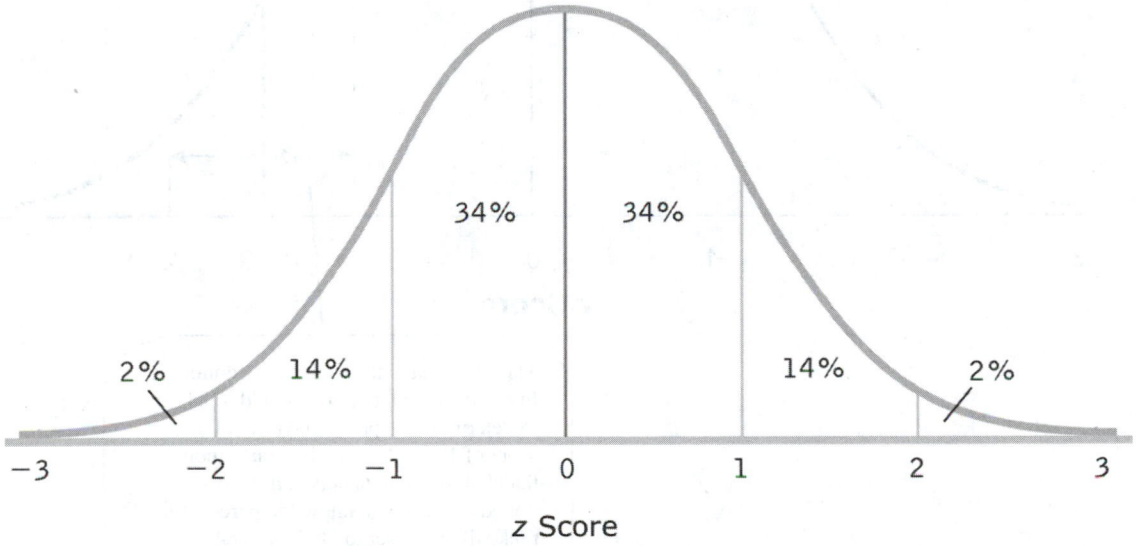

First, note that 50% (34% + 14% + 2% = 50%) of the scores are on either side of the mean of 0. Using the rounded percentages displayed in the figure, you can determine that a z score of 2 has a percentile rank of 98, because this score is greater than or equal to 50% + 34% + 14% = 98% of the scores in the population. Similarly, a z score of –1 has a percentile rank of 16 because this score equals or exceeds 2% + 14% = 16% of the scores in the population. The figure also shows that 34% + 34% = 68% of the scores are within 1 standard deviation of the mean, and 14% + 34% + 34% + 14% = 96% of the scores are within 2 standard deviations of the mean. Determining the percentile ranks of non-integer z scores such as 1.48 and 0.89 requires consulting Table B.1 in the appendix of your text. That exercise is postponed until the next chapter. However, by sketching the curve and locating the z scores on the horizontal axis, you can see that a z score of 1.48 is about 1.5 standard deviations above the mean and thus has a percentile rank that exceeds 84 (50% + 34% + ? > 84%), whereas a z score of 0.89 is a little less than 1 standard deviation above the mean and has a percentile rank much closer to 84 than to 50.

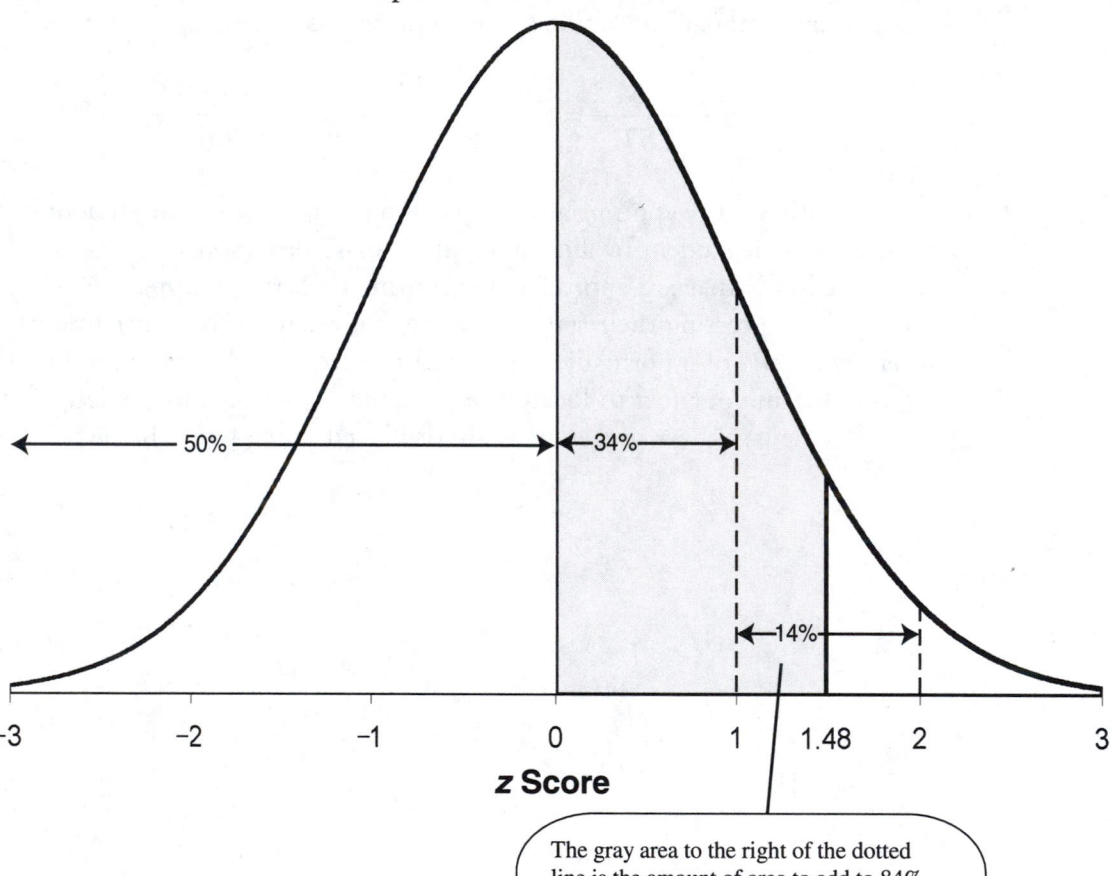

The gray area to the right of the dotted line is the amount of area to add to 84% to determine the percentile rank of a z score of 1.48. This area is clearly more than half of the area between the two dotted lines, so you know the percentile rank will be closer to 98 than to 84. Learning to conceptualize the problems in this way will remove some of the mystery from the curve and the percentages in Table B.1.

> The Central Limit Theorem: How Sampling Creates a Less Variable Distribution

The central limit theorem is so-named because of its central importance in mathematical statistics. However, the theorem is also very important in behavioral research. This single theorem explains why so many variables have a normal distribution, but it also specifies the conditions that guarantee a normal distribution of sample means when the population of individual scores is not normally distributed.

The term **distribution of means** refers to the population of means computed for all possible samples of a given size (e.g., $N = 20$ or $N = 50$) from a population. (Statisticians commonly refer to the distribution of means as the *sampling distribution of the mean*.) You can think of building a distribution of means by sampling randomly and repeatedly, with replacement, from a population until every possible combination of N participants is sampled. Each time you select a sample of participants, you obtain a measure of some characteristic for each participant (e.g., height, measured in inches), compute the mean of the measures, and continue in this manner until you have computed the means of an infinitely large number of samples.

Obviously, you cannot sample an infinitely large number of times from a population, but this little thought experiment should give you a better understanding of what is meant by a distribution of means and perhaps make the following paraphrase of the **central limit theorem** a little easier to understand as well:

Regardless of the shape of the distribution of individual scores in the population, the shape of the distribution of means from this population (the sampling distribution of the mean) will approach the shape of a normal curve as the size of the sample (N) grows large. In addition, the mean of the distribution of means is equal to the mean of the population, and the standard deviation of the distribution of means is equal to the standard deviation of the population divided by the square root of the sample size.

As an illustration of how the central limit theorem works, consider the possible sums that result when a pair of dice are tossed. As shown in the figure on the following page (left), there are only $6^2 = 36$ possible sums, so this example will allow us to avoid thinking about an infinitely large number of samples. The figure on the right is a probability histogram of the 36 possible sums.

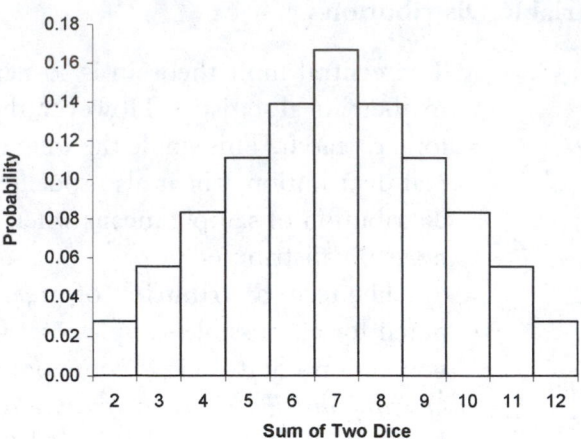

Each roll of the dice is analogous to randomly sampling 2 of the 6 die faces that comprise the entire population, and the probability histogram is the distribution of all possible sums of samples of $N = 2$ from this population. (We're using sums here instead of means but the distribution of sums has the same shape as a distribution of means. You may think of each sample sum as a sample mean multiplied by 2, the sample size.) The shape of the probability histogram is unimodal and symmetric, but it is not quite normal. According to the central limit theorem, we'll have to increase the sample size to get the shape of the probability histogram to look more like a normal curve.

Now notice what happens when the sample size is increased to 6. (With 6 dice, there are $6^6 = 46,656$ possible outcomes, so it is impractical to list them all.) In accord with the central limit theorem, the increase in the sample size from 2 to 6 results in a distribution of sums that is shaped more like a normal curve.

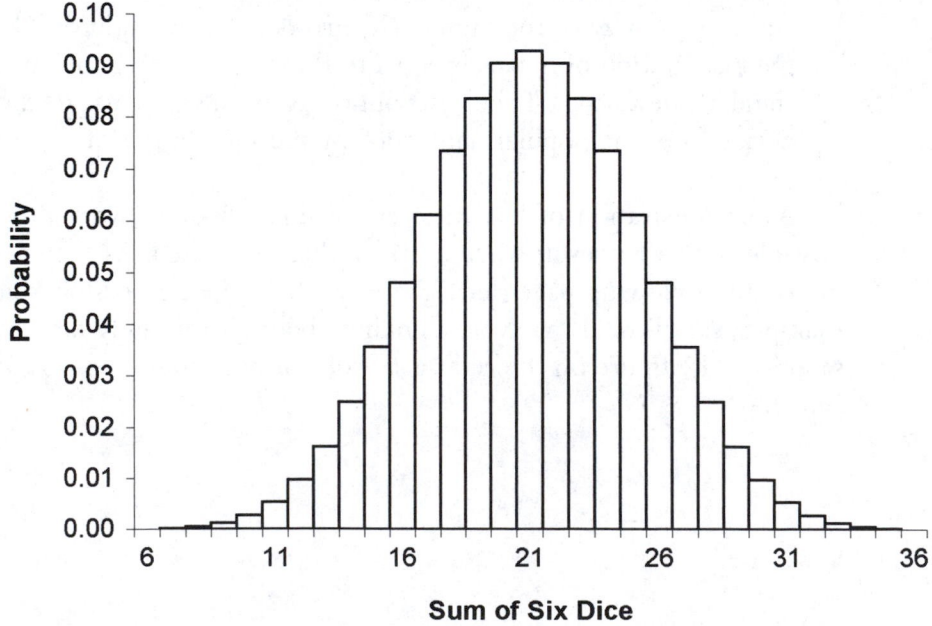

Please do not miss the point that the central limit theorem specifies the shape of the distribution of means (or sums) of *all possible samples* of a particular size. The central limit theorem is demonstrated by increasing the sample size (the number of dice in each roll), not the number of samples (rolls).

How large should the sample size be before the shape of the distribution of sums or means is sufficiently similar to the normal curve? The answer depends on the shape of the distribution of individual scores in the population. If the shape of the population distribution is not extremely skewed (e.g., the rectangular shape of a uniform distribution like the 6 dice in this example), then the distribution of sample means will be approximately normal for samples of size 30 or more ($N \geq 30$). For "heavy-tailed" (extremely skewed) distributions, the sample size must be larger, perhaps as large as $N = 100$.

Recall from the paraphrase of the central limit theorem above that it also specifies the mean and the standard deviation of the distribution of means. According to the central limit theorem, the mean of a distribution of sample means (the symbol is σ_M) is equal to the mean of the population (μ) from which the samples were selected. In symbols,

$$\mu = \mu_M$$

In the example of rolling 6 dice, the population mean may be computed by summing the 6 die faces and dividing by 6: $\mu = (6 + 5 + 4 + 3 + 2 + 1) / 6 = 21 / 6 = 3.5$. Converting the distribution of 46,656 sample sums to a distribution of sample means is accomplished by dividing each sum by the sample size (6). The mean of the distribution of means is then computed by dividing the sum of the means by the number of means: $\mu_M = 163,296 / 46,656 = 3.5$.

The central limit theorem also relates the standard deviation of the distribution of means (σ_M) to the standard deviation of the parent population (σ):

$$\sigma_M = \frac{\sigma}{\sqrt{N}}$$

To avoid potential confusion, the standard deviation of the distribution of means is called the *standard error of the mean*, usually shortened to **standard error**. As you can see from the formula, the standard error is much smaller than the standard deviation of the population because means are less variable than individual scores (see the explanation on p. 317 in the text). To return to the dice example, the population standard deviation (σ) is 1.71:

$$\sigma = \sqrt{\frac{\sum X^2 - \frac{(\sum X)^2}{N}}{N}} = \sqrt{\frac{(6^2 + 5^2 + 4^2 + 3^2 + 2^2 + 1^2) - \frac{(6+5+4+3+2+1)^2}{6}}{6}}$$

$$= \sqrt{\frac{(36+25+16+9+4+1) - \frac{21^2}{6}}{6}} = \sqrt{\frac{91 - \frac{441}{6}}{6}} = \sqrt{\frac{91-73.5}{6}}$$

$$= \sqrt{\frac{17.5}{6}} = \sqrt{2.91\overline{66}} = 1.71$$

The standard error (σ_M) of the means of all possible samples of 6 dice is 0.697:

$$\sigma_M = \sqrt{\frac{\sum M^2 - \frac{(\sum M)^2}{N}}{N}} = \sqrt{\frac{594,216 - \frac{163,296^2}{46,656}}{46,656}} = \sqrt{\frac{594,216 - \frac{26,665,583,616}{46,656}}{46,656}}$$

$$= \sqrt{\frac{594,216 - 571,536}{46,656}} = \sqrt{\frac{22,680}{46,656}} = \sqrt{0.486} = 0.697$$

Checking:

$$\sigma_M = \frac{\sigma}{\sqrt{N}} = \frac{1.708}{\sqrt{6}} = \frac{1.708}{2.449} = 0.697$$

In the next section, we will use the mean and standard error of the distribution of means to convert sample means to z statistics.

> How to Take Advantage of the Central Limit Theorem: Beginning With z Scores

The central limit theorem may be applied to virtually any variable, including scores from rating scales, achievement tests, personality inventories, and intelligence tests, as well as measures such as height, weight, response rate, and reaction time. In short, the central limit theorem may be applied to any variable of interest to behavioral scientists. The practical importance of the central limit theorem, as mentioned above, is that it enables researchers to compare the mean of a sample of scores to the standard normal distribution, even though the scores themselves are not distributed normally in the population. If the scores *are* normally distributed, then the sample size doesn't matter. But if we aren't sure about the shape of the population, then we'll need a sample size of at least 30 or so to enlist the aid of the central limit theorem. In either case, using the standard normal distribution requires that we standardize the sample mean. We do this by converting the mean (M) to a z statistic using the following formula:

$$z = \frac{M - \mu_M}{\sigma_M}$$

The formula is similar to the formula used to compute a z score, so make sure that you do not confuse them. The most common error is to divide by the standard deviation (σ) instead of the standard error (σ_M). As noted in the previous section, the standard error is computed by dividing the standard deviation of the population by the square root of the sample size:

$$\sigma_M = \frac{\sigma}{\sqrt{N}}$$

In the next chapter, we will use the table of normal curve percentages in the appendix of the text to determine the probability of observing a sample mean that is at least as extreme as certain criterion values. To use the percentages of the standard normal distribution, two requirements must be met: (1) The population parameters (μ and σ) must be known, and (2) the distribution of means must be approximately normal. If the population distribution is approximately normal, then the distribution of means will be approximately normal, regardless of the number of scores in the sample. However, if the population distribution is not normal, then the central limit theorem states that the distribution of means will be approximately normal if the sample size is sufficiently large ($N \geq 30$ or so).

STUDY QUESTIONS

1. Who among the following is credited with deriving the mathematical formula used to draw the normal curve?
   a. Abraham De Moivre
   b. Sir Isaac Newton
   c. Karl Pearson
   d. Karl Friedrich Gauss

2. The normal curve is *unimodal* which means that:
   a. there are as many scores above the mean as there are below the mean.
   b. most of the scores are in the middle with very few at the extremes.
   c. the areas to the left and right of the center are mirror images.
   d. probabilities may be computed from *z* scores.

3. The normal curve is *symmetric* which means that:
   a. there are as many scores above the mean as there are below the mean.
   b. most of the scores are in the middle with very few at the extremes.
   c. the areas to the left and right of the center are mirror images.
   d. probabilities may be computed from *z* scores.

4. The _____ of the normal curve indicates that the curve describes the approximate shape of the distributions of a large number of characteristics that vary.
   a. symmetry
   b. width
   c. ubiquity
   d. height

5. A(n) _____ is a type of statistical analysis that simultaneously examines as many studies as possible for a given research topic.

6. Micceri (1989) presented evidence that:
   a. deviations from the normal curve may be used to detect fraud.
   b. probability distributions of chance outcomes invariably evolve into a bell-shaped curve.
   c. the distributions of many measures commonly used in the behavioral sciences are very well approximated by a normal curve.
   d. the distributions of many measures commonly used in the behavioral sciences are not well approximated by a normal curve.

7. The process of **standardization** converts raw scores to:
   a. percentiles.
   b. z scores.
   c. means.
   d. standard deviations.

8. Although the mean, the median, and the mode are all located at the midpoint of the normal curve, the _____ define(s) the midpoint as the 50th percentile.
   a. mean
   b. median
   c. mode
   d. mean and the median

9. The **standard normal distribution** is a distribution of:
   a. z scores.
   b. raw scores with a mean of 0 and a standard deviation of 1.
   c. raw scores with a mean of 50 and a standard deviation of 10.
   d. raw scores with a mean of 100 and a standard deviation of 15.

10. If scores on the Stanford-Binet IQ test are normally distributed with mean = 100 and standard deviation = 16, what is the percentage of scores between 100 and 116?
    a. 14
    b. 16
    c. 34
    d. 68

11. If scores on the Stanford-Binet IQ test are normally distributed with mean = 100 and standard deviation = 16, which one of the following intervals contains the fewest scores?
    a. 100–116
    b. 116–132
    c. 68–84
    d. 132–148

12. About _____ percent of Stanford-Binet IQ test scores (mean = 100, standard deviation = 16) are between 116 and 132.
    a. 16
    b. 84
    c. 68
    d. 14

13. If scores on the Stanford-Binet IQ test are normally distributed with mean = 100 and standard deviation = 16, what is the minimum score in the top 2%?
    a. 116
    b. 132
    c. 84
    d. 68

14. If a variable is normally distributed then approximately _____ percent of the values of that variable are within one standard deviation of the mean.
    a. 14
    b. 34
    c. 50
    d. 68

15. A certain student was disappointed with her performance on a recent statistics exam because she answered only 75 percent of the questions correctly. She later learned that the scores on the exam were normally distributed, and the instructor awarded grades based on standard (z) scores rather than percent correct. If this student's standard (z) score is exactly 2, then she should be:
    a. pleased that her score was in the top 2% of the class.
    b. disappointed that her standard score is so small.
    c. relieved that her score was in the average range.
    d. disappointed that her score had a percentile rank of 2.

16. If the heights of female college students are normally distributed, with mean = 65 inches and standard deviation = 2.5 inches, what percentage of these students are taller than 65 inches?
    a. 35%
    b. 50%
    c. 65%
    d. 68%

17. For any normally distributed variable, what is the percentage of scores between 1 standard deviation below, and 2 standard deviations above, the mean?
    a. 68
    b. 34
    c. 82
    d. 48

18. If grades on a certain test are approximately normally distributed with a mean of 75 and a standard deviation of 10, what percentage of the students received grades less than 65?
    a. 8%
    b. 16%
    c. 60%
    d. 84%

19. If grades on a certain test are approximately normally distributed with a mean of 75 and a standard deviation of 10, what percentage of the students received grades either less than 55 or greater than 95?
    a. 4%
    b. 9%
    c. 68%
    d. 96%

20. If grades on a certain test are approximately normally distributed with a mean of 75 and a standard deviation of 10, what is the lowest grade in the top 2% of grades on the test?
    a. 50
    b. 80
    c. 90
    d. 95

21. If grades on a certain test are approximately normally distributed with a mean of 75 and a standard deviation of 10, what is the highest grade in the bottom 2% of grades on the test?
    a. 55
    b. 65
    c. 85
    d. 95

22. If grades on a certain test are approximately normally distributed with a mean of 75 and a standard deviation of 10, what is the lowest grade in the top 50% of grades on the test?
    a. 90
    b. 85
    c. 75
    d. 50

23. The Web site for the ACT College Entrance Exam reports that the mean composite score of the graduating class of 2007 is 21.2. In addition, the site provides the percentiles for the full range of scores, from 1 to 36. Interpolating, the score at the 84th percentile rounds to 26, whereas the score at the 16th percentile is roughly 16. What is the approximate standard deviation of the ACT scores?
    a. 68
    b. 34
    c. 10
    d. 5

24. Suppose that you are a statistician's research assistant and your task is to use a computer to simulate the random selection, with replacement, of a very large number of samples from a population in which there are just five values, 1, 2, 3, 4, and 5, each of which has the same probability of being selected. According to the **central limit theorem**:
    a. the shape of the distribution of sample means will be approximately normal as long as the sample size is sufficiently large.
    b. as the number of samples increases, the shape of the distribution of sample means becomes more like the shape of a normal curve.
    c. as the number of samples increases, the shape of the distribution of sample means becomes more like the shape of the population.
    d. the shape of the distribution of sample means will be the same as the shape of the population, regardless of the size of each sample.

25. A researcher has just computed the mean of a sample of 50 scores. The probability of obtaining a sample mean as extreme as the one that she computed is found by comparing her sample mean to a comparison distribution of _____ from the population.
    a. 50 scores selected at random
    b. 50 means selected at random
    c. means of all samples of 50 scores
    d. means of 50 samples selected at random

26. Which of the following is the more formal name of the **distribution of means**?
    a. sampling distribution of the mean
    b. standard distribution of means
    c. normal distribution of means
    d. standard error of the mean

27. A distribution of means is less variable than a distribution of individual scores because:
    a. means are insensitive to extreme scores.
    b. means pull extreme scores toward the center.
    c. outliers must be eliminated before computing the mean.
    d. samples almost never include extremely low or high scores.

28. Which of the following is correct regarding the distribution of means?
    a. The mean is the same as the mean of the population of individual scores from which the samples were taken.
    b. The standard error is the same as the standard deviation of the population of individual scores from which the samples were taken.
    c. The shape is approximately normal regardless of the shape of the population of individual scores and regardless of the sample size.
    d. The shape is normal only if the shape of the population of individual scores is normal.

29. Which of the following is (are) not needed to determine the mean, standard deviation, and shape of a distribution of means?
    a. the standard deviation of the population of individual scores
    b. the mean of the population of individual scores
    c. the number of scores in each sample
    d. samples from the population

30. You may compute the standard deviation of a distribution of means by:
    a. dividing the population standard deviation by the square root of the sample size.
    b. dividing the square of the population standard deviation by the sample size.
    c. dividing the square root of the population standard deviation and by the square root of the sample size.
    d. dividing the square of the population standard deviation by the square root of the sample size.

31. The **standard error** tells you how much _____ deviates from the mean of
_____.
    a. each score in a sample; the population
    b. each score in a sample; the sample
    c. each sample mean; the distribution of means
    d. each score in the population; the population

32. In a certain population of college-bound high school seniors, the mean ACT score is 22
and the standard deviation is 4. The standard error of the distribution of means of samples of $N = 25$ from this population is _____.
    a. 64
    b. 16
    c. 4
    d. 0.8

33. Which one of the following is the correct formula for converting a sample mean to a z
statistic?

    a. $\dfrac{X - \mu_M}{\dfrac{\sigma}{\sqrt{N}}}$
    b. $\dfrac{X - \mu_M}{\sigma}$
    c. $\dfrac{M - \mu_M}{\sigma}$
    d. $\dfrac{M - \mu_M}{\dfrac{\sigma}{\sqrt{N}}}$

34. A pizza delivery chain claims that it delivers its pizzas to any location within a 15 mile
radius within an average of 30 minutes, with a standard deviation of 12 minutes.
Suppose that a researcher employed by a competitor orders 16 pizzas to be delivered to
different locations within a 15 mile radius, and computes a sample mean delivery time
of 38 minutes. What is this mean delivery time expressed as a z statistic?
    a. 0.67
    b. −0.67
    c. 2.67
    d. −2.67

35. According to the Web site for the ACT College Entrance Exam, 1,300,599 high school
seniors took the ACT test in 2007, earning a mean composite score of 21.1, with a
standard deviation of 5.0. Suppose that the ACT is administered to a random sample of
100 students from the entire population of high school seniors and the sample mean is
computed to be 22. How many standard errors separate this sample mean from the
national mean?
    a. 0.16
    b. 0.5
    c. 1.6
    d. 4.02

ANSWERS TO CHAPTER 7 STUDY QUESTIONS

Question Number	Correct Answer	Question Number	Correct Answer
1	a, p. 299	19	a, pp. 310–311 (see Figure 7.6)
2	b, p. 299	20	d, pp. 310–311 (see Figure 7.6)
3	c, p. 299	21	a, pp. 310–311 (see Figure 7.6)
4	c, p. 299	22	c, pp. 310–311 (see Figure 7.6)
5	meta-analysis (p. 300)	23	d, pp. 310–311 (see Figure 7.6)
6	d, p. 305	24	a, p. 313 [This is a paraphrase of the central limit theorem.]
7	b, p. 307		
8	b, p. 308	25	c, p. 313
9	a, p. 308	26	a, p. 313
10	c, pp. 310–311 (see Figure 7.6)	27	b, pp. 317, 321
11	d, pp. 310–311 (see Figure 7.6)	28	a, pp. 317, 322
12	d, pp. 310–311 (see Figure 7.6)	29	d, pp. 320–321
13	b, pp. 310–311 (see Figure 7.6)	30	a, pp. 320–321
14	d, pp. 310–311 (see Figure 7.6)	31	c, pp. 320–321
15	a, pp. 310–311 (see Figure 7.6)	32	d, p. 321
16	b, pp. 310-311 (see Figure 7.6)	33	d, p. 324
17	c, pp. 310–311 (see Figure 7.6)	34	c, p. 324
18	b, pp. 310–311 (see Figure 7.6)	35	c, p. 324

CHAPTER EIGHT

HYPOTHESIS TESTING WITH *z* TESTS

Making Meaningful Comparisons

CHAPTER OUTLINE

The Versatile *z* Table: Raw Scores, *z* Scores, and Percentages
- From *z* Scores to Percentages: The Benefits of Standardization
- From Percentages to *z* Scores: The Benefits of Sketching the Normal Curve
- The *z* Table and Distributions of Means: The Benefits of Unbiased Comparisons

Hypothesis Tests: An Introduction
- Assumptions: The Requirements to Conduct Analyses
- The Six Steps of Hypothesis Testing: A Reliable Framework for Hypothesis Testing

Hypothesis Tests: The Single Sample *z* Test
- The *z* Test: When We Know the Population Mean and the Standard Deviation
- The *z* Test: The Six Steps of Hypothesis Testing

The Effect of Sample Size: A Means to Increase the Test Statistic
- Increasing Our Test Statistic through Sample Size: A Demonstration
- The Effect of Increasing Sample Size: What's Going On

Digging Deeper into the Data: What to Do with Dirty Data

LEARNING OBJECTIVES

After studying this chapter, you should be able to:

1. Define each of the following terms and provide examples that are not in the text: *assumptions*; *robust*; *parametric tests*; *nonparametric tests*, *critical values*, *critical region*; *p levels*, *statistically significant*, *one-tailed test*, and *two-tailed test*.

2. Provide solutions to problems and exercises that involve converting raw scores to standard scores and using the standard normal probability distribution (the *z* distribution) to determine percentile ranks and assign probabilities to values of normally distributed variables.

3. Provide solutions to problems and exercises that involve converting sample means to *z* statistics and using the standard normal probability

distribution to assign probabilities to intervals within a sampling distribution of normally distributed means.

4. Enumerate and explain the six steps of hypothesis testing.

5. Apply the six steps of hypothesis testing to conduct a *z* test of a null hypothesis about the value of a population mean when the population standard deviation is known.

6. Explain the role of sample size in hypothesis testing.

7. Identify three common categories of "dirty data" and discuss how a researcher may respond appropriately to problems within each category.

CHAPTER REVIEW

> The Versatile *z* Table: Raw Scores, *z* Scores, and Percentages

In this chapter, the six steps of traditional hypothesis testing are formally introduced in the context of conducting a one-sample *z* test. As background, you may wish to review the definition of hypothesis testing in Chapter 1 (text page 17) as well as the general logic underlying all hypothesis testing procedures in Chapter 4 (text pages 179-181).

To provide additional background for conducting the *z* test, this chapter begins with a continuation of the discussion of standardization that began in Chapter 7. Recall from that discussion that any raw score (*X*) may be standardized by converting it to a standard, or *z*, score. The practical utility of converting raw scores to *z* scores is to facilitate comparisons between measures of different variables—the "apples to oranges" comparisons that were described in Chapter 7. You also learned in Chapter 7 that the distributions of many variables of interest to behavioral scientists are well-approximated by a famous probability distribution called the normal curve. The *standardization* of a normally distributed variable places the values of that variable within the *standard* normal distribution, also known as the *z* distribution. After a normally distributed variable is standardized, its percentile rank may be determined from Table B.1 in the appendix of the text.

You also learned in Chapter 7 that standardization is not limited to raw scores but may be extended to the means of samples of raw scores as well. In addition, you learned that the means of samples selected from a population of normally distributed raw scores are themselves normally distributed, and this distribution of sample means is called the sampling distribution of the mean. Finally, you learned that the central limit theorem ensures that the sampling distribution of the mean of sufficiently large samples (*N* > 30 or so) is normal even if the population of raw scores is not. Converting a sample mean to a *z* statistic enables the researcher to determine the probability of observing a sample mean as extreme as the one observed if the null hypothesis is true. This assignment of probability values to *z* (and other test) statistics is the foundation of statistical inference and of most of the hypothesis testing procedures available to researchers.

First, we will use the standard normal curve (*z* distribution) to determine the percentile rank of a normally distributed variable value such as an individual's score on an IQ test. Then, we will reverse this process and use information in the form of percentages to determine individual scores. For both types of problems, it will often be helpful to sketch the curve to help you visualize the solution. In the first type of problem, you are given a raw score (X), as well as the mean (μ) and the standard deviation (σ) of the population or comparison group, and you are asked to determine:

- the percentage of raw scores greater than X, or
- the percentage of raw scores less than X (this percentage is called the percentile rank), or
- the percentage of scores between two raw scores, X_1 and X_2.

The solution to each of these problems involves three (3) general steps.

If you are asked to determine the percentage of raw scores *greater than X*, follow these steps:

Step 1. Convert the raw score to a *z* score:

$$z = \frac{(X - \mu)}{\sigma}$$

Step 2. Use the table of normal curve percentages (Table B.1 in the appendix of the text, pp. B1-B4) to find the value of *z* that you computed in Step 1. An excerpt from the table follows:

z	% MEAN TO z	% IN TAIL
.00	0.00	50.00
.01	0.40	49.60
.02	0.80	49.20
.03	1.20	48.80
.04	1.60	48.40
.05	1.99	48.01

Step 3. If *z* is a positive value, then look in the column labeled "% IN TAIL" to find the percentage of raw scores greater than X. If *z* is a negative value, then look in the column labeled "% MEAN TO *z*" and add the value from this column to 50%.

If you are asked to determine the percentage of raw scores *less than X*, follow these steps:

Step 1. Convert the raw score to a *z* score:

$$z = \frac{(X - \mu)}{\sigma}$$

Step 2. Use the table of normal curve percentages to find the value of z that you computed in Step 1.

Step 3. Look in the % MEAN TO z column to find the percentage of raw scores between the mean and z. If z is above the mean (i.e., if z is a positive value), then the solution is found by adding 50% to the value in the % MEAN TO z column. If z is below the mean (i.e., if z is negative), then the solution is found by subtracting the value from the % MEAN TO z column from 50%.

If you are asked to determine the percentage of raw scores between two raw scores, say, X_1 *and* X_2, follow these steps:

Step 1. Convert each raw score to a z score:

$$z_1 = \frac{(X_1 - \mu)}{\sigma} \qquad\qquad z_2 = \frac{(X_2 - \mu)}{\sigma}$$

Step 2. Use the table of normal curve percentages to find the values of z_1 and z_2 that you computed in Step 1.

Step 3. Look in the % MEAN TO z column to find the percentage of raw scores between the mean and z_1 and between the mean and z_2. If z_1 and z_2 are on opposite sides of the mean, the solution is simply to sum the two percentages. If z_1 and z_2 are on the same side of the mean, subtract the smaller percentage from the larger one.

Example Problem

Tom's IQ was measured to be 127. For Tom's comparison group, the mean IQ score is 100 and the standard deviation is 15. What is the percentile rank of Tom's IQ score—that is, what percentage of IQ scores in Tom's comparison group is less than Tom's score?

Solution

1. Tom's IQ score converts to a z score as follows:

$$z_{IQ} = \frac{(127 - 100)}{15} = \frac{27}{15} = 1.8$$

2. Look up $z = 1.8$ in Table B.1 and find % MEAN TO z to be 46.41%. This is the percentage of scores between Tom's score and the mean score of 100. Now add 50% to 46.41% to get the answer: Tom's IQ score has a percentile rank of **96.41**—that is, his score is greater than 96.41% of the scores in his comparison group.

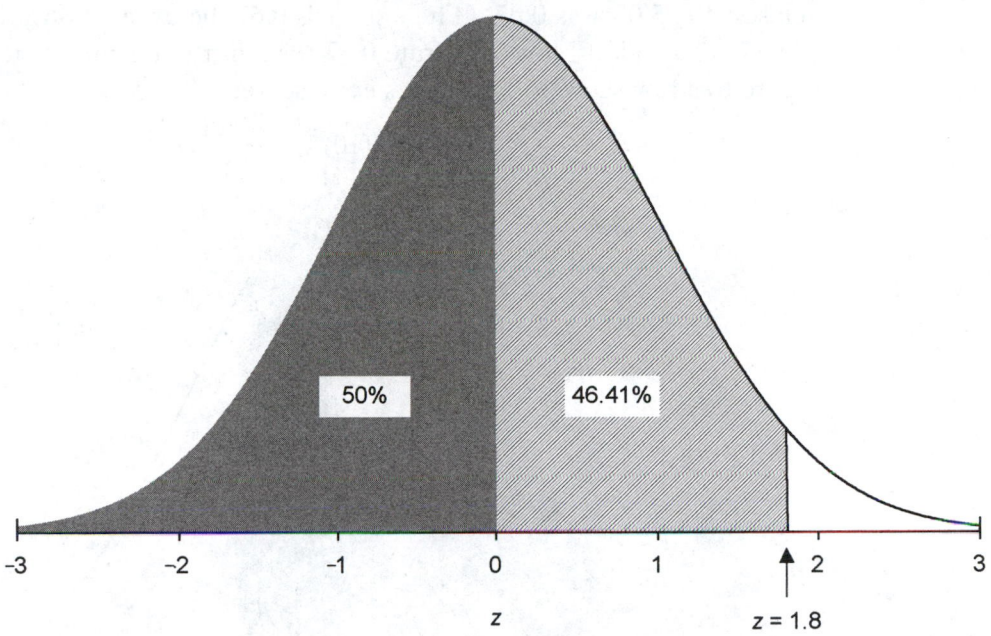

In the second type of normal curve problem, the mean and standard deviation of an appropriate comparison group of scores as well as a percentage of scores above or below a certain score are given. The problem requires that you find a *z* score that corresponds to this percentage, and may require that you convert the *z* score to a raw score. The solution to this type of problem involves just a few steps as well.

Step 1. Determine whether the percentage that you are given corresponds to a "% IN TAIL" or a "% MEAN TO *z*" and find the percentage in the appropriate column that is closest to the percentage that you are given.

Step 2. Find the *z* score that corresponds to this percentage.

Step 3. If the problem requires that you transform the *z* score to a raw score, then use the following formula to do so.

$$X = z(\sigma) + \mu$$

Example Problem

Tom's exam score is greater than 75% of the scores in his class. If the class mean and standard deviation are 75 and 10, respectively, what is Tom's exam score?

Solution

If Tom's score is greater than 75% of the scores, then it is greater than the scores below the mean, so it is greater than the scores represented by the left half of the normal curve. It is also greater than the next 25% of the scores, so look up "% MEAN TO *z*" = 25% to find the *z* score that corresponds to Tom's score. The *z* score that corresponds to the "% MEAN TO *z*" that is closest to 25.00% is 0.67. (The *z* score is 0.67, because 24.86% is closer than 25.17% to 25%.) Now substitute 0.67 for *z* in the formula that converts a *z* score to a raw score to find Tom's exam score:

$$X = 0.67(10) + 75 = \mathbf{81.7}$$

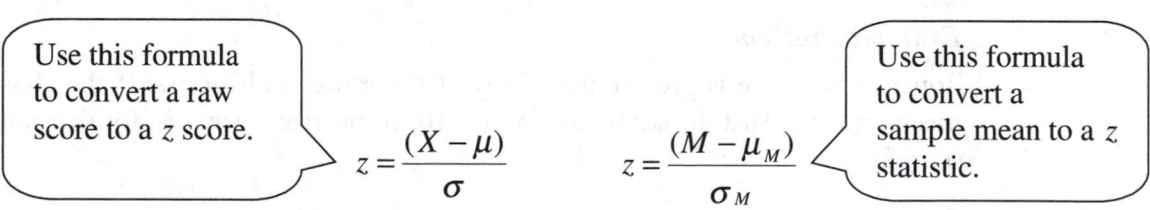

As noted in the previous graph, sample means may also be converted to *z* statistics and assigned a probability from Table B.1 in the appendix of the text. The formula used to convert a sample mean to a *z* statistic is similar to the formula used to convert a raw score to a *z* score. The most frequent error made by students is forgetting to use the standard error instead of the standard deviation in the denominator of the formula for converting a sample mean to a *z* statistic. The formulas are presented next for your convenience:

Use this formula to convert a raw score to a *z* score.

$$z = \frac{(X - \mu)}{\sigma}$$

Use this formula to convert a sample mean to a *z* statistic.

$$z = \frac{(M - \mu_M)}{\sigma_M}$$

Example Problem

In a certain population of individuals with fibromyalgia, the distribution of self-ratings of pain on a scale from 0 to 10 is approximately normal, with $\mu = 5.4$ and $\sigma = 3.2$. A sample of 50 individuals selected from this population participated in the second phase of the clinical trials of a new medication developed to relieve the pain associated with this condition. Following treatment, the mean pain rating in this sample was found to be 4.5. Determine the percentage of all samples of 50 individuals selected from this population expected to have a mean no greater than 4.5.

Solution

Convert the sample mean of 6.3 to a *z* statistic.

$$z = \frac{M - \mu_M}{\sigma_M} = \frac{4.5 - 5.4}{3.2 / \sqrt{50}} = \frac{-0.9}{0.453} = -1.99$$

Locate *z* = 1.99 in the left column of Table B.1 in the appendix of the text and find the % IN TAIL value to be **2.33**.

z	% MEAN TO *z*	% IN TAIL
1.95	47.44	2.56
1.96	47.50	2.50
1.97	47.56	2.44
1.98	47.61	2.39
1.99	47.67	2.33
2.00	47.72	2.28

The percentage of all samples of 50 individuals selected from this population who are expected to have a mean no greater than 4.5 is 2.33. We may also express this outcome as the percent chance (2.33), or probability (0.023), of randomly selecting a single sample of 50 individuals from this population and observing a mean less than or equal to 4.5.

> Hypothesis Tests: An Introduction

The process of selecting a statistical test requires that you determine whether the assumptions of the test are violated to a degree that would prohibit its use. The **assumptions** of a statistical analysis "are the requirements that the population from which we are sampling has specific characteristics that will allow us to make accurate inferences" (p. 352 in the text). The basic assumptions of the analysis procedures described in Chapters 5–12 of the text are as follows:

1. The dependent variable is measured on an interval or ratio scale.
2. The participants are randomly selected from the target population.
3. The values of the dependent variable (scores) are approximately normally distributed in the population.

In the practice of research, all three of these general assumptions are frequently compromised to some degree. For example, psychological variables such as anxiety, guilt, happiness, well-being, depression, extraversion, neuroticism, sensation-seeking, intelligence, attitudes, consideration of future consequences, and so forth are typically measured with paper-and-pencil instruments (scales) that are assumed to yield scores on an interval scale. However, this assumption is rarely, if ever, supported by empirical evidence. The assumption that participants are randomly selected from the population is routinely violated in the behavioral sciences in which convenience, not random, samples tend to be the rule. The cost of violating this assumption is paid in terms of limiting the extent to which the results may be generalized. Results determined for a convenience sample of participants may be generalized only to populations of individuals who are similar to the participants comprising the studied sample. The normality assumption may be ignored for large samples, thanks to the central limit theorem. For smaller samples, most statistical tests are relatively *robust* with respect to violations of this assumption. A statistical test is described as **robust** if the accuracy of the results is not markedly affected by the violation of one or more of its assumptions.

The statistical tests described in Chapters 5–11 are called **parametric tests** because they all assume that the dependent variable values are normally distributed in the population.[1] However, for small samples from populations with a nonnormal distribution, the parametric tests may be inappropriate. Under these conditions one of the **nonparametric tests**, which are required when the dependent variable is measured on a nominal or an ordinal scale, may be used instead of a parametric test. The nonparametric tests have more limited assumptions but in most cases are less sensitive than the parametric tests to the effects of the independent variable. Several of the nonparametric tests, or distribution-free tests as they are sometimes called, are described in Chapters 13 and 14.

The six steps of hypothesis testing are described on text pages 356–358 in terms that apply to each statistical test discussed in the text. The labels for each of these steps are listed next, and the application of the steps to the most basic hypothesis test, the one-sample *z* test, is outlined in the following section.

Step 1. Identify the populations, comparison distribution, and assumptions.

Step 2. State the null and research hypotheses.

Step 3. Determine the characteristics of the comparison distribution.

Step 4. Determine the critical, or cutoff, values of the test statistic.

Step 5. Calculate the test statistic.

Step 6. Make a decision regarding the status of the null hypothesis.

---

[1] The term *parametric* refers to the fact that the normal probability distribution is defined by *parameters*, two of which are μ and σ.

> Hypothesis Tests: The Single Sample z Test

A researcher believes that a new form of psychotherapy will increase the self-esteem scores of persons with low self-esteem. Accordingly, she obtains a sample of 16 individuals with low self-esteem, administers the form of psychotherapy over a six-week period, and evaluates the self-esteem of these clients using a suitably valid and reliable instrument. The researcher computes the mean (M) of the self-esteem scores in this sample of 16 clients and finds it to be 14. This single value is the researcher's best estimate of μ_1, the mean of the population of clients receiving the new psychotherapy. The mean self-esteem score in the population of *untreated* individuals with low self-esteem is known to be **12** ($\mu_2 = 12$), with a standard deviation of **4** ($\sigma = 4$). The question to be addressed by the hypothesis test is thus whether a sample mean of 14 is sufficiently greater than 12 to qualify as evidence that the new form of psychotherapy increases self-esteem in this population. The answer requires a test of the null hypothesis at the 0.05 level of statistical significance.

Step 1. Describe the populations and the comparison distribution, and make sure that the test is sufficiently robust with respect to any possible violations of its assumptions.

The population specified by the null hypothesis (Population 2) is the population of all persons with low self-esteem who have not been treated with this new form of psychotherapy. The population specified by the research hypothesis (Population 1) is the population of all individuals with low self-esteem who have been treated with the new psychotherapy. The comparison distribution is the distribution of means of all possible samples of 16 scores from Population 2. The one-sample z test is selected for this hypothesis test because the population standard deviation is known from prior research. The z test is a parametric test, so it requires that the self-esteem scores be measured on an interval or ratio scale and that the scores follow a normal distribution. The sample of clients is not a random sample, so the results may only be generalized to similar individuals.

Step 2. State the null and research hypotheses.

As you learned in Chapter 4, the hypothesis tested in a scientific study is not the researcher's hypothesis. Rather, it is the null hypothesis, a statement that is the logical opposite of the research hypothesis. The term *null* is from the Latin *nullus*, which means "not any." This term is aptly descriptive of the null hypothesis, which always states that there is "not any" effect of the independent variable and thus "not any" difference between the means of two or more populations. In the present example, a statement of the null hypothesis might read this way: "The new form of psychotherapy does *not* increase the self-esteem of persons with low self-esteem." Phrased more formally and in statistical terms, the null hypothesis states that "The mean score on a measure of self-esteem in the population of individuals with low self-esteem who are treated with this new form of psychotherapy is not higher than the mean self-esteem score in the population of individuals with low self-esteem who are not treated."

In symbols: H_0: $\mu_1 \leq \mu_2$.

where,

H_0 refers to the null hypothesis

μ_1 refers to the mean self-esteem score in the population of persons with low self-esteem treated with a new form of psychotherapy

μ_2 refers to the mean self-esteem score in the population of persons with low self-esteem who are not treated with the new form of psychotherapy

The research, or alternative, hypothesis may read as follows: "Psychotherapy increases the self-esteem of persons with low self-esteem." In more formal terms, "The mean score on a measure of self-esteem is higher in the population of individuals with low self-esteem who are treated with a new form of psychotherapy than in the population of individuals with low self-esteem who are not treated." In symbols: H_1: $\mu_1 > \mu_2$. Note the contrast between the symbolic expressions of the null and research hypotheses:

$$H_0\text{: } \mu_1 \leq \mu_2$$
$$H_1\text{: } \mu_1 > \mu_2$$

The null and research hypotheses must be *mutually exclusive* (that is, there can be no "middle ground" or overlap) and *exhaustive* (there can be no other possibilities). If this new form of psychotherapy *does not increase* self-esteem, then it must either *decrease* or *have no effect on* self-esteem.

The statement of the research hypothesis is a *directional* statement, because it declares that the new form of psychotherapy has a directional effect—that is, it increases levels of self-esteem. A directional statement of the research hypothesis requires a **one-tailed** test of the null hypothesis. A one-tailed test permits the rejection of the null hypothesis if the sample outcome is sufficiently extreme in the direction, or tail of the comparison distribution, predicted by the research hypothesis. A **two-tailed test** is required by a *nondirectional* null hypothesis: $\mu_1 = \mu_2$. A two-tailed test is so-named because it permits the rejection of the null hypothesis if the sample outcome is sufficiently extreme in either tail of the comparison distribution. A two-tailed test is more conservative (makes it more difficult to reject the null hypothesis) and for this reason is encountered more frequently in the literature of the behavioral sciences.

Step 3. Determine the characteristics of the comparison distribution.

The comparison distribution is the distribution of means of all possible samples of 16 scores from Population 2, the population specified by the null hypothesis. According to the null hypothesis, the new form of psychotherapy is without effect, so the mean of the population of individuals with low self-esteem who receive the new form of therapy is the same as the mean of the population of *untreated* individuals with low self-esteem. For the purpose of this example of hypothesis testing, we will assume that the mean of the population of untreated individuals with low esteem is known to be 12 ($\mu_2 = 12$), with a standard deviation of 4 ($\sigma = 4$). The mean of the comparison distribution is the same as the mean of the population of self-esteem scores specified by the null hypothesis:

$$\mu_M = \mu_2 = 12$$

The standard deviation of the comparison distribution (the standard error) is the population standard deviation divided by the square root of the sample size:

$$\sigma_M = \frac{\sigma}{\sqrt{N}} = \frac{4}{\sqrt{16}} = \frac{4}{4} = 1$$

The shape of the comparison distribution is normal, because we are assuming that self-esteem scores are normally distributed in the population. In actual research, we would need some evidence to support this assumption. Given the widespread belief among psychologists that most psychological and physical variables are normally distributed, this is a credible assumption. However, it is not a trivial assumption, particularly given Micceri's (1989) report that many measures routinely used in psychology and education are not normally distributed. Assuming a normal distribution of self-esteem scores in the population, the comparison distribution is also a normal distribution and may be sketched as follows:

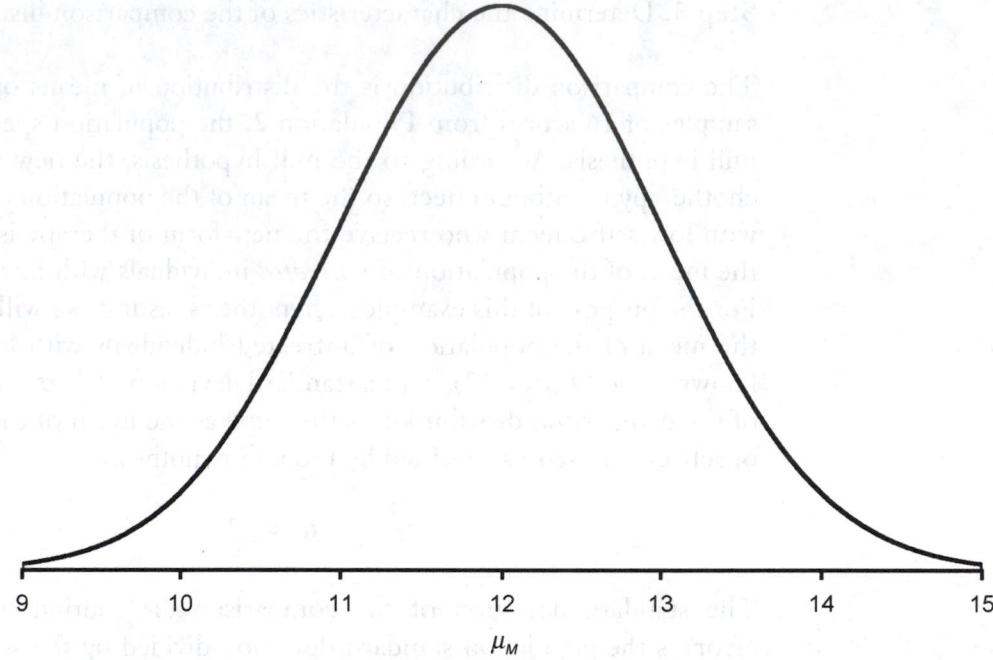

μ_M

The null hypothesis is assumed to be true and the "burden of proof" is on the researcher to show that this is not a reasonable assumption. The researcher accepts this burden of proof by agreeing to test the null hypothesis at the 0.05 p level.

Step 5. Determine the critical values of the test statistic.

The **critical values** of the test statistic (z in this example) are determined by the level of statistical significance, called the p level. The **p level** provides an answer to the question: How unusual or extreme must a sample mean be before the null hypothesized value of μ is rejected as implausible? If a sample mean has a probability of occurrence that is less than or equal to the p level, then the null hypothesis is considered to be implausible and may be rejected as such. The most commonly used p level is 0.05 (5%), so we will use this p level as well. In Table B.1 in the text, look up the percentage in the "% IN TAIL" column that is closest to the p level (5%, in this example). Two values, 4.95% and 5.05%, are equidistant from 5%, so the critical value of z is 1.645, the value midway between 1.64 and 1.65. The research hypothesis states that the mean self-esteem score in the population of treated individuals is greater than the mean of the population of untreated individuals, so the critical value of z is 1.645 instead of –1.645. The positive value is chosen because it defines ("cuts off") the *rejection region* of the comparison distribution. The upper tail of the comparison distribution is called the **rejection region,** because a sample mean that falls in this region will permit a rejection of the null hypothesis. If the researcher hypothesis stated that the mean of the population of treated individuals is *less than* the mean of the population of untreated individuals (i.e., $\mu_1 < \mu_2$), then the rejection region would be the *lower* 5% of the comparison distribution, and the critical value of *z* would be –1.645. The comparison distribution, with rejection region, looks like this:

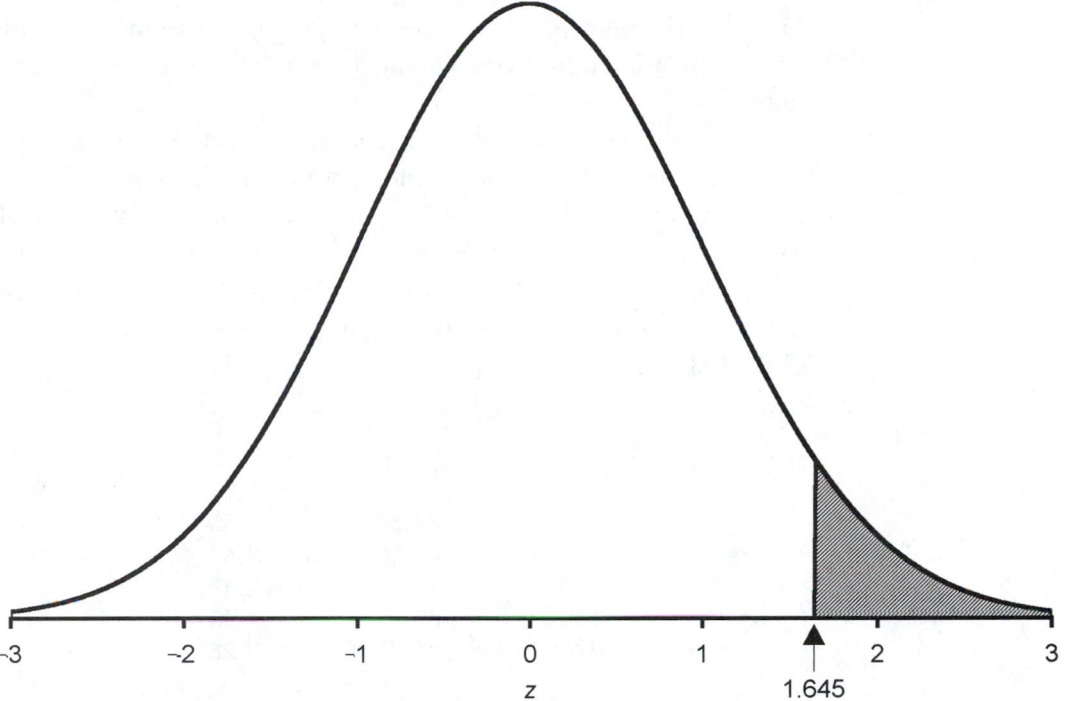

If this had been a *two*-tailed test, the critical values of the *z* statistic would have been determined by dividing the *p* level by 2 (0.05 / 2 = 0.025). From Table B.1 in the text, the *z* statistics that cut off the upper and lower 2.5% of the area under the comparison distribution are 1.96 and 1.96. This is why the two-tailed test is more conservative; it is easier to reject the null hypothesis when the critical value is 1.645 than when the critical value is farther out into the tails at 1.96.

Step 6. Convert the sample mean to a *z* statistic.

$$z = \frac{M - \mu_M}{\sigma_M} = \frac{M - \mu_M}{\sigma / \sqrt{N}} = \frac{14 - 12}{4 / \sqrt{16}} = \frac{2}{4/4} = 2$$

In hypothesis testing, *z* is called a ***test statistic***. It is necessary to convert the sample mean to a *z* statistic, because Table B.1 in the text provides percentages that correspond to values of *z* rather than sample means.

Step 7. Make a decision regarding the null hypothesis.

The null hypothesis should be rejected because the computed z statistic (z = 2) is more extreme than the critical value of z (1.645). Put another way, the null hypothesis may be rejected because the computed value of z falls in the rejection region. Having rejected the null hypothesis, we may conclude that the new form of psychotherapy appears to increase self-esteem in the population of individuals who are similar to the clients tested in this study.

You should be aware that published journal articles and statistical programs such as SPSS provide significance probabilities or p values, not critical values of test statistics such as z. The **p value** is the probability of observing a sample statistic at least as extreme as the one observed if the null hypothesis is true. You may determine the p value of the computed z statistic by consulting Table B.1 in the text. For z = 2.00, the p value is 2.28% (0.0228).

z	% MEAN TO z	% IN TAIL
1.95	47.44	2.56
1.96	47.50	2.50
1.97	47.56	2.44
1.98	47.61	2.39
1.99	47.67	2.33
⟶ 2.00	47.72	2.28

By the p-value method, then, the null hypothesis should be rejected because the probability (p value) of observing a mean of 14 or more for a sample of *untreated* persons with low self-esteem is less than the p level of 0.05 (5%).

Note that the *decision* is always to either *reject* or *fail to reject* the *null* hypothesis. The *conclusion* is that the sample evidence supports or does not support the *research* hypothesis. It is inappropriate to "accept," or "conclude support for," the null hypothesis. In addition, you should never use any forms of the words "prove" or "true" when interpreting the results of a hypothesis test. The results either "support" or "do not support" the research hypothesis.

When the null hypothesis is rejected, the sample outcome is typically described as **statistically significant**. In hypothesis testing, *significant* means *unlikely to have occurred by chance*; it does not mean *important*. A sample outcome that results in a failure to reject the null hypothesis is a *non-significant* result. Please note that it is inappropriate to refer to population parameters such as μ_1 and μ_2 as "significantly different." Statistical significance is a description of the outcome of a chance process, whereas the values of μ_1 and μ_2 are fixed and are forever either the same or different.

> The Effect of Sample Size: A Means to Increase the Test Statistic

The example used to illustrate the six steps of hypothesis testing with a z test used a sample of 16 clients. In this case, the sample size was based on convenience; that is, it was limited by the number of clients who consented to be in this study. Although the z statistic was significant at the 0.05 p level, one-tailed, the p value of 0.0228 would have been barely significant at the 0.05 level, two-tailed, and would not have been significant using the more conservative p level of 0.01 for either a one-tailed or a two-tailed test. If the researcher were to submit this study to the editor of a peer-reviewed journal for publication, she may be advised to replicate the study using a more stringent p level. Assuming that the effect of her new form of psychotherapy on low self-esteem is reliable—that is, the approximate 2-point increase in self-esteem scores would be observed if she were to repeat this study using different samples of clients—what can she do to virtually ensure that her results meet the more conservative criterion?

She can increase her sample size. The following table compares the results with a sample size of 16 with those that could be expected for samples of 25, 36, and 49 clients. Again, these outcomes were determined under the assumption that the effect of the psychotherapy intervention is constant across studies; that is, the numerator of the formula used to compute the z statistic is the same for each sample size.

Sample Size	σ_M	z	one-tailed p value	two-tailed p value
16	1.00	2.00	0.0228	0.0455
25	0.80	2.50	0.0062	0.0124
36	0.67	3.00	0.0013	0.0027
49	0.57	3.50	0.0002	0.0005

The table shows that increasing the size of the sample decreases the standard error which, in turn, increases the z statistic and lowers the p values for one- and two-tailed tests. The explanation is fairly straightforward: The standard error is the denominator of the formula used to compute the z statistic. The mathematical explanation is basic: As the denominator of any fraction decreases, the value of the fraction increases. But why does the size of the standard error decrease with an increase in sample size? As more participants from a normal population are added to the sample, the probability of adding participants with self-esteem scores near the mean is greater than for any other range of scores. The standard error is a measure of deviation from the mean, so this measure of deviation should be decreased by the addition of more participants whose scores are relatively close to the mean.

So, why not simply use a large sample size in each study that is submitted for publication? The most basic reason is cost: Exposing each participant to a treatment and measuring the resulting effect of the treatment on the dependent variable is expensive and time-consuming. The second reason reflects one of the primary goals of behavioral science, which is to disclose the existence of effects that have practical (applied) or theoretical importance. If the effect of a treatment is too small to be of any applied or theoretical value, then a statistically significant outcome that has been manufactured by a large sample size will not be of much interest to the community of researchers and practitioners. The issue of practical importance vs. statistical significance is discussed more completely in Chapter 12.

> Digging Deeper into the Data: What to Do with Dirty Data

The phrase "dirty data" refers generally to problems associated with representing a participant's behavior with a data value. These problems may be subsumed by three categories:

- missing data
- misleading data
- outliers

There are many reasons for missing data. Participants may simply neglect or even refuse to respond to questions or items in a printed instrument; responses may be unintelligible or they may become lost or misplaced by a research assistant; or participants may become ill, relocate, or even die over the course of a longitudinal study conducted over several weeks, months, or years.

The problem of misleading data occurs when participants enter bogus responses, either because they intend to undermine the research process or they exhibit some bias in their pattern of responses such as responding in accord with their perception of social norms (social desirability response bias) or consistently choosing responses near the center or one of the extremes of a rating scale regardless of the item content.

Outliers are data values that are some distance from the main body of data. Outliers may reflect a participant's attempt to mislead or they may result from something as trivial as hitting the wrong key on a numeric keypad. Of course, it is also possible that the outlier is a valid data value. After all, in any distribution of measures there will be some scores in the extreme range.

Specific remedies for each of these sources of dirty data are discussed on pages 368–372 in your text. Regardless of the specific remedy selected by the researcher, she or he is obligated to adhere to two ethical principles: (1) Decide in advance how such problems will be addressed, and (2) Describe the details of the remedial (data omission, or data replacement) procedure in the Method section of the research report. For example, a researcher may decide in advance to define an outlier according to the 1.5 X IQR criterion discussed in Chapter 2 and delete all values meeting this criterion. If the variable is distributed normally, a researcher may identify an outlier as any datum more than 3 standard deviations from the sample mean. In either event, the researcher's obligation is to adopt the criterion before any data are collected and to describe in the Method section the criterion as well as the number of data values omitted because of its application.

STUDY QUESTIONS

1. The table of normal curve percentages in the appendix of the text lists *z* scores in one column and the percentage of scores _____ in the second column.
   a. between any pair of *z* scores
   b. less than or equal to each *z* score
   c. greater than or equal to each *z* score
   d. between the mean ($z = 0$) and each *z* score

2. The percentage of scores between $z = -1.14$ and $z = +0.67$ on the standard normal curve is:
   a. 46.49.
   b. 37.85.
   c. 12.43.
   d. 62.15.

3. Scores on a certain mathematics achievement test are known to be normally distributed with a mean of 75 and a standard deviation of 12. If a minimum score of 90 is needed to qualify for membership in a high school math club, what percentage of the students taking this test are expected to qualify for membership?
   a. 2.5
   b. 1.25
   c. 10.57
   d. 89.44

4. In a certain population, the distribution of height follows the normal curve, with a mean of 5 feet 8 inches (68 inches) and a standard deviation of 3 inches. What is the percentile rank of an individual who is 6 feet (72 inches) tall?
   a. 90.82
   b. 9.18
   c. 69.74
   d. 30.26

5. In a certain population, the distribution of height follows the normal curve, with a mean of 5 feet 8 inches (68 inches) and a standard deviation of 3 inches. What is the percentile rank of an individual who is 5 feet (60 inches) tall?
   a. 0.38
   b. 99.62
   c. 68.75
   d. 31.25

6. In a certain population, the distribution of height follows the normal curve, with a mean of 5 feet 8 inches (68 inches) and a standard deviation of 3 inches. Determine the percentage of individuals in this population who are between 5 feet 6 inches and 5 feet 10 inches tall.
    a. 68.26
    b. 97.72
    c. 68.75
    d. 49.71

7. Kate's score on a chemistry exam is 62. If the scores on this exam are approximately normally distributed with a mean and standard deviation of 71 and 9, respectively, what is the percentile rank of Kate's score?
    a. 84.13
    b. 73.79
    c. 62
    d. 15.87

8. One of the tools used to diagnose mental retardation (MR) is the Wechsler IQ test, which yields scores that are approximately normally distributed with a mean of 100 and a standard deviation of 15. Approximately 85% of persons with MR are considered mildly retarded and have IQ scores ranging between 50 and 70. What is the percentile rank of an IQ score of 50?
    a. 4
    b. 0.04
    c. 0.96
    d. 96.96

9. One of the tools used to diagnose mental retardation (MR) is the Wechsler IQ test, which yields scores that are approximately normally distributed with a mean of 100 and a standard deviation of 15. Approximately 85% of persons with MR are considered mildly retarded and have IQ scores ranging between 50 and 70. What is the percentile rank of an IQ score of 70?
    a. 97.72
    b. 2.28
    c. 85
    d. 15

10. One of the tools used to diagnose mental retardation (MR) is the Wechsler IQ test, which yields scores that are approximately normally distributed with a mean of 100 and a standard deviation of 15. Approximately 85% of persons with MR are considered mildly retarded and have IQ scores ranging between 50 and 70. Approximately what percentage of all IQ scores are between 50 and 70?
    a. 85
    b. 20
    c. 2.23
    d. 1.33

11. The interquartile range, which may be expressed as $Q3 - Q1$ or as a phrase "____ to ____" (with the values for $Q1$ and $Q3$ inserted into the first and second blanks, respectively), is the middle 50% of the scores in a distribution. Assume that scores on the math and verbal subtests of the SAT are normally distributed with a mean of 500 and a standard deviation of 100. What is the interquartile range of scores on either subtest of the SAT?
    a. 433 to 567
    b. 475 to 525
    c. 400 to 600
    d. 450 to 550

12. A qualification for membership in the high-IQ society Mensa is an IQ score at the 98th percentile. If IQ test scores are normally distributed with a mean of 100 and a standard deviation of 15, what is the minimum score needed to qualify for membership?
    a. 144
    b. 169
    c. 131
    d. 123

13. The scores on a certain psychological test are known to be skewed with a mean of 62 and a standard deviation of 18. What is the probability that a sample of 50 scores randomly selected from this population will have a mean of 68 or more?
    a. < 0.01
    b. 0.37
    c. 0.63
    d. 0.99

14. A local pizzeria claims that it delivers its pizzas to any location within a 15-mile radius within an average of 30 minutes, with a standard deviation of 12 minutes. Suppose that a researcher working for a competitor orders 16 pizzas to be delivered to different locations within a 15-mile radius, and computes a sample mean delivery time of 38 minutes. Which one of the following is the *most* appropriate conclusion from this study?
    a. The research hypothesis is supported; the mean delivery time for this pizzeria is greater than 30 minutes.
    b. The research hypothesis is not supported; the mean delivery time for this pizzeria is fewer than or equal to 30 minutes.
    c. The research hypothesis is not supported; the mean delivery time for this pizzeria is 30 minutes.
    d. The research hypothesis is supported; the mean delivery time for this pizza chain is fewer than 30 minutes.

15. A sample mean that is 2 standard errors below the mean of a comparison distribution of means has a(n) _____ probability of having been selected from the null-hypothe-sized population.
    a. low (< 0.05)
    b. medium (around 0.5)
    c. high (> 0.95)
    d. unknown

16. In a test of the null hypothesis, $\mu_1 < \mu_2$, a researcher converts a sample mean to a z sta-tistic of –2.89. Assuming that the z statistic was computed correctly and the z test is appropriate for this research problem, which of the following decisions should this researcher make regarding the null hypothesis if the test was conducted at the conven-tional significance level of 0.05?
    a. Reject the null hypothesis because the sample mean is more than two standard errors from the mean of the comparison distribution (a two-tailed test).
    b. Fail to reject the null hypothesis because the sample mean is not in the predicted direction even though it is an extreme (unlikely) value.
    c. Fail to reject the null hypothesis because the p value of the z statistic is not less than 0.05.
    d. Reject the null hypothesis because the sample mean is more than two standard errors from the mean in the predicted direction (a one-tailed test).

17. Parametric analysis procedures such as the z test require that participants are sampled randomly from a population in which the values of the dependent variable are meas-ured on an interval scale and are approximately normally distributed. Such require-ments are called:
    a. ethical guidelines.
    b. assumptions.
    c. research protocol.
    d. critical values.

18. A **robust** hypothesis test is one that:
    a. frequently results in a rejection of the null hypothesis.
    b. is relatively free of assumptions about the shape of the distribution of scores in the sample.
    c. is relatively free of assumptions about the shape of the distribution of scores in the population.
    d. produces reasonably accurate results even when some its assumptions are not met.

19. Statistical analyses based on a set of assumptions about the population are:
    a. described as robust.
    b. called parametric tests.
    c. called nonparametric tests.
    d. conducted less frequently than analyses that are not based on any assumptions.

20. Which one of the following is *most* clearly an example of a null hypothesis? (*Hint: null* is from the Latin *nullus* which means "not any" as in "not any" effect of the experimental treatment and thus "not any" difference between two populations.)
    a. Most people cry when they are extremely happy.
    b. People who have and who have not previously used marijuana are equally likely to be regular users of "hard drugs" such as cocaine and heroin.
    c. Actors who have received training in "method acting" will get more roles than actors who have not received such training.
    d. Children who were physically abused by their parents are more likely to physically abuse their own children.

21. Which one of the following is *most* clearly an example of a research hypothesis?
    a. College graduates do not work a 40-hour week as is typical of the general population.
    b. CEO's have the same average cholesterol levels as the general population.
    c. The new drug is no more effective than the standard treatment.
    d. The new treatment has no effect on the cure rate.

22. The **critical values** are the:
    a. sample scores that are obtained if the null hypothesis is true.
    b. sample scores that are obtained if the null hypothesis is false.
    c. values of the test statistic that the computed values of the test statistic must exceed in order to reject the null hypothesis.
    d. values of the test statistic that the computed values of the test statistic must exceed in order to accept the null hypothesis.

23. The *cutoff score* on the comparison distribution is a score that is so extreme that it has only a 5% chance (or less) of occurring if the null hypothesis is true. In this example, "5%" is a:
    a. critical value.
    b. *p* level.
    c. statistically significant statistic.
    d. sample score.

24. A researcher's decision regarding the null hypothesis may be a Type I error. Which one of the following statements describes a Type I error?
    a. The research hypothesis should be rejected, but it is not rejected.
    b. The research hypothesis is rejected, but it should not be rejected.
    c. The null hypothesis should be rejected, but it is not rejected.
    d. The null hypothesis is rejected, but it should not be rejected.

25. In a study using 0.05 as the p level, a **statistically significant** finding is one that:
    a. has a probability of occurrence that is less than 5%, if the null hypothesis is true.
    b. has a probability of occurrence that is less than 5%, if the null hypothesis is false.
    c. is expected to occur by chance and thus requires that we fail to reject the null hypothesis.
    d. is so extreme that it results in the rejection of the research hypothesis.

26. A researcher predicted that an experimental treatment would alter participants' scores on a certain dependent variable. If the critical value of the z statistic is 1.96, and the computed value of the z statistic is 1.59, then this researcher should conclude that the results:
    a. do not support the null hypothesis.
    b. support the null hypothesis.
    c. support the research hypothesis.
    d. are not statistically significant.

27. A clinical psychologist hypothesized that women who have been physically abused by their husbands will score higher on a test of loyalty than women who have not been physically abused. If the population of physically abused women is labeled "Population 1," which one of the following is the null hypothesis to be tested by this psychologist?
    a. $\mu_1 < \mu_2$
    b. $\mu_1 \geq \mu_2$
    c. $\mu_1 \neq \mu_2$
    d. $\mu_1 = \mu_2$

28. Which one of the following statements requires a **one-tailed test** of the null hypothesis?
    a. Winning a one million dollar lottery will increase a person's relative happiness.
    b. Infants who receive special training will learn to walk at the same time as infants who do receive any special training.
    c. College graduates do not work a 40-hour work week as is typical of the general population.
    d. Compared to mice treated with a placebo, mice that receive daily injections of nicotine for a period of five weeks will show a different level of activity when both groups are injected with a stimulant drug.

29. The distribution of scores on the Beck Depression Inventory II following four weeks of a standard therapy in a certain population of outpatients is known to be normally distributed with mean $(\mu) = 27.82$ and standard deviation $(\sigma) = 9.55$. A researcher believes that the distribution of depression scores following four weeks of a new therapy differs from the distribution of scores obtained following the standard therapy. If Population 1 is the population of depression scores following four weeks of the new therapy, which one of the following is the null hypothesis being tested?
    a. $\mu_1 < \mu_2$
    b. $\mu_1 > \mu_2$
    c. $\mu_1 = \mu_2$
    d. $\mu_1 \geq \mu_2$

30. When conducting a **two-tailed test** of the null hypothesis at the 0.05 *p* level, the critical values of the *z* statistic are _____.
    a. −2.58 and +2.58
    b. −2.33 and +2.33
    c. −1.96 and +1.96
    d. −1.645 and +1.645

31. A school psychologist is convinced that the mean IQ score of the high school seniors in her district is greater than 100. Accordingly, she administered an IQ test to a random sample of 50 seniors in her district and determined the mean IQ score for her sample to be 104. Assume that IQ scores are normally distributed in the population with a mean of 100 and a standard deviation of 15. What is the computed value of the *z* statistic that this psychologist will use to test the null hypothesis?
    a. 0.27
    b. 0.04
    c. 1.89
    d. 13.33

32. A school psychologist is convinced that the mean IQ score of the high school seniors in her district is greater than 100. Accordingly, she administered an IQ test to a random sample of 50 seniors in her district and determined the mean IQ score for her sample to be 104. Assume that IQ scores are normally distributed in the population with a mean of 100 and a standard deviation of 15. What is the critical value of the *z* statistic for this test of the null hypothesis?
    a. 1.645
    b. 1.96
    c. −1.645
    d. −1.96

33. The distribution of scores on the Beck Depression Inventory II following four weeks of a standard therapy in a certain population of outpatients is normally distributed with mean (μ) = 27.82 and standard deviation (σ) = 9.55. A researcher hypothesized that the mean depression score following four weeks of a new therapy differs from the mean depression score following four weeks of the standard therapy. Suppose that the mean score for a sample of 36 patients following four weeks of the new therapy is 24.38. Which of the following is the most appropriate conclusion?
    a. Reject the null hypothesis because the computed *z* statistic is more extreme than the critical value of the *z* statistic, −1.645.
    b. Fail to reject the null hypothesis because the computed *z* statistic is not more extreme than the critical value of the *z* statistic, −1.645.
    c. Reject the null hypothesis because the computed *z* statistic is more extreme than the critical value of the *z* statistic, −1.96.
    d. Fail to reject the null hypothesis because the computed *z* statistic is not more extreme than the critical value of the *z* statistic, −1.96.

34. A school psychologist is convinced that the mean IQ score of the high school seniors in her district is greater than 100. Accordingly, she administered an IQ test to a random sample of 50 seniors in her district and determined the mean IQ score for her sample to be 104. Assume that IQ scores are normally distributed in the population with a mean of 100 and a standard deviation of 15. Assume also that the computed value of the *z* statistic is in the critical region. Which one of the following is the appropriate decision regarding the null hypothesis?
    a. The null hypothesis is proven to be true.
    b. The null hypothesis is proven to be false.
    c. The null hypothesis is not rejected.
    d. The null hypothesis is rejected.

35. A researcher predicted that an experimental treatment would alter participants' scores on a certain dependent variable. If the critical value of the *z* statistic is 1.96, and the computed value of the *z* statistic is 2.07, then this researcher should conclude that the results:
    a. prove that the research hypothesis is true.
    b. prove that the null hypothesis is true.
    c. are inconclusive.
    d. support the research hypothesis.

ANSWERS TO CHAPTER 8 STUDY QUESTIONS

Question Number	Correct Answer
1	d, p. 340
2	d, pp. 339–346
3	c, pp. 339–346
4	a, pp. 339–346
5	a, pp. 339–346
6	a, pp. 339–346
7	d, pp. 339–346
8	b, pp. 339–346
9	b, pp. 339–346
10	c, pp. 339–346
11	a, pp. 346–348
12	c, pp. 346–348 (Locate the percentage in the "% IN TAIL" column that is closest to 2 and find it to be 2.02. The corresponding value of z is 2.05, indicating that a score at the 98th percentile is 2.05 standard deviations above the mean. So, 2.05(15) + 100 = 130.75, the minimum IQ score required for Mensa membership.)
13	a, pp. 348–350 [The sample size is sufficiently large to use the normal curve percentages. Compute $z = (68 - 62) / (18 / \sqrt{50}) = 2.35$, then look up $z = 2.35$ in a table of normal curve percentages and find "% IN TAIL" to be 0.94%. The probability of observing a sample mean of 68 or more from a distribution of means of samples of $N = 50$ from the population described is 0.0094.]
14	a, pp. 360–364 (The computed z statistic = 2.67, and the critical z statistic is 1.645. Note that choice b is a statement of support for the null hypothesis, whereas choices c and d are statements of support for incorrect variations of the null hypothesis. The logic of hypothesis testing does not permit a conclusion of support for the null hypothesis.)

Question Number	Correct Answer
15	a [This is a very basic question about probabilities (p values) and z statistics; note that the cutoff z statistics for the 0.05 level of significance in a two-tailed test are 1.96 standard errors from the mean in either direction, so a sample mean that is 2 standard errors from the mean of the comparison distribution would be labeled "statistically significant" because the p value is less than 0.025.]
16	b, pp. 360–364 [Using the terminology of the six-step procedure described in the text, μ_1 always refers to the mean of the population of individuals receiving the experimental treatment, and in this example the research hypothesis is that the treatment will increase scores—that is, $\mu_1 > \mu_2$—so only those sample means that convert to z statistics more than 1.645 standard errors above the mean of the comparison distribution (positive z statistics) will enable this researcher to reject this directional null hypothesis. Because the z statistic is negative, the null hypothesis may not be rejected even though it is extreme.]
17	b, p. 352
18	d, p. 353
19	b, p. 354
20	b, p. 355 (Choice b is the only statement of no difference between two populations.)
21	a, p. 355 (Choice a is the only statement declaring a difference between two populations.)
22	c, p. 355

Question Number	Correct Answer
23	b, p. 356
24	d, p. 356
25	a, p. 356
26	d, p. 356
27	c, p. 361
28	a, p. 361
29	c, p. 361
30	c, p. 363
31	c, p. 363

Question Number	Correct Answer
32	a, p. 363 (The research hypothesis is directional, so a one-tailed test is required. The critical value of the z statistic defines, or cuts off, the most extreme 5% of the area in the right, or upper, tail of the comparison distribution.)
33	b, p. 363
34	d, pp. 363–364
35	d, p. 364

CHAPTER NINE

HYPOTHESIS TESTING WITH *t* TESTS

Comparing Two Groups

CHAPTER OUTLINE

The *t* Distributions: Distributions of Means When the Parameters Are Not Known
- Using *t* distributions: Estimating a Population Standard Deviation from the Sample
- Calculating a *t* Statistic for the Mean of a Sample: Using the Standard Error
- When *t* and *z* Are Equal: Very Large Sample Sizes
- The *t* Distributions: Distributions of Differences Between Means

Hypothesis Tests: The Single-Sample *t* Test
- The Single-Sample *t* Test: When We Know the Population Mean, But Not the Standard Deviation
- The *t* Table: Understanding Degrees of Freedom
- The *t* Test: The Six Steps of Hypothesis Testing

Hypothesis Tests: Tests for Two Samples
- The Paired-Samples *t* Test: Two Sample Means and a Within-Groups Design
- The Independent-Samples *t* Test: Two Sample Means and a Between-Groups Design

Digging Deeper into the Data: More Ways to Visualize Data
- The Stem-and-Leaf Plot: Searching for Outliers and Comparing Distributions
- The Dot Plot: Making it Easy on Your Eyes

LEARNING OBJECTIVES

After studying this chapter, you should be able to:

1. Define each of the following terms and provide examples that are not in the text: *t statistic*; *single-sample t test*; *degrees of freedom*; *paired-samples t test*, *independent-samples t test*, *pooled variance*; *stem-and-leaf plot*, and *dot plot*.

2. Distinguish between the formula used to compute the standard deviation as a descriptive statistic and the slightly adjusted formula used to compute the sample standard deviation as an estimate of the population standard deviation.

3. Discuss the problem with small samples that led William Gosset to develop the function used to generate the family of *t* distributions as models of the sampling distribution of the mean.

4. Explain the concept of *degrees of freedom* in the context of the family of Student's *t* distributions.

5. Carry out the six steps of hypothesis testing for a single-sample *t* test, a paired-samples *t* test, and an independent-samples *t* test.

6. Construct stem-and-leaf and dot plots and explain the advantages of each plot over a histogram.

CHAPTER REVIEW

> The *t* Distributions: Distributions of Means When the Parameters Are Not Known

The *t* statistic and its family of distributions made their first appearance in a famous paper entitled "The Probable Error of the Mean" by William S. Gosset, an Oxford-trained chemist and mathematician, who worked as a master brewer and statistician for the Guinness Brewing Company of Dublin, Ireland. In his daily work, Gosset faced a common problem in applied research: How can you make a reasonable inference about a population mean when (1) the standard deviation of the population is not known, and (2) the sample of data you have to work with is too small to provide a very stable estimate? Gosset (1908) considered the "usual method":

> The usual method of determining the probability that the mean of the population lies within a given distance of the mean of the sample is to assume a normal distribution about the mean of the sample with a standard deviation equal to $s/\sqrt{n}$, where s is the standard deviation of the sample, and to use the tables of the probability integral [a table of percentages under the normal curve such as Table B.1 in the appendix of the text].
>
> But, as we decrease the number of experiments [by "number of experiments," Gosset means the number of measurements, or scores, in each sample], the value of the standard deviation found from the sample of experiments [sample of scores] becomes itself subject to an increasing error, until judgments reached in this way may become altogether misleading. (p. 1)

In these opening paragraphs, Gosset laid out the problem that he will solve: The "usual method" of estimating the population mean—assuming a normal distribution of sample means and computing the standard error of the mean by substituting the sample standard deviation for the unknown population standard deviation—*won't work*. The problem, then, is determining the shape of the sampling distribution (the distribution of all possible means of samples of size N) when N is small and the sample standard deviation (s) must be used to estimate the population standard deviation (σ).

The sample standard deviation (s) that Gosset used to estimate the population standard deviation is not the same as the sample standard deviation (SD) that you learned to calculate in Chapter 2. When the population standard deviation (σ) is not known (a common situation), it must be *estimated* from the sample standard deviation. However, the formula used to compute the standard deviation as a descriptive statistic (SD, left, in the following equation,) is a *biased* estimate, because it consistently *underestimates* the value of the population standard deviation. An adjustment to the formula (s, right, in the following equation) makes the sample standard deviation an *unbiased* estimate of σ: it *overestimates* and *underestimates* the value of the population standard deviation equally often.

$$SD = \sqrt{\frac{\sum (X - M)^2}{N}} \qquad s = \sqrt{\frac{\sum (X - M)^2}{N-1}}$$

Using an estimate of σ changes the shape of the comparison (sampling) distribution:

- When the estimate of σ is too *small*, the value of the z statistic will be *higher*, than the z statistic computed when σ is known.
- When the estimate of σ is too *large*, the value of the z statistic will be *lower* than the z statistic computed when σ is known.

The upshot of all of this is that there are now more z statistics in the tails of the comparison distribution, and with more z statistics in the tails, there are fewer of them in the middle of the distribution, causing the peak to be flatter than the peak of a normal distribution.

So, Gosset suspected that the distribution of means of small samples, and thus the distribution of z's (as Gosset called them), would not be normal. The task he set for himself was to discover the shape of this distribution, and what he discovered was a family of distributions that has come to be called Student's t distributions.[1] The name "Student" is an interesting footnote in the history of statistics. For the duration of his professional life, Gosset published under this pseudonym, because Guinness employees were forbidden to publish papers in scientific journals after a master brewer was discovered to have published privileged information about the Guinness brewing process.

---

[1] According to Salsburg (2001), Gosset used the letter z instead of t to refer to the statistic that he developed. Over time the two letters appeared in textbooks to distinguish between the z statistic computed when σ is known and the t statistic computed when σ must be estimated from s.

The manner in which Gosset derived the function for Student's *t* distributions involved what has been called one of the first simulations of a random process (Stigler, 1999). Gosset described the simulation as follows:

Before I had succeeded in solving my problem analytically, I had endeavoured to do so empirically. The material used was a correlation table containing the height and left middle finger measurements of 3000 criminals, from a paper by W. R. Macdonnell (*Biometrika*, I, p. 219). The measurements were written out on 3000 pieces of cardboard, which were then very thoroughly shuffled and drawn at random. As each card was drawn its numbers were written down in a book, which thus contains the measurements of 3000 criminals in a random order. Finally, each consecutive set of 4 was taken as a sample—750 in all—and the mean, standard deviation, and correlation of each sample determined. The difference between the mean of each sample and the mean of the population was then divided by the standard deviation of the sample, giving us the *z* of Section III.

This provides us with two sets of 750 standard deviations and two sets of 750 *z*'s on which to test the theoretical results arrived at. The height and left middle finger correlation table was chosen because the distribution of both was approximately normal and the correlation was fairly high. (p. 14)

Without benefit of a modern calculating or computing device, Gosset determined an empirical approximation to the sampling distribution of the mean for samples of $N = 4$ measures of two variables, height and left middle finger length. His purpose was to examine the fit between the distribution whose function he derived mathematically ("analytically") and the distribution that he constructed from the 750 sample means that he computed, apparently by hand. His assessment? "A very close fit" (p. 19).

As noted, Gosset described a *family* of distributions, each one defined by a parameter called **degrees of freedom** (*df*) that is directly related to sample size (*N*). As *N* increases, *df* increases. The values of *df* are usually $N - 1$ or $N - 2$, depending on the type of *t* test used. Gosset also observed that the sample standard deviation, *s*, became a more accurate estimate of σ as the sample size grew larger; in fact, for large samples, the *t* and normal distributions have similar shapes. As you can see in the following figure, Student's *t* distributions look very much like normal distributions but with a flatter center and fatter tails. Again, as the size of the sample increases (and *df* increases), the sample standard deviation becomes a more stable estimate of the population standard deviation, and the *t* distribution looks progressively more like the normal distribution.

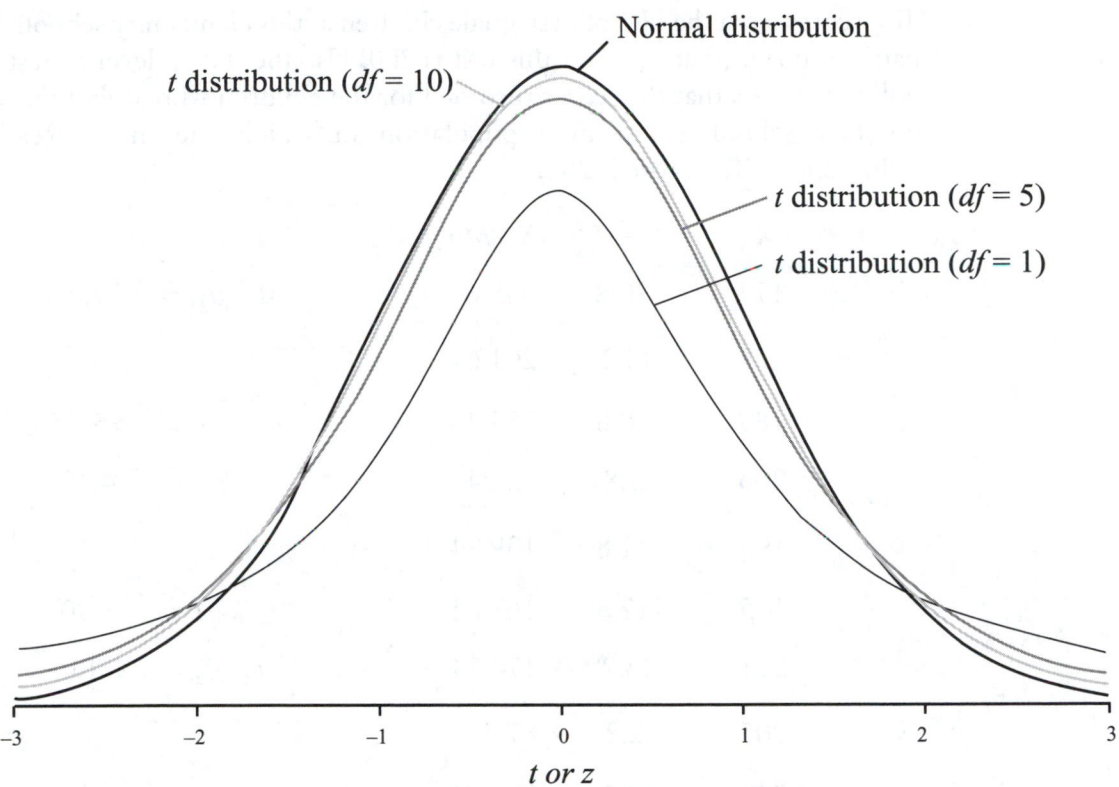

> Hypothesis Tests: The Single-Sample *t* Test

Testing the null hypothesis with a **single sample *t* test** is very similar to hypothesis testing with the single sample *z* test that you learned in the previous chapter. The statistic is identified by the letter *t* instead of *z*, and the standard error of the comparison distribution must be estimated using the sample standard deviation.

$$z = \frac{(M - \mu_M)}{\sigma / \sqrt{N}} \qquad t = \frac{(M - \mu_M)}{s / \sqrt{N}}$$

The six steps of the formal hypothesis testing procedure are illustrated in the next section for the paired-samples *t* test, so the following exercise is a shortened expression of the complete hypothesis testing procedure. The text provides an example of testing the null hypothesis with a single-sample *t* test that includes a discussion of all six steps (see pp. 397-399).

Example problem

A school psychologist believes that the one of the elementary schools in her school district consistently produces students with superior reading scores. Accordingly, she randomly selected the following 15 Reading Achievement

Test scores from the files of first-grade children at this elementary school. The national norm (that is, μ) on this test is 200. Use the 0.05 p level to test the null hypothesis that the scores recorded for the children who attend this elementary school are from a population in which the mean Reading Achievement Test score is 200.

X	$X-M$	$(X-M)^2$		
177	−30.8	948.64	$M - \mu_M =$	7.8
222	14.2	201.64		
189	−18.8	353.44	$s =$	15.87
206	−1.8	3.24	$s_M =$	4.10
196	−11.8	139.24		
195	−12.8	163.84	$t =$	1.90
221	13.2	174.24	$t_{critical} =$	2.145
205	−2.8	7.84		
222	14.2	201.64		
195	−12.8	163.84		
231	23.2	538.24		
204	−3.8	14.44		
232	24.2	585.64		
213	5.2	27.04		
209	1.2	1.44		

$$\Sigma = 3117 \qquad SS = 3524.4$$
$$N = 15 \qquad s^2 = 251.74$$
$$M = 207.8$$

Decision: The null hypothesis should not be rejected because the computed value of the t statistic (1.90) is not more extreme than the critical value of t (2.145) for a two-tailed test with 14 degrees of freedom conducted at the 0.05 p level.

> ## Hypothesis Tests: Tests for Two Samples

When there are two samples of scores to be compared, the choice is between the paired samples *t* test and the independent samples *t* test. This choice, in turn, depends on the experimental design. The **paired-samples *t* test** is used to analyze the data when the data are from *within-groups designs*, whereas the independent samples *t* test is used when the data are from *between-groups designs*. You may recall from Chapter 1 that a between-groups design includes two or more independent groups—that is, the individuals assigned to each group are unrelated to each other and to the individuals assigned to the other group(s). In contrast, the samples of scores analyzed for a within-groups design are *correlated*. The most commonly used within-groups design is a repeated-measures design. In this design, the same participants serve in all conditions of the study, so the correlation between the scores obtained from the same participants in different conditions is not surprising. The simplest form of a repeated measures design is called the *before-after* (or pretest-posttest) *design*. In this design, scores from a sample of participants are obtained before and after some treatment or intervention. Another type of within-groups design is called a matched-pairs (or matched-groups) design. Matched groups designs include samples of participants who are related in some way, either because they are from the same family (e.g., husbands and wives, brothers and sisters) or because the otherwise unrelated members of each pair of participants were matched on some variable related to the dependent variable before they were randomly assigned to the different conditions of the study.

So, a paired-samples *t* test should be used to analyze the data from a within-groups design because this test acknowledges the correlation, or dependency, between the scores obtained from the same group of participants who are measured under each condition of the study (repeated measures designs) or from different groups of participants who are either related in some way or matched on some variable (matched groups designs). It is not always possible to use a repeated-measures design; for example, the effect of the independent variable (treatment) may be long term and would thereby contaminate the scores obtained from participants under a second condition. However, a repeated measures design is more likely to detect the effect of an independent variable if there is one, because scores obtained from the same individuals are less variable than scores obtained from independent groups of participants. Thus, for a given treatment effect, the denominator of the paired-samples *t* statistic will be smaller than the denominator of an independent-samples *t* statistic, and the value of the paired-sample *t* statistic will be larger as a result. Larger *t* statistics have smaller *p* values and thus are more likely to meet the criterion of statistical significance. In Chapter 12, you will learn that this enhanced capacity to detect an effect of the independent variable may be quantified as a probability value called *statistical power*.

Example Problem

An educational psychologist designed a program to provide intensive training in the improvement of SAT scores for high school athletes who were recruited to play for NCAA Division I university football teams but did not qualify because of low SAT scores. A pilot test of the program was administered between the October and May SAT testing dates. Use the 0.05 p level to test the null hypothesis that the program has no effect on the SAT scores of high school football players like those participating in this study.

Step 1. Identify the populations, comparison distribution, and assumptions.

Both populations consist of the SAT scores of elite high school football players with Division I scholarships pending improvement of their SAT scores. Population 1 is the population of scores following the intensive training program and Population 2 is the population of scores prior to the intensive training program. The comparison distribution is the distribution of all possible mean difference scores obtained by subtracting the before scores from the after scores. SAT scores are assumed to be measured on an interval scale. The population distributions have not been well-studied, but are thought to be approximately normal or at least do not depart from normality enough to compromise the robustness of the paired-samples t test that will be used to analyze the sample of difference scores. The participants in the sample are volunteers, so the generalization of these results is limited to populations composed of individuals who are similar to the participants studied in this sample.

Step 2. State the null and research hypotheses.

The null hypothesis is that the mean the population of after scores (Population 1) is equal to the mean of the population of before scores (Population 2). The research (alternative) hypothesis is that the mean of the population of after scores is not equal to the mean of the population of before scores. In symbols,

$$H_0: \mu_1 = \mu_2$$
$$H_1: \mu_1 \neq \mu_2$$

Alternatively, the null and research hypotheses may be expressed in terms of mean difference scores as follows:

$$H_0: \mu_{Difference} = 0$$
$$H_1: \mu_{Difference} \neq 0$$

Step 3. Determine the characteristics of the comparison distribution.

The comparison distribution is the distribution of all possible mean difference scores for samples of $N = 8$ that might be obtained under the assumption that the null hypothesis is true. According to the null hypothesis, the mean of this distribution of difference scores must be 0, because the treatment (the intensive training program) is ineffective (*nullus = not any* effect).

Step 4. Determine the critical, or cutoff, values of the test statistic.

It is a t statistic from the distribution defined by $N - 1 = 8 - 1 = 7$ degrees of freedom. This is a two-tailed test conducted at the 0.05 p level, so there are two critical values of this t statistic: the negative value cuts off the lower 2.5% of the comparison distribution, and the positive value cuts off the upper 2.5% of the comparison distribution. From Table B.2 in the apprendix of the text, these values are –2.365 and 2.365.

Step 5. Calculate the test statistic.

SAT (before)	Treatment	SAT (after)	Difference	$\text{Diff} - M_{\text{Diff}}$	$(\text{Diff} - M_{\text{diff}})^2$
600		610	10	–10.625	112.891
610		600	–10	–30.625	937.891
640		690	50	29.375	862.891
720		750	30	9.375	87.891
710		710	0	–20.625	425.391
680		715	35	14.375	206.641
690		700	10	–10.625	112.891
740		780	40	19.375	375.391
		$\Sigma =$	165	$SS =$	3121.878
		$N =$	8	$s^2 =$	445.983
		$M_{\text{Diff}} = \Sigma / N =$	20.625	$s =$	21.118
				$s_M =$	7.466
				$t =$	2.763
				$t_{\text{Critical}} =$	2.365

Step 6. Make a decision regarding the status of the null hypothesis.

The null hypothesis may be rejected, because the computed value of the *t* statistic (2.763) is more extreme than the critical value (2.635). The educational psychologist's intensive training program is apparently effective in altering the SAT scores of elite high school football players like those who volunteered to participate in this study. However, this was a pilot program conducted with a small sample of athletes from one region of the country. Before even tentatively considering the program to be a success, the educational psychologist will replicate this study with a larger, more diverse, sample of athletes and will work to achieve a level of program effectiveness that enables student-athletes with subqualifying SAT scores to achieve qualifying scores.

Despite the advantages of using a within-groups design, between-groups designs are much more common in the research literature of the behavioral sciences. When there are two independent (unrelated) samples of participants, the independent samples *t* test is used to analyze the data. The discussion that follows develops the rationale for this analysis.

Population 1 is the distribution of scores represented by the research hypothesis. This distribution consists of the scores recorded for individuals who experience the treatment.

Population 2 is the distribution of scores represented by the null hypothesis. This distribution consists of the scores recorded for individuals who do not experience the treatment.

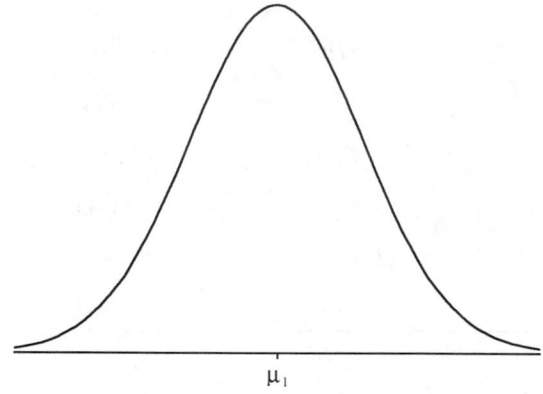 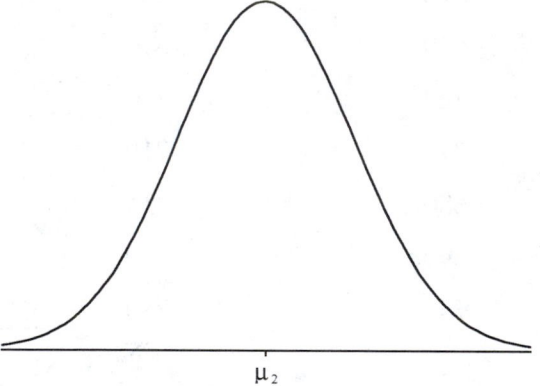

If the null hypothesis is correct, then the scores recorded for individuals receiving the experimental treatment have the same mean and variance as the scores recorded for individuals who do not receive the experimental treatment—that is, $\mu_1 = \mu_2$.

The following figures represent the distributions of means of samples of size N from each of these populations. Each distribution of means has the same mean as its parent population:

$$\mu_1 = \mu_{M_1} \text{ and } \mu_2 = \mu_{M_2}$$

And a variance equal to the common population variance divided by the sample size:

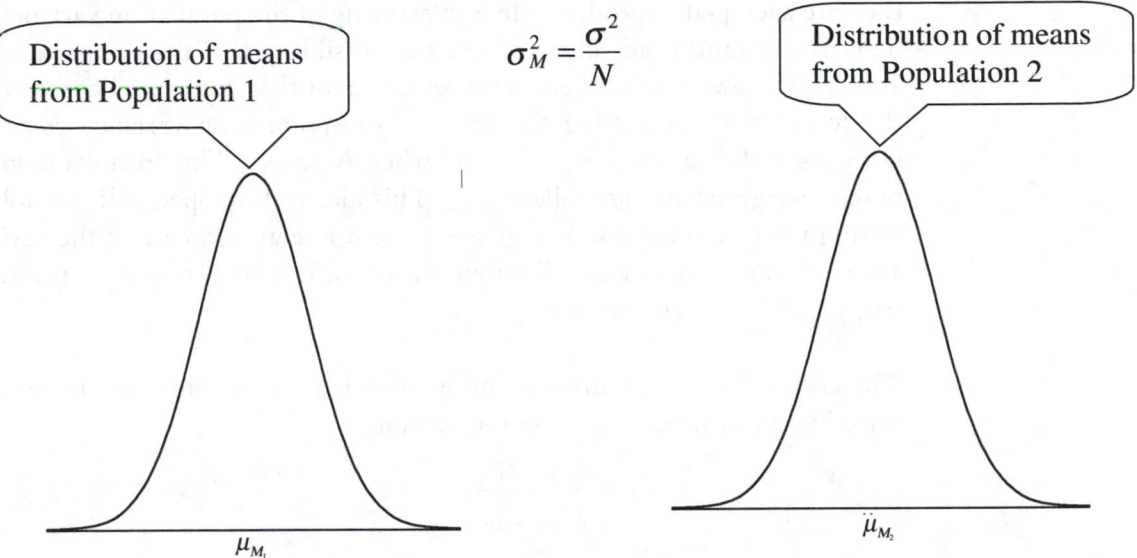

$$\sigma_M^2 = \frac{\sigma^2}{N}$$

Distribution of means from Population 1

Distribution of means from Population 2

μ_{M_1}

μ_{M_2}

The appropriate comparison distribution is constructed by randomly selecting one mean at a time from each distribution of means, and subtracting one from the other. The result is a distribution of all possible differences between means of samples of size N from each distribution of means.

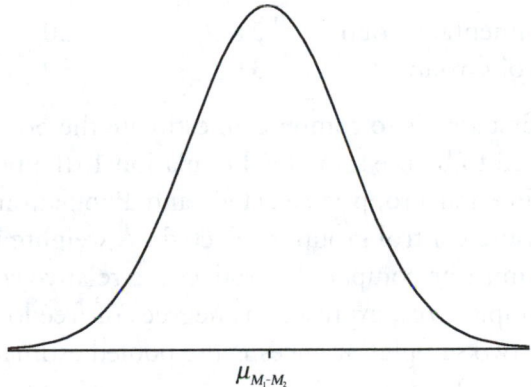

$\mu_{M_1-M_2}$

This comparison distribution of differences between means has a mean of zero and a variance equal to the sum of the variances of each distribution of means:

$$\sigma_{Difference}^2 = \sigma_{M_1}^2 + \sigma_{M_2}^2$$

However, the population variance (assumed to be the same for both populations) is not known, so it must be estimated from the variances of both samples. Thus, s_1^2 and s_2^2 are used to estimate σ^2 (the common population variance). Because the sample variances are not likely to be the same value, they are averaged to produce the best estimate of the population variance. This average must take into account the possibility that the two samples are equal in size, that is, there is no requirement that $N_1 = N_2$. Therefore, the formula for estimating the value of the population variance covers both possibilities: when $N_1 = N_2$ and when $N_1 \neq N_2$. This formula computes a weighted average called s_{Pooled}^2. This idea is developed with the following worked examples. The goal is to compute an estimate of the variance of the comparison distribution of differences between means ($\sigma_{Difference}^2$). This estimate is $s_{Difference}^2$.

The comparison distribution of differences between means may be converted to a t distribution, using the formula:

$$t = \frac{M_1 - M_2}{s_{Difference}}$$

This results in a t distribution with degrees of freedom based on both samples: $df_{Total} = df_1 + df_2 = N_1 + N_2 - 2$.

Use the group statistics in the following table to test the null hypothesis that $\mu_1 = \mu_2$.

	N	df	M	s^2
Experimental Group	21	20	95	60
Control Group	31	30	90	80

The first step is to compute an estimate the population variance, which is assumed to be the same for Population 1 (the population from which the experimental group is selected) and Population 2 (the population from which the control group is selected). A weighted average of the two variances must be computed to reflect the relative contributions of the different sample sizes, expressed as degrees of freedom. The weighted average of the two sample variances is the pooled estimate of the population variance (s_{Pooled}^2):

$$s_{Pooled}^2 = \frac{df_1}{df_{Total}} s_1^2 + \frac{df_2}{df_{Total}} s_2^2 = \frac{20}{50}(60) + \frac{30}{50}(80) = (.4)(60) + (.6)(80) = 24 + 48 = 72$$

The next step is to compute the variance of each distribution of means ($s_{M_1}^2$ and $s_{M_2}^2$). The pooled estimate of the population variance (72) is divided by the respective sample sizes (*not* the degrees of freedom) to produce the following values:

$$s_{M_1}^2 = \frac{s_{Pooled}^2}{N_1} = \frac{72}{21} = 3.429 \qquad s_{M_2}^2 = \frac{s_{Pooled}^2}{N_2} = \frac{72}{31} = 2.323$$

The variances of the two distributions of means are summed to produce an estimate of the variance of the distribution of differences between means:

$$s^2_{Difference} = s^2_{M_1} + s^2_{M_2} = 3.429 + 2.323 = 5.752$$

The standard deviation of the distribution of differences between means is computed as the square root of the variance of the distribution of differences between means.

$$s_{Difference} = \sqrt{s^2_{Difference}} = \sqrt{5.752} = 2.398$$

The t statistic may now be computed as follows:

$$t = \frac{M_1 - M_2}{s_{Difference}} = \frac{95 - 90}{2.398} = \frac{5}{2.398} = 2.09$$

The computed value of the t statistic (2.09) is compared to the t distribution for 20 + 30 = 50 degrees of freedom. Table B.2 in the appendix of the text does not include entries for 50 degrees of freedom, so the conservative choice is to use the critical value of t for 40 degrees of freedom, because this is the table value that is closest to, but less than, 50. The critical value of t for a two-tailed test conducted at a p level of 0.05 and 40 degrees of freedom is 2.021. The computed value of the t statistic is more extreme than the critical value, so the null hypothesis may be rejected. It may be concluded that the samples means are significantly different. The following figure is the comparison distribution of the t statistic, showing the two-tailed critical region for a p level of 0.05 and the shaded region corresponding to the p value of the computed statistic.

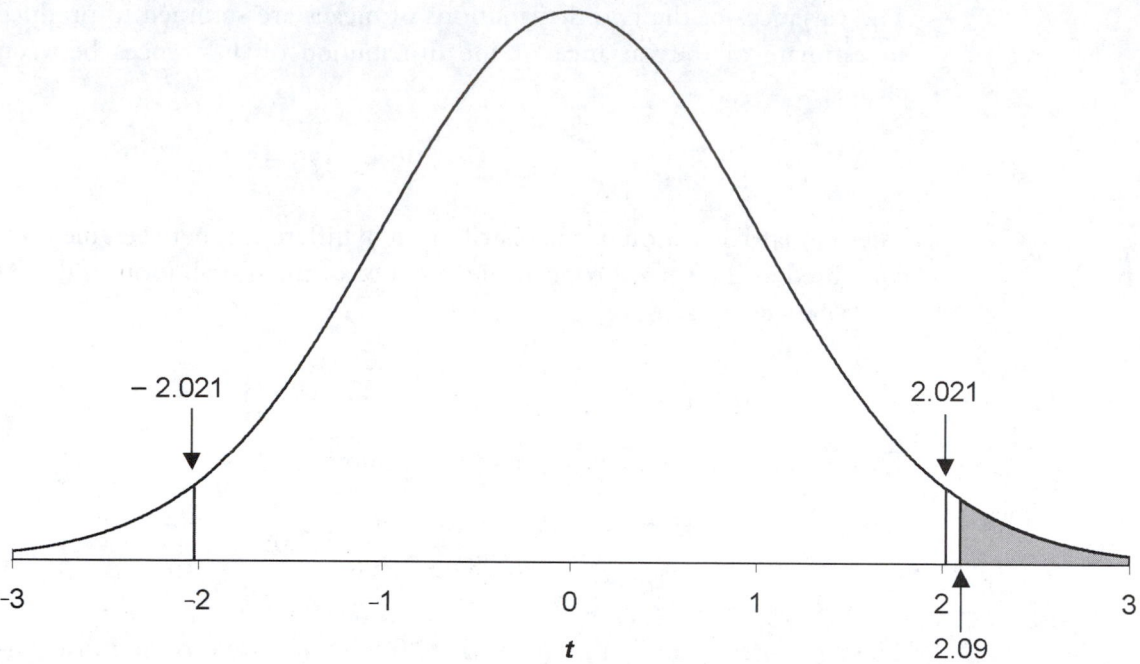

> **Digging Deeper into the Data: More Ways to Visualize Data**

Stem-and-leaf and dot plots are graphical methods of representing frequency distributions that include more information than the histograms or polygons described in Chapter 3. In addition to providing information about the shape of the distribution, a stem and leaf plot with a stem width of 10 (like the one that follows) includes information that may be used to derive all of the data values by: (1) multiplying the stem width by the stem value for a given row, and (2) adding this product to a given leaf. The place value of a leaf will always be 1 decimal position to the right of the place value of the stem width.

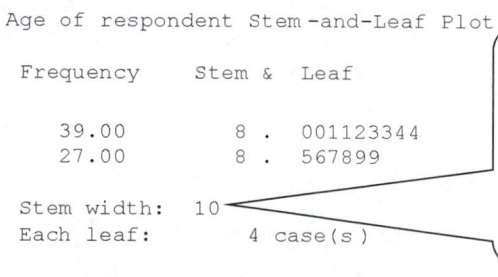

```
Age of respondent Stem-and-Leaf Plot

 Frequency      Stem &   Leaf

    39.00         8 .   001123344
    27.00         8 .   567899

Stem width:    10
Each leaf:       4 case(s)
```

The *stem width* is 10, so the place value of each *stem* is 10 and the place value of each *leaf* is 1. For example, the 9 in the bottom row represents 89; that is, stem width (10) **x** stem (8) + leaf (9) = 89. This is a portion of the stem-and-leaf plot displayed on the next page.

A histogram and stem-and-leaf plot of a grouped frequency distribution of age values from SPSS is displayed next. Note that rotating the stem-and-leaf plot 90 degrees counterclockwise provides a histogram-like display of group frequencies. Thus, *like* a histogram, a stem-and-leaf plot has "bars" composed of columns of digits that represent the frequency of scores within intervals. *Unlike* a histogram, a stem and leaf plot with a stem width of 10 (like the one following) includes information that may be used to derive all of the data values.

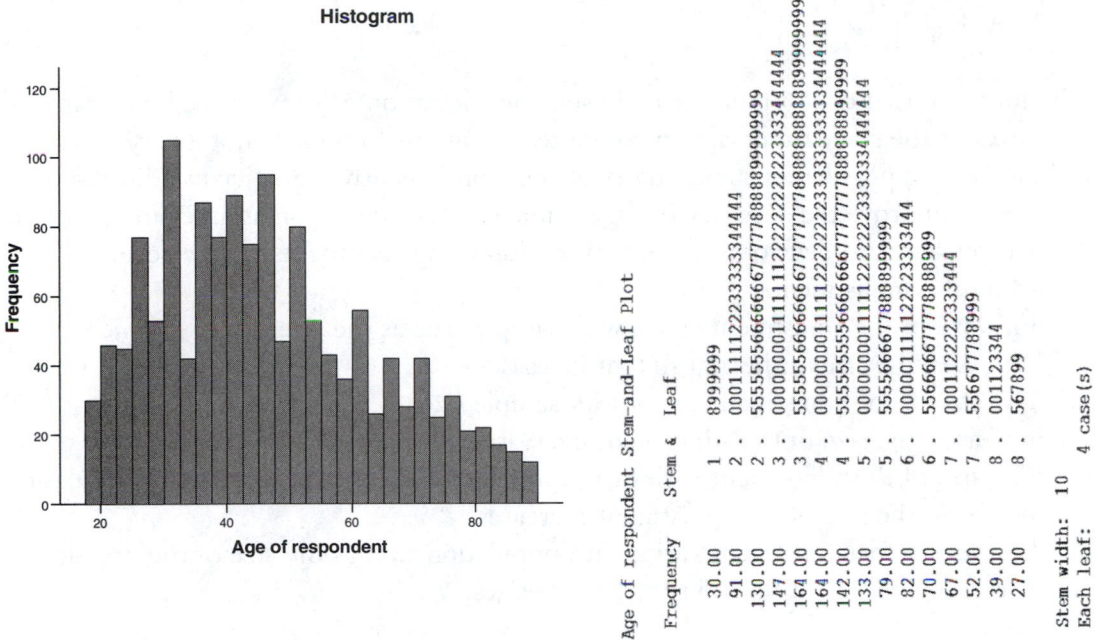

Dot plots provide much the same information as a stem-and-leaf plot. In a dot plot, a dot is placed above each data value for each occurrence of that value in the data set. The following dot plot is Figure 9.11 in the text (p. 416).

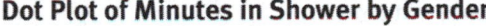
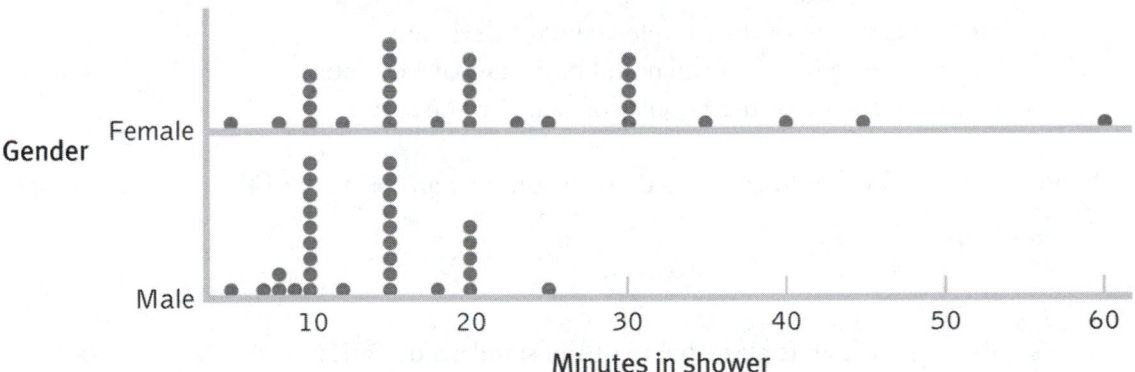

STUDY QUESTIONS

1. Who discovered the *t* distributions and developed the *t* tests?
   a. Abraham de Moivre
   b. W. S. Gosset
   c. J. A. Guinness
   d. R. A. Fisher

2. The formula used to compute a sample standard deviation was introduced in Chapter 2. However, the standard deviation computed using this formula is not a very accurate estimate of the population standard deviation. Consequently, statisticians adjusted the formula to improve the accuracy of the sample standard deviation as an estimate of the population standard deviation. Which of the following statements is *most* accurate regarding this adjustment?
   a. The size of the adjustment varies with sample size: as the size of the sample increases, the size of the adjustment increases.
   b. The size of the adjustment varies with sample size: as the size of the sample increases, the size of the adjustment decreases.
   c. The size of the adjustment varies with population size: as the size of the population increases, the size of the adjustment increases.
   d. The size of the adjustment varies with population size: as the size of the population increases, the size of the adjustment decreases.

3. Consider the following formula:

$$\sqrt{\frac{\sum (M - X)^2}{(N-1)}}$$

   What does this formula compute?
   a. the standard deviation
   b. a corrected estimate of the sample standard deviation
   c. an uncorrected estimate of the population standard deviation
   d. a corrected estimate of the population standard deviation

4. Which of the following formulas is used to compute an estimate of the standard error?
   a. $\dfrac{s}{\sqrt{N}}$ b. $\dfrac{s}{\sqrt{N-1}}$ c. $\dfrac{\sigma}{\sqrt{N}}$ d. $\dfrac{\sigma}{\sqrt{N-1}}$

5. The symbol s_M represents an estimate of the standard deviation of the:
   a. population specified by the research hypothesis.
   b. population specified by the null hypothesis.
   c. comparison distribution of means.
   d. scores in the sample.

6. Under what circumstances will the shape of the distribution of means *not* follow a normal curve even though the population distribution follows a normal curve? When the:
   a. null hypothesis is true.
   b. sample size is very large.
   c. sample size is very small.
   d. population standard deviation must be estimated.

7. How is a single-sample *t* test different from a *z* test?
   a. The comparison distribution for the *t* test is not a normal curve.
   b. Using the *z* test requires having to estimate the population standard deviation.
   c. Using the *t* test requires having to estimate the population mean.
   d. The *t* test is more likely to produce a statistically significant result.

8. The *t* statistic computed for a single-sample *t* test is a measure of the distance between:
   a. a sample mean and a population mean in terms of the standard deviation.
   b. a sample mean and a population mean in terms of the standard error.
   c. two population means in terms of the population standard deviation.
   d. two population means in terms of the standard error.

9. The shape of *t* distributions vary according to the:
   a. number of participants in the sample used to estimate the population standard deviation.
   b. standard deviation of the population from which the sample was taken.
   c. mean of the population from which the sample was taken.
   d. mean of the sample.

10. The shape of a *t* distribution differs most from the shape of the normal curve when the:
    a. sample size is large.
    b. sample size is small.
    c. population is large.
    d. population is small.

11. The author of the paper that first described the *t* distribution published anonymously under the name "Student" because he:
    a. was a very modest individual who did not wish to seek scientific notoriety.
    b. was a brewery employee who feared being fired if his employer discovered that he was conducting scientific experiments on the job.
    c. was forbidden by his employers to publish scientific papers because a scientist who worked for the company had revealed brewery secrets.
    d. wished to avoid the inevitable criticism from the mathematicians and scientists who held positions in prestigious universities while he toiled for a brewery.

12. To use a single-sample *t* test to decide whether a sample comes from a population with a specific mean, all of the following *except* the _____ must be known.
    a. sample mean
    b. population mean
    c. sample standard deviation
    d. population standard deviation

13. A single-sample *t* test is used:
    a. when the population standard deviation is known.
    b. to determine whether a sample is from a population with a known mean.
    c. to determine whether the means of unrelated samples are significantly different.
    d. to determine whether participants' scores change from one condition to another.

14. For any particular degrees of freedom, there is (are):
    a. an infinite number of *t* distributions, each determined by the population standard deviation.
    b. an infinite number of *t* distributions, each determined by the population mean.
    c. two *t* distributions, one for one-tailed tests and one for two-tailed tests.
    d. only one *t* distribution.

15. With respect to the family of *t* distributions, what is the relationship between sample size (N) and degrees of freedom (*df*)?
    a. as N increases, *df* increases
    b. as N increases, *df* decreases
    c. The relationship depends on the sample size.
    d. N and *df* are not related.

16. Because critical values are _____ extreme for a two-tailed test than for a one-tailed test, it is _____ likely that a two-tailed test will yield a significant result.
    a. less; more
    b. less; less
    c. more; less
    d. more; more

17. Excerpt from a *t* Table:

	One-Tailed Tests			Two-Tailed Tests		
df	0.10	0.05	0.01	0.10	0.05	0.01
18	1.330	1.734	2.552	1.734	2.101	2.878
19	1.328	1.729	2.539	1.729	2.093	2.861
20	1.325	1.725	2.528	1.725	2.086	2.845
21	1.323	1.721	2.518	1.721	2.080	2.831
22	1.321	1.717	2.508	1.717	2.074	2.819

A certain fifth-grade teacher believes, rather strongly, that her classes are always better prepared than those of her teaching colleagues for the Standards of Learning (SOL) tests given near the end of each academic year. This year, her class of 20 students earned a mean score of 107 with a standard deviation of 14. The teacher decides to conduct a *t* test using a *p* level of 0.01. What is the critical value of *t* for this proposed analysis?

a. 1.325

b. 1.725

c. 2.539

d. 2.861

18. A counseling psychologist hypothesized that having clients sign an agreement to attend a minimum number of counseling sessions increases the number of sessions attended. Suppose that the number of sessions attended at a certain university counseling center is approximately normally distributed with a mean (μ) of 4.6 and an unknown standard deviation (σ). Five students sign an agreement to attend at least 10 sessions. The number of sessions actually attended by these 5 students is as follows: 6, 4, 4, 14, and 12. The psychologist used the following formulas to analyze the data. Which one of the formulas is incorrect?

a. $M = \dfrac{\sum X}{N}$ b. $s = \sqrt{\dfrac{\sum (X-M)^2}{(N-1)}}$ c. $S_M = \dfrac{s}{\sqrt{N-1}}$ d. $t = \dfrac{M - \mu_M}{S_M}$

19. Refer to the previous question. The counseling psychologist prepared a manuscript for publication in a journal that requires all submitted manuscripts to be formatted according to the editorial guidelines of the American Psychological Association (APA). Which of the following sentences is formatted according to APA guidelines?

a. Clients who signed an agreement to attend at least 10 sessions (M = 8.00, SD = 4.69) did not attend more sessions than clients who did not sign such an agreement, t(4) = 1.62, p > 0.05.

b. Clients who signed an agreement to attend at least 10 sessions (*M* = 8.00, *SD* = 4.69) did not attend more sessions than clients who did not sign such an agreement, t(4) = 1.62, p > 0.05.

c. Clients who signed an agreement to attend at least 10 sessions (M = 8.00, SD = 4.69) did not attend more sessions than clients who did not sign such an agreement, *t*(4) = 1.62, *p* > 0.05.

d. Clients who signed an agreement to attend at least 10 sessions (*M* = 8.00, *SD* = 4.69) did not attend more sessions than clients who did not sign such an agreement, *t*(4) = 1.62, *p* > 0.05.

20. A research design in which each participant serves in both conditions of the study (e.g., in both the experimental condition and the control condition) is called a(n) _____ design.

a. between-groups

b. within-groups

c. mixed

d. independent-samples

21. The paired-samples (or dependent-samples) *t* test is almost exactly the same as the single-sample *t* test. The "difference" is that, whereas the individual raw scores from a single sample are analyzed by the single-sample *t* test, the paired-samples *t* test analyzes a single sample of _____ scores.
    a. *t*
    b. mean
    c. difference
    d. *z*

22. A nondirectional null hypothesis tested with a paired-samples *t* test is that the mean of:
    a. Population 1 is greater than or equal to the mean of Population 2.
    b. Population 1 is less than or equal to the mean of Population 2.
    c. the population of difference scores is not equal to zero.
    d. the population of difference scores is equal to zero.

23. A(n) _____ is used to test whether two population means are equal based on a design in which each participant is assigned to only one condition.
    a. single-sample *t* test
    b. paired-samples *t* test
    c. independent-samples *t* test
    d. *z* test

24. An independent-samples *t* test is used to:
    a. compare the scores in one group of participants to the scores in an unrelated group of participants.
    b. compare the scores obtained under two different conditions in the same group of participants.
    c. test the null hypothesis that two samples of scores have the same mean.
    d. compare the mean of a sample of scores to the mean of a population.

25. Which of the following is the comparison distribution for the independent-samples *t* test?
    a. distribution of sample means
    b. distribution of means of difference scores
    c. distribution of differences between sample means
    d. distribution of differences between population means

26. Conducting a(n) _____ requires two scores for each participant.
    a. single-sample *t* test
    b. paired-samples *t* test
    c. independent-samples *t* test
    d. *z* test

27. Beck, Steer, and Brown (1996) compared scores on the Beck Depression Inventory-II (BDI-II) administered to a sample of 26 outpatients at two therapy sessions one week apart and reported no significance difference between the mean total scores. Which of the following analyses was used to compare the two mean scores on the BDI-II?
    a. *z* test
    b. single-sample *t* test
    c. paired-samples *t* test
    d. independent-samples *t* test

28. Which of the following is NOT one of the assumptions that should be met before conducting an independent-samples *t* test?
    a. The dependent variable should be measured on an interval scale.
    b. The populations should be normally distributed.
    c. The samples should have the same number of participants.
    d. The samples should be randomly selected.

29. A psychologist hypothesized that sleep loss affects problem solving. First, she surveyed her large introductory psychology class to determine the number of hours that each student regarded as "a full night's sleep" and then asked how many hours they slept during the previous night. She then gave each student a set of problems to solve in a timed test and counted the number solved correctly by each student. She computed the following statistics on number of problems solved (out of 20) for a group of students who reported a difference of no more than 1 hour between a full night's sleep and how much they slept the previous night (control group: $N = 16$, $M = 16.45$, $s^2 = 24.12$) and a second group who reported getting at least three hours less than a full night's sleep during the previous night (sleep-deprived group: $N = 12$, $M = 12.29$, $s^2 = 19.96$). Which of the following is the most appropriate statement of the null hypothesis?
    a. The mean number of problems solved by students who get a "full night's sleep" is not different from the mean number of problems solved by students for whom a full night's sleep time is reduced by at least three hours.
    b. The mean number of problems solved by students who get a "full night's sleep" is significantly different from the mean number of problems solved by students for whom a full night's sleep time is reduced by at least three hours.
    c. The group of students who reported getting a "full night's sleep" will solve the same number of problems on average as the group of students who reported being sleep-deprived by at least three hours.
    d. The group of students who reported getting a "full night's sleep" will solve more problems on average than the group of students who reported being sleep-deprived by at least three hours.

30. A pooled estimate of the population variance (s^2_{pooled}) is determined by:
    a. computing the average of the variances of the samples from two populations.
    b. using the smaller of the two variances of the samples from two populations.
    c. using the larger of the two variances of the samples from two populations.
    d. pooling the two sample variances—that is, adding them together.

31. After obtaining scores from two groups of participants, a researcher computed an estimate of the population variance. Based on the following group statistics, what should her estimate of the population variance be?

	N	Variance
Group 1	11	40
Group 2	21	20

   a. $\dfrac{(10)(40)}{30}+\dfrac{(20)(20)}{30}=\dfrac{400+400}{30}=\dfrac{800}{30}=26.67$

   b. $\dfrac{40+20}{2}=\dfrac{60}{2}=30$

   c. $\dfrac{40+20}{2}+\dfrac{11+21}{2}=\dfrac{92}{2}=46$

   d. $\dfrac{(11)(40)}{32}+\dfrac{(21)(20)}{32}=\dfrac{440+420}{32}=\dfrac{860}{32}=26.875$

32. The estimated variance of the distribution of differences between means ($s^2_{Difference}$) is the:
   a. pooled estimate of the population variance.
   b. sum of the estimated variances of the two distributions of sample means.
   c. weighted average of the estimated variances of the two distributions of sample means.
   d. unweighted average of the estimated variances of the two distributions of sample means.

33. For each of two samples of scores, the squared standard errors are summed before the square root of their sum is taken. What has been computed?
   a. the estimated standard error of the distribution of mean difference scores
   b. the estimated standard error of the distribution of differences between means
   c. the pooled variance as an estimate of the common population variance
   d. the standard deviation of the population

34. For the independent-samples t test for independent means, degrees of freedom (df_{Total}) are computed as _____.
   a. $(N_1 + N_2 - 1)$
   b. $(N_1 - 1) + (N_2 - 1)$
   c. $(N_1 - 2) + (N_2 - 2)$
   d. $(N_1 + 1) - (N_2 + 1)$

35. You divide the difference between two sample means by $s^2_{Difference}$ to compute:
   a. a pooled estimate of $s^2_{Difference}$.
   b. the p value of a sample mean difference.
   c. a t statistic for an independent-samples t test.
   d. a t statistic for a paired-samples t test.

ANSWERS TO CHAPTER 9 STUDY QUESTIONS

Question Number	Correct Answer	Question Number	Correct Answer
1	b, p. 383	16	c, p. 394
2	b, pp. 384–385	17	c, p. 395
3	d, pp. 385–386	18	c, pp. 398–399
4	a, p. 387	19	d, pp. 399–400 (Symbols for descriptive statistics, test statistics, and probability values must be italicized.)
5	c, p. 387		
6	d, p. 387 (The distribution of means of small samples from normal populations in which the standard deviation is known is normal. Small samples per se do not influence the shape of the distribution of means as long as the parent population is a normal distribution.)	20	b, p. 402
		21	c, p. 404
		22	d, p. 404
		23	c, p. 406
		24	a, p. 406
		25	c, p. 407
		26	b, p. 408 (Table 9-2)
		27	c, p. 408 (Table 9-2)
7	a, pp. 387–388	28	c, p. 408
8	b, p. 388	29	a, p. 408
9	a, p. 388	30	a, pp. 409–410
10	b, p. 389	31	a, pp. 409–410
11	c, p. 391	32	b, pp 409–410
12	d, p. 393	33	b, pp. 409–410
13	b, p. 393	34	b, p. 410
14	d, p. 393	35	c, p. 412
15	a, pp. 393–394		

CHAPTER TEN

HYPOTHESIS TESTING WITH ONE-WAY ANOVA
Comparing Three or More Groups

CHAPTER OUTLINE

When to Use an *F* Distribution: Working With More Than Two Samples
- A Mnemonic for When to Use a *t* distribution or an *F* distribution: "*t*" for Two
- The *F* Distributions: Analyzing Variability to Compare Means
- Relation of *F* to *t* (and *z*): *F* as a Squared *t* for Two Groups and Large Samples

Analysis of Variance: Beyond *t* Tests
- The Problem of Too Many *t* Tests: Fishing for a Finding
- The Assumptions for ANOVA: The Ideal Conditions for the Perfect Study

The One-Way Between-Groups ANOVA: Applying the Six Steps of Hypothesis Testing
- Everything ANOVA but the Calculations: The Six Steps of Hypothesis Testing
- The *F* Statistic: Logic and Calculations
- Bringing It All Together: What's Our Decision?
- Why the ANOVA is Not Sufficient: Post-Hoc Tests

Digging Deeper into the Data: A Priori Post-Hoc Tests to Determine Which Groups Are Different
- Planned and A Priori Comparisons: When Comparisons between Pairs Are Guided by Theory
- Tukey *HSD*: An Honest Approach
- The Bonferroni Test: A More Stringent Post-Hoc Test

LEARNING OBJECTIVES

After studying this chapter, you should be able to:

1. Define each of the following terms and provide examples that are not in the text: *ANOVA*, *F statistic*, *between-groups variance*, *within-groups variance*, *one-way ANOVA*, *within-groups ANOVA*, *between-groups ANOVA*, *homoscedastic*, *heteroscedastic*, *source table*, *grand mean*, *post-hoc test*, *planned comparison*, *Tukey HSD test*, and *Bonferroni test*.

2. Explain the analogy between the numerator of the formulas used to compute the z and t statistics and the numerator of the formula used to the compute the F statistic—the between-groups estimate of the population variance. Do the same for the denominator of the formulas used to compute the z and t statistics and the denominator of the formula used to the compute the F statistic—the within-groups estimate of the population variance.

3. Relate the "problem of too many t tests" and what it means to "fish for a finding" to changes in the probability of committing a Type I error.

4. Explain the basic distinction between within-groups and between-groups ANOVAs as types of one-way ANOVAs and discuss the assumptions for these tests, including a reference to the distinction between *homoscedastic* and *heteroscedastic* populations (distributions).

5. Discuss the logic that underlies the computation of the ratio of the between-groups variance estimate to the within-group variance estimate in a one-way ANOVA.

6. Discuss the rationale for *planned comparisons* and *post-hoc tests* as well as the distinction between them. Include in your discussion an identification of some of the more commonly used post-hoc tests accompanied by a brief explanation of what it means for a test to be "stringent" or "conservative."

CHAPTER REVIEW

> ### When to Use an F Distribution: Working With More than Two Samples

This chapter introduced the **one-way analysis of variance (ANOVA)** for **between-groups** designs. The "one" in "one-way" refers to the inclusion of just one independent variable in the research design. The between-groups one-way ANOVA is like the independent-samples t test in this respect. In fact, the one-way ANOVA may be viewed as an extension of the t test. Whereas the independent-samples t test is limited to two levels of one independent variable, the one-way ANOVA may be used to analyze the data from research designs that include more than two levels of the independent variable. As was true for the t test, the independent variable in an ANOVA must be measured on a nominal scale and the dependent variable must be measured on an interval or ratio scale. The close relation between the independent-samples t test and the between-groups one-way ANOVA is reflected in the fact that squaring the t statistic produces the F statistic that would be computed if the data used to compute the t statistic were subjected to a one-way ANOVA instead—that is, $t^2 = F$, and $t = \sqrt{F}$. As mentioned, the independent-samples t test can not be used to analyze the data from a study with three or more groups of scores, so the comparison is limited to the relatively simple two-sample designs.

The close kinship between the independent-samples t test and the one-way ANOVA for between-groups designs may be illustrated further by a comparison of the formulas used to compute the t and F statistics, respectively:

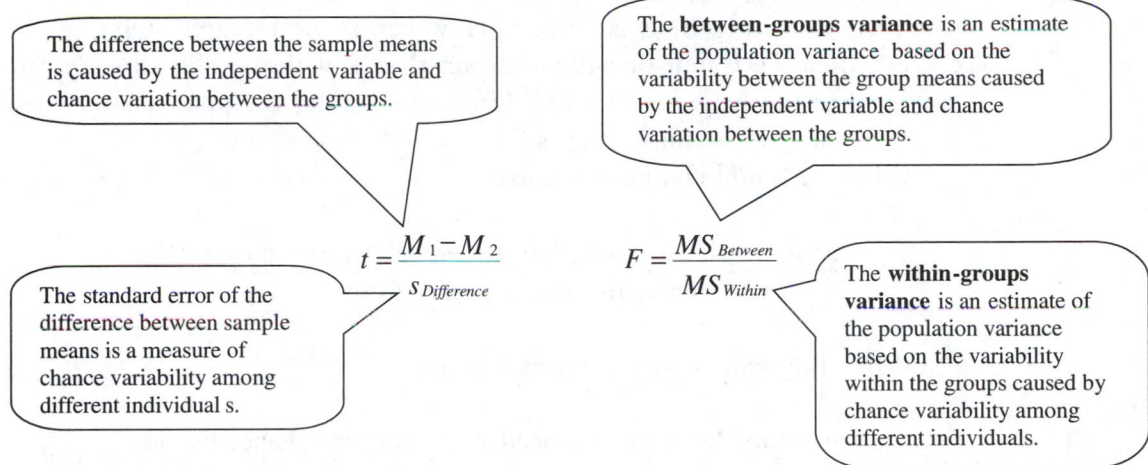

The difference between the sample means is caused by the independent variable and chance variation between the groups.

The **between-groups variance** is an estimate of the population variance based on the variability between the group means caused by the independent variable and chance variation between the groups.

$$t = \frac{M_1 - M_2}{S_{Difference}}$$

$$F = \frac{MS_{Between}}{MS_{Within}}$$

The standard error of the difference between sample means is a measure of chance variability among different individual s.

The **within-groups variance** is an estimate of the population variance based on the variability within the groups caused by chance variability among different individuals.

The null hypothesis tested by an ANOVA is that all of the population means are equal. If there are three groups (samples) of scores in a study, then the null hypothesis may be expressed in symbols as follows:

$$H_0 : \mu_1 = \mu_2 = \mu_3$$

The research hypothesis is that the population means are not all the same; that is, at least one of the population means differs from at least one of the others. Note that this statement of the research hypothesis may not be efficiently expressed in symbols.

The formula for the F statistic is a ratio of two sources of variability. The **between-groups variance** computed in the numerator of the formula is a measure of the variability between the sample means. If the null hypothesis is correct, then this source of variability reflects nothing more than the fact that different samples from the same population will have different means just by chance. (Statisticians use the term *sampling error* to refer to this chance variability among sample means.) However, if the research hypothesis is correct, then the between-groups variance is a measure of the variability caused by the effect of the independent variable as well as chance factors. In contrast, the **within-groups variance** is a measure of the spread among scores in the different samples. The major source of differences among scores within any given sample is an enduring source of variability called individual differences; that is, participants differ from on another because of the operation of genetic and environmental influences on behavior. *Unlike* between-groups variance, within-groups variance is unaffected by the status of the null hypothesis.

Understanding the sources of variability that contribute to the between- and within-groups variances should lead you to the following realization: When the null hypothesis is correct, both the between-groups variance and within-groups variance are products of nothing more than the random variation among scores in the population and have approximately the same value. This means that, on average, the value of the F statistic will be about 1.00 when the null hypothesis is correct. However, if the research hypothesis is correct, then the F statistic will be greater than 1, with its value directly proportional to the magnitude of the differences among the population means. These points may be illustrated as follows:

When the *null* hypothesis is correct:

$$F = \frac{\text{Variability due to } \sout{\text{the independent variable and }} \text{chance factors}}{\text{Variability due to chance factors}} > 1$$

When the *research* hypothesis is correct:

$$F = \frac{\text{Variability due to the independent variable and chance factors}}{\text{Variability due to chance factors}} > 1$$

The comparison distribution for an ANOVA is called an F distribution. In contrast to the bell-shape and symmetry of the normal and t distributions, an F distribution has a pronounced positive skew. The positive skew is a consequence of the fact that the F statistic is a ratio of variances. You learned how to compute the sample variance (s^2) as an estimate of the population variance (σ^2) in Chapter 9 as a step in the calculation of the t statistic. So you know that computing the sample variance as an estimate of the population variance requires subtracting each score from the mean, squaring the resulting deviation scores, and averaging them by dividing by $N - 1$. It is this squaring operation that produces the positive skew in the F distribution. As a ratio of two estimates of the population variance, the F statistic cannot have a negative value, so lower values of this statistic are bunched at the left end of the distribution, exhibiting a kind of floor effect.

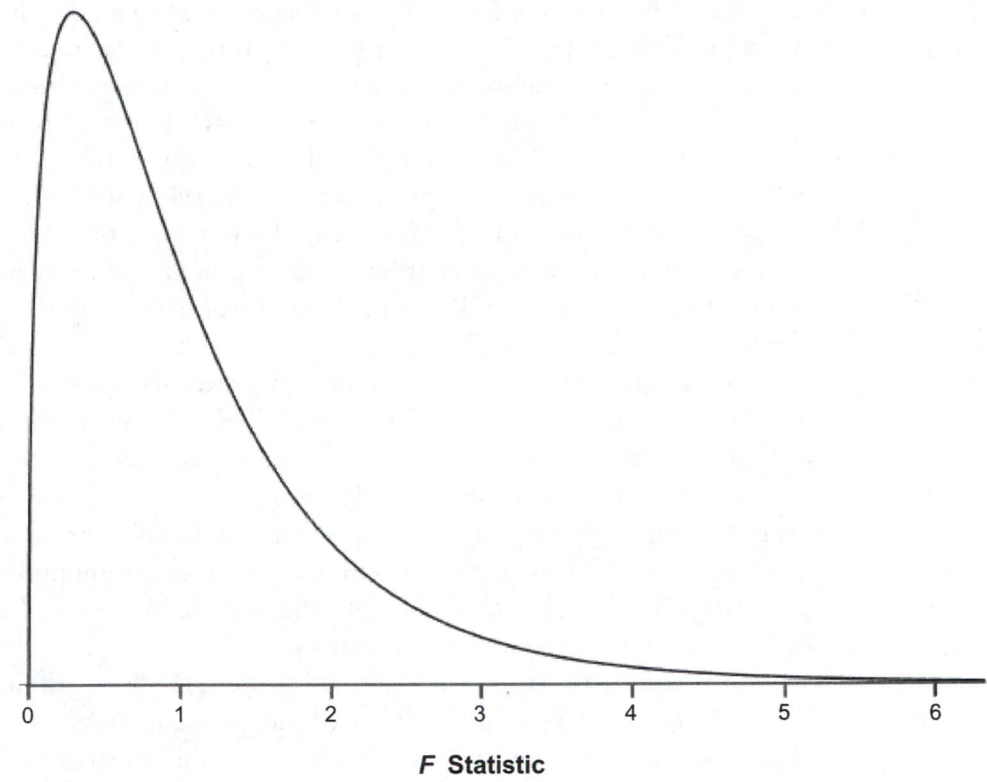

F Statistic

> Analysis of Variance: Beyond *t* Tests

You may be wondering why researchers need to compute a one-way ANOVA rather than multiple independent-samples *t* tests. For example, instead of conducting a one-way ANOVA to test the null hypothesis that the three population means are equal, why not conduct three separate *t* tests: one comparing Group 1 to Group 2, one comparing Group 1 to Group 3, and one comparing Group 2 to Group 3? Conducting multiple *t* tests on the same set of data is identified in the text as the "problem of too many *t* tests" because this practice increases the probability of detecting a significant difference between group means based on chance alone. This tactic results in an increase in the probability of committing a Type I error. In other words, the more tests conducted at the 0.05 *p* level, the more likely it is that one of them will turn out to be significant even though there is no difference between the population means. Type I errors are generally considered to be more serious than Type II errors. You may recall the maxim from the criminal justice system that "it is better that 10 guilty men go free than one innocent man be convicted." Statisticians and research scientists express a similar philosophy in setting the maximum probability of a Type I error at 0.05, while advocating that the probability of a Type II error not exceed 0.20.

The inflated probability of making at least one Type I error when multiple *t* tests are conducted may be estimated as follows. If there are *j* groups in a study, then there are $j (j - 1) / 2$ possible t tests, so a study with four groups would include $(4) (3) / 2 = 12 / 2 = 6$ t tests. If the t tests are completely independent, then the chance that at least 1 of the 6 t statistics is found to be statistically significant may be determined using the binomial probability function, $1 - (1 - \alpha)^c$, where α is the p level and c is the number of t tests. Thus, when $c = 6$ and $\alpha = 0.05$, the probability of observing at least one statistically significant difference is $1 - 0.95^6 = 0.265$. However, all of the 6 t tests can not be independent because each group mean appears in more than one comparison. The probability of at least one Type I error is thus higher than the value returned by the formula.

The solution to the problem of too many t tests is a one-way ANOVA followed by post hoc tests. The ANOVA will disclose whether there are any significant differences among the sample means and post hoc tests will reveal which sample means are significantly different. As we will see, post hoc tests were designed to protect against Type I error inflation. First, we will examine the one-way ANOVA in more detail, including its assumptions and applications to different research designs. In the last section, we will explore some alternatives for conducting post hoc tests.

As mentioned at the beginning of this review, the "one" in the name "one-way ANOVA" refers to the number of independent variables in the design. The practice of naming an ANOVA in terms of the research design for which it is used is further illustrated in the following table.

		Number of Independent Variables	
		1	2 or more
Number of Conditions Experienced by Participants	1	One-Way Between-Groups ANOVA	Factorial Between-Groups ANOVA
	All	One-Way Within-Groups ANOVA	Factorial Within-Groups ANOVA
	More than 1 but not all		Factorial Mixed ANOVA

The factorial ANOVAs listed in the right column of the table are discussed in Chapter 11. The one-way within-groups (also called repeated-measures) ANOVA is also described further in chapter. For our purposes in this chapter, we will simply note, again, that *one*-way designs, and thus *one*-way ANOVAs, are so-named because they include *one* independent variable. The other major term used to identify an ANOVA refers to whether the study is based on a between-groups design or a within-groups design. This distinction was introduced in Chapter 1 (text page 26) and reintroduced in Chapter 9 in the descriptions of the independent-samples and paired-samples t tests. To review, a between-groups design is one in which each participant is assigned to experience only one condition of the experiment, where a *condition* refers to a level of the independent variable. This means that different groups of participants will be exposed to different levels of the independent variable, and any differences between the scores across the different levels will thus be differences *between* different *groups*. Such differences are analyzed using a one-way **between-groups ANOVA**. In contrast, a within-groups design is one in which each participant experiences all of the conditions of an experiment. Thus each participant is repeatedly measured on the dependent variable— once for each level of the independent variable—and any difference between the levels is thus a difference *within* the same *group*. These differences are analyzed using a one-way **within-groups ANOVA**.

The one-way between-groups ANOVA was described earlier as an extension of the independent-samples t test. The parallels between the t tests and the one-way ANOVAs are further illustrated in the following table.

		Number of Levels of the Independent Variable	
		2	2 or more
Number of Conditions Experienced by Participants	1	Independent-Samples t Test	One-Way Between-Groups ANOVA
	All	Paired-Samples t Test	One-Way Within-Groups ANOVA

The assumptions for the one-way ANOVA are the same as the assumptions for the z and t tests: The dependent variable should be normally distributed and the samples should be randomly selected from populations with equal variances. The results of an ANOVA are relatively robust with respect to a violation of the normality assumption, particularly if the sample size is large enough to invoke the central limit theorem. The criteria for satisfying the equal-variances assumption depends on whether the sample sizes are equal. If the sample sizes are equal, the largest variance should be no more than five times larger than the smallest variance. When the sample sizes are *not* equal, the largest variance should be no more than twice as large as the smallest variance. The terms **homoscedastic** and **heteroscedastic** refer to populations with equal and unequal variances, respectively.

The third assumption, that some method of random sampling is used to select participants, is routinely violated because random sampling is usually impractical. When samples are not randomly selected, the results may be generalized only to individuals who are similar to the participants.

> The One-Way Between-Groups ANOVA: Applying the Six Steps of Hypothesis Testing

Based on the findings of many studies that "mental imagery training has beneficial effects on motor learning and performance," Ozel, Larue, and Molinaro (2004) "hypothesized that athletes ought to perform mental rotation tasks better than nonathletes. Also, athletes trained to react quickly to constantly changing environments should be faster at processing the information in a mental rotation task than athletes operating in more settled environments" (p. 49). All of the participants stated that they had no experience with mental rotation training or testing of any kind prior to the study.

Step 1. Identify the populations, comparison distribution, and assumptions.

The participants were "36 right-handed male undergraduate unpaid volunteers from the University of Caen between the ages of 18 and 37 years." (p. 52). Ozel et al. tested a "nonathlete" group of 12 male university students who "had to have occupations and spare time activities involving no strong spatial component such as computer sciences, mathematics, or engineering drawing" (p. 53) and compared their scores to two other groups of 12 male students. One group was composed of "athletes engaged in open skills activities" (this group engaged in sporting activities such as handball, rugby, basketball, and soccer, activities that required quick reactions to a changing environment), and the second group "consisted of athletes engaged in closed-skills activities" such as track and field, swimming, gymnastics, and archery—activities that did not require quick responses to a rapidly changing environment (p. 53). Based on these descriptions, we may identify Population 1 as the population of all male nonathletes, aged 18 to 37 years, with limited experience in activities involving visuospatial skills, Population 2 as the population of all male athletes, aged 18 to 37 years, competing in sports requiring quick reactions to rapidly changing environments, and Population 3 as the population of all male athletes, aged 18 to 37 years, competing in sports that involve more settled environments. Please note that the participants do *not* comprise random samples from these populations, so the results of the study may be generalized only with great caution.

The mental rotation task involves simultaneous presentations of two-dimensional representations of three-dimensional geometric figures that are either congruent or mirror images.

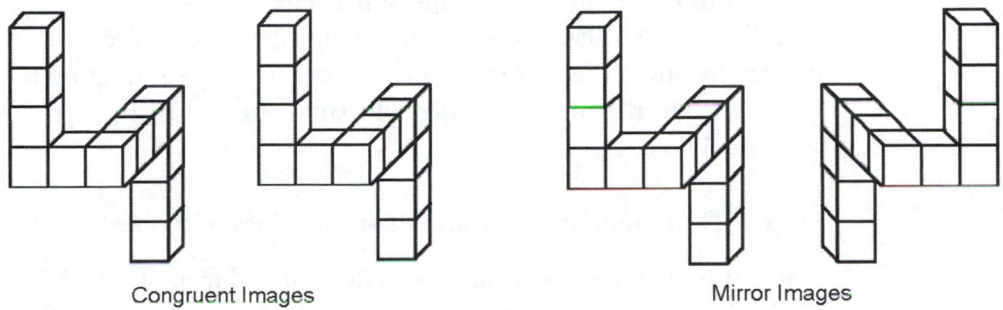

Congruent Images   Mirror Images

Ozel et al. measured mental rotation time as the time (in milliseconds) required for each participant to press one of two response keys to indicate that the images were either the same (congruent) or different (mirror images). The researchers manipulated the number of degrees required to mentally rotate the target stimulus (always the stimulus on the right) as well as the complexity (number of blocks comprising each) of the stimuli. Each participant completed four trials at each of four angles of rotation (45°, 90°, 135°, and 180°) for simple and complex pairs of stimuli. Ozel et al. determined the median response time for each of the four trials determined for each angle and each stimulus type. To simplify the example, we will use fictional data representing the mean of each participant's eight (4 angles of rotation × 2 levels of stimulus complexity) median response times. Although the data are fictional, the group means and standard deviations are very close to those reported by Ozel et al. (2004).

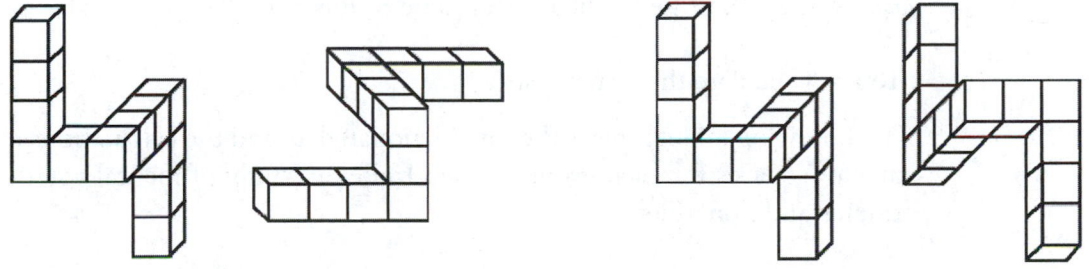

Congruent Images 90 Degrees Out of Phase   Congruent Images 180 Degrees Out of Phase

Step 2. State the null and research hypotheses.

The null hypothesis states that the mean rotation speeds in the three populations are the same. In symbols: $\mu_1 = \mu_2 = \mu_3$. The research hypothesis states that the population means are not all the same; at least one of the population means differs from at least one of the other two.

Step 3. Determine the characteristics of the comparison distribution.

The comparison distribution is an F distribution based on 2 and 33 degrees of freedom. The smaller value is the between-groups degrees of freedom

($df_{Between}$). The between-groups degrees of freedom is determined by subtracting 1 from the number of groups of participants: $df_{Between} = N_{Groups} - 1 = 3 - 1 = 2$. The larger value is the within-groups degrees of freedom (df_{Within}). The within-groups degrees of freedom is determined by subtracting the number of groups from the total number of participants: $df_{Within} = N - N_{Groups} = 36 - 3 = 33$.

Step 4. Determine the critical, or cutoff, values of the test statistic.

The critical value of the F statistic is determined from Table B.3 in the appendix of the text according to three values: the between-groups degrees of freedom ($df_{Between}$), the within-groups degrees of freedom (df_{Within}), and the significance (p) level. For this analysis, $df_{Between} = 2$, $df_{Within} = 33$, and the p level is 0.05. A portion of Table B.3 is displayed next to illustrate how to locate the critical value of the F statistic.

WITHIN-GROUPS df	SIGNIF-ICANCE (p) LEVEL	BETWEEN-GROUPS DEGREES OF FREEDOM	
		1	2
30	.01	7.56	5.39
	.05	4.17	3.32
	.10	2.88	2.49

> The critical value of the F statistic is located at the intersection of three values: $df_{Between}$, df_{Within}, and the p level.

Please note that the table does not include 33 as a value of df_{Within}, so the next *lower* value, 30, is used. The critical value of F is 3.32.

Step 5. Calculate the test statistic.

The following table displays the raw (fictional) data and the calculations of the sums of squares for each group in the Ozel et al. study of mental rotation in athletes and nonathletes.

Sample	X	$(X - M)^2$	$(M - GM)^2$	$(X - GM)^2$
Open-Skills Athletes	252	4749.506944	2149.373	13289.017
	276	8633.506944	2149.373	19398.361
	49	17978.34028	2149.373	7695.149
	178	25.84027778	2149.373	1703.873
	196	166.8402778	2149.373	3513.881
	269	7381.673611	2149.373	17497.469
$M = 183.08$	44	19344.17361	2149.373	8597.369
	282	9784.506944	2149.373	21105.697
	274	8265.840278	2149.373	18845.249
	41	20187.67361	2149.373	9162.701
	296	12750.17361	2149.373	25369.481
	40	20472.84028	2149.373	9355.145
Closed-Skills Athletes	215	5763.340278	5.576	6127.445
	270	17139.17361	5.576	17763.025
	226	7554.506944	5.576	7970.561
	173	1150.340278	5.576	1316.093
	142	8.506944444	5.576	27.857
	53	7410.340278	5.576	7009.373
$M = 139.08$	44	9040.840278	5.576	8597.369
	40	9817.506944	5.576	9355.145
	188	2392.840278	5.576	2629.433
	25	13015.00694	5.576	12481.805
	265	15855.00694	5.576	16455.245
	28	12339.50694	5.576	11820.473
Nonathletes	60	784	2373.833	5886.265
	88	0	2373.833	2373.833
	74	196	2373.833	3934.049
	144	3136	2373.833	52.969
	36	2704	2373.833	10144.921
	47	1681	2373.833	8050.037
$M = 88.00$	96	64	2373.833	1658.281
	103	225	2373.833	1137.173
	62	676	2373.833	5583.377
	158	4900	2373.833	452.753
	44	1936	2373.833	8597.369
	144	3136	2373.833	52.969

$GM = 136.722$ $SS_{\text{Within}} = 250665.8333$ $SS_{\text{Between}} = 54345.384$ $SS_{\text{Total}} = 305011.212$

The last three columns of the table include the values that are summed to compute the three sums of squares in the one-way between-groups ANOVA.

- The sum of the values in the column labeled $(X - M)^2$ is the within-groups sum of squares (SS_{Within}); that is, $SS_{Within} = \sum(X - M)^2$.
- The sum of the values in the column labeled $(M - GM)^2$ is the between-groups sum of squares ($SS_{Between}$); that is, $SS_{Between} = \sum(M - GM)^2$. The symbol **GM** represents the **grand mean**, which is computed as the mean score for all of the participants in the study without regard to group membership.
- The sum of the values in the column labeled $(X - GM)^2$ is the total sum of squares (SS_{Total}); that is, $SS_{Total} = \sum(X - GM)^2$.

The first two sums of squares, SS_{Within} and $SS_{Between}$, are used to compute the two independent estimates of the population variance, the within-groups variance and the between-groups variance, respectively. The total sum of squares (SS_{Total}) may be used to check the values computed for SS_{Within} and $SS_{Between}$; that is, $SS_{Total} = SS_{Within} + SS_{Between}$. The following formula shows the relation between SS_{Within} and $SS_{Between}$ and the F statistic:

$$F = \frac{MS_{Between}}{MS_{Within}} = \frac{SS_{Between}/df_{Between}}{SS_{Within}/df_{Within}}$$

The sums of squares, degrees of freedom, mean squares, and the F statistic are typically presented in an ANOVA **source table**. The previous source table includes the formulas used to compute the values displayed in the source table that follows for the results of the study of mental rotation.

Source	SS	df	MS	F
Between	$\sum(M - GM)^2$	$N_{Groups} - 1$	$\dfrac{SS_{Between}}{df_{Between}}$	$\dfrac{MS_{Between}}{MS_{Within}}$
Within	$\sum(X - M)^2$	$N_{Total} - N_{Groups}$	$\dfrac{SS_{Within}}{df_{Within}}$	
Total	$\sum(X - GM)^2$	$N_{Total} - 1$		

Source	SS	df	MS	F
Between	54345.384	2	27172.692	3.577
Within	250665.8333	33	7595.934	
Total	305011.217	35		

Step 6. Make a decision regarding the status of the null hypothesis.

The null hypothesis may be rejected, because the computed value of the test statistic ($F = 3.577$) is greater than the critical value ($F_{Critical} = 3.32$) for $df_{Between} = 3$, $df_{Within} = 30$, and a p level of 0.05. The results support the research hypothesis: the mean speed of mental rotation is not the same in the populations of open-skills athletes, closed-skills athletes, and nonathletes who spend very little time in activities with a spatial component.

To determine which group means are significantly different from each other, a post-hoc test must be conducted. Post-hoc tests are discussed in the next section.

> Digging Deeper into the Data: Post-Hoc Tests to Determine Which Groups Are Different

Some researchers have been outspoken critics of the overall, or *omnibus*, analysis of variance (ANOVA). Their criticism is based on the fact that a rejection of the omnibus null hypothesis (which states that all of the population means are equal) is not very informative: The researcher still must determine which of three or more population means differ from each other. According to these authors, the solution is to bypass the omnibus test and instead conduct **planned comparisons** between specific pairs of group means. This is a rather radical approach and has not yet been adopted by mainstream research psychologists, who prefer instead to conduct the omnibus ANOVA and then conduct either planned comparisons or **post-hoc tests**.

The difference between planned and post-hoc comparisons is this: Planned comparisons are based on specific hypotheses that were formally expressed before any data were collected. Such comparisons are described as *confirmatory* analyses because they are employed to test and thus either confirm or fail to confirm specific hypotheses. Post-hoc tests, in contrast, are *exploratory* analyses because they are not planned in advance. These tests explore all possible pairwise differences by comparing all unique pairs of group means.

A researcher using the **Bonferroni test** (also called the *Dunn Multiple Comparison* test or simply *Dunn's test*) protects against inflating the probability of making a Type I error by dividing the p level by the number of comparisons to be made. Thus, when there are five groups and 10 possible comparisons, the Bonferroni procedure adjusts the p level for each comparison to $0.05/10 = 0.005$. To be considered "significant," a difference between two group means would have to be large enough to have a p value less than or equal to 0.005. A researcher using the Bonferroni procedure could use the t test for independent means to make all of her comparisons and not worry about inflating the Type I error rate. However, when the number of comparisons is "large" (more than 5), the Bonferroni procedure has been described as "intolerably conservative" (Hays, 1981, p. 435) and, for this reason, is not favored by researchers who conduct post-hoc, as opposed to planned, comparisons. The phrase "intolerably conservative" refers to the increased probability of committing a Type II error when the Bonferroni test is used for more than a few comparisons.

Researchers can choose among several post-hoc tests that are less conservative than the Bonferroni procedure. Because it is considered neither too liberal nor too conservative, the **Tukey HSD test** is widely used and will be illustrated here.

$$HSD = \frac{M_1 - M_2}{\sqrt{\dfrac{MS_{Within}}{N}}} = \frac{183.083 - 88}{\sqrt{\dfrac{7595.934}{12}}} = \frac{95.083}{\sqrt{632.995}} = \frac{95.083}{25.159} = 3.779$$

where,

M_1 and M_2 are two group means,

MS_{Within} is the within-groups estimate of the population variance from the one-way ANOVA, and

N is the number of participants in each group

If the groups have different numbers of participants, then the harmonic mean of the unequal sample sizes returned by the formula:

$$N' = \frac{N_{Groups}}{\sum \dfrac{1}{N}}$$

is substituted for the number in each group (N in the HSD formula).

The critical value of the HSD statistic is found in Table B.5 (in the appendix of the text) by first locating the column value that corresponds to the number of groups (treatment levels) and then finding the row value that corresponds to the within-groups degrees of freedom (df_{Within}) and the p level. The value found at the intersection of the appropriate column and row is $HSD_{critical}$. Each computed value of HSD that exceeds $HSD_{critical}$ indicates an "honestly significantly different" pair of means.

WITHIN-GROUPS *df*	SIGNIF-ICANCE (*p*) LEVEL	\(k\) = NUMBER OF TREATMENTS (LEVELS)					
		2	3	4	5	6	7
.							
.							
.							
30	.05	2.89	3.49	3.85	4.10	4.30	4.46
	.01	**3.89**	**4.45**	**4.80**	**5.05**	**5.24**	**5.40**

From the table, the critical value of *HSD* for this comparison is 3.49. Because the computed value of *HSD* (3.78) exceeds the critical value, the means are significantly different. Athletes whose competitive activities are mostly of the open-skills type exhibited a significantly higher rate of mental rotation than nonathletes. No other comparisons were significant.

REFERENCE

Ozel, S., Larue, J., & Molinaro, C. (2004). Relation between sport and spatial imagery: Comparison of three groups of participants. *The Journal of Psychology*, *138*(1), 49–63.

STUDY QUESTIONS

1. Suppose there are three populations with the same bell-shape, the same mean, and the same relatively small variance, that is, there is relatively little variation in the scores within each of these three identical populations. Suppose further that a sample is selected from each of these three populations. Which one of the following is most accurate?
   a. The sample means will be the same.
   b. The sample variances will be very different.
   c. The sample means will be similar to each other.
   d. The sample means will be very different from each other.

2. Which one of the following best expresses what an analysis of variance is about?
   a. a comparison of two different ways of estimating population variances
   b. a comparison of estimates of the true values of three or more population means
   c. a comparison of estimates of the true values of three or more population variances
   d. a comparison of three or more estimates of the true value of a single population mean

3. Hazan and Shaver (1987) compared mean responses to the statement, "My relationship with [name of present or past romantic partner] made/makes me very happy." among samples of college students representing three populations defined according to attachment style, that is, students were categorized as having attachment styles that were either "secure," "avoidant," or "anxious-ambivalent." If the mean "happiness" scores in the three populations are the same, then the within-groups variance is _____ it is when the population mean happiness scores are not the same.
   a. the same as
   b. higher than
   c. lower than

4. An analysis of variance is conducted to determine whether the _____ differ more than you would expect if the null hypothesis were true.
   a. means of the samples
   b. variances of the samples
   c. means of the populations
   d. variances of the populations

5. Although an analysis of variance is conducted to answer the question of whether the _____ of the samples differ more than you would expect if the null hypothesis were true, this question is addressed by analyzing _____.
   a. means; variances
   b. variances; means
   c. variances; sample sizes
   d. variances; population variances

6. The **within-groups variance** tells you how much:
   a. the means vary among the samples.
   b. the means vary among the populations.
   c. the scores within each sample (group) vary.
   d. each sample mean differs from the true population mean.

7. The variances (s^2) for each of five (5) groups of 20 scores are as follows: 64, 121, 144, 169, and 81. If you averaged these five variances, you would have computed the:
   a. between-groups estimate of the population variance.
   b. within-groups estimate of the population variance.
   c. population variance.
   d. F statistic.

8. How are the within-groups variance and the status of the null hypothesis related, if at all?
   a. If the null hypothesis is true, then the within-groups variance will be larger than it would be if the null hypothesis is false.
   b. If the null hypothesis is true, then the within-groups variance will be smaller than it would be if the null hypothesis is false.
   c. The relation between the within-groups variance and the status of the null hypothesis depends on the size of the samples in the study.
   d. Within-groups variance and the status of the null hypothesis are not related.

9. Which one of the following statements most accurately describes the relation between the F statistic and the t statistic?
   a. The two statistics are not related, either to each other, or to any other statistic.
   b. Both statistics are related to the z statistic, but they are not related to each other.
   c. For a study of two independent groups of participants, the square root of the F statistic is equal to the t statistic.
   d. For a study of any number of independent groups of participants, the square root of the F statistic is equal to the t statistic.

10. What is the "problem of too many t tests"?
    a. Researchers too often use the t test when they should be using other statistical tests.
    b. When researchers use a large number of t tests in the same study, the chance of committing a Type I error is less than the p level.
    c. When researchers use a large number of t tests in the same study, the chance of committing a Type I error is greater than the p level.
    d. There are three types of t tests—the single-sample t test, the paired-samples t test, and the independent-samples t test—which leads to confusion.

11. A(n) _____ ANOVA is a hypothesis test in which there are more than two samples, and each sample is composed of different participants.
    a. one-way
    b. within-groups
    c. repeated-measures
    d. between-groups

12. Which of the following is *not* an assumption for an analysis of variance?
    a. The populations should follow a normal curve.
    b. The variances of the populations should be equal.
    c. The samples should have the same number of participants.
    d. The participants should be randomly selected from the population.

13. When conducting an analysis of variance, the researcher:
    a. knows the true value of the population variance.
    b. estimates the population variance from the scores in samples.
    c. knows that each of three or more populations have different variances.
    d. assumes that each of three or more populations have different variances.

14. Populations that have the same variance are called _____ populations.
    a. normal
    b. heteroscedastic
    c. homoscedastic
    d. heterogeneous

15. When the sizes of the groups are *not* close to equal, the analysis of variance is more sensitive to a violation of the assumption that:
    a. participants were randomly selected from the population.
    b. the scores are normally distributed in the population.
    c. the scores are from populations with equal variances.
    d. the dependent variable was measured on an interval scale.

16. An analysis of variance (ANOVA) is commonly used to test the null hypothesis that:
    a. three or more population means are equal.
    b. three or more population means differ from each other.
    c. at least one of three or more population means differs from the others.
    d. the variance between different groups is equal to the variance within each of the groups.

17. You are interested in comparing four methods of teaching. You randomly assign 20 students to each of the four methods and then administer a standardized test at the end of the study. The null hypothesis that you are interested in testing is:
    a. teaching method and intelligence are independent in the population.
    b. the mean standardized test scores differ for the four teaching methods.
    c. the mean standardized test scores are the same for the four teaching methods.
    d. the sample means for the four groups assigned to the different teaching methods are equal.

18. In a comparison of the average number of hours worked per week for five different levels of education (e.g., no HS degree, HS graduate, some college, college graduate, graduate degree), the research hypothesis would state that:
    a. there is no difference in the average hours worked for people in the five education categories.
    b. any differences in the average hours worked in the five groups are attributable to chance.
    c. the means for the different levels of education are not all the same in the population.
    d. the population means for all five levels of education are the same.

19. In an analysis of variance, the between-groups degrees of freedom is computed as the:
    a. sum of the degrees of freedom ($n - 1$) for each group.
    b. total number of participants in the study (N) minus 1.
    c. number of scores in each group (n) minus 1.
    d. number of groups minus 1.

20. In an analysis of variance, the within-groups degrees of freedom is computed as the:
    a. sum of the degrees of freedom ($n - 1$) for each group.
    b. total number of participants in the study (N) minus 1.
    c. number of scores in each group (n) minus 1.
    d. number of groups minus 1.

21. A researcher reported the following results of a study conducted to investigate whether there are differences among the anxiety test scores recorded for college students who have been diagnosed with panic disorder, generalized anxiety disorder, and social phobia. A group of students with no diagnosis of an anxiety disorder was included for comparison purposes.

Group	M	SD	n
Panic Disorder	24	5	22
Generalized Anxiety Disorder	20	9	34
Social Phobia	18	6	29
No Diagnosis	10	8	30

The comparison distribution for an analysis of the data in the table just shown is an F distribution with _____ degrees of freedom.
a. 3 and 111
b. 4 and 115
c. 3 and 112
d. 21, 33, 28, and 29

22. A(n) _____ is used to locate a critical value of the F statistic and to determine how extreme a computed F statistic must be in order to reject the null hypothesis at a given p level.
a. F distribution
b. normal distribution
c. F table
d. ANOVA table

23. Excerpt from the F Table:

Within-Groups df	Significance (p) Level	Between-Groups Degress of Freedon					
		1	2	3	4	5	6
10	0.01	10.05	7.56	6.55	6.00	5.64	5.39
	0.05	4.97	4.10	3.71	3.48	3.33	3.22
	0.10	3.29	2.93	2.73	2.61	2.52	2.46
11	0.01	9.65	7.21	6.22	5.67	5.32	5.07
	0.05	4.85	3.98	3.59	3.36	3.20	3.10
	0.10	3.23	2.86	2.66	2.54	2.45	2.39
12	0.01	9.33	6.93	5.95	5.41	5.07	4.82
	0.05	4.75	3.89	3.49	3.26	3.11	3.00
	0.10	3.18	2.81	2.61	2.48	2.40	2.33
13	0.01	9.07	6.70	5.74	5.21	4.86	4.62
	0.05	4.67	3.81	3.41	3.18	3.03	2.92
	0.10	3.14	2.76	2.56	2.43	2.35	2.28

If the null hypothesis is tested at the 0.01 p level, what is the critical value of the F statistic for an ANOVA with 4 groups, each with 15 participants?
a. 3.89
b. 5.21
c. 5.74
d. The value is not in the table.

24. An F distribution is:
a. bell-shaped like a normal curve.
b. positively skewed.
c. negatively skewed.
d. shaped like a rectangle.

25. An F statistic is a ratio of an estimate of the population variance based on variation among the _____ to an estimate of the population variance based on variation among the _____.
a. scores in each sample; means of each sample
b. means of each sample; scores in each sample
c. scores in each population; means of each population
d. means of each population; scores in each population

26. Consider the following figure from the text (Figure 10-3):

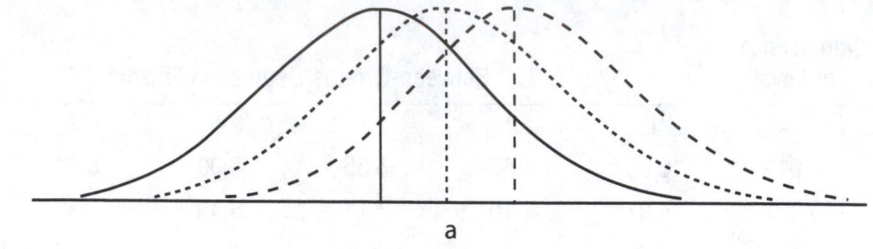

a

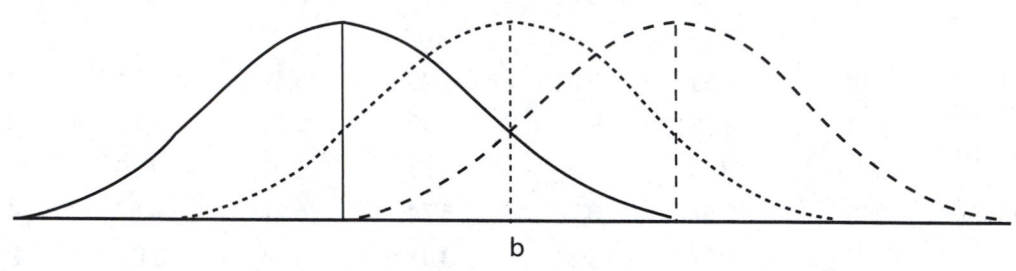

b

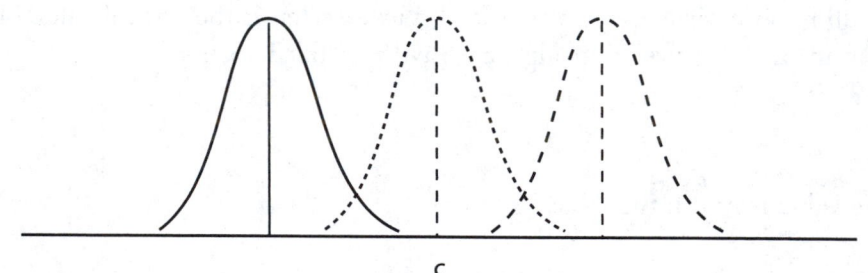

c

For which of the three sets of distributions is the ratio of between-groups variance to within-groups variance largest?
  a. the top set of distributions (a)
  b. the middle set of distributions (b)
  c. the bottom set of distributions (c)
  d. The ratio is approximately the same in the three sets of distributions.

27. The between-groups variance is based solely on the variability among the:
  a. means of each sample.
  b. scores in each sample.
  c. scores in each population.
  d. means in each population.

28. The within-groups variance and the between-groups variance will be about the same when:
    a. the null hypothesis is true.
    b. the research hypothesis is true.
    c. either the null or the research hypothesis is true, depending on the number of groups.
    d. False premise: The within-groups and between-groups variance estimates are never approximately the same.

29. The ratio of the between-groups variance to the within-groups variance is _____ when the null hypothesis is true.
    a. 0
    b. approximately 1
    c. extremely large
    d. undefined

30. The F statistic is a ratio of the:
    a. within-groups to the between-groups variance estimate.
    b. between-groups to the within-groups variance estimate.
    c. mean of the group means to the overall (grand) mean.
    d. between-groups degrees of freedom to the within-groups degrees of freedom.

31. Which one of the following is *not* included in an analysis of variance **source table**?
    a. SS_{Total}
    b. $df_{Between}$
    c. n
    d. F

32. An incomplete source table for an analysis of variance:

Source	SS	df	MS	F
Between Groups	150.000	3		
Within Groups	600.000	50		
Total	750.000	53		

Use the information in the source table to determine which of the following is $MS_{Between}$.
    a. 150
    b. 50
    c. 6
    d. 600

33. If $SS_{Between} = 150$, $SS_{Within} = 600$, $df_{Between} = 3$, and $df_{Within} = 50$, what is the value of the F statistic?
    a. 4.167
    b. 4
    c. 0.25
    d. 0.06

34. In an analysis of variance, the **grand mean** is:
    a. the mean of all of the scores without regard to group membership.
    b. the mean of the variances of each group.
    c. the ratio of $MS_{Between}$ to MS_{Within}.
    d. not computed unless the research hypothesis is true.

35. Which of the following completely ignore(s) the group a score is in?
    a. $SS_{Between}$
    b. SS_{Within}
    c. SS_{Total}
    d. $SS_{Between}$ and SS_{Within}

36. Which of the following is the sum of the squared deviations of each score from the grand mean?
    a. SS_{Within}
    b. $SS_{Between}$
    c. SS_{Total}
    d. MS_{Within}

37. The sum of the squared deviations of each score from its group mean is the:
    a. within-groups sum of squares (SS_{Within}).
    b. between-groups sum of squares ($SS_{Between}$).
    c. total sum of squares (SS_{Total}).
    d. within-groups mean square (SS_{Within}).

38. Which one of the following formulas expresses the fact that $SS_{Total} = SS_{Within} + SS_{Between}$?

    a. $\sum(X - GM)^2 = \sum(X - M)^2 + \sum(M - GM)^2$

    b. $\sum(M - GM)^2 = \sum(X - M)^2 + \sum(X - GM)^2$

    c. $\sum(X - M)^2 = \sum(X - GM)^2 + \sum(M - GM)^2$

    d. $\sum(X - M)^2 = \sum(M - GM)^2 + \sum(X - GM)^2$

39. The sum of the squared deviations of each score's group mean from the grand mean is the:
    a. within-groups sum of squares (SS_{Within}).
    b. between-groups sum of squares ($SS_{Between}$).
    c. total sum of squares (SS_{Total}).
    d. within-groups variance (MS_{Within}).

40. In a test of the null hypothesis that three populations have identical means, a researcher computed the value of an F statistic to be 3.14 based on the scores obtained from 3 groups of 21 participants (63 participants in all). If the p level was set at 0.05, which one of the following is the correct decision?
    a. The null hypothesis should be rejected because $F(3, 21) = 3.07$.
    b. The null hypothesis should not be rejected because $F(2, 21) = 3.47$.
    c. The null hypothesis should be rejected because $F(3, 60) = 2.76$.
    d. The null hypothesis should not be rejected because $F(2, 60) = 3.15$.

41. Which one of the following statements regarding post hoc and planned comparisons is most accurate?
    a. A post-hoc test may be conducted only after the result of an analysis of variance permits a rejection of the null hypothesis.
    b. A planned comparison may be conducted only after the result of an analysis of variance permits a rejection of the null hypothesis.
    c. Both post-hoc and planned comparisons require some adjustment of the probability of committing a Type I error.
    d. Both post-hoc and planned comparisons require some adjustment of the probability of committing a Type II error.

42. The Tukey HSD test is a frequent choice of researchers as a:
    a. more structured alternative to the one-way analysis of variance.
    b. means of reducing the probability of committing a Type II error.
    c. post-hoc test that is considered neither too liberal nor too conservative.
    d. post-hoc test that offers more protection than the Bonferroni test during "fishing" expeditions.

43. The **Bonferroni test** is:
    a. limited to planned comparisons.
    b. more conservative than the Tukey HSD test.
    c. another name for an independent-samples t test.
    d. the only post-hoc test that may be used with unequal sample sizes.

ANSWERS TO CHAPTER 10 STUDY QUESTIONS

Question Number	Correct Answer
1	c, pp. 430–431 (If the populations are identical, and there is very little variability within them, then samples from each of the populations will have little variability within them and are very likely to have similar means. Selecting samples with identical means is extremely unlikely.)
2	a, pp. 430–431
3	a, p. 431
4	a, p. 431
5	a, p. 431
6	c, p. 431
7	b, pp. 430–431
8	d, p. 431
9	c, pp. 432–433
10	b, pp. 435–437
11	d, p. 439
12	c, p. 440
13	b, p. 440
14	c, p. 440
15	c, p. 440
16	a, p. 445
17	c, p. 445
18	c, p. 445
19	d, p. 445
20	a, p. 445
21	a, pp. 445–446
22	c, p. 446

Question Number	Correct Answer
23	d, pp. 445–446 [The between-groups df = the number of groups $- 1 = 4 - 1 = 3$, and the within-groups df = the number of participants in each group minus 1 = 15 $- 1 + 15 - 1 + 15 - 1 + 15 - 1 = (4)(14) = 56$; alternatively, df_{Within} = the total number of participants minus the number of groups = 60 $- 4 = 56$.]
24	b, p. 447
25	b, p. 448
26	c, pp. 448–449
27	a, p. 450
28	a, p. 450
29	b, p. 450
30	b, p. 450
31	c, pp. 451–452
32	b, p. 453
33	a, p. 453
34	a, p. 453
35	c, p. 454
36	c, p. 454
37	a, p. 455
38	a, pp. 455–457
39	b, p. 457
40	d, pp. 458–459
41	a, pp. 459, 462
42	c, pp. 463–467
43	b, pp. 466–467

CHAPTER ELEVEN

TWO-WAY ANOVA

Understanding Interactions

CHAPTER OUTLINE

LEARNING OBJECTIVES

After studying this chapter, you should be able to:

1. Define each of the following terms and provide examples that are not in the text: *two-way ANOVA, factorial analysis of variance, factor, cell, main effect, interaction, quantitative interaction, qualitative interaction, marginal means, residual, mixed-design ANOVA, multivariate analysis of variance (MANOVA), covariate, analysis of covariance (ANCOVA),* and *multivariate analysis of covariance (MANCOVA)*.

2. Distinguish between a one-way and a two-way ANOVA and explain the advantages of a two-way ANOVA over a one-way ANOVA.

3. Explain the difference between a 2 × 2 and a 3 × 2 factorial ANOVA as well as the difference between the between-groups and within-groups versions of each. In addition, you should be able to determine the number of cells in a two-way ANOVA identified in this way.

4. Provide explanations and examples that distinguish between (a) main and interaction effects, (b) quantitative and qualitative interactions, and (c) the relative importance of main and interaction effects.

5. Construct tables of cell and marginal means for a two-way ANOVA and manipulate the means to indicate any combination of main and interaction effects that you may then depict in bar graphs.

6. Describe the six steps of the hypothesis-testing procedure as it applies to a two-way ANOVA and explain the elements of an ANOVA source table that results from the analysis.

7. Describe the computational procedure that results in a more precise interpretation of an interaction by removing the contributions of the main effects.

CHAPTER REVIEW

> ### Two-Way ANOVA: When the Outcome Depends on More Than One Variable

This chapter introduces the **two-way analysis of variance (ANOVA)** as an extension of the one-way ANOVA described in Chapter 10. The "two" in the name of the ANOVA refers to the inclusion of two independent variables (called **factors**) in the design and analysis. The two-way ANOVA, in turn, is a member of the class of analyses called factorial ANOVAs. A **factorial ANOVA** is used to analyze the data from a factorial design. The most commonly used factorial design is called a *between-groups design*. This term was introduced in Chapter 1 and reviewed in Chapter 9. In a between-groups design, participants are randomly assigned to experience only one level of one factor. The most basic factorial ANOVA, and the one discussed at length in this chapter, is a two-way ANOVA for a between-groups design; so this ANOVA is most completely described as a *two-way between-groups ANOVA*.

All between-groups factorial designs include:

• two or more independent variables (factors), each of which has two or more levels.

• one interval- or ratio-scaled dependent variable, which is the same for all participants.

- conditions or **cells** defined as the combination of one level of one factor with one level of the other factor(s); each cell identifies a different group of participants.
- random assignment of 10-20 participants to each cell of the design.
- one possible **main effect** of each factor and one possible **interaction** for each unique combination of factors. *These* are further described later in this discussion.
- a name specified by the number of factors, and the number of levels of each factor. For example, a **2 × 2 design (read "two-by-two")** has two factors and two levels in each one; a 3 × 2 design also has two factors, with 3 levels of the first factor and 2 levels of the second factor; a 3 × 2 × 3 design has 3 factors, and so forth.
- a number of cells determined by the product of the number of levels of each factor. For example, in a 2 × 2 design, there are (2) (2) = 4 cells; in a 3 × 2 design, there are (3) (2) = 6 cells; in a 3 × 2 × 3 design, there are (3) (2) (3) = 18 cells, etc.
- at least three null hypotheses that are tested by a factorial ANOVA. The ANOVA is identified by the number of factors in the design: if there are two factors, the ANOVA is termed a "two-way" ANOVA; if there are three factors, the ANOVA is termed a "three-way" ANOVA, etc.

In a 2 × 2 factorial design, the factors may be generically identified as Factor A and Factor B. Each factor has two levels, which may be designated using the notation A_1, A_2, B_1, and B_2. Using this notation, there are four unique combinations of levels (cells) in a 2 × 2 design: A_1B_1, A_1B_2, A_2B_1, and A_2B_2. These are identified in the following annotated figure.

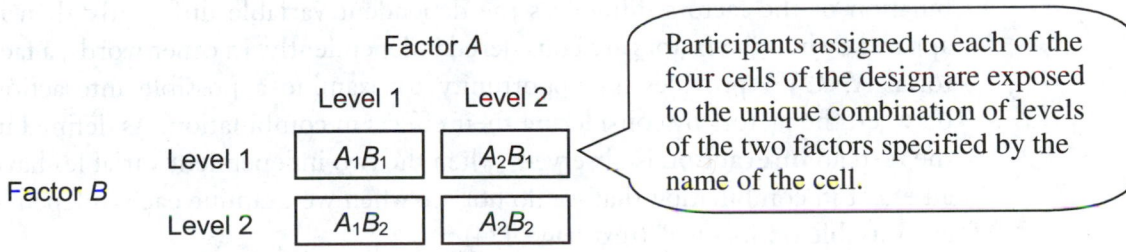

The influence of any single factor on the dependent variable is called a main effect. Thus, a **main effect** occurs when the different levels of one factor produce significantly different effects on the dependent variable, *irrespective of the other factor(s)*. For example, a main effect of Factor A occurs when the mean of level A_1 (the first column mean) differs significantly from the mean of level A_2 (the second column mean), ignoring the specific cell means for the levels of Factor B. Similarly, a main effect of Factor B is observed when the mean of level B_1 (the first row mean) differs significantly from the mean of level B_2 (the second row mean), ignoring the specific cell means for the levels of Factor A. The following figure illustrates the cell, row, and column means for the generic 2 × 2 ANOVA. The row and column means are also called **marginal means**; the marginal means are compared in a test of main effects.

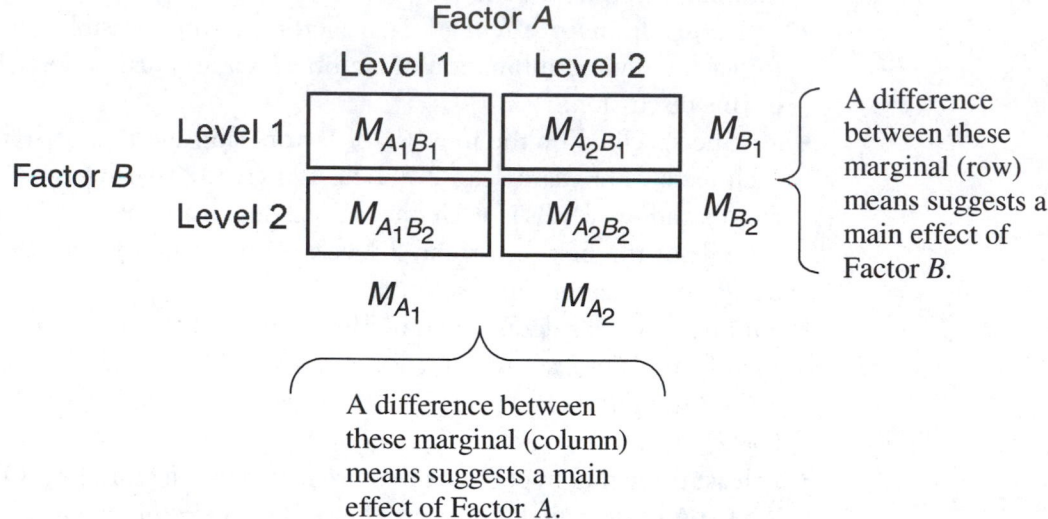

There are as many potential main effects as there are factors in a factorial design. For example, in a 2 × 2 design there are two possible main effects: using conventional notation, we would say that there may be a "main effect of *A*," a "main effect of *B*," or "main effects for both *A* and *B*."

A factorial ANOVA is more efficient than a one-way ANOVA in that it provides simultaneous tests of the effects of more than one factor. In addition, and more importantly, a factorial ANOVA includes a test of whether the combination of the factors influences the dependent variable differently than is apparent when the factors are considered independently. In other words, a factorial ANOVA provides an opportunity to examine a possible interaction between the factors by considering their effects in combination. As defined in the text, an **interaction** is observed "when the two independent variables have an effect in combination that we do not see when we examine each independent variable on its own" (text page 484).

> The Layers of ANOVA: Understanding Interactions

Interactions may be described as quantitative or qualitative, according to whether the effects of the levels of one factor vary in magnitude or vary in direction over the levels of the other factor. A **quantitative interaction** is suggested in the previous example in that the effect of gender on income increases in magnitude—it does not change direction—over the levels of the age factor. A **qualitative interaction** would be evident if the income gap reversed direction from younger to older workers—that is, if older female workers earned more than older male workers.

Researchers typically conduct studies based on a factorial design because they are interested in interaction effects. Put another way, the primary rationale for employing a factorial design is at least one research hypothesis that predicts an interaction effect. However, even in the absence of any interaction effects, the factorial design is valued as an efficient method of analyzing the main effects of two or more factors, because the design is, in effect, a combination of two or more one-way designs conducted at the same time.

> The Expanded Source Table: Conducting a Two-Way Between-Groups ANOVA

Now we'll be reviewing our six steps of hypothesis testing for a two-way ANOVA. Let's start with a simple example that will guide us through the entire process. Imagine that we are working for a company that is developing a new type of shampoo. We want to figure out if people prefer the shampoo compared to the current best-seller. We also want to figure out if we should market the shampoo to men or women, and so we want to see if there's a difference in preference for the shampoo between genders. In our marketing study, male and female testers were either given the new shampoo or the best-seller and after using the shampoo, we asked them to rate how much they liked it on a scale of 1 (hated it) to 10 (best shampoo ever). For the purposes of our example, we'll only put four testers in each group but know that if this was a real study, we'd probably want to use more than only 16 total testers!

Experimental Condition	Data for Testers	Mean Liking of Product
Females, Best-Seller	5, 5, 6, 6	5.50
Females, New Product	9, 9, 9, 10	9.25
Males, Best-Seller	4, 5, 6, 8	5.75
Males, New Product	6, 6, 7, 7	6.50
		Grand Mean (GM) = 6.75

Now that we have our data in hand, let's go through the steps necessary for the ANOVA.

Step 1. Identify the populations, distributions, and assumptions.

For our example, we have four populations with four raters in each population. Population 1 refers to females who received the best-seller. Population 2 refers to females who received the new product. Population 3 refers to males who received the best-seller. Lastly, population 4 refers to males who received the new product. Now would also be a good opportunity to discuss our independent variables. Our first independent variable is gender with two levels (male or female), and our second independent variable is the product type (best-seller or new product).

We now need to look at the distribution to which we will compare our sample. Because we have more than 2 groups, we will need to use the F distribution, which means we'll use an ANOVA. Because we're looking at two independent variables, we know that this is a two-way ANOVA. Because our groups are not related to one another in any way, we also know that this is a between-groups ANOVA.

Our assumptions in a two-way ANOVA are the same as our one-way ANOVA. First, our sample should be randomly selected. Second, the populations should be normally distributed. Third, the population variances should be equal or show **homoscedasticity**. For our marketing study, our sample is not random because the testers come from our pool of product testers rather than the general population. We also don't know about the normal distribution or homoscedasticity of our population. So, we want to be cautious about any conclusions that we make (although with only three testers in each group, we would want to be very cautious no matter what).

Step 2. State the null and research hypotheses.

For a two-way ANOVA we have three sets of hypotheses—one for each of the main effects and one for the interaction. For the main effects, in our case because we have two levels in each of our two independent variables, we can say that the two levels are not equal:

Gender Main Effect

Null Hypothesis: On average, males and females will not differ in shampoo liking, $H_0 = \mu_m = \mu_f$.

Research Hypothesis: On average, males and females will differ in shampoo liking, $H_1 = \mu_m \neq \mu_f$.

Shampoo Main Effect

Null Hypothesis: On average, there will be no difference in liking between the best-seller and the new product, $H_0 = \mu_b = \mu_n$.

Research Hypothesis: On average, the best-seller will differ in liking than the new product, $H_1 = \mu_b \neq \mu_n$.

If we had more than two levels in any of our independent variables, our research hypothesis would state that any two levels of the independent variable are not equal to one another.

For our interaction, we state the hypotheses in words rather than symbols. The null hypothesis is that the effect of one independent variable does not depend on the level of the other independent variable, whereas the research hypothesis is that the effect of one independent variable does depend on the level of the other independent variable. In our example:

Null Hypothesis: The effect of gender does not depend on the type of shampoo.

Research Hypothesis: The effect of gender depends on the type of shampoo.

Step 3. Determine the characteristics of the comparison distribution.

For our two-way ANOVA, we need to provide degrees of freedom for each of the three comparison distributions. There will be two sets of degrees of freedom for our main effects and one for our interaction. Each of our three F statistics will be a ratio between the between-groups variance and within-groups variance. We will have three between-groups variance estimates for each of our three effects, and each one will have separate degrees of freedom. Our within-groups estimate is the same for all three.

The between-groups degrees of freedom for the two-way ANOVA for both of our main effects are the same as for a one-way ANOVA. It is just the number of groups minus 1. In our example, there were two groups for gender so: $df_{Rows(gender)} = N_{Rows} - 1 = 2 - 1 = 1$. There were also two groups for product type so: $df_{Columns(product\ type)} = N_{Columns} - 1 = 2 - 1 = 1$. For the between-groups degrees of freedom for *the interaction, we multiply the degrees of freedom for the two main effects so:* $df_{interaction} = (df_{Rows(gender)})(df_{Columns(product\ type)}) = (1)(1)$.

We calculate the between-groups degrees of freedom in the same way as we did for a one-way ANOVA. Specifically, we calculate the sum of the degrees of freedom in each cell. If you recall, there are four testers in each of cell, so $4 - 1 = 3$. Then, there are four cells for each of our groups: $3 + 3 + 3 + 3 = 12$. Therefore, $df_{within} = 12$.

If we calculate the total degrees of freedom, we will be able to do a quick check of our work. The total degrees of freedom are the same in a two-way ANOVA as a one-way—the total number of participants minus 1. We had 12 product testers in total so our total degrees of freedom equal 11. If we add up our three between-groups degrees of freedom (the two for the main effect and the one for the interaction) and the within-groups degrees of freedom, they should equal the total degrees of freedom. For our example, $1 + 1 + 1 + 12 = 15$.

Step 4. Determine critical values, or cutoffs.

There are three critical values or cutoffs, for each of the F ratios. We'll determine our critical values the same way that we did for a one-way ANOVA using Appendix B of your text. We look up the within-groups degrees of freedom on the left-hand side of the table (which is the same for all of our main effects and our interaction) and then look up our between-groups degrees of freedom across the top. The spot on the grid where they intersect will contain three numbers for our significance level. Generally, we want the significance level at 0.05; however, if we choose 0.01 or 0.10 we can find that there as well.

Using our example, our within-groups degrees of freedom was 12 and each of our between-groups degrees of freedom was 1. If we want a p level of 0.05, our cut-off is 4.75. If any of our obtained F ratios exceeds 4.75 for our main effects and/or the interaction, we will be able to reject the associated null hypothesis.

Step 5. Calculate the test statistic.

If you remember for our one-way ANOVA, we needed to calculate one F statistic. As you may have already guessed, for a two-way ANOVA we'll need to calculate three F statistics—one for each main effect and one for the interaction.

Our first step is to calculate the total sum of squares. The formula for the total sum of squares is: $SS_{total} = \sum(X - GM)^2$. Just as we did for our one-way ANOVA, this means that we subtract the grand mean (the overall mean of our entire sample) from every score, square the deviation, and add up all of the deviations. You may remember that when we first introduced the data, the grand mean (GM) was 6.75. This process is elaborated in the following table:

	Liking ratings for each participant in each group (X)	Subtract grand mean from each score ($X - GM$)	Square the deviations, $(X - GM)^2$
Female, Best-Seller	5	$(5 - 6.75) = -1.75$	3.06
	5	$(5 - 6.75) = -1.75$	3.06
	6	$(6 - 6.75) = -0.75$	0.56
	6	$(6 - 6.75) = -0.75$	0.56
Female, New Product	9	$(9 - 6.75) = 2.25$	5.06
	9	$(9 - 6.75) = 2.25$	5.06
	9	$(9 - 6.75) = 2.25$	5.06
	10	$(10 - 6.75) = 3.25$	10.56
Male, Best-Seller	4	$(4 - 6.75) = -2.75$	7.56
	5	$(5 - 6.75) = -1.75$	3.06
	6	$(6 - 6.75) = -0.75$	0.56
	8	$(8 - 6.75) = 1.25$	1.56
Male, New Product	6	$(6 - 6.75) = -0.75$	0.56
	6	$(6 - 6.75) = -0.75$	0.56
	7	$(7 - 6.75) = 0.25$	0.06
	7	$(7 - 6.75) = 0.25$	0.06
			Total Sum of Squares (SS_{total}) = 46.96

Next, let's work on the between-groups sum of squares for our main effects. This is not different from the between-groups sum of squares for the one-way ANOVA. The difference is that now we need to do two of them. We'll start with calculating the sum of squares for gender. We calculate this by subtracting the grand mean from the mean for each level of gender for each score.

	Liking ratings for each participant in each group (X)	Mean for gender level, $M_{row(gender)}$	Subtract grand mean from mean for each level of the variable $(M_{row(gender)} - GM)$	Square the deviations, $(M_{row(gender)} - GM)^2$
Female, Best-Seller	5 5 6 6		$(7.38 - 6.75) = 0.63$ $(7.38 - 6.75) = 0.63$ $(7.38 - 6.75) = 0.63$ $(7.38 - 6.75) = 0.63$	0.40 0.40 0.40 0.40
Female, New Product	9 9 9 10	7.38	$(7.38 - 6.75) = 0.63$ $(7.38 - 6.75) = 0.63$ $(7.38 - 6.75) = 0.63$ $(7.38 - 6.75) = 0.63$	0.40 0.40 0.40 0.40
Male, Best Seller	4 5 6 8		$(6.13 - 6.75) = -0.62$ $(6.13 - 6.75) = -0.62$ $(6.13 - 6.75) = -0.62$ $(6.13 - 6.75) = -0.62$	0.38 0.38 0.38 0.38
Male, New Product	6 6 7 7	6.13	$(6.13 - 6.75) = -0.62$ $(6.13 - 6.75) = -0.62$ $(6.13 - 6.75) = -0.62$ $(6.13 - 6.75) = -0.62$	0.38 0.38 0.38 0.38
				Sum of Squares for Gender $(SS_{row\,(gender)}) = 6.24$

We'll do the same thing for our column variable—product type. The table has been slightly rearranged to make it easier to read.

	Liking ratings for each participant in each group (X)	Mean for product type level, $M_{column(product)}$	Subtract grand mean from mean for each level of the variable ($M_{column(product)} - GM$)	Square the deviations, $(M_{column(product)} - GM)^2$
Female, Best-Seller	5 5 6 6		$(5.63 - 6.75) = -1.12$ $(5.63 - 6.75) = -1.12$ $(5.63 - 6.75) = -1.12$ $(5.63 - 6.75) = -1.12$	1.25 1.25 1.25 1.25
Male, Best-Seller	4 5 6 8	5.63	$(5.63 - 6.75) = -1.12$ $(5.63 - 6.75) = -1.12$ $(5.63 - 6.75) = -1.12$ $(5.63 - 6.75) = -1.12$	1.25 1.25 1.25 1.25
Female, New Product	9 9 9 10		$(7.88 - 6.75) = 1.13$ $(7.88 - 6.75) = 1.13$ $(7.88 - 6.75) = 1.13$ $(7.88 - 6.75) = 1.13$	1.28 1.28 1.28 1.28
Male, New Product	6 6 7 7	7.88	$(7.88 - 6.75) = 1.13$ $(7.88 - 6.75) = 1.13$ $(7.88 - 6.75) = 1.13$ $(7.88 - 6.75) = 1.13$	1.28 1.28 1.28 1.28
				Sum of Squares for Gender ($SS_{column\ (product)}$) = 20.24

Our next step is to calculate the within-groups sum of squares, which is the same as what we did for the one-way ANOVA. For each of our 16 scores, we will subtract the cell mean from that individual score, then square and sum the deviations. This has been elaborated in the following table:

	Liking ratings for each participant in each group (X)	Cell Mean (M_{Cell})	Subtract grand mean from each score ($X - M_{Cell}$)	Square the deviations ($X - M_{Cell}$)^2
Female, Best-Seller	5 5 6 6	5.50	(5 − 5.50) = −0.5 (5 − 5.50) = −0.5 (6 − 5.50) = 0.5 (6 − 5.50) = 0.5	0.25 0.25 0.25 0.25
Female, New Product	9 9 9 10	9.25	(9 − 9.25) = −0.25 (9 − 9.25) = −0.25 (9 − 9.25) = −0.25 (10 − 9.25) = 0.75	0.063 0.063 0.063 0.56
Male, Best Seller	4 5 6 8	5.75	(4 − 5.75) = −1.75 (5 − 5.75) = −0.75 (6 − 5.75) = 0.25 (8 − 5.75) = 2.25	3.06 0.56 0.063 5.06
Male, New Product	6 6 7 7	6.50	(6 − 6.50) = −0.5 (6 − 6.50) = −0.5 (7 − 6.50) = 0.5 (7 − 6.50) = 0.5	0.25 0.25 0.25 0.25
				Sum of Squares Within (SS_{within}) = 11.49

We now just have one more sum of squares to calculate—that for the interaction. The simplest way to find this is to remember that the total sum of squares is the sum of the sum of squares for our main effects, the interaction, and within. In other words, $SS_{interaction} = SS_{Total} - (SS_{Rows} + SS_{Columns} + SS_{Within})$. For our example, we can calculate this by: $SS_{interaction} = SS_{Total} - (SS_{Gender} + SS_{Product} + SS_{Within})$ or $SS_{interaction} = 46.96 - (6.24 + 20.24 + 11.49) = 46.96 - (37.97) = 8.99$.

With this information, we can go ahead and put together our source table with all of the various pieces of our puzzle. Remember that to calculate the mean squares for each piece, we'll need to divide each sum of squares by its corresponding degrees of freedom. Each of our F statistics is calculated in the same way as with the one-way ANOVA, that is, by dividing the mean square between by the mean square within.

Source	SS	Df	MS	F
Gender	6.24	1	6.24	6.50
Product	20.24	1	20.24	21.08
Gender × Product	8.99	1	8.99	9.36
Within	11.49	12	0.96	
Total	46.96	15		

Step 6. Make a decision.

As previously mentioned, if any of our test statistics exceeds 4.75, we can reject the null hypothesis. If we can reject the null hypothesis for our interaction, we will want to draw the pattern of our data on a graph which will allow us to interpret our data. If we have more than two levels in any of our groups, we will want to conduct post-hoc tests. In general, we will also focus on the interaction rather than on any significant main effects. However, if the interaction is not statistically significant, we will focus our attention on our main effects.

In our example, all three F statistics exceed 4.75. As a result, we can conclude that the interaction effect is significant as well as both of our main effects. At this point, it is a good idea to graph our findings to visualize what exactly is going on. We can also draw lines to confirm that there is an interaction. If we extend the lines, we would see that the lines intersect.

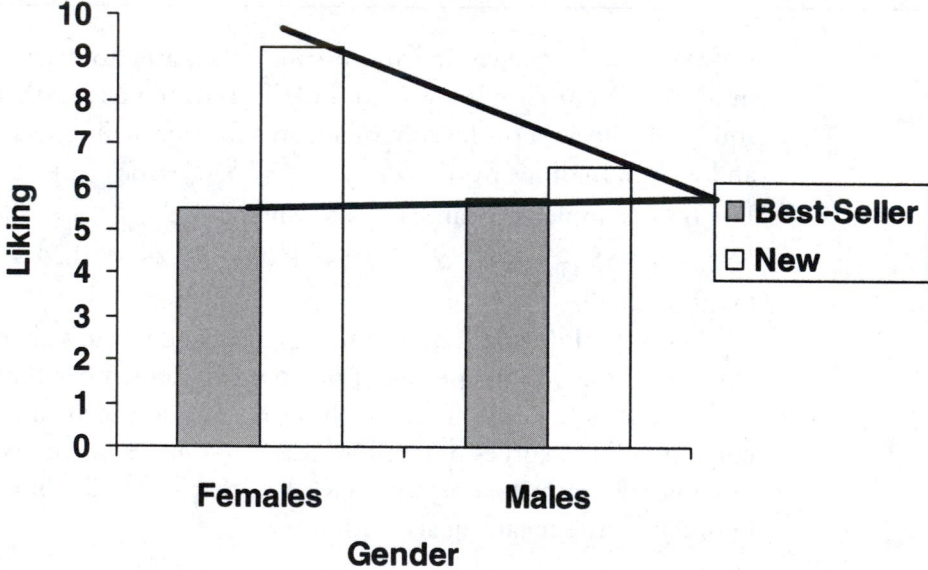

Now that we've done our analyses and confirmed the presence of our interaction through a graph, we can go ahead and interpret the data. So, do our raters prefer the new shampoo and should we market this to men or women? Our main effect for product tells us that overall, our raters did prefer the new product compared to the best-seller. However, this doesn't tell us the whole story. If we look closely at our interaction, female testers especially liked the new product. As a result, we'd be wise to market the new product to women in particular if we want to sell the most shampoo!

> Interactions: A More Precise Interpretation

In the previous section, we reviewed the traditional method for interpreting interactions. In this section, we'll discuss a more precise method. The traditional method involves reporting the cell means; however, it is more precise when examining interactions to remove the contributions of the two main effects before interpreting the interaction.

Using this new method, we calculate the **residuals**—what is left after the main effects have been removed. To do this involves the following three steps:

1. Subtract the grand mean from each of the marginal means for the rows and then for each of the marginal means of the columns. This will leave us with row effects and column effects.
2. Subtract the row effects and column effects from the cell means, which results in the removal of the main effects.
3. Subtract the grand mean from each of the cell means.

Let's go through our previous example to interpret the interaction using the new method:

	Best-Seller	New Product	Marginal Means
Female	5.50	9.25	7.38
Male	5.75	6.50	6.13
Marginal Means	5.63	7.88	6.75

Now that all of the means are in our table, let's take step one and subtract the grand mean (6.75) from each of our marginal means to determine our row and column effects:

	Best-Seller	New Product	Marginal Means	Row Effects
Female	5.50	9.25	7.38	0.63
Male	5.75	6.50	6.13	−0.62
Marginal Means	5.63	7.88	6.75	
Column Effects	−1.12	1.13		

In our second step, we subtract the row effects and column effects from each of the cell means:

	Best-Seller	New Product	Marginal Means	Row Effects
Female	5.99	7.49	7.38	0.63
Male	7.49	5.99	6.13	−0.62
Marginal Means	5.63	7.88	6.75	
Column Effects	−1.12	1.13		

Finally, we subtract the grand mean from these new cell means:

	Best-Seller	New Product	Marginal Means	Row Effects
Female	**−0.76**	**0.74**	7.38	0.63
Male	**0.74**	**−0.76**	6.13	−0.62
Marginal Means	5.63	7.88	6.75	
Column Effects	−1.12	1.13		

To graph the interaction, we should go back one step and graph the means once we have subtracted the row and column effects but not the grand mean:

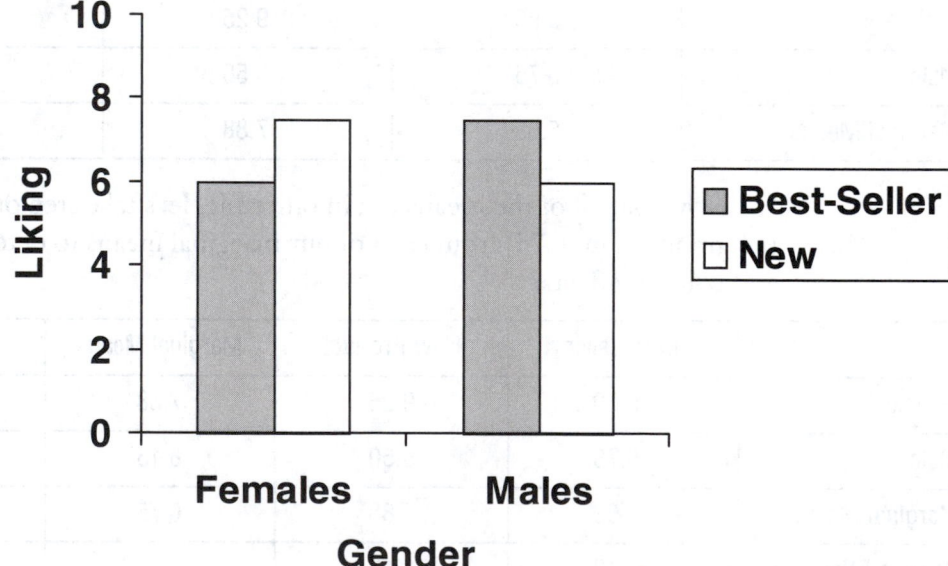

> **Digging Deeper into the Data: Variations on ANOVA**

In this chapter, two-way ANOVAs have been the focus. However, there are several variations on the ANOVA that can be used. First, the authors refer to the **mixed-design ANOVA,** which is an ANOVA that uses at least one within-groups independent variable and one between-groups independent variable. For this design, the independent variables should be nominal variables and the dependent variables should be interval variables. If you remember, within-groups designs refer to research designs in which participants experience all research conditions.

For example, imagine that we want to test a new drug for depression to see if it improves mood. We measure mood before and after administration of the drug. We also want to see if the time of day (morning or evening) affects mood. So, some people will be instructed to take the drug in the morning and others will be instructed to take it at night. This would be an example of a mixed-design ANOVA because there is a between-groups variable (when participants take the drug: morning or evening) and a within-groups variable that everyone experiences (before administration of the drug and after administration of the drug).

However, variations on the ANOVA don't stop at mixed-design ANOVAs. If we have a design with more than one dependent variable, we would use a **multivariate analysis of variance (MANOVA)**. A regular ANOVA can look at multiple independent variables but not at multiple dependent variables. When using a MANOVA, we want our multiple dependent variables to be related in some way. For example, if we're testing that new depression drug, we could look at a variety of measures related to positive mood such as ratings of happiness, excitement, and joy.

Another type variation of an ANOVA is an **analysis of covariance (ANCOVA)**. We use an ANCOVA when we worry that a third-interval variable or **covariate** might be affecting our dependent variable. The ANCOVA allows us to statistically remove the effect of the third variable from our analysis. Examples of covariates include age, years of education, or household income. A **multivariate analysis of covariance (MANCOVA)** is just like the ANCOVA, except we're now looking at multiple dependent variables, just like our MANOVA.

In order to sort out all of these different statistical tests, your text includes the following table:

TABLE 11-24. VARIATIONS ON ANOVA

There are many variations on ANOVA that allow us to analyze a variety of research designs. A MANOVA allows us to include more than one dependent variable. An ANCOVA allows us to include covariates to correct for third variables that might influence our study. A MANCOVA allows us to include both more than one dependent variable and a covariate.

	INDEPENDENT VARIABLES	DEPENDENT VARIABLES	COVARIATE
ANOVA	Any number	Only one	None
MANOVA	Any number	More than one	None
ANCOVA	Any number	Only one	At least one
MANCOVA	Any number	More than one	At least one

STUDY QUESTIONS

1. A **two-way ANOVA** includes:
   a. one independent variable with at least two levels.
   b. one independent variable with no more than two levels.
   c. two independent variables.
   d. two dependent variables.

2. A study comparing freshmen, sophomores, juniors, and seniors on some dependent measure:
   a. has four independent variables.
   b. would be termed a four-way factorial ANOVA.
   c. is a two-way ANOVA, with two levels of each independent variable.
   d. has one independent variable with four levels.

3. Langer, Blank, and Chanowitz (1978) conducted a field experiment in which a confederate of the researchers approached individuals who were about to make copies in a university library with a request to allow them to make copies first. In making the request, the confederate stated that she or he needed to make either (1) 5 copies or (2) 20 copies and accompanied the request with either (1) no information, (2) "placebic" information ("because I have to make copies"), or (3) "real" information ("because I am in a rush"). Langer et al. were interested in the extent to which people would comply with the confederate's request under these conditions. How many independent variables are in this study?
   a. 1
   b. 2
   c. 3
   d. 5

4. A **factorial analysis of variance:**
   a. includes at least one nominal independent variable.
   b. includes at least three levels of each independent variable in the analysis.
   c. examines the effects of two or more independent variables in one study.
   d. uses factor analysis to examine the effect of an experimental manipulation.

5. The advantage of a two-way ANOVA over conducting separate one-way ANOVAs is that it allows the researcher to:
   a. study more variables using fewer participants.
   b. study the effects of combining two or more variables.
   c. save money by assigning participants to more than one group.
   d. combine independent and dependent variables in one experiment.

6. Each unique combination of levels of the factors in a factorial design is called a(n):
   a. marginal mean.
   b. interaction.
   c. cell.
   d. factor.

7. The following shows the design of the Langer, Blank, and Chanowitz (1978) field experiment:

Information Accompanying Request

		No Information	Placebic Information	Real Information
Size of Request	Small (5 copies)	$n = 15$	$n = 15$	$n = 16$
	Large (20 Copies)	$n = 25$	$n = 25$	$n = 24$

The statistical procedure used to analyze the results of this study is most accurately described as a:
   a. one-way between-groups ANOVA.
   b. one-way within-groups ANOVA.
   c. 3 × 2 between-groups ANOVA.
   d. 3 × 2 within-groups ANOVA.

8. Niedenthal and Setterlund (1994) used a factorial design to study the effects of word type (*happy, positive, neutral, negative,* and *sad*) and mood (*happy, sad*) on decision latencies in a lexical decision task. How many cells are in this design?
   a. 2
   b. 5
   c. 7
   d. 10

9. A **main effect** is observed when:
   a. one of the independent variables has an influence on the dependent variable.
   b. the effect of one variable is much greater than the effect(s) of the other variable(s).
   c. at least one cell mean is significantly different from at least one other cell mean.
   d. there is no interaction effect.

10. An **interaction** occurs when:
   a. the independent variables influence each other but not the dependent variable.
   b. only one independent variable has an effect on the dependent variable.
   c. the effect of one variable depends on the level of another variable.
   d. both independent variables affect the dependent variable.

11. How many main and interaction effects are possible in a 2 × 3 factorial ANOVA?
    a. 2 main effects and 1 interaction effect
    b. 2 main effects and 3 interaction effects
    c. 3 main effects and 2 interaction effects
    d. 6 main effects and 2 interaction effects

12. Consider the following table of means:

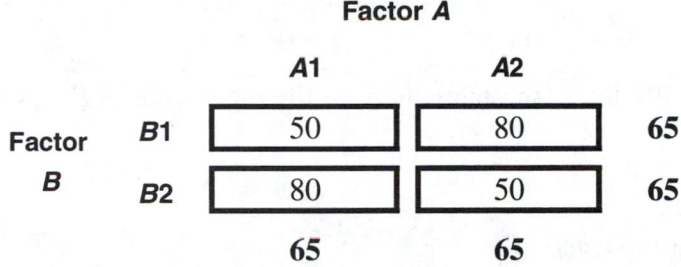

    The table shows that the effect of Factor *A* reverses direction across the levels of Factor *B*. This pattern would be most specifically described as a:
    a. main effect of Factor *A*, but no main effect of Factor *B*.
    b. main effect of Factor *B*, but no main effect of Factor *A*.
    c. quantitative interaction effect.
    d. qualitative interaction effect.

13. Consider the following table of means:

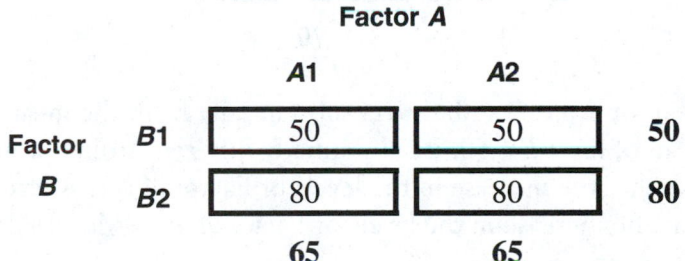

    The row and column means are:
    a. used to identify the presence of a quantitative interaction.
    b. used to identify the presence of a qualitative interaction.
    c. called marginal means.
    d. called cell means.

14. Consider the following table of means:

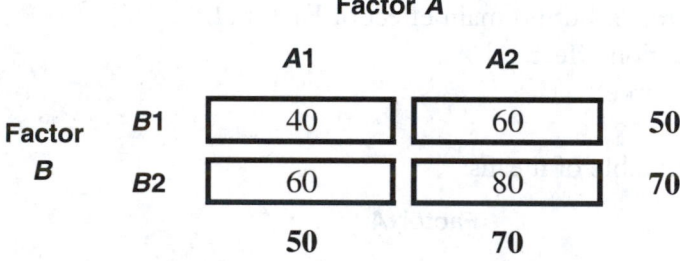

Factor A

		A1	A2	
Factor	B1	50	50	50
B	B2	80	80	80
		65	65	

The mean of level B1 (50) differs substantially from the mean of level B2 (80), indicating a(n):

a.   main effect of Factor A.
b.   main effect of Factor B.
c.   interaction between the levels of Factor A.
d.   interaction between the levels of Factor B.

15. Consider the following table of means:

Factor A

		A1	A2	
Factor	B1	40	60	50
B	B2	60	80	70
		50	70	

Notice that the mean of level $A1$ (50) differs substantially from the mean of level $A2$ (70), just as the mean of level $B1$ (50) is substantially different from the mean of level $B2$ (70). Notice also that the increase in the levels of Factor A across level $B1$ (from 40 to 60) is the same as the increase in the levels of Factor A across level $B2$ (from 60 to 80). This pattern of means indicates:

a.   the main effects of Factors A and B but no interaction.
b.   the main effects of Factors A and B and an interaction.
c.   a quantitative interaction but no main effects.
d.   a qualitative interaction but no main effects.

16. Consider the following table of means:

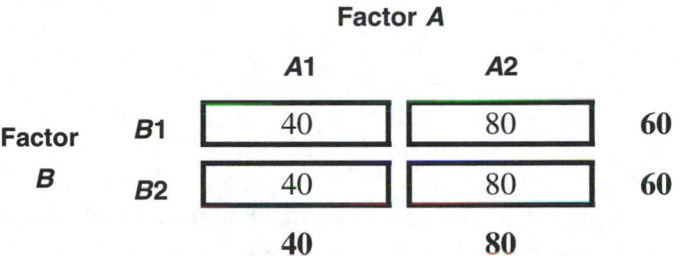

Factor A

		A1	**A2**	
Factor	**B1**	40	80	**60**
B	**B2**	40	80	**60**
		40	**80**	

Notice that the mean of level $A1$ (40) differs substantially from the mean of level $A2$ (80), but the mean of level $B1$ (60) is the same as the mean of level $B2$ (60). Notice also that the increase in the levels of Factor A across level $B1$ (from 40 to 80) is the same as the increase in the levels of Factor A across level $B2$ (from 40 to 80). This pattern of means indicates:

a. the main effects of Factors A and B but no interaction.
b. the main effects of Factors A and B and an interaction.
c. a main effect of Factor A, but no other effects.
d. an interaction, but no other effects.

17. Consider the following table of means:

Factor A

		A1	**A2**	
Factor	**B1**	40	80	**60**
B	**B2**	60	80	**70**
		50	**80**	

Notice that the mean of level $A1$ (50) differs substantially from the mean of level $A2$ (80), and the mean of level $B1$ (60) differs quite a bit from the mean of level $B2$ (70). Notice also that the increase in the levels of Factor A across level $B1$ (from 40 to 80) is not the same as the increase in the levels of Factor A across level $B2$ (from 60 to 80). This pattern of means indicates:

a. the main effects of Factors A and B but no interaction.
b. the main effects of Factors A and B and an interaction.
c. a main effect of Factor A, but no other effects.
d. a main effect of Factor B, but no other effects.

18. You should inspect the _____ means to determine whether there is likely to be an interaction in a two-way ANOVA.
    a. row
    b. column
    c. pattern of cell
    d. row and column

19. The following figure displays a hypothetical result of a study in which students read a brief description of a woman before they use a scale to rate the likelihood that the woman would be sexually harassed. The independent variables were the gender of the student rater and the length of the woman's hair ("short" vs. "mid-length" vs. "long").

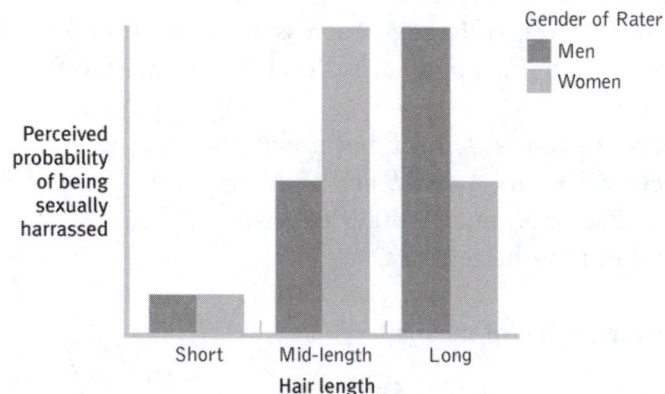

Identify the effect(s) displayed in the figure.
    a. There is a main effect of gender but no other effects.
    b. There is a main effect of hair length but no other effects.
    c. There are main effects of both gender and hair length but no interaction.
    d. There is an interaction but no main effects.

20. The following figure displays a hypothetical result of a study in which students read a brief description of a woman before they use a scale to rate the likelihood that the woman would be sexually harassed. The independent variables were the gender of the student rater and the length of the woman's hair ("short" vs. "mid-length" vs. "long").

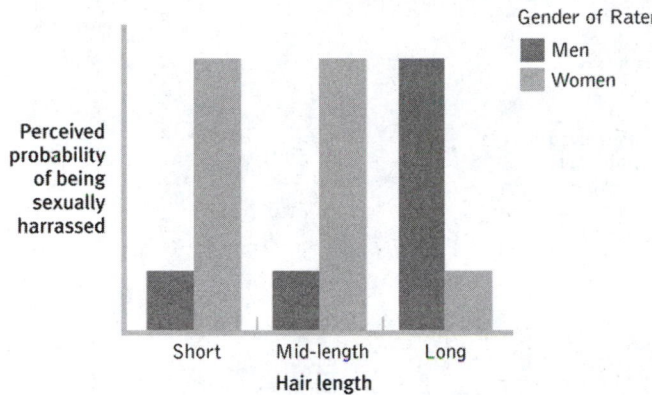

Identify the effect(s) displayed in the figure.
a. There is a main effect of gender and an interaction.
b. There is a main effect of hair length and an interaction.
c. There are main effects of both gender and hair length but no interaction.
d. There is an interaction but no main effects.

21. The following figure displays a hypothetical result of a study in which students read a brief description of a woman before they use a scale to rate the likelihood that the woman would be sexually harassed. The independent variables were the gender of the student rater and the length of the woman's hair ("short" vs. "mid-length" vs. "long").

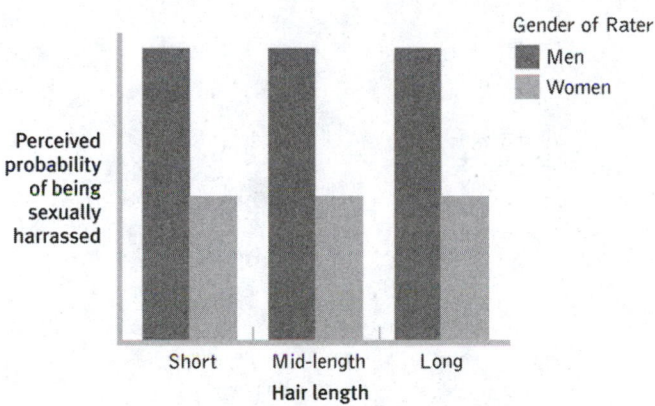

Identify the effect(s) displayed in the figure.
a. There is a main effect of hair length but no other effects.
b. There is a main effect of gender but no other effects.
c. There are main effects of both gender and hair length but no interaction.
d. There is an interaction but no main effects.

22. The following figure displays a hypothetical result of a study in which students read a brief description of a woman before they use a scale to rate the likelihood that the woman would be sexually harassed. The independent variables were the gender of the student rater and the length of the woman's hair ("short" vs. "mid-length" vs. "long").

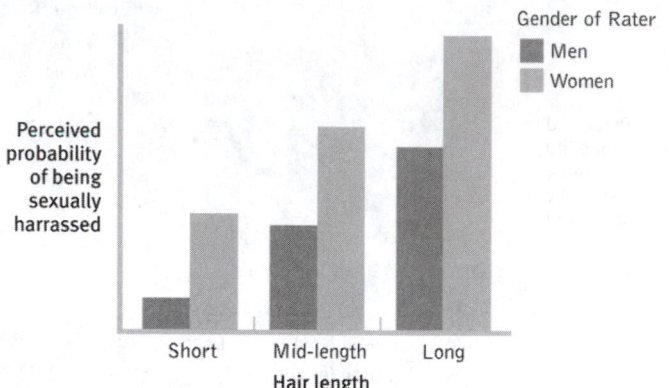

Identify the effect(s) displayed in the figure.
a. There is a main effect of gender but no other effects.
b. There is a main effect of hair length but no other effects.
c. There are main effects of both gender and hair length but no interaction.
d. There is an interaction but no main effects.

23. The following figure displays a hypothetical result of a study in which students read a brief description of a woman before they use a scale to rate the likelihood that the woman would be sexually harassed. The independent variables were the gender of the student rater and the length of the woman's hair ("short" vs. "mid-length" vs. "long").

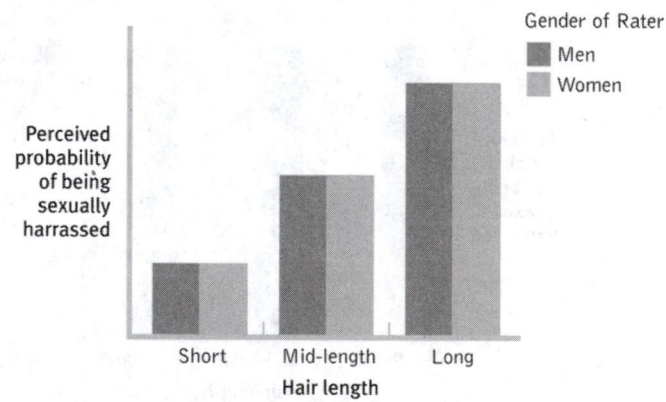

Identify the effect(s) displayed in the figure.
a. There is a main effect of gender but no other effects.
b. There is a main effect of hair length but no other effects.
c. There is a main effect of hair length and an interaction.
d. There are no main effects and no interaction.

24. In a two-factor ANOVA, there is (are) _____ hypothesis(es) to be tested.
    a. one
    b. two
    c. three
    d. The number of hypotheses depends on the number of levels of each factor.

25. The following table shows the number of participants in each cell of the 3 × 2 factorial design used by Langer et al. (1978):

Information Accompanying Request

		No Information	Placebic Information	Real Information
Size of Request	Small (5 copies)	$n = 15$	$n = 15$	$n = 16$
	Large (20 Copies)	$n = 25$	$n = 25$	$n = 24$

Which one of the following is the correct method of determining, and the correct number of, degrees of freedom for the effect of the information (column) factor?
    a. number of cells – number of columns = 6 – 3 = 3
    b. (number of columns – 1) (number of rows – 1) = (2) (1) = 2
    c. number of cells – 1 = 6 – 1 = 5
    d. number of columns – 1 = 3 – 1 = 2

26. The following table shows the number of participants in each cell of the 3 × 2 factorial design used by Langer et al. (1978):

Information Accompanying Request

		No Information	Placebic Information	Real Information
Size of Request	Small (5 copies)	$n = 15$	$n = 15$	$n = 16$
	Large (20 Copies)	$n = 25$	$n = 25$	$n = 24$

Which one of the following is the correct method of determining, and the correct number of, degrees of freedom for the information × request interaction?
    a. number of cells – number of columns = 6 – 3 = 3
    b. (number of columns – 1) (number of rows – 1) = (2) (1) = 2
    c. number of cells – 1 = 6 – 1 = 5
    d. number of columns – 1 = 3 – 1 = 2

27. The following table shows the number of participants in each cell of the 3 × 2 factorial design used by Langer et al. (1978):

		Information Accompanying Request		
		No Information	Placebic Information	Real Information
Size of Request	Small (5 copies)	$n = 15$	$n = 15$	$n = 16$
	Large (20 Copies)	$n = 25$	$n = 25$	$n = 24$

Which one of the following is the correct method of determining, and the correct number of, the within-groups degrees of freedom?
a. Find the cell with the smallest number of participants and multiply this value by the number of cells: (15) (6) = 90.
b. Subtract 1 from the number of participants in each cell and sum: 14 + 14 + 15 + 24 + 24 + 23 = 114.
c. Average the number of participants in each cell: (15 + 15 + 16 + 25 + 25 + 24) / 6 = 120 / 6 = 20.
d. Sum the number of participants in the cells and subtract 1: 120 − 1 = 119.

28. How many sources of variability are in a two-way ANOVA?
a. four
b. three
c. two
d. The number varies, depending on the number of levels of each factor.

29. Analysis of Variance Source Table for the Langer et al. (1978) Study:

Source	SS	df	MS	F	p
Information	1.288	2	0.644	3.593	0.031
Request	7.805	1	7.805	43.563	0.000
Information X Request	0.521	2	0.261	1.454	0.238
Error	20.424	114	0.179		
Total	60.000	120			

Refer to the previous table. Which of the following describes the results?
a. There are two main effects and an interaction.
b. There are two main effects.
c. There is one main effect.
d. There is an interaction.

30. With respect to interactions, the term _____ refers to what is left after the effects of the two independent variables have been removed.
    a. degrees of freedom
    b. residual
    c. error
    d. marginal mean

31. The term **mixed-design ANOVA** refers to a factorial design that includes:
    a. at least one manipulated factor and at least one nonmanipulated factor.
    b. one or more between-groups factors and one or more within-groups factors.
    c. one or more nominal independent variables and one or more interval independent variables.
    d. at least one qualitative interaction and at least one quantitative interaction.

32. A **multivariate analysis of variance** is used to analyze the data from a study that includes:
    a. multiple independent variables and one dependent variable.
    b. one within-subjects variable and several between-subjects variables.
    c. one between-subjects variable and several within-subjects variables.
    d. at least one independent variable and more than one dependent variable.

33. As she was designing a study of the effects of three types of reinforcement on learning in children, a developmental psychologist realized that older children would learn more material at a faster rate than younger children, so she decided to hold age constant by including this interval variable in a type of ANOVA called a(n):
    a. analysis of covariance.
    b. multivariate analysis of variance.
    c. mixed-design ANOVA.
    d. within-groups ANOVA.

Refer to the following study description to answer the next two review questions.

Study Description. In a study by Lambert, Khan, Lickel, and Fricke (1997), participants were asked to play the role of a job interviewer and form a preliminary evaluation of the fitness of a job applicant for the position of flight attendant. More specifically, each participant read a description of the job followed by a vita of the applicant that included personal information as well as a prominently displayed black and white photograph of an attractive woman in her twenties. After reading the job description and the vita, each participant used a 10-point scale to rate the likelihood that he or she would hire the applicant. Half of the participants rated the applicant after being asked to imagine a personal episode of their lives that made them feel very sad whenever they thought of it and half rated the applicant in a mood-neutral condition. In addition, half of the participants in each mood condition (sad versus neutral) rated the applicant based on a job description that emphasized customer relations and the positive role of physical attractiveness in passenger satisfaction (stereotype-appropriate condition), while the other half made their ratings based on a job description that emphasized rational and analytical problem-solving skills (stereotype-inappropriate condition).

34. Refer to the **Study Description**.

Mood

		Sad	Neutral	
Job Description	Stereotype-Appropriate	8.4	6.8	**7.6**
	Stereotype-Inappropriate	6.4	4.6	**5.5**
		7.4	**5.7**	

The table of means shows that sad participants were more willing to hire the applicant than mood-neutral participants, and participants who read the job description that valued physical attractiveness (the stereotype-appropriate job description) were also more willing to hire the applicant than participants who read the job description that valued analytical, problem-solving skills (the stereotype-inappropriate job description). However, these effects do not influence each other; that is, the effect of being sad on the likelihood-of-hiring ratings is not altered by the appropriateness of the stereotype for the job description and vice versa. This is an example of:

a. a main effect of mood but no other effects.

b. a main effect of job description but no other effects.

c. main effects of mood and job description but no interaction.

d. an interaction between mood and job description but with no main effects.

35. Refer to the **Study Description**.

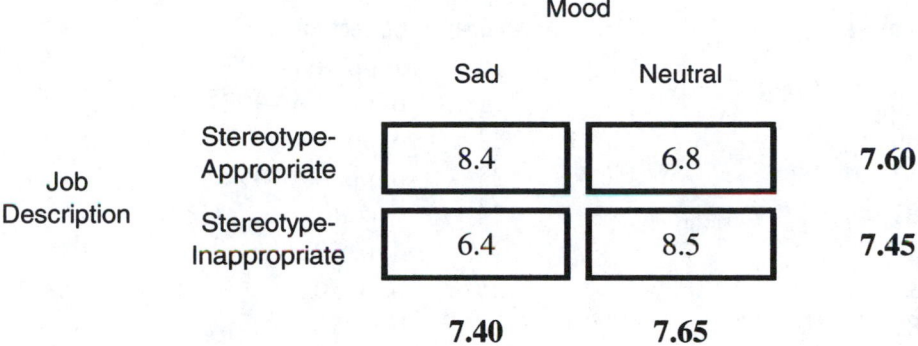

		Mood		
		Sad	Neutral	
Job Description	Stereotype-Appropriate	8.4	6.8	**7.60**
	Stereotype-Inappropriate	6.4	8.5	**7.45**
		7.40	**7.65**	

The table of means shows that sad participants were less likely to hire the applicant when the stereotype was inappropriate (the job description valued analytical problem-solving skills), whereas the participants in a neutral mood were more likely to hire the applicant when the stereotype was inappropriate. This is an example of:

a. a qualitative interaction but no main effects.

b. a quantitative interaction but no main effects.

c. two main effects but no interaction.

d. the effects of the factors canceling each other, so there are no effects of any kind.

ANSWERS TO CHAPTER 11 STUDY QUESTIONS

Question Number	Correct Answer	Question Number	Correct Answer
1	c, p. 480	20	a, pp. 496–497
2	d, p. 480	21	b, pp. 496–497
3	b, p. 480	22	c, pp. 496–497
4	c, p. 480	23	b, pp. 496–497
5	b, p. 481	24	c, p. 499
6	c, p. 482	25	d, p. 502
7	c, p. 482	26	b, p. 502
8	d, p. 482	27	b, p. 502
9	a, p. 483	28	a, pp. 504–505
10	c, p. 484	29	b, pp. 507–508
11	a, pp. 483–484	30	b, p. 511
12	d, p. 488	31	b, p. 515
13	c, p. 488	32	d, p. 516
14	b, p. 488	33	a, p. 517
15	b, pp. 488–494	34	c (review of main and interaction effects)
16	c, pp. 488–494	35	a (review of main and interaction effects)
17	b, pp. 488–494		
18	c, p. 494		
19	d, pp. 496–497		

CHAPTER TWELVE

BEYOND HYPOTHESIS TESTING

Confidence Intervals, Effect Size, and Power

CHAPTER OUTLINE

Beyond Hypothesis Testing: Reducing Misinterpretations
- Men, Women, and Math: An Accurate Understanding of Differences
- Beyond Hypothesis Testing: The "Telling" Details in Our Samples' Stories

Confidence Intervals: An Alternative to Hypothesis Testing
- Interval Estimation: A Range of Plausible Means
- z Distributions: Calculating Confidence Intervals
- t Distributions: Calculating Confidence Intervals

Effect Size: Just How Big is the Difference?
- Misunderstandings from Hypothesis Testing: When "Significant" Isn't Very Significant
- What Effect Size Is: Standardization Across Studies
- Cohen's d: The Effect Size for a z Test or a t Test
- R^2: The Effect Size for ANOVA

Statistical Power and Sensitivity: Correctly Rejecting the Null Hypothesis
- Calculation of Statistical Power: How Sensitive is a z Test?
- Beyond Sample Size: Other Factors that Affect Statistical Power

Digging Deeper into the Data: Meta-Analysis
- Meta-Analysis: A Study of Studies
- The Steps for Calculating a Meta-Analysis
- The File Drawer Statistic: What Are All the Null Results?

LEARNING OBJECTIVES

After studying this chapter, you should be able to:

1. Define each of the following terms and provide examples that are not in the text: *point estimate, interval estimate, confidence interval, effect size, Cohen's d, R^2, statistical power, alpha, Institutional Review Board (IRB), meta-analysis,* and *file drawer statistic.*

2. Distinguish between *statistical significance* and *practical importance* and discuss this distinction with regard to the issue of gender differences in mathematics reasoning ability.

3. Discuss the concept of *confidence intervals* as an estimation procedure as well as an alternative to traditional hypothesis testing. Include in your discussion references to point and interval estimates and relate the level of confidence to the *p* level used in hypothesis testing.
4. Explain the relation between a confidence interval and the phrase "margin of error" that frequently accompanies media reports of political poll results.
5. Calculate a 95% confidence interval for a single-sample *z* test and an independent-samples *t* test.
6. Discuss the concept of *effect size* and include in your discussion a distinction between the *size* of an effect and the *statistical significance* of an effect. In addition, you should know how to compute effect size statistics for *z* and *t* tests (Cohen's *d* statistic) and an analysis of variance (the R^2 statistic).
7. Discuss the concept of *statistical power*, including its (a) formal definition, (b) relation to the probability of committing either a Type I or Type II error; (c) calculation for a single-sample *z* test; and (d) susceptibility to the influence of effect size (as determined by the difference between population means as well as the size of the population standard deviation), sample size, alpha (the *p* level), and one-tailed vs. two-tailed tests.
8. Explain how a researcher would conduct a *meta-analysis* of research reports on a given topic of interest.

CHAPTER REVIEW

> **Beyond Hypothesis Testing: Reducing Misinterpretations**

A research outcome that is *statistically significant* may be of substantial or very limited *practical importance*. A statistically significant difference between two sample means (e.g., a gender difference between the mean scores on a standardized test of math reasoning ability) is simply a difference that has a very low probability of having occurred by chance. However, the difference may be so small as to be of almost no practical importance. Benbow and Stanley (1980) found a statistically significant difference in mean scores on the quantitative subtest of the SAT in a sample of approximately 10,000 male and female students in the 7th through the 10th grades who were tested as part of a national talent search (for a more complete discussion, see pp. 529–531 in the text). A sample size this large virtually guarantees that even a tiny difference between the mean scores in the samples of male and female students will be found to be statistically significant. So, do not assume that a result labeled "statistically significant" is also high in practical significance. Such results may, or may not, be noteworthy in terms of informing policy decisions.

> Confidence Intervals: An Alternative to Hypothesis Testing

You were introduced to the six steps of hypothesis testing in Chapter 8. Recall that the most basic hypothesis test, a z test, involved converting a sample mean to a z statistic to determine the probability of observing a sample mean as extreme as the one observed under the assumption that the null hypothesis is true. The z test provided an answer to the question, "What is the probability of observing a sample mean at least this extreme if the population mean is the value specified by the null hypothesis?" If the z statistic was associated with a probability (p value) less than or equal to the p level (usually 0.05), then the null hypothesis was rejected. More specifically, the null hypothesized value of the population mean was rejected as the true value of the mean of the population represented by the sample.

Now compare the strategy of hypothesis testing with a different strategy—one in which a researcher wishes to estimate the true value of the mean of the population with no specific null-hypothesized value in mind. The research question is, "What is the value of the population mean?" instead of "Can I reject the null–hypothesized value of the population mean?" The best answer to this question is what statisticians call the *expected value* of the population mean. The expected value of the population mean is the sample mean, so the researcher's best estimate of the value of the population mean is the sample mean. The sample mean is termed a **point estimate**, because it may be located as a point on the scale used to measure the dependent variable. To quote the text, a point estimate is "just one number" used to estimate the population parameter (p. 534). Of course, the researcher knows that she would almost certainly compute a different sample mean each time she selected a sample from this population, so each use of the sample mean as a point estimate of the population mean is accompanied by error. In Chapter 7, you learned that the comparison distribution of sample means is the distribution of all possible means of samples of a given size (denoted by N) from the population of interest. You also learned that the mean of the distribution of sample means (μ_M) is equal to the mean of the population (μ) and you learned to calculate the standard error (μ_M) as the standard deviation of this distribution of sample means. Now, perhaps it is easier to see why the standard error is conceptualized as an "error"; it is a measure of error associated with using the sample mean as a point estimate of the population mean.

The researcher could accompany the sample mean with the standard error and thereby provide an **interval estimate** of the unknown value of the population mean. She could report, for example, that her best estimate of the population mean is given by the interval $M \pm \sigma_M$. From Chapter 7, you know that approximately 68% of the sample means in the comparison distribution are within 1 standard error of the population mean. This means that the interval $M \pm \sigma_M$ will include the unknown value of the population mean in about 68% of the samples from the population. This is not the same as saying that there is a 68% chance that any one particular interval includes the population mean. The population mean is a fixed value, so it is either in a given interval or it isn't. The thing that varies from sample to sample is the interval, not the population mean. So, instead of saying that there is about a 68% chance that any specific $M \pm \sigma_M$ interval includes the population mean, we would say that 68% of all $M \pm \sigma_M$ intervals derived from samples of this size from this population will include the population mean.

But why limit ourselves to an interval that will include ("cover" or "trap") the population mean just 68% of the time? To increase our confidence that the interval constructed around the sample mean includes the population mean, we could extend the interval an additional standard error in each direction. Now, we could say that roughly 95% of the intervals that extend from $M - 2\sigma_M$ to $M + 2\sigma_M$ will include the population mean. This is, in fact, the convention adopted by statisticians and researchers, with one small adjustment. The level of confidence is specified to be exactly, rather than approximately, 95%. And the interval is, appropriately enough, called a **confidence interval**. To make the interval a 95% confidence interval, the standard error is multiplied by 1.96 instead of 2. You may recall from Chapter 8 that 1.96 and −1.96 were introduced as the critical values of z that define, or "cut off," the upper and lower 2.5% of the sample means in the comparison distribution. The values +1.96 and −1.96 are thus the critical values of z for a two–tailed test of any null hypothesis conducted at a p level of 0.05. This means that a given level of confidence is the additive inverse of the p level used in traditional hypothesis testing. For the frequently used p level of 0.05 (5%),

Level of confidence = 100% − p level = 100% − 5% = 95%

So now, instead of testing a single null-hypothesized value of the population mean, you can construct an interval using a sampling procedure that includes the actual value of the population mean 95% of the time. The upshot is this: Any null-hypothesized value of the population mean that is *not* within a given confidence interval may be rejected at the 0.05 p level.

In constructing a 95% confidence interval, you are in effect saying the following: "I know that the chances are not good that my sample mean will have the same value as the true population mean. I am simply using my sample mean as an *estimate* of the true value of population mean. However, if I construct a 95% confidence interval around my sample mean, I will have an interval that was produced by a sampling procedure that includes the true, but unknown, value of the population mean 95% of the time. I am 95% confident because the interval will extend exactly 1.96 standard errors above and below my sample mean, and for all normal distributions of sample means, 95% of the means are within 1.96 standard errors of the center of the distribution."

Here is an example. You (for this exercise you are a licensed clinical psychologist) may think that the IQ of the average college student is higher than 100, the scale score identified as the average IQ score in the general population. The standard deviation is arbitrarily assigned to be 15 on the Wechsler Adult Intelligence Scale (WAIS) and 16 on the Stanford-Binet IQ test. We'll use the WAIS value of 15 as the population standard deviation, that is, $\sigma = 15$. So, rather than test the null hypothesis which states that the IQ of the average college student is the same as the mean IQ in the general population ($\mu_{College\ Students} = \mu_{General\ Population} = 100$), you decide to gather a sample of 36 college students, administer the WAIS to them, compute the sample mean IQ score, and use this sample mean to construct a 95% confidence interval.

You compute the sample mean IQ score and find that it is 109—i.e., $M = 109$. Now you are ready to construct the limits of a 95% confidence interval.

1. Compute the standard error of the mean (the standard deviation of the comparison distribution of sample means). This is the population standard deviation (15) divided by the square root of the sample size (36). So, the standard error (σ_M) is 15 / 6 = 2.5.

2. You are constructing a 95% confidence interval, so the values of z are -1.96 and $+1.96$. (For a 90% confidence interval, the two z values would be -1.645 and $+1.645$; for a 99% confidence interval, the two values of z would be -2.58 and $+2.58$.)

3. The upper limit of the confidence interval is $1.96(\sigma_M) + M$; thus,

$$M_{Upper} = 1.96(2.5) + 109 = 4.9 + 109 = 113.9.$$

4. The lower limit of the confidence interval is $-1.96(\sigma_M) + M$; thus,

$$M_{Lower} = -1.96(2.5) + 109 = -4.9 + 109 = 104.1.$$

If the value of the population mean specified by the null hypothesis (100) is within the CI, then the null hypothesis may *not* be rejected. In this example, however, the null hypothesis may be rejected, because 100 is not within the limits of the confidence interval. Neither is 115, nor 95, nor 120, nor 102, within the interval, so we may reject all of these values as well, if they were specified by other null hypotheses. Being able to simultaneously reject a large number of null-hypothesized values of a population parameter is an advantage of using a confidence interval over traditional hypothesis testing.

The level of confidence in any particular interval estimate is based on the long-run relative frequency interpretation of probability. More specifically, to say that we are 95% confident that a given interval includes the true value of the mean IQ score in the population of college students is to say that 95% of the confidence intervals constructed from samples of this size from this population include the true value of the population mean. This is worth repeating: If a very large number of studies were conducted just as this one was, and a 95% confidence interval were constructed for each sample, then about 95% of these confidence intervals would include the value of the population mean. One more time: For 95% of all samples of this size that are selected in this way, the interval from 1.96 standard errors below the sample mean to 1.96 standard errors above the sample mean will include the population mean.

To review a point made earlier, please note that it is incorrect to state the probability is 0.95 that any specific confidence interval contains the true value of the population mean. The population parameter is a fixed value and does not vary from sample-to-sample as the confidence interval does. Each time we sample from a population and construct a confidence interval based on a new sample mean, the limits of the interval change. It should be clear that different intervals could not all have the same probability of including the population mean. Any correct probability statement must refer to the sampling process, not to any one interval. The level of confidence we have in any one interval is based on a very large number of repetitions of the sampling process. For a 95% confidence interval, this *process* has a 0.95 probability of producing an interval that will include the true value of the population mean. In other words, if this sampling process were repeated *a very large number of times*, each time resulting in a new mean around which is constructed a new confidence interval, then we can say (with confidence) that *approximately* 95% of these confidence intervals will include the true value of the population mean. If this sampling process were repeated *an infinitely large number of times*, then *exactly* 95% of the confidence intervals constructed as this one was would include the true value of the population mean.

Here is a second example. Suppose that a polling organization obtained a representative sample of 1,000 likely voters, and 480 of them said they would vote for a particular candidate. A statistician employed by the polling organization may then determine the lower and upper limits of a 95% confidence interval for the percentage of voters in the population who favor this candidate as follows:

$$M_{Lower} = -z(\sigma_M) + M_{Sample} = -1.96(.0158) + 0.48 = 0.449, \text{ or } \mathbf{44.9\%}$$

$$M_{Upper} = z(\sigma_M) + M_{Sample} = 1.96(.0158) + 0.48 = 0.511, \text{ or } \mathbf{51.1\%}$$

where,

$M_{Sample} = p$, the proportion of voters in the sample favoring the candidate[1]

$$\sigma_M = \sqrt{\frac{p(1-p)}{N}}$$

A media report would typically include the percentage of likely voters favoring the candidate as well as the margin of error. The *margin of error* is $z(\sigma M)$ or one half of the confidence interval. In the previous example, the margin of error is 1.96(.0158) = .031, or 3.1%. The poll result would thus be reported as 48% with a margin of error of 3.1% (or 48 ± 3.1%). If the same poll found that a competing candidate was favored by 45% of likely voters,

---

[1] In a sample of values that includes only 0 (does not favor the candidate) and 1 (favors the candidate), the proportion of voters favoring the candidate is the mean of the sample.

then the candidates would be said to be in a "statistical tie." This term refers to the fact that the difference between the percentages of likely voters favoring the two candidates is less than the margin of error. The figure below shows a 95% confidence interval centered around the sample percentage of voters favoring the hypothetical candidate.

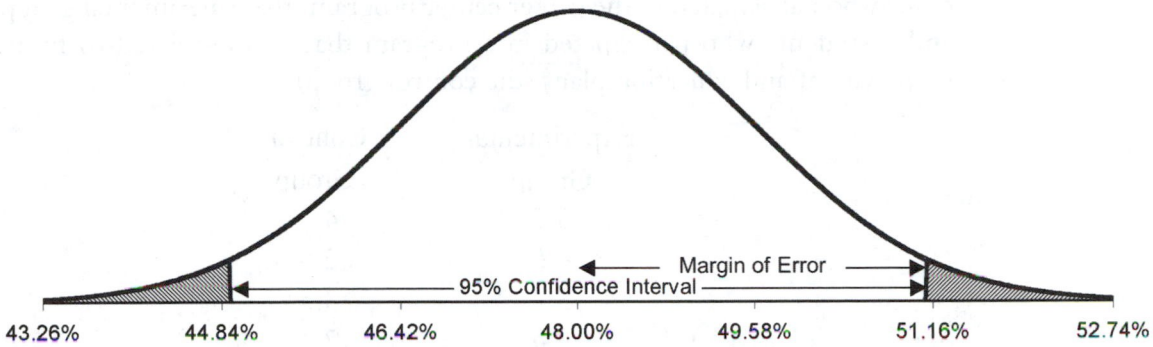

| 43.26% | 44.84% | 46.42% | 48.00% | 49.58% | 51.16% | 52.74% |

If a higher level of confidence is desired—say, 99%—then the width of the interval must increase from one that is bounded by 1.96 and −1.96 to one that extends from −2.58 to 2.58, the values of z that define the lower and upper 0.5% of the comparison distribution. The following shows a 99% confidence interval for the sample percentage of voters:

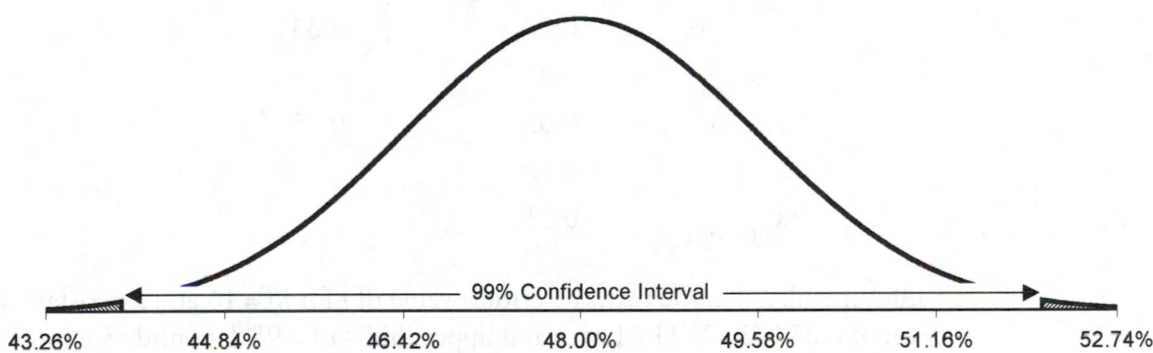

| 43.26% | 44.84% | 46.42% | 48.00% | 49.58% | 51.16% | 52.74% |

We may also construct confidence intervals for the t tests introduced in Chapter 9. The following example is for the independent-samples t test. The logic is the same, but the normal distribution is replaced by a t distribution specified by $N_X + N_Y - 2$ degrees of freedom and the parameter we are estimating is the difference between two population means, $\mu_X - \mu_Y$. The 95% confidence interval computed to estimate the value of $\mu_X - \mu_Y$ depends upon the two sample means (M_X and M_Y), the standard error of the difference between the sample means ($s_{Difference}$), and the critical value of t for $N_X + N_Y - 2$ degrees of freedom and a p level determined by subtracting the desired level of confidence from 1 (e.g., $1 - 0.95 = 0.05$).

Following an example from Chapter 4, we will construct a 95% confidence interval for the difference between the mean consideration of future consequences (CFC) scale scores in two populations of second-year students: those who do and those who do not participate in a semester-long program administered by the university career center that "exposes students to the many graduate school and career options available to them" (p. 179 in the text). At the end of the semester, the following results were obtained for 9 students who participated in the career center program (the experimental group) and 9 students who participated in a program that was unrelated to future employment and education plans (the control group).

	Experimental Group	Control Group
	3.5	4
	4.5	2.5
	3	3.5
	3.5	2
	4	3.5
	3.5	3.5
	3	4
	3.5	3.5
	4	2
M	3.61	3.17
s^2	0.24	0.63
s^2_{Pooled}	0.43	
s^2_M	0.05	0.05
$s^2_{Difference}$	0.10	
$s_{Difference}$	0.31	

From Appendix C in the text, the critical value of t for $df = 16$ and a two-tailed p level of 0.05 is 2.12. The lower and upper limits of a 95% confidence interval for the difference between the population means is thus:

$$(M_X - M_Y)_{Lower} = -2.12 \, (s_{Difference}) + (M_X - M_Y) = -2.12 \, (0.31) + 0.44 = \mathbf{-0.22}$$
$$(M_X - M_Y)_{Upper} = +2.12 \, (s_{Difference}) + (M_X - M_Y) = 2.12 \, (0.31) + 0.44 = \mathbf{1.1}$$

Because this interval includes the null-hypothesized value of 0 as the difference between the population means, we would fail to reject the null hypothesis and conclude that there is no evidence from this study that the difference between the population mean CFC scale scores is other than 0.

> Effect Size: Just How Big is the Difference?

An **effect size** is "a standardized value that indicates the size of a difference with respect to a measure of spread, but is not affected by sample size"

(p. 543). Cohen's *d* is a statistic commonly used as a measure of effect size for studies in which a *z* test or a *t* test is used to test the null hypothesis. In these studies, effect size refers to the capacity of an experimental treatment (independent variable manipulation) to separate two population means. Because the mean of the population described by the null hypothesis is the only "known" population mean, the mean of the alternative (research) population must be estimated from the sample mean. So, for studies in which the null hypothesis is tested with a *z* test, Cohen's *d* is a measure of the number of standard deviations separating the sample mean from the null-hypothesized population mean:

$$d = \frac{M - \mu}{\sigma}$$

To return to the previous example in which you (as a licensed clinical psychologist) hypothesized that the mean IQ in the population of college students differs from the mean IQ in the general population, Cohen's *d* would be computed as follows:

$$d = \frac{109 - 100}{15} = \frac{9}{15} = \frac{3}{5} = 0.6$$

The overlap between the populations of IQ scores represented by the null and research hypotheses as just described is shown in the following figure:

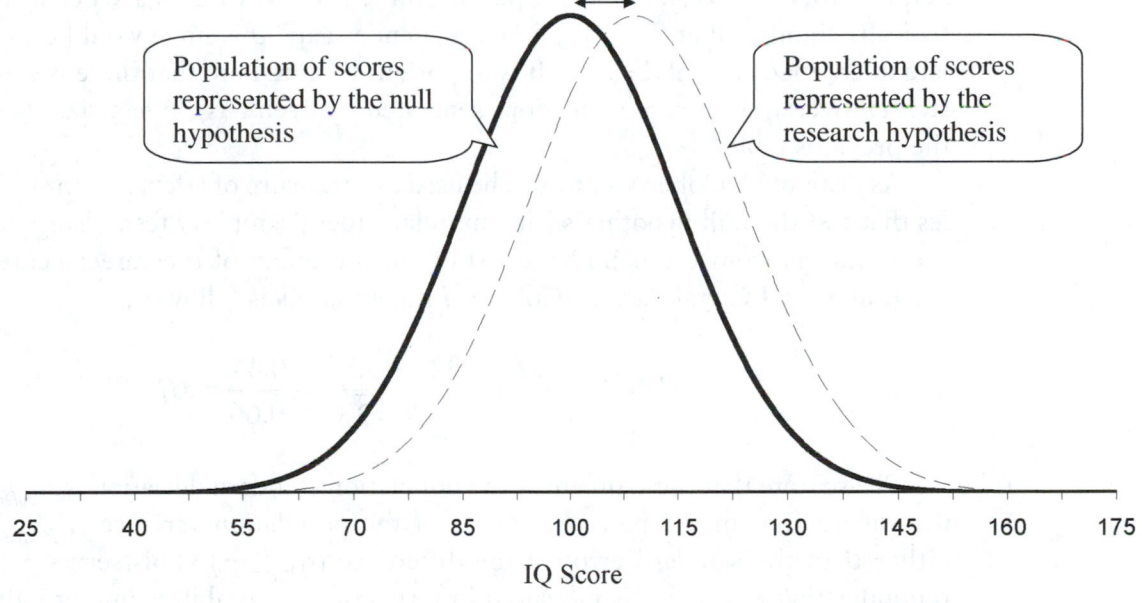

According to the guidelines originally proposed by Cohen (1969, 1977, 1988), this estimated difference of 0.6 standard deviations between the population means is just a bit above a medium effect size, as shown in Table 12-1 in the text:

TABLE 12-1. COHEN'S CONVENTIONS FOR EFFECT SIZES: *d*

Jacob Cohen has published guidelines (or conventions), based on the overlap between two distributions, to help researchers determine whether an effect is small, medium, or large. These numbers are not cutoffs, merely rough guidelines to aid researchers in their interpretation or results.

EFFECT SIZE	CONVENTION	OVERLAP
Small	0.2	85%
Medium	0.5	67%
Large	0.8	53%

Notice that, because the estimated difference between the population means is measured in terms of the population standard deviation, effect size is completely independent of sample size. This means, of course, that you cannot increase the size of an effect by increasing the number of participants. On the other hand, you *can* increase the likelihood of obtaining a statistically significant result by increasing the number of participants in your study. Recall that the Benbow and Stanley (1980) report of a statistically significant gender difference in mathematics reasoning ability (measured by scores on the math section of the SAT; SAT-M) was based on a sample size of approximately 10,000 students. Given this sample size and the pooled variance (computed from the standard deviations provided in Table 1 of the Benbow and Stanley report), a gender difference as small as 3.23 points on the SAT-M would have been statistically significant at the 0.05 *p* level. A "gender gap" this small would translate to an effect size of *d* = 0.04. It is important to note here that there is substantial overlap between populations separated by even large effect sizes (see the previous table).

As just noted, Cohen's *d* can also be used as a measure of effect size in studies that test the null hypothesis with an independent samples *t* test. Using the group means from the hypothetical study of the effect of the career center program on CFC scale scores, Cohen's *d* is computed as follows:

$$d = \frac{M_X - M_Y}{s_{Pooled}} = \frac{3.61 - 3.17}{\sqrt{0.43}} = \frac{0.44}{0.66} = .67$$

Please note that the estimate of the population standard deviation is s_{Pooled}, the square root of the pooled estimate of the population variance (s^2_{Pooled}), rather than the standard error of the difference ($s_{Difference}$). This serves as a reminder that effect size is measured in terms of the variability among individual scores rather than the variability among sample means. In this example, the effect size is in the medium-to-large range, despite the inclusion of the null-hypothesized value of the population mean difference in the confidence interval. We will explore this apparent discrepancy in the discussion of power next.

The statistic R^2 (or, equivalently, "eta squared," η^2) is typically used to measure the effect size in studies that test the null hypothesis with a one-way ANOVA. R^2 is a measure of the proportion of variability in the dependent variable that is explained by the independent variable. The total variability in the dependent variable is expressed in the total sum of squares (SS_{Total}) from the ANOVA source table, whereas the variability attributed to the effect of the independent variable is expressed in the between-groups sum of squares ($SS_{Between}$). The measure of effect size for a one-way ANOVA is thus computed as:

$$R^2 = \frac{SS_{Between}}{SS_{Total}}$$

R^2 is interpreted by examining the guidelines in Table 12-3 in the text:

TABLE 12-3. COHEN'S CONVENTIONS FOR EFFECT SIZES: R^2

The following guidelines, called conventions by statisticians, are meant to help researchers decide how important an effect is. These numbers are not cutoffs, merely rough guidelines to aid researchers in their interpretation of results.

EFFECT SIZE	CONVENTION
Small	0.01
Medium	0.06
Large	0.14

> Statistical Power and Sensitivity: Correctly Rejecting the Null Hypothesis

The effect size for the hypothetical study of the effect of the career center program on CFC scores was just computed to be 0.67, a little past the midpoint between a medium effect size and a large effect size. So why were the results of a study based on a medium-to-large effect size found to be insignificant? The answer is found by examining the statistical power of the study. **Statistical power** is the probability of rejecting a false null hypothesis. In other words, power is the proportion of times a false null hypothesis will be rejected in replications of a study designed to test that hypothesis. It is in every researcher's interest to maximize the statistical power of each test of a false null hypothesis, just as it is in her or his interest to minimize the opposite probability—that of failing to reject a false null hypothesis—a Type II error. Power is thus the additive inverse of the probability of committing a Type II error. The four possible outcomes of a hypothesis test may be compared in the following decision matrix:

Status of the Null Hypothesis

Researcher's Decision	The null hypothesis is true	The null hypothesis is false
Reject the null hypothesis	Type I Error	Power
Do not reject the null hypothesis	Correct Decision	Type II Error

Note that power and its complement, the probability of making a Type II error, may be determined only when the null hypothesis is false. However, because the null hypothesis is believed to be false in each study that includes one or more hypothesis tests, it is important to identify the factors that increase power in order to maximize the likelihood of detecting a false null hypothesis.

1. Power is increased by a large effect size. Effect size, in turn, is a function of two factors—the capacity of the independent variable to separate the means of two or more populations, and the variability within the populations. This is perhaps best understood by inspecting Figures 12-8 and 12-9 in the text. In the following figure (Figure 12-8), the variability in the four populations is the same, so the larger effect size illustrated by the bottom pair of distributions is due to the greater difference between the means.

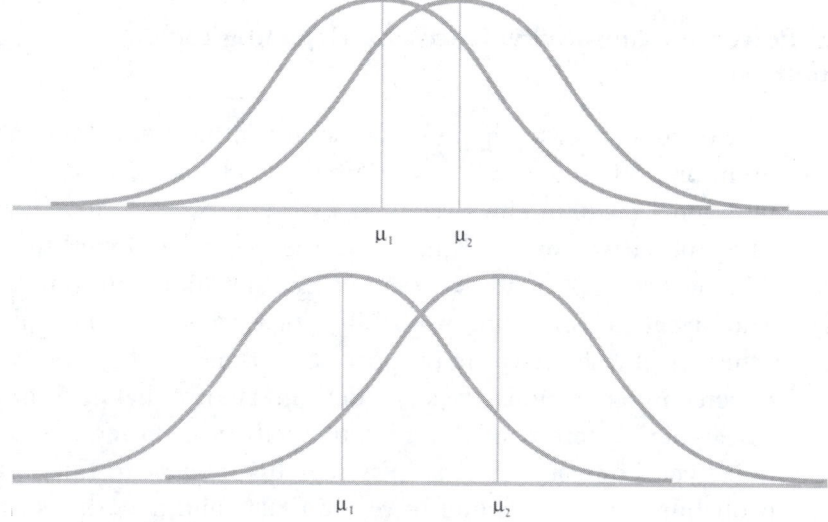

In contrast, the differences between the means of the four populations illustrated in Figure 12-9 are the same, but the lower variability in the bottom pair results in less overlap and a larger effect size.

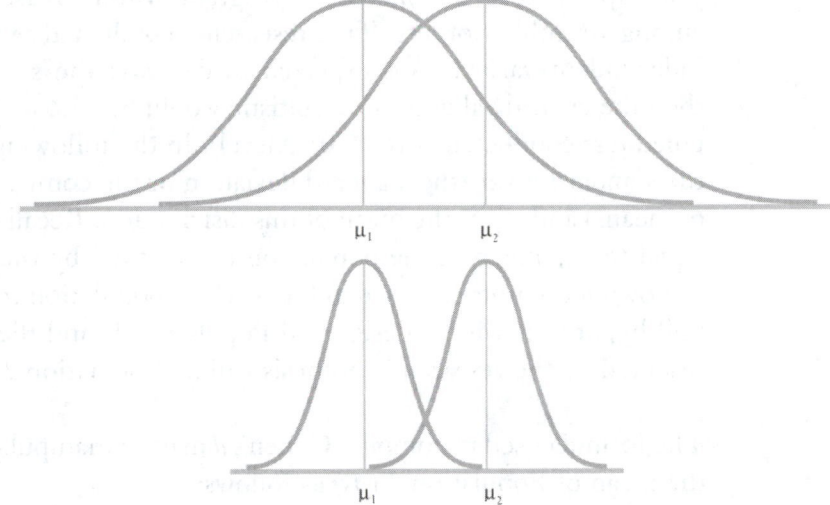

2. Power is increased by a large sample size: As N increases, power increases.
3. Power is increased by a higher p level (also known as **alpha**): A study conducted at a p level of 0.05 is more powerful than a study conducted at a p level of 0.01.
4. Power is increased by a one-tailed test: A one-tailed test is more powerful than a two-tailed test.

These points will be illustrated in the following power calculations for a one-tailed z test.

An industrial-organizational psychologist hypothesizes that assembly workers would display a higher level of job satisfaction if they were given a new kind of incentive program. He consults the literature on the effect of incentive programs on job satisfaction and decides that his new program will have a medium effect size. Assessment of the job satisfaction of assembly workers at this company over many years has resulted in a distribution that is approximately normal, with $\mu = 82$ and $\sigma = 7$ on a standard job satisfaction scale. The psychologist plans to provide the new incentive program to 25 randomly selected assembly workers.

    a. What is the power of this study if the null hypothesis is tested at a p level of 0.05?

    b. What is the power of this study if the sample size is increased from 25 to 36 assembly workers?

Step 1. Determine the critical values of z for the given p level (alpha) and a one-tailed test of the null hypothesis. Alpha (α) is 0.05, so the critical value of the z statistic (z_α) is the value that cuts off the upper 5% of the comparison distribution: $z_\alpha = 1.645$. The upper (right) tail of the distribution is the rejection region for the null hypothesis because the psychologist expects that the incentive program will increase job satisfaction among assembly workers. If the researcher conducted a study in which the independent variable was expected to decrease the sample mean score, then the critical value of the z statistic would be -1.645 (again, for a one-tailed test conducted at the 0.05 p level). In the following formulas, σ_M is the standard error (the standard deviation of the comparison distribution of means) and μ_M is the mean of this distribution. Recall that μ_M is always equal to the mean of the population represented by the null hypothesis. Following the notation used in the text, the population represented by the null hypothesis will be designated Population 1, and the population represented by the research hypothesis will be Population 2.

The formula used to compute Cohen's d may be manipulated to determine the mean of Population 2 (μ_2) as follows:

$$\mu_2 = d\sigma + \mu_1 = 0.5(7) + 82 = 3.5 + 82 = 85.5$$

The mean of any distribution of means is always equal to the mean of the parent population, so the mean of Population 2 is the same as the mean of the distribution of means represented by the research hypothesis: $\mu_2 = \mu_{M2}$. Because calculations of power are based on distributions of means, the latter symbol is used. The subscript "2" reminds us that this is the mean of the distribution of all possible means of samples of size N from the population represented by the research hypothesis.

The standard error is computed as follows:

$$\sigma_M = \frac{\sigma}{\sqrt{N}} = \frac{7}{\sqrt{25}} = \frac{7}{5} = 1.4$$

You have the means of the two distributions of means as well as the standard error, so you may sketch the two curves as follows:

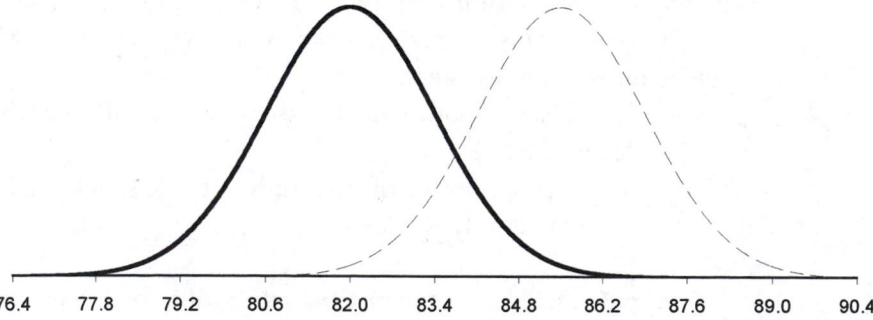

| 76.4 | 77.8 | 79.2 | 80.6 | 82.0 | 83.4 | 84.8 | 86.2 | 87.6 | 89.0 | 90.4 |

Step 2. Convert the critical value of the z statistic to a sample mean:

$$M_\alpha = z_\alpha \sigma_M + \mu_M = 1.645(1.4) + 82 = 2.303 + 82 = 84.303$$

The area to the right of M_α under the distribution of means represented by the research hypothesis corresponds to power. This area is shaded in the following figure:

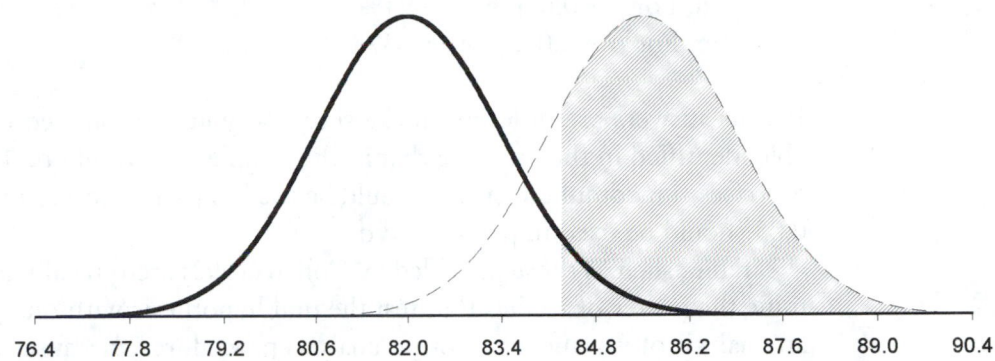

| 76.4 | 77.8 | 79.2 | 80.6 | 82.0 | 83.4 | 84.8 | 86.2 | 87.6 | 89.0 | 90.4 |

Step 3. The remaining step is to look up the shaded area in the previous figure in the table of normal curve percentages in Appendix B in the text. First, we'll have to express the sample mean computed in Step 2 (M_α) as a z statistic. This z statistic is labeled z_{Power} in the following formula.

$$z_{Power} = \frac{M_\alpha - \mu_{M_2}}{\sigma_M} = \frac{84.303 - 85.5}{1.4} = \frac{-1.197}{1.4} = -.855$$

When power is to the right of a negative value of z_{Power}, power is always equal to the area between the mean and z ("%MEAN to z") added to the area to the right of the mean (50%). The power of this study is the sum of the value in the %MEAN to z column for $z = 0.86$ (30.51%) and the area to the right of the mean (50%), so power = **80.51%**.

To figure power for part b, first determine the new value for the standard error:

$$\sigma_M = \frac{\sigma}{\sqrt{N}} = \frac{7}{\sqrt{36}} = \frac{7}{6} = 1.167$$

Then follow the previous steps:

Step 2. $\qquad M_\alpha = z_\alpha \sigma_M + \mu_M = 1.645(1.167) + 82 = 1.92 + 82 = 83.92$

Step 3. $\qquad z_{Power} = \frac{M_\alpha - \mu_{M_2}}{\sigma_M} = \frac{83.92 - 85.5}{1.167} = \frac{-1.58}{1.167} = -1.35$

$$\text{Power} = \%\text{MEAN to } z + 50\% = 41.15\% + 50\% = \textbf{91.15\%}$$

As additional exercises, manipulate:

c. the sample size (e.g., try a smaller sample size of 16).
d. the effect size (e.g., try a large effect size).
e. alpha (e.g., use 0.01 instead of 0.05).

The solutions are:

c. For $N = 16$, power = 63.87%.
d. For $d = 0.8$, power = 94%.
e. For $\alpha = 0.01$, power = 37.07%.

If your answers are different, make sure that you manipulated only the variable identified in the exercise; that is, the sample size should be 16 in all three exercises, a medium effect size should be used in parts c and e, and an alpha of 0.05 should be used in parts c and d.

Tables such as those provided by Cohen (1992) are typically used to determine the power of studies that test the null hypothesis with one of the t tests, an analysis of variance, and other analysis procedures. Because sample size is the most easily manipulated of the factors that influence power, researchers typically consult power tables to determine the minimum sample size required to achieve power of 80% (0.8), the level recommended by Cohen and others. Software found on Web sites may also be used to determine the power of a completed study or the sample size needed to achieve a desired level of power. The G*Power program described on page 561 in the text may be downloaded to run from your computer. Remember the confidence interval for the independent samples t test that failed to reject the null hypothesis despite a medium-to-large effect size? The G*Power program returned a sample size of 74 (37 in each group) to achieve power of 80%. With just 9 participants assigned to each group, this study had little chance to reject the null hypothesis; the G*Power program returned a value of 0.267038 (26.7%) for the power of this study.

> Digging Deeper into the Data: Meta-Analysis

A **meta-analysis** is "a study that involves the calculation of a mean effect size from the individual effect sizes of many studies" (text page 563). Put another way, a meta-analysis is a review of studies on a selected topic based on a statistical analysis of the effect sizes reported for each one. A meta-analysis, then, may be thought of as an analysis in which the results of a large number of published studies, expressed as effect sizes, are treated as data values. The following figure may help to show the conceptual similarities between the analysis of data in a single study and a meta-analysis of the effect sizes of many studies:

Single Study		Meta-Analysis	
Participant	Score on Dependent Variable	Study	Effect Size (Cohen's d)
1	X_1	1	d_1
2	X_2	2	d_2
3	X_3	3	d_3
4	X_4	4	d_4
.	.	.	.
.	.	.	.
.	.	.	.
N	X_N	N	d_N

The steps involved in conducting a meta-analysis are enumerated in the text as follows:

1. Select the topic of interest and decide on a set of rules for which articles to include *before* beginning your search of the literature. For example, you should decide on a criterion for the range of scores on the dependent variable as well as whether your meta-analysis will include all categories of studies or will be limited to experiments.

2. Search the literature, including electronic databases such as PsycINFO as well as conference proceedings and unpublished studies that represent the "gray" or "fugitive" literatures.

3. Record the effect size for every study that meets the criteria that you established in Step 1. If the author(s) did not include an effect size, then you may calculate the effect size from group statistics.

4. Analyze the effect sizes, using the arsenal of statistical procedures presented in this text. These options include (a) descriptive methods such as presenting tables of effect sizes that fall within a specified range, graphical summaries of effect sizes such as histograms, boxplots, or stem-and-leaf plots, and summary statistics such as the mean, median, and standard deviation; (b) inferential analyses such as a test of the null hypothesis that the mean effect size is zero, as well as a confidence interval around the mean effect size. A measure of center such as the mean effect size (or the median, if there are clear outliers among the effect sizes) is perhaps the best single measure of the overall effect of a class of related independent variables on a class of related dependent variables.

The most time-consuimg task in Step 2 is chasing down unpublished results that comprise a large part of the fugitive literature. These results are as important, if not more important, than the published literature, but they remain unpublished mostly because they failed to result in a rejection of the null hypothesis. Because unpublished results are likely to be nonsignificant, their inclusion in a meta-analysis typically reduces the mean effect size. The filing away of unpublished, but potentially important, findings has been dubbed the "file drawer problem," a solution to which was proposed by Rosenthal (1991). Rosenthal advocates conducting a statistic called the **file drawer statistic** that estimates the number of studies with nonsignificant results that would be required to reduce the mean effect size computed for published results to a value that would no longer be statistically significant. A low value of the file drawer statistic would mean that an effect size based on published studies is likely to be an inflated estimate of the true effect size in the population, whereas a large file drawer statistic would increase confidence in the reliability of a significant effect size.

In the final analysis, carefully conducted meta-analyses may go a long way toward improving the public image of research in the behavioral sciences, much of which is regarded by policy-makers and the lay public alike as fraught with uncertainty and contradictions.

STUDY QUESTIONS

1. A sample statistic used to estimate the value of a population parameter is called a(n):
   a. measure of effect size.
   b. confidence limit.
   c. interval estimate.
   d. point estimate.

2. A(n) _____ is a range of values that is likely to include the value of a population parameter.
   a. point estimate
   b. interval estimate
   c. significance test
   d. hypothesis test

3. The phrase "margin of error" is most closely associated with which of the following?
   a. point estimate
   b. interval estimate
   c. confidence interval
   d. effect size

4. A **confidence interval** is centered around the mean of the:
   a. population represented by the research hypothesis.
   b. population represented by the null hypothesis.
   c. comparison distribution.
   d. sample.

5. A researcher constructed a 95% confidence interval from a random sample of 25 scores. Which of the following is the correct interpretation of this confidence interval?
   a. There is a 95% chance that the sample mean is within the confidence interval.
   b. There is a 95% chance that the population mean is within the confidence interval.
   c. There is a 95% chance that the interval does not include the null-hypothesized mean.
   d. The population mean is within 95% of the confidence intervals generated as this one was.

6. A researcher obtains a sample of 25, 90-day-old male rats from the A-1 Animal
    Breeding Farm and observes the time it takes each one to reach the goal box in a rela-
    tively simple maze that she also obtained from the breeding farm. The breeder assures
    her that the average 90-day-old male A-1 rat runs this maze in 17.6 seconds with a
    standard deviation of 4.5 seconds. Suppose the researcher computes a mean of 21.4 sec-
    onds for her sample of 25 rats. What are the limits of a 95% confidence interval for the
    true mean running time for the population of A-1 rats?
    a. 15.84 to 19.36
    b. 16.12 to 19.08
    c. 19.92 to 22.88
    d. 19.64 to 23.16

7. The results section of a certain research article reported a 95% confidence interval for
    the mean to be 0.5583 ± 0.0348. What can you conclude from this result?
    a. The true value of the population mean is 0.5583.
    b. The true value of the population mean is not likely to be 0.5.
    c. The null hypothesis should be rejected because 0.0348 is less than 0.05.
    d. The null hypothesis should not be rejected, because 0.0348 is less than 0.05.

8. If a confidence interval does *not* include the mean specified by the null hypothesis, then
    the null hypothesis:
    a. may be rejected.
    b. may not be rejected.
    c. is false.
    d. is true.

9. According to the null hypothesis, the number of hours worked in the previous week by
    college graduates is not different from the mean number of hours worked in the previ-
    ous week by the population in general (thought to be 40). What decision regarding the
    validity of the null hypothesis, if any, may be made based on a 95% confidence interval
    that extends from 46.16 to 49.30 hours as an estimate of the mean number of hours
    worked the previous week by college graduates?
    a. The null hypothesis is not rejected because the interval does not include the value 40.
    b. The null hypothesis is rejected because the interval does not include the value 40.
    c. The null hypothesis is not rejected because the level of confidence is not < 5%.
    d. There is no way to evaluate the null hypothesis from a confidence interval.

10. A result that is statistically significant is not necessarily an important result. Under
    which of the following conditions would a significant result be *least* likely to be a result
    of practical importance?
    a. Effect size and sample size are large.
    b. Effect size and sample size are small.
    c. Effect size is large but sample size is small.
    d. Effect size is small but sample size is large.

11. A standardized measure of effect size discloses the extent to which:
    a. two samples differ in terms of the distance between their respective means.
    b. an increase in sample size is correlated with an increase in the probability of obtaining a statistically significant outcome.
    c. two populations differ in terms of the distance between their respective means.
    d. two populations differ in terms of the variability of the scores around their respective means.

12. As the _____ increases, effect size increases.
    a. size of the sample
    b. population standard deviation
    c. difference between two sample means
    d. difference between two population means

13. Computing the statistic that measures effect size, Cohen's d, is most similar to _____.
    a. converting a raw score to a standard (z) score
    b. computing the population standard deviation
    c. finding an area under the normal curve
    d. computing the population mean

14. Which of the following is the formula for computing effect size?
    a. $\dfrac{M_1 - M_2}{SD}$
    b. $\dfrac{\mu_1 - \mu_2}{\dfrac{\sigma}{\sqrt{N}}}$
    c. $\dfrac{\mu_{M_1} - \mu_{M_2}}{\dfrac{\sigma}{\sqrt{N}}}$
    d. $\dfrac{\mu_1 - \mu_2}{\sigma}$

15. You have just computed Cohen's d to be 0.47. This means that:
    a. the means of two distributions of means are 0.47 standard deviations apart.
    b. the means of two populations are 0.47 standard deviations apart.
    c. the ratio of two population standard deviations is 0.47.
    d. there is a 47% chance of rejecting the null hypothesis.

16. Suppose that the Cohen's d statistics computed for two different studies are 0.5 (Study 1) and 1.5 (Study 2). This means that the:
    a. effect sizes of the two studies are comparable if they used the same measure.
    b. effect sizes of the two studies are comparable if they used the same sample size.
    c. effect size for Study 2 is one standard error greater than the effect size for Study 1.
    d. effect size for Study 2 is one standard deviation greater than the effect size for Study 1.

17. How are effect size and sample size related?
    a. negatively: as effect size increases, sample size decreases
    b. positively: as effect size increases, sample size increases
    c. Effect size and sample size are completely unrelated.
    d. The relationship is strong but not linear.

18. For research designed to test a null hypothesis involving two population means, Cohen's effect size conventions are:
    a. small = 0.25; medium = 0.50; large = 0.75
    b. small = 0.30; medium = 0.60; large = 0.90
    c. small = 0.20; medium = 0.50; large = 0.80
    d. Conventions vary depending on other factors.

19. When you have the results of a completed study of two independent samples of scores, you estimate the effect size as the difference between the _____ divided by the

    _____.

    a. two populations means; population standard deviation
    b. null-hypothesized population mean and the sample mean; standard error of the mean
    c. two sample means; pooled estimate of the population standard deviation
    d. research-hypothesized population mean and the sample mean; standard error of the mean

20. Which of the following is used to estimate an effect size in an analysis of variance and indicates the proportion of variance in the dependent variable accounted for (predicted or explained) by the independent variable?
    a. F
    b. f
    c. R
    d. R^2

21. The **statistical power** of a study is the probability that the study will:
    a. not have a significant result if the null hypothesis is true.
    b. have a significant result if the research hypothesis is true.
    c. have a significant result if the null hypothesis is true.
    d. not have a significant result if the research hypothesis is true.

22. The traditional minimum requirement for conducting a study is that:
    a. alpha = beta.
    b. beta is less than alpha.
    c. power is greater than beta.
    d. power is at least 0.80.

23. Based on a number of published studies, the mean self-esteem score in the general population is 50, and the standard deviation is 10 (i.e., $\mu = 50$, $\sigma = 10$). If a researcher predicts that her new program designed to increase a person's self-esteem has a small effect size, then what value would she predict to be the mean of the population of individuals who go through her program of self-esteem improvement?
    a. 48
    b. 55
    c. 60
    d. 52

24. A team of personality psychologists predict that people who experienced a disaster during their childhood will score slightly higher on a measure of fear of disasters (that is, the researchers predict a small positive effect size). It is known from extensive previous testing, using this measure with the population in general, that scores are normally distributed, with a mean of 58 and a standard deviation of 6. The researchers then test their prediction by giving the measure to 120 people who grew up in an area that experienced a devastating forest fire when they were children.

    If the p level is set at 0.05, what is the power of this study?
    a. 0.548
    b. 0.707
    c. − 0.546
    d. 0.546

25. **Alpha** is another name for:
    a. p value.
    b. p level.
    c. power.
    d. effect size.

26. Which of the following would *not* result in an increase the power of a study?
    a. increase the sample size
    b. use a one-tailed instead of a two-tailed hypothesis test
    c. use a more stringent p level (alpha)
    d. exaggerate the levels of the independent variable

27. At a practical level, researchers are most likely to determine power to help them decide:
    a. how many participants to include in their study.
    b. whether to conduct a one-tailed or a two-tailed test.
    c. whether to set alpha higher or lower than 0.05 (5%).
    d. how large their effect size must be.

28. You and a colleague each conduct a t test for independent means to determine whether there is a difference in the sizes (as determined by number of employees) of companies that offer extended maternity leave plans and those that do not. Your results, based on a total of 50 companies, indicate that there is not a significant size difference between companies that do and do not offer extended maternity leave plans, whereas the results reported by your colleague, based on her sample of 150 companies, show that larger companies are significantly more likely to offer an extended maternity leave plan. Is this possible? Choose the best answer and explanation.
    a. No, because as the sample size increases, variability increases and power will decrease as a result.
    b. Yes, because as the sample size increases, variability increases and power will increase as a result.
    c. Yes, because as the sample size increases, variability decreases and power will increase as a result.
    d. No, because statistical significance is unrelated to sample size, and there are no other differences in the designs of the two studies that could account for the different results.

29. How does sample size affect power?
    a. As sample size increases, the standard deviation of the comparison distribution increases, resulting in less overlap between the two populations.
    b. As sample size increases, the standard deviation of the comparison distribution decreases, resulting in less overlap between the two distributions of means.
    c. As sample size increases, the standard deviation of the comparison distribution increases, resulting in less overlap between the two distributions of means.
    d. As sample size increases, the standard deviation of the comparison distribution decreases, resulting in less overlap between the two populations.

30. How is sample size related to power?
    a. It depends on the effect size.
    b. It depends on the standard deviation.
    c. As sample size increases, power increases.
    d. As sample size increases, power decreases.

31. How is effect size related to power?
    a. positively: as the effect size increases, power increases
    b. negatively: as the effect size increases, power decreases
    c. depends on the size of the population standard deviation
    d. depends on the size of the sample

32. Sampling from a more homogeneous group in which participants' responses are more likely to be similar increases power by:
    a. increasing the standard deviation of the population.
    b. decreasing the standard deviation of the population.
    c. inflating the probability of committing a Type I error.
    d. increasing the standard error of the distribution of means.

33. A(n) _____ is a committee that institutions are legally mandated to have to vet research that uses human or animal participants prior to beginning the study. This committee may require researchers at the institution to accompany their research proposal with a power analysis.

34. Which of the following involves the calculation of a mean effect size from the individual effect sizes of many studies?
    a. a meta-analysis
    b. a power analysis
    c. an alpha analysis
    d. a file-drawer statistic

35. Which of the following refers to a calculation of the number of studies with null results that would have to exist so that a mean effect size is no longer statistically significant?
    a. meta-analysis
    b. alpha
    c. file-drawer statistic
    d. power

ANSWERS TO CHAPTER 12 STUDY QUESTIONS

Question Number	Correct Answer	Question Number	Correct Answer
1	d, p. 534	19	c, p. 548
2	b, p. 534	20	d, p. 548
3	c, p. 535	21	b, p. 551
4	d, p. 535	22	d, pp. 551–552
5	b, p. 535	23	d, p. 553
6	d, pp. 536–537	24	b, pp. 552–556
7	b, pp. 537–538	25	b, p. 556
8	a, p. 538	26	c, p. 557
9	b, p. 538	27	a, p. 557
10	d, pp. 542–543	28	c, pp. 558–559
11	c, p. 543	29	b, p. 559
12	c, p. 543	30	c, p. 559
13	a, p. 546	31	a, p. 560
14	d, p. 546	32	b, p. 560
15	b, p. 546	33	institutional review board, p. 562
16	d, p. 546	34	a, p. 563
17	c, p. 546	35	c, p. 566
18	c, p. 547 (see Table12-1)		

CHAPTER THIRTEEN

CHI SQUARE

Expectations Versus Observations

CHAPTER OUTLINE

Nonparametric Statistics: When We're Not Even Close to Meeting the Assumptions
- Nonparametric Tests: Using the Right Statistical Tool for the Right Statistical Job
- Nonparametric Tests: When to Use Them
- Nonparametric Tests: Why to Avoid Them Whenever Possible

Chi-Square Test for Goodness-of-Fit: When We Have One Nominal Variable
- Chi-Square Test for Goodness-of-Fit: The Six Steps of Hypothesis Testing
- A More Typical Chi-Square Test for Goodness-of-Fit: Evenly Divided Expected Frequencies

Chi-Square Test for Independence: When We Have Two Nominal Variables
- Chi-Square Test for Independence: The Six Steps of Hypothesis Testing
- Cramer's V: The Effect Size for Chi Square
- Graphing Chi-Square Percentages: Depicting the Relation Visually
- Relative Risk: How Much Higher Are the Chances of an Outcome?

Digging Deeper into the Data: A Deeper Understanding of Chi Square
- Standardized Residuals: A Post-Hoc Test for Chi Square
- Chi-Square Controversies: Expectations About Expected Frequencies

LEARNING OBJECTIVES

After studying this chapter, you should be able to:

1. Define each of the following terms and provide examples that are not in the text: *chi-square test for goodness-of-fit*, *chi-square test for independence*, *Cramer's V*, *relative risk*, and *adjusted standardized residual*.
2. Know under what circumstances you would want to use a nonparametric test rather than a parametric test.
3. Distinguish between a chi-square test for goodness-of-fit and a chi-square test for independence and know when you'd want to use each one.

4. Calculate a chi-square test for goodness-of-fit and a chi-square test for independence based on observed and expected frequencies.
5. Determine effect size using Cramer's V and relative risk.

CHAPTER REVIEW

> ### Nonparametric Statistics: When We're Not Even Close to Meeting the Assumptions

So far in the text we've worked with parametric statistics. In this chapter, we are introduced to nonparametric statistics. We need to use nonparametric statistics when our research design falls under one of three circumstances:

1. When our dependent variable is nominal
2. When either the independent or dependent variable is ordinal
3. When the sample size is small and we suspect that the underlying population of interest is skewed.

Let's talk about some examples of these previous three situations. For the first situation, imagine that we want to examine the number of people in your class who own pets. We could compare the number of people who own pets compared to those who don't. Unlike a *t*-test, our dependent variable is not an interval variable—either students own a pet or they don't—which means that we need to use a parametric test.

For the second example, we'd need to use an ordinal variable or a ranked variable. For example, imagine we are looking at scores on a midterm based on how much time people spent studying. We could rank the amount of time people in the class spent studying (most time—1st place, 2nd place, 3rd place, etc.) and compare scores on the exam.

Our last example would occur if the sample size is small and the underlying population is skewed. In other words, the sample is somewhat unusual in nature. For example, imagine we wanted to look at the reaction times of male runners who won a gold medal in the Olympics. In this case, there are not a lot of male gold medal runners, so we would end up with a small sample size. Further, the underlying population would probably not be normal.

Although nonparametric tests are useful because they allow us to perform statistical tests when we ordinarily could not, they have a number of limitations. For one thing, we cannot calculate confidence intervals and effect-size measures. In addition, we are more likely to make a Type II error because such tests have less statistical power than parametric tests. Lastly, it is almost always best to use interval data to explain our findings rather than nominal or ordinal data.

> ## Chi-Square Test for Goodness-of-Fit: When We Have One Nominal Variable

In this chapter, we will discuss two different types of chi-square nonparametric hypothesis tests. The first is the **chi-square test for goodness-of-fit,** which we use when we have one nominal variable. This test examines whether the pattern of observed data deviates from what we would expect by chance. If our data is different enough than what we would expect by chance, we can reject the null hypothesis. For this test, we'll be using the chi-square statistic, χ^2, which is based on the chi-square distribution. This is similar to when we used the F statistic and the F distribution for our ANOVAs and the t statistic and t distribution for a t-test.

For this test, we only have one variable that's categorical with two or more categories into which participants are placed. The chi-square goodness-of-fit test gives us a measure of how good the fit is between the observed data in the various categories of a single nominal variable and what we would expect based on the null hypothesis.

Before we discuss how to calculate a chi-square test for goodness of fit, let's discuss an example. Imagine that we want to know whether students in our class are more likely (or less) to have pets than would be expected by chance. Let's say that we have 100 total students in the class, and 65 have pets whereas 35 do not. So, let's go through the six-step process.

Pet Category	Number of Classmates
Students with at least 1 pet	65
Students with no pets	35

Step 1. Identify the populations, distribution, and assumption.

There are two populations when conducting a chi-square: the frequency of participants in the cells based on what we have observed for our study and the frequency of participants in cells based on what we would expect by chance, the null hypothesis. Because we're looking at frequencies and we have just one variable, we know that our distribution is a chi-square distribution and the particular test is the goodness-of-fit.

For this test we have four different assumptions. We first assume that we are working with a nominal variable. For our example, we are looking at the number of pet owners compared to those without pets, so we know that we fall under this assumption. The second assumption is that each observation must be independent of all other observations. In other words, we can't have the same observation in more than one category. For example, no student in the class can be both a pet owner and not a pet owner—you can be one or the other. So, this assumption will be no problem. The third assumption is that all participants should be randomly selected. Although our sample is not randomly selected because all participants are coming from the same classroom, if we meet all of the other assumptions, we could still go forward with the test. This will just limit our ability to generalize beyond our sample. Lastly, we need a minimum of at least 5 (preferably 10) participants in each cell. For our sample, we have 65 with pets and 35 without—both numbers are greater than 10, so we can go ahead with the chi-square test.

Step 2. State the null and research hypotheses.

For chi-square tests, we state the hypothesis in words rather than words and symbols. So, in this case:

> Null hypothesis: The number of students with pets compared to those without pets is what we would expect by chance.

> Research hypothesis: The number of students with pets compared to those without pets is different than what we would expect by chance.

Step 3. ■ Determine the characteristics of the comparison distribution.

Our next step is to determine our degrees of freedom. For chi-square hypothesis tests, degrees of freedom are based on the number of categories, or cells, in which participants can be counted rather than the number of participants overall. In our case, we have two categories—those who own pets and those who do not. The formula to *calculate the degrees of freedom in a chi-square is the number of categories minus 1: $df_{\chi^2} = k - 1$*. In this case, k is the number of categories, and in our case, $df_{\chi^2} = 2 - 1 = 1$.

Step 4. Determine critical values or cutoffs.

We use the chi-square table to determine the cutoff or critical value. Because a chi-square can never be negative, there is only one critical value, even when we have a two-tailed test. The full table can be found in Appendix B of the text. All we need is to find our degrees of freedom in the first column (which is 1 for our example) and then look for the p value, which is usually 0.05. For our example then, our critical value is 3.84.

Step 5. Calculate the test statistic.

To calculate the test statistic, we need to know our formula which is: $\chi^2 = \Sigma [(O - E)^2 / E]$. The O in the formula refers to the observed frequencies (or the data we've collected), and the E refers to the expected frequencies. In some examples, you will be told what the expected frequencies would be. In our example, let's assume that students in the class are equally likely to have a pet as they are to not have a pet. In other words, let's say that either having or not having a pet is equally likely. Alternatively, you could have been given the proportion of the general population with pets and go with that instead. However, assuming it's equally likely, we could create the following table:

Pet Category	Observed (O)	Expected (E)
Students with at least 1 pet	65	50
Students with no pets	35	50

Now that we have our observed and expected frequencies, we can work with our formula. We will need to subtract the expected frequencies from the observed frequencies and square the difference. Finally, we'll divide that value by the expected frequency (in our case, divide the obtained value by 50). We can work out these steps in another table such as the following:

Pet Category	Observed (O)	Expected (E)	$O - E$	$(O - E)^2$	$(O - E)^2/E$
Students with at least 1 pet	65	50	15	225	4.5
Students with no pets	35	50	−15	225	4.5

Our final step is to sum the numbers in the right-most column, which is: $4.5 + 4.5 = 9.0$. This is our test statistic, which we will use to compare with our cutoff.

Step 6. Make a decision.

Because our test statistic, 9.0, is greater than our critical value, 3.84, we can reject the null hypothesis. In this case, we can say that students in the class have significantly more pets than would be expected by chance. To report the results, we provide the degrees of freedom, the value of the test statistic, and whether the p value was greater or less than the value of the cutoff. We also provide the sample size with our degrees of freedom. For our example, we would provide the following, $\chi^2 = (1, N = 100) = 9.0, p < 0.05$.

> ## Chi-Square Test for Independence: When We Have Two Nominal Variables

The chi-square test for independence is used when we have more than one nominal variable. The test allows us to determine whether the two variables are independent of one another. Imagine we want to know if getting into the elite state junior orchestra depends on whether students received special music lessons from a tutor. To find out, we design a study so that some students who are planning on trying out for the orchestra get lessons while others do not.

We then look to see who was accepted into the orchestra. Based on our results, imagine that we construct the following table:

	Accepted into Orchestra	Not Accepted into Orchestra	Totals
Received music lessons	22	53	75
No lessons	8	67	75
Totals	30	120	

We would use a chi-square test for independence because we have two nominal variables (orchestra status and music lessons). Our frequencies refer to observed frequencies. The test will allow us to determine if getting accepted into the orchestra depends on whether the students received special lessons. Just like our previous tests, we have six steps of hypothesis testing, which we will review:

Step 1. Identify the populations, distribution, and assumptions.

Population 1 refers to students who received music lessons, and population 2 refers to students who did not receive music lessons. Because these are nominal variables, we know that we will need to use the chi-square distribution. Further, there is more than one nominal variable, so we know that we will need to use the chi-square test of independence.

As with the chi-square test for goodness-of-fit, we have four assumptions. First, we know that we are working with two nominal variables. We also pass our second assumption because each participant is only in one cell—there is no overlap. Third, all participants should be randomly selected. In our case, participants were not randomly selected from all students trying out for the orchestra. We concentrated on one school district. As a result, we will need to be cautious about our conclusions. Finally, because we have more than five times as many participants as cells (150 total), we have a large enough sample size.

Step 2. State the null and research hypotheses.

As with our chi-square for goodness-of-fit, we state our hypotheses in words rather than with words and symbols. Because the chi-square test for independence tests for whether one variable depends on the other test, we will use such words in our hypotheses. So, for our example:

Null Hypothesis: Getting accepted into the state orchestra is independent of whether students received special music lessons.

Research Hypothesis: Getting accepted into the state orchestra depends on whether students received special music lessons.

Step 3. Determine the characteristics of the comparison distribution.

The formula to determine the degrees of freedom for the chi-square test for independence is: $df_{\chi^2} = (k_{Row} - 1)(k_{Column} - 1)$. For our example, the row variable is whether students received music lessons, and there are two levels. So, we calculate for the row variable as: $(k_{Row} - 1) = 2 - 1 = 1$. Our column variable is whether students were accepted into the orchestra, and there are also two levels, $(k_{Column} - 1) = 2 - 1 = 1$. When we put both together, we know that $df_{\chi^2} = 1$.

Step 4. Determine the critical values, or cutoffs.

Now that we know our degrees of freedom, we can determine our critical value. For our example, we'll keep the p level at 0.05 and look at the table in Appendix B of the text under 1 degree of freedom. When we do that, we'll find that our critical value is 3.84. As a result, to reject the null hypothesis, our test statistic must be greater than 3.84, as pictured in the following figure from the text:

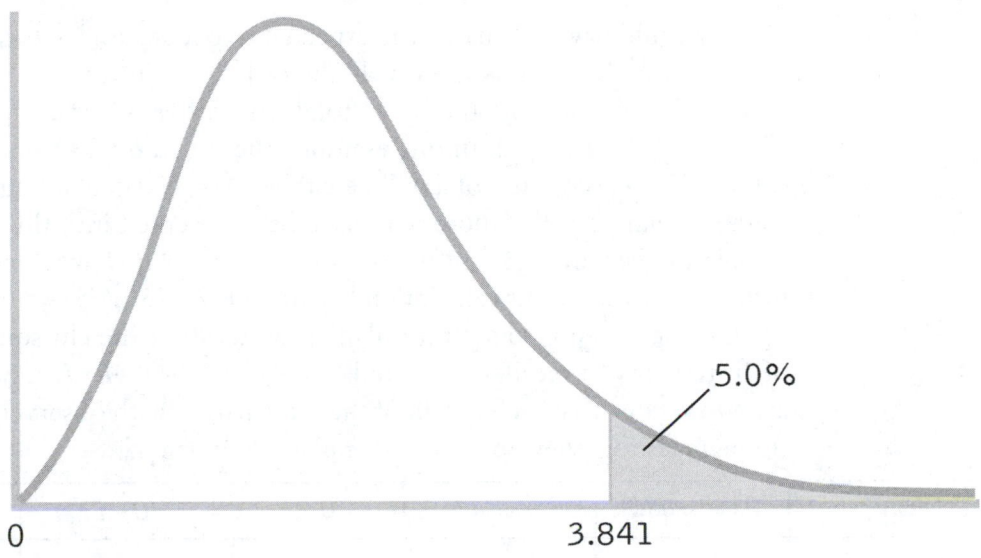

0   3.841

Step 5. Calculate the test statistic.

For this step, we will need to determine what the expected frequencies will be. For our example, we can look at the total number of students who made it into the orchestra (30) and divide that number by the total number of students who tried out for the orchestra (150). This means that the acceptance rate is 20.0% (30/150) for our sample. If receiving music lessons does not affect the outcome, then we would expect the same percentage regardless of the music-lesson condition. We also know that 80% of people did not gain acceptance into the orchestra. Therefore, we expect that 80% of people regardless of the music condition would not get into the orchestra. Because we would expect 20% of the 75 people who received lessons to get accepted, our expected frequency becomes: $(0.20)(75) = 15$. This is also the same frequency for those who did not receive lessons. Now, we expect 80% of the students in each music condition group to not get into the orchestra, so this expected frequency becomes: $(0.80)(75) = 60$. Now, we can go ahead and create a table of expected frequencies based on this information.

	EXPECTED		
	Accepted into orchestra	Not accepted into orchestra	Totals
Received music lessons	15	60	75
No lessons	15	60	75
Totals	30	120	

We could have calculated the expected frequency for each cell using a formula instead. To do this, we divide the cell's column total by the grand total and multiply that by the row total. In other words, the formula is: $(Total_{Column}/N)(Total_{Row})$. In our example, the grand total (N) is 150. Our row total is 75. Our column total will be either 30 or 120 depending on which cell we are looking at. For those who have been accepted into the orchestra, our calculation becomes: $(30/150)(75) = 15$. For those who have not been accepted into the orchestra, our calculation becomes: $(120/150)(75) = 60$.

Our next step is to use formula that we used for the chi-square goodness-of-fit test. If you recall, our formula was: $\chi^2 = \Sigma\,[(O - E)^2/E]$. So, we can create a new table that includes all of the information with observed and expected frequencies together, so we can complete the formula.

Category	Observed (O)	Expected (E)	O – E	(O – E)²	(O – E)²/ E
Lessons, accepted	22	15	7.0	49	3.27
Lessons, not accepted	53	60	–7.0	49	0.82
No lessons, accepted	8	15	–7.0	49	3.27
No lessons, not accepted	67	60	7.0	49	0.82

Then, we can add up everything in our right-most column: $(3.27 + 0.82 + 3.27 + 0.82) = 8.18$.

Step 6. Make a decision.

Because 8.18 is greater than 3.84, we can reject the null hypothesis. This means that getting into the orchestra depends on the whether the students received music lessons. When reporting the findings, we would use the same format as the chi-square goodness-of-fit and include the degrees of freedom, the total number of participants, the test statistic, and whether the test statistic is greater or less than the critical value, $\chi^2 = (1, N = 150) = 8.18, p < 0.05$.

Even if we are able to reject the null hypothesis, the results of the hypothesis test alone do not tell us how large the effect is. Before we can say that our findings are important, we need to calculate **Cramer's V or Cramer's phi, ϕ,** which is the standard effect size used with the chi-square for independence. The formula for *Cramer's V* is:

$$\sqrt{\frac{\chi^2}{(N)(df_{Row\,/\,Column})}}$$

For this formula, χ^2 is the test statistic that was calculated, N is the total number of participants in the study, and $df_{Row/Column}$ is the smaller of either the degrees of freedom for the row or column variable.

Let's calculate Cramer's V for our example. In our previous example, $\chi^2 = 8.18$, there were 150 participants, and the degrees of freedom for both variables was 1. If we plug these numbers into the formula:

$$\sqrt{\frac{\chi^2}{(N)(df_{Row\,/\,Column})}} = \sqrt{\frac{8.18}{(150)(1)}} = \sqrt{0.0545} = 0.23$$

We can use the Table 13-10 from the text to determine how large the effect is.

TABLE 13-10. CONVENTIONS FOR DETERMINING EFFECT SIZE BASED ON CRAMER'S V

Jacob Cohen (1992) developed guidelines to determine whether particular effect sizes should be considered small, medium, or large. The effect-size guidelines vary depending on the size of the contingency table. There are different guidelines based on whether the smaller of the two degrees of freedom (row or column) is 1, 2, or 3.

EFFECT SIZE	WHEN $df_{ROW/COLUMN} = 1$	WHEN $df_{ROW/COLUMN} = 2$	WHEN $df_{ROW/COLUMN} = 3$
Small	0.10	0.07	0.06
Medium	0.30	0.21	0.17
Large	0.50	0.35	0.29

Based on this information, because Cramer's V is larger than guidelines for a small effect but smaller than a medium effect, we would probably say that we have a small-to-medium effect. Cramer's V would then get added at the end when we report our results: $\chi^2 = (1, N = 150) = 8.18, p < 0.05$, Cramer's $V = 0.23$.

Another way to understand our findings with greater depth is to graph the data. When graphing a chi square, it makes more sense to graph proportions or percentages rather than frequencies. To determine the proportions, let's review the breakdown for participants in each group for our study:

	Accepted into Orchestra	Not Accepted into Orchestra	Totals
Received music lessons	22	53	75
No lessons	8	67	75
Totals	30	120	

From our example, we evenly divided the 150 total participants into 75 who received music lessons and 75 who did not. As a result, when calculating proportions to get graphed, our denominator will be 75.

Received Music Lessons: Accepted into orchestra (22/75) = 0.29
not accepted into orchestra (53/75) = 0.71

No Music Lessons: Accepted into orchestra (8/75) = 0.11
Not accepted into orchestra (67/75) = 0.89

We can put this information into the following table and see that the proportions for each condition should add up to 1.00 or if we had used percentages, 100%.

	Accepted into orchestra	Not accepted into orchestra	
Received music lessons	0.29	0.71	1.00
No lessons	0.11	0.89	1.00

With this information, we can then graph our proportions. When using proportions, our y-axis should range from 0 to 1.0.

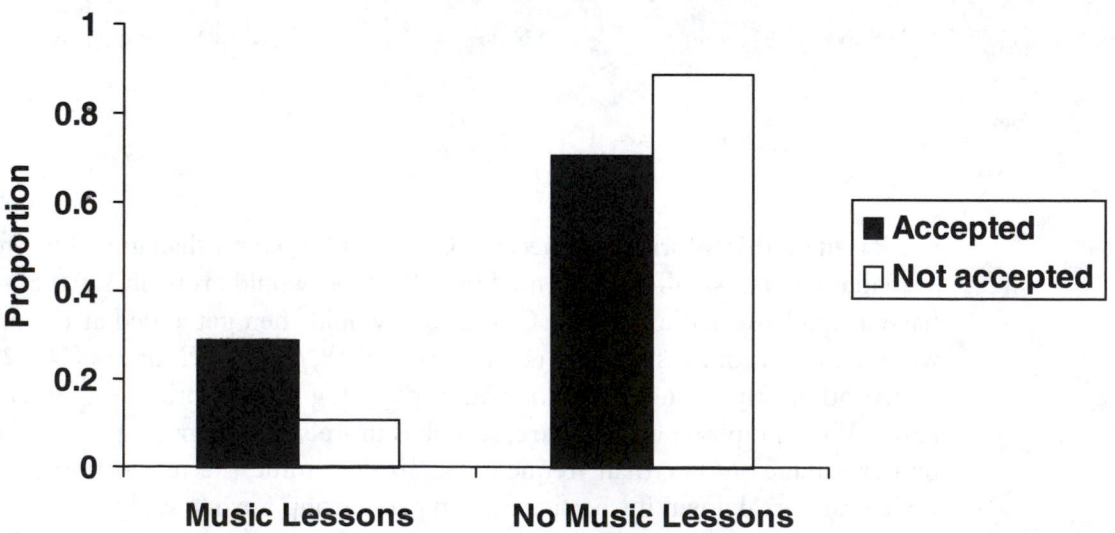

Aside from using Cramer's V to determine effect size, we can also use **relative risk**, which is a measure created by making a ratio of two conditional proportions. We tend to refer to relative risk when we're looking at the probabilities of contracting diseases or other negative outcomes. When we're working with outcomes that are not as serious and negative, we refer to this measure as **relative likelihood** or **relative chance.**

For our example with music lessons, we could look at the relative likelihood of getting accepted. To do this, we could first take the proportion of getting accepted with lessons $(22/75) = 0.29$ and divide this by the proportion of those who got accepted without lessons $(8/75) = 0.11$. This would leave us with a relative likelihood of $0.29/0.11 = 2.64$. We would interpret this by indicating that the chance of students who receive special music lessons getting accepted is 2.64 times higher than for students not receiving special lessons. We could also reverse this ratio for $0.11/0.29 = 0.38$, meaning that when students do not receive lessons they are 0.38 times less likely to get into the orchestra than if they receive lessons.

You always want to be aware of base rates when using or reading about relative risks. Although something might be twice or three times as likely to occur, this may not really be a meaningful difference. For example, imagine that the rate of contracting a disease is 0.001% (1 in 100,000). But, we find out that those who wear glasses are three times as likely to contract the disease or 0.003% (3 in 100,000). It sounds like wearing glasses would be risky if we want to avoid contracting this disease; however, when we look more closely at the numbers, we can see that we're not really talking about a meaningful increase in risk.

> ## Digging Deeper into the Data: A Deeper Understanding of Chi Square

If you remember, when we calculated ANOVAs and were able to reject the hypothesis, we knew that there was a difference between our groups somewhere, but we needed to calculate post-hoc tests to determine exactly where that difference was. We have a similar problem with chi-square tests. When we have a significant chi-square test, we know that some of the cells' observed frequencies are different from what we would expect by chance. However, we don't know which cell frequencies are different.

We can make this determination using the **adjusted standardized residual,** or the difference between the observed frequency and the expected frequency for a cell in a chi-square research design, divided by the standard error. It is a measure of the number of standard errors that an observed frequency falls from its associated expected frequency. In a way, it's a lot like a z score. Just like a z score, it also doesn't matter whether the adjusted standardized residual is positive or negative. In general, if the adjusted standardized residual for a particular cell is greater than 2 or 3, we can say that the cell's observed frequency is significantly different from what we would expect by chance. Because the adjusted standardized residual is too complicated to calculate by hand, you'll want to use a computer program to perform the analysis. The following table is a copy of a printout for our study of the correlation between music lessons and admission to the orchestra:

Receiving Lessons ٭ Acceptance into Orchestra Crosstabulation

			Orchestra		Total
			No	Yes	No
Lessons	None	Count	67	8	75
		Expected Count	60.0	15.0	75.0
		Adjusted Residual	**2.9**	**–2.9**	
	Lessons	Count	53	22	75
		Expected Count	60.0	15.0	75.0
		Adjusted Residual	**–2.9**	**2.9**	
Total		Count	120	30	150

Looking at the table, we can see the adjusted standardized residuals are bolded. Because the adjusted standardized residuals are 2.9 and –2.9, this means that each cell is different than what would be expected by chance. In other words, all four observed frequencies are farther from the expected frequencies than would occur if the null hypothesis were true.

Lastly, the text discusses some controversies regarding chi squares. We had previously discussed that the minimum expected frequency per cell should be 5. However, if you cannot meet this, Cochran's rule states that an expected value can be as low as 1 if no more than 20% of the expected values are less than 5. We could also look to see whether the total number of participants is more than five times the number of cells. We can probably use a chi-square test if both of these criteria are met.

STUDY QUESTIONS

1. The chi-square tests are a part of the legacy of _____.
   a. Karl Pearson
   b. Ronald Fisher
   c. William Gosset
   d. Francis Galton

2. The chi-square statistic is based on a comparison between the:
   a. mean scores of two independent samples of observations.
   b. median ranks of two independent samples of observations.
   c. frequency of an observation and the frequency expected by chance.
   d. number of interval variables in two or more nonoverlapping categories.

3. A researcher may use an analysis of variance to determine whether three or more groups of participants are from populations with identical means. In contrast, a researcher may use a chi-square test to determine whether:
   a. the different categories of a nominal variable have the same mean.
   b. a single group of participants is from a population with a specified mean.
   c. two or more groups of participants are from populations with identical means.
   d. an observed frequency distribution is the same as an expected frequency distribution.

4. A nonparametric test should be used when the dependent variable is measured on a(n) _____ scale.
   a. nominal or an ordinal
   b. nominal or an interval
   c. ordinal or an interval
   d. nominal, ordinal, or interval

5. Which of the following is the best advice to give a researcher whose sample size is small and who suspects that the population distribution of dependent variable values is extremely skewed?
   a. Use a parametric test.
   b. Use a nonparametric test.
   c. Use either a parametric test or a nonparametric test.
   d. Re-design the study, because there are no appropriate statistical tests for this research situation.

6. Which of the following is a (are) consequence(s) of analyzing your data with a nonparametric test?
   a. Estimates of differences are less precise and therefore less trustworthy.
   b. There is an increase in the probability of making a Type II error.
   c. There is a decrease in statistical power.
   d. All of these are consequences.

7. To maximize statistical power and minimize the probability of committing a Type II error, researchers should measure the dependent variable on a(n) _____ scale whenever possible.
   a. nominal
   b. ordinal
   c. interval
   d. nonparametric

8. For cases in which the assumptions of a parametric test are clearly violated:
   a. the equivalent nonparametric test is often more powerful.
   b. the equivalent, but less powerful, nonparametric test should be conducted.
   c. the parametric test should be conducted to avoid sacrificing statistical power.
   d. there is no alternative but to replace the independent and dependent variables.

9. The **chi-square test for goodness-of-fit** is used to test hypotheses about _____ variable(s).
   a. one ordinal
   b. one nominal
   c. two ordinal
   d. two nominal

10. The **chi-square test for independence** is used to test hypotheses about _____ variable(s).
    a. one ordinal
    b. one nominal
    c. two ordinal
    d. two nominal

11. Which of the following is/are an assumption(s) for the chi-square tests?
    a. Groups must have equal variances.
    b. Observations must be independent.
    c. Variables must be measured on an interval scale.
    d. Observations must be sampled from a normal population.

12. According to Delucchi (1983), which of the following is the most important principle regarding low expected cell frequencies in the chi-square tests?
    a. There should be at least five times as many individuals (participants) as there are cells.
    b. The tests should not be used if any of the expected cell frequencies is less than 10.
    c. The tests should not be used if any of the expected cell frequencies is less than 5.
    d. The tests have adequate power even with expected frequencies as low as 1.

13. Which of the following is the formula for finding the degrees of freedom associated with a chi-square test for goodness-of-fit?
    a. (number of columns – 1) (number of rows – 1)
    b. (number of columns – 1) / (number of rows – 1)
    c. number of categories – 1
    d. number of participants – 1

14. Suppose that the results of a large national survey showed the following prevalence of psychological disorders in the adult population of the United States:

Anxiety disorders	15%
Drug and alcohol dependence	20%
Affective disorders	10%
Psychosis	2%
No diagnosed disorder	53%

    To test whether these disorders are distributed among college students as they are among adults, a clinical psychologist gathers information from a representative sample of 1000 students from U.S. colleges. In this example, the expected frequency distribution is:
    a. the number of students in each of the diagnostic categories.
    b. the number of students in each of the diagnostic categories, expressed as percentages.
    c. the distribution of percentages reported for adults, converted to frequencies per 1000.
    d. impossible to determine from the information provided.

15. Steinman (2006) compared the rate of twinning in mothers who do not consume animal products (a vegan diet) to that of mothers in the general population. Suppose that 2% of mothers in the general population give birth to twins. Suppose further that Steinman studied the birth records of 1000 vegan mothers and observed just five (5) births of twins. What is the expected frequency of twins in the sample of vegan mothers?
    a. (0.02)(1000) = 20
    b. (0.05)(1000) = 50
    c. 1000 / 5 = 200
    d. (0.02)(0.05)(1000) = 1

16. Chi-square distributions are:
    a. negatively skewed.
    b. positively skewed.
    c. approximately bell-shaped.
    d. composed of positive and negative values.

17. How is a chi-square table used in hypothesis testing?
    a. A computed chi-square statistic is compared to a critical value of chi-square from the table.
    b. The table provides estimates of power for different significance levels and effect sizes.
    c. The table provides estimates of effect size for different levels of power and significance.
    d. A p value for a computed chi-square statistic is compared to the appropriate p level for the specified degrees of freedom.

18. Which of the following is the formula for computing the chi-square statistic?

    a. $\chi^2 = \dfrac{Total_{Column}}{N}(Total_{Row})$ b. $\chi^2 = \Sigma\left[\dfrac{(O-E)^2}{E}\right]$

    c. $\chi^2 = \Sigma\left[\dfrac{(O-E)^2}{O}\right]$ d. $\chi^2 = \Sigma\sqrt{\dfrac{(O-E)^2}{O}}$

19. Portion of a Chi-Square Table

df	Significance Level		
	0.10	0.05	0.01
1	2.706	3.841	6.635
2	4.605	5.992	9.211
3	6.252	7.815	11.345
4	7.780	9.488	13.277
5	9.237	11.071	15.087

Suppose that a researcher computed the chi-square statistic in a test of the null hypothesis that four brands of a product are equally preferred in a population of potential consumers. If the test is conducted at the 0.01 level of significance and the computed value of chi-square is 10.07, then the null hypothesis should:
    a. be rejected because 10.07 is greater than 6.252.
    b. be rejected because 10.07 is greater than 7.780.
    c. not be rejected because 10.07 is less than 11.345.
    d. not be rejected because 10.07 is less than 13.277.

20. In a market survey of 99 respondents, a researcher tested the null hypothesis that three brands are equally preferred in the population. The researcher found that 40 respondents preferred Brand A, 35 stated a preference for Brand B, and 24 preferred Brand C. Which of the following represents an appropriate step in the calculation of the chi-square statistic?
    a. $(40 - 35)2 / 35$
    b. $(40 - 35)2 / 24$
    c. $(40 - 33)2 / 33$
    d. $(40 - 33)2 / 40$

21. A student at a Canadian university conducted a survey of the food preferences (vegetarian, vegan, or neither) and country of origin (Canada, the United States, or other) of 100 students at her university. To test whether food preference and country of origin are related in the population, she should conduct a(n) _____.
    a. chi-square test for independence
    b. independent-samples t test
    c. one-way between-groups analysis of variance
    d. chi-square test for goodness of fit

22. The table of cells for a chi-square test for independence is called a:
    a. χ^2 summary table.
    b. cross-tabulation.
    c. chi-square distribution.
    d. contingency table.

23. For any cell in a contingency table, the expected frequency is the number of observations you would expect in that cell if the:
    a. variables are independent.
    b. variables are not independent.
    c. population means are the same.
    d. population means are not the same.

24. *Unlike* a chi-square for goodness-of-fit, a chi-square test for independence requires that you compute differences between observed and expected frequencies for each combination of categories, that is, for each _____ of the contingency table.
    a. cell
    b. row
    c. column
    d. variable

25. The following formula is used to compute the _____ in a contingency table.

$$\frac{Total_{Column}}{N}(Total_{Row})$$

a. degrees of freedom
b. expected frequency of a cell
c. observed frequency of a cell
d. chi-square statistic

26. The _____ may be computed by dividing the column total ($Total_{Column}$) by the total number of participants (N) and multiplying this quotient by the row total ($Total_{Row}$).
a. observed frequency for a given cell
b. effect size for a chi-square test
c. chi-square test statistic
d. expected frequency for a given cell

27. Which of the following is the formula for determining degrees of freedom for the chi-square test for independence?
a. $N-1$
b. number of cells -1
c. $(k_{Column}-1)(k_{Row}-1)$
d. $(N)(df_{Row/Column})$

28. A researcher hypothesized that the most intense facial displays of emotion are negative emotions expressed on the left side of the face. Accordingly, the researcher made full-face photographs of an actor either displaying a happy or an angry expression, then used imaging software to create composite photographs of the left and right sides of each face. A total of 68 participants selected one of the four composite photographs identified in the following table as the most intense facial display of emotion. The expected frequencies are in parentheses.

	Expression		
Photograph	Happy	Angry	Total
Left Side	8	26	34
Right Side	20	14	34
Total	28	40	68

What is the expected frequency in the cell that corresponds to the *Happy* expression displayed on the *Left Side* of the face?
a. 8
b. (8 / 28)(68) = 19.43
c. (28 / 68)(34) = 14
d. (8 / 20)(28) = 11.2

29. Which of the following is the standard effect size used for a chi-square test for independence?
    a. the adjusted standardized residual
    b. the phi coefficient
    c. R^2
    d. Cramer's V

30. Which of the following is the formula used to compute the measure of effect size for a chi-square test for independence?

    a. $\sqrt{\dfrac{\chi^2}{df}}$ b. $\sqrt{\dfrac{\chi^2}{N}}$

    c. $\sqrt{\dfrac{\chi^2}{(N)(df_{Row\,/\,Column})}}$ d. $\dfrac{\sqrt{\chi^2}}{(N)(df_{Row\,/\,Column})}$

31. In a chi-square research design, the measure called **relative risk** is computed as the:
    a. ratio of two conditional proportions.
    b. square root of the quotient determined by dividing the chi-square statistic by the product of the sample size and the smaller of the row and column degrees of freedom.
    c. ratio of the sum of the expected cell frequencies to the sum of the observed cell frequencies.
    d. difference between an expected frequency and an observed frequency divided by the standard error.

32. A significant chi-square hypothesis test means that:
    a. at least some of the cells' observed frequencies are significantly different from their corresponding expected frequencies.
    b. the variability among the scores for one nominal variable is significantly different from the variability among the scores for at least one other nominal variable.
    c. the number of participants is at least five times greater than the number of cells in the contingency table.
    d. the expected frequencies in any given column of cells are significantly different from the expected frequencies in any given row of cells.

33. Which of the following refers to a measure of the number of standard errors that an observed frequency falls from its associated expected frequency?
    a. Cramer's V
    b. relative risk
    c. chi square
    d. adjusted standardized residual

34. The major source of controversy in chi-square hypothesis tests is the assumption regarding the minimum expected frequencies for each cell. According to the text, it is probably safe to use the chi-square test as long as:
    a. the minimum expected frequency is at least 10.
    b. no more than 20% of the cells have an expected frequency below 10.
    c. the minimum expected frequency for a given cell is greater than or equal to the observed frequency for that cell.
    d. no more than 20% of the cells have an expected frequency below 5 and the number of participants is at least 5 times the number of cells.

35. What is the primary problem with very low expected cell frequencies in a chi-square test?
    a. There is an increased risk of committing a Type I error.
    b. there is an increased risk of committing a Type II error.
    c. Very low expected cell frequencies usually mean that there are too few participants in the study.
    d. Power may be inflated to the point of rejecting the null hypothesis when it should not be rejected.

ANSWERS TO CHAPTER 13 STUDY QUESTIONS

Question Number	Correct Answer	Question Number	Correct Answer
1	a, p. 579	19	c, pp. 588–591
2	c, p. 579	20	c, p. 592
3	d, p. 579	21	a, pp. 594–595
4	a, pp. 581–582	22	d, p. 595
5	b, p. 582	23	a, p. 596
6	d, p. 583	24	a, p. 596
7	c, p. 584	25	b, p. 597
8	a, p. 584	26	d, p. 597
9	b, p. 586	27	c, p. 596
10	d, p. 586	28	c, p. 597
11	b, p. 587	29	d, p. 599
12	a, p. 588	30	c, p. 599
13	c, p. 588	31	a, p. 601
14	c, p. 589	32	a, p. 603
15	a, p. 589	33	d, pp. 603–604
16	b, p. 589	34	d, p. 605
17	a, p. 589	35	b, p. 605
18	b, p. 590		

CHAPTER FOURTEEN

BEYOND CHI SQUARE

Nonparametric Tests with Ordinal Data

CHAPTER OUTLINE

Nonparametric Statistics: When the Data Are Ordinal
- Hypothesis Tests with Ordinal Data: A Nonparametric Equivalent for Every Parametric Test
- Examining the Data: Deciding to Use a Nonparametric Test for Ordinal Data

Spearman Rank-Order Correlation Coefficient: Quantifying the Association Between Two Ordinal Variables
- Calculating Spearman's Correlation: Converting Interval Observations to Rank-Ordered Observations
- Eyeballing the Data: Using Your Scientific Common Sense

Nonparametric Hypothesis Tests: Comparing Groups Using Ranks
- The Wilcoxon Signed-Rank Test for Matched Pairs: A Nonparametric Test for Within-Groups Designs
- The Mann-Whitney U Test: Comparing Two Independent Groups Using Ordinal Data
- Kruskal-Wallis H Test: Comparing the Mean Ranks of Several Groups

Digging Deeper into the Data: Transforming Skewed Data, the Meaning of Interval Data, and Bootstrapping
- Coping with Skew: Data Transformations
- Controversies in Nonparametric Hypothesis Tests: What Really Is an Interval Variable?
- Bootstrapping: When the Data Do the Work Themselves

LEARNING OBJECTIVES

After studying this chapter, you should be able to:

1. Define each of the following terms and provide examples that are not in the text: *Spearman rank-order correlation coefficient, Wilcoxon signed-rank test, Mann-Whitney U test, Kruskal-Wallis H test, square root transformation, log transformation, logarithm,* and *bootstrapping.*

2. Distinguish between subjective and objective approaches to assessment and evaluation, and explain the role of the normal curve in objective assessment.

3. Distinguish between a Spearman rank-order correlation coefficient, Wilcoxon signed-rank test, Mann-Whitney U test, or a Kruskal-Wallis H test, and know when you'd want to use each one.

4. Convert interval data to ordinal data to calculate a Spearman rank-order correlation coefficient, a Wilcoxon signed-rank test, a Mann-Whitney U test, or a Kruskal-Wallis H test.

5. Recognize when you would want to transform your data using a square root or log transformation.

CHAPTER REVIEW

> Nonparametric Statistics: When the Data Are Ordinal

We cannot use parametric tests when data are ordinal. If you recall from previous chapters, ordinal data are rank-ordered. For example, we might want to look at variables from individuals who were in the top 10 in a race. Based on such data, we can't have a normal distribution that is bell-shaped because there will only be one individual at every value (e.g., one person in first place, one person in second place, etc.). In this chapter, we'll be learning about four different alternatives to the parametric tests when we have ordinal data. These nonparametric tests aren't any more difficult than the parametric tests. We just need to know when to use them and recognize when we are working with ordinal data.

The best thing about these tests is that they allow us to conduct a hypothesis test when we otherwise could not because we do not have a normal distribution. Unfortunately, when using these nonparametric tests, there are no effect size estimates. Plus, it can be tricky to calculate confidence intervals unless we use the median rather than the mean. Because this creates a less than ideal situation, we only want to use nonparametric tests when we have no other choice.

There are actually two situations when we use nonparametric tests for ordinal data. The most obvious one is when our data are ordinal. However, we may also consider using these nonparametric tests when our underlying population distribution is greatly skewed due to a small sample size. When this happens, we may want to consider transforming our data from interval to ordinal.

For example, imagine that we're looking at the SAT verbal scores of students in a particular class:

500   525   475   530   450   510   540   430   490   750

Based on this data, we have a severe outlier with an SAT verbal score of 750 compared to the rest of the class. If we placed these data in order from lowest to highest score, we could then assign ranks, as the following table shows.

Original Score (Interval)	430	450	475	490	500	510	525	530	540	750
Ranked Score (Ordinal)	10	9	8	7	6	5	4	3	2	1

With this adjustment, the 750 is no longer an outlier but becomes the first ranking.

> Spearman Rank-Order Correlation Coefficient: Quantifying the Association Between Two Ordinal Variables

In this section, we'll be discussing the **Spearman rank-order correlation coefficient,** which is a nonparametric statistic that quantifies the association between two ordinal variables. The Spearman rank-order correlation coefficient is also known as Spearman's rho and is symbolized by the coefficient, r_s.

As an example, imagine we want to know whether the class ranking of students is related to their SAT verbal scores. For the purposes of our example, let's stick to a sample of 12 students. We receive the class rankings, which are ordinal by nature. However, the SAT verbal scores are not ordinal. Because a Spearman correlation can only be used if both variables are ordinal, we will need to transform the SAT verbal scores to ranking as well.

To transform the scores to rankings, we should organize the SAT verbal scores from highest to lowest and rank them. If there are students that share the same SAT verbal score, we take the average of the two ranks that the participants would hold, as the following table shows.

Student	SAT Verbal Score	SAT Rank
Emily	710	1
Jacob	680	2
Danielle	660	3
Tyra	630	4
Simeon	570	5
Natasha	560	6.5
Max	560	6.5
Christopher	510	8
Tabitha	500	9
Gordon	490	10
Gwendolyn	470	11
Sam	450	12

In this table, we can see that both Natasha and Max earned a 560 on the SAT verbal. So, we'd take the average of the two ranks that they would hold if the scores were different $(6 + 7)/2 = 6.5$. As you can see, both students would receive a rank of 6.5. Now that we have converted our score to ranks, we can combine this information with the class-ranking data.

Student	SAT Rank	Class Rank
Emily	1	1
Jacob	2	5
Danielle	3	3
Tyra	4	7
Simeon	5	2
Natasha	6.5	9
Max	6.5	11
Christopher	8	4
Tabitha	9	12
Gordon	10	6
Gwendolyn	11	8
Sam	12	10

Now that our data are ready we can work toward calculating the correlation. Just like we did with a Pearson correlation, we test the null hypothesis that the correlation coefficient is 0. If we reject the null hypothesis, it means that the correlation is significantly different from 0. We can also think of the Spearman correlation coefficient as a descriptive statistic.

To calculate the correlation, we will need the formula which is:

$$r_s = 1 - \frac{6(\sum D^2)}{N(N^2 - 1)}$$

For this formula, D refers to the difference in rank and N refers to the sample size, which is 12 for our example. This means that we need to calculate D and square it for each participant.

Student	SAT Rank	Class Rank	Difference (D)	Squared Difference (D^2)
Emily	1	1	0	0
Jacob	2	5	−3	9
Danielle	3	3	0	0
Tyra	4	7	−3	9
Simeon	5	2	3	9
Natasha	6.5	9	−2.5	6.25
Max	6.5	11	−4.5	20.25
Christopher	8	4	4	16
Tabitha	9	12	−3	9
Gordon	10	6	4	16
Gwendolyn	11	8	3	9
Sam	12	10	2	4

Now that we've calculated D and D^2 we can go back to our formula and take the sum of these differences: $D^2 = (0 + 9 + 0 + 9 + 9 + 6.25 + 20.25 + 16 + 9 + 16 + 9 + 4) = 107.5$. Then, we plug this into our formula:

$$r_s = 1 - \frac{6(\Sigma D^2)}{N(N^2 - 1)}$$

$$= 1 - \frac{6(107.5)}{12(12^2 - 1)} = 1 - \frac{645}{12(144 - 1)} = 1 - \frac{645}{1716} = 1 - 0.376 = 0.62$$

Based on our example, the Spearman correlation coefficient is 0.62. The Spearman correlation is similar to the Pearson correlation in that it can range from –1 to 1. The sign indicates the direction of the correlation rather than the strength of the correlation. Because we have obtained a positive correlation, we know that as one ranking increases so does the other ranking. In our example, as class rankings increase, so do SAT rankings.

Also remember that whenever we are working with any correlation—whether it is a Pearson correlation or a Spearman correlation coefficient—that we cannot infer causation. Even though in our example we have a fairly strong correlation, indicating that class rankings positively correlate with SAT rankings, we cannot say that one variable caused the other one to occur. As you probably recall, we can never know with a correlation whether variable A caused variable B, variable B caused variable A, or whether some other variable causes the others. In our example, probably some other variable such as IQ or overall time spent studying caused the rankings in class and SAT scores.

> Nonparametric Hypothesis Tests: Comparing Groups Using Ranks

In this section, we'll learn how to use three different nonparametric inferential statistics that provide an alternative to the parametric tests we've learned previously. First, we'll start with the **Wilcoxon signed-rank test,** which is a nonparametric hypothesis test used when we have two groups, a within-groups design, and an ordinal dependent variable. In other words, the Wilcoxon signed-rank test provides a nonparametric alternative to the dependent-samples t-test.

Let's describe an example. Imagine that we have our verbal SAT data and we want to know if the students' verbal SAT scores will change when they take the exam the second time around. The following are the data from our class for both tests and the difference score for the two tests:

Student	First SAT Score	Second SAT Score	Difference
Emily	710	700	10
Jacob	680	720	−40
Danielle	660	610	50
Tyra	630	730	−100
Simeon	570	510	60
Natasha	550	520	30
Max	560	580	−20
Christopher	510	420	90
Tabitha	500	420	80
Gordon	490	600	−110
Gwendolyn	470	540	−70
Sam	450	570	−120

To perform the test, we are going to continue to use the six steps of hypothesis testing that we've used so far.

Step 1. Determine the assumptions.

For this test, we have three different assumptions. First, we assume that the differences between pairs must be able to be ranked. Since our data are currently interval, we will need to convert the data, which we can easily do. Second, we should use random selection. Our participants all came from the same class and were not randomly selected; however, this should not prevent us with moving forward. Third, difference scores should come from a symmetric population distribution. It is also hard to know whether the difference scores are from a symmetric population, but we will still move forward with the test.

Step 2. State the null and research hypotheses.

Our null and research hypotheses are stated in words rather than symbols. For our example, the null hypothesis is that the SAT scores taken the second time will not be different from the first time. Our research hypothesis is that SAT scores taken the second time will differ from the first time.

Step 3. Determine the characteristics of the comparison distribution.

The Wilcoxon signed-rank test compares an obtained T statistic with the T distribution. This means that we will now need to decide on a cutoff level (0.05 for our purposes). We also need to decide on a one or two-tailed test. Because we just want to see if the scores will differ the second time around, we will use a two-tailed test. However, if we thought that scores would be either higher or lower the second time around, we would have a one-tailed test. Lastly, we need to determine our sample size, which is 12.

Step 4. Determine the critical values, or cutoffs.

In the appendix using Table B.9 (text pages B-16–B-17), we can determine the critical value. The biggest difference with the parametric t test is that we can reject the null hypothesis if our test statistic is equal to or smaller than the critical value. Using this table and given that our p level is 0.05, we have a two-tailed test, with 12 participants, our cutoff will be 13. When we calculate our hypothesis test, we will calculate two statistics. We want the smaller of the test statistics to be equal to or smaller than 13.

Step 5. Calculate the test statistic.

The first thing that we'll want to do is organize our difference scores from highest to lowest in terms of absolute value and rank them based on the absolute value as you'll see in the following table:

Student	Difference	Rank
Sam	−120	1
Gordon	−110	2
Tyra	−100	3
Christopher	90	4
Tabitha	80	5
Gwendolyn	−70	6
Simeon	60	7
Danielle	50	8
Jacob	−40	9
Natasha	30	10
Max	−20	11
Emily	10	12

Once we've done this, we need to expand our table and include two more columns. We need to split up the ranks based on positive differences and negative differences.

Student	Difference	Rank	Ranks for Positive Differences	Ranks for Negative Differences
Sam	−120	1		1
Gordon	−110	2		2
Tyra	−100	3		3
Christopher	90	4	4	
Tabitha	80	5	5	
Gwendolyn	−70	6		6
Simeon	60	7	7	
Danielle	50	8	8	
Jacob	−40	9		9
Natasha	30	10	10	
Max	−20	11		11
Emily	10	12	12	

We can now go and calculate the test statistic by summing the ranks for the positive scores and summing the ranks for the negative scores.

$$\Sigma R_+ = (4 + 5 + 7 + 8 + 10 + 12) = 46$$
$$\Sigma R_- = (1 + 2 + 3 + 6 + 9 + 11) = 32$$

The smaller of these is the test statistic, T. In our case, the smaller is $\Sigma R_+ = 32$.

Step 6. Make a decision.

Because our test statistic, 32, is not smaller than the critical value of 13, we fail to reject the null hypothesis. In other words, there was no significant difference between the second set of test scores and the first. There are no degrees of freedom so this gets reported as $T = 32$, $p > 0.05$.

When we have two groups that are not related, we would usually use the independent-samples t test. However, if we do not meet the assumptions of an independent-samples t test, we need to use a nonparametric test. In this case, we would use the **Mann-Whitney U test,** which is a nonparametric hypothesis test used when there are two groups, a between-groups design, and an ordinal dependent variable. Our parametric independent-samples t test was symbolized with t; for a Mann-Whitney U test, it is symbolized with U.

For our example, imagine that we want to compare the SAT verbal scores of males and females in our class. Although our data are interval, our sample is too small and not normally distributed so we should use a nonparametric test. We will need to convert our data into ranks. Let's first divide our data into the two groups for male and female students.

Female Students	SAT Score
Emily	710
Danielle	660
Tyra	630
Natasha	560
Tabitha	500
Gwendolyn	470

Male Students	SAT Score
Jacob	680
Simeon	570
Max	560
Christopher	510
Gordon	490
Sam	450

We'll now continue with our six steps of hypothesis testing just like we did for our parametric tests.

Step 1. Determine the assumptions.

For a Mann-Whitney U test, there are three assumptions. First, our data must be ordinal. At the moment, our data is interval, which we will need to convert to ordinal once we are prepared to calculate the test statistic. Second, we should have random selection. Because our data are not randomly selected, we will want to be very cautious about generalizing from our results. Third, no ranks should be tied. Although not ideal, there is only one tie in our data. As a result, it is probably safe to proceed with our example.

Step 2. State the null and research hypotheses.

For a Mann-Whitney U test, we state the null and research hypotheses in words rather than symbols. So for our example:

> Null Hypothesis: Male and female students do not differ in SAT verbal scores.

> Research Hypothesis: Male and female students differ in SAT verbal scores.

Step 3. Determine the characteristics of the comparison distribution.

The Mann-Whitney U test compares the two distributions of our two samples. In our case, we compare the SAT verbal scores of the six female students to the six male students. There is no comparison distribution in the sense of a parametric test.

Step 4. Determine critical values or cutoffs.

We can determine the critical values by looking at Table B.9 in the appendix of the textbook. There are two versions of the table—one for a one-tailed test and one for a two-tailed test. Based on our research hypothesis and since we don't have a more specific hypothesis regarding the verbal SAT scores, we'll go with a two-tailed test. We also only have critical values for a p level of 0.05. Next, to determine the critical value, we'll need the sample size of each group. In this table, we find the sample size for the first group across the top row and the sample size for the second group in the left-hand column. With this information, our cutoff is 5. For a nonparametric test, we want our test statistic to be equal to or smaller than our critical value. For our example, this means that we want our test statistic to be equal to or smaller than 5.

Step 5. Calculate the test statistic.

To calculate our test statistic, we first need to organize our data. We need to list our data from highest to lowest in a single column and then rank the data. Note that we had one set of tied scores (those of Natasha and Max), and we needed to average the ranks of the two scores.

Student	SAT Score	SAT Rank
Emily	710	1
Jacob	680	2
Danielle	660	3
Tyra	630	4
Simeon	570	5
Natasha	560	6.5
Max	560	6.5
Christopher	510	8
Tabitha	500	9
Gordon	490	10
Gwendolyn	470	11
Sam	450	12

Next, we'll want to list which group (Male or Female) each rank belongs to and then separate the ranks by group.

Student	SAT Score	SAT Rank	Gender (F vs. M)	F Ranks	M Ranks
Emily	710	1	F	1	
Jacob	680	2	M		2
Danielle	660	3	F	3	
Tyra	630	4	F	4	
Simeon	570	5	M		5
Natasha	560	6.5	F	6.5	
Max	560	6.5	M		6.5
Christopher	510	8	M		8
Tabitha	500	9	F	9	
Gordon	490	10	M		10
Gwendolyn	470	11	F	11	
Sam	450	12	M		12

Our next step is to sum up the ranks for each group, including subscripts (F and M) to indicate which group is which.

$$\Sigma R_F = 1 + 3 + 4 + 6.5 + 9 + 11 = 34.5$$

$$\Sigma R_M = 2 + 5 + 6.5 + 8 + 10 + 12 = 43.5$$

Now, we'll need our formula for our test statistic. We calculate separate test statistics for each group. For our first group (F), the test statistic is calculated by:

$$U_F = (n_f)(n_m) + \frac{(n_F)(n_F + 1)}{2} - \Sigma R_F$$

$$= (6)(6) + \frac{6(6+1)}{2} - 34.5 = 36 + \frac{6(7)}{2} - 34.5 = 36 + 21 - 34.5 = 22.5$$

The test statistic for our second group (M) is calculated by:

$$U_M = (n_M)(n_F) + \frac{(n_M)(n_M + 1)}{2} - \Sigma R_M$$

$$= (6)(6) = \frac{6(6+1)}{2} - 43.5 = 36 + \frac{6(7)}{2} - 43.5 = 36 + 21 - 43.5 = 13.5$$

Our test statistic for our first group, U_F, is 22.5, and our test statistic for our second group, U_M, is 13.5.

Step 6. Make a decision.

We then compare only our smaller test statistic, 13.5, to the critical value of 5. Because our test statistic is not smaller than our critical value, we fail to reject the null hypothesis. We cannot conclude that the SAT verbal scores of the female students are different from those of the male students. When writing this up, we report only the smaller test statistic and we do not include the subscript. The statistic will read, $U = 13.5$, $p > 0.05$.

For our last nonparametric test with ordinal data, we'll be using a **Kruskal-Wallis H test,** which is a nonparametric test used when there are more than two groups, a between-groups design, and an ordinal dependent variable. In other words, the Kruskal-Wallis H test can serve as a nonparametric alternative to the one-way ANOVA.

For our example, let's say that our 12 students who took the verbal SAT were in three different English classes in their high school, and we want to see whether there is a difference in their performance on the verbal SAT based on which class they attended. The following table shows our SAT data broken down by the three classes that the students are in:

Class A	SAT Score
Emily	710
Danielle	660
Max	560
Sam	450
Class B	
Jacob	680
Natasha	560
Gordon	490
Gwendolyn	470
Class C	
Tyra	630
Simeon	570
Christopher	510
Tabitha	500

Just with our other tests, we'll use the six steps of hypothesis testing:

Step 1. Determine the assumptions.

First, our data must be ordinal. When we are ready to calculate the test statistic, we will go ahead and convert our data. Second, we should use random selection. If our students were not randomly selected, we would be cautious about generalizing our results.

Step 2. State the null and research hypotheses.

Again, we'll state the null and research hypotheses in words rather than symbols.

> Null Hypothesis: The population distributions for SAT verbal scores for our three classes are the same.

> Research Hypothesis: The population distributions for SAT verbal scores for our three classes are different.

Step 3. Determine the characteristics of the comparison distribution.

The Kruskal-Wallis H test compares the three distributions presented by our three samples. Because the H distribution, our test statistic, is close enough to the chi-square distribution, we can use the chi-square table. For our test, we'll use a p value of 0.05 and we'll also need the degrees of freedom. The degrees of freedom is equal to the number of groups minus 1. Because we have three groups and 3 minus 1 equals 2, our degrees of freedom is 2.

Step 4. Determine critical values, or cutoffs.

Using the chi-square table, 2 degrees of freedom, and a p level of 0.05, our critical value, or cutoff is 5.991.

Step 5. Calculate the test statistic.

To calculate the test statistic, we'll need to organize our data. We'll use a similar technique that we used for the Mann-Whitney U test such that we'll organize the raw scores from lowest to highest in a single column and rank the data; then we'll mark which class the data belongs to and separate the ranks by group, as the following table shows.

Student	SAT Score	SAT Rank	Class (A, B, or C)	A Ranks	B Ranks	C Ranks
Emily	710	1	A	1		
Jacob	680	2	B		2	
Danielle	660	3	A	3		
Tyra	630	4	C			4
Simeon	570	5	C			5
Natasha	560	6.5	B		6.5	
Max	560	6.5	A	6.5		
Christopher	510	8	C			8
Tabitha	500	9	C			9
Gordon	490	10	B		10	
Gwendolyn	470	11	B		11	
Sam	450	12	A	12		

The formula for the test statistic is:

$$H = \left[\frac{12}{N(N+1)}\right]\left[\Sigma n(M - GM^2)\right]$$

This means that we'll need to take the mean of the ranks of each group and the grand mean (*GM*). First, let's take the mean of each group differentiating them with a subscript.

$$M_A = \frac{\Sigma R_A}{n} = (1+3+6.5+12)/4 = 5.625$$

$$M_B = \frac{\Sigma R_B}{n} = (2+6.5+10+11)/4 = 7.375$$

$$M_C = \frac{\Sigma R_C}{n} = (4+5+8+9)/4 = 6.5$$

$$GM = \frac{\Sigma R}{N} = (1+2+3+4+5+6.5+6.5+8+9+10+11+12)/12 = 6.5$$

Now that we have the pieces of the equation, we can go ahead and calculate our test statistic. For the first part of the equation, 12 is a constant and N refers to the total number of students, 12. For the second part with the sigma, Σ, we'll need to make that calculation for each of our three groups using n, the number of students in each group. So, let's go ahead and plug in our numbers:

$$H = \left[\frac{12}{N(N+1)}\right]\left[\Sigma n(M - GM)^2\right]$$

$$= \left[\frac{12}{12(12+1)}\right]\left[(4(5.625 - 6.5)^2) + (4(7.375 - 6.5)^2) + (4(6.5 - 6.5)^2)\right]$$

$$= [12/(12 \times 13)]\left[4(-0.875)^2(4(0.875)^2) + (4(0)^2)\right]$$

$$= [12/156][(4)(0.766) = (4)(0.766) + (4)(0)]$$

$$= [0.077][3.064 + 3.064 + 0]$$

$$H = 0.47$$

Step 6. Make a Decision.

We compare our test statistic, 0.47, to our critical value of 5.991. Because the test statistic is not larger than the critical value, we cannot reject the null hypothesis. There is no difference in SAT verbal scores by English class. In our write up, the statistics would read, $H = 0.47, p > 0.05$.

If we had found a significant difference, we would need to determine where the difference is between our groups. All we would know is that a difference exists somewhere. To determine where the difference lies, we would need to use a post-hoc test. Because we are using nonparametric tests, we'd want to follow-up with separate Mann-Whitney U tests to determine which groups are different.

> Digging Deeper into the Data: Transforming Skewed Data, the Meaning of Interval Data, and Bootstrapping

When our underlying population distribution is not normal, we could use a nonparametric test. However, there are three other ways that we could work with our data, which are discussed in this section.

First, we could transform skewed data into a normal distribution. When we convert our data from interval to ordinal, if we have skewed data, it will no longer be skewed. However, when we convert our data to ordinal, we need to use a nonparametric test, and as discussed previously, nonparametric tests have limitations. Instead of transforming our interval data to ordinal data, we could use a **square root transformation** which reduces skewness by compressing the negative and positive sides of the transformation.

For example, recall when we listed the skewed SAT scores in the beginning of the chapter with our outlier score of 750:

430   450   475   490   500   510   525   530   540   750

If we take the square root of these scores, our outlier score of 750 is now much less extreme and closer to the other scores:

20.74   21.21   21.79   22.13   22.36   22.58   22.91   23.02   23.24   27.39

A square root transformation is only one type of transformation. We could also decide to do a **log transformation,** which compresses the positive side of a skewed distribution and extends the smaller values on the negative side of the distribution. When values are less than 1, we must add a constant to the entire distribution so that the lowest value is 1.

To review, we can deal with skewed data in three ways:

1. Transform an interval variable to an ordinal variable and conduct a nonparametric test.
2. Use a square root transformation, which compresses the data on both ends to make it more normal.
3. Use a log transformation to normalize heavily skewed data, adding a constant if necessary so that the lowest value is equal to or greater than 1.

Our second way to work with a distribution that is not normal is to consider what is an interval variable. For example, some researchers believe that few scales that psychologists use are actually interval because the distance between two scores is not always the same. Others believe that while this may be true, data from these scales are not ordinal either. Newton and Rudestam (1999) provide suggestions for dealing with data that are hard to characterize as either interval or ordinal. First, use measures that are valid and reliable. Second, use the maximum amount of information possible by avoiding converting interval scales or nominal scales unless there is no alternative. Third, look for skew and outliers by graphing the data. Newton and Rudestam suggest using a nonparametric test when the distribution is far from normal, when the data are nominal or ordinal to begin with, when sample sizes are small, or the number of participants in each cell is far from equal.

The third option is to use **bootstrapping**, a statistical process by which the original sample data are used to represent the entire population, and we repeatedly take samples from the original sample data to form a confidence interval. We may need to use bootstrapping if certain circumstances limit our opportunity to collect vital data. When bootstrapping data, we treat the sample data as if they constituted the entire population. We do this through sampling with replacement. We first take the mean of the entire population. Then, we keep calculating the mean from samples of the number of the total number of participants with replacement. In other words, if we have five participants in our sample, we keep taking the mean of five participants. However, each time we choose one participant for our mean, the participant gets thrown back into the group of five participants and could be chosen again to calculate our mean. Because we would want to do this over and over thousands of times, we can use a computer program to help us with this. We only use bootstrapping when we have no other choice, but when we have a very limited sample, it is a fair way to work with our data and obtain a larger sample.

STUDY QUESTIONS

1. Imagine you run an ice-cream store, and you want to determine whether the rankings of your ten flavors are related to the rankings of your ten ice-cream toppings (e.g., whipped cream, hot fudge, etc.). Based on this data, it would be best to choose a _____ test. More specifically, we should use a _____.
   a. parametric test; Pearson correlation coefficient
   b. nonparametric test; Wilcoxon signed-rank test
   c. nonparametric test; Spearman rank-order correlation coefficient
   d. parametric test; paired-samples t test

2. Imagine that you are the coach of a high-school baseball team, and you want to analyze whether the rankings of your teammates differ this month compared to last month. Based on these data, it would be best to choose a _____ test. More specifically, we should use a _____.
   a. nonparametric test; Wilcoxon signed-rank test
   b. parametric test; paired-samples t test
   c. nonparametric test; Kruskal-Wallis H test
   d. parametric test; one-way between-groups ANOVA

3. As an avid-fan of NASCAR racing, you want to determine whether American cars ranked higher in the race than non-American cars. Based on this information, it would be best to choose a _____ test. More specifically, we should use a(n)_____.
   a. parametric test; independent-samples t test
   b. parametric test; Pearson correlation coefficient
   c. nonparametric test; Spearman rank-order correlation coefficient
   d. nonparametric test; Mann-Whitney U test

4. Using a test of short-term memory, you are investigating whether there are differences in rankings on the test based on whether the test-takers are in early adulthood, middle adulthood, or later adulthood. Based on this information, it would be best to choose a _____ test. More specifically, we should use a(n) _____.
   a. nonparametric test; Mann-Whitney U test
   b. nonparametric test; Kruskal-Wallis H test
   c. parametric test; independent-samples t test
   d. parametric test; one-way between-groups ANOVA

5. Deciding to transform interval data to ordinal data is a good idea when our underlying population is skewed with a severe outlier because:
   a. the outlier will be transformed to one of the rankings and will no longer stand out as an outlier.
   b. we can still use a parametric test with the statistical transformation.
   c. our sample size will increase when we transform the data, making it easier to reject the null hypothesis.
   d. transforming the data will give more statistical weight to the outlier.

6. The **Spearman rank-order correlation coefficient** is a nonparametric statistic that quantifies the association between:
   a. two interval variables.
   b. two nominal variables.
   c. two ordinal variables.
   d. two independent variables.

7. What would the following data look like if we converted these IQ scores to rankings (from lowest to highest)? The raw data are: 72, 98, 98, 105, 115, 137.
   a. 1, 2, 3, 4, 5, 6
   b. 1, 2.5, 2.5, 4, 5, 6
   c. 1, 2, 3, 4.5, 4.6, 6
   d. 1, 2, 2, 4, 5, 6

8. The formula for Spearman's correlation coefficient, r_s, is:
   a. $1 - \dfrac{\sum D}{N(N^2 - 1)}$

   b. $\dfrac{6(\sum D^2)}{N(N^2 - 1)}$

   c. $1 - \dfrac{N(\sum D^2)}{N - 1}$

   d. $1 - \dfrac{6(\sum D^2)}{N(N^2 - 1)}$

9. Imagine you want to calculate the Spearman's correlation coefficient of rankings of height and weight for a group of five individuals. Although you have their rankings for heights, you will need to convert the weight data into ordinal data. Be sure to rank the weights from highest to lowest.

Participant	Height	Weight
A	1	205
B	2	189
C	3	210
D	4	142
E	5	110

a. 0.30
b. 0.52
c. 0.15
d. 0.70

10. Which of the following statements is NOT true about the Spearman correlation coefficient?
    a. It ranges from –1 to 1.
    b. If the sign is negative, it means that the relationship between the two variables is weak.
    c. A correlation of 0 indicates that there is no relationship between the two variables.
    d. If the ranks of one variable are the same as the ranks of the second variable, Spearman's correlation coefficient would equal 1.

11. The **Wilcoxon signed-rank test** is used when there are two groups, a _____ - groups design, and an _____ variable.
    a. within; interval
    b. between; interval
    c. within; ordinal
    d. between; ordinal

12. Which of the following is NOT an assumption of the Wilcoxon signed-rank test?
    a. The differences between pairs must be able to be ranked.
    b. The difference scores should come from a symmetric population distribution.
    c. There must be at least 10 differences scores.
    d. We should use random selection.

13. Using a Wilcoxon signed-rank test with $N = 15$, a p level of 0.05, and a two-tailed test, our cutoff would be:
    a. 25.
    b. 15.
    c. 30.
    d. 19.

14. In a Wilcoxon signed-rank test, the formula $T = \Sigma R_{smaller}$ means that:
    a. We use the sum of the smaller of the ranks for the positive and negative scores to determine whether we can reject the null hypothesis.
    b. We use the sum of the bottom half of the ranks to determine whether we can reject the null hypothesis.
    c. We use the sum of all of our ranks, which should be smaller than the critical value, to reject the null hypothesis.
    d. We use the sum of the difference scores, which should be smaller than the critical value, to reject the null hypothesis.

15. Imagine that you administer a test of self-esteem to 10 individuals and then again five years later to the same people. You want to determine whether scores on the test will differ over the five-year span. After scoring the tests, you obtain the following difference scores: -7.5, -6.2, -5.1, -4.7, -3, 3.0, -2.5, 2.1, -1.9, 1.1. Using this information, T equals:
    a. 31.
    b. 24.
    c. 55.
    d. 7.

16. Participants are given a test of short-term memory before and after they receive tips of improving their memory skills. You want to see whether giving the memory tips affects their performance on the test. For the eight participants you obtain the following pairs of scores:

Before	After
91.1	96.2
90.2	97.3
85.7	91.4
83.5	79.9
77.4	81.9
71.2	75.0
68.9	72.1
65.1	66.0

Based on this information, T equals:

a. 36.
b. 30.
c. 16.
d. 6.

17. In a Wilcoxon signed-rank test, if our $N = 30$ and $T = 130$ with a p level of 0.05 and a two-tailed test, we would:

a. fail to reject the null hypothesis.
b. be unable to make a decision regarding the outcome of the test.
c. reject the null hypothesis.
d. need to look at the ratio of our ranks.

18. The **Mann-Whitney U test** is used when there are two groups, a _____ -groups design, and an _____ variable.

a. within; interval
b. between; interval
c. within; ordinal
d. between; ordinal

19. Which of the following is NOT an assumption for the Mann-Whitney U test?

a. We should use random selection.
b. Difference scores should come from a symmetric population distribution.
c. The data must be ordinal.
d. Ideally, no ranks are tied.

20. In a Mann-Whitney U test with 7 participants in each group, a p level of 0.05 and a two-tailed test, our critical value is:

a. 8.
b. 11.
c. 10.
d. 13.

21. Which of the following is the formula for calculating U in a Mann-Whitney U test for the first group?

a. $U_1 = (n_1)(n_1) + \dfrac{n_1(n_1+1)}{2} - \sum R_1$

b. $U_1 = (n_1)(n_2) + \dfrac{n_1(n_1+1)}{2} - \sum R_1$

c. $U_1 = (n^2) + \dfrac{n_1(n_1+1)}{2} - \sum R_1$

d. $U_1 = \dfrac{n_1(n_1+1)}{2} - \sum R_1$

22. You administer a test of math abilities to two groups of 6 students and will analyze the data using a Mann-Whitney U test. Group 1 earns the following scores: 19, 17, 16, 13, 12, 7. Group 2 earns the following scores: 16, 14, 12, 11, 9, 5. Based on this information, ΣR_1 and ΣR_2 would be, respectively:
    a. 31; 47.
    b. 30; 48.
    c. 47; 31.
    d. 48; 30.

23. You measure the amount of time that it takes two groups of rats to run through a maze and analyze the data using a Mann-Whitney U test. Group 1 earns the following times: 5.2, 5.7, 6.1, 6.2, 6.8, 7.3, 7.7. Group two earns the following times: 6.5, 6.6, 7.2, 7.8, 8.4, 8.8, 8.9. Based on this information, U would equal:
    a. 36.
    b. 69.
    c. 8.
    d. 41.

24. In a Mann-Whitney U test, if we have 12 people in each group and $\underline{U} = 40$ with a p level of 0.05 and a two-tailed test, we would:
    a. reject the null hypothesis.
    b. be unable to make a decision regarding the outcome of the test.
    c. need to compare ΣR_1 and ΣR_2 first.
    d. fail to reject the null hypothesis.

25. The **Kruskal-Wallis H test** is used when there are _____ two groups, a between-groups design, and an _____ variable.
    a. more than; ordinal
    b. more than; interval
    c. less than; ordinal
    d. less than; interval

26. If we are comparing four samples and using the Kruskal-Wallis H test, the number of degrees of freedom would be:
    a. 1.
    b. 2.
    c. 3.
    d. 4.

27. If our degrees of freedom equals 4 and we use a p level of 0.05 for our Kruskal-Wallis H test, the critical value would be:
    a. 7.780.
    b. 9.488.
    c. 13.277.
    d. 7.815.

28. The formula for H in the Kruskal-Wallis H test is:

   a. $\sum n(M - GM)^2$.

   b. $\left[\dfrac{12}{N(N+1)}\right]\left[\sum n(M - GM)^2\right]$.

   c. $\dfrac{\sum R}{N}$.

   d. $\left[N(N+1)\right]\left[(M - GM)^2\right]$.

29. Imagine that three groups of three separate individuals take a confidence scale. You want to analyze the scores using a Kruskal-Wallis H test. Group 1 earns scores of 55, 52, and 48. Group 2 earns scores of 53, 50, and 48. Group 3 earns scores of 54, 44, and 38. After converting this information to ranks, the grand mean would equal:
   a. 15.
   b. 11.
   c. 5.
   d. 10.

30. Using the Kruskal-Wallis H test, you want to analyze the reading speeds of a group of young adults, middle aged adults, and older adults. The young adult ranks are 1, 4, and 6.5. The middle-aged adult ranks are 3, 5, and 6.5. The older adult ranks are 2, 8, and 9. Using this information, H would equal:
   a. 9.50.
   b. 0.13.
   c. 4.08.
   d. 1.26.

31. Using a Kruskal-Wallis H test, you analyze whether liking scores differ for three groups of participants asked to drink three beverages. The participants in the first group score their drink as: 20, 19, and 18. Group two scores their drink as: 19, 17, and 16. Lastly, group three scores their drink as 10, 8, and 6. Based on this information, H would equal:
   a. 6.18.
   b. 46.5.
   c. 0.13.
   d. 18.75.

32. In a Kruskal-Wallis H test, if we have three groups and $H = 7.52$ with a p level of 0.05, we would:
    a. reject the null hypothesis.
    b. first need to know how many participants are in each group.
    c. need to know what the grand mean equals to make a determination about the null hypothesis.
    d. fail to reject the null hypothesis.

33. A **square root transformation** reduces skewness by:
    a. compressing only the negative sides of a skewed distribution.
    b. compressing only the positive sides of a skewed distribution.
    c. compressing the negative and positive sides of a skewed distribution.
    d. flattening out the middle of skewed distribution.

34. A **log transformation:**
    a. compresses the negative side of skewed distribution and extends the larger values on the positive side of the distribution.
    b. compresses the negative and positive sides of a skewed distribution.
    c. extends the negative and positive sides of a skewed distribution.
    d. compresses the positive side of a skewed distribution and extends the smaller values on the negative side of the distribution.

35. **Bootstrapping** is performed by using what technique?
    a. a log transformation
    b. a square root transformation
    c. sampling with replacement
    d   a post-hoc test

ANSWERS TO CHAPTER 14 STUDY QUESTIONS

Question Number	Correct Answer	Question Number	Correct Answer
1	c, p. 621	19	b, p. 636
2	a, p. 621	20	a, p. 637
3	d, p. 621	21	b, p. 638
4	b, p. 621	22	a, p. 638
5	a, p. 623	23	c, p. 638
6	c, p. 624	24	d, p. 638
7	b, p. 626	25	a, p. 639
8	d, p. 628	26	c, p. 639
9	d, p. 628	27	b, p. 640
10	b, p. 628	28	b, p. 641
11	c, p. 633	29	c, p. 641
12	c, p. 633	30	d, p. 641
13	a, p. 634	31	a, p. 641
14	a, p. 635	32	a, p. 641
15	b, p. 635	33	c, p. 644
16	d, p. 635	34	d, p. 644
17	c, p. 635	35	c, p. 646
18	d, p. 636		

SPSS Manual

CHAPTER 1

AN INTRODUCTION TO STATISTICS AND RESEARCH DESIGN

The Basic Elements of Statistical Reasoning

EXERCISE 1
NAMING VARIABLES AND DATA ENTRY

The goal in this first exercise is to become familiar with the program by getting some practice with naming variables and data entry.

- Launch SPSS. You may either select the SPSS icon from the 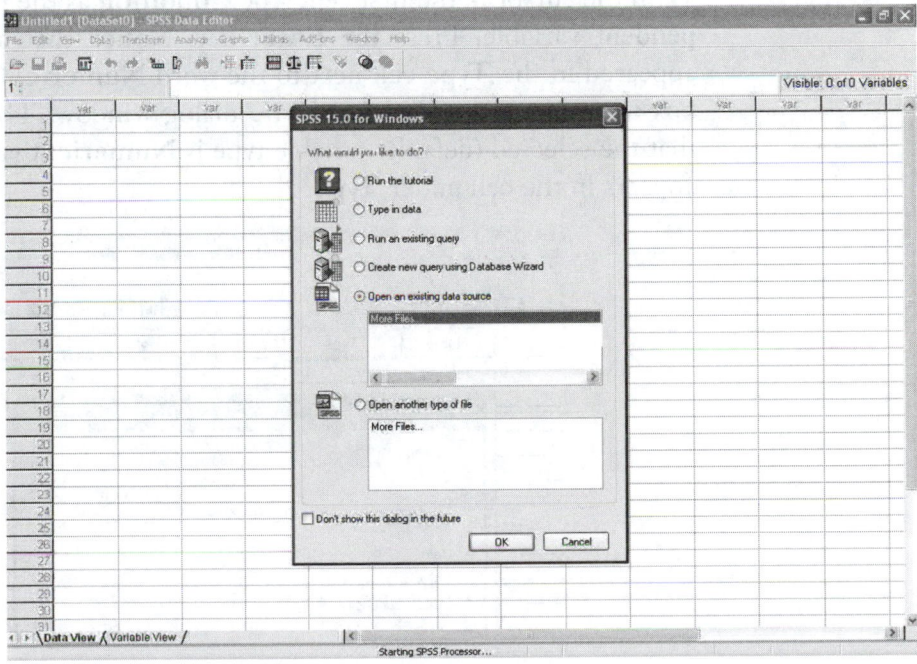 menu at the lower left corner of the screen or you may double-click the SPSS shortcut icon on your desktop. When the application has finished loading, the screen should be similar to the one below. The window in the center of the display is called a dialog window (or dialog box) in SPSS. You may opt to skip this one by checking the box in the lower left corner of the window.

- From the list of options under "What would you like to do?" select the round radio button next to **Type in data**, and click **OK** to cause this dialog window to disappear.

You are now looking at the spreadsheet–like **Data View** window of the SPSS **Data Editor**. The cell in the upper left corner of the window should be highlighted (outlined with a bold border), indicating that it is the active cell. We could enter a data value in this cell and others, but we would be getting ahead of ourselves. First, we'll name and define the variables.

THE VARIABLE VIEW WINDOW

- There are two tabs at the lower left corner of the screen. Select the **Variable View** tab to access the **Variable View** window. The cell in the upper left corner should be the active (highlighted) cell:

	Name	Type	Width	Decimals	Label	Values	Missing	Columns	Align	Measure

Naming and coding the independent variable

- With the cursor in the first cell, type **Condition** as the name of the independent variable. Press the **Enter** key. Notice that a small gray box appeared in the **Type** cell next to the word **Numeric**. Click on the gray box to produce the **Variable Type** dialog window. The window shows that the selected (default) variable type is **Numeric**; that's why this word appears in the cell under **Type**.

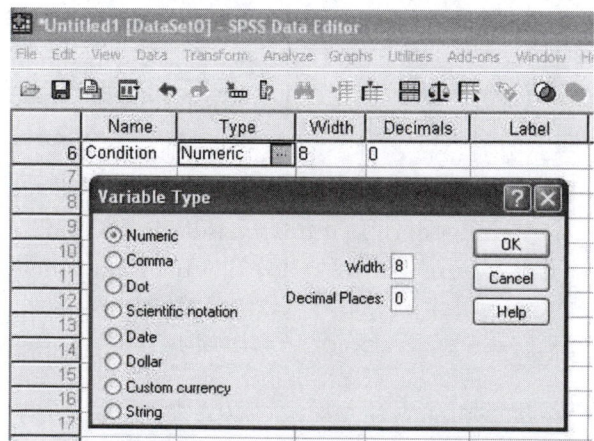

You will rarely, if ever, need to use any of the other choices, so leave the default selection as it is and click **OK** to return to the Variable View window. Leave the **Width** set at 8 but change the **2** in the **Decimals** column to **0**, because the values that you'll enter for the condition variable will be whole–number codes that represent the names of the two conditions (levels of the independent variable).

- Click in the cell under **Label** and type a descriptive label for the condition variable (without the quotation marks): "1 = intruder; 2 = no intruder." Click in the first cell in the **Values** column; a gray box should appear. Click on the gray box to produce the **Value Labels** dialog window. Enter "1" as the first **Value:** and press the Tab key on the keyboard [Tab ⇄] to move the cursor to the **Label:** field. Type "intruder" (without the quotation marks) and click the **Add** button to enter the value and its label. The value and its label should appear as **1 = "intruder"** in the large field below. Now repeat the process, entering "2" as the second Value: and "no intruder" as its label. Again, click the **Add** button to enter the code value and label. When you have completed both labels, the Value Labels dialog window should appear as follows:

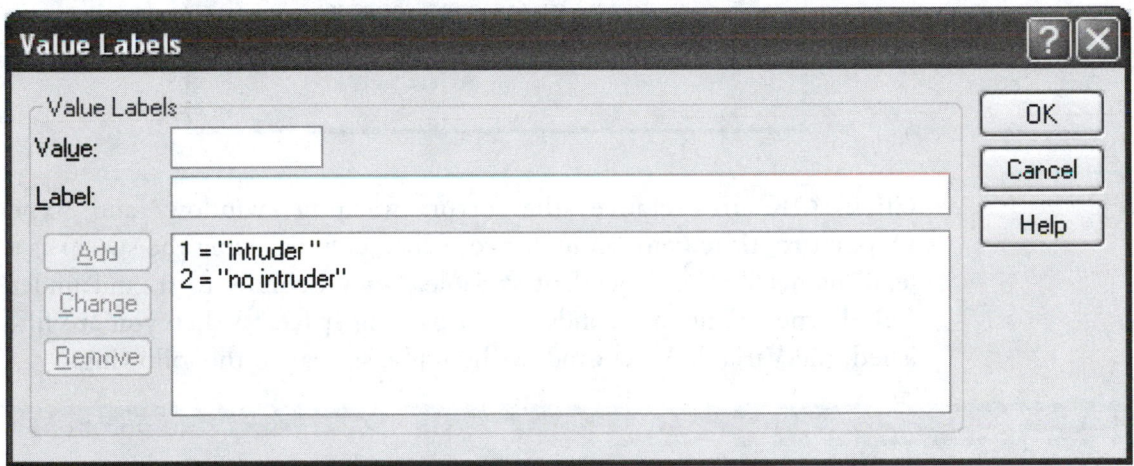

- Click **OK** to return to the **Variable View** window.

We may ignore the **Missing** and **Columns** menu options for now. By default the values that you enter in the Data Editor will be aligned in the right side of each cell. If you like, you may replace "Right" with "Center" (or "Left") by typing a **c** (or an **l**) in the first cell under **Align**. The last column heading, **Measure**, allows you to identify the scale (**Scale, Ordinal,** or **Nominal**) used to measure the variable entered in that row. Select **Nominal** to indicate that the codes you'll enter represent the names of the two levels of the independent variable. Note, however, that the analysis is not affected by the choices displayed in this column; they are useful only as reminders of the types of variables entered in each row.

Naming the dependent variable

• In the second row under **Name** type **Departure time** as the name of the dependent variable. Unless you encounter an error of some sort, your screen should look like this.

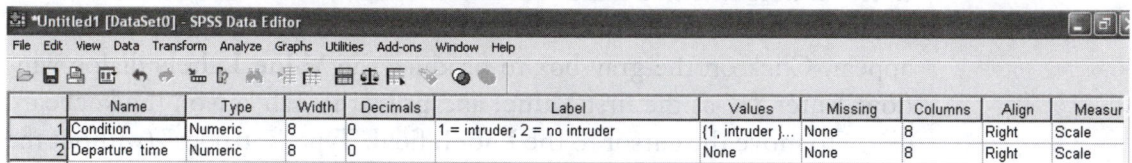

Well, I set you up to encounter an "error of some sort." As you discovered, the space that you typed between "Departure" and "time" is an "illegal character."

• Click **OK** to remove the error warning window and type **Departure_time** (with an underscore character replacing the space) as a legal name for the dependent variable. Set **Decimals** to **0,** and under **Label** type "Time in seconds to exit parking space." When you are finished, the Variable View window should be similar to the following:

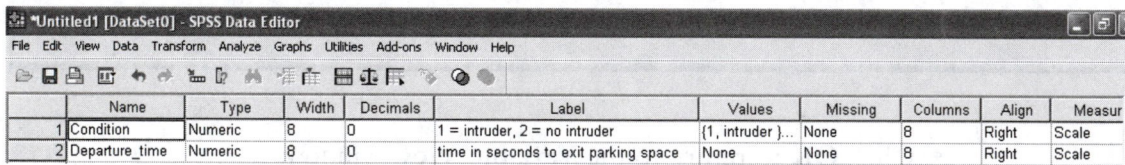

Click on the **Data View** tab to return to the Data View window of the Data Editor. Before entering data, you should save the data file by selecting **Save As...** from the **File** menu at the top left corner of the menu bar.

*Untitled1 [DataSet0] - SPSS Data
File
Edit
View
Data
Transform
Analyze
New
Open
Open Database
Open Dimensions Data...
Read Text Data...
Close
Ctrl+F4
Save
Ctrl+S
Save As...

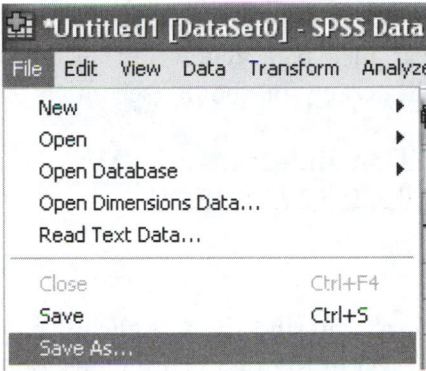

When the **Save Data As** dialog window appears, the cursor should be blinking in the **File name:** field at the bottom of the window. Follow the steps in the figure to save the file.

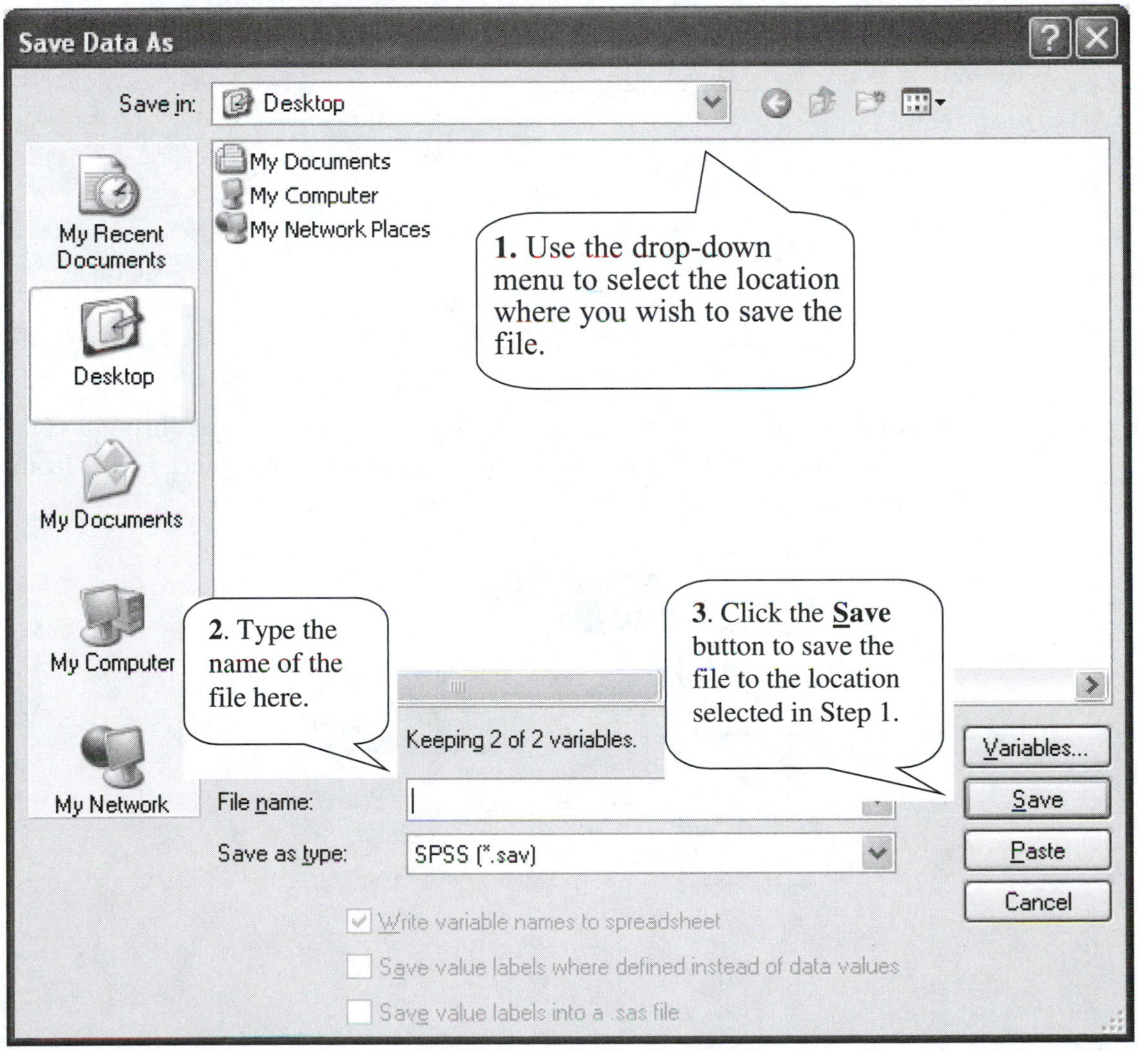

Save Data As
Save in:
Desktop
My Documents
My Computer
My Network Places
My Recent Documents
Desktop
My Documents
My Computer
My Network
1. Use the drop-down menu to select the location where you wish to save the file.
2. Type the name of the file here.
3. Click the Save button to save the file to the location selected in Step 1.
Keeping 2 of 2 variables.
File name:
Save as type:
SPSS (*.sav)
Variables...
Save
Paste
Cancel
Write variable names to spreadsheet
Save value labels where defined instead of data values
Save value labels into a .sas file

THE DATA VIEW WINDOW OF THE DATA EDITOR

You should see **Condition** and **Departure_time** displayed as the first two variable ("var") names at the top of the window.

- Move the cursor until it is directly over **Condition**; the variable label should appear in a pale yellow box just below the variable name and remain on the screen for about 5 seconds.

	Condition	Departure_time	var	var	var
1	1 = intruder, 2 = no intruder				
2					

- As a shortcut to entering the **Condition** codes, type a "1" (without the quotation marks) in the first cell under Condition, then press the Enter key to enter the value. Now click on the cell that you just entered the "1" in, right–click, and select Copy from the drop-down menu.

	Condition	Departure_time
1	1	
2		Cut
3		Copy
4		Paste
5		Clear
6		Grid Font

- Hold down the left mouse button as you drag the cursor through cells 2–25. Release the left mouse button, right–click, and select **Paste** from the drop-down menu to paste the "1" into those cells.

25		
26		Cut
27		Copy
28		Paste
29		Clear
30		Grid Font

- Type a "2" in cell 26 and repeat the previous sequence (p. 1-6) to paste a "2" into cells 27–50.

The data that you will enter (below) are a subset of the data collected by student observers in a quasi–replication of the first two studies reported by Ruback and Juieng (1997).

Condition	Departure_time	Condition	Departure_time	Condition	Departure_time	Condition	Departure_time
1	31	1	28	2	27	2	65
1	24	1	25	2	45	2	35
1	63	1	41	2	17	2	25
1	32	1	18	2	19	2	29
1	22	1	7	2	17	2	43
1	36	1	15	2	12	2	13
1	34	1	27	2	38	2	17
1	74	1	14	2	26	2	18
1	12	1	56	2	34	2	19
1	40	1	45	2	25	2	7
1	20	1	75	2	58	2	76
1	20	1	22	2	16	2	20
1	17			2	12		

- Now enter the values for the dependent variable **Departure_time** in the order shown. When you've finished entering the data, the first 10 rows of your Data View window should be similar to the one below.

	Condition	Departure_time
1	1	31
2	1	24
3	1	63
4	1	32
5	1	22
6	1	36
7	1	34
8	1	74
9	1	12
10	1	40

Ruback & Juieng Data for SPSS Exe
File   Edit   View   Data   Transform   Analyze

1 : Condition   1

Although typing numbers into the **Data Editor** may seem to be a dull task, you should not underestimate the importance of careful data entry. Common data entry errors include:

1. Double data entry—that is, entering the same data value on consecutive data entries.

2. Skipping a data entry.

3. Either pressing too lightly, or forgetting to press, the Enter key between data entries.

4. Confusing digits that are similar in appearance such as "3" and "8."

5. Repeating a digit—that is, typing "933" instead of "93."

USING THE EXPLORE PROCEDURE TO IDENTIFY OUTLIERS

The last error will show up as a data entry with too many digits. For example, suppose that the value "76" (case 49) was mistakenly entered as "766." We'll use the Explore procedure to look for possible outliers.

From the **Analyze** menu, select **Descriptive Statistics ▶ Explore...** .

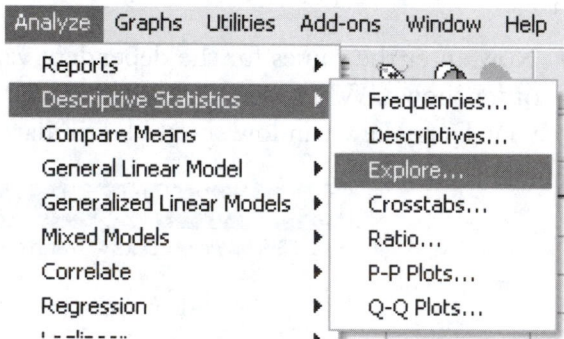

- When the **Explore** dialog window appears, select **Departure_time** and click the ▶ button to move this variable into the **Dependent List:** field. Locate the **Display** section in the lower left corner of the window and click on the round radio button next to **Statistics**.

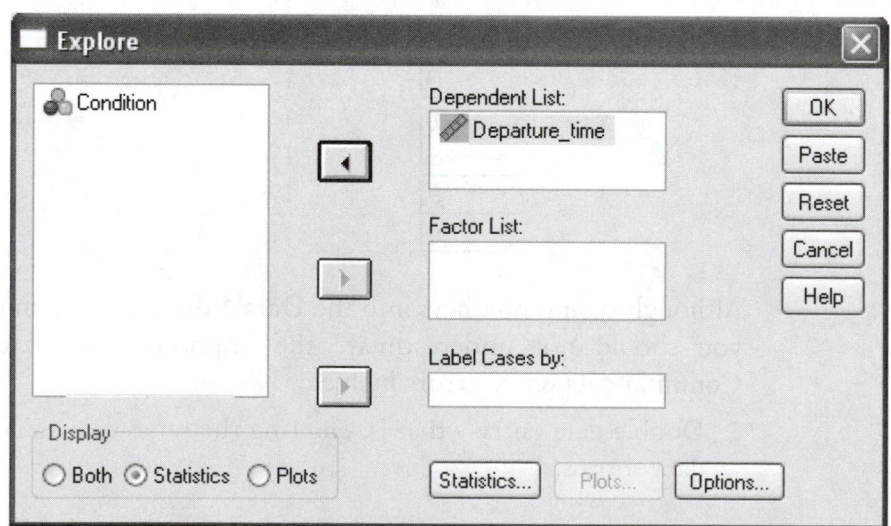

- When the dialog window looks like the one at the bottom of the previous page, click on the **Statistics...** button (in the center of the window on the bottom row) to produce the **Explore: Statistics** dialog window.

- In the **Explore: Statistics** dialog window, select **Outliers** as shown below. Then click **Continue** to return to the **Explore** dialog window.

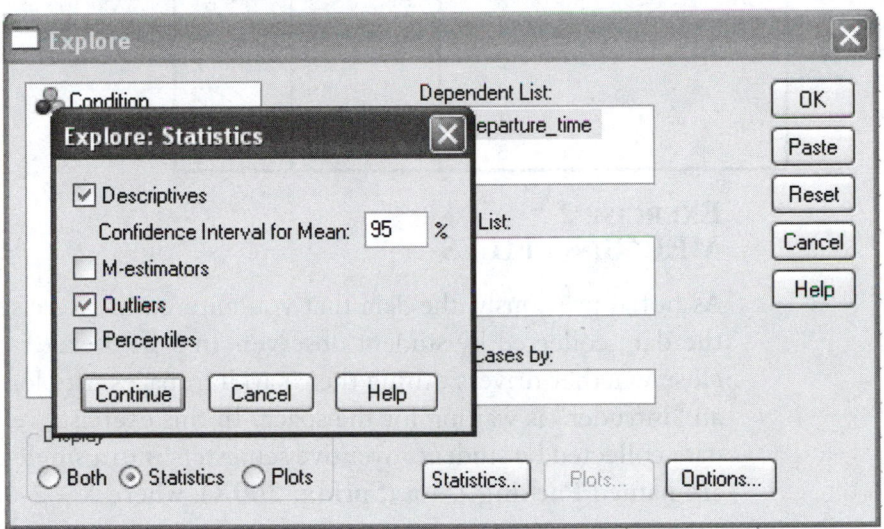

- Now click **OK** to produce the output.

You should see a **Descriptives** table followed by an **Extreme Values** table in the Output pane of the SPSS Viewer. You can use the Descriptives table to check the **Minimum** and **Maximum** data values to see if either is outside the range of the data values. Outliers may be more easily identified in the Extreme Values table, where they may be compared with the highest and lowest 5 values in the dataset.

Descriptives

			Statistic	Std. Error
Departure_time	Mean		44.02	14.920
	95% Confidence Interval for Mean	Lower Bound	14.04	
		Upper Bound	74.00	
	5% Trimmed Mean		28.96	
	Median		25.00	
	Variance		1130.306	
	Std. Deviation		105.500	
	Minimum		7	
	Maximum		766	
	Range		759	
	Interquartile Range		22	
	Skewness		6.804	.337
	Kurtosis		47.404	.662

If you know the range of the data, the presence of outliers may be detected by inspecting the minimum and maximum values in the Descriptives table.

Extreme Values

			Case Number	Value
Departure_time	Highest	1	49	766
		2	24	75
		3	8	74
		4	39	65
		5	3	63
	Lowest	1	48	7
		2	18	7
		3	38	12
		4	31	12
		5	9	12

> Outliers are perhaps more easily detected in a list of the highest and lowest values in a dataset.

EXERCISE 2
MERGING FILES

As noted previously, the data that you entered in Exercise 1 are a subset of the data collected by student observers in a field exercise designed to disclose whether drivers exiting their parking spaces take longer to leave when an "intruder" is waiting for the space. In this exercise we will merge all the data collected by students over five semesters into a single data file. The files are named **Parking Data (Spring, 200X)**, where X = 2-6.

- Open the file named **Parking Data (Spring, 2002)**.

- From the **Data** menu, select **Merge Files ▶ Add Cases...**

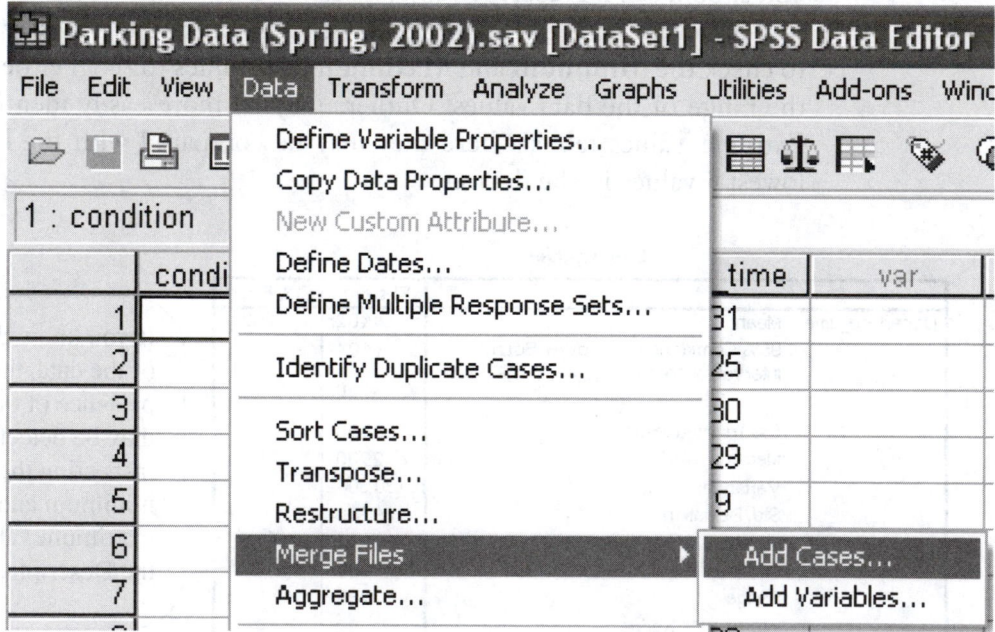

- When the **Add Cases to** dialog window appears, select the radio button next to **An external SPSS data file** then click on the **Browse…** button.

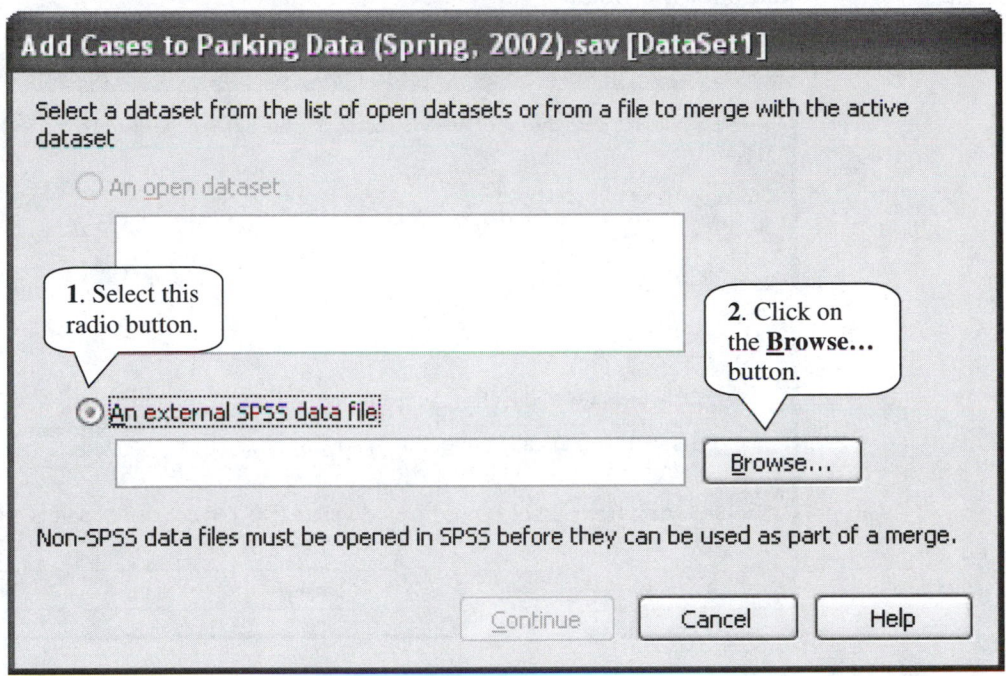

- From the **Add Cases: Read File** dialog window, select **Parking Data (Spring, 2003)** and click the **Open** button.

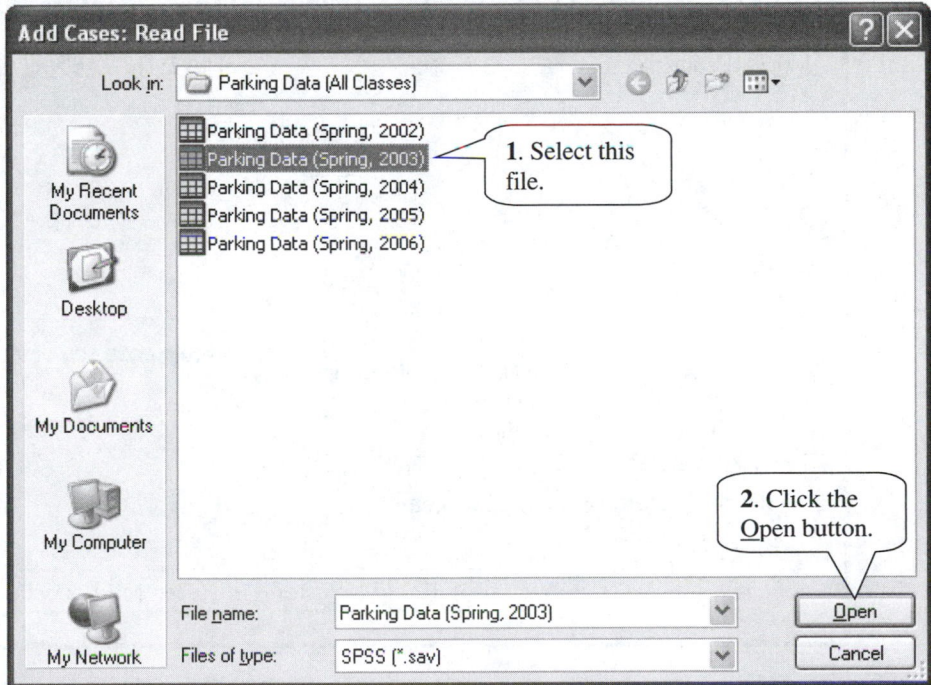

- Clicking the **Open** button returns you to the **Add Cases to** dialog window. The **Parking Data (Spring, 2003)** file should be listed in the external data file field.

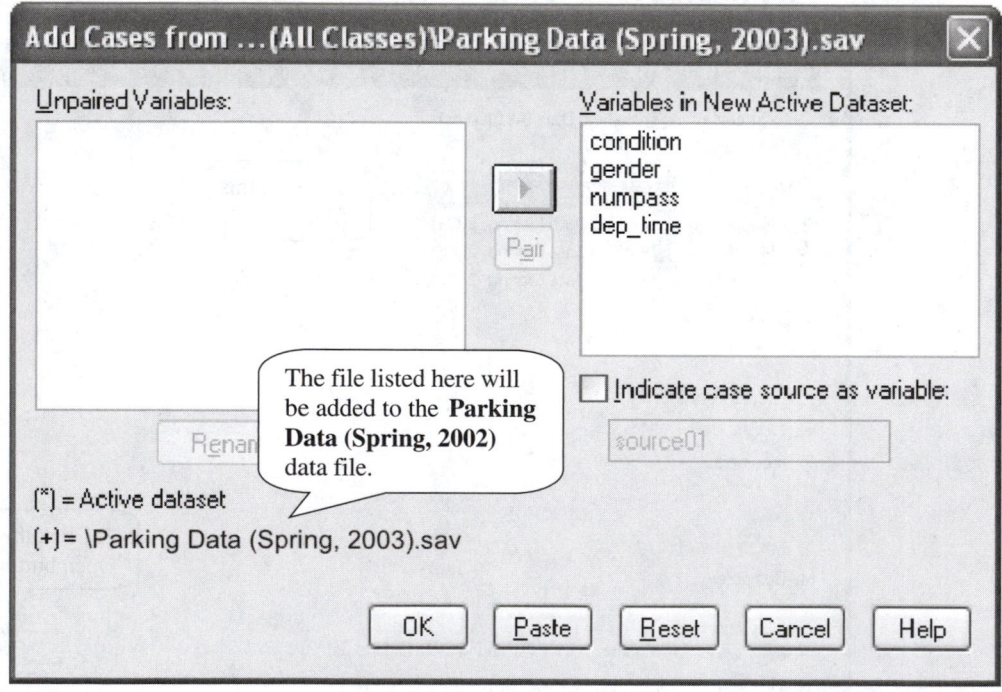

- Click **Continue** to produce the **Add Cases from ...** dialog window.

- Click **OK** to add **Parking Data (Spring, 2003).sav** to the Parking Data (Spring, 2002) data file.
- Now repeat the 6 steps below to add each of the remaining three data files to the open dataset.

    1. From the **Data** menu, select **Merge Files ▶ Add Cases...**

    2. When the **Add Cases to** dialog window appears, select the radio button next to **An external SPSS data file**, and then click on the **Browse...** button.

    3. From the **Add Cases: Read File** dialog window, select **Parking Data (Spring, 200X)** and click the **Open** button.

    4. Clicking the Open button returns you to the **Add Cases to** dialog window. The Parking Data (Spring, 200X) file should be listed in the external data file field.

    5. Click **Continue** to produce the **Add Cases from ...** dialog window.

    6. Click **OK** to add **Parking Data (Spring, 200X).sav** to the Parking Data (Spring, 2002) data file.

- When you have merged all five files, save the merged files under a new name such as **Parking Data (Merged Files)**.

EXERCISE 3
USING SELECT CASES TO DELETE "DIRTY DATA"

In this exercise we will remove unwanted data from the merged parking data files.

- From the **Data** menu, select the **Select Cases...** option.

- When the **Select Cases** dialog window appears, click on the radio button next to **If condition is satisfied**. Then click on the **large If...** button to produce the **Select Cases: If** dialog window. (*Note*: The window was cropped to fit on the page.)

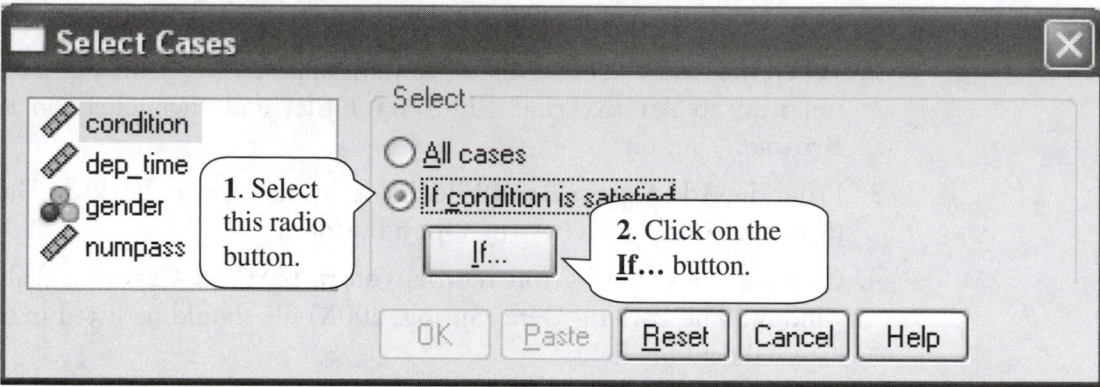

- When the **Select Cases: If** dialog window appears, select **dep_time**, then click the ▶ button to move the dep_time variable into the field at the top of the window. Now position the cursor to the right of dep_time and type "**<= 120**" (without the quotation marks). The command instructs SPSS to select the cases whose departure times were not more than 2 minutes. This selection criterion is based on the original study by Ruback and Juieng (1997):

  The three drivers who waited in their car for more than 2 min were not included in the data because the researchers assumed those drivers had certain time-consuming tasks to complete before leaving (e.g., waiting for another shopper or looking at a map). (p. 823)

- The window should now appear as follows:

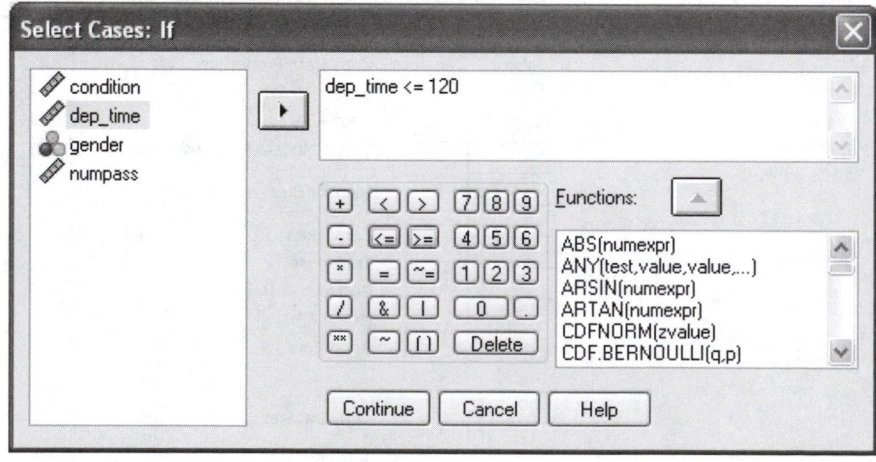

- Click **Continue** to return to the **Select Cases** dialog window. Locate the Output section near the bottom of the window and select the radio button next to **Delete unselected cases**. This will remove all cases with departure times longer than 2 minutes from the data set.

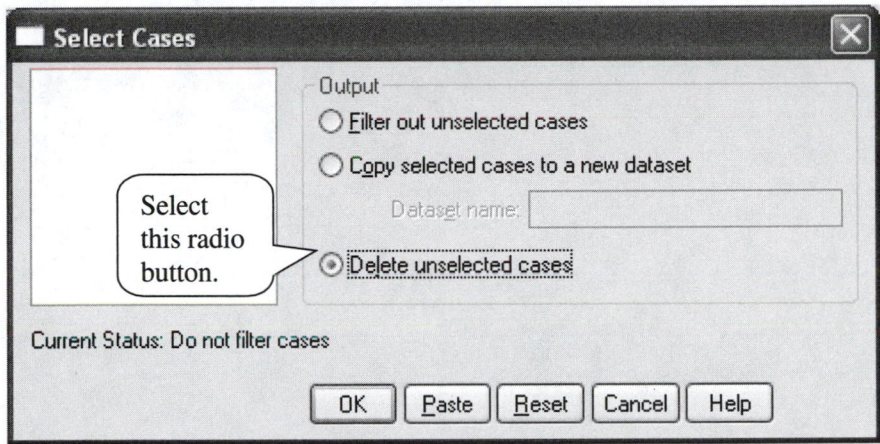

- Click **OK** to execute the case selection command. **Save** the file. We will use this file to complete exercises in other chapters.

CHAPTER 2

DESCRIPTIVE STATISTICS

Organizing, Summarizing, and Graphing Individual Variables

1. Go to http://www.norusis.com/ and download the "corrected data CD for release 15." Launch SPSS and open the file **gssnet.sav** from the downloaded folder. This file contains a random subset of cases from the General Social Survey, a national survey of randomly selected households that has been conducted every two years since 1972.

From the **Analyze** menu, **select Descriptive Statistics ▶ Frequencies...** . When the **Frequencies** dialog window appears, select **Age of respondent** and move this variable into the **Variable(s):** field as shown:

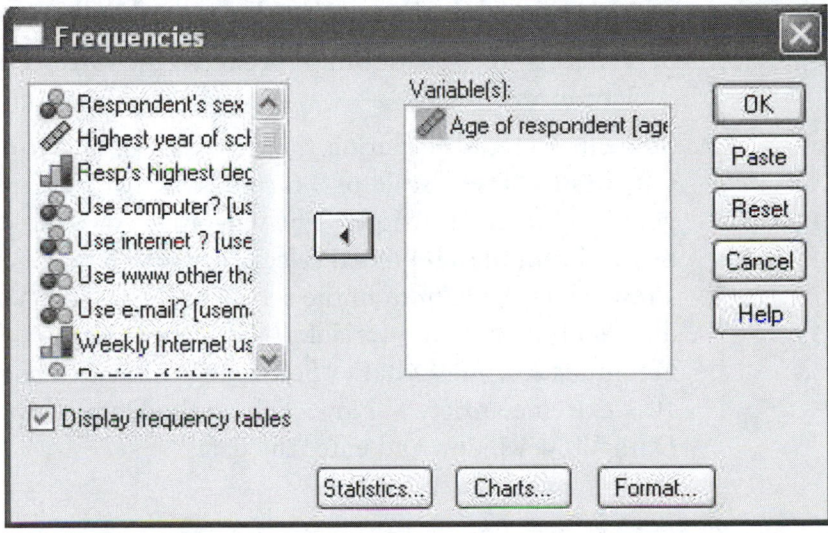

Click on the **Statistics...** tab to open the **Frequencies: Statistics** dialog window. Find the **Central Tendency** section and select **Mean, Median,** and **Mode,** then locate the **Dispersion** section and select **Std. deviation, Variance,** and **Range.** Finally, under **Distribution** select **Skewness** and **Kurtosis** before clicking **Continue** to return to the **Frequencies** window.

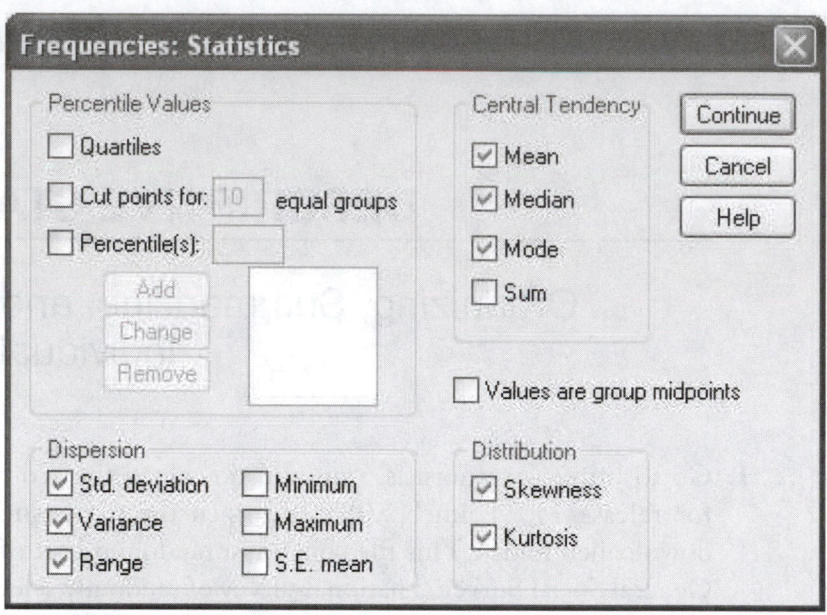

Deselect the **Display Frequencies** option, that is, make sure this option is NOT checked. Otherwise, the output will include a frequency table listing all of the ages from 18 to 89. Click **OK** to produce the output.

a. Explain how the sign of the **Skewness** statistic may be predicted by comparing the values of the **Mean**, the **Median**, and the **Mode**.

b. What is the relationship between the **Std. Deviation** and the **Variance**?

2. Students were asked during the first class of an introductory course in statistics to "Use a scale of 0 (*no anxiety*) to 10 (*extreme anxiety*) to rate your level of math anxiety." The self-ratings of 87 students are displayed below. From the **File** menu select **New ▶ Data**. Click on the **Variable View** tab at the bottom of the screen to display the **Variable View** window and define the variable as follows: **Name** = "Math_Anxiety," **Decimals** = 0, and **Label** = "Self-ratings of math anxiety (0 = no anxiety, 10 = extreme anxiety)." Now click on the **Data View** tab to display the **Data View** window and enter the data.

4	1	8	7	8	6	8	8	6
6	5	3	3	7	9	4	6	8
7	5	7	6	8	5	6	7	3
5	5	10	2	7	5	7	6	7
9	4	3	8	3	4	4	5	10
4	4	7	2	7	2	7	8	10
8	2	0	8	8	1	4	5	7
2	0	6	10	2	8	1	8	
7	3	10	6	5	7	6	8	
7	6	6	5	10	4	4	5	

The **Bar Charts** option in SPSS should be used when the variable is measured on a nominal or ordinal scale, whereas the **Histograms:** option is selected when the variable is measured on an interval or ratio scale. Rating scales such as this one are generally regarded as an interval scale of measurement.

3. Select **Analyze ... Descriptive Statistics ▶ Frequencies...** to display the **Frequencies** dialog window. Make sure that the **Display frequency tables** option (lower left corner) is selected. Select the variable displayed in the left field and either click the triangle (**▶**) or double-click the variable name to move it into the **Variable(s):** field on the right side of the window. Select the **Statistics...** tab at the bottom of the window to display the **Frequencies: Statistics** dialog window. Find the **Percentile Values** section and select **Quartiles**, then **Continue** to return to the Frequencies dialog window. Now select the **Charts ...** tab to display the **Frequencies: Charts** dialog window. Under **Chart Type** select **Histograms:** then click **Continue** to return to the Frequencies dialog window. Click **OK** to produce the output.

4. **a.** Identify the score at the **75th percentile**.

   b. The 75th percentile is also known as _____.

   c. Identify the score at the **25th percentile**.

   d. The 25th percentile is also known as _____.

5. **a.** Compute the **interquartile range**.

   b. Describe the interquartile range in a way that does not refer to any of the terms from question 4 above.

6. **a.** Identify the score at the **50th percentile**.

   b. Provide two other names for the **50th percentile**.

ANSWERS

1.

  a. In all positively skewed distributions, the value of the mean exceeds that of the median, whereas in all negatively skewed distributions, the value of the median exceeds that of the mean.

  b. The standard deviation is the square root of the variance.

2.

Statistics

Math_anxiety

N	Valid	87
	Missing	0
Percentiles	25	4.00
	50	6.00
	75	8.00

Math_anxiety

		Frequency	Percent	Valid Percent	Cumulative Percent
Valid	0	2	2.3	2.3	2.3
	1	3	3.4	3.4	5.7
	2	6	6.9	6.9	12.6
	3	6	6.9	6.9	19.5
	4	10	11.5	11.5	31.0
	5	11	12.6	12.6	43.7
	6	12	13.8	13.8	57.5
	7	15	17.2	17.2	74.7
	8	14	16.1	16.1	90.8
	9	2	2.3	2.3	93.1
	10	6	6.9	6.9	100.0
	Total	87	100.0	100.0	

Histogram

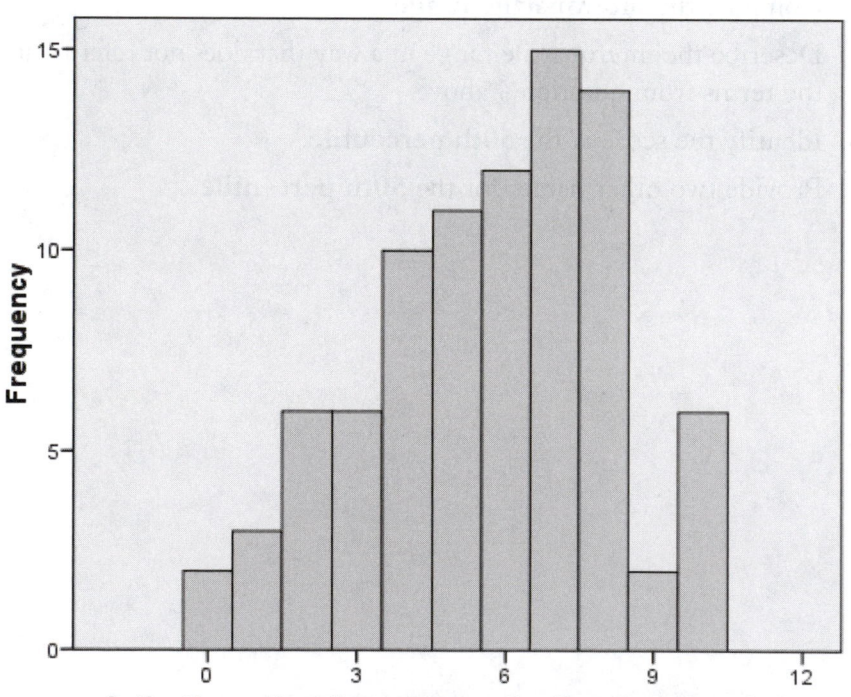

Mean =5.69
Std. Dev. =2.47
N =87

Self ratings of math anxiety on the first day of statistics class (0 = no anxiety, 10 = extreme anxiety)

4. **a.** The score at the 75th percentile is **8**.

   b. The 75th percentile is also known as the **third quartile** (or **Q3**).

   c. The score at the 25th percentile is **4**.

   d. The 25th percentile is also known as the **first quartile** (or **Q1**).

5. **a.** The interquartile range is computed by subtracting Q1 from Q3: 8 − 4 = **4**.

   b. The interquartile range is the **middle 50%** of the scores in a distribution.

6. **a.** The score at the 50th percentile is **6**.

   b. Two other names for the 50th percentile are the **second quartile (Q2)** and the **median**.

CHAPTER 3

VISUAL DISPLAYS OF DATA

Graphs That Tell a Story

In this exercise we will use SPSS to create a graph. We will create this visual display of data, we will observe the 10 points listed in the section *How to Build a Graph: Dos and Don'ts* on p. 118 in the text as well as the guidelines for the preparation of figures from the *Publication Manual of the American Psychological Association* (2001).

CONSTRUCTING A HISTOGRAM TO DISPLAY FREQUENCY DATA

Launch SPSS. If you have not yet disabled the opening **What Do You Want To Do?** dialog window, then click **OK** to open an existing data source. If you have disabled the opening window, then select **File, Open ▶ Data...** from the SPSS Data Editor menu. Either method will produce the **Open Data** dialog window (on the next page). Click on the button to access the **Look in:** drop-down menu of drives and folders. Navigate to the folder where you saved the merged data file from the Chapter 1 exercises, and click the **Open** button to access the contents of the folder.

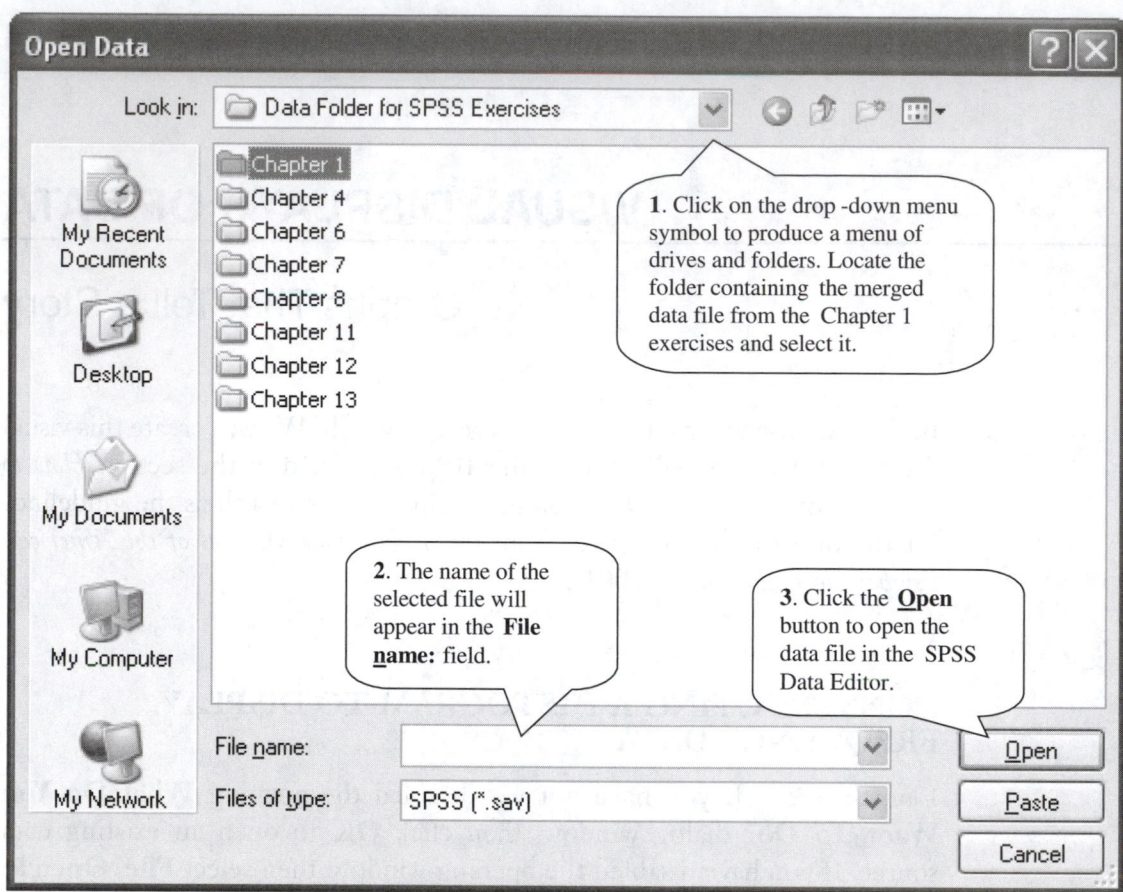

- Select **Graphs, Chart Builder…**

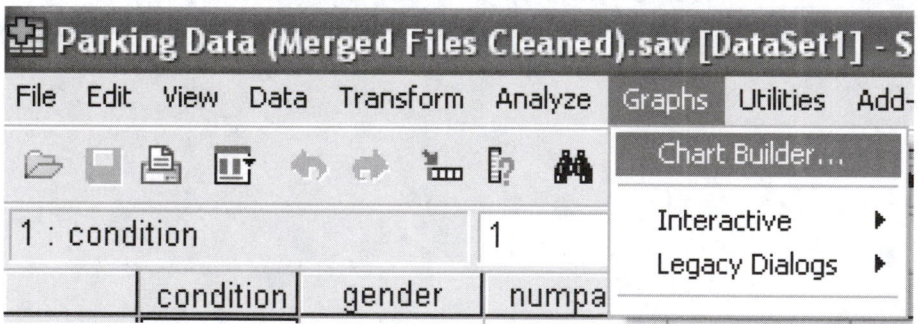

- ... to produce the first **Chart Builder** dialog window. If the variable properties were defined when they were first entered in the **Variable View** window, it will not be necessary to define them at this step.

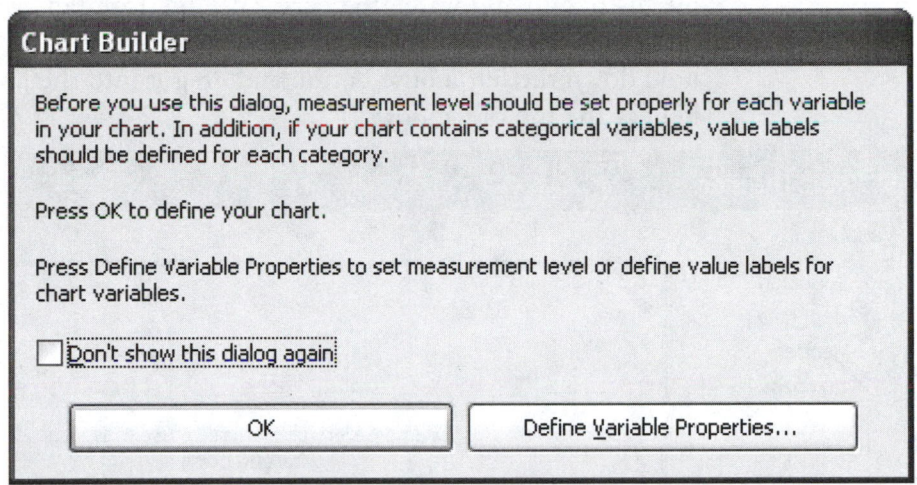

- Click the box next to **Don't show this dialog again**. If you should ever need to access the **Define Variable Properties...** dialog window, you may do so by selecting it from the Data menu in the Data Editor.

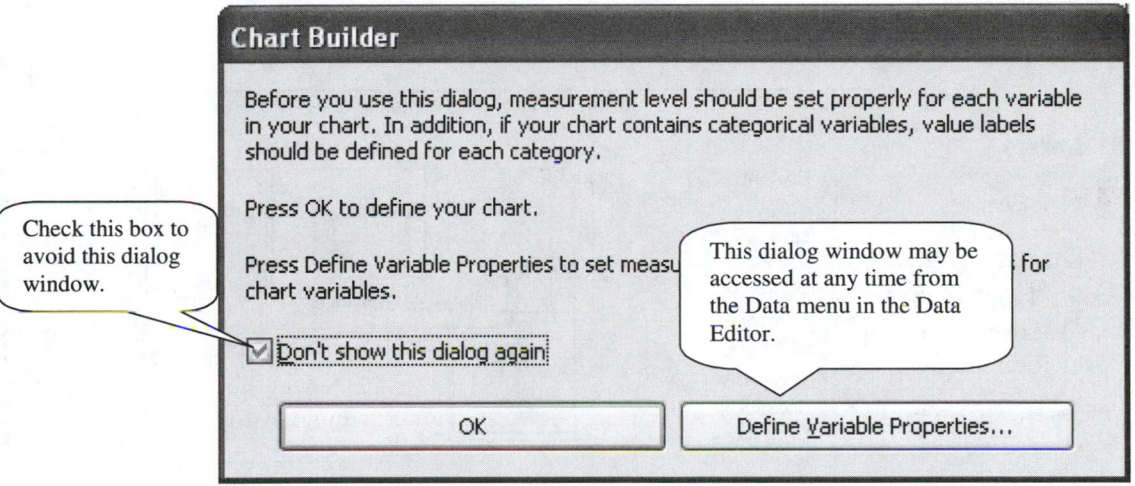

- Click **OK** to access the second **Chart Builder** dialog window. Selecting **Histogram** from the **Choose from:** list produces an array of histograms in the chart gallery window on the right. Move the cursor over the simple histogram and watch the cursor change from an arrow to a pointing hand. Select the simple histogram from the chart gallery as shown, then hold down the left mouse button and drag it into the large chart preview field at the top of window.

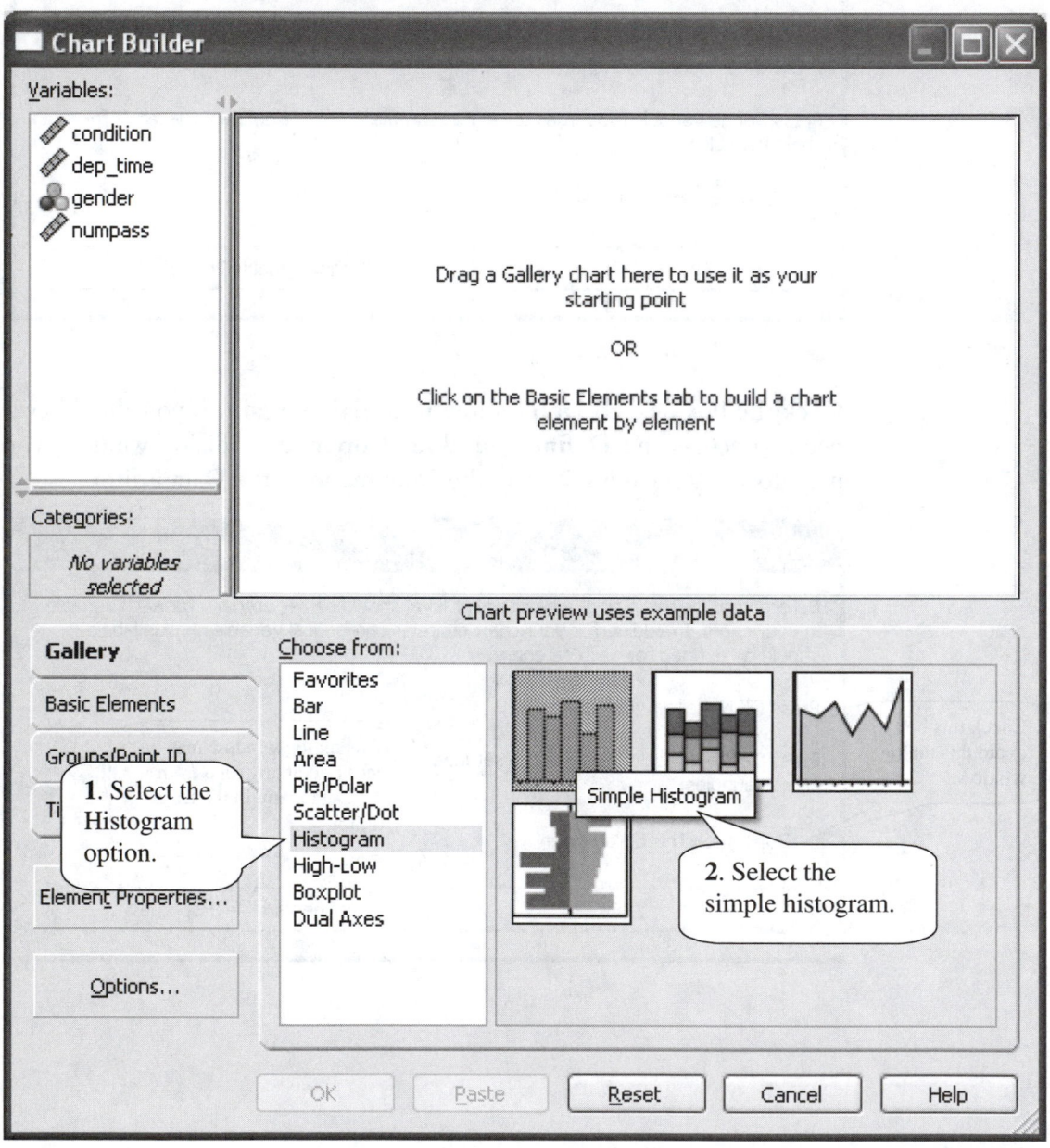

- Select **dep_time** from the list of **Variables:** and drag this variable into the **x-axis?** field in the chart preview area.

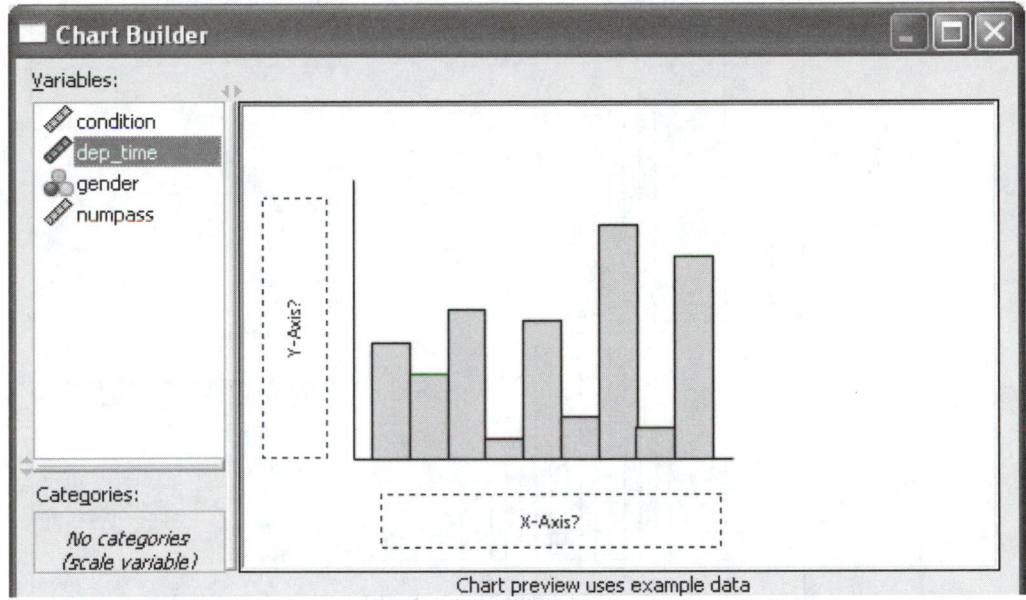

- Click the **OK** button to produce the histogram. The default chart options in SPSS result in a histogram like the one below. The annotations identify the elements of the chart that should be edited or deleted.

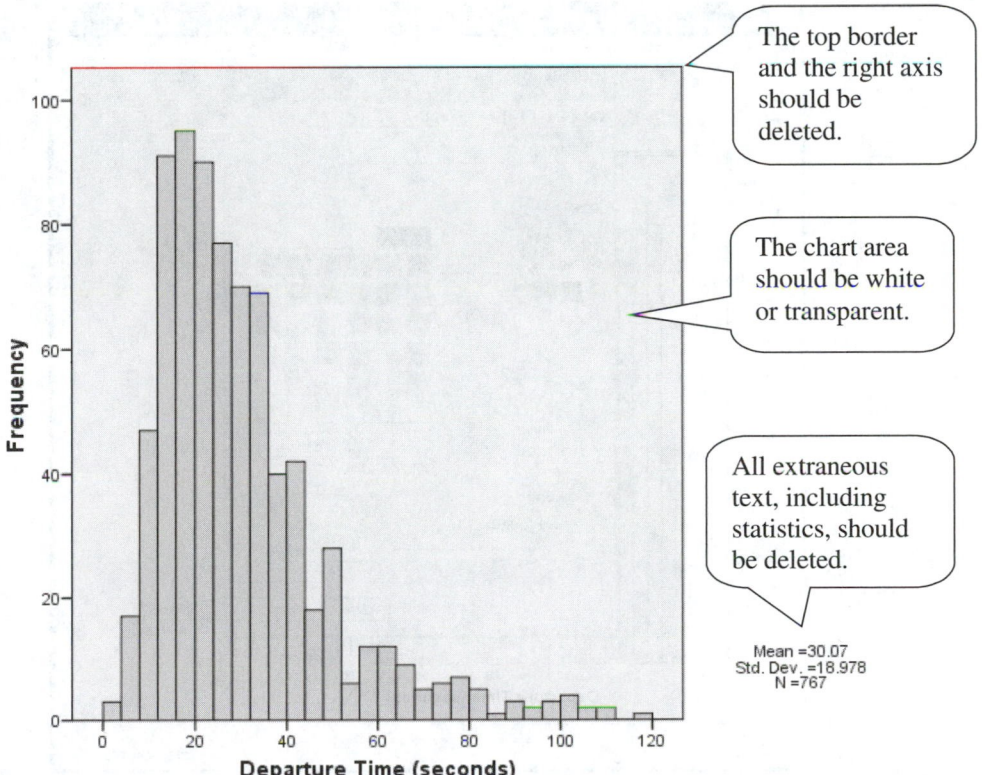

- To access the SPSS **Chart Editor**, you may double-click on any part of the chart or right-click and select **SPSS Chart Object ▶ Open**.

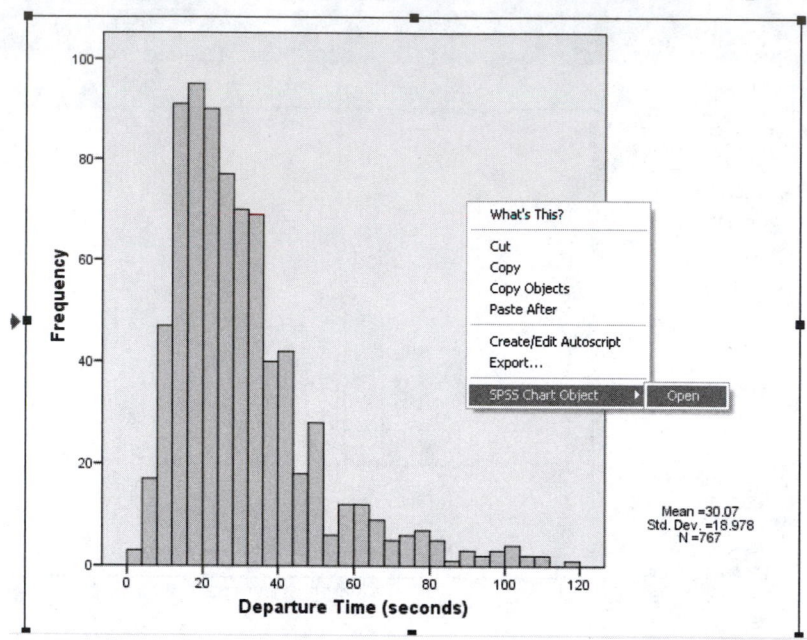

- In the **Chart Editor** double click on the chart to produce the **Properties** dialog window.

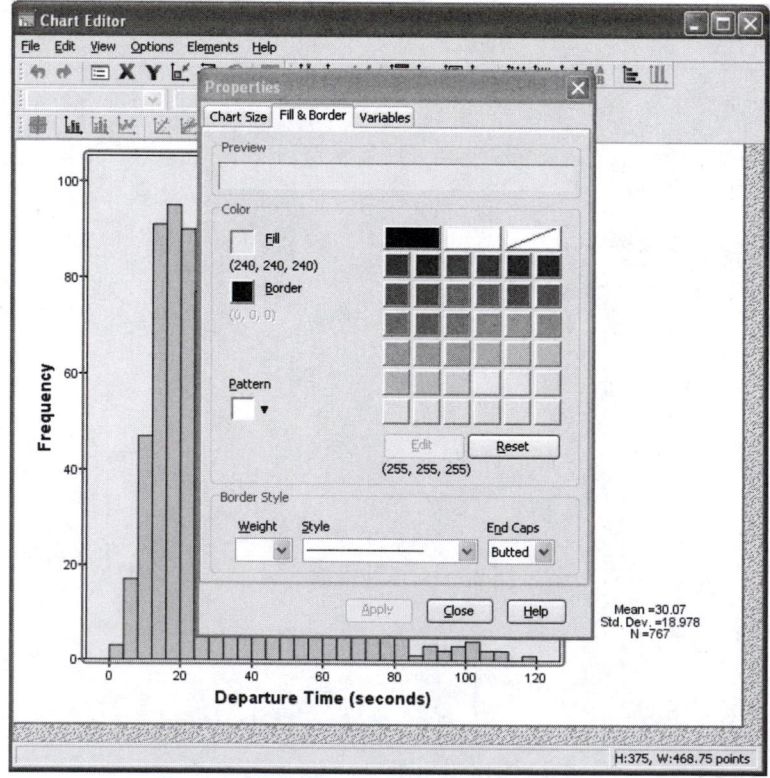

- In the **Properties** window, click on the box to the left of <u>**Fill**</u>, then select **Transparent** to replace the light gray background with a transparent background. Now click on the box to the left of <u>**Border**</u>, then select Transparent to remove the top border and right axis of the chart. Click on the **Apply** button, then the <u>**Close**</u> button to close the window and return to the **Chart Editor**.

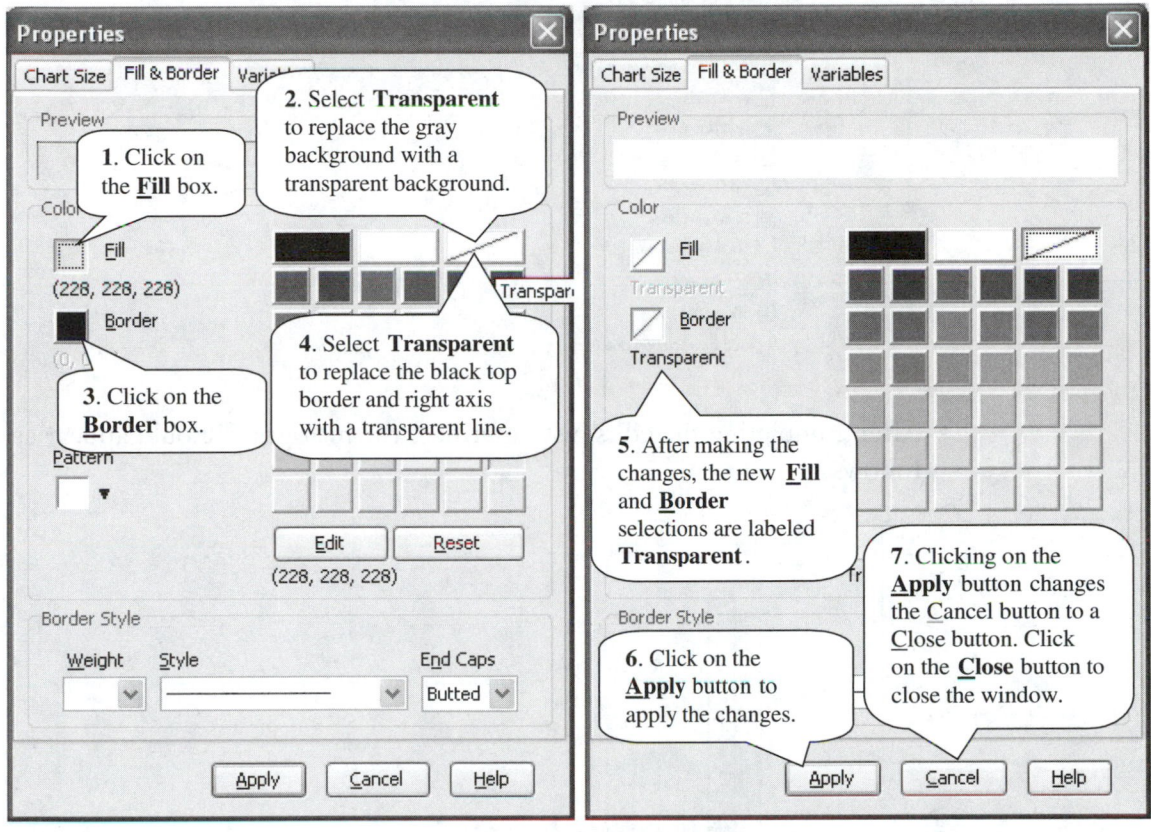

- Right-click on the statistics text and select **Delete** from the menu.

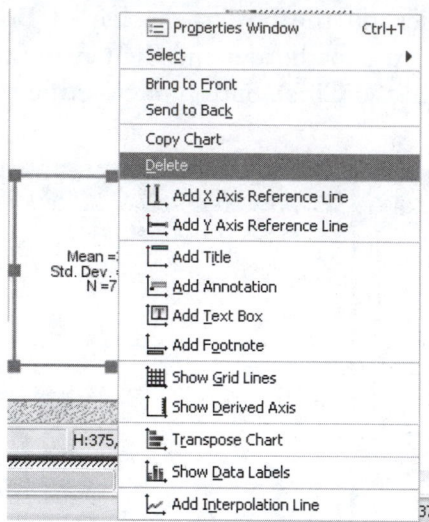

- After completing the edits just described, the histogram should appear as follows.

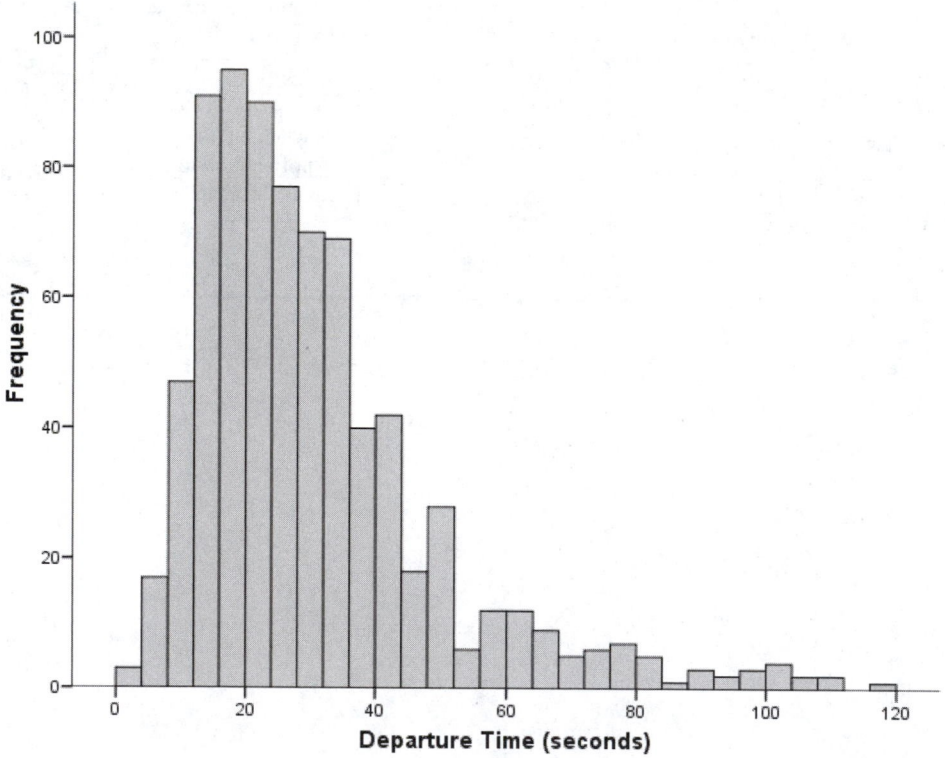

- You may continue to edit the chart to change the color and or border of the bars. Double-click the chart (or right-click and select **SPSS Chart Object ▶ Open**) to access the **Chart Editor**. Then either double-click on one of the bars (or right-click and **Select ▶ All Histogram Bar**) to bring up the Properties dialog window.

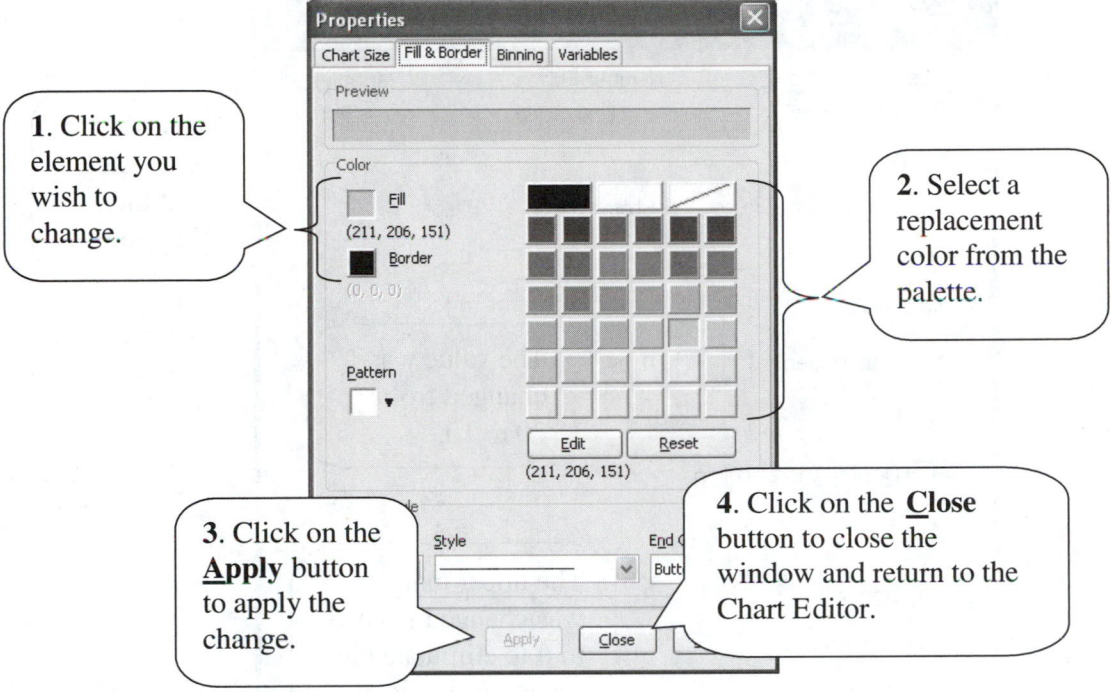

1. Click on the element you wish to change.

2. Select a replacement color from the palette.

3. Click on the **Apply** button to apply the change.

4. Click on the **Close** button to close the window and return to the Chart Editor.

- To change any element of any chart within the **Chart Editor**, double-click on that element to access the **Properties** dialog window, then select the tab for that element. For example, to change either the horizontal or vertical axis scale, double-click on the axis or one of the axis labels to bring up the Properties dialog window, then select the **Scale** tab.

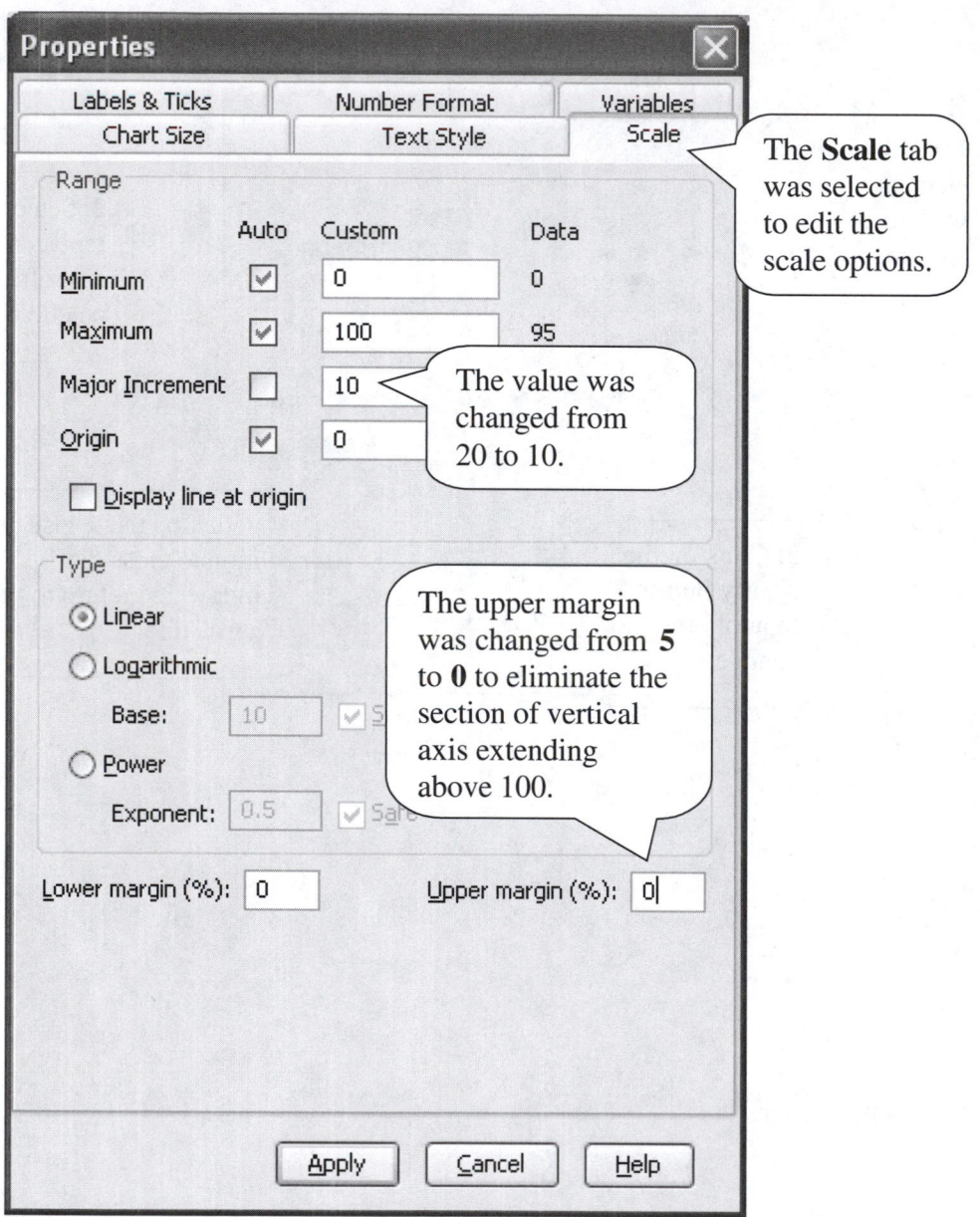

- After changing the vertical and horizontal axes, your completed histogram should be similar to the one below:

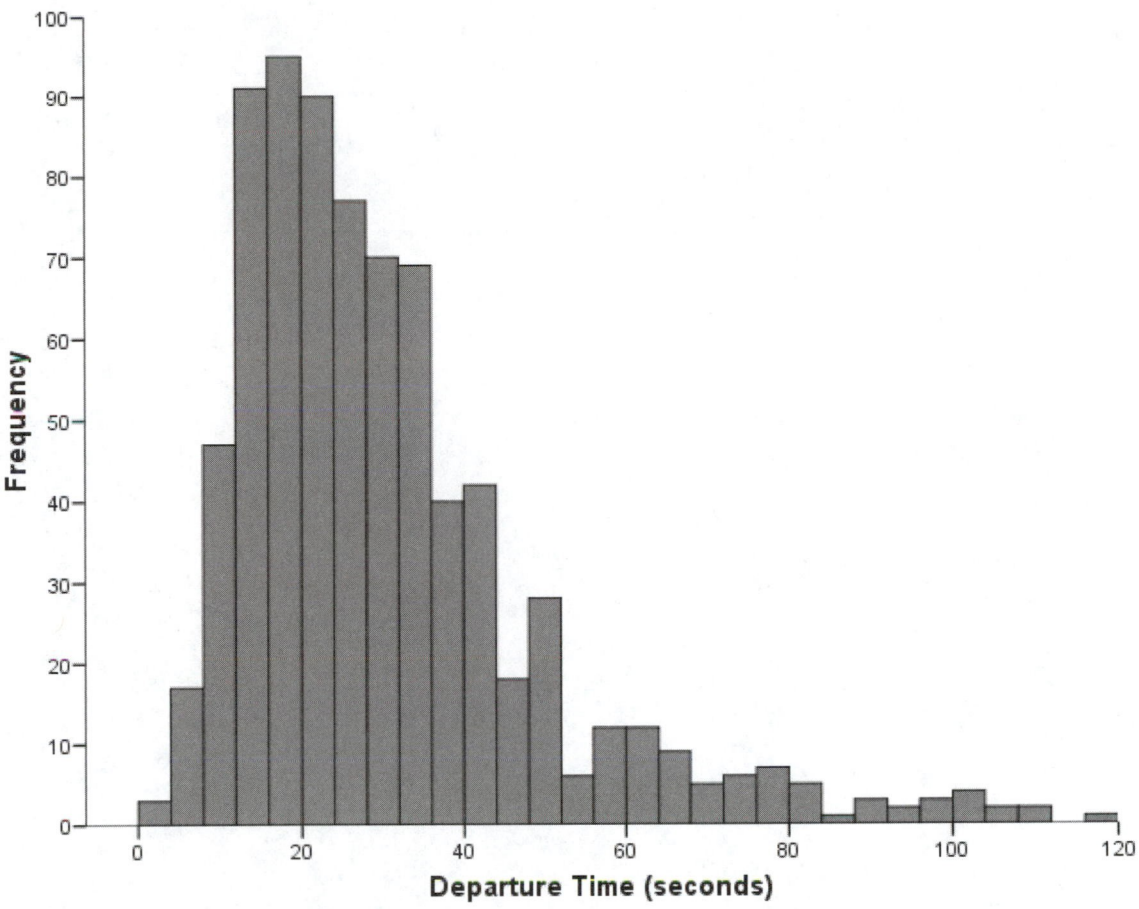

CHAPTER 4

PROBABILITIES AND RESEARCH

The Risks and Rewards of Scientific Sampling

EXPECTED RELATIVE-FREQUENCY PROBABILITY

EXERCISE 1

Launch SPSS and select **Type in data** from the list of "What would you like to do?" options. First, we'll do some things "by hand" and then use the syntax language of SPSS to do them for us.

Go to the **Variable View** window and enter the names of four variables: **Trial**, **Outcome**, **Sum**, and **Proportion**. The **Type** of each variable is **Numeric** and **Decimals** should be set to **2** for *Proportion*, zero for the others as shown below.

	Name	Type	Width	Decimals	Label
1	Trial	Numeric	8	0	
2	Outcome	Numeric	8	0	
3	Sum	Numeric	8	0	
4	Proportion	Numeric	8	2	

- Go to the **Data View** window. You should see *Trial*, *Outcome*, *Sum*, and *Proportion* listed as the names of the first four variables. Type **1** in the first row under Trial. Press the Enter key until the cursor is on Row 100 (this is the "by hand" part); type **100** in the first column in that row.

- From the **Transform** menu, select **Compute Variable...** to produce the **Compute Variable** dialog window. Type **Trial** in the **Target Variable:** field, then type **lag(trial) + 1** in the **Numeric Expression:** field.

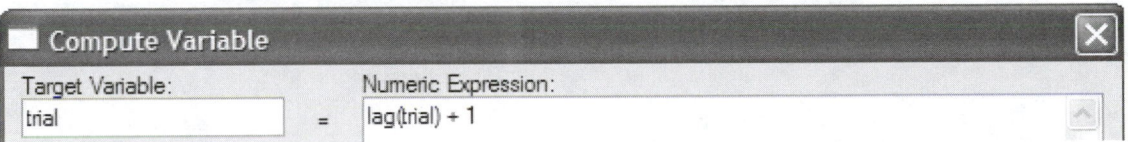

- Now click the **If... (optional case selection condition)** button (it's in the bottom left corner of the window and looks like this: [If...]) to produce the **Compute Variable: If Cases** window. Click the radio button next to **Include if case satisfies condition:** and type **missing(trial)** in the condition field.

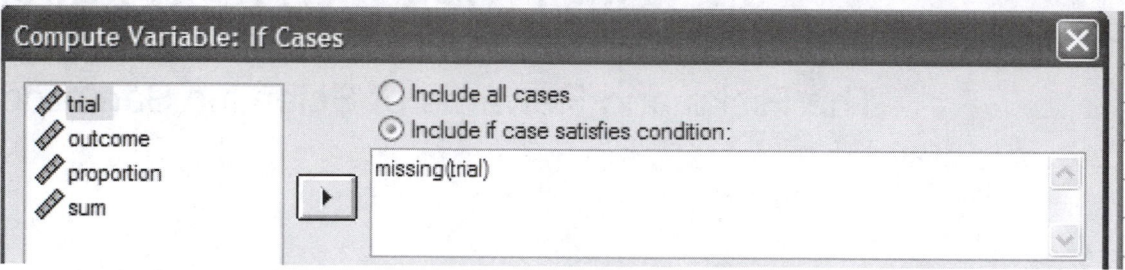

The only two values of Trial so far are 1 and 100, so 98 of them are "missing." The expression **lag(trial) + 1** adds 1 to the value of trial in the previous row, the row that "lags" behind by 1. So, the combination of lag(trial) + 1 and missing(trial) will fill the blank ("missing") cells under Trial with the values 2 through 99.

- Click **OK** to produce the **Change existing variable?** query, then click **OK** to fill the blank cells under Trial.

- Open the **Compute Variable...** window again and type **Outcome** in the **Target Variable:** field. Scroll down the **Function group:** window and select **Random Numbers** to access the **Functions and Special Variables:** list. Select **Rv.Binom** and click the [▲] button to move this function into the **Numeric Expression:** window. Replace the first **?** with **1** and the second **?** with **.5 or 0.5** (typing the zero makes it easier to see the decimal). The expression should read **RV.BINOM(1,0.5)**.

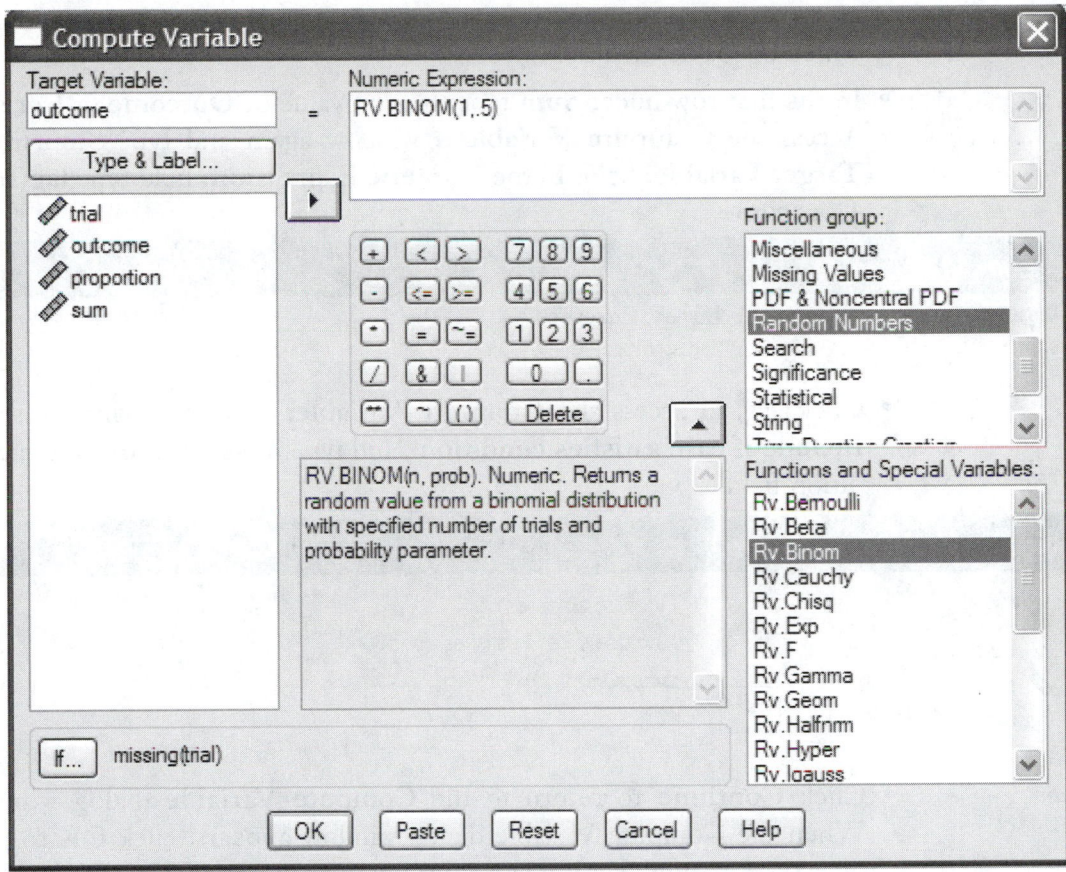

You may skip the selection of the Rv.Binom function and just type the function and arguments into the numeric expression window. The first argument specifies the number of trials (1) and the second argument specifies the probability of observing a success on that trial (0.5). So, you are using RV.BINOM to simulate a single coin toss. Because there are 100 values of the Trial variable, you are simulating 100 coin tosses in all. Notice that the **If... (optional case selection condition)** radio button has the phrase **missing(trial)** instead of **(optional case selection condition)** printed to the right of the button. This means that the **Compute Variable: If Cases** dialog window is set to **Include if case satisfies condition:** from a previous step in this exercise.

- Click (what is now) the **If... missing(trial)** button to produce the **Compute Variable: If Cases** window and click the radio button next to **Include all cases**. Click **Continue** to return to the **Compute Variable** window. You should see the default phrase **(optional case selection condition)** next to the **If...** button.

- Click **OK** to produce the **Change existing variable?** query, then click **OK** to generate 100 outcomes of a coin tossing experiment. Each **1** that appears under **Outcome** is a success (e.g., a head or a tail, depending on which one is defined as a success).

- In the first row under **Sum** type the first value of **Outcome** (a 1 or a 0). Access the **Compute Variable...** window again and type **Sum** in the **Target Variable:** field. In the **Numeric Expression:** field type **lag(sum) + outcome**.

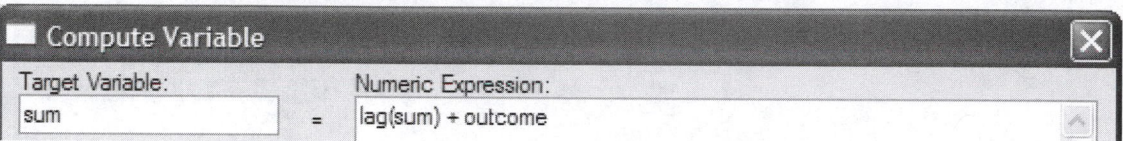

- Click [If...] to access the **Compute Variable: If Cases** window, select **Include if case satisfies condition:**, and type **missing(sum)** in the condition field.

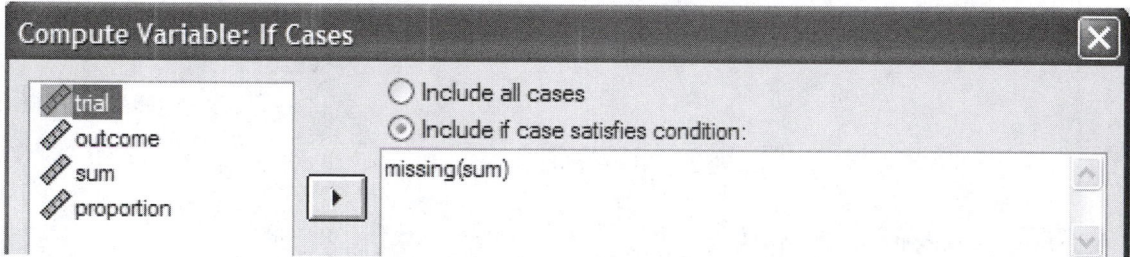

- Click **Continue** to return to the **Compute Variable** dialog window. When the Compute Variable dialog window appears, click **OK** to produce the **Change existing variable?** query, then click **OK** to fill the blank cells under **Sum**. The Sum variable maintains a running total of the number of successes (outcomes that equal 1). Check the values in this column to make sure you understand the values of the Sum variable.

- Access the **Compute Variable...** window again and type **Proportion** in the **Target Variable:** field. In the **Numeric Expression:** field type **sum/trial**. Click [If...] to access the **Compute Variable: If Cases** window, and click the radio button next to **Include all cases**.

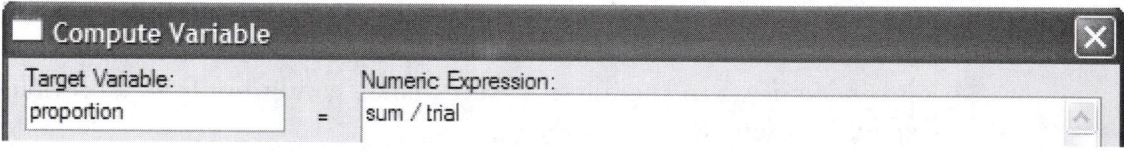

- Click **Continue** to return to the **Compute Variable** window, then click **OK** to produce the **Change existing variable?** query, then click OK again to fill the cells under **Proportion**. If the values of Proportion are single digits, go to the **Variable View** window and make sure that **Decimals** is set to **2**. Each value of proportion is the proportion of successful trials to that point.

Assignment 1

Make a line graph of the change in proportion of successes over trials. From the **Graphs** menu select **Chart Builder...** to produce the Chart Builder dialog window. The first Chart Builder dialog window offers an opportunity to define the variable properties if you have not already done so. That won't be necessary in this exercise, so click **OK** to produce the second Chart Builder dialog window. From the **Gallery** of chart types (bottom half of the window), select **Line** and drag the **Simple Line** template (it's the leftmost template in the gallery; you'll see the label "Simple Line" appear when you move the cursor over the template) into the large chart preview field at the top of the window.

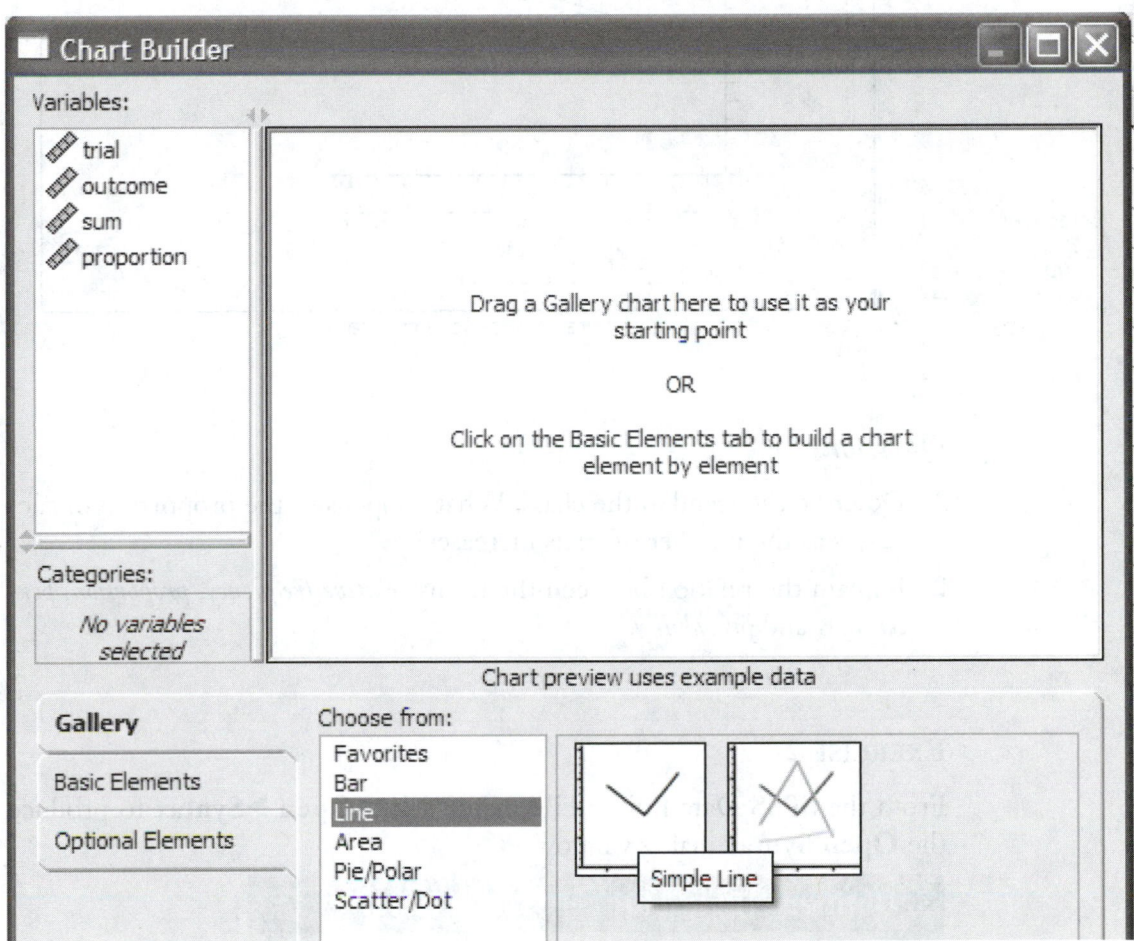

Select **Trial** and drag this variable to the **X-Axis?** field, then select **Proportion** and drag it to the **Y-Axis?** field. Click **OK** to generate the chart.

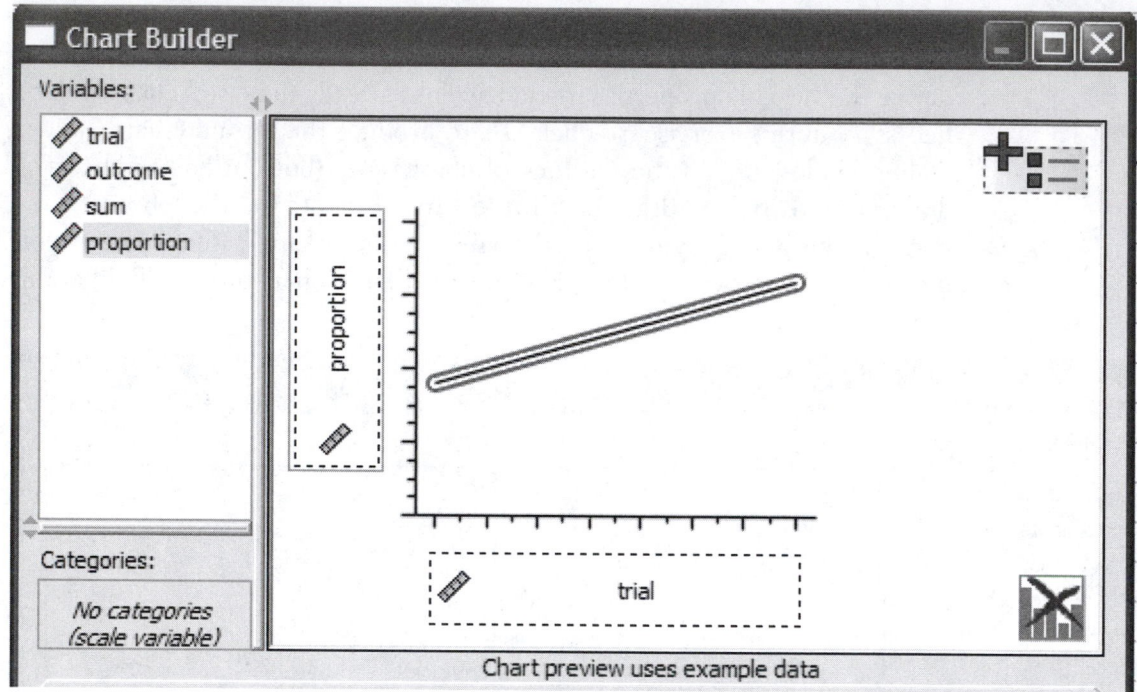

Questions

1. Describe the trend in the chart. What happens to the proportion of successes as the number of trials increases?

2. Explain the relation between the terms *relative frequency*, *proportion*, *percentage*, and *probability*.

EXERCISE 2

From the SPSS Data Editor **File** menu, select **Open ▶Syntax** to produce the **Open Syntax** dialog window.

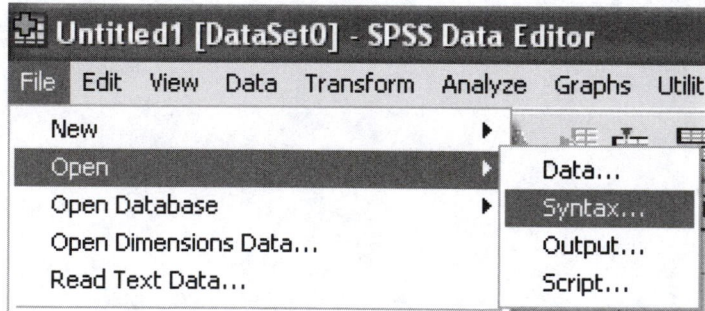

The current folder is identified in the **Look in:** drop-down menu at the top of the **Open Syntax** window:

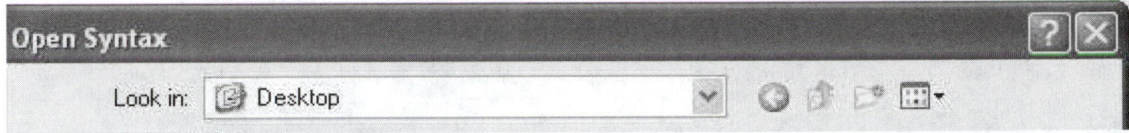

Click the ⌄ button on the right to access the menu of accessible drives and folders. Navigate to the data folder and open the syntax file named **1000 trials of a coin-toss experiment**. You will see the following lines of syntax appear in the SPSS Syntax Editor window. Locate the **set seed = ######** line and replace each **#** character with a random digit.

```
new file.
* This program creates a new SPSS data file with four variables:
* trial, outcome, sum, and proportion. Each of the trials uses
* RV.BINOM(1,0.5) to simulate the outcome of a coin toss. Sum
* stores a running total of successful outcomes (e.g. "heads"),
* and proportion expresses sum as a proportion of trials.
* IMPORTANT: Replace the # characters below with a 6-digit random
* number to produce a unique sequence of outcomes each time you
* run the file.
set seed = ######.
input program.
* Need initial values of variables for lag function.
compute trial = 1.
compute outcome = rv.binom(1,.5).
compute sum = outcome.
compute proportion = sum.
end case.
      loop #trial = 2 to 1000.
            compute trial = #trial.
            compute outcome = rv.binom(1,0.5).
            compute sum = lag(sum) + outcome.
            compute proportion = sum/trial.
      end case.
      end loop.
      end file.
end input program.
formats proportion (f8.2).
execute.
```

To execute the syntax code, select **Run, All** from the **SPSS Syntax Editor** menu as shown below.

The syntax program will create a new file with the same four variables that you created in Exercise 1. The first 5 rows of your file should be similar to the one below.

	trial	outcome	sum	proportion
1	1	1	1	1.00
2	2	1	2	1.00
3	3	0	2	.67
4	4	1	3	.75
5	5	1	4	.80

Assignment 2

Follow the instructions for Assignment 1 to make a line graph for the new sequence of 1000 trials.

Question

3. Imagine that you are a gambler and you've made a wager with another individual about the outcomes of coin-toss experiments. You decide before the first coin toss who bets *heads* and who bets *tails* and each person defines that outcome as a success on every trial. Here's the wager: The person who bets *heads* has to pay the other person a dollar for every hundredth of a percentage point (0.01%) that the percentage of heads is below 50, whereas the person who bets tails has the same obligation if the percentage of tails is below 50. So, if the percentage of heads turns out to be 52.87, the person who bet tails would owe $287.

Would you rather define the length of the game as 100 trials or 1000 trials? Write a brief explanation of your answer. Be sure to refer to the graphs that you constructed for Assignments 1 and 2.

EXERCISE 3

Open and run the syntax file named **100,000 trials of a coin-toss experiment** and save the data file. Use the values in the data file to complete Assignment 3. Instead of scrolling down in this very large data file, use the **Go to Case…** command to quickly locate the cases (rows) that correspond to the trial numbers in the table. From the **Edit** menu, select the **Go to case…** command to produce the **Go To Case** dialog window. Type a trial number in the **Case Number:** field. Click **OK** to cause the requested row to appear at the top of the **Data Editor** window.

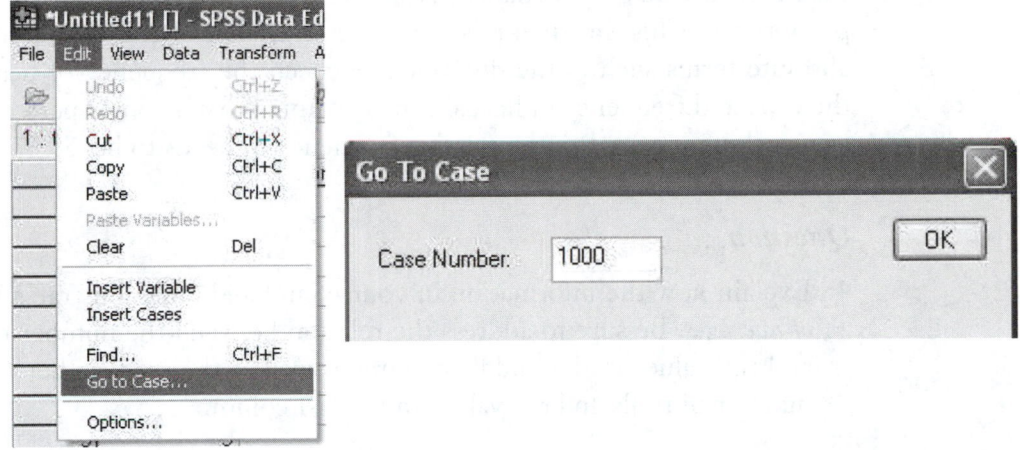

Assignment 3

Use the values in the data to complete the following table.

Trials	Sum	abs_error	rel_error
1	_____	_____	_____
10	_____	_____	_____
100	_____	_____	_____
1,000	_____	_____	_____
10,000	_____	_____	_____
100,000	_____	_____	_____

Individuals who exhibit the **gambler's fallacy** often support their belief by appealing to something called "the law of averages." After losing several games in a row, they may say something like, "I'm due for a win; it's just the law of averages." In mathematical statistics, the law of averages is more often called the *law of large numbers* or, more precisely, *the weak law of large numbers*. A paraphrase of the formal statement of the law of large numbers might read as follows: As the number of independent trials of a random process grows large, the deviation from expectation approaches zero. If the random process is tossing a coin, then the proportion of successes (e.g., heads) that you observe approaches the expected relative frequency probability as the number of coin tosses grows large. This is true, whether the expected relative frequency probability of success is exactly .5, or some other value such as .495 or .505.

The deviation from expectation is sometimes called *chance error*. You might express the law of averages in terms of chance error by stating that chance error decreases as the number of trials increases. Note, however, that this statement is true only if chance error is measured as a relative frequency or proportion. This statement is not true if chance error is measured in absolute terms such as the difference between the frequency of heads and the expected frequency of heads. If it is assumed that a coin is perfectly balanced, then one expects the relative frequency of heads to be .5

Question

4. Explain how the information in your completed table illustrates the *law of averages*. Be sure to address the relation between the number of trials and the values in the middle column as well as the relation between the number of trials and the values in the last column.

ANSWERS

1.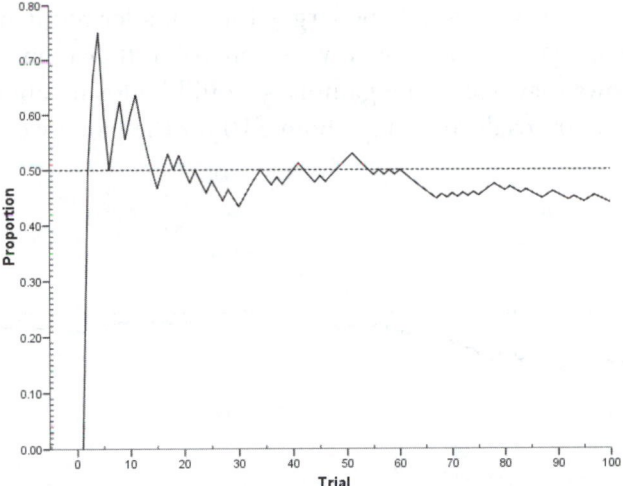

The above graph shows the proportion of successes becoming less variable as the number of trials increases. However, the proportion of successes also appears to be deviating away from .5 (50%). Although the deviation away from .5 reflects a random process that may or may not be apparent in your chart, you should observe a similar reduction in variability. The reduction in variability is a function of sample size; as the size of the sample (number of trials) increases, variability decreases.

2. The terms *relative frequency* and *proportion* are interchangeable. In this context, both terms express the frequency of some outcome as a fraction of the total number of trials. A proportion may be expressed as a percentage by multiplying by 100. A *percentage* is simply the relative frequency with which an outcome occurs per 100 trials. These three terms may be used to express the *probability* of observing a particular outcome. When a percentage of outcomes is used to express the probability of an outcome, the phrase "percent chance" is typically used: "If you flip a coin enough times, the percent chance of observing a head is close to 50."

3. If you are a gambler, then you are probably a risk-taker so you'd rather base your wager on a game of 100 trials. That's because the deviation from the expected relative frequency of a successful outcome (.5) will usually be larger for a smaller number of trials. So, you stand to either win or lose more if you wager on 100 rather than 1000 trials. The line graph below shows that one of the gamblers would be losing about $600 if the game were limited to 100 trials, but only about $100 if the game were extended to 1,000 trials.

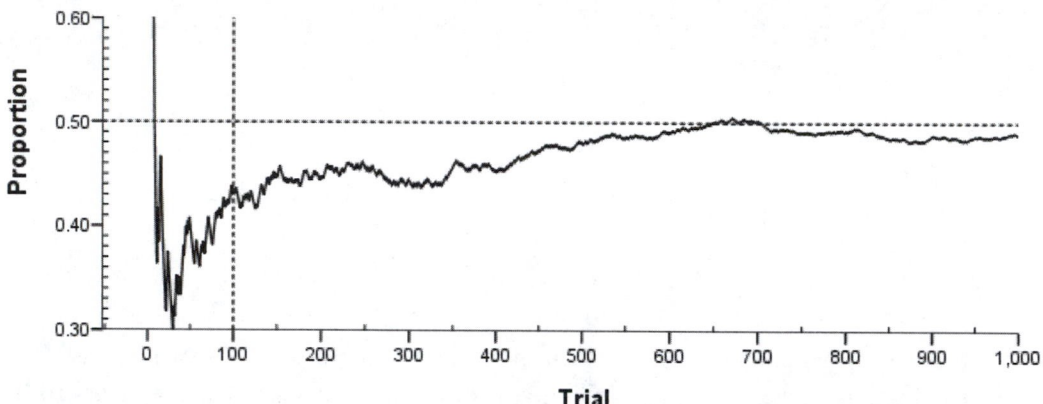

4. The numbers in the table will vary, of course, but the values in the last column should decrease with the number of trials as required by the "law of averages."

Trials	Sum	abs_error	rel_error
1	0	0.5	0.5
10	2	3	0.3
100	44	6	0.06
1,000	482	18	0.018
10,000	4961	39	0.0039
100,000	50020	20	0.0002

The law of averages states that the deviation from an expected frequency decreases as the number of trials grows large. However, this deviation must be expressed relative to the total number of trials—that is, as a relative frequency (last column) rather than a frequency (middle column).

CHAPTER 5

CORRELATION

Quantifying the Relation Between Two Variables

A graduate student assigned to teach her first class in introductory statistics for psychology majors wondered whether student performance on an exam would be related to class attendance. Accordingly, she kept a careful record of class absences before the first of three examinations in her class.

SPSS DATA ENTRY

Launch SPSS and select **Type in data** near the top of the list of menu options:

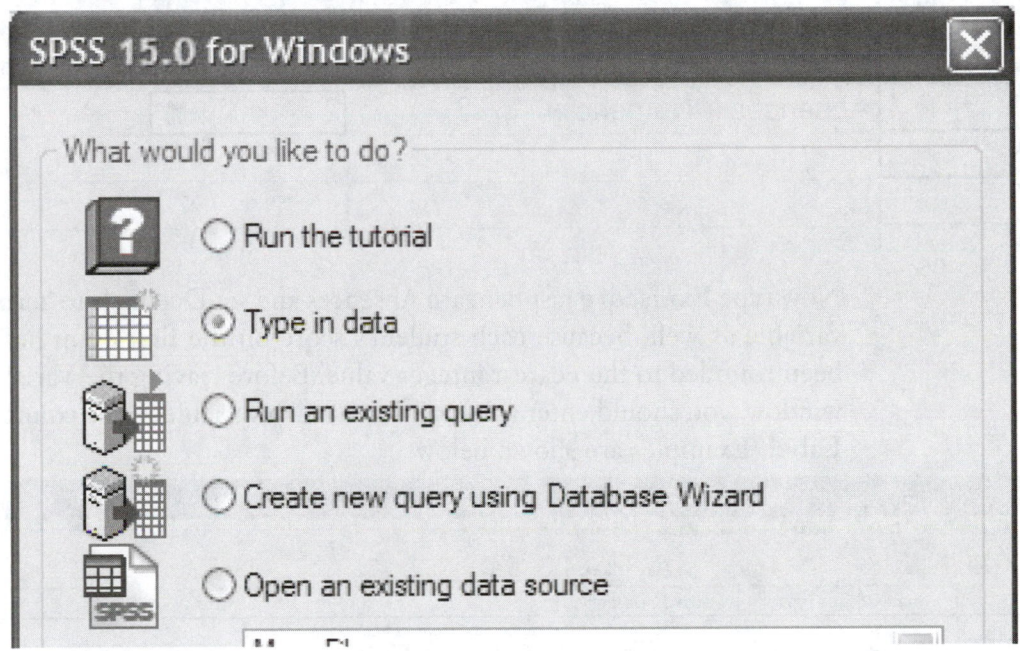

SPSS is fully launched when the spreadsheet–like **Data Editor** window appears. Click on the **Variable View** tab at the bottom of the screen to display the **Variable View** window:

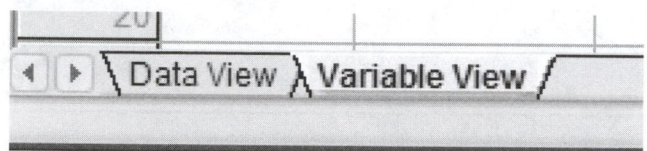

Type **Absences** in the first row of the first column of the Variable View window (under **Name**) and press the Enter key. Your screen should look like the one below, showing the default variable **Type** as **Numeric** and the default value of **Decimals** as "2." Do not change the variable type, but change the value of Decimals by clicking on the bottom arrow or just highlight the **2** and replace it by typing a **zero**. This value should be set to zero, because the number of class absences for each student is a **discrete** variable (one whose values can only be positive integers).

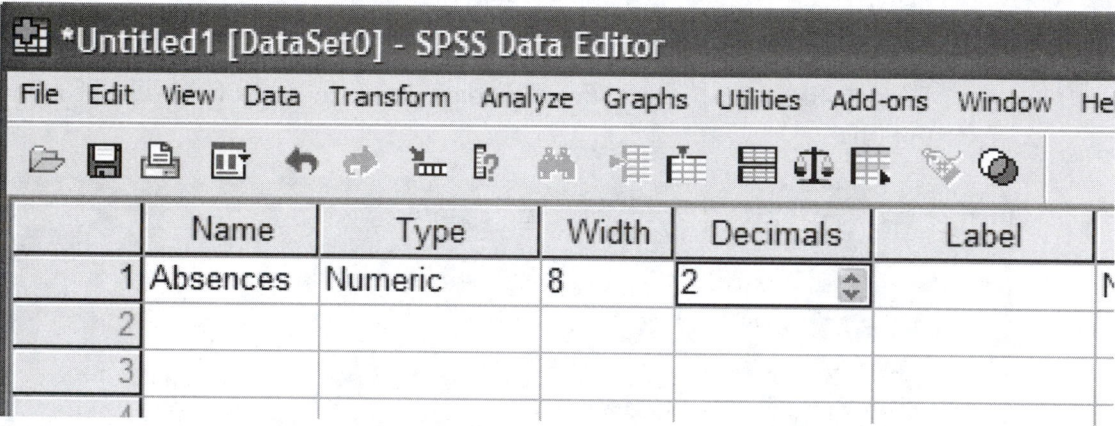

Now type **Exmscore** just beneath Absences and set Decimals to zero for this variable as well, because each student's score on the first exam has already been rounded to the nearest integer value. Before leaving the Variable View window, you should enter a description of each variable in the column under **Label**. Examples are shown below:

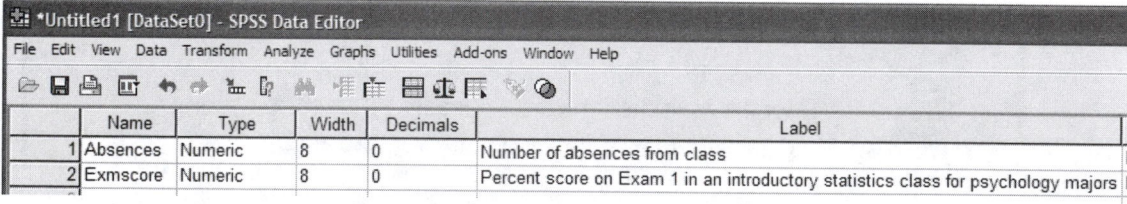

Now select the **Data View** window tab to return to the **Data Editor** window. You should see the names of the variables as headings for the first two columns (see below). If you do not see these names, review the previous steps and make sure that you've entered the names of the variables as instructed.

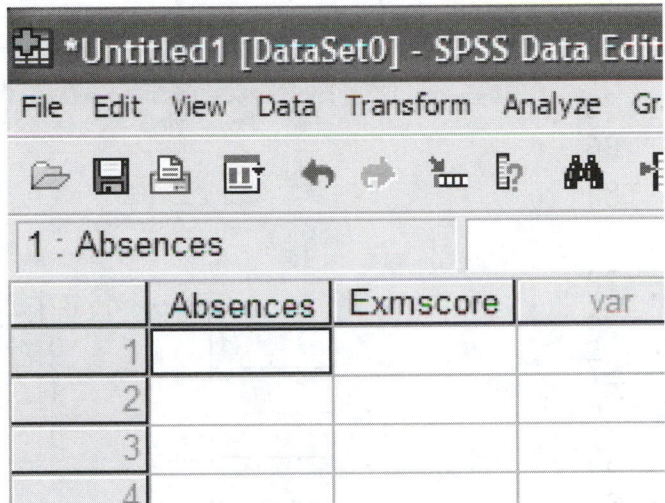

The data that you will type into the Data Editor window are displayed in the two columns on the next page. Absences is conceptualized as the "X" or **predictor** variable, because the instructor's interest is in determining whether a student's attendance record can be used to predict his or her exam score. The "Y" variable, Exmscore, is called the **criterion**, or dependent, variable.

The values in the X column should be typed in the Data Editor window in the column under Absences, and the values in the Y column should entered in the column under Exmscore. After entering all of the values, check to make sure that you entered them correctly in the order shown. When the data entry is complete, your screen should look like the one below on the right.

X	Y
0	86
1	85
0	81
0	79
0	78
0	75
1	67
1	65
2	63
0	63
2	61
1	60
1	52
2	51
2	48
2	47
1	43
2	43
2	40

*Untitled1 [DataSet0] - SPSS Data Edi

File   Edit   View   Data   Transform   Analyze   G

8 :

	Absences	Exmscore	var
1	0	86	
2	1	85	
3	0	81	
4	0	79	
5	0	78	
6	0	75	
7	1	67	
8	1	65	
9	2	63	
10	0	63	
11	2	61	
12	1	60	
13	1	52	
14	2	51	
15	2	48	
16	2	47	
17	1	43	
18	2	43	
19	2	40	
20			

EXERCISE 1

1. Select **Graphs, Scatter/Dot...** to access the **Scatter/Dot** dialog window.

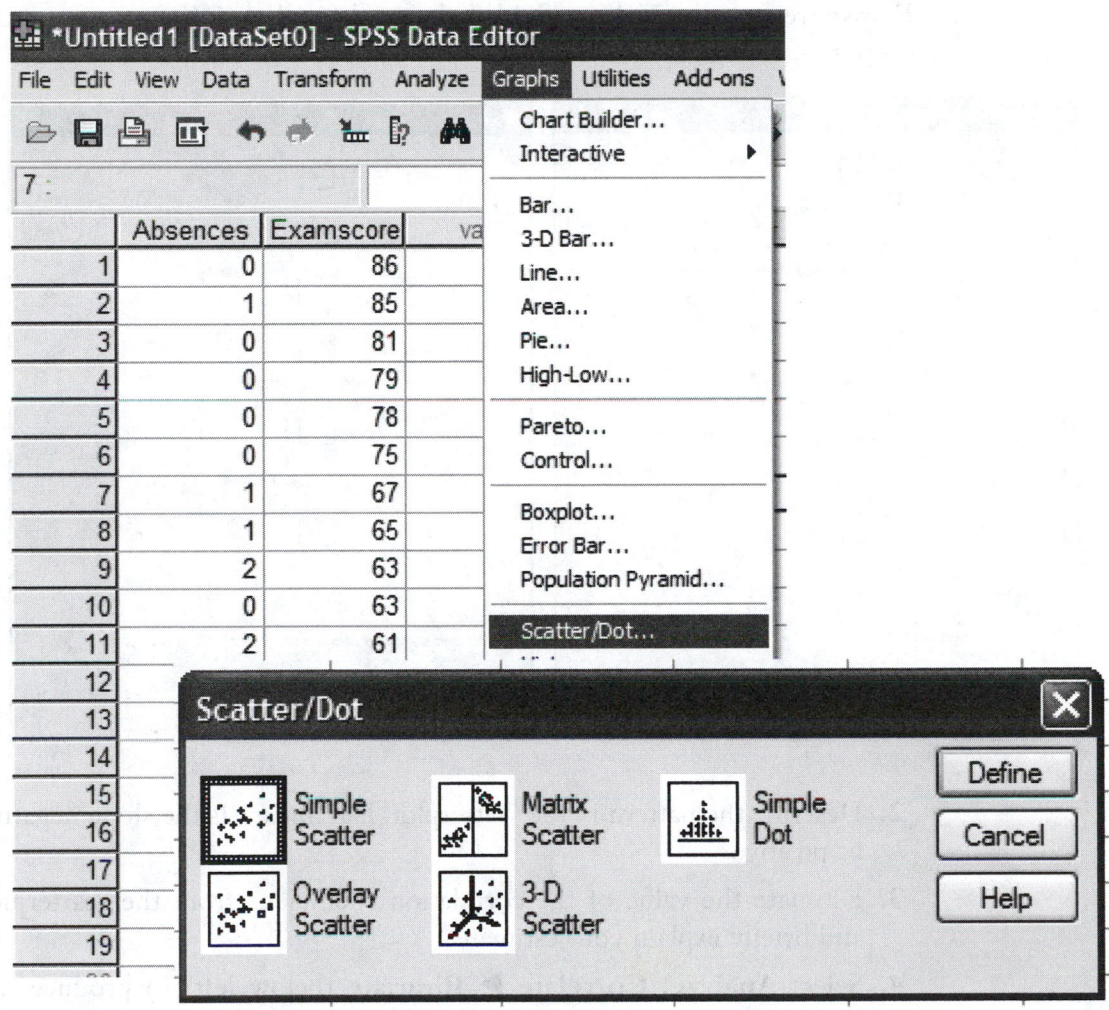

Select **Simple Scatter**, then click **Define** to bring up the **Simple Scatterplot** dialog window (below left). Now select **Absences** and click on the ▶ symbol to move this variable into the **X Axis:** field, then move **Exmscore** into the **Y Axis: field** (below right). Click **OK** to generate the output.

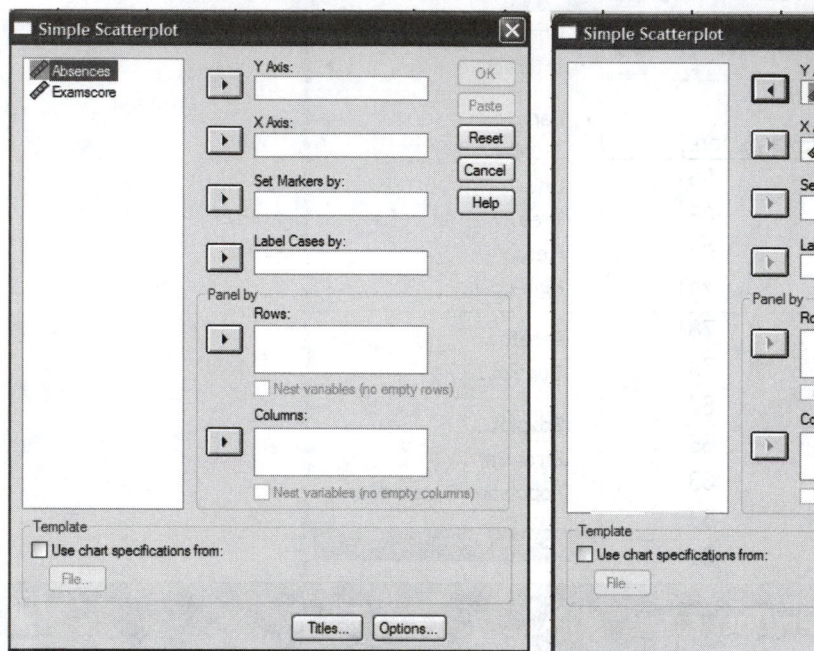

2. Describe the pattern in the scatterplot. Is it linear? Is the slope negative or positive?

3. Estimate the value of the correlation coefficient from the scatterplot and briefly explain your estimate.

4. Select **Analyze, Correlate ▶ Bivariate** (below left) to produce the **Bivariate Correlations** dialog window (below right).

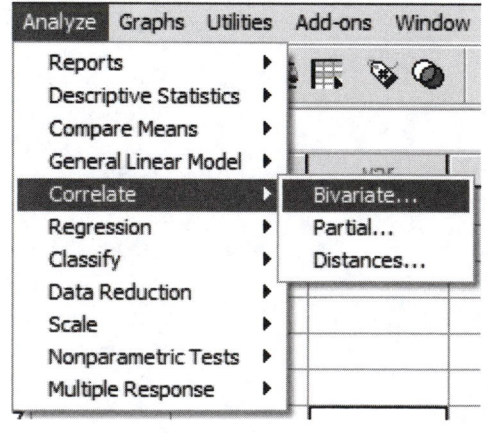
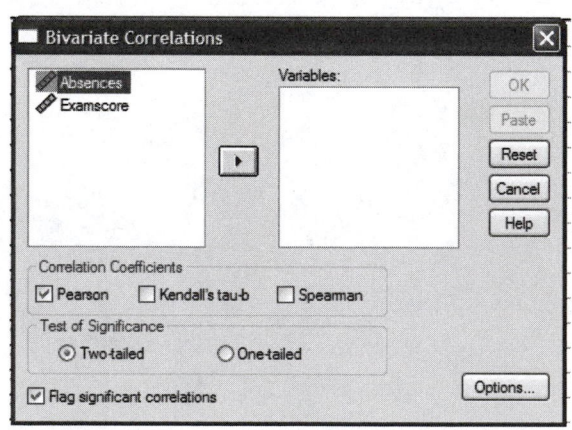

In the **Bivariate Correlations** dialog window, select both variables and move them into the **Variables:** field on the right side of the window. Make sure that the **Pearson** option under **Correlation Coefficients** is selected (see below). Click **OK** to generate the output.

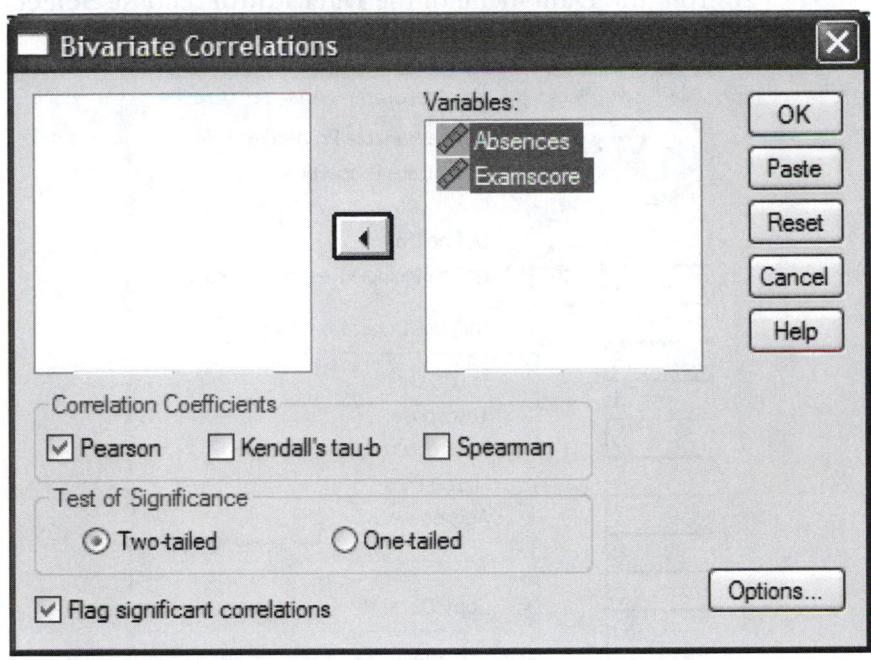

5. What is the value of the correlation coefficient? Was your estimate close? If your estimate wasn't close, revisit your explanation in **3** and explain how you went wrong.

6. What does the *magnitude* of the correlation coefficient reveal about the relationship between the two variables? What does the *sign* of the correlation coefficient reveal about the relationship?

EXERCISE 2

7. Add the following data values for the 20th student: **9** absences (she came to the first class and did not show up again until the day of the exam) and an exam score of **98**. Follow the instructions from Exercise 1-1 to produce a scatterplot of the data with this student added.

8. What term is used to describe the point that represents the added student?

9. Select **Analyze, Correlate ▶ Bivariate...** to compute the correlation coefficient for the data with this student added.

10. What is the effect of the addition of the new student's data on the sign and strength of the correlation coefficient?

EXERCISE 3

In this exercise, we'll exclude the cases with 2 or more absences before generating a scatterplot of the data with these cases removed.

- From the **Data** menu of the **Data Editor**, choose **Select Cases...**

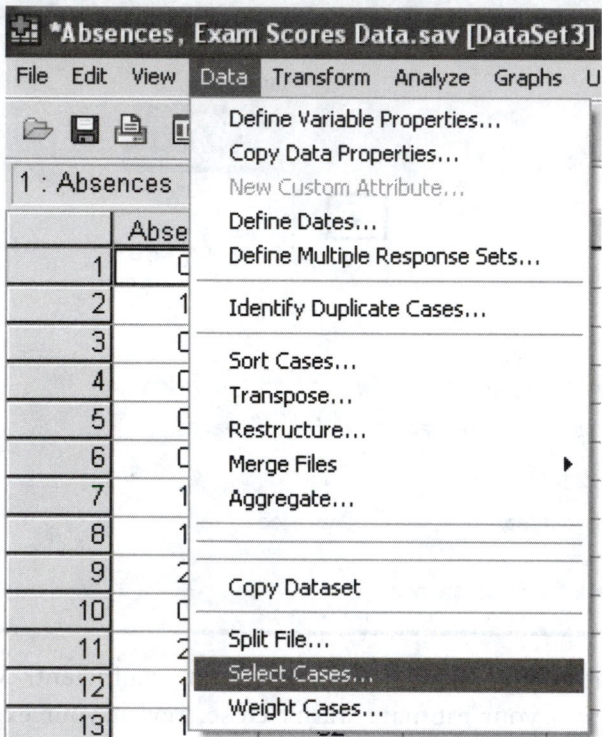

- This will produce the **Select Cases** dialog window. Click on the radio button next to **If condition is satisfied** as shown. Then click on the **If...** button (If...) just below.

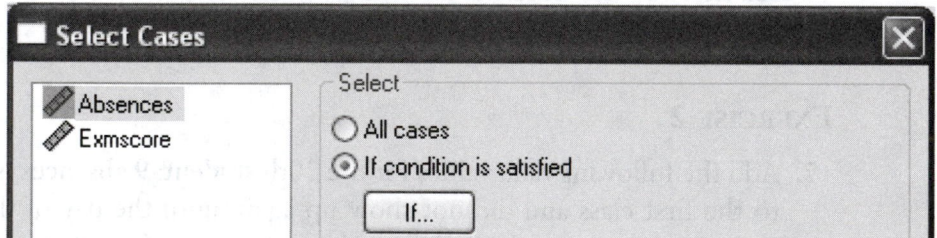

Clicking on the If... button produces the **Select Cases: If** dialog window. Type **Absences <= 1** as shown, then click **Continue** to return to the **Select Cases** dialog window.

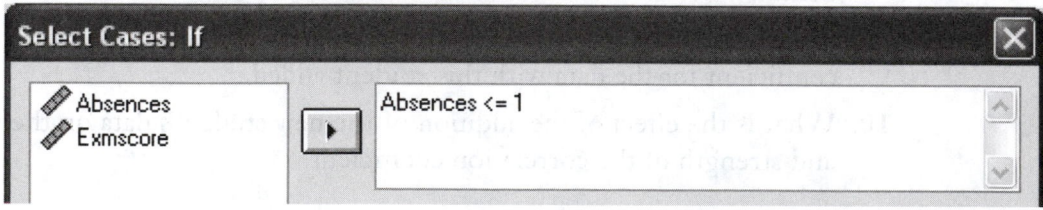

The **Select Cases** dialog should display **Absences <= 1** as the **If...** condition. If your dialog window looks like the one below, then click **OK** to return to the Data Editor.

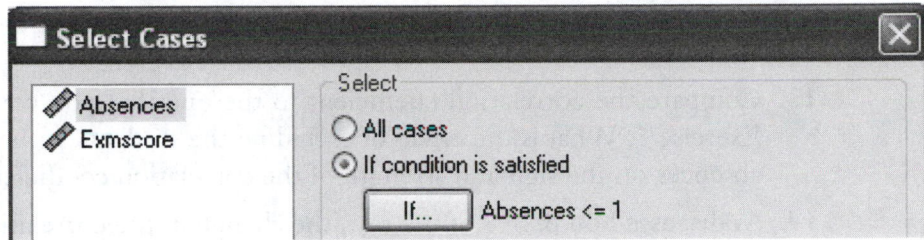

The Data Editor should be similar to the following. The forward slash (![slash]9) marks the cases with 2 or more absences that have been filtered (temporarily excluded) from the data set.

	Absences	Exmscore	filter_$
1	0	86	1
2	1	85	1
3	0	81	1
4	0	79	1
5	0	78	1
6	0	75	1
7	1	67	1
8	1	65	1
9	2	63	0
10	0	63	1
11	2	61	0
12	1	60	1
13	1	52	1
14	2	51	0
15	2	48	0
16	2	47	0
17	1	43	1
18	2	43	0
19	2	40	0
20	9	98	0

*Absences, Exam Scores Data.sav [DataSet3]

File   Edit   View   Data   Transform   Analyze   Graphs

1 : Absences   0

11. Follow the instructions from Exercise 1 to produce a scatterplot of the data with students with 2 or more absences removed.

12. Select **Analyze, Correlate ▶ Bivariate...** to compute the correlation coefficient for the data after removing the students with 2 or more absences.

13. Compare the correlation coefficient to the one that you computed in Exercise 2. What is the effect of excluding the students with 2 or more absences on the sign and strength of the correlation coefficient?

14. As discussed on p. 228 of the text, the change in the correlation coefficient occurred because the _____ of values of the absences variable was _____.

15. Does the correlation coefficient that you computed in Exercise 1 show that missing class causes students to make lower exam grades? Explain your answer.

ANSWERS

EXERCISE 1

1.

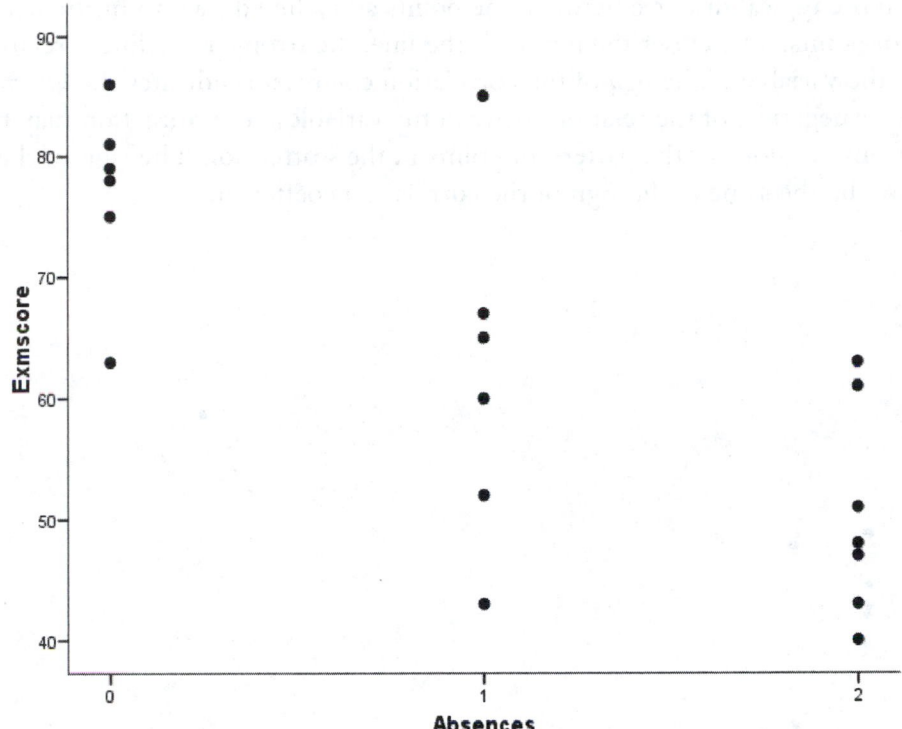

2. There is an apparent trend for students with fewer absences to earn higher exam scores, as may be expected. The relation between the variables is negative because a line drawn to fit the three columns of points would slope downward from left to right. You can visualize this pattern by connecting the middle of each cluster of points with an imaginary line.

3. The easiest part of the estimate is the sign, because estimating the magnitude (strength) of a linear relation from a scatterplot requires practice associating scatterplots with correlation coefficients, but a good estimate will be between –.5 and –.75.

4.

Correlations

		Absences	Exmscore
Absences	Pearson Correlation	1	-.747**
	Sig. (2-tailed)		.000
	N	19	19
Exmscore	Pearson Correlation	-.747**	1
	Sig. (2-tailed)	.000	
	N	19	19

** Correlation is significant at the 0.01 level (2-tailed).

5. From the SPSS output table, the correlation coefficient is –.747.

6. The *magnitude* of the correlation coefficient indicates the *strength* of the linear relationship between the variables. The strength of the relation may be roughly estimated by noting the typical distance between the points and a line drawn to fit the overall pattern of points. The closer the points to the line, the stronger the linear relation between the variables. The *sign* of the correlation coefficient indicates the *direction* (positive or negative) of the relation between the variables. This direction may be discerned from the slope of the pattern of points in the scatterplot. The sign of the slope will always be the same as the sign of the correlation coefficient.

EXERCISE 2

7.

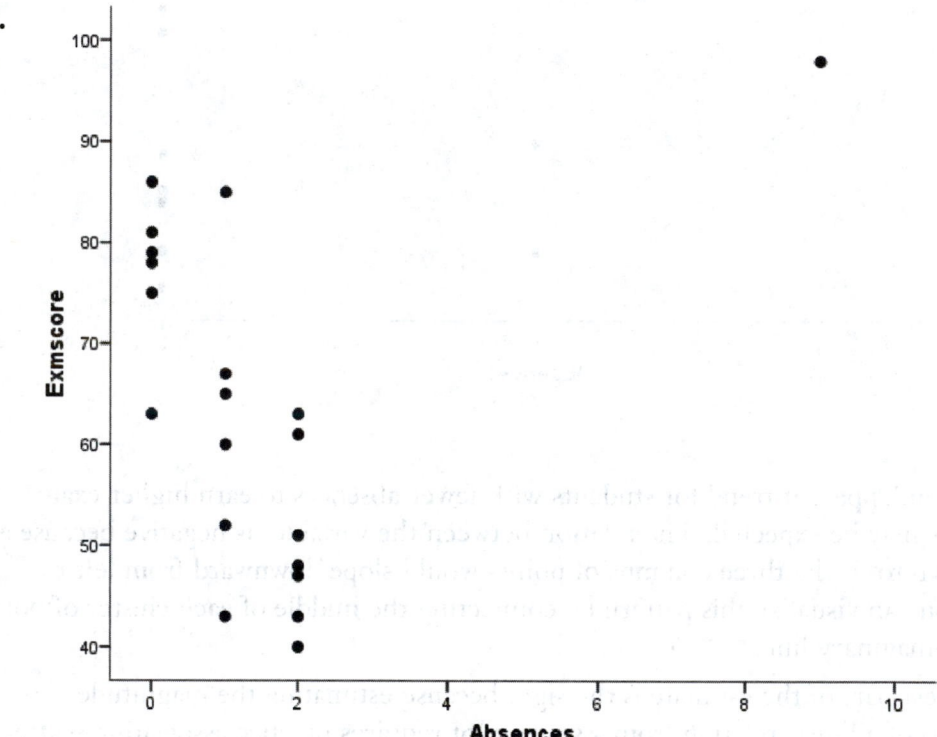

8. The added point is called an **outlier**.

9.

Correlations

		Absences	Exmscore
Absences	Pearson Correlation	1	.156
	Sig. (2-tailed)		.511
	N	20	20
Exmscore	Pearson Correlation	.156	1
	Sig. (2-tailed)	.511	
	N	20	20

10. The addition of the point representing the new student markedly reduced the strength and reversed the direction of the linear relation between the variables. The relation between the variables is grossly distorted by the outlier.

EXERCISE 3

11.

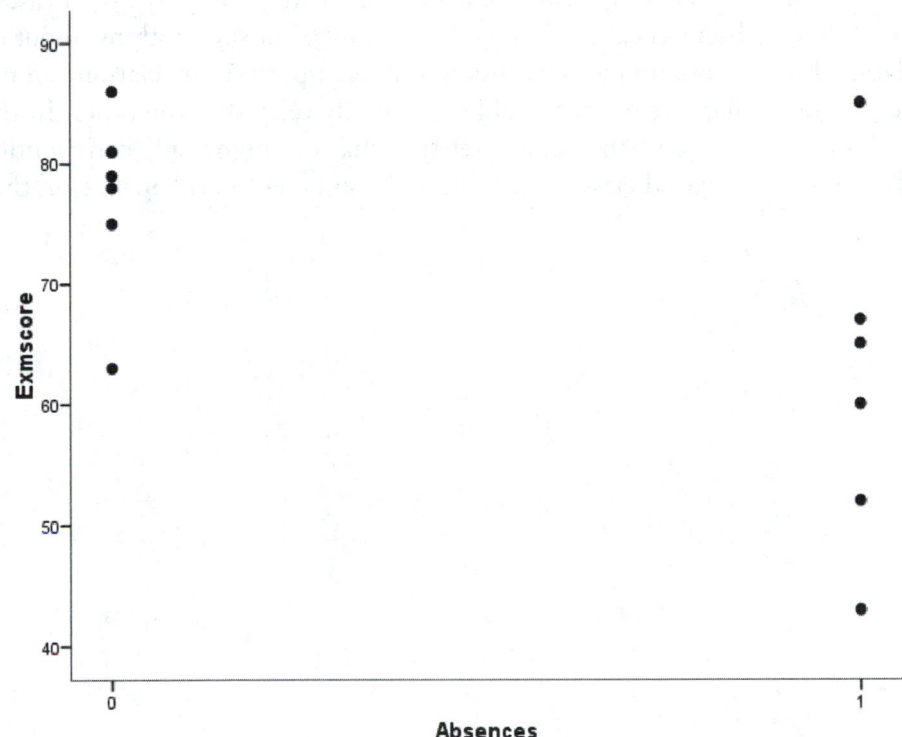

12.

Correlations

		Absences	Exmscore
Absences	Pearson Correlation	1	-.580*
	Sig. (2-tailed)		.048
	N	12	12
Exmscore	Pearson Correlation	-.580*	1
	Sig. (2-tailed)	.048	
	N	12	12

* Correlation is significant at the 0.05 level (2-tailed).

13. The removal of the students with two or more absences reduced the correlation coefficient from $-.74$ to $-.58$, indicating a reduction in the strength, but with no change in the direction, of the relation between the variables.

14. The change in the correlation coefficient occurred because the **range** of values of the absences variable was **restricted**.

15. The strong negative correlation between class absences and exam scores indicates that students with fewer absences earned higher exam scores, but says nothing about a causal relationship. Correlation is not causation. Even a perfect correlation can not be interpreted to mean that one of the variables is causally related to the other. In this example, a third variable, perhaps a character trait that we might call "conscientiousness," is responsible for good class attendance and competent performance on the exams.

REGRESSION

Tools for Predicting Behavior

EXERCISE 1
PRODUCING A CORRELATION MATRIX

Launch SPSS. The default **"What would you like to do?"** menu option is **Open an existing data source**. Leave this option selected and access the **Statistics Grades (N = 72)** file on the data CD. The file includes scores on six variables for each of 72 students enrolled in an introductory statistics course. Four of the variables will be used in this exercise: scores on the verbal section of the SAT, scores on the math section of the SAT, self-reported ratings of math anxiety, and the final grade in the course. The values of these four variables for the first 15 cases from this file are displayed below.

SAT_Verbal	SAT_Math	Math_Anxiety	Final_Grade
560	540	4	92.42
680	690	5	94.29
590	420	9	91.31
580	470	4	88.57
580	480	8	82.63
700	720	2	95.69
480	450	7	85.72
600	630	5	91.69
460	410	5	71.69
630	600	4	96.39
600	600	2	94.83
750	710	0	83.80
510	430	3	71.52
660	580	6	84.21
570	570	8	85.01

Select **Analyze, Correlate, Bivariate...** to access the **Bivariate Correlations** dialog window.

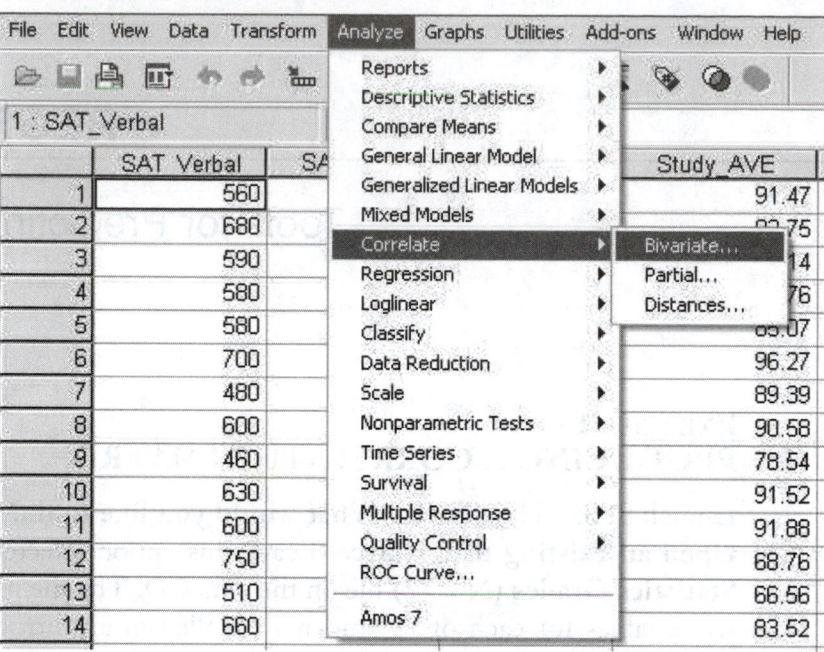

Select all four variables and click the ![button] button to move them into the **Variables:** field.

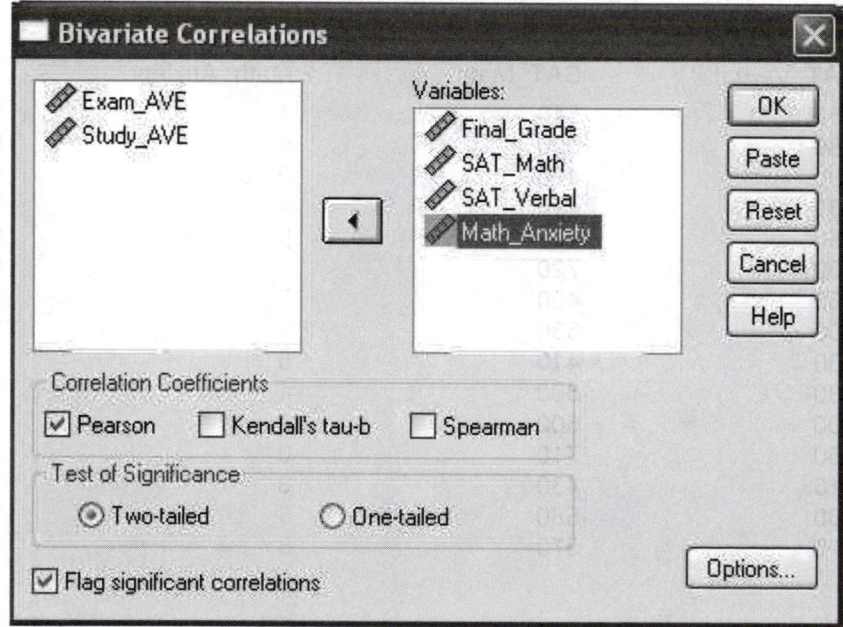

Click **OK** to generate the output. A table of correlation coefficients like the one produced by SPSS for this set of variables is called a *correlation matrix*. The correlations in the matrix are termed *zero-order correlations* to distinguish them from the higher-order correlations computed using the partial correlation procedure. In the social and behavioral sciences, the strength of a correlation was described by Cohen (1988) as follows: *strong* (r = .5 and above), *moderate* (r = .3 to .49), and *weak* (r = .10 to .29). The sign of r is ignored when assessing the strength of a correlation.

Questions

1. How many *unique* zero-order correlations are displayed in the correlation matrix?

2. Identify all of the unique pairs of variables by listing their names separated by a comma (e.g., SAT_Math, Final_Grade). In the column next to each pair of variables, identify the strength of the correlation between them by writing either "strong," "moderate," or "weak."

EXERCISE 2
SIMPLE LINEAR REGRESSION

In this exercise, you will run a simple linear regression to predict a student's final statistics grade from her or his score on the math section of the SAT. Score on the math section of the SAT (SAT_Math) was selected as the predictor, or independent, variable because this variable was most strongly correlated with the criterion, or dependent, variable, final statistics grade (Final_Grade). *Remember:* Correlations reveal potential, not actual, causal relations among variables. A high correlation, alone, can not tell us that having a higher score on the math section of the SAT causes a person to receive a higher final grade in statistics.

Select **Analyze, Regression ▶ Linear** to produce the **Linear Regression** dialog window.

In the **Linear Regression** dialog window, the term **Dependent:** appears at the top near the center of the window, and the term **Independent(s):** appears a little farther down. In simple linear regression, the values of the independent (or predictor) variable (X) are used to predict the values of the dependent (or criterion) variable, Y. Select **Final_Grade** and click the button to move this variable into the **Dependent:** field. Now move **SAT_Math** into the **Independent(s):** field. Click **OK** to generate the regression output.

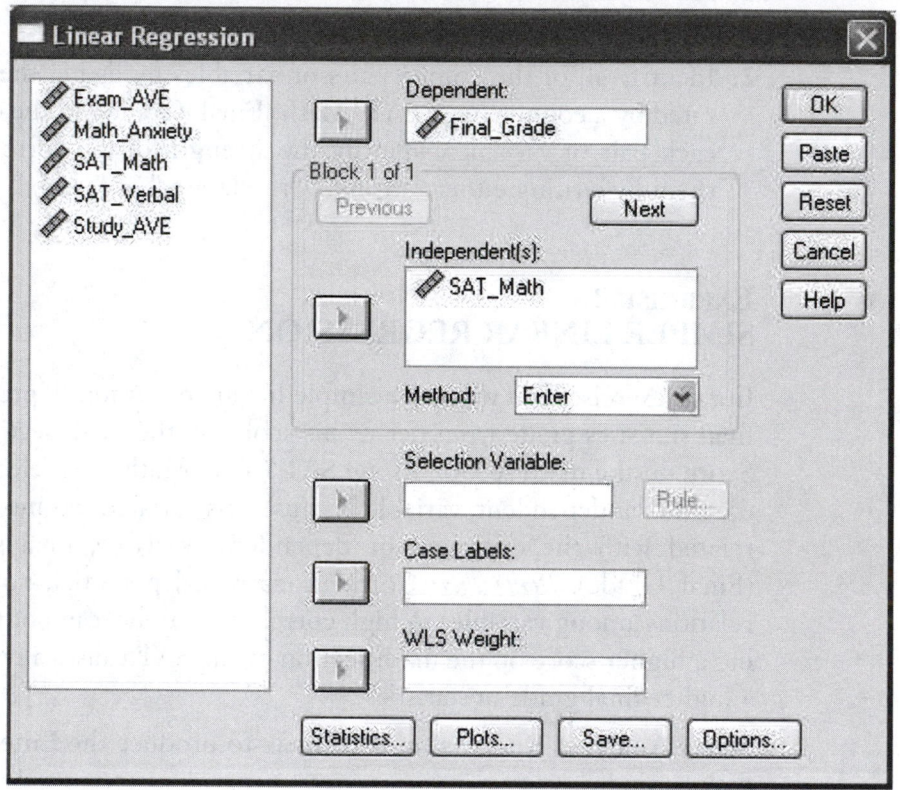

Questions

3. What is the name of the statistic whose symbol is R?

4. What is the value of R?

5. Interpret R; that is, describe what this statistic measures.

6. What is the name of the statistic whose symbol is R^2 (R Square in the Model Summary table)?

7. What is the value of R^2?

8. Interpret R^2; that is, describe what this statistic measures.

9. For each 1-point increase in a student's score on the math section of the SAT (SAT_Math) what is the change in the student's final grade in statistics (Final_Grade)?

10. Identify the name of the statistic whose value is the same as R.

EXERCISE 3
MULTIPLE REGRESSION

In this exercise, you will run a multiple linear regression to predict a student's final statistics grade from scores on the math and verbal sections of the SAT as well as self-reported ratings of math anxiety.

Select **Analyze, Regression ▶ Linear** to produce the **Linear Regression** dialog window. In the **Linear Regression** dialog window, **Final_Grade** should be in the **Dependent:** field and **SAT_Math** should be in the **Independent(s):** field. Select **SAT_Verbal** and **Math_Anxiety** and click the [▶] button to add these variables to the **Independent(s):** field. Click **OK** to generate the regression output.

Questions

11. Compare the values of R and R^2 from the simple and multiple regression analyses. What is the general effect of adding independent variables to the regression model?

12. Rank the three independent variables according to their relative strength in predicting final grade in statistics. (*Hint*: Look at the standardized regression coefficients.)

ANSWERS

Exercise 1

1. The correlation coefficients above the diagonal of autocorrelations (the 1's) are a mirror image of the correlations below the diagonal, so there are just 6 unique zero order correlations in the matrix.

		Final_Grade	SAT_Math	SAT_Verbal	Math_Anxiety
Final_Grade	Pearson Correlation	1	.557**	.547**	-.175
	Sig. (2-tailed)		.000	.000	.141
	N	72	72	72	72
SAT_Math	Pearson Correlation	.557**	1	.709**	-.497**
	Sig. (2-tailed)	.000		.000	.000
	N	72	72	72	72
SAT_Verbal	Pearson Correlation	.547**	.709**	1	-.330**
	Sig. (2-tailed)	.000	.000		.005
	N	72	72	72	72
Math_Anxiety	Pearson Correlation	-.175	-.497**	-.330**	1
	Sig. (2-tailed)	.141	.000	.005	
	N	72	72	72	72

**. Correlation is significant at the 0.01 level (2-tailed).

2.

Variables	Description of Relation
SAT_Math, Final_Grade	Strong
SAT_Verbal, Final_Grade	Strong
Math_Anxiety, Final_Grade	Weak
SAT_Math, SAT_Verbal	Strong
SAT_Math, Math_Anxiety	Moderate
SAT_Verbal, Math_Anxiety	Moderate

EXERCISE 2

Model Summary

Model	R	R Square	Adjusted R Square	Std. Error of the Estimate
1	.557[a]	.310	.300	5.68251

a. Predictors: (Constant), Score on the Math section of the SAT

ANOVA[b]

Model		Sum of Squares	df	Mean Square	F	Sig.
1	Regression	1015.876	1	1015.876	31.460	.000[a]
	Residual	2260.362	70	32.291		
	Total	3276.238	71			

a. Predictors: (Constant), Score on the Math section of the SAT

b. Dependent Variable: Final average in an introductory statistics course

Coefficients[a]

Model		Unstandardized Coefficients		Standardized Coefficients	t	Sig.
		B	Std. Error	Beta		
1	(Constant)	61.980	4.535		13.666	.000
	Score on the Math section of the SAT	.047	.008	.557	5.609	.000

a. Dependent Variable: Final average in an introductory statistics course

3. R is the symbol for the **multiple correlation coefficient**.

4. From the Model Summary Table, the value of R is **.557**.

5. The multiple correlation coefficient is a measure of the degree of linear relation among all of the independent variables and the dependent variable. R is computed as the correlation between the actual and predicted values of the dependent variable and thus can never be a negative value. In simple linear regression, R is the absolute value of the Pearson correlation coefficient computed for the independent and dependent variables.

6. The statistic R^2 is called the **coefficient of determination**.

7. From the Model Summary Table, the value of $R^2 = $ **.31**.

8. The coefficient of determination is a measure of the proportion of the total variability in the dependent variable that is "explained" or "determined" by the independent variable.

9. For each 1-point increase in a student's score on the math section of the SAT (SAT_Math), a student's final grade in statistics (Final_Grade) increases by **.047** points, the value of the slope (regression coefficient).

10. The value of the standardized regression coefficient (beta) is the same as that of the multiple correlation coefficient. This will always be the case when there is only one independent (predictor) variable.

EXERCISE 3

Model Summary

Model	R	R Square	Adjusted R Square	Std. Error of the Estimate
1	.607[a]	.369	.341	5.51586

a. Predictors: (Constant), SAT_Verbal, Math_Anxiety, SAT_Math

ANOVA[b]

Model		Sum of Squares	df	Mean Square	F	Sig.
1	Regression	1207.360	3	402.453	13.228	.000[a]
	Residual	2068.878	68	30.425		
	Total	3276.238	71			

a. Predictors: (Constant), SAT_Verbal, Math_Anxiety, SAT_Math

b. Dependent Variable: Final_Grade

Coefficients[a]

Model		Unstandardized Coefficients		Standardized Coefficients	t	Sig.
		B	Std. Error	Beta		
1	(Constant)	51.618	6.563		7.865	.000
	Math_Anxiety	.354	.312	.126	1.135	.260
	SAT_Math	.034	.012	.407	2.736	.008
	SAT_Verbal	.027	.012	.300	2.194	.032

a. Dependent Variable: Final_Grade

11. The value of the multiple correlation coefficient R increased from **.557** to **.607**, whereas the coefficient of determination R^2 increased from **.31** to **.369**. Adding independent variables to the multiple regression model always increases the values of R and R^2.

12. The strongest predictor of a student's final statistics grade is her or his score on the math section of the SAT ($\beta = .407$), followed by the score on the verbal section of the SAT ($\beta = .3$), and the student's self-reported rating of math anxiety ($\beta = .126$). It is important to remember that these are *relative* measures of predictive strength. The value of each standardized coefficient change with the addition of each new predictor variable.

CHAPTER 7

INFERENTIAL STATISTICS

The Surprising Story of the Normal Curve

STANDARDIZING A VARIABLE

In this set of exercises you will request that SPSS create a standardized variable by transforming raw scores (self-ratings of math anxiety) to **standard**, or **z**, **scores**. The formula for converting a raw score to a z score is:

$$z = \frac{X - \mu}{\sigma}$$

where,

X is a raw score
μ is the mean of the raw scores
σ is the standard deviation of the raw scores

A z score expresses a raw score in terms of the number of standard deviations between the raw score and the mean of the raw scores. Just as a yardstick measures distance in inches and feet, a z score measures distance in standard deviation units. The mean of the raw scores depicted in the figure below is 38, and the standard deviation is 4.

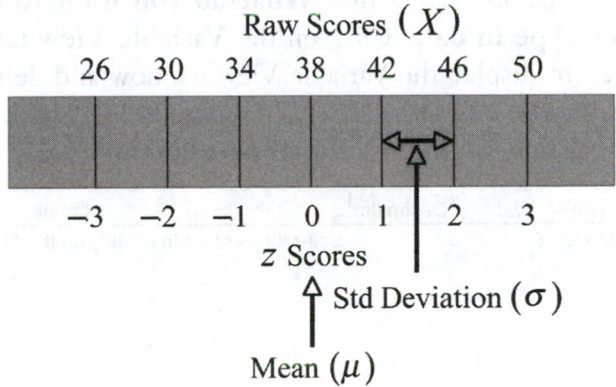

When raw scores represent measures of different variables it is necessary to standardize them before you can make meaningful comparisons between them. For example, it would be inappropriate to compare exam scores from an English class and a math class, because the content differs substantially and the classes may not be equally difficult. Thus, a seemingly low exam score in a difficult class may be relatively better than a higher score in a less difficult class. Standardizing the two exam scores enables a direct comparison between them. Here is an example. Suppose an English major is beaming after receiving a score of 93 on a midterm exam in her English literature course. Her best friend, a math major, is a little down after receiving a score of 77 on her midterm exam in a linear algebra course. Here are the relevant descriptive statistics for the two classes:

Class	μ	σ
English Literature	85	8
Linear Algebra	67	10

Is the English major's exam score better than her friend's score on the linear algebra exam?

Solution. Convert both scores to standard scores and compare them.

$$z_{English} = \frac{93 - 85}{8} = \frac{8}{8} = 1$$

$$z_{Math} = \frac{77 - 67}{10} = \frac{10}{10} = 1$$

As you can see, both scores are one standard deviation above the class mean, so they are equivalent.

EXERCISE 1

Launch SPSS. When the "**What do you want to do?**" window appears, select **Type in data**. Click on the **Variable View** tab at the bottom of the screen to display the Variable View window and define the variable as follows: **Name** = "Math_anxiety," **Decimals** = 0, and **Label** = "Self-ratings of math anxiety on the first day of statistics class."

	Name	Type	Width	Decimals	Label
1	Math_anxiety	Numeric	8	0	Self-ratings of math anxiety on the first day of statistics class

Click on the **Data View** tab to display the Data Editor and enter the following data.

4	1	8	7	8	6	8	8	6
6	5	3	3	7	9	4	6	8
7	5	7	6	8	5	6	7	3
5	5	10	2	7	5	7	6	7
9	4	3	8	3	4	4	5	10
4	4	7	2	7	2	7	8	10
8	2	0	8	8	1	4	5	7
2	0	6	10	2	8	1	8	
7	3	10	6	5	7	6	8	
7	6	6	5	10	4	4	5	

- From the **Analyze** menu, select **Descriptive Statistics** ▶ **Descriptives...** to produce the **Descriptives** dialog window.
- Select **Math_anxiety** and click the triangle (▶) to move the variable into the **Variable(s):** field.
- Click **Options** to produce the **Descriptives: Options** dialog window.
- Make sure that **Mean** and **Std. deviation** are the only statistics selected and click **Continue** to return to the Descriptives dialog window.
- Select the **Save standardized values as variables** option in the lower left corner of the window.
- Click **OK** to produce the output.
- Return to the **Data Editor** and notice the addition of the standardized variable.
- Use **Analyze, Descriptive Statistics** ▶ **Descriptives...** to determine the mean and standard deviation of the standardized variable. (Remember to *deselect* the **Save standardized values as variables** option in the lower left corner of the window; otherwise SPSS will generate a new variable named **ZZMath_anxiety**.)

Questions

1. What is the mean of the standardized variable?
2. What is the standard deviation of the standardized variable?
3. Do all samples of standard scores have the same mean and standard deviation? Put another way, are the mean and standard deviation the same for all distributions of z scores? Explain your answer.

SCALE SCORES

Any raw score may be standardized, then converted to a scale score using the formula:

$$\text{Scale Score} = z(\sigma) + \mu$$

where,

> z is the standardized equivalent of a raw score
> μ is the arbitrary mean of the scale scores
> σ is the arbitrary standard deviation of the scale scores

The **T score scale** was developed to convert standard scores to a scale in which negative scores would almost never be observed. The arbitrary mean of the T score scale is 50 and the arbitrary standard deviation is 10. The following formula may be used to convert a z score to a T score:

$$T = z(10) + 50$$

EXERCISE 2

- From the **Transform** menu, select **Compute Variable...** to produce the **Compute Variable** dialog window.

- Locate the **Target Variable:** field in the upper left corner of the window and type **T_score**. Select **ZMath_anxiety** and click the triangle (▶) to move this variable into the **Numeric Expression:** field.

- Position the cursor to the right of ZMath_anxiety and type *** 10 + 50**. The Numeric Expression: field should look like this when you are finished:

  ZMath_anxiety * 10 + 50

- Click **OK** to produce the new variable **T_score**.

- Use **Analyze, Descriptive Statistics ▶ Descriptives...** to determine the mean and standard deviation of the T scores. (Remember to *deselect* the **Save standardized values as variables** option in the lower left corner of the window; otherwise SPSS will generate a new variable named ZT_score.)

Questions

4. What is the mean of the T_score variable?

5. What is the standard deviation of the T_score variable?

6. Are there any negative T scores? Why or why not? (*Hint:* Think of a negative T score in terms how far it would be from the mean.)

EXERCISE 3

In this exercise you will use the steps from Exercise 2 to express the self–ratings of anxiety on a new scale that has a mean of 200 and a standard deviation of 25. Choose a name for your new scale and type this name in the **Target Variable:** field. In the **Numeric Expression:** field, replace the mean and standard deviation of the T score scale with the mean and standard deviation of the new scale.

Question

7. What values on this new scale were assigned to individuals with self–reported anxiety scores of:

   a. 0?   **b.** 5?   **c.** 10?

THE CENTRAL LIMIT THEOREM

The purpose of this exercise is to use SPSS to conduct a series of exercises suggested by the *Experience It For Yourself* exercise described on pages 315 to 317 in the text. To demonstrate the central limit theorem (CLT), you will sample with replacement from a population of 140 student heights.

EXERCISE 4

From the **SPSS Data Editor**, select **File, Open ▶ Data...** . When the **Open Data** dialog window appears, navigate to the data CD and open the file **Height Data**. From the **Graphs** menu, select **Legacy Dialogs ▶ Histograms...** as shown:

When the **Histogram** dialog window appears, select **height** and click on the triangle (▶) to move this variable into the **Variable:** field. Click on the box next to **Display normal curve** to request a normal curve superimposed on the histogram of height data. Before clicking **OK** make sure that your window looks like the one displayed below:

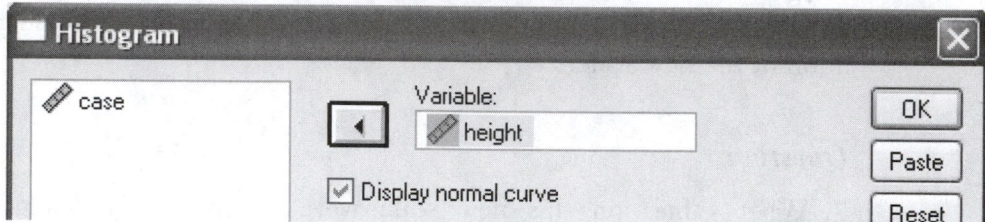

The histogram will appear in the **SPSS Viewer**. Notice that the shape of the histogram is not very closely approximated by the superimposed normal curve. However, regardless of the shape of the population distribution, the CLT guarantees that the distribution of all possible means from the population will be normal as long as the sample size is sufficiently large. We'll begin with 1,000 samples of size $N = 3$ to get an idea of what the sampling distribution of the mean looks like for a limited number of very small samples. Then we'll increase the sample size as well as the number of samples. The most efficient way to generate a large number of samples very quickly is to use SPSS syntax commands.

EXERCISE 5

From the SPSS Data Editor **File** menu, select **Open ▶ Syntax...**

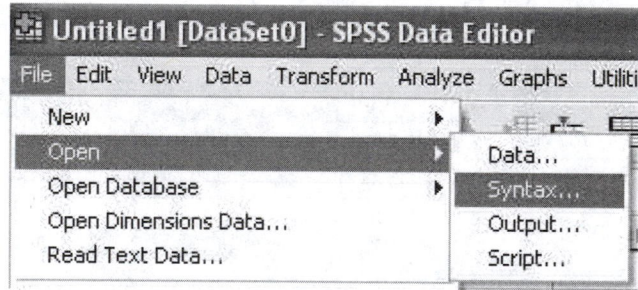

When the **Open Syntax** dialog window appears, navigate to the data CD and open the syntax file named **Sampling with replacement**. When the file is loaded into the syntax editor, you should see the following lines:

```
* This program creates 1000 samples of size n = 3, by sampling with
* replacement from an SPSS data file. Replace the # characters
* in the next line with random digits to generate unique samples.
```

```
set seed = ######.
input program.
loop sample = 1 to 1000.
     loop #case = 1 to 3.
           compute case = trunc(uniform(140))+1.
           end case.
       end loop.
       leave sample.
end loop.
end file.
end input program.
execute.
sort cases by case.

* IMPORTANT: The drive letter following the table subcommand line may
* have to be changed, depending on the location of the data file. The
* syntax is based on an assumption that the height data file is
* accessed from the data CD in drive D:\.

match files file = * /table = 'D:\Chapter 7\height data.sav' /by case.
sort cases by sample.
execute.

* The aggregate outfile = * command will replace the active dataset
* created by the program. If you wish to save the file produced by
the
* program, replace the asterisk with a file name.

aggregate outfile = *
     /break = sample
     /height_mean = mean(height).
```

To run the syntax program select **Run, All** from the Syntax Editor menu:

Executing these syntax commands will produce an aggregated data file with two variables, **sample** and **height_mean**. *Sample* has 1,000 values (from the second executable line of the syntax program) and *height_mean*

is the mean of each sample of 3 cases (specified in the third executable line in the program). The first five lines of the Data Editor should be similar to the following:

	sample	height_mean
1	1	62.33
2	2	62.33
3	3	67.00
4	4	63.33
5	5	63.67

Repeat the steps from Exercise 3 to construct a histogram of means of samples of 3 students. For this exercise the variable to be graphed is named **height_mean**. Move this variable into the **Variable:** field and be sure to request the normal curve before clicking **OK** to produce the histogram of sample means.

Questions

8. Compare the shapes of the population distribution and the distribution of 1,000 sample means. Which appears to be more similar to the normal curve?

9. Compare the mean of the distribution of sample means to the mean of the population. Are they similar or different? Now compare the population standard deviation to the standard deviation of the distribution of sample means (called the *standard error of the mean*, or just *standard error*). Explain your findings.

EXERCISE 6

Repeat Exercise 5, but before executing the syntax commands change the number of cases from 3 to 30 as follows:

```
loop #case = 1 to 30.
```

Questions

10. Compare the shape of distribution of means of samples of 3 students to the one that you just generated, based on samples of 30 students. Which appears to be more similar to the normal curve?

11. You should find that the mean of this distribution of sample means is very similar to the one based on samples of 3 students. However, the estimate of the standard error is different. Describe, then explain, this difference.

EXERCISE 7

Repeat Exercise 6, but this time change the number of samples from 1,000 to 10,000.

```
loop sample = 1 to 10000.
```

Ten thousand samples is appreciably closer to the infinitely large "all possible samples" required to build the sampling distribution of the mean. With a much larger number of samples, you should see a better fit of the normal curve to the sampling distribution of means. If you want to see a still better fit, increase the sample size to 60.

```
loop sample = 1 to 10000.
loop #case = 1 to 60.
```

As you increase the sample size, you should find that the shape of the sampling distribution of the mean becomes progressively more similar to the shape of the normal curve.

ANSWERS

1. The mean of the standardized variable is **0**.

2. The standard deviation of the standardized variable is **1**.

3. Just as all yardsticks are scaled in feet and inches, all z distributions are scaled in standard deviation units. Thus all distributions of standardized variables, regardless of the original scale of measurement, will have a mean of 0 and a standard deviation of **1**.

4. The mean of the T_score variable is **50**.

5. The standard deviation of the T_score variable is **10**.

6. Although not impossible, negative T scores are very rarely observed because such scores would be more than 5 standard deviations ($5 \times 10 = 50$) below the mean. Because most variables are approximately normally distributed, roughly **99%** of such distributions are within 3 standard deviations of the mean.

7. The values on the new scale assigned to individuals with self-reported anxiety scores of 0, 5, and 10 are shown in parentheses.

   a. 0? **(142)**   b. 5? **(193)**   c. 10? **(245)**

8. The normal curve is more perhaps a little more similar to the shape of the distribution of means of samples of 3 students than to the population distribution.

9. The mean of the distribution of sample means (64.89) is very similar to the mean of the population (64.84). This is in accord with the CLT. The population standard deviation (4.086) is almost double the standard deviation of the distribution of sample means (2.339). The latter value is an estimate of the standard error of the mean ($\sigma_M = \sigma / \sqrt{N} = 4.086 \sqrt{3} = 2.359$). The influence of extreme values is reduced when means replace individual scores, so the variability among means will always be less than the variability among individual scores.

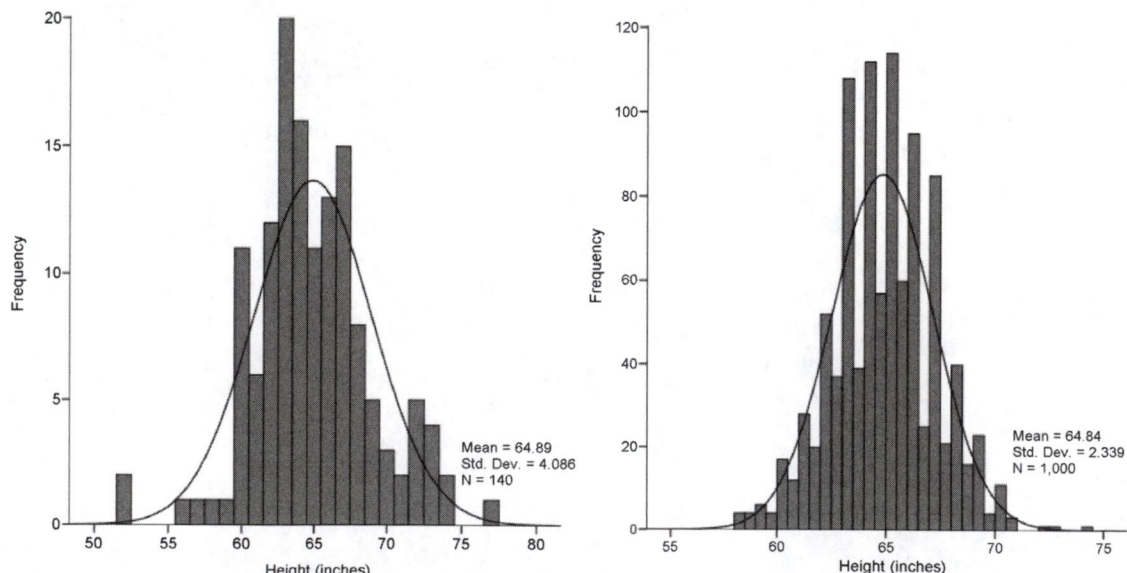

10. The normal curve is more similar to the shape of the distribution of means of samples of 30 students (below right) than to the shape of the distribution of means of samples of 3 students (below left). This is in accord with the CLT.

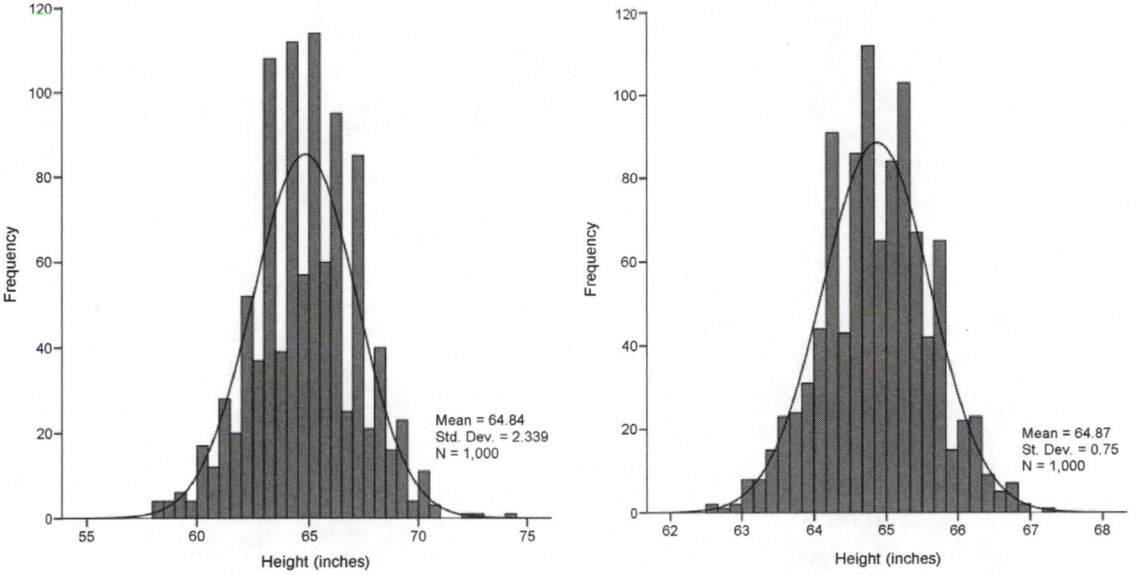

11. The estimate of the standard error is much smaller because the sample size is larger by a factor of 10. As sample size increases, variability decreases.

The histogram below was generated for 10,000 samples of $N = 100$ measures of height.

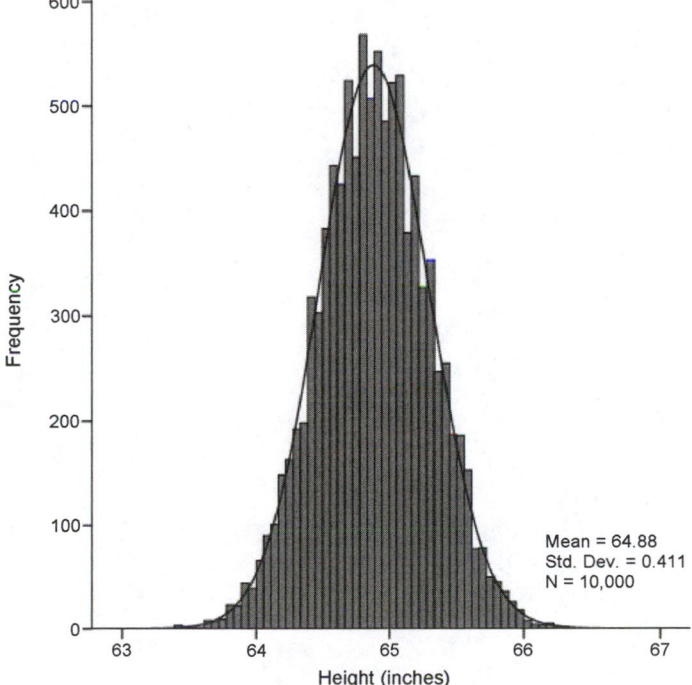

CHAPTER 8

HYPOTHESIS TESTING WITH *z* TESTS

Making Meaningful Comparisons

The general purpose of this set of exercises is to provide some hands-on experience testing the null hypothesis with z tests as described on pages 354–356 of the text. More specifically, we will examine the effect of increasing the sample size on the probability of rejecting the null hypothesis (see pages 356–358 in the text). We will use an SPSS syntax file to generate 1000 samples of hypothetical data from a normally distributed population with mean (μ) = 3.51 and standard deviation (σ) = 0.61. The syntax file simulates randomly selecting samples of different numbers of participants from this population, administering the Consideration of Future Consequences (CFC) scale to each participant in each sample, and recording the mean for each sample. The CFC scale was introduced on pages 14 and 15 of the text. Briefly, responses to each of the 12 items comprising the CFC scale range from 1 (*extremely uncharacteristic*) to 5 (*extremely characteristic*). Each respondent's CFC score is determined by summing the responses (1 to 5) to the items and dividing this sum by 12 to produce a mean score. Seven of the items are reverse scored, so higher scores indicate greater consideration of future consequences.

EXERCISE 1

- Launch SPSS. Select **Type in data** and click **OK**. From the **File** menu, select **Open ▶ Syntax…**

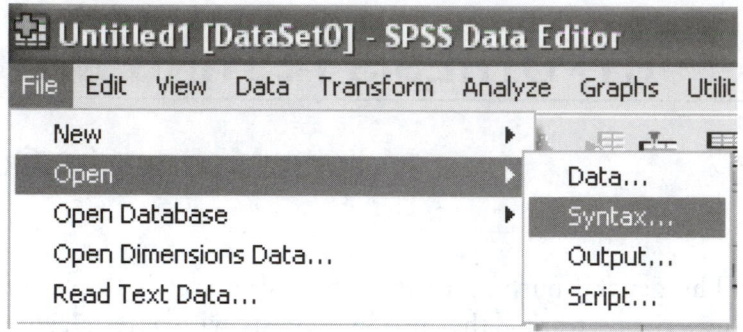

to produce the **Open Syntax** dialog window. Click the ⌄ button to access the **Look in:** drop-down menu and navigate to the folder named **Chapter 8**. Select the syntax file as shown in the truncated image of the window below, then click on the **Open** button to open the file in the SPSS Syntax Editor.

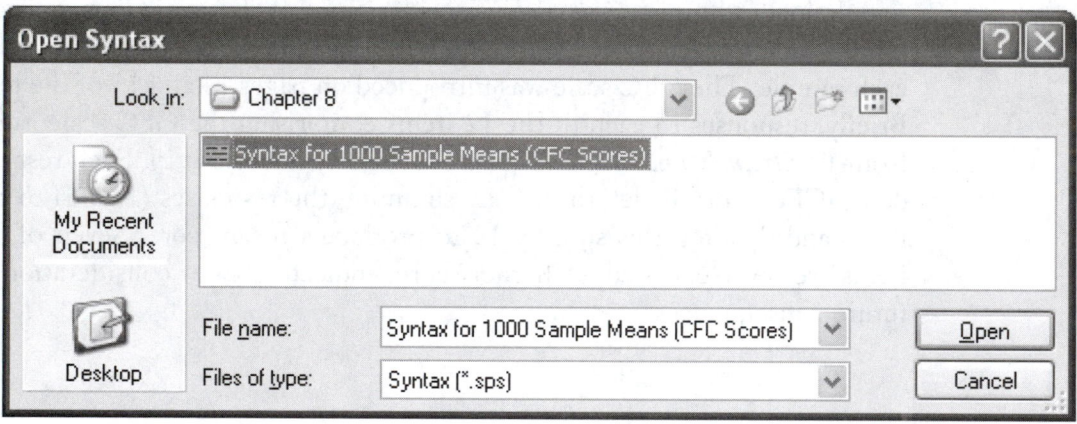

- You should see the following syntax file. Replace the # characters with a sequence of random digits. This will ensure that your samples of hypothetical CFC scores will be unique each time you execute the syntax code. The **input program** produces 1000 randomly selected samples of 5 CFC scores from a normal population with $\mu = 3.7$ and $\sigma = 0.61$. The **aggregate** command at the bottom of file computes the mean of each sample and stores this mean in a new file along with the number of the sample.

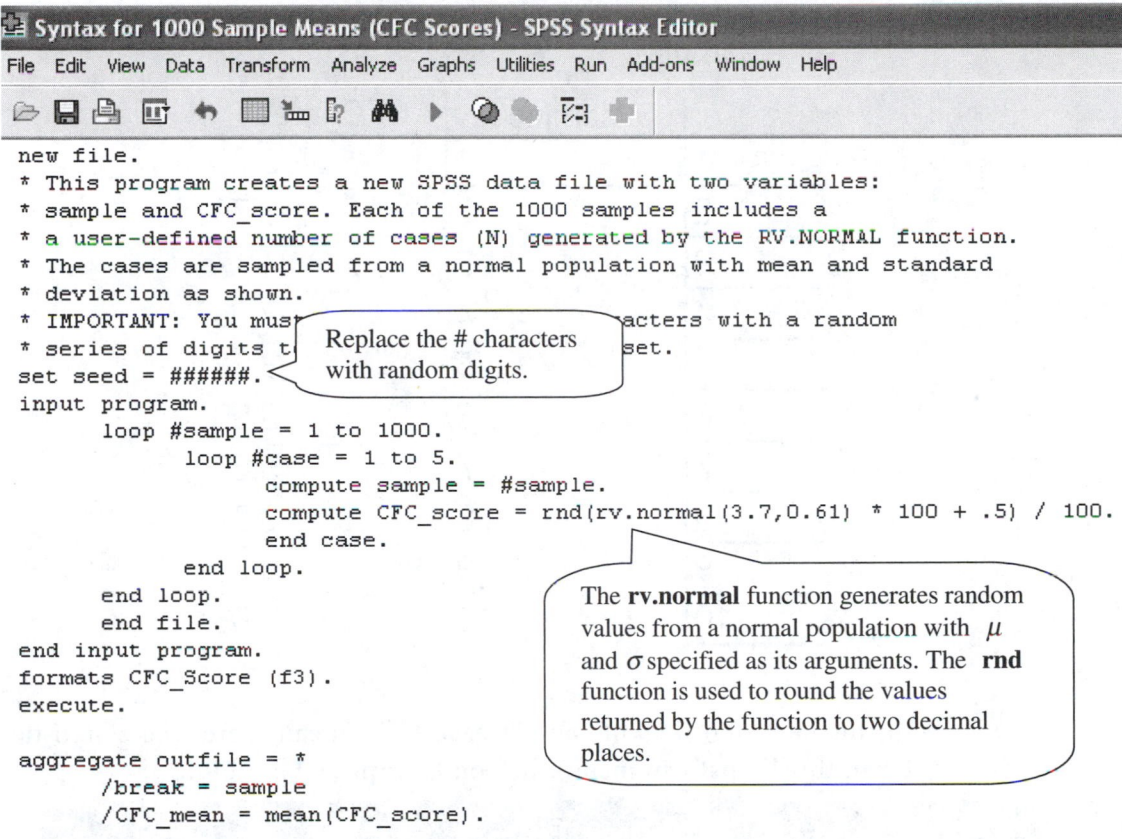

```
new file.
* This program creates a new SPSS data file with two variables:
* sample and CFC_score. Each of the 1000 samples includes a
* a user-defined number of cases (N) generated by the RV.NORMAL function.
* The cases are sampled from a normal population with mean and standard
* deviation as shown.
* IMPORTANT: You must                    acters with a random
* series of digits t                     set.
set seed = ######.
input program.
      loop #sample = 1 to 1000.
            loop #case = 1 to 5.
                  compute sample = #sample.
                  compute CFC_score = rnd(rv.normal(3.7,0.61) * 100 + .5) / 100.
                  end case.
            end loop.
      end loop.
      end file.
end input program.
formats CFC_Score (f3).
execute.

aggregate outfile = *
      /break = sample
      /CFC_mean = mean(CFC_score).
```

> Replace the # characters with random digits.

> The **rv.normal** function generates random values from a normal population with μ and σ specified as its arguments. The **rnd** function is used to round the values returned by the function to two decimal places.

- Click on **Run** in the menu bar, select **All** and press the left mouse button to produce a new SPSS data file of 1000 means computed for samples of 5 CFC scores.

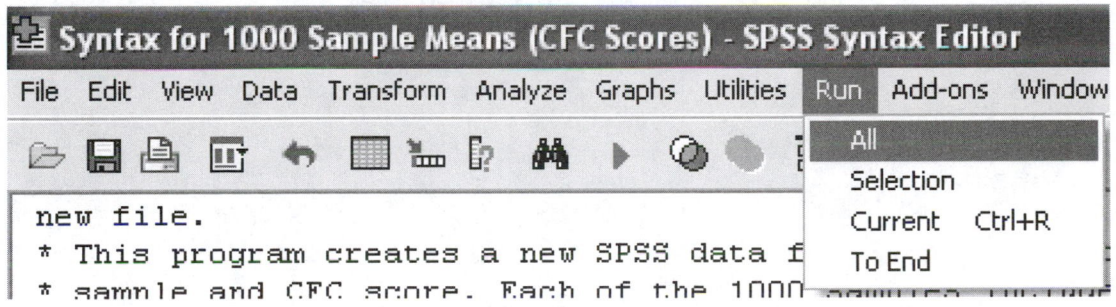

The first 10 rows of the **Data View** window of the **Data Editor** should be similar to following:

	sample	CFC_mean
1	1	3.79
2	2	3.79
3	3	4.17
4	4	3.89
5	5	3.75
6	6	3.90
7	7	3.88
8	8	3.72
9	9	3.73
10	10	3.63

- In this next step we will convert each CFC mean score to a z statistic. From the **Transform** menu, click on **Compute Variable...**

... to produce the **Compute Variable** dialog window. The image below has been cropped to fit on the page.

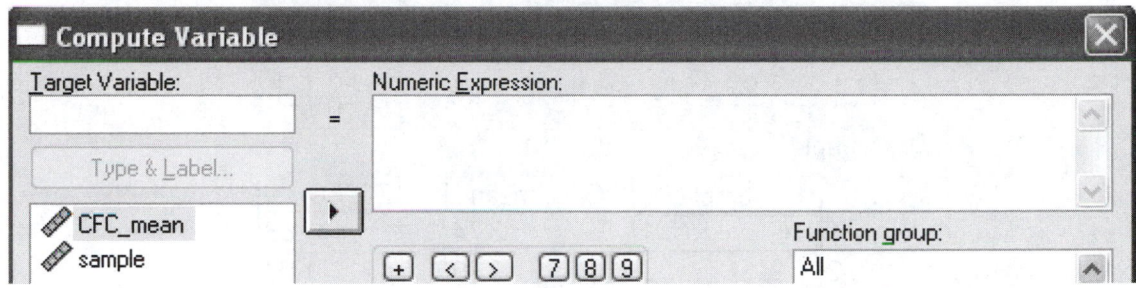

- Position the cursor in the **Target Variable:** field and type **Z_CFC**. Now place the cursor in the **Numeric Expression:** field and type the following formula:

```
(CFC_mean − 3.51) / (0.61 / SQRT(5))
```

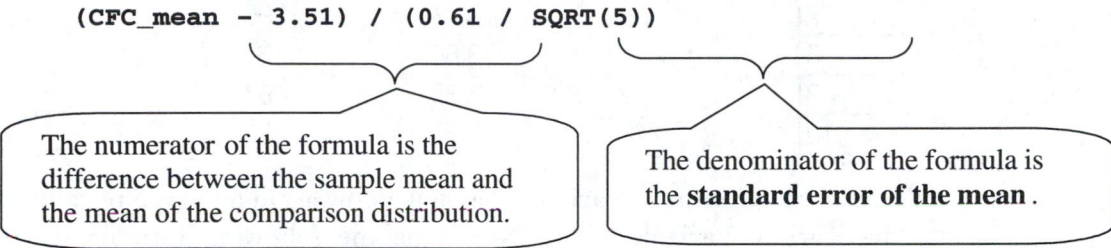

The numerator of the formula is the difference between the sample mean and the mean of the comparison distribution.

The denominator of the formula is the **standard error of the mean**.

The formula converts each CFC mean score to a *z* statistic. Check to make sure that your screen looks like the following, then click **OK**.

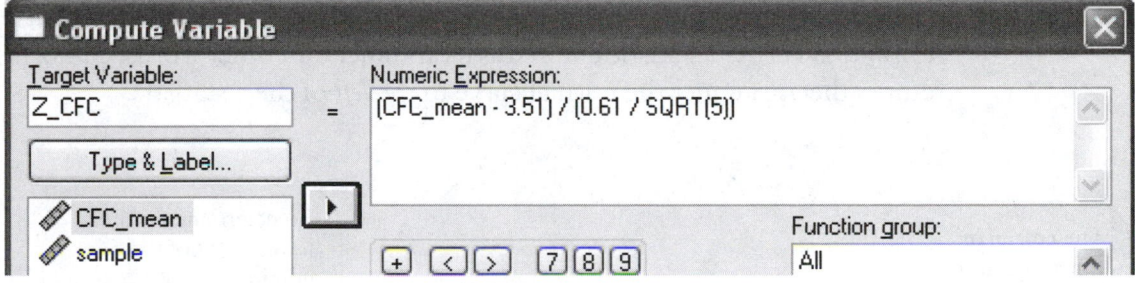

Your Data View window should be similar to the following.

	sample	CFC_mean	Z_CFC
1	1	3.74	.83
2	2	3.79	1.03
3	3	3.95	1.63
4	4	3.46	-.17
5	5	4.22	2.62
6	6	3.83	1.17
7	7	3.77	.95
8	8	3.60	.32
9	9	3.33	-.67
10	10	3.53	.07

- Access the **Compute Variable** dialog window again and type **p_value** in the **Target Variable:** field. Now type the following formula in the **Numeric Expression:** field:

```
2 * (1 - cdfnorm(abs(Z_CFC)))
```

The **cdfnorm** function returns the probability of observing a z statistic *less than or equal to* the z statistic entered as its argument. In other words, cdfnorm returns the area under the normal curve to the *left* of the z statistic.

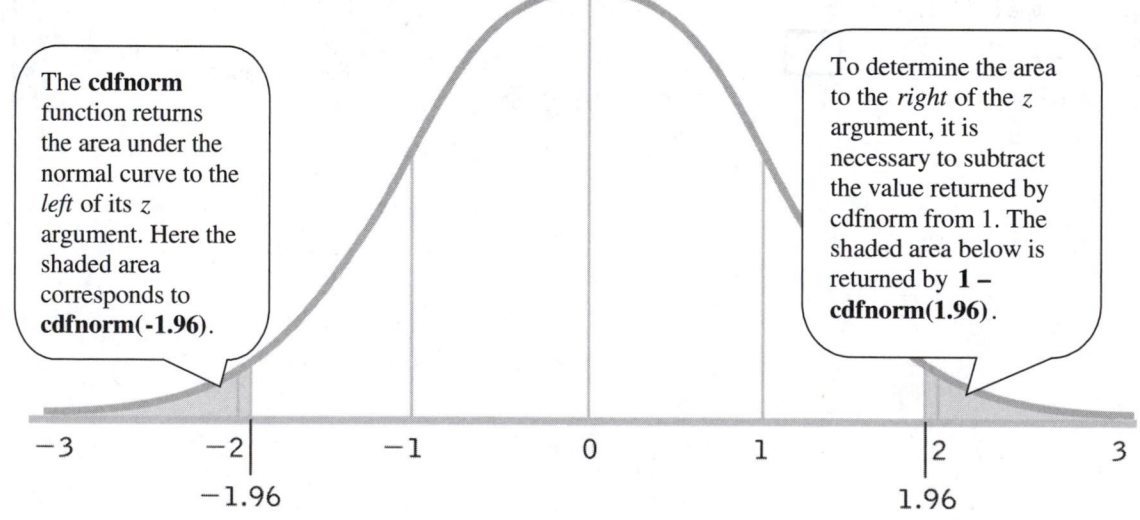

The **cdfnorm** function returns the area under the normal curve to the *left* of its z argument. Here the shaded area corresponds to **cdfnorm(-1.96)**.

To determine the area to the *right* of the z argument, it is necessary to subtract the value returned by cdfnorm from 1. The shaded area below is returned by **1 – cdfnorm(1.96)**.

Because the cdfnorm function returns the area to the left of its z argument, you will get different areas under the curve for positive and negative z statistics:

```
cdfnorm(-1.96) = .0228
cdfnorm (1.96) = .9772
```

Therefore, to return the area to the left of a negative z argument *or* the area to the right of that same z argument expressed as a positive value, it is necessary to take the absolute value of z and subtract the value returned by cdfnorm(abs(z)) from 1:

```
1 - cdfnorm(abs(z))
```

To return the area to the left of a negative z argument *and* the area to the right of that same z argument expressed as a positive value, it is necessary to subtract the value returned by cdfnorm(abs(z)) from 1 and multiply this difference by 2:

```
2 * (1 - cdfnorm(abs(z)))
```

The value returned by 2 * (1 – cdfnorm(abs(z))) is set equal to the variable p_value, so each **p_value** is the probability of observing a z score as extreme (in either tail of the normal distribution) as the one recorded in that row of the **Data Editor**. Put another way, the p_value of each z statistic is the likelihood of observing a mean CFC score as different from the population mean of 3.51 as the one recorded in that row. A p value that includes the area in both tails of the normal distribution is called a two-tailed p value.

- Click **OK** to generate a column of p_values in the **Data View** window.

  Go to the **Variable View** window and set **Decimals** equal to **2** for the **Z-CFC** variable and equal to **4** for the **p_value** variable. Your screen should be similar to the one below.

⊞ *Untitled4 [] - SPSS Data Editor

File   Edit   View   Data   Transform   Analyze   Graphs   Utilities   Add-ons   Windo

1 : sample   1

	sample	CFC_mean	Z_CFC	p_value
1	1	3.74	.83	.4074
2	2	3.79	1.03	.3013
3	3	3.95	1.63	.1036
4	4	3.46	-.17	.8661
5	5	4.22	2.62	.0089
6	6	3.83	1.17	.2408
7	7	3.77	.95	.3406
8	8	3.60	.32	.7470
9	9	3.33	-.67	.5000
10	10	3.53	.07	.9474

Notice that the p value for the mean CFC score of the first sample is .4074. This means that there is about a 41% chance of observing a mean as extreme as 3.74 ($\geq$ 3.74 and $\leq$ 3.28) if this sample is from a population with μ = 3.51 and σ = .61—that is, if the null hypothesis is true.

Our next step is to treat each sample mean as the outcome of a different experiment designed to test the null hypothesis that the population mean CFC score is 3.51. This is a nondirectional expression of the null hypothesis, so each test is two-tailed. We will conduct each test at the .05 level of significance

- From the **Transform** menu, select **Compute Variable...** to access the **Compute Variable** dialog window. In the **Target Variable:** field, type **reject_null** as the name of a new variable. In the **Numeric Expression:** field, type **p_value <= .05** as shown in the figure.

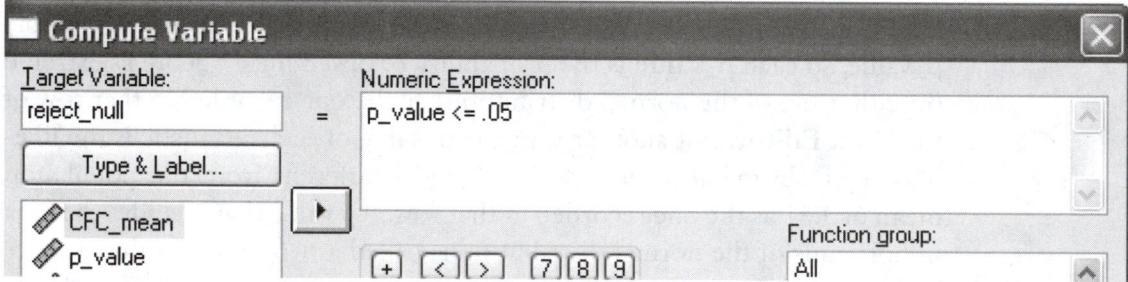

If the value of p_value is less than or equal to .05, then the value **1** will be assigned to **reject_null**; otherwise the value **0** will be assigned. Each **1** thus represents a rejection of the null hypothesis.

- Click the **OK** button to return to the **Data Editor**. The first 10 rows of the **Data View** window should be similar to the following.

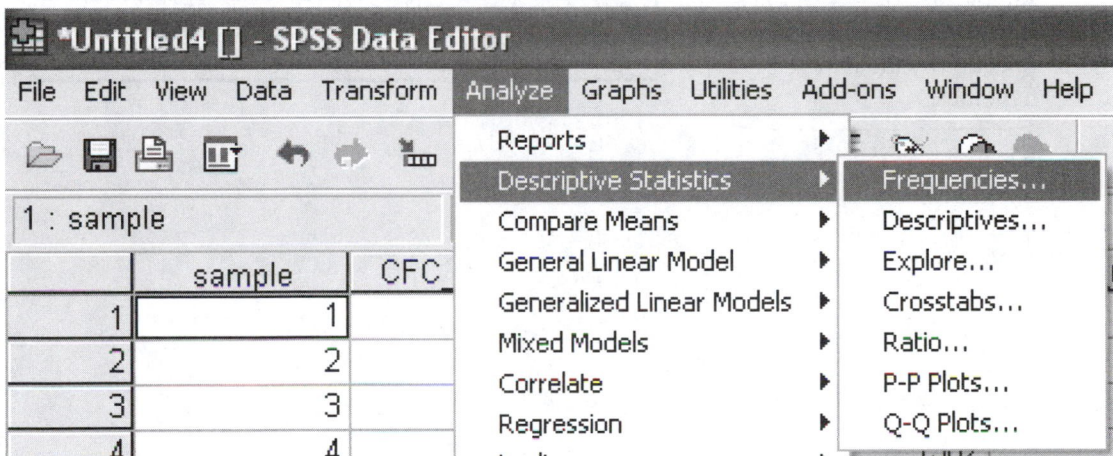

	sample	CFC_mean	Z_CFC	p_value	reject_null
1	1	3.74	.83	.4074	0
2	2	3.79	1.03	.3013	0
3	3	3.95	1.63	.1036	0
4	4	3.46	-.17	.8661	0
5	5	4.22	2.62	.0089	1
6	6	3.83	1.17	.2408	0
7	7	3.77	.95	.3406	0
8	8	3.60	.32	.7470	0
9	9	3.33	-.67	.5000	0
10	10	3.53	.07	.9474	0

- Now click on **Analyze** in the menu bar and select **Descriptive Statistics** ▶ **Frequencies...** from the drop-down menu.

• When the **Frequencies** dialog window appears, select **reject_null** and click the [▸] button to move this variable into the **Variable(s):** field as shown.

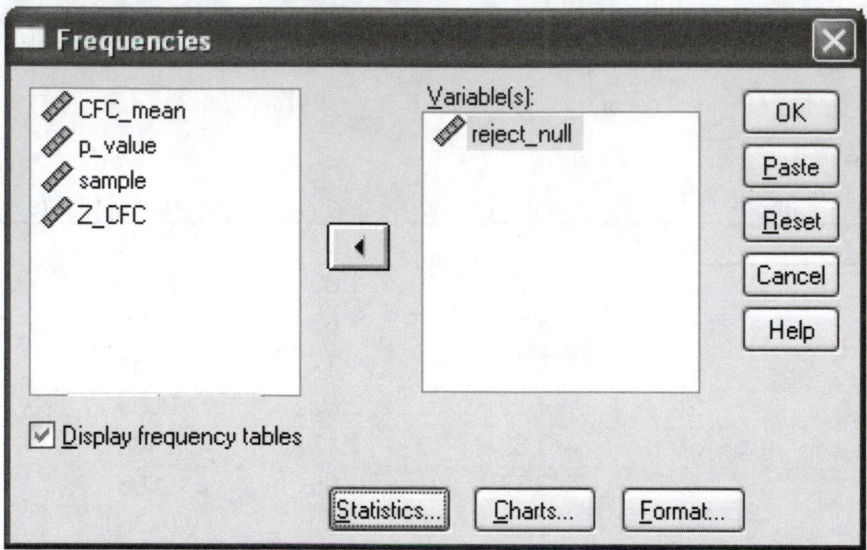

• Click **OK** to produce a frequency output table like the one below.

Of 1000 samples (experiments) based on a sample size of $N = 5$, only 107 (10.7%) resulted in a rejection of the null hypothesis.

reject_null

		Frequency	Percent	Valid Percent	Cumulative Percent
Valid	0	893	89.3	89.3	89.3
	1	107	10.7	10.7	100.0
	Total	1000	100.0	100.0	

- Click on **File** in the menu bar and select **Save As…** from the drop-down menu. When the **Save Output As** dialog window appears, type a name in the **File name:** field and click the **Save** button to save the file to the location named in the **Save in:** field at the top of the window. In the next exercise, we will repeat Exercise 1 for samples of 10, 20, 40, 80, and 160. At the conclusion of each series of steps, we will save the file.

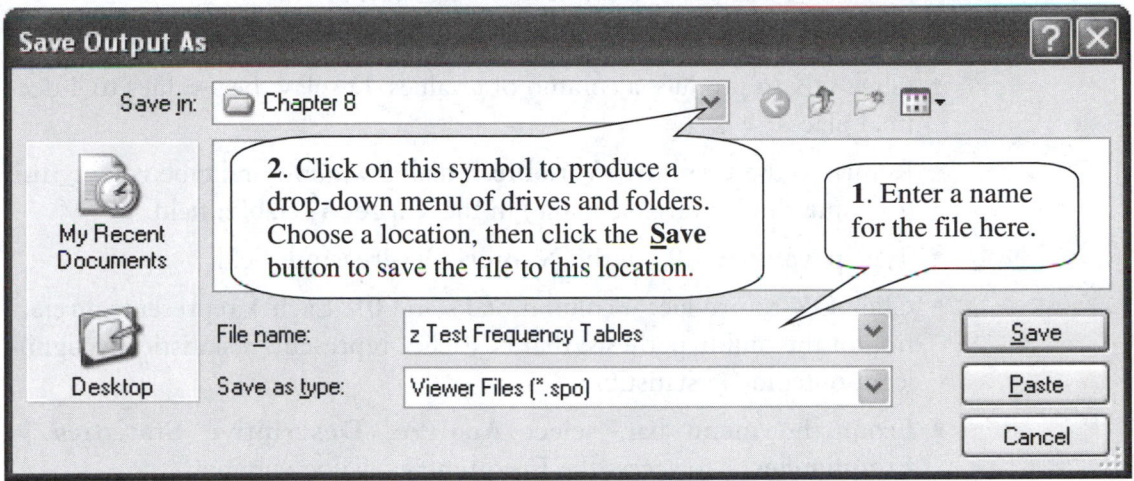

EXERCISE 2

- Access the **SPSS Syntax Editor** and open the syntax file named **Syntax for 1000 Sample Means (CFC Scores)**.

- Replace the # characters with a sequence of random digits.

- Double the size of the sample by changing the following line in the syntax file.

```
loop #case = 1 to 5
```
Double this value to double the sample size.

- From the menu of the Syntax Editor, click on **Run**, then **All** to run the syntax program.

- From the **Transform** menu, select **Compute Variable…** to access the **Compute Variable** dialog window.

- Type **Z_CFC** (or some name that identifies this variable as a *z* statistic) in the **Target Variable:** field.

- Type the following expression in the **Numeric Expression:** field:
```
CFC_mean – 3.51) / (0.61 / SQRT(N)
```
where, N = the size of the sample.

- Click **OK** to produce a column of z statistics. Display the z statistics to 2 decimal places.
- Access the **Compute Variable...** dialog window again and type **p_value** in the **Target Variable:** field.
- Type the following expression in the **Numeric Expression:** field:

      `2 * (1 - cdfnorm(abs(Z_CFC)))`

  where, Z_CFC refers to the name of the z statistic.
- Click **OK** to produce a column of p values. Display the p values to 4 decimal places.
- Return to the **Compute Variable...** dialog window and type **reject_null** (or some similar variable name) in the **Target Variable:** field.
- Type **p_value <= .05** in the **Numeric Expression:** field.
- Click **OK** to produce a column of **1**'s and **0**'s. Each **1** represents a rejection of the null hypothesis; that is, each **1** represents a statistically significant outcome (z statistic).
- From the menu bar, select **Analyze**, **Descriptive Statistics ▶ Frequencies...** to access the **Frequencies** dialog window.
- Move **reject_null** into the **Variable(s):** field and click **OK** to produce a frequency table in the SPSS **Viewer** (output) window.
- **Save** the viewer file to preserve the addition of each frequency table.

Repeat these steps for samples of **20**, **40**, **80** and **160** cases.

Assignment

Go to the **Data View** window and select **File, New ▶ Data** to produce a new DataSet.

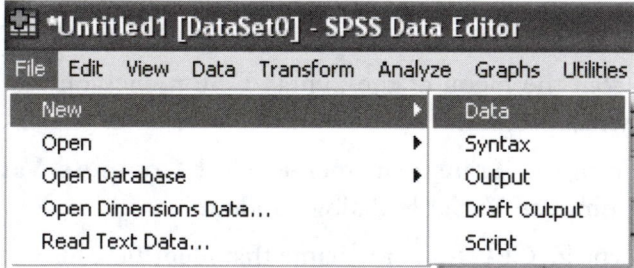

Go to the **Variable View** window and enter **Sample_size** and **Percent_sig** as two new variable names.

Return to the Data View window and enter **5, 10, 20, 40, 80,** and **160** as the values of the **Sample_size** variable.

The values to be entered under **Percent_sig** are the percentages of each set of 1,000 samples that resulted in statistically significant outcomes. These are listed in the frequency tables that you saved in the viewer file.

From the **Graphs** menu, select **Legacy Dialogs** ▶ **Bar...** to produce the **Bar Charts** dialog window.

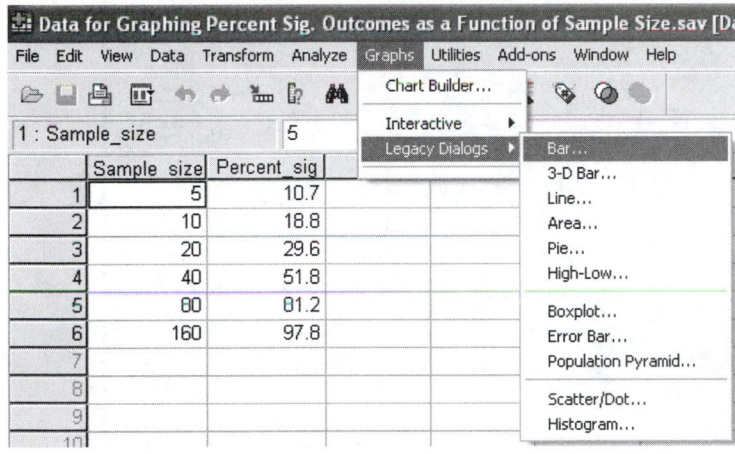
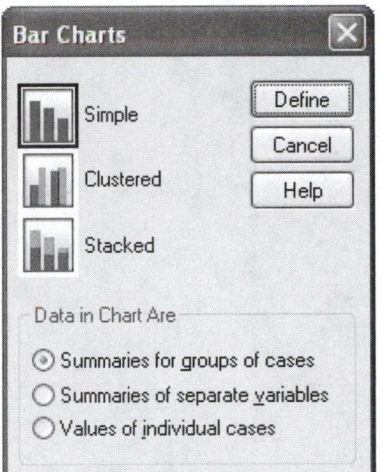

In the **Bar Charts** dialog window, select **Simple**, then click **Define** to produce the **Define Simple Bar: Summaries for Groups of Cases** dialog window.

Select **Sample_size** and move this variable into the **Category Axis:** field.

Click on the radio button next to **Other statistic (e.g., mean)** to activate the **Variable:** field, then move the **Percent_sig** variable into this field.

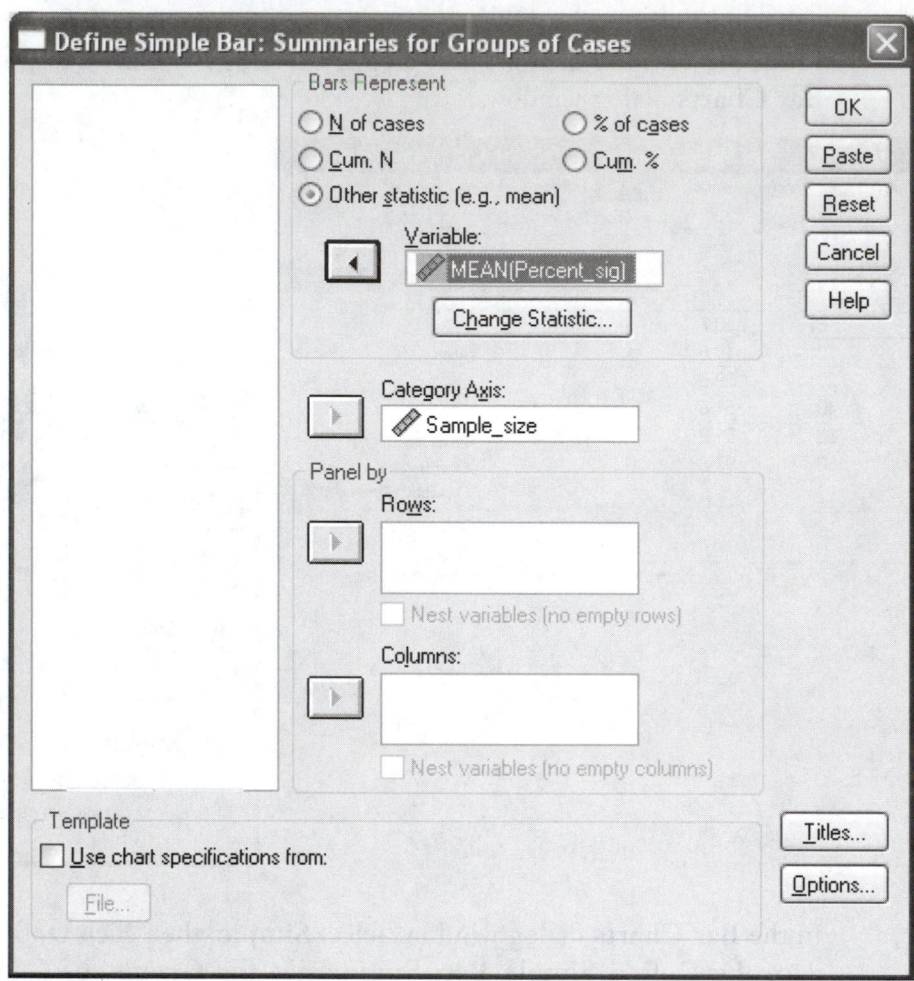

Click **OK** to produce the bar chart.

Questions

1. Describe the relation between sample size, the size of the standard error, the size of the z statistic, and the probability of obtaining a statistically significant outcome (i.e., rejecting the null hypothesis). Support your answer with the frequency tables and bar chart.

2. Given these sampling conditions (i.e., sampling from a normal population with $\mu = 3.7$ and $\sigma = 0.61$), about how large should the sample size be in order to correctly reject the null hypothesis at least 80 percent of the time?

ANSWERS

1. As sample size increases, the standard error decreases, and the size of the *z* statistic increases. The larger the value of the *z* statistic, the smaller the *p* value, increasing the likelihood of obtaining a *p* value less than or equal to the significance criterion, .05.

reject_null

		Frequency	Percent	Valid Percent	Cumulative Percent
Valid	0	893	89.3	89.3	89.3
	1	107	10.7	10.7	100.0
	Total	1000	100.0	100.0	

reject_null

		Frequency	Percent	Valid Percent	Cumulative Percent
Valid	0	482	48.2	48.2	48.2
	1	518	51.8	51.8	100.0
	Total	1000	100.0	100.0	

reject_null

		Frequency	Percent	Valid Percent	Cumulative Percent
Valid	0	812	81.2	81.2	81.2
	1	188	18.8	18.8	100.0
	Total	1000	100.0	100.0	

reject_null

		Frequency	Percent	Valid Percent	Cumulative Percent
Valid	0	188	18.8	18.8	18.8
	1	812	81.2	81.2	100.0
	Total	1000	100.0	100.0	

reject_null

		Frequency	Percent	Valid Percent	Cumulative Percent
Valid	0	704	70.4	70.4	70.4
	1	296	29.6	29.6	100.0
	Total	1000	100.0	100.0	

reject_null

		Frequency	Percent	Valid Percent	Cumulative Percent
Valid	0	22	2.2	2.2	2.2
	1	978	97.8	97.8	100.0
	Total	1000	100.0	100.0	

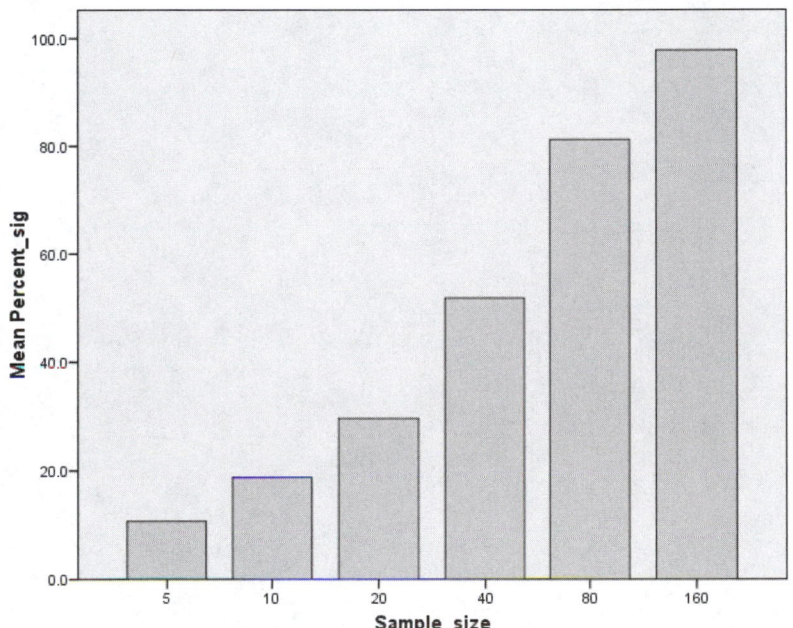

2. According to the histogram, a sample size of at least 80 is required to correctly reject the null hypothesis at least 80 percent of the time. (We know the null hypothesis is false, because we sampled from a population whose mean, 3.7, differs from the mean specified by the null hypothesis, 3.51.)

CHAPTER 9

HYPOTHESIS TESTING WITH *t* TESTS

Comparing Two Groups

INDEPENDENT-SAMPLES *t* TEST

A psychologist believes that a moderate dose of caffeine can improve memory. She designed an experiment in which she randomly assigned half of her available pool of 40 college students to the caffeine condition and half to the placebo condition. Thirty minutes after drinking a cup of fruit juice containing either caffeine (150 mg) or a placebo, participants in both groups studied the same list of 30 words for 30 minutes before being challenged with a test of free recall.

Launch SPSS, select **Type in data** and click **OK.** Go to the **Variable View** window and enter the names of the variables and other settings as shown below.

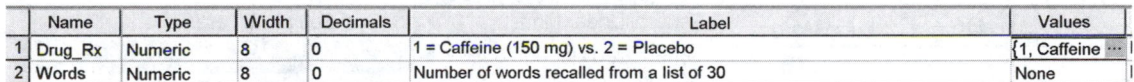

	Name	Type	Width	Decimals	Label	Values
1	Drug_Rx	Numeric	8	0	1 = Caffeine (150 mg) vs. 2 = Placebo	{1, Caffeine ⋯
2	Words	Numeric	8	0	Number of words recalled from a list of 30	None

Clicking on the cell under **Values** will cause the gray box to appear, and clicking on the gray box will produce the **Value Labels** dialog window (below). Enter **1** for **Value:** and **Caffeine (150 mg)** as the **Label:** for that value. Click the **Add** button to move the Value: and Label: pair into the field below. Now enter **2** as the second **Value:** and **Placebo** as its **Label:**. The **Value Labels** window should look like this:

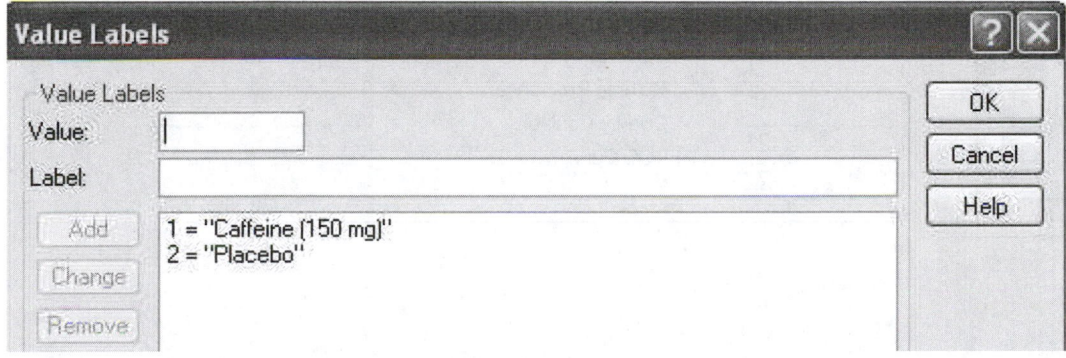

Click **Add** then **OK** to return to the Variable View window. Now go back to the **Data View** window and enter the data from the following table.

Drug_Rx	Words	Drug_Rx	Words	Drug_Rx	Words	Drug_Rx	Words
1	18	1	16	2	21	2	17
1	19	1	21	2	19	2	19
1	21	1	22	2	15	2	21
1	26	1	18	2	17	2	15
1	20	1	16	2	18	2	18
1	20	1	24	2	12	2	22
1	22	1	19	2	21	2	16
1	23	1	26	2	18	2	24
1	15	1	25	2	25	2	23
1	21	1	22	2	21	2	23

After checking the data entry for accuracy, save the file. (Use a name that identifies the contents of the file—something like "Caffeine and Memory Data." We'll use this file to complete the set of exercises for Chapter 10.

From the **Analyze** menu, select **Compare Means** ▶ **Independent–Samples T Test...**

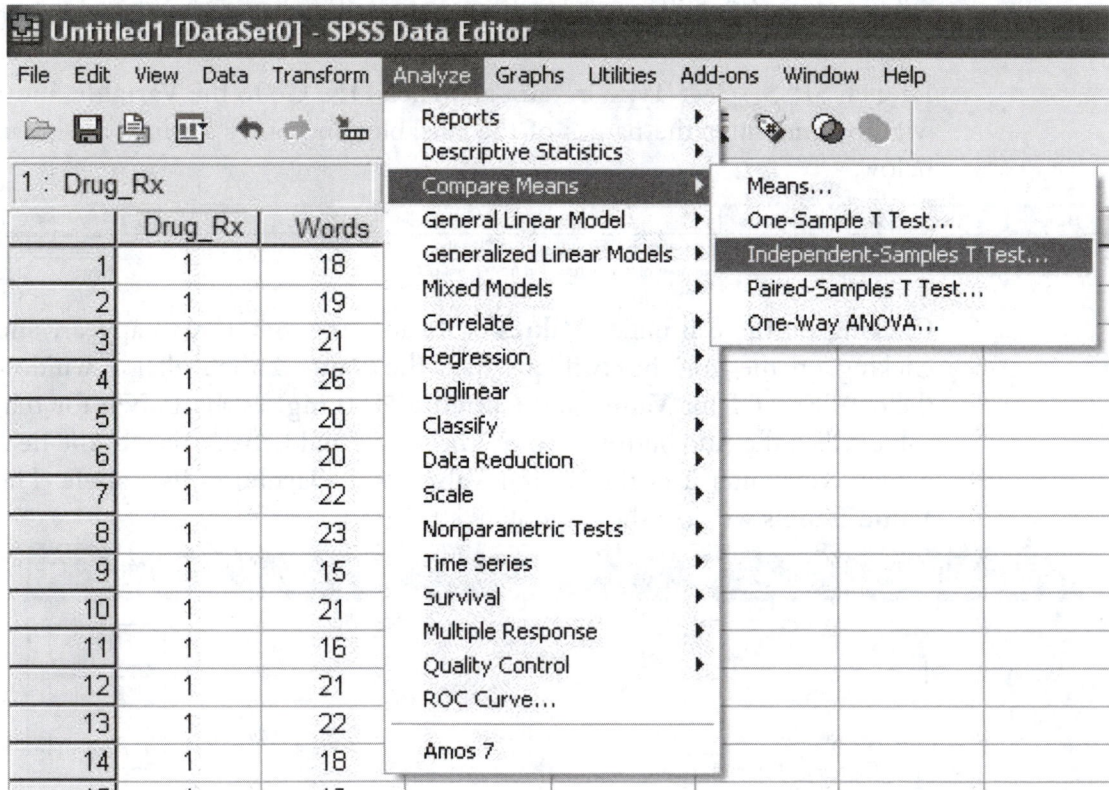

… to produce the **Independent–Samples T Test** dialog window.

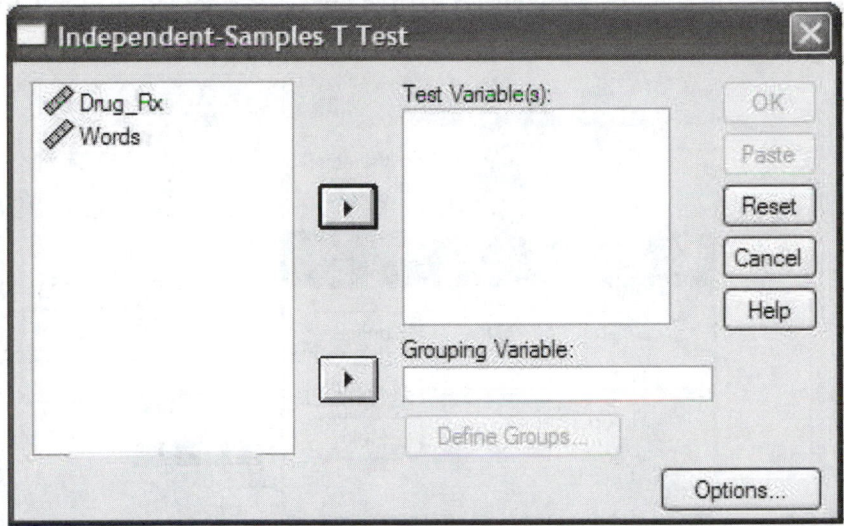

Select **Words** and click the ▶ button to move this variable into the **Test Variable(s):** field. Now move the **Drug_Rx** variable into the **Grouping Variable:** field.

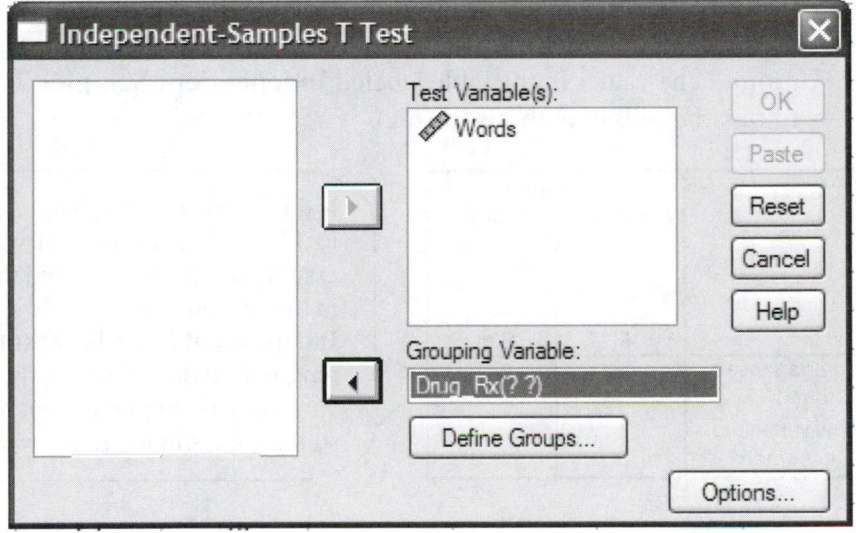

Click on **Define Groups...** to produce the **Define Groups** window. Make sure that the **Use specified values** option is selected. Enter **1** for **Group 1:** and **2** for **Group 2:** as shown.

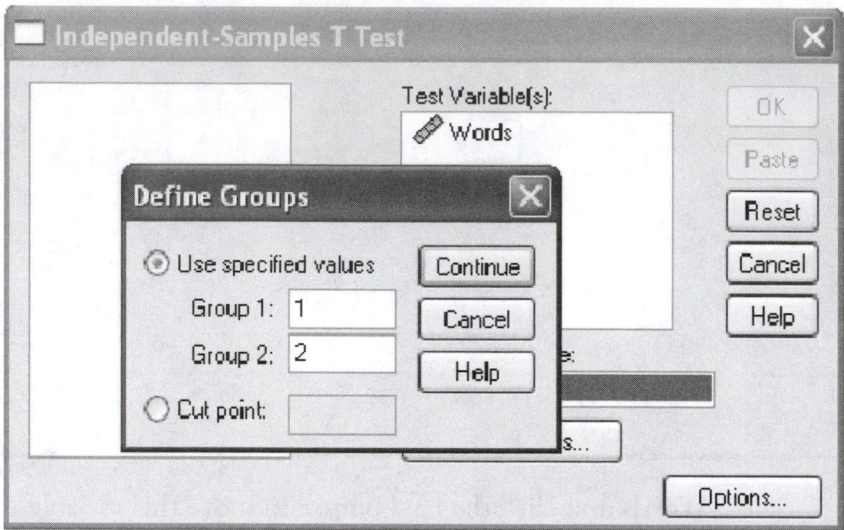

Click **Continue,** then **OK** to produce the **T-Test** output tables. The **Group Statistics** table includes the name of the dependent variable as well as the sample size, mean, standard deviation, and standard error for each group. The values in the table labeled **Independent Samples Test** are used to test the null hypothesis (below).

		Levene's Test for Equality of Variances	
		F	Sig.
Words	Equal variances assumed	.176	.678
	Equal variances not assumed		

> If this *p* value is less than or equal to .05, then the equality of variances assumption is rejected, and the values in the second row of the **Independent Samples Test** table are reported. In this example, the equal variances assumption is not rejected, so the values in the first row are

An important assumption of the independent-samples *t* test is that the variances of the two populations are equal. This equality of variances assumption is the null hypothesis tested by **Levene's test**, the results of which are on the left side of the **Independent Samples Test** table. If the **Sig.** value is greater than or equal to .05, then the equal variances assumption is not rejected, and the **t**, **df**, and **Sig. (2-tailed)** values in the *first* row in the table are used to test the null hypothesis about the effect of caffeine on memory; otherwise, the values in the second row must be used.

Recall that the psychologist hypothesized that a moderate dose of caffeine would improve memory, so the null hypothesis must be expressed as a *directional* hypothesis requiring a *one-tailed test*. The **t–test for Equality of Means** section of the Independent Samples Test output table (below) includes only two-tailed *p* values in the column under **Sig. (2-tailed)**, so you must divide the two-tailed *p* value by 2 to produce the one-tailed *p* value.

		t-test for Equality of Means		
t	df	Sig. (2-tailed)	Mean Difference	Std. Err. Difference
1.393	38	.172	1.450	1.041
1.393	37.876	.172	1.450	1.041

> Divide this two-tailed *p* value by 2 to get the *p* value for a one-tailed test.

PRESENTING THE RESULTS, APA-STYLE

The *Publication Manual of the American Psychological Association* (5th ed.) prescribes a format for reporting the results of all statistical analyses. The following is an example from the study of the interaction between language and memory by Loftus and Palmer (1974). In this study, participants watched a very brief film of an automobile accident before receiving a questionnaire which included the critical question, "About how fast were the cars going when they _____ into each other?" One group of 50 participants read the word *smashed* in the blank while a second group of 50 participants read the word *hit*. Loftus and Palmer reported the results as follows:

> The mean estimate of speed for subjects interrogated with *smashed* was 10.46 mph; with *hit* the estimate was 8.00 mph. These means are significantly different, $t(98) = 2.00$, $p < .05$. (p. 587)

The phrase in which the statistical results are detailed is presented below with comments:

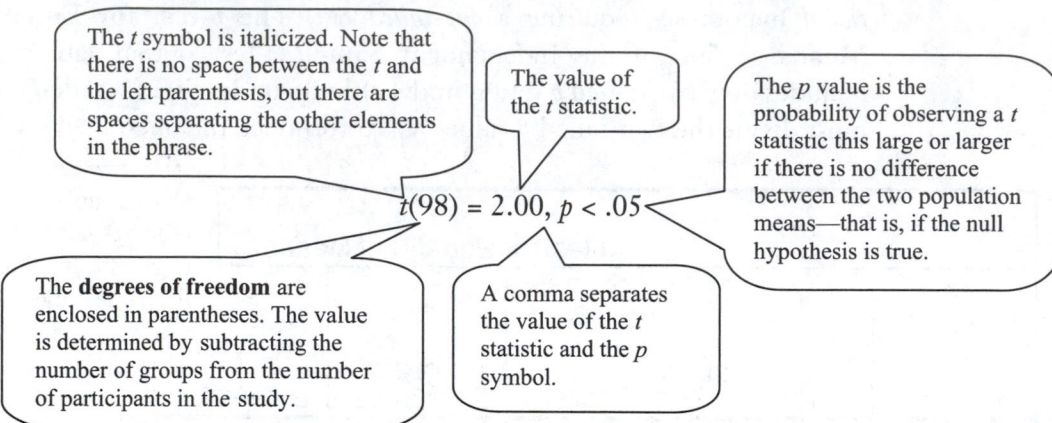

The *t* symbol is italicized. Note that there is no space between the *t* and the left parenthesis, but there are spaces separating the other elements in the phrase.

The value of the *t* statistic.

The *p* value is the probability of observing a *t* statistic this large or larger if there is no difference between the two population means—that is, if the null hypothesis is true.

$t(98) = 2.00, p < .05$

The **degrees of freedom** are enclosed in parentheses. The value is determined by subtracting the number of groups from the number of participants in the study.

A comma separates the value of the *t* statistic and the *p* symbol.

Ruback and Juieng's (1997) study of territorial defense in parking lots offers another example of reporting the results of an independent–samples *t* test according to APA formatting guidelines. Although these researchers were primarily interested in whether the presence of a waiting driver (an "intruder") affected the time to exit a parking space (departure time), they realized that this relation might be moderated by other variables. After reporting a significant positive correlation between departure time and the number of passengers in the departing vehicle, Ruback and Juieng used independent samples *t* tests to determine whether number of passengers moderated the relation between departure time and a driver's gender or ethnicity. They reported as follows:

> Male drivers had significantly more passengers in the car with them ($M = 1.10$) than did female drivers ($M = 0.68$), $t(198) = 3.14$, $p < .01$, but male drivers and female drivers did not differ in their departure times. Although African American drivers ($M = 1.00$) had more passengers than did White drivers ($M = 0.65$), $t(180) = 3.00$, $p < .01$, the two groups did not differ significantly in their departure times. (p. 824)

One may assume that the two studies just cited reported the results of two-tailed tests, because the reported values of the *t* statistics were greater than the cutoff values for two-tailed tests conducted at the reported significance levels. Had Loftus and Palmer conducted a one-tailed test of the null hypothesis, they may have reported the result as follows: The estimate of the speed of the cars by subjects interrogated with *smashed* ($M = 10.46$ mph) was significantly greater than the estimate of the subjects in the *hit* condition ($M = 8.00$ mph), $t(98) = 2.00$, $p < .05$, one-tailed.

Assignment

1. Use APA formatting guidelines to report the results of the independent–samples *t* test that you conducted to test the null hypothesis that caffeine does not improve recall from verbal memory. Be sure to report the group means and standard deviations as well as the *t* statistic, degrees of freedom, *p* value, and the number of tails in the test. State whether the results were statistically significant and supplement your report with the tables from the SPSS output.

PAIRED-SAMPLES *t* TEST

The same researcher decided to replicate her caffeine study with a repeated measures design. Accordingly, she recruited 20 participants, randomly assigned 10 to the caffeine condition and 10 to the placebo condition, administered the treatments, and recorded the number of words recalled in both groups. The study continued at the same time the next day, but this time each participant switched conditions. A new list of words, matched for length and difficulty with the first list, was studied, and the number of words recalled was recorded.

Go to the **Variable View** window and enter **Caffeine** and **Placebo** as two new variable names. Make sure that **Type** is **Numeric** and **Decimals** is set to **0**. The **Label** entries are optional, but it is generally useful to have more complete descriptions of variables, particularly when a label identifies the codes applied to different values of a nominal variable.

	Name	Type	Width	Decimals	Label	Values
1	Drug_Rx	Numeric	8	0	1 = Caffeine (150 mg) vs. 2 = Placebo	{1, Caffeine ⋯
2	Words	Numeric	8	0	Number of words recalled from a list of 30	None
3	Caffeine	Numeric	8	0	Caffeine condition (half received this treatment on Day 1 and half on Day 2)	None
4	Placebo	Numeric	8	0	Placebo condition (half received this treatment on Day 1 and half on Day 2)	None

Now go to the **Data Editor** and enter, in the order shown, the following data values:

Caffeine: 18, 19, 21, 26, 20, 20, 22, 23, 15, 21, 16, 21, 22, 18, 16, 24, 19, 26, 25, 22

Placebo: 25, 12, 21, 21, 21, 17, 19, 24, 16, 19, 18, 15, 23, 15, 18, 18, 17, 21, 22, 23

After entering the data, the Data Editor should look like this:

	Drug Rx	Words	Caffeine	Placebo
1	1	18	18	25
2	1	19	19	12
3	1	21	21	21
4	1	26	26	21
5	1	20	20	21
6	1	20	20	17
7	1	22	22	19
8	1	23	23	24
9	1	15	15	16
10	1	21	21	19
11	1	16	16	18
12	1	21	21	15
13	1	22	22	23
14	1	18	18	15
15	1	16	16	18
16	1	24	24	18
17	1	19	19	17
18	1	26	26	21
19	1	25	25	22
20	1	22	22	23

From the **Analyze** menu, select **Compare Means ▶ Paired–Samples T Test...** to produce the **Paired–Samples T Test** dialog window.

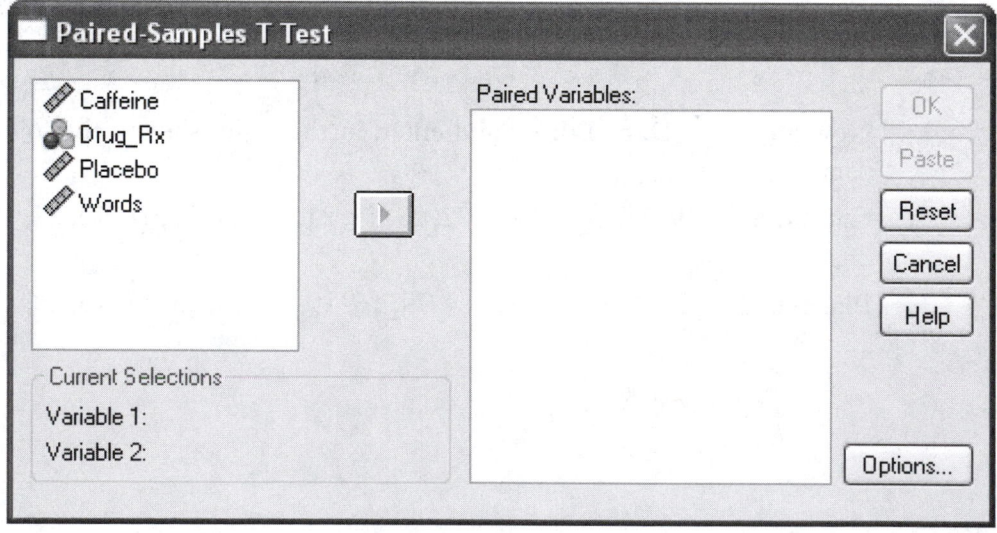

Select **Caffeine** then hold down the Control key on the keyboard as you select **Placebo**. When both variables are selected they will appear under **Current Selections** in the lower left corner of the dialog window:

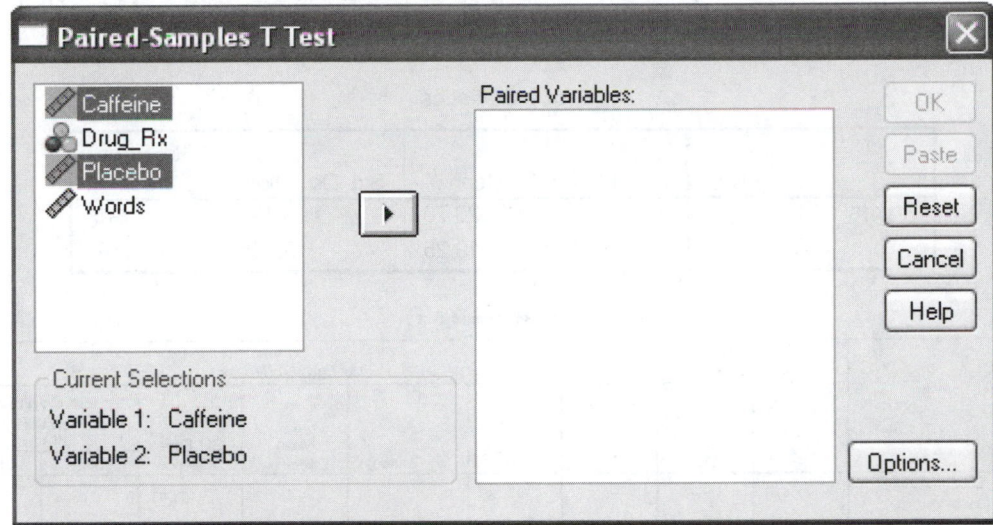

Now click on the ▶ button to move these variables into the **Paired Variable(s):** window. When the dialog window looks like the one below, click **OK** to produce the **T-Test** output tables.

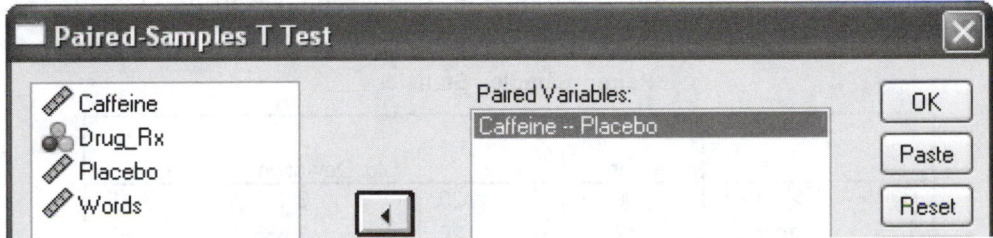

Assignment

2. Describe the results of the paired-samples *t* test according to the formatting guidelines of the APA. Your description should include the means and standard deviations of the dependent variable well as the *t* statistic, degrees of freedom, *p* value, and number of tails in the test. State whether the results were statistically significant and supplement your report with the tables from the SPSS output.

3. The paired-samples *t* test and independent-samples *t* test resulted in different decisions regarding the null hypothesis, despite the fact that the data values (number of words recalled) in the two studies were identical. Explain why the result of the paired-samples *t* test was significant, whereas the result of the independent-samples *t* test was not. (*Hint*: The paired-samples *t* test was used to analyze data from a within-groups design, whereas the independent-samples *t* test was conducted on data from a between-groups design.)

ANSWERS

1. The number of words recalled in the caffeine condition ($M = 20.7$, $SD = 3.2$) was not significantly greater than the number recalled in the placebo condition ($M = 19.25$, $SD = 3.39$), $t(38) = 1.393$, $p = .086$, one-tailed.

Group Statistics

	Drug Rx	N	Mean	Std. Deviation	Std. Error Mean
Words	1	20	20.70	3.197	.715
	2	20	19.25	3.385	.757

Independent Samples Test

		Levene's Test for Equality of Variances		t-test for Equality of Means						95% Confidence Interval of the Difference	
		F	Sig.	t	df	Sig. (2-tailed)	Mean Difference	Std. Error Difference		Lower	Upper
Words	Equal variances assumed	.176	.678	1.393	38	.172	1.450	1.041		-.658	3.558
	Equal variances not assumed			1.393	37.876	.172	1.450	1.041		-.658	3.558

2. The number of words recalled in the caffeine condition ($M = 20.7$, $SD = 3.2$) was significantly greater than the number recalled in the placebo condition ($M = 19.25$, $SD = 3.39$), $t(38) = 1.393$, $p = .04$, one-tailed.

Paired-Samples Statisics

		Mean	N	Std. Deviation	Std. Error Mean
Pair 1	Caffeine	20.70	20	3.197	.715
	Placebo	19.25	20	3.385	.757

Paired-Samples Correlations

		N	Correlation	Sig.
Pair 1	Caffeine & Placebo	20	.430	.058

Paired-Samples Test

		Paired Differences							
					95% Confidence Interval of the Difference				
		Mean	Std. Deviation	Std. Error Mean	Lower	Upper	t	df	Sig (2-tailed)
Pair 1	Caffeine - Placebo	1.450	3.517	.786	-.196	3.096	1.844	19	.081

3. The result of the paired-samples, but not the independent-samples, t test was significant because the variability among scores in a within-groups (repeated-measures) design is less than the variability among scores in a between-groups design. The variability among scores in a within-groups design is lower because a major source of variability, individual differences, is eliminated when the same participants serve in both conditions of the study.

CHAPTER 10

HYPOTHESIS TESTING WITH ONE-WAY ANOVA

Comparing Three or More Groups

The **one-way analysis of variance (ANOVA) for between-subjects (independent-samples) designs** may be used to analyze interval or ratio (scale) data from a study that includes at least two independent samples of participants. However, because an independent-samples t test is traditionally used when there are only two groups of scores, the one-way ANOVA is typically reserved for studies that include at least three groups of participants.

EXERCISE 1
COMPARING THE OUTPUT OF THE INDEPENDENT-SAMPLES t TEST AND A ONE-WAY ANOVA

In this first one-way ANOVA exercise, we will compare the results of the independent-samples t test from a previous exercise to the results of a one-way ANOVA. This will be followed by a one-way ANOVA to test a null hypothesis after adding a third group of scores to the data set. Launch SPSS, and open the file containing the caffeine and memory data from the Chapter 9 exercises. The file contains hypothetical data for 40 participants who were randomly assigned to a caffeine or a placebo condition.

First, we will repeat the independent-samples t test of the null hypothesis that the mean difference between the number of words recalled in Populations 1 (the caffeine population) and 2 (the placebo population) is zero, that is, $\mu_1 - \mu_2 = 0$. From the **Analyze** menu, select **Compare Means** ▶ **Independent–Samples T Test...** to produce the **Independent–Samples T Test** dialog window. Select **Words** and move this variable into the **Test Variable(s):** field. Now move the **Drug_Rx** variable into the **Grouping Variable:** field. Click on **Define Groups...** to produce the **Define Groups** window. Enter **1** for **Group1:** and **2** for **Group 2:**. Click **Continue** to return to the **Independent-Samples T Test** dialog window, then **OK** to produce the **T-Test output** tables.

Now we will conduct a one–way ANOVA to test the null hypothesis that was tested with the independent-samples t test.

From the **Analyze** menu, select **Compare Means ▶ One-Way ANOVA…** .

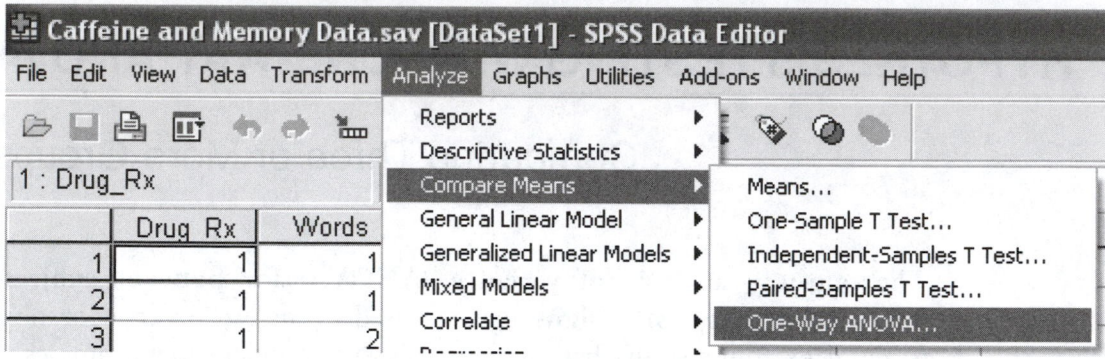

- This will produce the **One-Way ANOVA** dialog window.

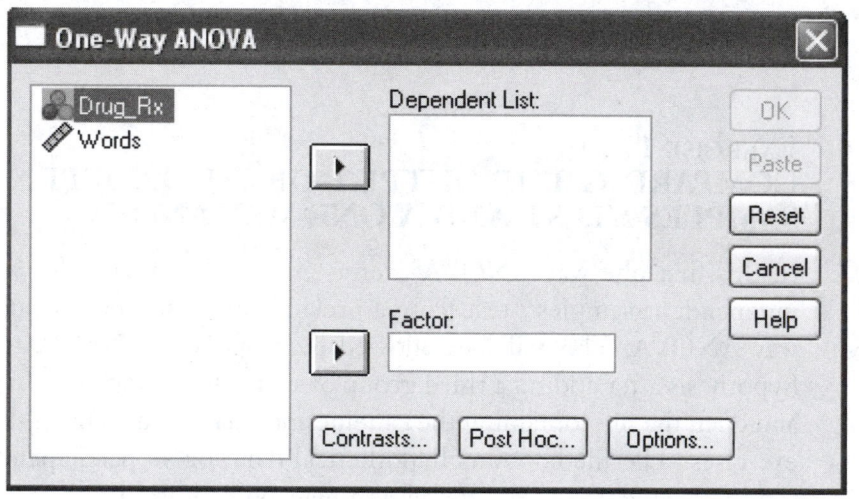

- Select **Words** and move this variable into the **Dependent List:** field. Move the **Drug_Rx** variable into the **Factor:** field. (*Factor* is a synonym for *independent variable*.)

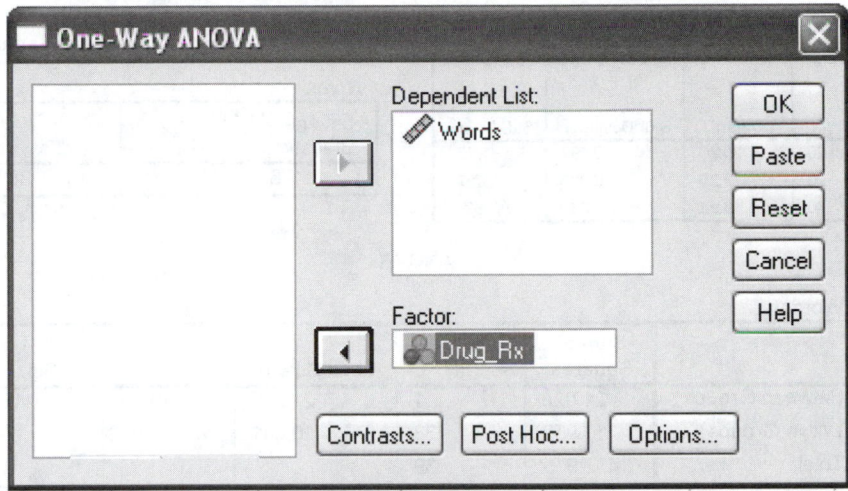

- Now click on the **Options:** tab to produce the **One-Way ANOVA: Options** dialog window. Select the **Descriptive** and **Homogeneity of variance test** (Levene's test) options as shown.

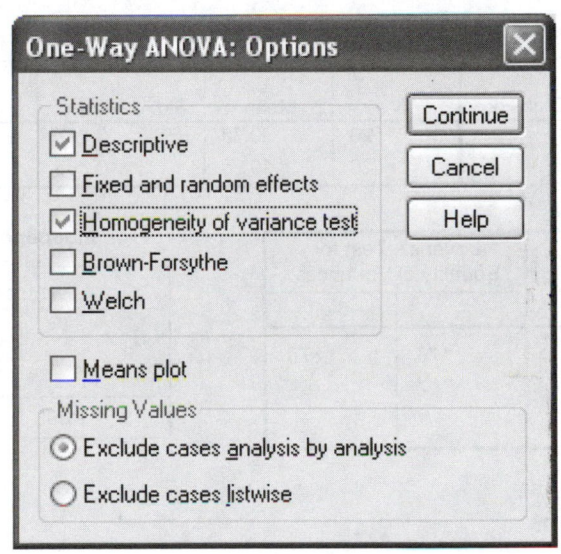

Click **Continue** to return to the **One-Way ANOVA** dialog window, then **OK** to produce the **Descriptives, Test of Homogeneity of Variances** and **ANOVA** output tables.

Descriptives

Words

	N	Mean	Std. Deviation	Std. Error
1	20	20.70	3.197	.715
2	20	19.25	3.385	.757
Total	40	19.98	3.332	.527

Test of Homogeneity of Variances

Words

Levene Statistic	df1	df2	Sig.
.176	1	38	.678

ANOVA

Words

	Sum of Squares	df	Mean Square	F	Sig.
Between Groups	21.025	1	21.025	1.939	.172
Within Groups	411.950	38	10.841		
Total	432.975	39			

These one-way ANOVA output tables may be compared to the tables produced by the independent-samples *t* test procedure that you performed on these data in the Chapter 9 exercise.

Group Statistics

	Drug Rx	N	Mean	Std. Deviation	Std. Error Mean
Words	1	20	20.70	3.197	.715
	2	20	19.25	3.385	.757

		Levene's Test for Equality of Variances	
		F	Sig.
Words	Equal variances assumed	.176	.678
	Equal variances not assumed		

Independent-Samples Test

t-test for Equality of Means		
t	df	Sig. (2-tailed)
1.393	38	.172

Questions

1. Compare the *p* values (the values under "Sig.") from the two Levene tests of the equal variances assumption. Did you expect that they would be the same or different? Explain.

2. Compare the values of the *t* and *F* statistics from the independent samples *t* test and the ANOVA, respectively. Explain how they are related. (*Hint*: You can perform an arithmetic operation on the *t* statistic to produce the *F* statistic.)

3. Compare the p values from the independent-samples t test and the ANOVA. Did you expect that they would be the same or different? Explain.

EXERCISE 2
CONDUCTING A ONE-WAY ANOVA ON DATA FROM THREE GROUPS

In this exercise, we will add a third group of participants. The researcher's decision to add a third group of participants was motivated by her disappointment with the nonsignificant outcome of the independent-samples t test. She believes that adding a higher dose of caffeine (300 mg; roughly equivalent to two cups of brewed coffee) will result in support for her hypothesis that caffeine facilitates recall from verbal memory.

Instructions for entering data for Group 3

- Click on the **Data View** tab to access the **Data Editor**.

- Place the cursor in the first blank cell in the column under **Drug_Rx** and type a **3** in this cell.

40	2	23
41	3	.
42		

- Copy the **3** that you just typed (right-click and select **Copy**).

40	2	23
41	3	
42	Cut	
43	Copy	
44	Paste	
45	Clear	
46	Grid Font	

- Highlight the next 19 cells, that is, just hold down the left mouse button and drag the cursor through the next 19 cells, stopping when the cell in row **60** is highlighted.

- Right-click and select **Paste**.

59		
60	Cut	
61	Copy	
62	Paste	
63	Clear	
64		
65	Grid Font	

- Starting with row **41** in the column under **Words,** type the data values in the order shown.

  19, 24, 22, 20, 28, 21, 22, 24, 25, 26, 24, 20, 22, 23, 23, 29, 23, 24, 22, 15

Now, we will conduct a one-way ANOVA to test the null hypothesis that the means of the populations of words recalled following the administration of a placebo, a low caffeine dose (150 mg), and a moderate caffeine dose (300 mg) are identical.

- From the **Analyze** menu, select **Compare Means ▶ One-Way ANOVA...** to produce the **One-Way ANOVA** dialog window. Verify that **Words** is in the **Dependent List:** field and **Drug_Rx** variable is in the **Factor:** field.

- Click on the **Options:** tab to produce the **One-Way ANOVA: Options** dialog window. Make sure that the **Descriptive** and **Homogeneity of variance test** options are selected, then click **Continue** to return to the **One-Way ANOVA** dialog window, and **OK** to produce the **Descriptives, Test of Homogeneity of Variances** and **ANOVA** output tables.

Descriptives

Words

	N	Mean	Std. Deviation	Std. Error
1	20	20.70	3.197	
2	20	19.25		
3	20	22.80	3.105	.694
Total	60	20.92	3.500	.452

> A comparison of the group means shows that the high-dose caffeine group remembered more words than the low-dose and placebo groups. The one-way analysis of variance is conducted to determine whether these differences are statistically significant.

Test of Homogeneity of Variances

Words

Levene Statistic	df1	df2	Sig.
.411	2	57	.665

> The equal variances assumption is not rejected, because the *p* value is not less than .05.

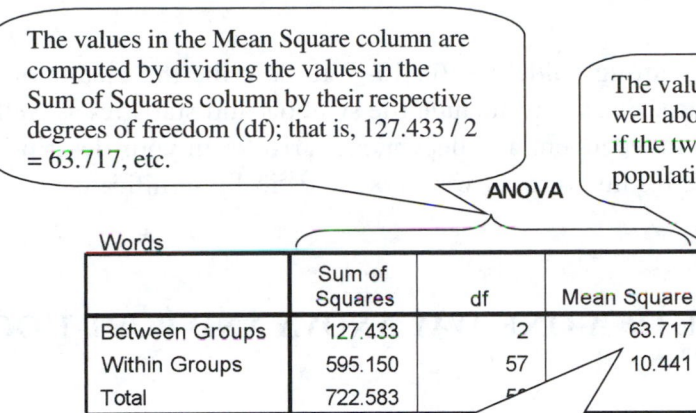

The values in the Mean Square column are computed by dividing the values in the Sum of Squares column by their respective degrees of freedom (df); that is, 127.433 / 2 = 63.717, etc.

The value of the F statistic is well above the value expected if the two estimates of the population variance are equal.

ANOVA

Words

	Sum of Squares	df	Mean Square	F	Sig.
Between Groups	127.433	2	63.717	6.102	.004
Within Groups	595.150	57	10.441		
Total	722.583				

The mean square between groups (63.717) and the mean square within groups (10.441) are estimates of the population variance. If there is no treatment effect, these estimates should be similar in value.

The p value indicates that an F statistic as large as 6.102 occurs only 4 times in 1,000 experiments like this one, if the null hypothesis is true.

PRESENTING THE RESULTS, APA-STYLE

As noted in the exercises for Chapter 9, the *Publication Manual* of the APA prescribes a format for reporting the results of all statistical analyses. The following is an example from the study of territorial defense in parking lots by Ruback and Juieng (1997, p. 828):

> The first analysis was designed to test whether or not the four levels of intrusion differed significantly. This one-way ANOVA, involving the high intrusion (honking), the low intrusion (no honking), and the two control groups (no intrusion and distraction), indicated a significant difference among the four groups, $F(3, 236) = 13.50$, $p < .001$.

The phrase in which the statistical results are detailed is presented below with comments:

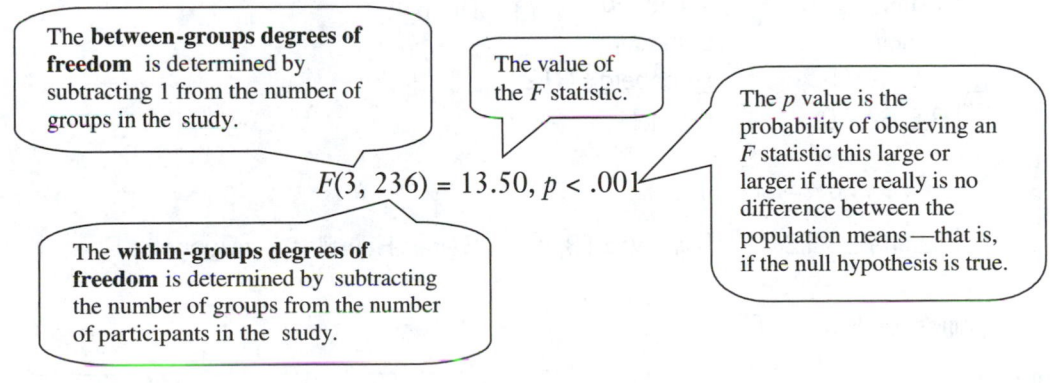

The **between-groups degrees of freedom** is determined by subtracting 1 from the number of groups in the study.

The value of the F statistic.

The p value is the probability of observing an F statistic this large or larger if there really is no difference between the population means —that is, if the null hypothesis is true.

$$F(3, 236) = 13.50, p < .001$$

The **within-groups degrees of freedom** is determined by subtracting the number of groups from the number of participants in the study.

Assignment

Use the APA formatting guidelines (p. 10-7) to describe the results of the analysis of variance. Be sure to include the symbols and statistics as well as the names of the independent and dependent variables in your description. State whether the results were, or were not, statistically significant.

EXERCISE 3
AN EXAMPLE OF A ONE-WAY ANOVA AND POST-HOC COMPARISONS

A significant result for an analysis of variance tells you that the population means are not all the same, but it does not disclose which ones are different. For that, you need to conduct **post-hoc comparisons** (also called *a posteriori comparisons*). These are follow-up analyses designed to identify statistically significant differences between pairs of group means.

First, we will repeat the one-way ANOVA that we conducted in the previous exercise, but this time we'll add some **simple** (i.e., **pairwise**) post hoc comparisons.

- Select **Analyze, Compare Means ▶One-Way ANOVA...** to produce the **One-Way ANOVA** dialog window. Make sure that **Words** is in the **Dependent List:** field and **Drug_Rx** is in the **Factor:** field.

- Now click on the **Options:** tab to produce the **One-Way ANOVA: Options** dialog window and click on the **Post Hoc...** tab to produce the **One-Way ANOVA: Post Hoc Multiple Comparisons** window.

- There are 14 options listed in the section under Equal Variances Assumed at the top of the window. Select the box to the left of **Tukey** and click **Continue** to return to the **One-Way ANOVA** dialog window. Click **OK** to produce the **Multiple Comparisons** output tables.

Multiple Comparisons

Dependent Variable: Words
Tukey HSD

(I) Drug_Rx	(J) Drug_Rx	Mean Difference (I - J)	Std. Error	Sig.
1	2	1.450	1.022	.338
	3	-2.100	1.022	.109
2	1	-1.450	1.022	.338
	3	-3.550*	1.022	.003
3	1	2.100	1.022	.109
	2	3.550*	1.022	.003

*. The mean difference is significant at the .05 level.

> The first two rows of the table show that the mean of the low-dose caffeine group (Group 1) is not significantly different from either the mean of the placebo group (p = .338) or the mean of the moderate-dose caffeine group (p = .109).

> The third row is a repeat of the test in the first row (the positions of the means are just reversed) and is thus redundant. The fourth row shows that the mean of the placebo group (Group 2) is significantly different from the mean of the high-dose caffeine group (p = .003). Note that significant mean differences are indicated by an asterisk.

> The last two rows are redundant and may be ignored.

> The "Sig." column lists the p values for each post hoc test.

The **Tukey *HSD*** (honestly significantly different) test is frequently selected as a post-hoc test because it is considered neither too conservative nor too liberal. The results of a one-way analysis of variance and post-hoc comparisons for this hypothetical study may be reported as follows.

A one-way analysis of variance revealed a significant effect of drug treatment on the number of words remembered in a test of free recall, $F(2, 57) = 6.102$, $p = .004$. Post-hoc comparisons (Tukey *HSD*) showed that participants in the high-dose caffeine group remembered significantly more words ($M = 22.8$, $SD = 3.1$) than participants in the placebo group ($M = 19.25$, $SD = 3.39$), $p = .003$. There were no other significant group differences.

A second example is from a study by Ruback, Pape, and Doriot (1989) of users of public telephones in a shopping mall in Atlanta. The researchers manipulated the number of individuals waiting to use the phone by having either zero, one, or two male confederates approach the area within 30 seconds of the time each subject lifted the receiver to make a call. Because the researchers could not locate a single public telephone with enough traffic to conduct an experiment, a public station with two adjacent telephones was used, and one of the confederates in the two-confederate condition used the other phone while the second confederate stood a little to the side and behind, but within 3 feet of, the caller. The authors used an analysis of variance to examine the effect of the subject's gender and the number of confederate "intruders" on the amount of time each subject remained at the telephone. They used the Newman-Keuls post-hoc test to identify differences between group means. Ruback et al. reported their findings as follows:

> The only significant effect was for number of confederates, $F(2, 50) = 3.23$, $p < .05$. A post-hoc Newman-Keuls test of the means ($p < .05$) revealed that subjects intruded on by two confederates were at the phone longer ($M = 237.4$ secs) than were subjects intruded on by one confederate ($M = 107.0$ secs) and subjects not intruded on by a confederate ($M = 81.5$ secs). The latter two conditions did not differ significantly from each other. (p. 239)

EXERCISE 4
ONE-WAY ANOVA AND POST-HOC COMPARISONS WITH FOUR GROUPS

In this exercise, you will add a fourth group of participants to the design. The researcher's decision to add a fourth group of participants representing a *zero control group* (no treatment of any kind, not even a placebo) was motivated by a colleague's disbelief in the *placebo effect*. A **placebo effect** is a manifestation of the power of suggestion. For example, roughly half of the participants in a randomized clinical trial of a new medication designed to relieve pain may be given a placebo, a capsule that looks, feels, and tastes like the capsule that includes the new medication but which does not include the medication. A double-blind procedure is usually employed such that neither the participants nor the individuals administering the capsules know whether the participant is receiving the medication or a placebo. A sizable percentage of the participants given the placebo may report pain relief—an outcome that is, by definition, a placebo effect. Kirsch and Sapirstein (1999) estimated that 50% of the response to antidepressant medication is due to the placebo effect, with 25% attributable to the pharmacological properties of the medication, and 25% to other factors such as the physician-patient relationship.

- Add the following data values (number of words recalled) for Group 4:

  14, 20, 19, 17, 23, 13, 18, 18, 21, 16, 15, 19, 16, 11, 17, 22, 14, 21, 24, 10.

- Conduct a one-way ANOVA on the data from this four-group design and follow the omnibus ANOVA with a set of Tukey *HSD* post-hoc comparisons.

Questions

4. Use the APA formatting guidelines to describe the results of the analysis of variance. Be sure to include the appropriate statistical symbols and statistics as well as the names of the independent and dependent variables in your description of the results of the overall analysis of variance, and support your description with copies of the appropriate SPSS output tables. Report the results of the Tukey post-hoc tests. For all significant mean differences, enclose group means and standard deviations in parentheses and provide the p value from the Tukey test. For each report that involves a p value, state whether the results were, or were not, statistically significant.

5. Describe any evidence of a possible placebo effect. (*Hint*: Think of the logic of hypothesis testing and the fact that the zero control group was added to the design to disclose a possible placebo effect.)

ANSWERS

1. The p values from the two Levene tests of the equal variances assumption are identical as should be the case when the same test is used more than once to analyze the same set of data.

2. Squaring the t statistic produces the F statistic—that is, $t^2 = F$, and $t = \sqrt{F}$.

3. The p values from the t test and the ANOVA are identical. This follows from the relation between the t and F statistics identified in the answer to Question 2. Put another way, when there are two groups of scores the independent samples t test and the one-way ANOVA are algebraically equivalent, so the p values should be the same.

4. A one-way ANOVA revealed a significant caffeine treatment effect, $F(3, 76) = 9.03$, $p < .0005$. Follow-up group comparisons using Tukey's HSD test revealed that memory performance following the higher (300 mg) dose of caffeine ($M = 22.8$, $SD = 3.11$) was significantly different from both the placebo ($M = 19.25$, $SD = 3.39$, $p = .008$) and zero control ($M = 17.4$, $SD = 3.89$, $p < .0005$) conditions. The number of words recalled following the lower (150 mg) dose of caffeine ($M = 20.7$, $SD = 3.2$) was significantly greater than the number recalled following the zero control condition ($p = .015$) but not following the placebo treatment ($p = .535$). Finally, there were no significant differences between either the placebo and zero control conditions ($p = .320$) or the two caffeine conditions ($p = .215$).

Descriptives

Words

	N	Mean	Std. Deviation
1	20	20.70	3.197
2	20	19.25	3.385
3	20	22.80	3.105
4	20	17.40	3.858
Total	80	20.04	3.883

Test of Homogeneity of Variances

Words

Levene Statistic	df1	df2	Sig.
.693	3	76	.559

ANOVA

Words

	Sum of Squares	df	Mean Square	F	Sig.
Between Groups	312.938	3	104.313	9.030	.000
Within Groups	877.950	76	11.552		
Total	1190.888	79			

Multiple Comparisons

Dependent Variable: Words

Tukey HSD

(I) Drug_Rx	(J) Drug_Rx	Mean Difference (I - J)	Std. Error	Sig.
1	2	1.450	1.075	.535
	3	-2.100	1.075	.215
	4	3.300*	1.075	.015
2	1	-1.450	1.075	.535
	3	-3.550*	1.075	.008
	4	1.850	1.075	.320
3	1	2.100	1.075	.215
	2	3.550*	1.075	.008
	4	5.400*	1.075	.000
4	1	-3.300*	1.075	.015
	2	-1.850	1.075	.320
	3	-5.400*	1.075	.000

*. The mean difference is significant at the .05 level.

5. The null hypothesis tested to determine whether there is evidence of a placebo effect is as follows:

> The mean number of words recalled following treatment with a placebo is the same as the mean number of words recalled in the absence of any systematic treatment.

> In symbols, $\mu_{placebo} = \mu_{zero\ control}$

This hypothesis was not rejected ($p = .320$), so there is no evidence of a placebo effect in this study. The research hypothesis states that the mean number of words recalled following treatment with a placebo is not the same as the mean number of words recalled in the absence of any systematic treatment. A rejection of the null hypothesis would provide support for this hypothesis.

You may be thinking that the absence of a significance difference between the placebo and low-dose caffeine group ($p = .535$) provides evidence of a placebo effect. However, the logic of hypothesis testing does not regard a failure to reject the null hypothesis as evidence supporting it.

CHAPTER 11

TWO-WAY ANOVA

Understanding Interactions

Do drivers "defend their territory" by taking longer to leave a parking space when another driver is waiting to take it? This question was addressed in a replication of parts of two studies reported by Ruback and Juieng (1997). In this set of exercises you will analyze the data from this replication by conducting two factorial ANOVAs. A **factorial ANOVA** is used when the experimental design includes at least two independent variables, each with two or more levels.

The data file for this exercise is entitled "Parking Data for Exercise 11" on the data CD. Double-clicking on this file will launch SPSS and load the file into the **Data Editor** window. The first 10 cases are shown below:

Parking Data.sav [DataSet1] - SPSS Data Editor

File Edit View Data Transform Analyze Graphs Utilities Add-ons Window Help

1 : Intruder_cond   1

	Intruder cond	gender	numpass	dir_exit	dep_time
1	1	1	1	2	29
2	1	2	0	1	31
3	1	2	1	1	12
4	1	2	1	1	31
5	1	1	0	1	24
6	1	2	1	2	14
7	1	2	3	1	21
8	1	2	0	1	15
9	1	1	0	2	60
10	1	2	0	1	80

From the **Analyze** menu, select **General Linear Model** ▶ **Univariate…**

	Intruder_cond	gender	numpass	dir_exit	dep_time
1	1	1	1	2	29
2	1	2	0	1	31
3	1	2	1	1	12
4	1	2	1	1	31
5	1	1	0	1	24
6	1	2	1	2	14
7	1	2	3	1	21
8	1	2	0	1	15
9	1	1	0	2	60
10	1	2	0	1	80

to produce the **Univariate** dialog window (below). Select **dep_time** and click on the ▶ button to move this variable into the **Dependent Variable:** box on the right. Now select **Intruder_cond** and move this independent variable into the **Fixed Factor(s):** field; do the same with the **gender** variable. After moving the variables, the Univariate window should look like this:

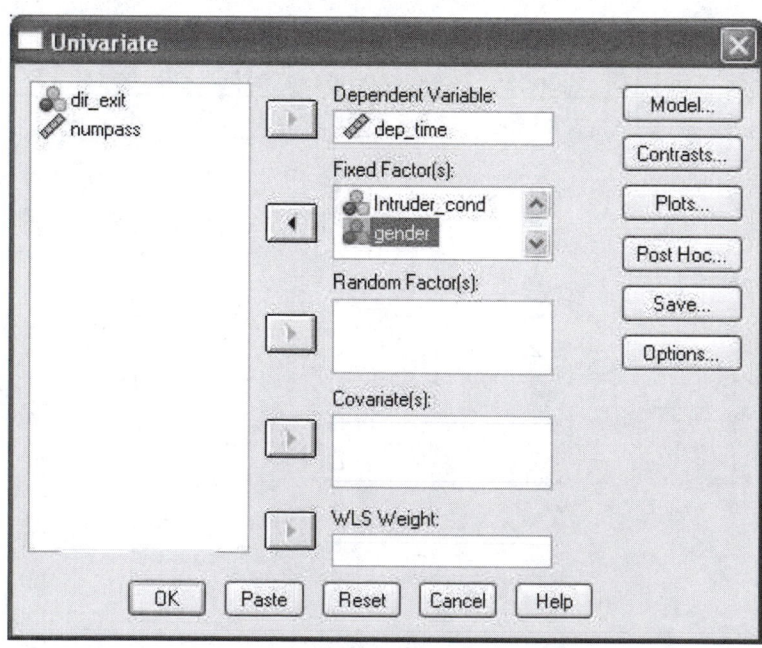

Now click on the **Options...** tab (bottom tab on the right side of the window) to produce the **Univariate: Options** dialog window; click in the box to the left of **Descriptive statistics** (under **Display** on the left side of the window), and click **Continue** to return to the Univariate dialog window.

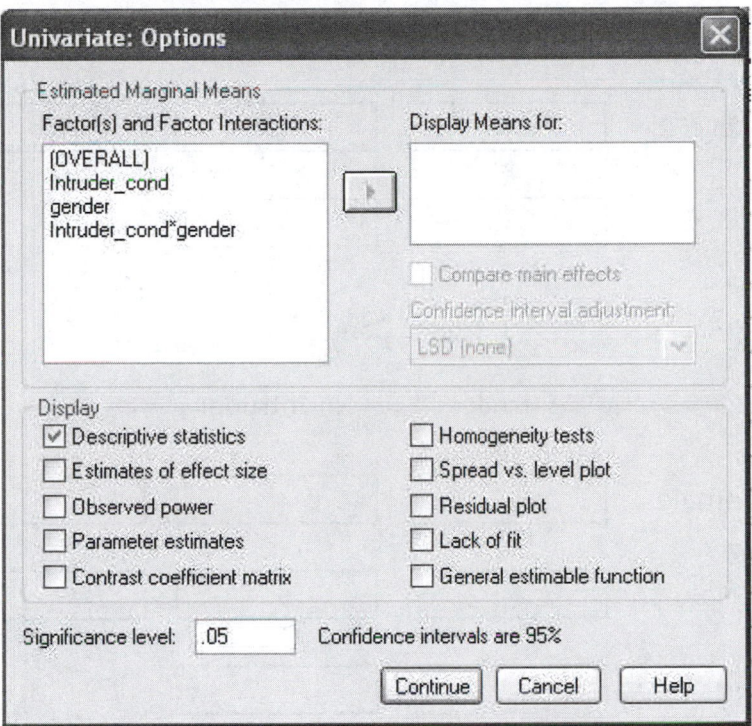

Now click **OK** to close the Univariate window and produce the output.

The first of three output tables is labeled **Between-Subjects Factors** and lists each of the factors in the analysis as well as the numbers of participants representing each level of each factor. For example, the first two rows tell us that 96 drivers were in the intruder condition (code = 1), and 95 drivers were in the no-intruder condition (code = 2). The next two rows tell us that there were 91 female drivers (code = 1) and 100 male drivers (code = 2)

The table labeled **Descriptive Statistics** lists the means, standard deviations, and number of drivers in each condition (cell or combination of intruder condition and gender of driver) of the study. For example, the two rows list the statistics for female and male drivers in the intruder condition. The statistics in the rows labeled "Total" are for the factor listed in the first column, ignoring the levels of the factor listed in the second column. The last row in the table lists the statistics for the combination of all levels of all factors. A more traditional format for presenting the means for a 2×2 factorial design is shown on the next page. A generic form of the table is presented first followed by a blank table.

Factor A

	Level 1	Level 2	
Factor B			
Level 1	A_1B_1	A_2B_1	B_1
Level 2	A_1B_2	A_2B_2	B_2
	A_1	A_2	

Intruder Condition

	Intruder	No Intruder	
Gender of Driver			
Female			
Male			

You may wish to fill in the blanks in the second table with the appropriate means from the SPSS output. The table may be particularly helpful as you answer the following questions.

1. Which condition resulted in the lowest mean departure time? The highest?

2. Compare the intruder vs. no-intruder conditions. Which condition resulted in the slower departure time?

3. Now compare the means for the female and male drivers. Which group had the slower departure time?

The third table in the output, labeled **Tests of Between-Subjects Effects**, includes the results of a 2 (Intruder Condition: intruder vs. no intruder) × 2 (Gender: male vs. female drivers) between-groups factorial ANOVA. The column labeled **Source** lists the different sources of variance. You may ignore the first two rows, labeled "Corrected Model" and "Intercept." The next three rows list the names of the factors as well as the intruder condition × gender of the driver interaction. The column labeled **Type III Sum of Squares** lists the between-groups sums of squares (SS_B) for the two factors and their interaction as sources of variance or "treatments." The bottom row in this column, labeled **Error**, lists the within-groups sum of squares (SS_W). The **df**, **Mean Square**, **F**, and **Sig.** columns include the degrees of freedom, population variance estimates, F statistics, and p values, respectively, for each of the sources of variance.

4. For each of the following questions, provide the appropriate evidence to support your answer. Be sure to present the results in the editorial style of the American Psychological Association.

   a. Was there a main effect of intruder condition?

   b. Was there a main effect of gender?

   c. Was there an interaction effect? If so, was it *qualitative* or *quantitative*?

   d. Interpret the result of the test for an interaction effect.

In the Results section of Study 1, Ruback and Juieng (1997) wrote: "Because number of people in the departing car was related to time it took to depart, $r(198) = .24$, $p < .001$, we used this variable as a grouping factor in subsequent analyses. A 2×2 ANOVA of the departure times was conducted using intrusion and number of people in the departing car as grouping variables, with number in the car being dichotomized into (a) only one person in the car or (b) more than one person in the car" (pp. 824–825).

A correlation between number of passengers and departure time was also observed in this study, $r(190) = .148$, $p = .041$. In this next exercise, you will follow the example of Ruback and Juieng by dichotomizing the number of passengers variable before conducting a 2 (Intruder Condition: intruder vs. no intruder) $\times$ 2 (number of passengers: 0 vs. 1 or more) ANOVA for just the male drivers. This ANOVA will not include female drivers because their departure times were similar in the intruder and no-intruder conditions.

The first part of this exercise requires that you select just the male drivers for analysis. First, click on **Data … Select Cases …** to produce the **Select Cases dialog window**. In the Select Cases dialog window, click on the radio button next to **If condition is satisfied**, then click on the large **If** button to produce the **Select Cases: If** dialog window. In the Select Cases: If dialog window, select gender from the list of variables and click on the ▶ button to move this variable into the box on the right. Type **= 2** so that the expression in the box now reads **gender = 2**. Click **Continue** to return to the Select Cases dialog window, then **OK** to return to the **Data Editor** window. Your screen should look like this, with slashes through the cases that correspond to female drivers:

	Intruder_cond	gender	numpass	dir_exit	dep_time	filter_$
1	1	1	1	2	29	0
2	1	2	0	1	31	1
3	1	2	1	1	12	1
4	1	2	1	1	31	1
5	1	1	0	1	24	0
6	1	2	1	2	14	1
7	1	2	3	1	21	1
8	1	2	0	1	15	1
9	1	1	0	2	60	0
10	1	2	0	1	80	1
11	1	2	1	1	90	1
12	1	1	1	1	38	0
13	1	2	1	2	107	1
14	1	2	2	2	33	1
15	1	1	0	1	45	0

The next task is to recode the numpass variable into a different variable (call it numpass2) with two values: 1 = 0 passengers, 2 = 1 or more passengers. From the **Transform** menu options select **Recode into Different Variables**… to produce the Recode into Different Variables dialog window. When this window appears, select **numpass** from the list of variables and click the ▶ button to move this variable into the field on the right. Place the cursor in the **Name:** box under **Output Variable** and type the name of the recoded variable (**numpass2**). In the **Label:** box, type **1 = 0 passengers, 2 = 1 or more passengers**. Now click on the **Old and New Values** box near the center of the window to produce the **Recode into Different Variables: Old and New Values** dialog window. The cursor should be blinking in the **Value:** box under **Old Value** in the upper left corner of the window. The first old value to be recoded is 0, so type **0** in this box, then position the cursor in the **Value:** box under **New Value** and type **1** as the new value. Now click the **Add** button to enter the recode request to the **Old -->New** list. To recode the rest of the values of numpass, click the **Range, value through HIGHEST**: button (the next-to-last radio button on the left side of the window) and type **1** in the box. Type **2** in the Value: box under **New Value** and click the **Add** button to cause all values of numpass that are 1 and higher to be recoded as **2**. Click **Continue** to return to the Recode into Different Variables dialog window. When the Recode into Different Variables dialog window appears, click the **Change** button to execute the recode requests, and click **OK** to return to the Data Editor window. Your Data Editor window should now include numpass2 as a new variable with two values: 1 to indicate drivers with no passengers and 2 to denote drivers with at least one passenger:

*Parking Data.sav [DataSet1] - SPSS Data Editor

File Edit View Data Transform Analyze Graphs Utilities Add-ons Window Help

1 : Intruder_cond | 1

	Intruder_cond	gender	numpass	dir_exit	dep_time	filter_$	numpass2
1	1	1	1	2	29	0	2
2	1	2	0	1	31	1	1
3	1	2	1	1	12	1	2
4	1	2	1	1	31	1	2
5	1	1	0	1	24	0	1
6	1	2	1	2	14	1	2
7	1	2	3	1	21	1	2
8	1	2	0	1	15	1	1
9	1	1	0	2	60	0	1
10	1	2	0	1	80	1	1
11	1	2	1	1	90	1	2
12	1	1	1	1	38	0	2
13	1	2	1	2	107	1	2
14	1	2	2	2	33	1	2
15	1	1	0	1	45	0	1

5. Conduct a 2 (Intruder Condition: intruder vs. no intruder) × 2 (number of passengers: 0 vs. 1 or more) ANOVA and interpret the output by answering the following questions. Be sure to support your answers by citing the appropriate statistics from the SPSS output.

   a. Was there a main effect of intruder condition?

   b. Was there a main effect of number of passengers?

   c. Was there an interaction? If so, was it qualitative or quantitative?

   d. Interpret the result of the test for an interaction effect.

In the brief introduction to their naturalistic observation study (Study 1), Ruback and Juieng (1997) observed that "Because a parking space has minimal value to a departing driver, intrusion should facilitate a speedier departure. However, because concerns with identity and control are so tied to driving, it was predicted that intrusion would induce territorial defense." (p. 823). In their discussion of the results of this study, they wrote:

> In this observational study, departing drivers took longer to leave their parking spaces when they were intruded upon by another driver than when they were not. Although longer departure times following intrusion may indicate territorial behavior, causality cannot be inferred with this

observational study because other factors may be operating. For instance, the presence of the intruding cars may have distracted the departing drivers, causing them to need more time to leave the parking space. A related possibility is that departing drivers took longer to leave when intruded upon because they wanted to be careful to avoid a collision with the intruding car. (p. 825)

In their follow-up field experiment (Study 2), Ruback and Juieng (1997) attempted to separate intrusion from distraction by having a confederate drive slowly past drivers who were about to leave. They reported that ". . . drivers who were intruded upon ($M = 36.78$ s) did not stay significantly longer than did those who were distracted ($M = 31.09$ s), $F(1, 236) = 2.09$, ns" (p. 828). In their discussion of this finding, Ruback and Juieng noted that "the distraction condition may not have been a pure manipulation of distraction, in that even though the distracting car was not waiting for the departing driver, the presence of the distracting car could have primed departing drivers about the value of the space they were about to leave" (p. 829).

Ruback and Juieng did not record the direction of exit of the departing drivers they observed. If drivers were distracted by the presence of another vehicle, or if "they wanted to be careful to avoid a collision with the intruding car," then one may reasonably assume that they would have been more distracted, or would have exercised more caution, when backing toward than away from that vehicle. See the figure below.

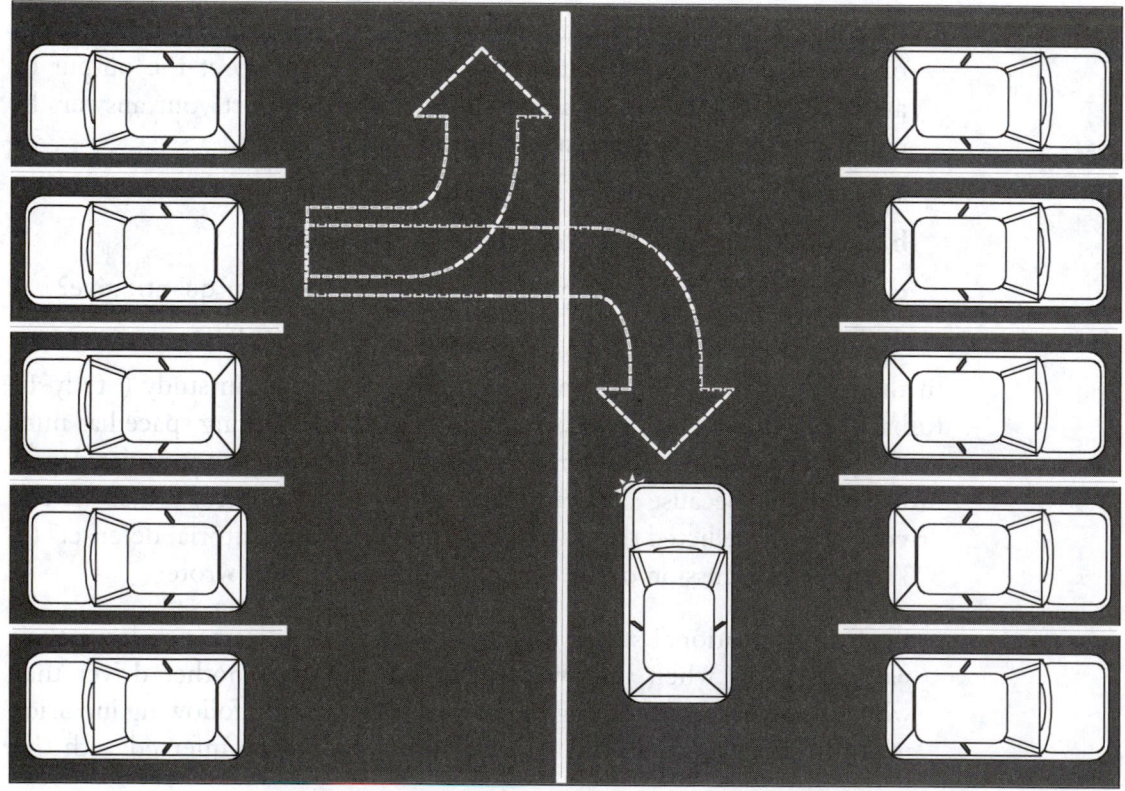

6. Use an independent-samples t test to analyze the effect of the variable dir_exit (direction of exit: 1 = toward, 2 = away) on departure time. Report the results in the style of the American Psychological Association by following a brief statement of the result of the t test with a comma and the following syntax: $t(\mathrm{df}) = \mathrm{x.xx}$, $p = \mathrm{.xxx}$, 2-tailed.

7. Do the results of these exercises support the hypothesis that drivers exhibit territorial defense of parking spaces by taking longer to exit in the presence of an intruder? Explain your answer.

ANSWERS

1. The lowest mean was recorded for male drivers in the no-intruder condition ($M = 21.45$ s, $SD = 11.808$ s, $n = 47$), whereas the highest mean was for female drivers in the no-intruder condition ($M = 35.23$ s, $SD = 22.644$ s, $n = 48$).

2. The slowest departure times were observed in the intruder ($M = 31.45$ s, $SD = 21.704$ s, $n = 96$) condition. Drivers in the no-intruder condition ($M = 28.41$ s, $SD = 19.302$ s, $n = 95$) exited their spaces about 3 seconds sooner.

3. Female drivers had slower departure times ($M = 33.88$ s, $SD = 21.296$ s, $n = 91$). Male drivers ($M = 26.35$ s, $SD = 19.253$ s, $n = 100$) exited parking spaces around 7.5 seconds faster than female drivers.

4. **a.** There was no main effect of intruder condition, $F(1, 187) = 1.207$, $p = .273$.

   b. There was a main effect of gender, $F(1, 187) = 7.053$, $p = .009$. The departure times of male drivers ($M = 26.35$ s) were significantly faster than those of female drivers ($M = 33.88$ s).

   c. There was a significant intruder condition x gender interaction, $F(1, 187) = 4.328$, $p = .039$. This is a *qualitative* interaction, because the effect of intruder condition was opposite for male and female drivers.

   d. The significant interaction effect indicates that the effect of the intruder condition depended upon the gender of the departing driver. When an intruder was present, female drivers left about 3 seconds sooner than in the no-intruder condition. In contrast, male drivers remained in "their" parking spaces about 9 seconds *longer* when an intruder was present vs. when there was no intruder.

5. **a.** There was a main effect of intruder condition, $F(1, 96) = 6.923$, $p = .01$. Male drivers exited "their" parking spaces significantly more slowly in the presence of an intruder.

   b. There was also a main effect of number of passengers, $F(1, 96) = 10.194$, $p = .002$. Male drivers accompanied by one or more passengers took significantly longer to leave the parking spaces ($M = 32.08$ s, $SD = 22.117$ s, $n = 50$) than those who were not accompanied by passengers ($M = 20.62$ s, $SD = 13.883$ s, $n = 50$).

   c. There was no interaction between intruder condition and number of passengers, $F(1, 96) = .464$, $p = .497$.

   d. The absence of an interaction effect means that male drivers were not differentially influenced by the presence of passengers in the intruder and no–intruder conditions.

6. The departure times when backing toward ($M = 30.52$ s, $SD = 18.021$ s, $n = 54$) vs. away ($M = 32.64$ s, $SD = 25.866$ s, $n = 42$) from an intruder were not significantly different, $t(94) = -0.474$, $p = .637$, 2-tailed.

7. Male, but not female, drivers took longer to leave parking spaces when an intruder was present and when they were accompanied by one or more passengers, but there is no evidence that the effect of intrusion was affected by the presence of passengers. These

results offer tentative support for the territoriality hypothesis, although it is difficult to separate the effect of an intruder as a "threat" to one's "property" from the effect of an intruder as a distraction when one is leaving a parking space. However, one may argue as follows: If the presence of a waiting driver causes drivers to exit more slowly because they are distracted or because they are concerned about having an accident, then it is reasonable to suppose that those concerns would be magnified for drivers exiting toward rather than away from an intruder. However, this study provided no evidence that drivers may have been more distracted or may have exercised extra caution when backing toward a waiting driver. This result does not support the argument that longer departure times in the presence of an intruder may be explained by an appeal to distraction or the exercise of additional caution while backing out.

CHAPTER 12

BEYOND HYPOTHESIS TESTING

Confidence Intervals, Effect Size, and Power

The purpose of this set of exercises is to demonstrate a statistical inference procedure called **interval estimation**. As an alternative to hypothesis testing, a researcher may compute a **confidence interval** that is centered around the sample mean (M), and use this interval to simultaneously test a number of null hypothesized values of a population mean (μ).

EXERCISE 1

Launch SPSS and navigate to the data CD. Locate the syntax file named **Syntax for 1000 Sample means (100,15)** and open it. Now select **Run**, then **All** (as shown below) to execute the syntax program and create the data file.

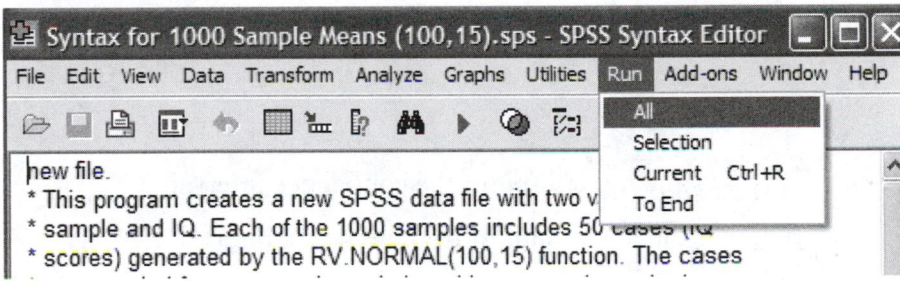

The syntax program generated an SPSS data file that includes two variables, **sample** and **IQ_mean**. The values of the sample variable are simply the sample numbers (1 to 1000), and the values of the IQ_mean variable are means of samples of 50 values randomly selected from a normal population with μ 100 and σ 15. The **Data Editor** should be similar to this:

	sample	IQ_mean	var	var	var
1	1	100.60			
2	2	101.16			
3	3	101.14			
4	4	99.66			
5	5	97.30			

Untitled16 [] - SPSS Data Editor
File Edit View Data Transform Analyze Graphs Utilities Add-ons Window Help
1 : sample   1

We will construct a **95% confidence interval** around each of the sample means in the IQmeans data file. Each confidence interval (CI) is defined by its lower and upper limits. The formulas for the lower and upper limits are as follows:

$$CI_{UL} = M + z_{\frac{\alpha}{2}}(\sigma_M) = M + 1.96\left(\frac{\sigma}{\sqrt{N}}\right) = M + 1.96\left(\frac{15}{\sqrt{50}}\right)$$

$$CI_{LL} = M - z_{\frac{\alpha}{2}}(\sigma_M) = M - 1.96\left(\frac{\sigma}{\sqrt{N}}\right) = M - 1.96\left(\frac{15}{\sqrt{50}}\right)$$

where,

CI_{UL} is the upper limit of the confidence interval

CI_{LL} is the lower limit of the confidence interval

M is the sample mean

$\pm z_{\frac{\alpha}{2}}$ are the critical z scores that define the two-tailed rejection region of the null hypothesis tested at a significance level of $\alpha = .05$; when $\alpha = .05$, $\pm z = \pm1.96$

σ_M is the standard error of the mean

From the **Transform** menu, select **Compute Variable...** to produce the **Compute Variable** dialog window and create a new variable named **CI95_LL**. Type **CI95_LL** in the **Target Variable:** field, then move **IQ_mean** into the **Numeric Expression:** field and complete the expression so that it reads as follows:

IQ_mean – 1.96 * 15 / SQRT(50)

Click **OK**. The formula computes the **lower** limit of a 95% confidence interval for each of the sample means in the data file.

Use **Transform, Compute Variable...** to create a new variable named **CI95_UL**. In the **Target Variable:** box type **CI95_UL** (the name CI95_LL should still be in the field, so just change the "U" to an "L"). Edit the expression in the **Numeric Expression:** field (this should require nothing more than changing the minus sign to a plus sign) to read:

$$\text{IQ\_mean} + 1.96 * 15 / \text{SQRT}(50)$$

Click **OK**. The formula computes the **upper** limit of a 95% confidence interval for each of the sample means.

Each of the 95% confidence intervals that you just computed is an interval estimate of the true value of the population mean. Each interval estimate is centered around a sample mean (M), which is your best estimate of the true value of the population mean (μ). The intervals are **95% confidence intervals** because the level of confidence is computed as the **additive inverse** of the significance level: **CI% = 100% − alpha% = 100% − 5% = 95%**. We are permitted to say that we are 95% confident that any given interval contains the true value of the population mean. In the next step, we will count the number of confidence intervals that include the true value of the population mean.

Use **Transform, Compute Variable...** to produce the **Compute Variable** dialog window and create a new variable named **decision**. Type **decision** in the **Target Variable:** field. In the **Numeric Expression:** field, type:

$$\text{CI95\_UL} >= 100 \ \& \ \text{CI95\_LL} <= 100$$

and click **OK**. For each pair of confidence limits the expression will return **1** if the population mean is within the interval, **0** if it is not. Go to the **Variable View** window and set **Decimals** to zero for the decision variable.

If you typed the formulas correctly, the first 10 rows of the **Data Editor** window should be similar to this:

	Sample	IQ_mean	CI95_LL	CI95_UL	decision
1	1	100	96	104	1
2	2	104	100	108	1
3	3	101	97	105	1
4	4	100	96	104	1
5	5	101	97	105	1
6	6	95	91	99	0
7	7	98	94	102	1
8	8	98	94	102	1
9	9	103	99	107	1
10	10	100	96	104	1

From the **Analyze** menu, select **Descriptive Statistics ▶ Frequencies...** to produce a count of the number of 95% confidence intervals that include the true value of the population mean. When the **Frequencies** window appears, move **decision** into the **Variable(s):** field and click **OK**.

We know the true value of the population mean in this and all other computer simulati on exercises, because we set up the population to have a mean of 100 and a standard deviation of 15. Because we know the population parameters we can detect whether each of the confidence intervals that we constructed really includes the true value of the population mean ($\mu = 100$).

Questions

1. Assuming that the null hypothesis is true, what is the *expected* percentage of 95% confidence intervals that include the value 100?

2. What is the *actual* percentage of confidence intervals that include the value 100? Support your answer with the SPSS output.

3. Suppose that a school psychologist in a certain school district believes that the 8th-grade students in her district are unusual but she isn't sure how their relative difference might be expressed on a standard IQ test. She hypothesizes that the mean IQ score in this population of 8th-grade students is not 100.

   State the **null hypothesis** that the school psychologist is interested in testing.

4. Now suppose that the samples of IQ scores in the IQMeans data file are samples of 8th-grade students from this psychologist's district. Thus each confidence interval represents a test of the null hypothesis (the one that you wrote as your answer to Question 3, if you are correct). Based on the confidence intervals that you constructed, what percentage of the time will this school psychologist conclude that she is correct—that is, what percentage of the time will she conclude that the mean IQ in the population of 8th-graders in her district really is different from 100? Put another way: Of this large number of tests of the null hypothesis, what percentage of them will allow the school psychologist to reject the null hypothesis and conclude that the mean IQ score among 8th grade students in her school district is not 100?

5. You may wish to reread the text box on top of this page before you answer this question: What percentage of the school psychologist's rejections of the null hypothesis are correct rejections? Explain your answer.

EXERCISE 2

Repeat Exercise 1, but this time use the syntax file named **Syntax for 1000 Sample means (110,15)**. Execute each step of this exercise exactly as you did in Exercise 1.

Questions

6. What is the *actual* percentage of confidence intervals that include the value 100? Support your answer with the SPSS output.

7. Each confidence interval is a test of the null hypothesis that you identified in Question 3. Of this large number of confidence intervals, what percentage of them will allow the school psychologist to reject the null hypothesis and conclude that the mean IQ score among 8th-grade students in her school district is not 100?

8. Recall that this is a computer simulation as you answer this question: What percentage of the school psychologist's rejections of the null hypothesis are correct rejections? Explain your answer.

9. Assuming that your answer to Question 6 above is a number greater than zero, what does this percentage represent?

   A. correct decisions   B. Type I errors   C. Type II errors

10. Explain your answer to Question 9.

ANSWERS

EXERCISE 1

1. Expect 950, or 95%, of the confidence intervals to include the null-hypothesized value of the population mean (100).

2. Answers will vary because of the random number seed. According to the output table below, **94.1 percent** of the confidence intervals included the population mean, 100. This is reasonably close to the expected rate of 95 percent.

decision

		Frequency	Percent	Valid Percent	Cumulative Percent
Valid	0	59	5.9	5.9	5.9
	1	941	94.1	94.1	100.0
	Total	1000	100.0	100.0	

3. The null hypothesis that the school psychologist is interested in testing is as follows: **The mean IQ score in the population of 8th-grade students in her district is 100.** Note that the null hypothesis is always the opposite of the research hypothesis.

4. According to the output table above, the school psychologist will conclude that she is correct—that is, she will conclude that the average IQ in the population of 8th-graders in her district really is different from 100—about **5.9 percent** of the time. In other words, the school psychologist will reject the null hypothesis about 5.9 percent of the time.

5. Each time the school psychologist rejects the null hypothesis she is making a Type I error, so **none** of her rejections are correct. We know that all of her rejections are Type I errors because we set up the population mean to be 100—the value specified by the null hypothesis.

EXERCISE 2

6. According to the output table below, **0.1 percent** of the confidence intervals include the population mean, 100. This is not surprising given that the population mean for this exercise is 110.

decision

		Frequency	Percent	Valid Percent	Cumulative Percent
Valid	0	999	99.9	99.9	99.9
	1	1	.1	.1	100.0
	Total	1000	100.0	100.0	

7. According to the previous output table, the school psychologist will conclude that she is correct—that is, she will conclude that the average IQ in the population of 8th-graders in her district really is different from 100—about **99.9 percent** of the time. In other words, the school psychologist will reject the null hypothesis about 99.9 percent of the time.

8. Each time the school psychologist rejects the null hypothesis she is making a correct decision, so **all** her rejections are correct. We know that all her rejections are correct decisions because we set up the population mean in this exercise to be 110 instead of 100 as it was in Exercise 1. We set up the null hypothesis to be false, so each decision to reject it is a correct decision.

9. Each of the confidence intervals that contain the null-hypothesized value of the population mean (100) is a Type II error (choice C).

10. The confidence intervals that resulted in a failure to reject the null hypothesis are Type II errors because the null hypothesis was set up to be false in this exercise. A Type II error occurs when the researcher fails to reject a false null hypothesis.

CHAPTER 13

CHI SQUARE

Expectations Versus Observations

THE CHI-SQUARE TEST FOR GOODNESS OF FIT

Chi-square tests are conducted when the variables of interest are measured on a **nominal** scale. Examples of such variables, also termed **categorical variables**, include *gender, political party affiliation, ethnicity, religious preference, diagnostic category, favorite color*, and so forth. There are two chi-square tests. In this set of exercises we will use the **chi-square test for goodness of fit** to test the null hypothesis that the frequency distributions of the values of *a single* nominal variable in two populations are the same. The research hypothesis states that the distributions of frequencies in the two populations are not the same.

EXERCISE 1

A large national of adult respondents, aged 25 to 65, were asked whether they preferred coffee, tea, soft drinks, or some other caffeinated beverage. The results are displayed in the table on the left. A survey of the preferences of 1,000 college students yielded the observed frequencies (f_o) displayed in the table on the right. Use the **.01** level of significance to test the null hypothesis that the two frequency distributions are from identical populations.

Adult Sample		Sample of College Students	
Beverage Preference	Percent	Beverage Preference	f_o
Coffee	40	Coffee	320
Tea	25	Tea	190
Soft drinks	30	Soft drinks	485
Other	5	Other	5
Total	100	Total	1000

- Launch SPSS and select **Type in data** from the opening "What would you like to do" menu options. Click the **Variable View** tab to access the

Variable View window. In the **Name** column, type **Bev_pref** as the name of the category variable and **Observed_Freq1** as the name of the observed frequencies variable. Both variables should be **Numeric** with **Decimals** set to **0**.

- Click in the first cell under **Values** to produce a gray box on the right side of the cell. Click on the gray box to access the **Value Labels** dialog window. Enter "1" in the **Value:** field, then **Tab** into the **Label:** field, type "Coffee," and either click the **Add** button or press the **Enter** key to complete the entry.

Click the **Add** button to move the **Value:** and the **Label:** into the list field at the bottom of the window.

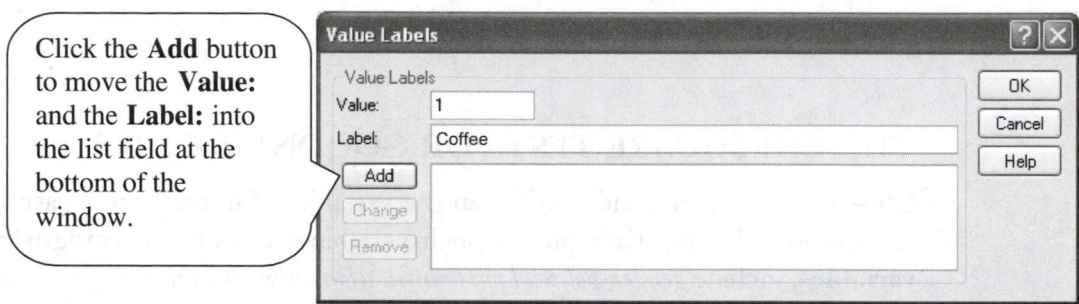

- Use "2," "3," and "4" as the values for "Tea," "Soft drinks," and "Other," respectively. There are two options to correct entry errors. Clicking on an incorrect entry will cause the **Value:** and **Label:** to be displayed in the Value Labels fields. The first option is to click on the **Remove** button to erase the entry; the second is to edit the entry by typing a new Value: or Label: and clicking the **Change** button. When the **Value Labels** dialog window looks like the one below, click **OK** to return to the **Variable View** window.

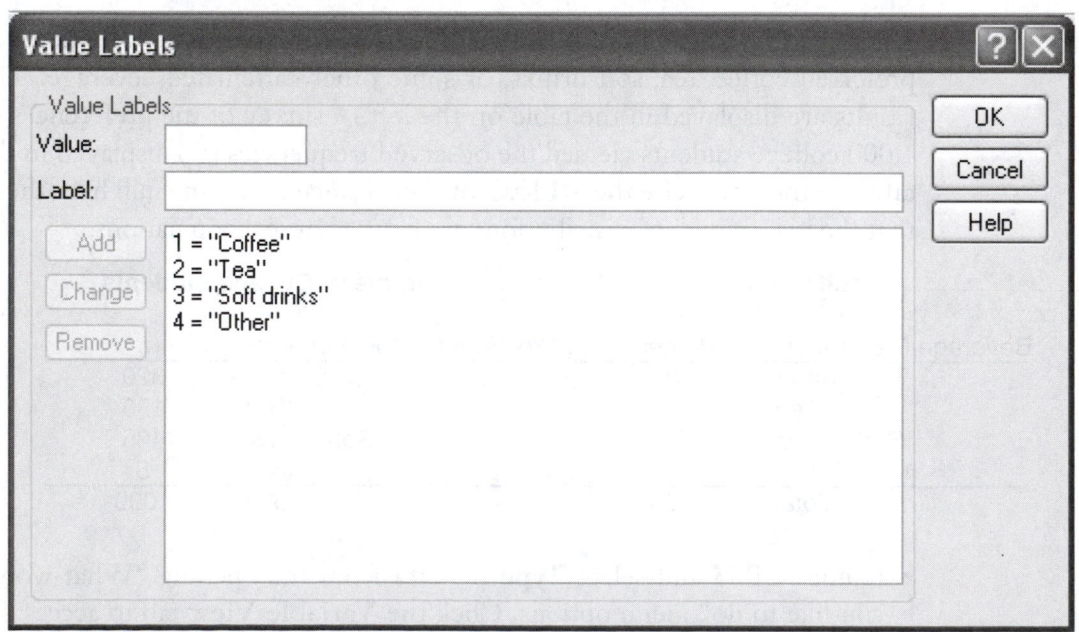

The Variable View window should look like this.

	Name	Type	Width	Decimals	Label	Values	Missing	Columns	Align	Measure
1	Bev_pref	Numeric	8	0		{1, Coffee}...	None	11	Right	Nominal
2	Observed_Freq1	Numeric	8	0		None	None	11	Right	Scale

- Select the **Data View** tab to access the **Data Editor** window. Enter the label values (**1**, **2**, **3**, and **4**) under **Bev_pref.** and enter the observed frequencies for the sample of college students (under f_O in the table on p. 13-1) in the **Observed_Freq1** column.

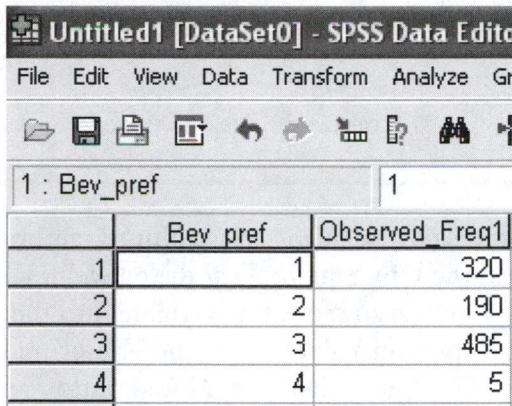

- From the **Data** menu, select **Weight Cases...** to access the **Weight Cases** dialog window.

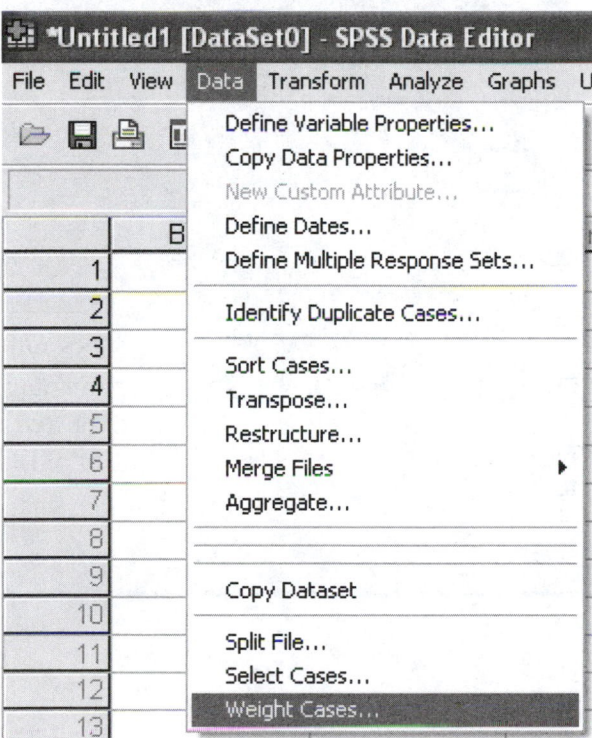

- Select the **Weight cases by** radio button and click the ▸ button to move **Observed_Freq1** into the **Frequency Variable:** field. Click **OK** to return to the **Data Editor** window.

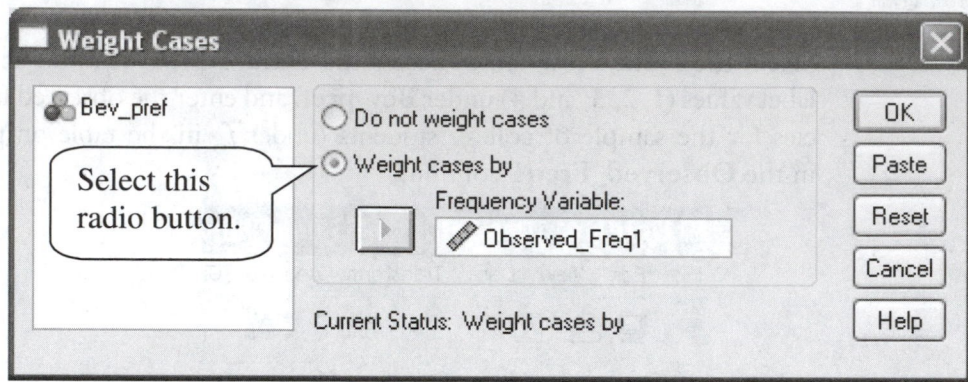

- From the **Analyze** menu, select **Nonparametric Tests ▶ Chi-Square...** to access the **Chi-Square Test** dialog window. Select **Bev_pref** and click the ▸ button to move this variable into the **Test Variable List:** field. Under **Expected Values** select the **Values:** radio button. Enter **40** in the field to the right of the **Value:** radio button and click the **Add** button to complete the entry. (SPSS will convert the percentages into relative frequencies.)

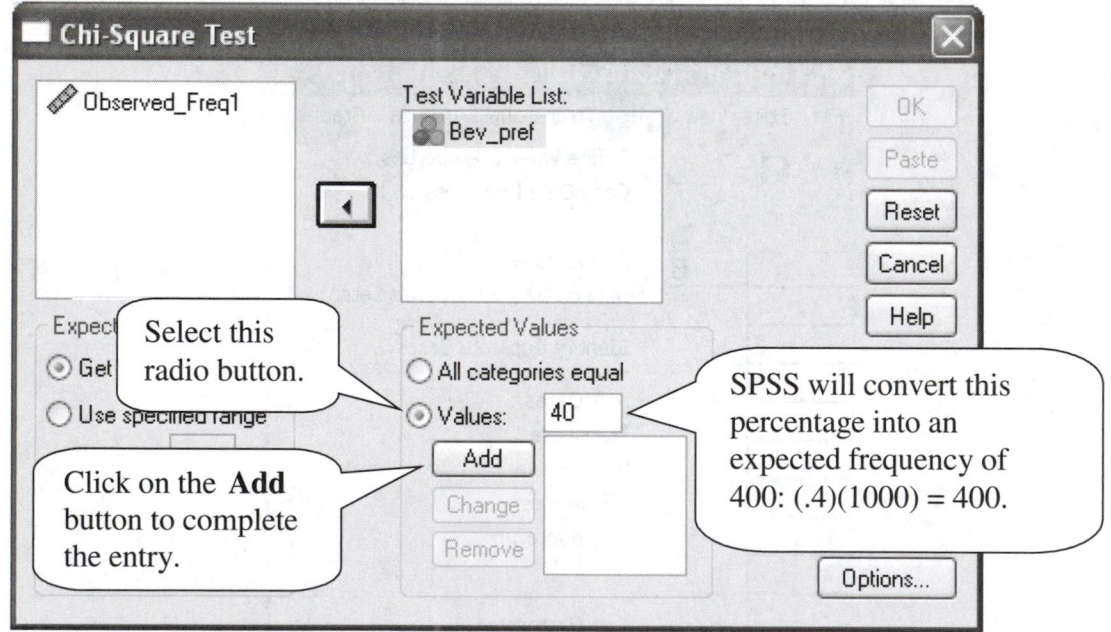

When all of the expected values have been entered, the **Expected Values** section of the dialog window should look like this:

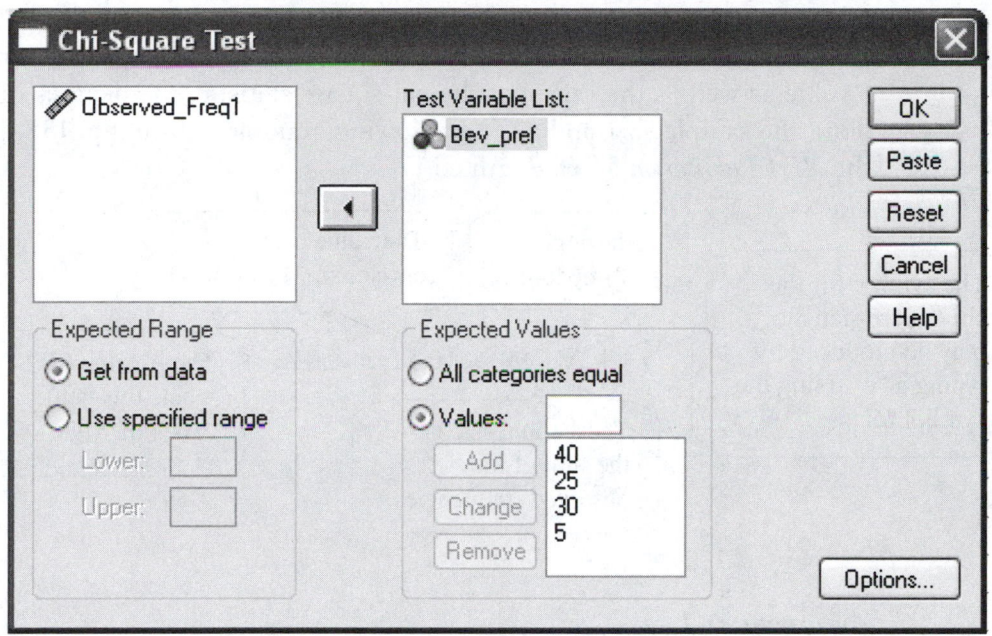

- Click **OK** to produce the two chi-square output tables.

Bev_pref

	Observed N	Expected N	Residual
1	320	400.0	-80.0
2	190	250.0	-60.0
3	485	300.0	185.0
4	5	50.0	-45.0
Total	1000		

The value of Total is the sample size N.

Each residual is the difference between the observed and expected frequency.

Test Statistics

	Bev_pref
Chi-Square [a]	184.983
df	3
Asymp. Sig.	.000

a. 0 cells (.0%) have expe
   5. The minimum expecte

The magnitude of the chi-square statistic is proportional to the differences between the observed and expected frequencies listed in the Residual column in the table above.

The p value is the probability of observing a chi-square statistic at least as large as the one observed (184.983) if the null hypothesis is true. If the p value is less than the significance criterion, then the null hypothesis is assumed to be false and rejected accordingly. SPSS reports p values less than .0005 as ".000."

PRESENTING THE RESULTS OF A CHI-SQUARE ANALYSIS, APA-STYLE

The APA editorial style requires that a report of the results of a chi-square analysis include the symbols for the chi-square statistic, sample size, and the p value as well as the values of the chi-square statistic, the degrees of freedom, the sample size, and p. The following example is from pp. 138–139 of the *APA Publication Manual* (5th ed.):

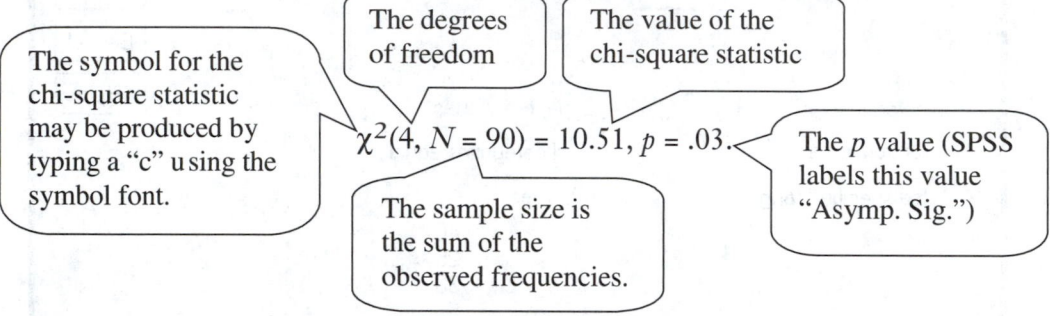

The symbol for the chi-square statistic may be produced by typing a "c" using the symbol font.

The degrees of freedom

The value of the chi-square statistic

$$\chi^2(4, N = 90) = 10.51, p = .03.$$

The sample size is the sum of the observed frequencies.

The p value (SPSS labels this value "Asymp. Sig.")

Assignment 1

1. Use the editorial style of the APA to describe the result of the chi-square analysis. Be sure to include all the elements in the example above and state whether the result does or does not support the research hypothesis.

EXERCISE 2

In a brand-blind preference test, 135 participants were asked to select a preferred laundry detergent after using four of the market-leading brands for a 1-week trial period. The results, expressed as the number of participants favoring each of the four brands, are displayed below. Use the .05 level of significance to test the null hypothesis that the four brands are equally preferred in the population.

Brand	f_o
A	46
B	31
C	27
D	31

- Go to the **Variable View** window and enter **Brand_pref** as the name of the category variable and **Observed_Freq2** as the name of the observed frequencies variable. Both variables should be **Numeric** with **Decimals** set to **0**.

- Access the **Value Labels** dialog window and enter the labels displayed in the table on p. 13-6 (i.e., 1 = Brand A, 2 = Brand B, etc.). After entering the values and labels, click **OK** to return to the **Variable View** window.

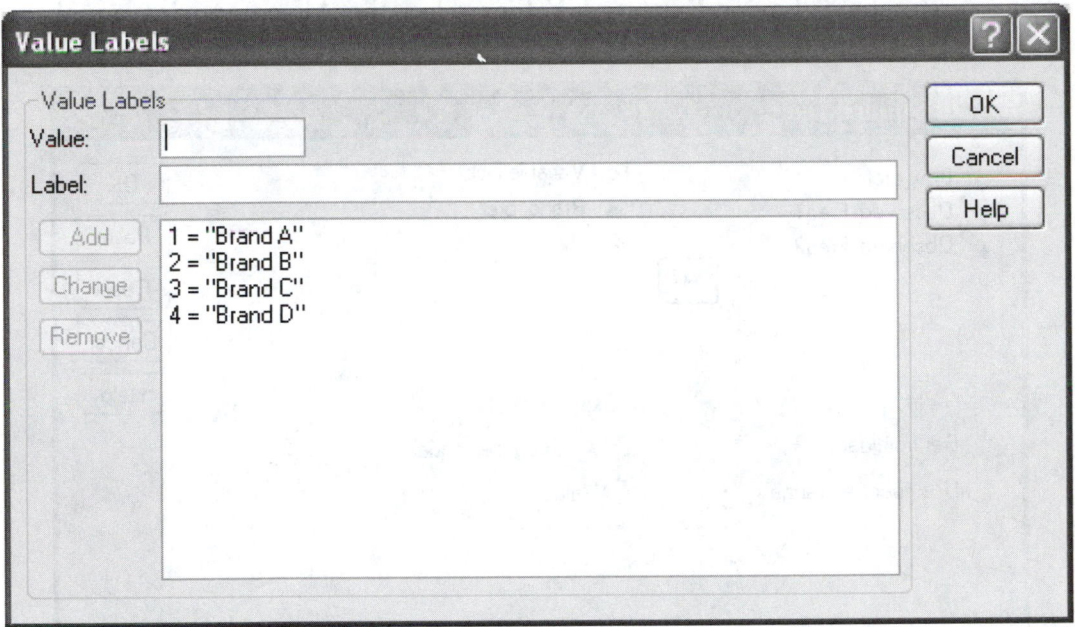

- Go to the **Data Editor** window and enter the label values (**1, 2, 3**, and **4**) under **Brand_pref**, then enter the observed frequencies for the sample of participants (under f_o in the table on p. 13-6) in the **Observed_Freq2** column.

- From the **Data** menu, select **Weight Cases...** to access the **Weight Cases** dialog window. Select the **Weight cases by** radio button and move **Observed_Freq2** into the **Frequency Variable:** field. Click **OK** to return to the **Data Editor** window.

- From the **Analyze** menu, select **Nonparametric Tests ▶ Chi-Square...** to access the **Chi-Square Test** dialog window. Select **Brand_pref** and click the ▶ button to move this variable into the **Test Variable List:** field. Under **Expected Values** select the **All categories equal:** radio button.

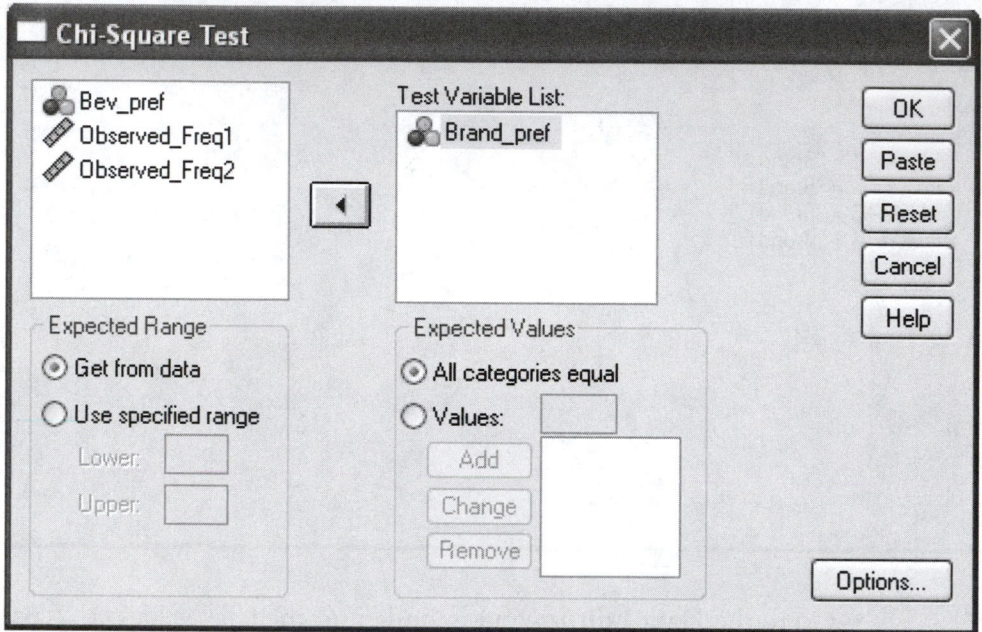

- Click **OK** to produce the SPSS output tables.

Assignment

2. Use the editorial style of the APA to describe the results of the chi-square analysis. Be sure to include all the elements in the example on p. 13-6 and state whether the result does or does not support the research hypothesis.

EXERCISE 3

The faculty handbook at a small liberal arts college advises faculty to teach their courses at a level of difficulty that produces the following symmetrical grade distribution: A's (10%), B's (20%), C's (40%), D's (20%), and F's (10%). The midterm grade distribution for Dr. Smith's most difficult course (enrollment of 50 students) is as follows: A's (20%), B's (40%), C's (32%), D's (6%), F's (2%). Use the .05 level of significance to test the null hypothesis that Dr. Smith's grade distribution does not differ from the distribution described in the faculty handbook.

Follow the steps in Exercise 1 to produce the SPSS output tables. These are summarized as follows:

- Go to the **Variable View** window and enter the **Grade** as the name of the category variable and **Observed_Freq3** as the name of the observed frequencies variable. Both variables should be **Numeric** with **Decimals** set to **0**.

- Access the **Value Labels** dialog window and enter the labels displayed in the table (i.e., 1 = A, 2 = B, etc.). After entering the values and labels, click **OK** to return to the **Variable View** window.

- Go to the **Data Editor** window and enter the label values (**1, 2, 3, 4,** and **5**) under **Grade**. Convert the percentages for the 50 students to frequencies (i.e., multiply each proportion by 50) and enter these in the **Observed_Freq3** column.

- From the **Data** menu, select **Weight Cases...** to access the **Weight Cases** dialog window. Select the **Weight cases by** radio button and move **Observed_Freq3** into the **Frequency Variable:** field. Click **OK** to return to the **Data Editor** window.

- From the **Analyze** menu, select **Nonparametric Tests** ▶ **Chi-Square...** to access the **Chi-Square Test** dialog window. Select **Grade** and click the ▶ button to move this variable into the **Test Variable List:** field. Under **Expected Values** select the **Values:** radio button. Enter the recommended grade distribution percentages (**10, 20, 40, 20,** and **10**) in the field to the right of the **Value:** radio button and click the **Add** button to complete each entry. (SPSS will convert the percentages into relative frequencies.)

- Click **OK** to produce the SPSS output tables.

Assignment3

3. Use the editorial style of the APA to describe the results of the chi-square analysis. Be sure to include all of the elements in the example on p. 13-6 and state whether the result does or does not support the research hypothesis.

CHI-SQUARE TEST FOR INDEPENDENCE

In this set of exercises we will conduct a **chi-square test for independence** to test a null hypothesis which states that two nominal variables are independent (unrelated) in the population.

The data for this exercise are based on results reported by Loftus and Palmer (1974). Participants in their study watched a brief film of a multi-car accident before completing a questionnaire about the film. The manipulated variable was the phrasing of a question that asked each participant to estimate the speed of the cars when they "hit" vs. "smashed into" each other. Fifty participants were assigned to each experimental condition, and 50 were assigned to a control condition that did not include this question. One week later participants from all three groups were invited back to the laboratory to complete a second questionnaire that included the question, "Did you see any broken glass?"

Launch SPSS, and select the **Type in data** option. Navigate to the data CD and load the file **Memory Reconstruction Data.** The values of the variable **Verb_condition** are as follows: 1 = *smashed*, 2 = *hit*, and 3 = *control*. The values of the **Response** variable are responses to the question, "Did you see any broken glass?" (1 = yes, 2 = no).

- From the **Analyze** menu, select **Descriptive Statistics ▶ Crosstabs…**

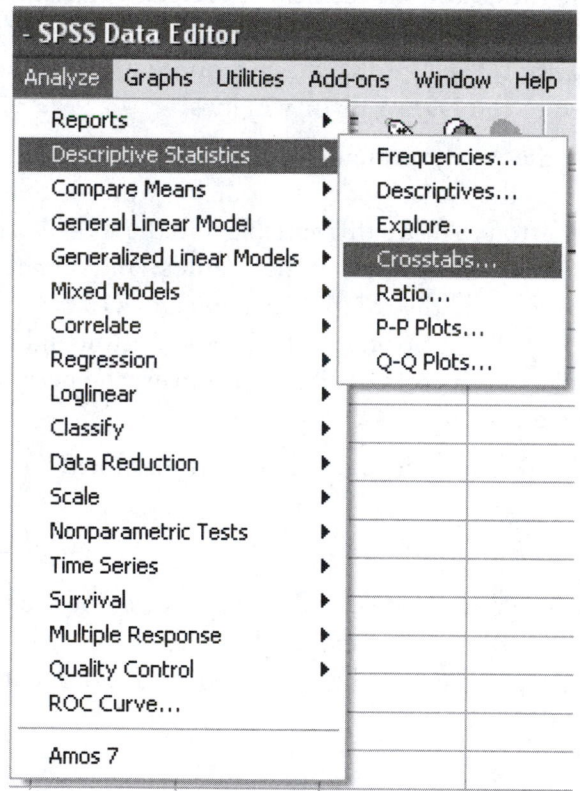

- When the **Crosstabs** dialog window appears, select **Response** and move this variable into the **Row(s):** field, then select **Verb-condition** and move this variable in the **Column(s):** field.

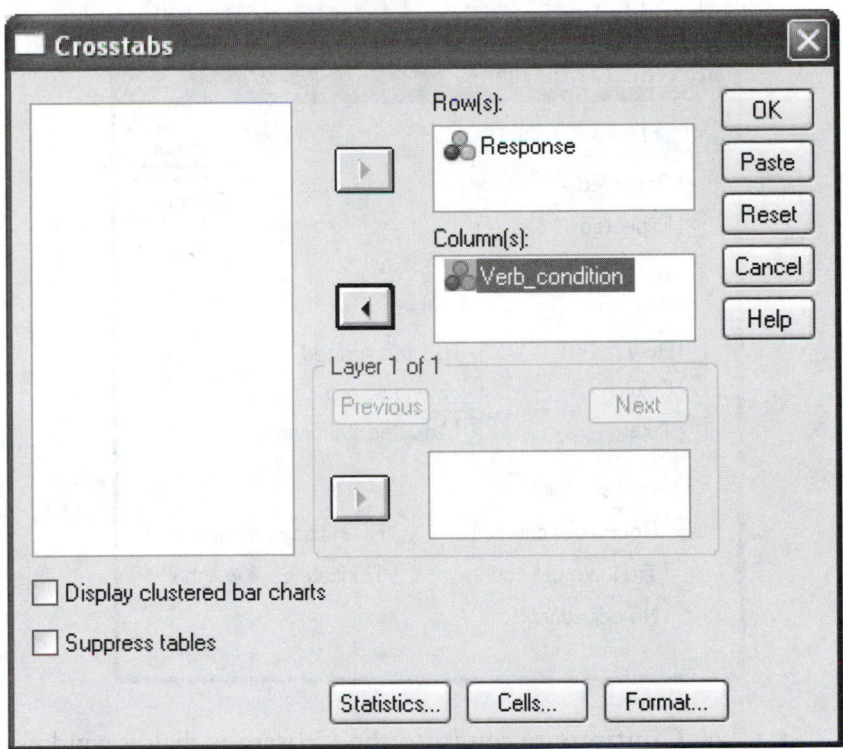

- Click on the **Statistics...** button to produce the **Crosstabs: Statistics** dialog window. Select **Chi-square** and **Phi and Cramér's V**, then click **Continue** to return to the **Crosstabs** dialog window.

- Now click on the **Cells...** button to produce the **Crosstabs: Cell Display** window. Select the **Observed** and **Expected** options under **Counts,** as well as the **Row** and **Column** options under **Percentages.** The window displayed below is a truncated version of the full window.

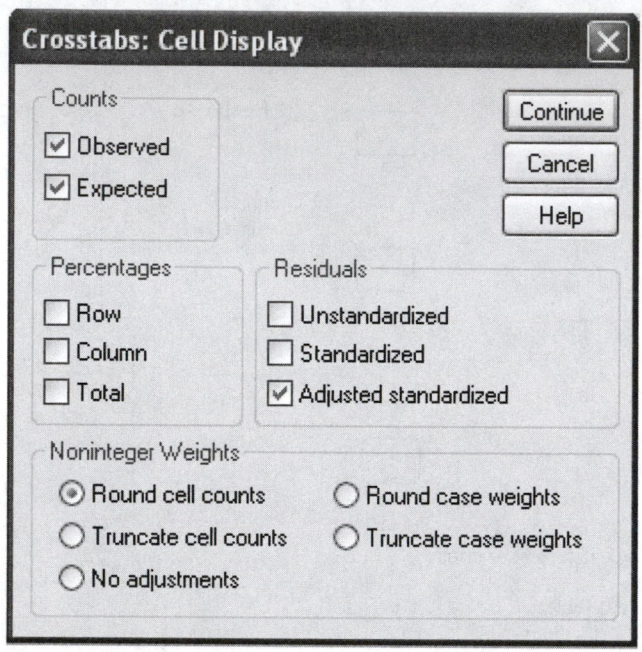

- Click **Continue** to return to the **Crosstabs** dialog window, then **OK** to produce the output.

The **Case Processing Summary** table includes information about sample size (N) and missing data. A second table, labeled **Response * Verb_condition Crosstabulation**, is better known as a **2 × 3 contingency table.** This table lists the **observed** (labeled **Count**) and **expected** (**Expected Count**) **frequencies,** as well as the **adjusted standardized residuals** for each cell of the table.

PRESENTING THE RESULTS OF THE HYPOTHESIS TEST, APA STYLE

The following table, labeled **Chi-Square Tests**, lists three statistics and their associated p values. The test that is most commonly used is the **Pearson Chi-Square**, named for its inventor, Karl Pearson.

Chi-Square Tests

	Value	df	Asymp. Sig. (2-sided)
Pearson Chi-Square	7.780[a]	2	.020
Likelihood Ratio	7.430	2	.024
Linear-by-Linear Association	6.369	1	.012
N of Valid Cases	150		

a. 0 cells (.0%) have expected count less than 5. The minimum expected count is 9.67.

The value of the chi-square statistic is **7.780**. The p value (**.020**) is the probability of observing a chi-square statistic this extreme under the assumption that the null hypothesis is true. Degrees of freedom for the chi-square test for independence are determined by computing the product of (the number of rows − 1) and (the number of columns − 1). For this example, **df = (3 − 1) (2 − 1) = 2(1) = 2**.

Loftus and Palmer (1974) described the result as follows:

> An independence chi-square test on these responses was significant beyond the .025 level, $\chi^2(2) = 7.76$. The important result ... is that the probability of saying "yes," $P(Y)$, to the question about broken glass is .32 when the verb *smashed* is used, and .14 with *hit*. Thus *smashed* leads both to more "yes" responses and to higher speed estimates. (p. 587)

Assignment

4. Review the example of reporting the results of a chi-square analysis on p. 13-6, and edit the paragraph from the report by Loftus and Palmer (1974) to conform to current APA guidelines.

5. Look at the footnote in the above output table labeled **Chi–Square Tests**. Following Lewis and Burke (1949), the majority of statisticians have advised that the results of a chi-square test for independence are valid to the extent that each of the expected frequencies in a chi-square contingency table is at least 5. However, in a more recent review of the literature, Delucchi (1983) concluded that very low expected frequencies for each cell could be tolerated (that is, would not inflate the Type I error

rate) as long as the total number of participants was at least 5 times the number of cells in the contingency table.

Based on this more recent guideline, are the results of this chi-square analysis valid? Defend your answer.

6. Review the discussion (pp. 603–604 in the text) pertaining to **adjusted standardized residuals**. Identify the cells in the contingency table whose observed frequencies are different from their expected frequencies.

7. What is the **effect size** for this study? Use the table below (from p. 599 in the text) to label the effect size.

TABLE 13-10.   CONVENTIONS FOR DETERMINING EFFECT SIZE BASED ON CRAMER'S V

Jacob Cohen (1992) developed guidelines to determine whether particular effect sizes should be considered small, medium, or large. The effect-size guidelines vary depending on the size of the contingency table. There are different guidelines based on whether the smaller of the two degrees of freedom (row or column) is 1, 2, or 3.

EFFECT SIZE	WHEN $df_{ROW/COLUMN} = 1$	WHEN $df_{ROW/COLUMN} = 2$	WHEN $df_{ROW/COLUMN} = 3$
Small	0.10	0.07	0.06
Medium	0.30	0.21	0.17
Large	0.50	0.35	0.29

ANSWERS

CHI-SQUARE TEST FOR GOODNESS OF FIT

1. The research hypothesis is supported. In the population of college students like those observed in this sample, the distribution of preferences for caffeinated beverages is different from the distribution of preferences in the adult population, $\chi^2(3, N = 1000) = 184.983$, $p < .0005$.

2. There is no evidence from this study to support the hypothesis that one brand of laundry detergent is preferred over another, $\chi^2(3, N = 135) = 6.244$, $p = .100$.

Test Statistics

	Brand_pref
Chi-Square [a]	6.244
df	3
Asymp. Sig.	.100

a. 0 cells (.0%) have expected frequencies less than 5. The minimum expected cell frequency is 33.8.

3. The research hypothesis is supported: The distribution of grades in Dr. Smith's class is almost certainly different from the distribution of grades recommended in the faculty handbook, $\chi^2(4, N = 50) = 23.9$, $p < .0005$.

Test Statistics

	Grade
Chi-Square [a]	23.900
df	4
Asymp. Sig.	.000

a. 0 cells (.0%) have expected frequencies less than 5. The minimum expected cell frequency is 5.0.

CHI-SQUARE TEST FOR INDEPENDENCE

4. Compared to participants who were not asked to estimate the speed of the cars in the accident and those who read a question that included the verb *hit*, participants who read the word *smashed* were more than twice as likely to recall seeing broken glass in the scene, $\chi^2(2, N = 150) = 7.78$, $p = .020$.

5. There were 150 participants in the study, and this number is greater than 5 times the number of cells ($5 \times 6 = 30$). According to this criterion, the results of this chi-square analysis are valid.

6. The absolute values of the adjusted standardized residuals in the cells that correspond to the *smashed* condition (Verb_condition = 1) exceed 2.5. According to criteria discussed in the text, the observed frequencies for these cells are different from the expected frequencies.

Response * Verb_condition Crosstabulation

			Verb_condition			
			1	2	3	Total
Response	1	Count	16	7	6	29
		Expected Count	9.7	9.7	9.7	29.0
		Adjusted Residual	2.8	-1.2	-1.6	
	2	Count	34	43	44	121
		Expected Count	40.3	40.3	40.3	121.0
		Adjusted Residual	-2.8	1.2	1.6	
Total		Count	50	50	50	150
		Expected Count	50.0	50.0	50.0	150.0

7. The effect size is .228. According to Cohen's criteria, this is between a small and a medium effect size.

CHAPTER 14

BEYOND CHI SQUARE

Nonparametric Tests with Ordinal Data

As discussed in the text, nonparametric analyses are used primarily under two conditions: (1) when the data are measured on an ordinal scale, and (2) when "the underlying population distribution is greatly skewed, a situation that often develops when we have a small sample size" (p. 622 in the text). You were introduced to the most commonly used nonparametric tests in the previous chapter: the chi-square tests for goodness of fit and independence. In this set of exercises, we will use SPSS to compute three alternatives to the parametric statistics described in Chapters 5 and 9. First, we will compute Spearman's rho, the nonparametric alternative to the Pearson correlation described in Chapter 5. Then we will use SPSS to compute the Wilcoxon signed ranks statistic as a nonparametric alternative to the paired-samples t test introduced in Chapter 9. Finally, we will compute the Mann-Whitney U statistic as a nonparametric alternative to the independent-samples t tests that were also introduced in Chapter 9.

EXERCISE 1
COMPUTING THE SPEARMAN RANK-ORDER CORRELATION COEFFICIENT

- Launch SPSS. If you have not disabled the opening window, select **Type in data**, click the **OK** button, and click on the **Variable View** tab to access the **Variable View** window.

- Type **Country** as the name of the first variable. Click in the cell under **Type**, then click on the gray box to access the **Variable Type** dialog window. In the Variable Type window, click on the radio button next to **String**. The default setting for the **Width** of the variable name is **8** characters. There are 13 characters in "United States," so change the number of **Characters:** in the string variable to **15** as shown.

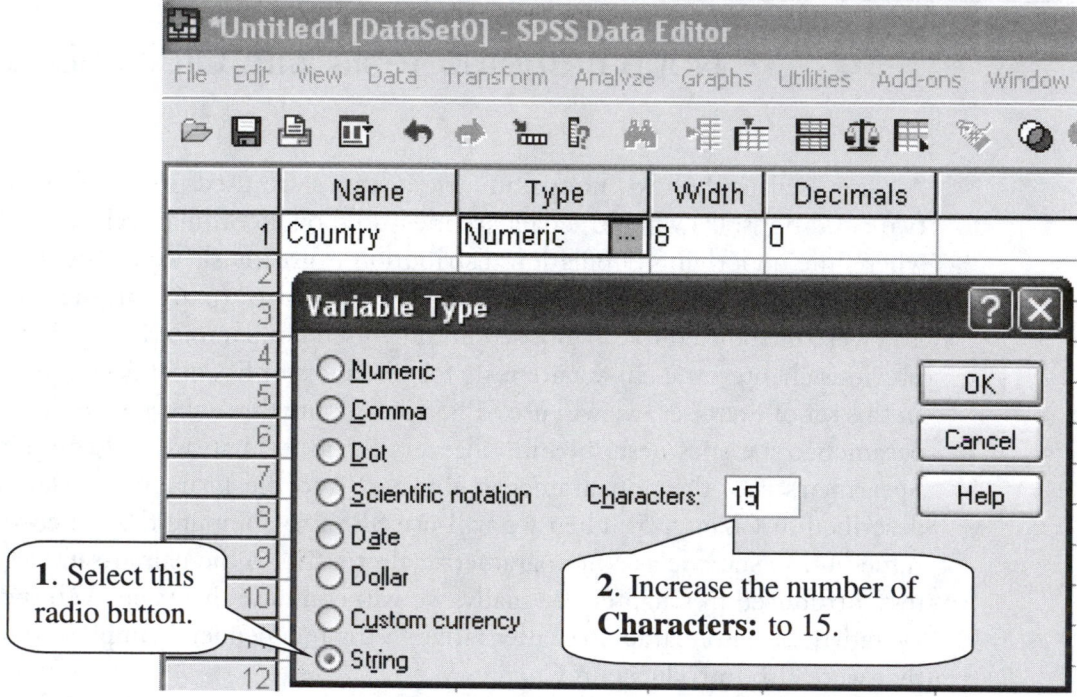

- Click the **OK** button to return to the **Variable View** window.

- Enter **Pride_Score** and **Compet_Rank** as shown.

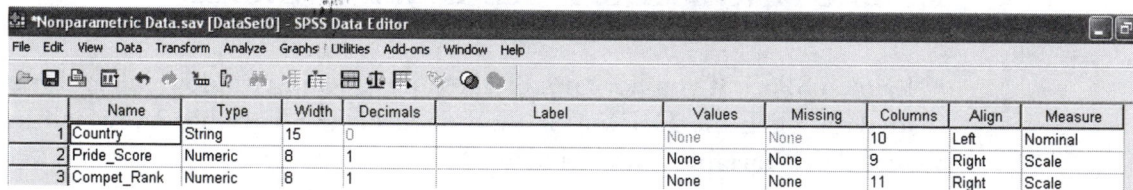

	Name	Type	Width	Decimals	Label	Values	Missing	Columns	Align	Measure
1	Country	String	15	0		None	None	10	Left	Nominal
2	Pride_Score	Numeric	8	1		None	None	9	Right	Scale
3	Compet_Rank	Numeric	8	1		None	None	11	Right	Scale

- Enter the following data into the **Data Editor**.

COUNTRY	PRIDE SCORE	COMPETITIVENESS RANK
United States	4.0	1
South Africa	2.7	10
Austria	2.4	2
Canada	2.4	3
Chile	2.3	5
Japan	1.8	7
Hungary	1.6	8
France	1.5	6
Norway	1.3	4
Slovenia	1.1	9

- When you are finished, the **Data View** window should look like the one below.

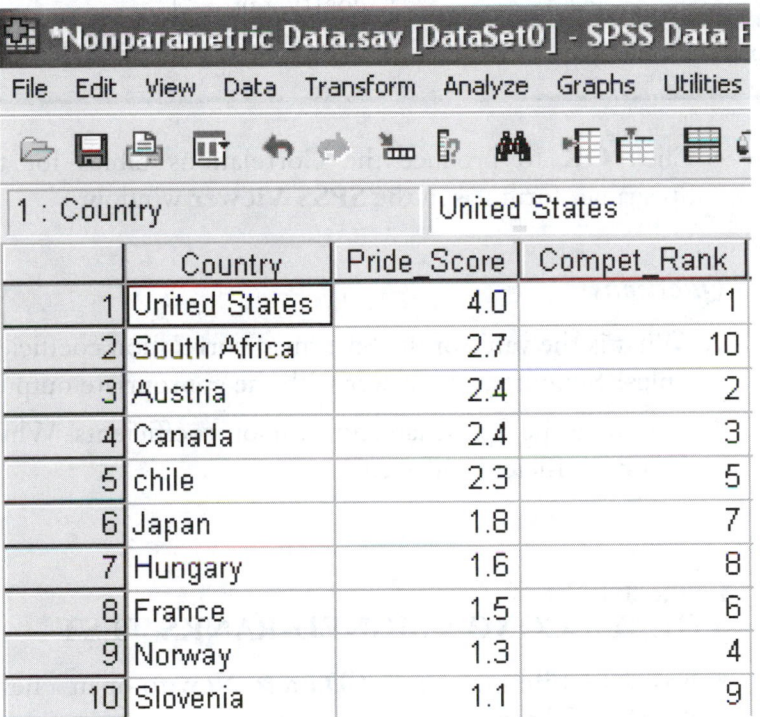

- From the **Analyze** menu select **Correlate ▶ Bivariate...** to produce the **Bivariate Correlations** dialog window. Click on the box next to **Spearman**, then move the variables, **Pride_Score** and **Compet_Rank**, into the **Variables:** field. (It is not necessary to convert the values of Pride_Score to ranks. SPSS will do this for us.)

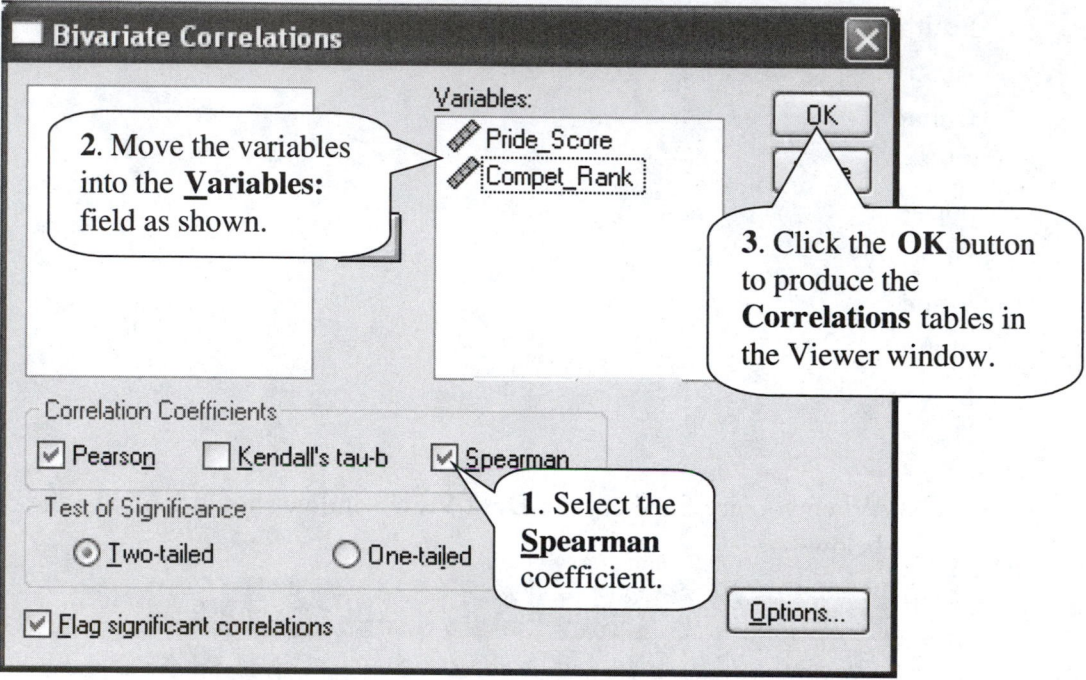

- Click **OK** to produce the Correlations tables for the Pearson and Spearman formulas in the **SPSS Viewer** window.

Questions

1. What is the value of the Spearman correlation coefficient for these variables? Support your answer with the appropriate output table.

2. Compare the Spearman and Pearson coefficients. Why are these correlation coefficients different?

EXERCISE 2
THE WILCOXON SIGNED-RANKS TEST

- From the **File** menu, select **Data ▶ New** to open a new data window in the Data Editor.

- Go to the **Variable View** window and enter the variables as follows:

	Name	Type	Width	Decimals	Label	Values	Missing	Columns	Align	Measure
1	Country	String	15	0		None	None	10	Left	Nominal
2	Period_1	Numeric	8	2	1995-1996	None	None	8	Right	Scale
3	Period_2	Numeric	8	2	2003-2004	None	None	8	Right	Scale

- Go to the **Data View** window and enter the data from the table:

COUNTRY	1995–1996	2003–2004
United States	3.11	4.00
Australia	2.10	2.90
Ireland	3.36	2.90
New Zealand	2.62	2.60
Canada	2.56	2.40
Great Britain	2.09	2.20

- After completing the data entry, the **Data Editor** should look similar to this:

	Country	Period_1	Period_2
1	United States	3.11	4.00
2	Australia	2.10	2.90
3	Ireland	3.36	2.90
4	New Zealand	2.62	2.60
5	Canada	2.56	2.40
6	Great Britain	2.09	2.20

It is not necessary to convert these interval measures to ranks. SPSS will compute the difference between each pair of variable values, rank the differences from smallest to largest, and assign a rank of 1 to the smallest difference, 2 to the next-smallest difference, etc.

From the **Analyze** menu, select **Nonparametric Tests** ▶ **2 Related Samples...**

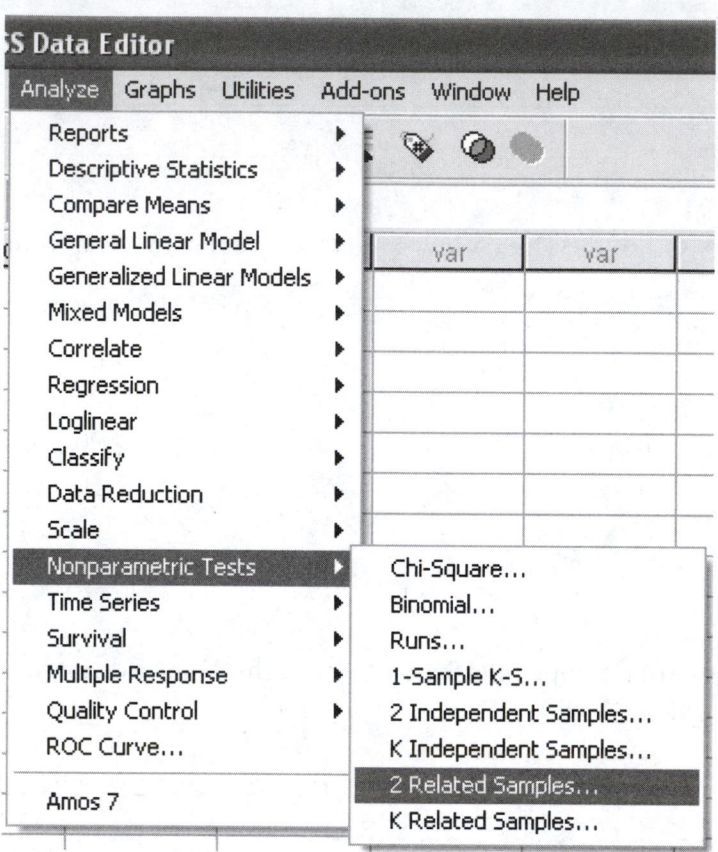

- In the **Two-Related-Samples Tests** dialog window, select **Period_1**, then hold down the Shift key or the Control (Ctrl) key while you select **Period_2**. Both variables should now appear under **Current Selections** in the lower left corner of the window.

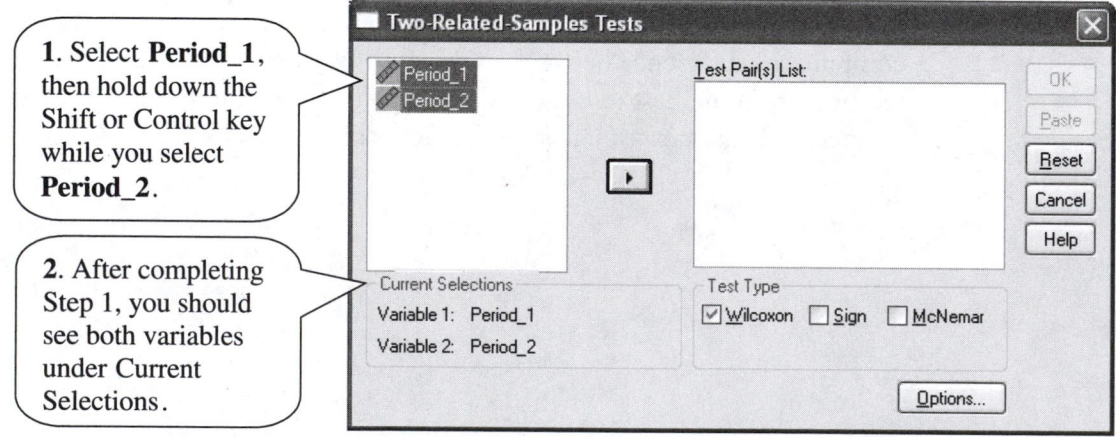

1. Select **Period_1**, then hold down the Shift or Control key while you select **Period_2**.

2. After completing Step 1, you should see both variables under Current Selections.

- Click the ▸ button to move the pair of variables into the **Test Pair(s) List:** field. Locate the Test Type section of the window and make sure that the box next to **Wilcoxon** is checked.

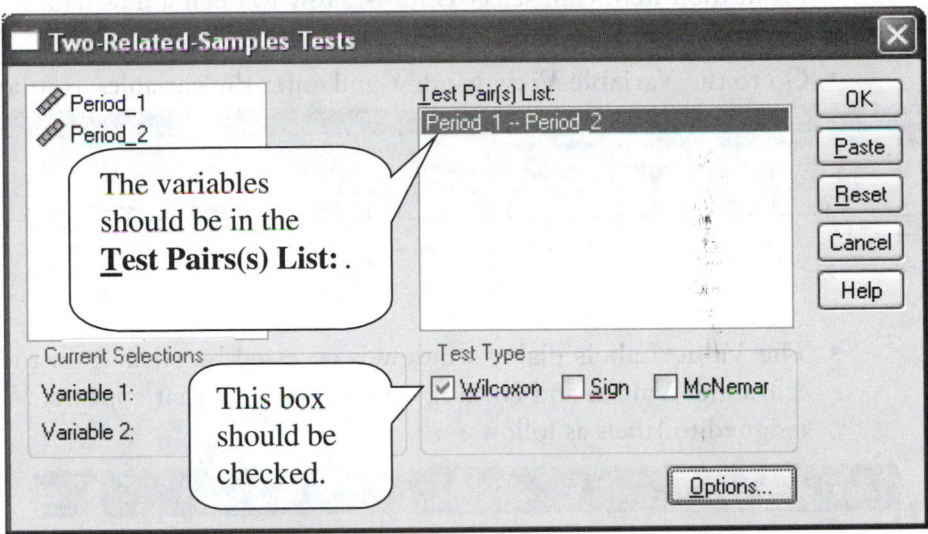

- Click the **OK** button to generate the two output tables.

Ranks

		N	Mean Rank	Sum of Ranks
Period_2 - Period_1	Negative Ranks	3[a]	2.67	8.00
	Positive Ranks	3[b]	4.33	13.00
	Ties	0[c]		
	Total	6		

a. Period_2 < Period_1
b. Period_2 > Period_1
c. Period_2 = Period_1

The result of a Wilcoxon signed ranks test is traditionally reported using T as the symbol for the Wilcoxon statistic. T is the smallest of the two sums of difference ranks.

Test Statistics[b]

	Period_2 - Period_1
Z	-.524[a]
Asymp. Sig. (2-tailed)	.600

a. Based on negative ranks.
b. Wilcoxon Signed Ranks Test

z is related to T by the formula,

$$z = \frac{T - \dfrac{N(N+1)}{4}}{\sqrt{\dfrac{N(N+1)(2N+1)}{24}}}$$

The denominator of the formula is adjusted for tied ranks.

The two-tailed p value is the probability of observing a z statistic as extreme as -.524 in either tail if the null hypothesis is true. The distribution of this z statistic is approximately normal as long as $N(N+1)/2 > 20$. In this example, $N = 6$, so $6(7)/2 = 42/2 = 21$.

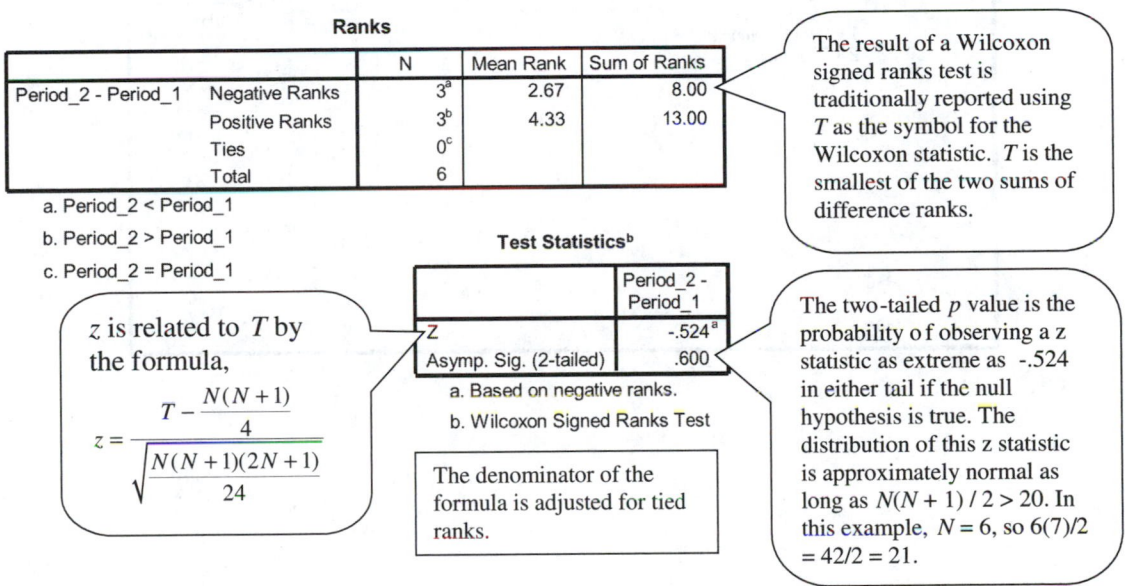

Question

3. Are the accomplishment-related national pride rankings different in the two periods? Explain your answer.

Exercise 3
THE MANN-WHITNEY *U* TEST

- From the **File** menu, select **Data ▶ New** to open a new data window in the **Data Editor**.

- Go to the **Variable View** window and enter the variables as follows:

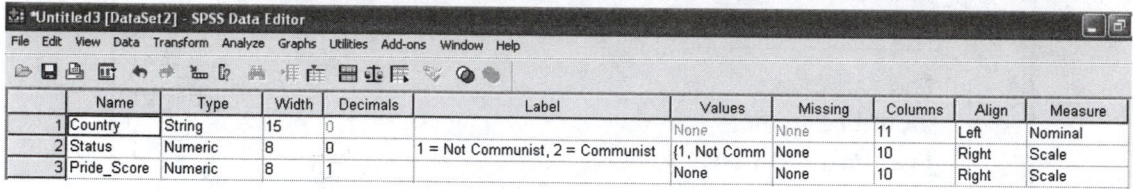

	Name	Type	Width	Decimals	Label	Values	Missing	Columns	Align	Measure
1	Country	String	15	0		None	None	11	Left	Nominal
2	Status	Numeric	8	0	1 = Not Communist, 2 = Communist	{1, Not Comm	None	10	Right	Scale
3	Pride_Score	Numeric	8	1		None	None	10	Right	Scale

- The **Value Labels** dialog window is accessed by clicking in the second cell under **Values** and clicking on the gray box that appears. Values are assigned to labels as follows:

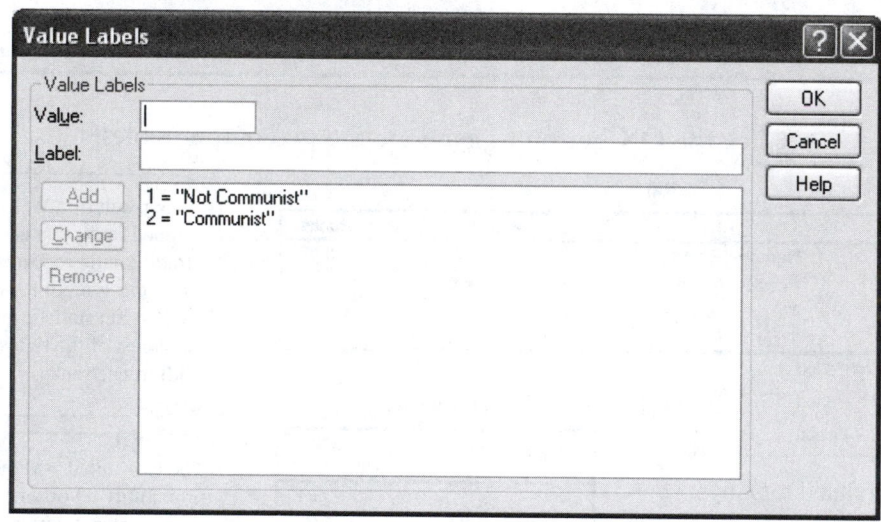

- Go to the **Data View** window and enter the data from the table:

COUNTRY	STATUS CODE	PRIDE SCORE
Not Communist		
Ireland	1	2.90
Austria	1	2.40
Spain	1	1.60
Portugal	1	1.60
Sweden	1	1.20
Communist		
Hungary	2	1.60
Czech Republic	2	1.30
Slovenia	2	1.10
Slovakia	2	1.10
Poland	2	0.90

- After completing the data entry, the Data Editor should look similar to this:

	Country	Status	Pride_Score
1	Ireland	1	2.9
2	Austria	1	2.4
3	Spain	1	1.6
4	Portugal	1	1.6
5	Sweden	1	1.2
6	Hungary	2	1.6
7	Czech Republic	2	1.3
8	Slovenia	2	1.1
9	Slovakia	2	1.1
10	Poland	2	.9

It is not necessary to convert the values of Pride_Score to ranks. SPSS will combine the values of Pride_Score for the two groups, rank the scores from smallest to largest, and compute the average rank for the two groups.

- From the **Analyze** menu, select **Nonparametric Tests** ▶ **2 Independent Samples...**

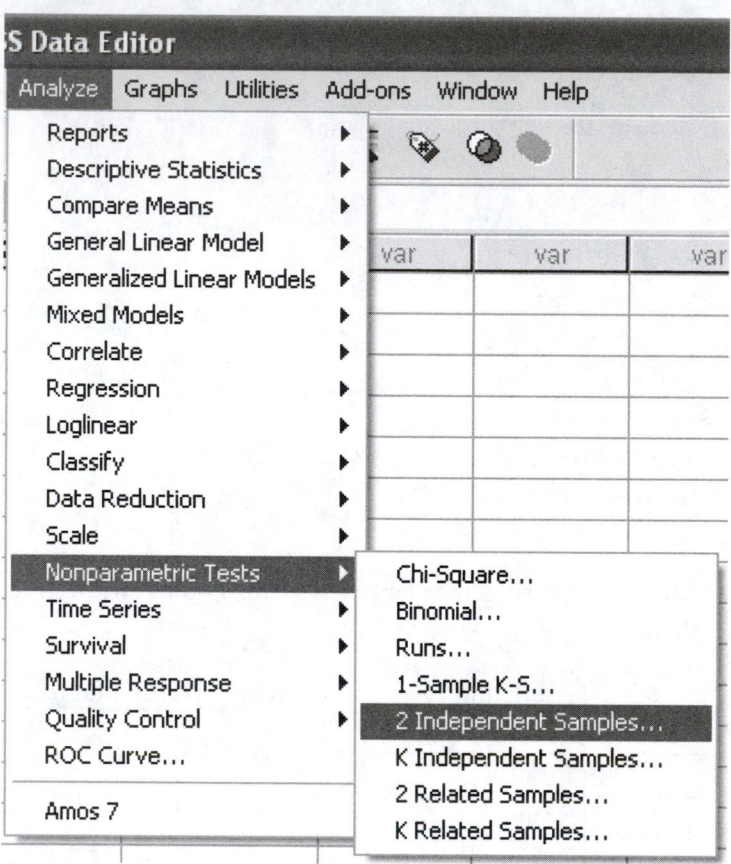

- In the **Two-Independent-Samples Tests** dialog window, select **Pride_Score** and move this variable into the **Test Variable List:** field. Select **Status** and move this variable into the **Grouping Variable:** field.

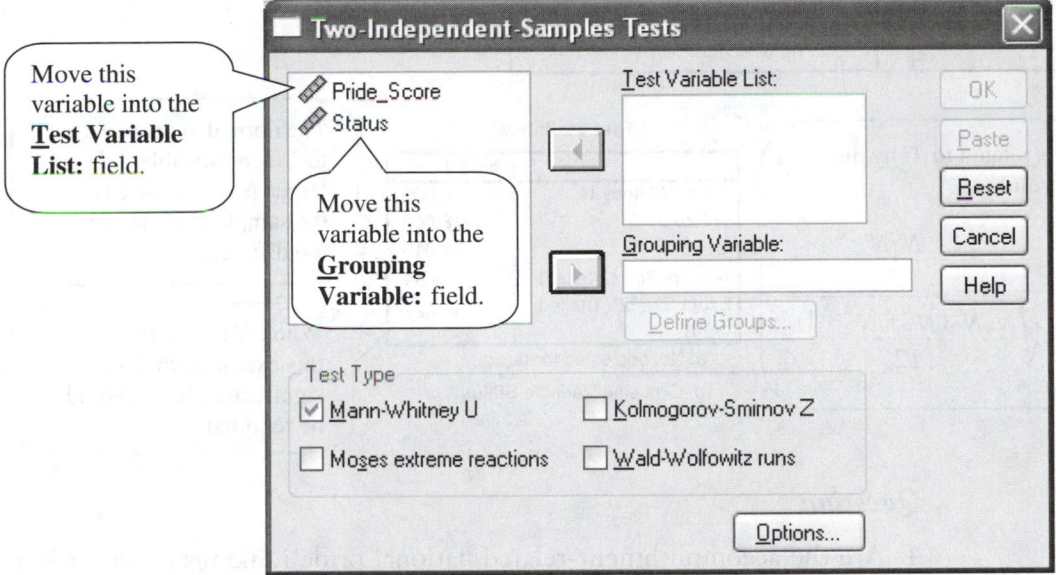

- Click on **Define Groups...** to access the **Two-Independent-Samples Tests: Define Groups** dialog window.

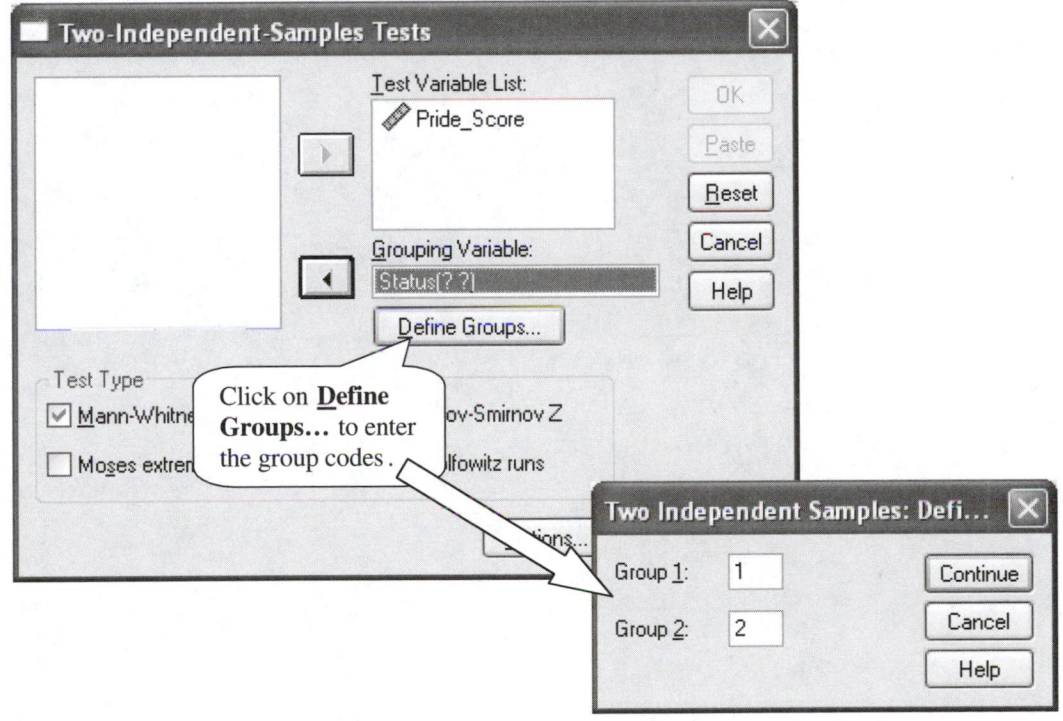

- Click the **OK** button to generate the two output tables.

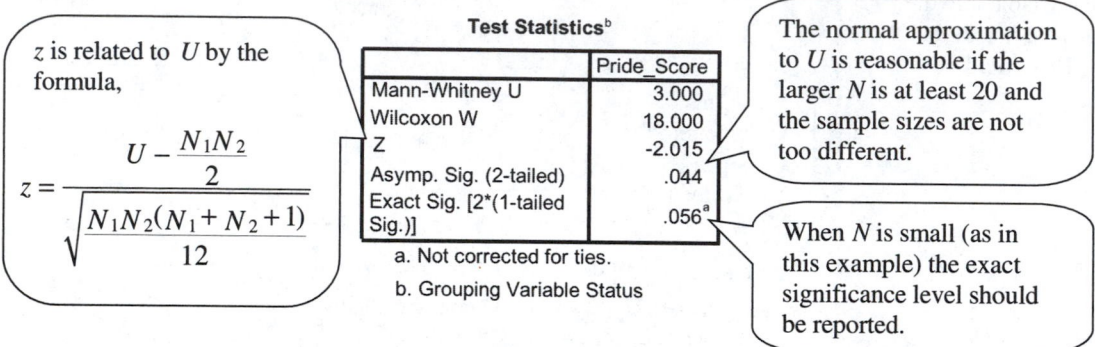

Ranks

	Status	N	Mean Rank	Sum of Ranks
Pride_Score	1	5	7.40	37.00
	2	5	3.60	18.00
	Total	10		

z is related to U by the formula,

$$z = \frac{U - \dfrac{N_1 N_2}{2}}{\sqrt{\dfrac{N_1 N_2 (N_1 + N_2 + 1)}{12}}}$$

Test Statistics[b]

	Pride_Score
Mann-Whitney U	3.000
Wilcoxon W	18.000
Z	-2.015
Asymp. Sig. (2-tailed)	.044
Exact Sig. [2*(1-tailed Sig.)]	.056[a]

a. Not corrected for ties.

b. Grouping Variable Status

The normal approximation to U is reasonable if the larger N is at least 20 and the sample sizes are not too different.

When N is small (as in this example) the exact significance level should be reported.

Question

4. Are the accomplishment-related national pride rankings different in the populations of recently communist and recently noncommunist countries? Explain your answer.

ANSWERS

1. As shown in the table, the Spearman correlation coefficient is .401.

Correlations

			Compet_Rank	Pride_Score
Spearman's rho	Compet_Rank	Correlation Coefficient	1.000	.401
		Sig. (2-tailed)	.	.250
		N	10	10
	Pride_Score	Correlation Coefficient	.401	1.000
		Sig. (2-tailed)	.250	.
		N	10	10

2. The Pearson and Spearman correlations are not the same because SPSS does not convert the values of Pride_Score to ranks before computing the Pearson correlation coefficient. However, the Pearson and Spearman formulas are interchangeable when the values of both variables are entered as ranks.

Correlations

		Compet_Rank	Pride_Score
Compet_Rank	Pearson Correlation	1.000	-.519
	Sig. (2-tailed)	.	.124
	N	10	10
Pride_Score	Pearson Correlation	-.519	1.000
	Sig. (2-tailed)	.124	.
	N	10	10

3. According to the Wilcoxon signed ranks test, the hypothesis that the accomplishment-related national pride rankings in the two periods are different is not supported. The p value is .6, considerably above the significance criterion of .05.

4. According to the Mann Whitney U test for independent ranks, the hypothesis that the accomplishment-related national pride rankings in recently communist and noncommunist countries are different is not supported, although this outcome would be described as "marginally significant" by most researchers. The p value is .056, just above the significance criterion of .05.